LICHENS

by

Annie Lorrain Smith

New Introductory Matter
and Supplementary Index

by

D. L. Hawksworth

Rp

THE RICHMOND PUBLISHING CO. LTD.

Note
Lichens first published by Cambridge University Press in 1921
Reprinted by permission of Cambridge University Press
© Syndics of the Cambridge University Press. England 1921
New introductory matter
and supplementary index ©   D. L. Hawksworth 1975

SBN 85546 192 6

Republished in 1975 by
The Richmond Publishing Co. Ltd., Richmond, Surrey, England.

Reprinted in Great Britain by Kingprint Limited, Richmond, Surrey.

FOREWORD

Annie Lorrain Smith's *Lichens*, first published in 1921, is one of the most outstanding works on lichens ever to have appeared in English. Miss Smith was born on 25 October 1854 in Dumfriesshire and from about 1889 until her eightieth birthday devoted much of her time to the study of cryptogamic botany as an "unofficial worker" in the Cryptogamic Herbarium of the British Museum (Natural History), London. Following the death of the Rev. J. M. Crombie in 1906 she turned her attention from the marine algae and fungi with which she had been mainly concerned up to that time to lichens, completing the second volume of Crombie's *A Monograph of Lichens found in Great Britain* (issued in 1911). Later she produced a second edition of this monumental work under the title *A Monograph of British Lichens* (vol. 1, 1918; vol. 2, 1926) and, in the same year as *Lichens*, published a *Handbook of British Lichens* comprising keys to the British species. Miss Smith was President of the British Mycological Society in 1907 and 1918 and an O.B.E. was conferred on her in 1934. She passed away in London on 7 September 1937. A detailed account of her career is provided by A. Gepp and A. B. Rendle (*J. Bot., Lond.* **75**: 328–330, 1937).

Miss Smith worked in a period when the number of people interested in lichens was small. In the last two decades in particular, however, there has been a dramatic upsurge of interest in the group and a corresponding increase in the number of books and papers produced. Despite this many aspects of the subject still lack the thorough in-depth reviews included in *Lichens* and, 54 years after its first publication, the work remains the only work in English providing a comprehensive account of the group.

In his review of this book when it first appeared, R. Paulson (*Trans. Br. mycol. Soc.* **7**: 300–301, 1922) considered it a "... very complete and exceedingly able treatement" and emphasised the value of the exhaustive bibliography and method of citation as "... a veritable mine of wealth". Today this remains an extremely useful key to the earlier literature on lichens as the developments of various concepts are carefully traced in all chapters. This book is not by any means merely to be regarded as of historical interest, however, as the very detailed account of the history of lichenology and the keys to the world's families and genera of lichens in particular, remain the only comparable treatments in English. Some sections, especially those concerned with chemistry, ecology and physiology, are now dated but nevertheless serve to provide interesting historical insights into the development of concepts in these fields. In order to enable users of this book to locate more modern accounts of various aspects a short list of titles for further reading, arranged by Chapter, is included after this Foreword. The names of lichens, are, as is the case with all other organisms, continually in a state of flux and for this reason many of the names employed by Miss Smith will not be familiar to newcomers to lichenology in the 1970's. A list of currently accepted names where these differ from ones used in the main text has consequently been added as a Supplementary Index which follows the main Index to the book.

Lichenologists will be indebted to the Richmond Publishing Co. for making this long out of print mine of information readily available once more. *Lichens* has proved to be of continuing value to students, amateurs and research workers alike and will certainly remain so for many decades to come. Indeed it is doubtful if it would now be possible to provide a modern similarly comprehensive account of the group in a single volume.

D. L. Hawksworth

KEW, *February* 1975

FURTHER READING

General

[The works listed under this section include data relevant to three or more of the Chapters in *Lichens*; they should be used in conjunction with this book.]

Des Abbayes, H. (1951). *Traité de Lichénologie.* [*Encycl. Biol.* **41:** i − x, 1− 217.] Paris: Lechevalier.

Ahmadjian, V. and Hale, M. E., eds. (1974) ["1973"]. *The Lichens.* New York and London: Academic Press.

Brown, D. H. Hawksworth, D. L. and Bailey, R. H., eds.(1976). *Lichenology: Progress and Problems.* [Systematics Association Special Volume no. 8.] London, New York and San Francisco: Academic Press. [In press.]

Hale, M. E. (1974). *The Biology of Lichens.* 2nd edition. London: Arnold.

Hawksworth, D. L. (1973). Some advances in the study of lichens since the time of E. M. Holmes. *Bot. J. Linn. Soc.* **67:** 3 − 31.

Henssen, A. and Jahns, H. M. (1973) ["1974"]. *Lichenes. Eine Einführung in die Flechtenkunde.* Stuttgart: Thieme.

Chapter II [See under Chapter V for references on physiological aspects.]

Ahmadjian, V. (1967a). *The Lichen Symbiosis.* Waltham, Mass.: Blaisdell.

Ahmadjian, V. (1967b). A guide to the algae occurring as lichen symbionts: isolation, culture, cultural physiology, and identification. *Phycologia* **6:** 127 − 160.

Ahmadjian, V. and Heikkilä, H. (1970). The culture and synthesis of *Endocarpon pusillum* and *Staurothele clopima. Lichenologist* **4:** 259 − 267.

Jacobs, J. B. and Ahmadjian, V. (1969) The ultrastructure of lichens. I. A general survey. *J. Phycol.* **5:** 227 − 240.

Chapter III

Ozenda, P. (1963). Lichenes. In *Handbuch der Pflanzenanatomie* (K. Linsbauer, ed.) **6** (9): 1 − 199. Berlin: Borntraeger.

Chapter IV

Letrouit-Galinou, M.−A. (1968). The apothecia of the Discolichens. *Bryologist* **71:** 297 − 327.

Letrouit-Galinou, M.−A. (1973). Les asques des Lichens et le type archaescé. *Bryologist* **76:** 30–47.

Richardson, D. H. S. (1970). Ascus and ascocarp structure in lichens. *Lichenologist* **4:** 350 − 361.

Richardson, D. H. S. and Morgan-Jones, G. (1964). Studies on lichen asci I. The bitunicate type. *Lichenologist* **3:** 205 − 224.

Chapter V

Culberson, C. F. (1969). *Chemical and Botanical Guide to Lichen Products*. Chapel Hill, N. C.: University of North Carolina Press.

Culberson, W. L. (1969). The use of chemistry in lichen systematics. *Taxon* **18**: 152 – 166.

Culberson, W. L. and Culberson, C. F. (1970). A phylogenetic view of chemical evolution in the lichens. *Bryologist* **73**: 1 – 31.

Farrar, J. F. (1973). Lichen physiology: progress and pitfalls. In *Air Pollution and Lichens* (B. W. Ferry, M. S. Baddeley and D. L. Hawksworth, eds.): 238 – 282. London: Athlone Press of the University of London.

Harris, G. P. (1971). The ecology of corticolous lichens. II. The relationship between physiology and the environment. *J. Ecol.* **59**: 441 – 452.

Richardson, D. H. S., Hill, D. J. and Smith, D. C. (1968). Lichen physiology XI. The role of the alga in determining the pattern of carbohydrate movement between lichen symbionts. *New Phytol.* **67**: 469 – 486.

Smith, D. C. (1962). The biology of lichen thalli. *Biol. Rev.* **37**: 536 – 570.

Smith, D. C. (1973). *The Lichen Symbiosis.* [Oxford Biology Readers no. 42.] London: Oxford University Press.

Chapter VI

Armstrong, R. A. (1973). Seasonal growth and growth rate – colony size relationships in six species of saxicolous lichens. *New Phytol.* **72**: 1023 – 1030.

Bailey, R. H. (1967). Studies on the dispersal of lichen soredia. *J. Linn. Soc., Bot.* **59**: 479 – 490.

Beschel, R. E. (1961). Dating rock surfaces by lichen growth and its application to glaciology and physiography (lichenometry). In *Geology of the Arctic* (G. O. Raasch, ed.) **2**: 1044 – 1062. Toronto: University of Toronto Press.

Frey, E. (1959). Die Flechtenflora und -vegetation des Nationalparks im Unterengadin. II. Die Entwicklung der Flechtenvegetation auf photogrammetrisch kontrollierten Dauerflächen. *Ergebn. wiss. Unters. schweiz. NatnParks* **6**: 241 – 319.

Grummann, V. (1960). Die Cecidien auf Lichenen. *Bot. Jb.* **80**: 101 – 144.

Keissler, K. A. von (1930). Die Flechtenparasiten. *Rabenh. Krypt.-Fl.* **8**: i–xi, 1 – 712.

Santesson, R. (1967). On taxonomical and biological relations between lichens and non-lichenized fungi. *Bot. Notiser* **120**: 497 – 498.

Webber, P. J. and Andrews, J. T. (1973). Lichenometry: a commentry. *Arctic Alp. Res.* **5**: 295 – 302.

Chapter VII

Ahmadjian, V. (1970). The lichen symbiosis: its origin and evolution. In *Evolutionary Biology* (T. Dobzhansky, M. K. Hecht and W. C. Steere, eds.) **4**: 163 – 184. New York: Meredith Corporation.

Chapter VIII

Ainsworth, G. C. (1971). *Ainsworth & Bisby's Dictionary of the Fungi.* 6th Edition. Kew: Commonwealth Mycological Institute.

Duncan, U. K. (1970). *Introduction to British Lichens.* Arbroath: Buncle. [Sole agents: Richmond Publishing Co. Ltd.]

Hale, M. E. (1969). *How to Know the Lichens.* Dubuque, Iowa: Brown.

Hawksworth, D. L. (1970). Guide to the literature for the identification of British lichens. *Bull. Br. mycol. Soc.* **4:** 73 – 95.

Hawksworth, D. L. (1974). *Mycologist's Handbook.* Kew: Commonwealth Mycological Institute.

Poelt, J. (1969). *Bestimmungsschlüssel europäischer Flechten.* Lehre: Cramer.

Seaward, M. R. D., ed. (1976). *Lichen Ecology and Biogeography.* London, New York and San Francisco: Academic Press. [In preparation.]

Chapter IX

Barkman, J. J. (1958). *Phytosociology and Ecology of Cryptogamic Epiphytes.* Assen: Van Gorcum.

Ferry, B. W., Baddeley, M. S. and Hawksworth, D. L., eds. (1973). *Air Pollution and Lichens.* London: Athlone Press of the University of London.

Hawksworth, D. L. (1973). Ecological factors and species delimitation in the lichens. In *Taxonomy and Ecology* (V. H. Heywood, ed.): 31–69. [Systematics Association Special Volume No. 5.] London and New York: Academic Press.

Hawksworth, D. L., Coppins, B. J. and Rose, F. (1974). Changes in the British lichen flora. In *The Changing Flora and Fauna of Britain* (D. L. Hawksworth, ed.): 47–78. [Systematics Association Special Volume No. 6.] London and New York: Academic Press.

Fletcher, A. (1973a). The ecology of marine (littoral) lichens on some rocky shores of Anglesey. *Lichenologist* **5:** 368–400.

Fletcher, A. (1973b). The ecology of maritime (supralittoral) lichens on some rocky shores of Anglesey. *Lichenologist* **5:** 401–422.

Seaward, M. R. D., ed. (1976). *Lichen Ecology and Biogeography.* London, New York and San Francisco: Academic Press. [In preparation.]

Chapter X

Gerson, U. (1973). Lichen-Arthropod associations. *Lichenologist* **5:** 434–443.

Kok, A. (1966). A short history of the orchil dyes. *Lichenologist* **3:** 248–272.

Llano, G. A. (1944). Lichens. Their biological and economic significance. *Bot. Rev.* **10:** 1–63.

Richardson, D. H. S. (1975). *The Vanishing Lichens.* Newton Abbot, London and Vancouver: David and Charles.

Cambridge Botanical Handbooks

Edited by A. C. Seward and A. G. Tansley

LICHENS

CAMBRIDGE UNIVERSITY PRESS

C. F. CLAY, Manager

LONDON : FETTER LANE, E.C. 4

LONDON : H. K. LEWIS AND CO., Ltd.,
136, Gower Street, W.C. 1
LONDON : WHELDON & WESLEY, Ltd.,
28, Essex Street, Strand, W.C. 2
NEW YORK : THE MACMILLAN CO.
BOMBAY ⎫
CALCUTTA ⎬ MACMILLAN AND CO., Ltd.
MADRAS ⎭
TORONTO : THE MACMILLAN CO. OF
CANADA, Ltd.
TOKYO : MARUZEN-KABUSHIKI-KAISHA

LICHENS

BY

ANNIE LORRAIN SMITH, F.L.S.

ACTING ASSISTANT, BOTANICAL DEPARTMENT, BRITISH MUSEUM

CAMBRIDGE:
AT THE UNIVERSITY PRESS
1921

PREFACE

THE publication of this volume has been delayed owing to war conditions, but the delay is the less to be regretted in that it has allowed the inclusion of recent work on the subject. Much of the subject-matter is of common knowledge to lichenologists, but in the co-ordination and arrangement of the facts the original papers are cited throughout. The method has somewhat burdened the pages with citations, but it is hoped that, as a book of reference, its value has been enhanced thereby. The Glossary includes terms used in lichenology, or those with a special lichenological meaning. The Bibliography refers only to works consulted in the preparation of this volume. To save space, etc., the titles of books and papers quoted in the text are generally translated and curtailed: full citations will be found in the Bibliography. Subject-matter has been omitted from the index: references of importance will be found in the Table of Contents or in the Glossary.

I would record my thanks to those who have generously helped me during the preparation of the volume: to Lady Muriel Percy for taking notes of spore production, and to Dr Cavers for the loan of reprints. Prof. Potter and Dr Somerville Hastings placed at my disposal their photographs of the living plants. Free use has been made of published text-figures which are duly acknowledged.

I have throughout had the inestimable advantage of being able to consult freely the library and herbarium of the British Museum, and have thus been able to verify references to plants as well as to literature. A special debt of gratitude is due to my colleagues Mr Gepp and Mr Ramsbottom for their unfailing assistance and advice.

A. L. S.

LONDON,
February, 1920

CONTENTS

CHAPTER III

MORPHOLOGY

I. GENERAL ACCOUNT OF LICHEN STRUCTURE

ORIGIN OF LICHEN STRUCTURES

II. STRATOSE THALLUS

1. CRUSTACEOUS LICHENS

2. SQUAMULOSE LICHENS

3. FOLIOSE LICHENS

III. RADIATE THALLUS

1. CHARACTERS OF RADIATE THALLUS
2. INTERMEDIATE TYPES OF THALLUS
3. FRUTICOSE AND FILAMENTOUS THALLUS

IV. STRATOSE-RADIATE THALLUS

1. STRATOSE OR PRIMARY THALLUS

3. SOREDIA

4. ISIDIA

VI. HYMENOLICHENS

CHAPTER IV

REPRODUCTION

I. REPRODUCTION BY ASCOSPORES

1. DISCOLICHENS

CHAPTER V

PHYSIOLOGY

I. CELLS AND CELL PRODUCTS

II. GENERAL NUTRITION

CHAPTER VII

PHYLOGENY

I. GENERAL STATEMENT

II. THE REPRODUCTIVE ORGANS

III. THE THALLUS

CHAPTER VIII

SYSTEMATIC

I. CLASSIFICATION

II. NUMBER AND DISTRIBUTION

1. ESTIMATES OF NUMBER
2. GEOGRAPHICAL DISTRIBUTION

III. FOSSIL LICHENS

CHAPTER IX

ECOLOGY

CHAPTER X

ECONOMIC AND TECHNICAL

GLOSSARY

Acrogenous, borne at the tips of hyphae; see spermatium, 312.

Allelositismus, Norman's term to describe the thallus of Moriolaceae (mutualism), 313.

Amorphous cortex, formed of indistinct hyphae with thickened walls; cf. decomposed cortex.

Amphithecium, thalline margin of the apothecium, 157.

Antagonistic symbiosis, hurtful parasitism of one lichen on another, 261 *et seq.*

Apothecium, open or disc-shaped fructification, 11, 156 *et passim.* Veiled apothecium, 169. Closed or open at first, 182.

Archilichens, lichens in which the gonidia are bright green (Chlorophyceae), 52, 55 *et passim.*

Ardella, the small spot-like apothecium of Arthoniaceae, 158.

Areola (areolate), small space marked out by lines or chinks on the surface of the thallus, 73 *et passim.*

Arthrosterigma, septate tissue-like sterigma (spermatiophore), 197.

Ascogonium, the cell or cells that produce ascogenous hyphae, 180 *et seq.*

Ascolichens, lichens in which the fungus is an Ascomycete, 159, 173 *et passim.*

Ascus, enlarged cell in which a definite number of spores (usually 8) are developed; cf. theca, 157, 184.

Ascyphous, podetia without scyphi, 119 *et passim.*

Biatorine, apothecia that are soft or waxy, and often brightly coloured, as in *Biatora*, 158.

Blasteniospore, see *polarilocular spore.*

Byssoid, slender, thread-like, as in the old genus *Byssus.*

Campylidium, supposed new type of fructification in lichens, 191.

Capitulum, the globose apical apothecium of Coniocarpineae; cf. mazaedium, 319.

Carpogonium, primordial stage of fructification, 160, 164 *et passim.*

Cephalodium, irregular outgrowth from the thallus enclosing mostly blue-green algae; or intruded packet of algae within the thallus, 11, 133 *et passim.*

Chrondroid, hard and tough like cartilage, a term applied to strengthening strands of hyphae, 104, 114.

Chroolepoid, like the genus *Chroolepis* (*Trentepohlia*).

Chrysogonidia, yellow algal cells (*Trentepohlia*).

Cilium, hair-like outgrowth from surface or margin of thallus, or margin of apothecium, 91.

Consortium (consortism), mutual association of fungus and alga (Reinke); also termed "mutualism," 31, 313.

Corticolous, living on the bark of trees, 363.

Crustaceous, crust-like closely adhering thallus, 70–79.

Cyphella, minute cup-like depression on the under surface of the thallus (*Sticta*, etc.), 11, 126.

Decomposed, term applied to cortex formed of gelatinous indistinct hyphae (amorphous), 73–81 *et passim*, 357.

Determinate, thallus with a definite outline, 72.

Dimidiate, term applied to the perithecium, when the outer wall covers only the upper portion, 159.

Discoid, disc-like, an open rounded apothecium, 156.
Discolichens, in which the fructification is an apothecium, 160 *et seq.*
Dual hypothesis, the theory of two organisms present in the lichen thallus, 27 *et seq.*

Effigurate, having a distinct form or figure; cf. placodioid, 80, 201.
Endobasidial, Steiner's term for sporophore with a secondary sporiferous branch, 200.
Endogenous, produced internally, as spores in an ascus, 179; see also under thallus.
Endolithic, embedded in the rock, 75.
Endosaprophytism, term used by Elenkin for destruction of the algal contents by enzymes of the fungus, 36.
Entire, term applied to the perithecium when completely surrounded by an outer wall, 159.
Epilithic, growing on the rock surface, 70.
Epiphloeodal, thallus growing on the surface of the bark, 77.
Epiphyllous, growing on leaves, 363.
Epithecium, upper layer of thecium (hymenium), 158.
Erratic lichens, unattached and drifting, 259.
Exobasidial, Steiner's term for sporophore without a secondary sporiferous branch, 200.
Exogenous, produced externally, as spores on tips of hyphae; see also under thallus.

Fastigiate cortex, formed of clustered parallel hyphal branches vertical to long axis of thallus, 82.
Fat-cells, specialized hyphal cells containing fat or oil, 75, 215 *et passim.*
Fibrous cortex, formed of hyphae parallel with long axis of thallus, 82.
Filamentous, slender thallus with radiate structure, 101 *et seq.*
Foliose, lichens with a leafy form and stratose in structure, 82–97.
Foveolae, Foveolate, pitted, 373.
Fruticose, upright or pendulous thallus, with radiate structure, 101 *et seq.*
Fulcrum, term used by Steiner for sporophore, 200.

Gloeolichens, lichens in which the gonidia are *Gloeocapsa* or *Chroococcus*, 284, 373, 389.
Gonidium, the algal constituent of the lichen thallus, 20–45 *et passim.*
Gonimium, blue-green algal cell (Myxophyceae), constituent of the lichen thallus, 52.
Goniocysts, nests of gonidia in Moriolaceae, 313.
Gyrose, curved backward and forward, furrowed fruit of *Gyrophora*, 184.

Hapteron, aerial organ of attachment, 94, 122.
Haustorium, outgrowth or branch of a hypha serving as an organ of suction, 32.
Helotism, state of servitude, term used to denote the relation of alga to fungus in lichen organization, 38, 40.
Heteromerous, fungal and algal constituents of the thallus in definite strata, 13, 68, 305 *et passim.*
Hold-fast, rooting organ of thallus, 109, 122 *et passim.*
Homobium, interdependent association of fungus and alga, 31
Homoiomerous, fungal and algal constituents more or less mixed in the thallus, 13, 68, 305 *et passim.*
Hymenial gonidia, algal cells in the hymenium, 30, 314, 315, 327.
Hymenium, apothecial tissue consisting of asci and paraphyses; cf. thecium, 157.
Hymenolichens, lichens of which the fungal constituent is a Hymenomycete, 152–154, 342.
Hypophloeodal, thallus growing within the bark, 78, 364.
Hypothallus, first growth of hyphae (proto- or pro-thallus) persisting as hyphal growth at base or margin of the thallus, 70, 257 *et passim.*
Hypothecium, layer below the thecium (hymenium), 157.

Intricate cortex, composed of hyphae densely interwoven but not coalescent, 83.
Isidium, coral-like outgrowth on the lichen thallus, 149–151.

Lecanorine, apothecium with a thalline margin as in *Lecanora*, 158.
Lecideine, apothecium usually dark-coloured or carbonaceous and without a thalline margin, 158.
Leprose, mealy or scurfy, like the old form genera, *Lepra, Lepraria*, 191.
Lichen-acids, organic acids peculiar to lichens, 221 *et seq.*
Lignicolous, living on wood or trees, 366.
Lirella, long narrow apothecium of Graphideae, 158.

Mazaedium, fructification of Coniocarpineae, the spores lying as a powdery mass in the capitulum, 176.
Medulla, the loose hyphal layer in the interior of the thallus, 88 *et passim.*
Meristematic, term applied by Wainio to growing hyphae, 48.
Microgonidia, term applied by Minks to minute greenish bodies in lichen hyphae, 26.
Multi-septate, term applied to spores with numerous transverse septa, 316 *et seq.*
Murali-divided, Muriform, term applied to spores divided like the masonry of a wall, 187.

Oidium, reproductive cell formed by the breaking up of the hyphae, 189.
Oil-cell, hyphal cell containing fat globules, 215.
Orculiform, see polarilocular.
Orthidium, supposed new type of fructification in lichens, 192.

Palisade-cells, the terminal cells of the hyphae forming the fastigiate cortex, 82, 83.
Panniform, having a felted or matted appearance, 260.
Paraphysis, sterile filament in the hymenium, 157.
Parasymbiosis, associated harmless but not mutually useful growth of two organisms, 263.
Parathecium, hyphal layer round the apothecium, 157.
Peltate, term applied to orbicular and horizontal apothecia in the form of a shield, 336.
Perithecium, roundish fructification usually with an apical opening (ostiole) containing ascospores, 158 *et passim.*
Pervious, referring to scyphi with an opening at the base (*Perviae*), 118.
Phycolichens, lichens in which the gonidia are blue-green (Myxophyceae), 52 *et passim.*
Placodioid, thallus with a squamulose determinate outline, generally orbicular; cf. effigurate, 80.
Placodiomorph, see polarilocular.
Plectenchyma (Plectenchymatous), pseudoparenchyma of fungi and lichens, 66 *et passim.*
Pleurogenous, borne laterally on hyphal cells; see spermatium, 312.
Pluri-septate, term applied to spores with several transverse septa, 321 *et seq.*
Podetium, stalk-like secondary thallus of Cladoniaceae, 114, 293 *et seq.*
Polarilocular, Polaribilocular, two-celled spores with thick median wall traversed by a connecting tube, 188, 340–341.
Polytomous, arising of several branches of the podetium from one level, 118.
Proper margin, the hyphal margin surrounding the apothecium, 157.
Prothallus, Protothallus, first stages of hyphal growth; cf. hypothallus, 71.
Pycnidiospores, stylospores borne in pycnidia, 198 *et passim.*
Pycnidium, roundish fructification, usually with an opening at the apex, containing sporophores and stylospores; cf. spermogonium, 192 *et seq.*
Pyrenolichens, in which the fructification is a closed perithecium, 173 *et passim.*

Radiate thallus, the tissues radiate from a centre, 98 *et seq.*

Rhagadiose, deeply chinked, 74 ; cf. rimose.
Rhizina, attaching "rootlet," 92-94.
Rimose, Rimulose, cleft or chinked into areolae, 73.
Rimose-diffract, widely cracked or chinked, 74.

Scutellate, shaped like a platter, 156.
Scyphus, cup-like dilatation of the podetium, 111, 117.
Signature, a term in ancient medicine to signify the resemblance of a plant to any part of the human body, 406, 409.
Soralium, group of soredia surrounded by a definite margin, 144.
Soredium, minute separable particle arising from the gonidial tissue of the thallus, and consisting of algae and hyphae, 141.
Spermatium, spore-like body borne in the spermogonium, regarded as a non-motile male cell or as a pycnidiospore, 201.
Spermogonium, roundish closed receptacle containing spermatia, 192.
Sphaeroid-cell, swollen hyphal cell, containing fat globules, 215.
Squamule, a small thalline lobe or scale, 74 *et passim.*
Sterigma, Nylander's term for the spermatiophore, 197.
Stratose thallus, where the tissues are in horizontal layers, 70.
Stratum, a layer of tissue in the thallus, 70.
Symbiont, one of two dissimilar organisms living together, 32.
Symbiosis, a living together of dissimilar organisms, also termed commensalism, 31, 32 *et seq.*

Tegulicolous, living on tiles, 369.
Terebrator, boring apparatus, term used by Lindau for the lichen "trichogyne," 179.
Thalline margin, an apothecial margin formed of and usually coloured like the thallus ; cf. amphithecium.
Thallus, vegetative body or soma of the lichen plant, 11, 421. Endogenous thallus in which the alga predominates, 68. Exogenous thallus in which the fungus predominates, 69.
Theca, enlarged cell containing spores ; cf. ascus.
Thecium, layer of tissue in the apothecium consisting of asci and paraphyses ; cf. hymenium, 157.
Trichogyne, prolongation of the egg-cell in Florideae which acts as a receptive tube ; septate hypha in lichens arising from the ascogonium, 160, 177–181, 273.

Woronin's hypha, a coiled hypha occurring in the centre of the fruit primordium, 159, 163.

ERRATA

p. 24. *For* Baranetsky *read* Baranetzky.
p. 277. For *Ascolium* read *Acolium.*
p. 318. For *Lepolichen coccophora* read *coccophorus.*

INTRODUCTION

LICHENS are, with few exceptions, perennial aerial plants of somewhat lowly organization. In the form of spreading encrustations, horizontal leafy expansions, of upright strap-shaped fronds or of pendulous filaments, they take possession of the tree-trunks, palings, walls, rocks or even soil that afford them a suitable and stable foot-hold. The vegetative body, or thallus, which may be extremely long-lived, is of varying colour, white, yellow, brown, grey or black. The great majority of lichens are Ascolichens and reproduction is by ascospores produced in open or closed fruits (apothecia or perithecia) which often differ in colour from the thallus. There are a few Hymenolichens which form basidiospores. Vegetative reproduction by soredia is frequent.

Lichens abound everywhere, from the sea-shore to the tops of high mountains, where indeed the covering of perpetual snow is the only barrier to their advance; but owing to their slow growth and long duration, they are more seriously affected than are the higher plants by chemical or other atmospheric impurities and they are killed out by the smoke of large towns: only a few species are able to persist in somewhat depauperate form in or near the great centres of population or of industry.

The distinguishing feature of lichens is their composite nature: they consist of two distinct and dissimilar organisms, a fungus and an alga, which, in the lichen thallus, are associated in some kind of symbiotic union, each symbiont contributing in varying degree to the common support: it is a more or less unique and not unsuccessful venture in plant-life. The algae—Chlorophyceae or Myxophyceae—that become lichen symbionts or "gonidia" are of simple structure, and, in a free condition, are generally to be found in or near localities that are also the customary habitats of lichens. The fungus is the predominant partner in the alliance as it forms the fruiting bodies. It belongs to the Ascomycetes[1], except in a few tropical lichens (Hymenolichens), in which the fungus is a Basidiomycete. These two types of plants (algae and fungi) belonging severally to many different genera and species have developed in their associated life this new lichen organism, different from themselves as well as from all other plants, not only morphologically but physiologically. Thus there has arisen a distinct class, with families, genera and species, which through all their varying forms retain the characteristics peculiar to lichens.

---

[1] E. Acton (1909) has described a primitive lichen *Botrydina vulgaris*, in which there is no fruiting stage, and in which the fungus seems to show affinity with a Hyphomycete.

In the absence of any "visible" seed, there was much speculation in early days as to the genesis of all the lower plants and many opinions were hazarded as to their origin. Luyken[1], for instance, thought that lichens were compounded of air and moisture. Hornschuch[2] traced their origin to a vegetable infusorium, *Monas Lens*, which became transformed to green matter and was further developed by the continued action of light and air, not only to lichens, but to algae and mosses, the type of plant finally evolved being determined by the varying atmospheric influences along with the chemical nature of the substratum. An account[3] is published of Nees von Esenbeck, on a botanical excursion, pointing out to his students the green substance, *Lepraria botryoides*, which covered the lower reaches of walls and rocks, while higher up it assumed the grey lichen hue. This afforded him sufficient proof that the green matter in that dry situation changed to lichens, just as in water it changed to algae. An adverse criticism by Dillenius[4] on a description of a lichen fructification is not inappropriate to those early theorists : " Ex quo apparet, quantum videre possint homines, si imaginatione polleant."

A constant subject of speculation and of controversy was the origin of the green cells, so dissimilar to the general texture of the thallus. It was thought finally to have been established beyond dispute that they were formed directly from the colourless hyphae and, as a corollary, *Protococcus* and other algal cells living in the open were considered to be escaped gonidia or, as Wallroth[5] termed them, "unfortunate brood-cells," his view being that they were the reproductive organs of the lichen plant that had failed to develop.

It was a step forward in the right direction when lichens were regarded as transformed algae, among others by Agardh[6], who believed that he had followed the change from *Nostoc lichenoides* to the lichen *Collema limosum*. Thenceforward their double resemblance, on the one hand to algae, on the other to fungi, was acknowledged, and influenced strongly the trend of study and investigation.

The announcement[7] by Schwendener[8] of the dual hypothesis solved the problem for most students, though the relation between the two symbionts is still a subject of controversy. The explanation given by Schwendener, and still held by some[9], that lichens were merely fungi parasitic on algae, was indeed a very inadequate conception of the lichen plant, and it was hotly contested by various lichenologists. Lauder Lindsay[10] dismissed the theory as " merely the most recent instance of German transcendentalism applied

---

[1] Luyken 1809. [2] Hornschuch 1819. [3] Raab 1819. [4] Dillenius 1741, p. 200.
[5] Wallroth 1825. [6] Agardh 1820. [7] See p. 27. [8] Schwendener 1867.
[9] Fink 1913. [10] Lindsay 1876.

to the Lichens." Earlier still, Nylander[1], in a paper dealing with cephalodia and their peculiar gonidia, had denounced it: " Locum sic suum dignum occupat algolichenomachia inter historias ridiculas, quae hodie haud paucae circa lichenes, majore imaginatione quam scientia, enarrantur." He never changed his attitude and Crombie[2], wholly agreeing with his estimate of these "absurd tales," translates a much later pronouncement by him[3]: "All these allegations belong to inept Schwendenerism and scarcely deserve even to be reviewed or castigated so puerile are they—the offspring of inexperience and of a light imagination. No true science there." Crombie[4] himself in a first paper on this subject declared that " the new theory would necessitate their degradation from the position they have so long held as an independent class." He scornfully rejected the whole subject as "a Romance of Lichenology, or the unnatural union between a captive Algal damsel and a tyrant Fungal master." The nearest approach to any concession on the algal question occurs in a translation by Crombie[5] of one of Nylander's papers. It is stated there that a saxicolous alga (*Gongrosira* Kütz.) had been found bearing the apothecia of *Lecidea herbidula* n. sp. Nylander adds: "This algological genus is one which readily passes into lichens." At a later date, Crombie[6] was even more comprehensively contemptuous and wrote: " whether viewed anatomically or biologically, analytically or synthetically, it is instead of being true science, only the Romance of Lichenology." These views were shared by many continental lichenologists and were indeed, as already stated, justified to a considerable extent: it was impossible to regard such a large and distinctive class of plants as merely fungi parasitic on the lower algae.

Controversy about lichens never dies down, and that view of their parasitic nature has been freshly promulgated among others by the American lichenologist Bruce Fink[7]. The genetic origin of the gonidia has also been restated by Elfving[8]: the various theories and views are discussed fully in the chapter on the lichen plant.

Much of the interest in lichens has centred round their symbiotic growth. No theory of simple parasitism can explain the association of the two plants: if one of the symbionts is withdrawn—either fungus or alga—the lichen as such ceases to exist. Together they form a healthy unit capable of development and change: a basis for progress along new lines. Permanent characters have been formed which are transmitted just as in other units of organic life.

A new view of the association has been advanced by F. and Mme Moreau[9]. They hold that the most characteristic lichen structures—more particularly

---

[1] Nylander 1869.   [2] Crombie 1891.   [3] Nylander 1891.   [4] Crombie 1874.
[5] Crombie 1877.   [6] Crombie 1885.   [7] Fink 1913.   [8] Elfving 1913.
[9] Moreau 1918.

the cortex—have been induced by the action of the alga on the fungus. The larger part of the thallus might therefore be regarded as equivalent to a gall: "it is a cecidium, an algal cecidium, a generalized biomorphogenesis."

The morphological characters of lichens are of exceptional interest, conditioned as they are by the interaction of the two symbionts, and new structures have been evolved by the fungus which provides the general tissue system. Lichens are plants of physiological symbiotic origin, and that aspect of their life-history has been steadily kept in view in this work. There are many new requirements which have had to be met by the lichen hyphae, and the differences between them and the true fungal hyphae have been considered, as these are manifested in the internal economy of the compound plant, and in its reaction to external influences such as light, heat, moisture, etc.

The pioneers of botanical science were of necessity occupied almost exclusively with collecting and describing plants. As the number of known lichens gradually accumulated, affinities were recognized and more or less successful efforts were made to tabulate them in classes, orders, etc. It was a marvellous power of observation that enabled the early workers to arrange the first schemes of classification. Increasing knowledge aided by improved microscopes has necessitated changes, but the old fundamental "genus" *Lichen* is practically equivalent to the Class *Lichenes*.

The study of lichens has been a slow and gradual process, with a continual conflict of opinion as to the meaning of these puzzling plants—their structure, reproduction, manner of subsistence and classification as well as their relation to other plants. It has been found desirable to treat these different subjects from a historical aspect, as only thus can a true understanding be gained, or a true judgment formed as to the present condition of the science. It is the story of the evolution of lichenology as well as of lichens that has yielded so much of interest and importance.

The lichenologist may claim several advantages in the study of his subject: the abundant material almost everywhere to hand in country districts, the ease with which the plants are preserved, and, not least, the interest excited by the changes and variations induced by growth conditions; there are a whole series of problems and puzzles barely touched on as yet that are waiting to be solved.

In field work, it is important to note accurately and carefully the nature of the substratum as well as the locality. Crustaceous species should be gathered if possible along with part of the wood or rock to which they are attached; if they are scraped off, the pieces may be reassembled on gummed paper, but that is less satisfactory. The larger forms are more easily secured;

they should be damped and then pressed before being laid away : the process flattens them, but it saves them from the risk of being crushed and broken, as when dry they are somewhat brittle. Moistening with water will largely restore their original form. All parts of the lichen, both thallus and fruit, can be examined with ease at any time as they do not sensibly alter in the herbarium, though they lose to some extent their colouring : the blue-grey forms, for instance, often become a uniform dingy brownish-grey.

Microscopic examination in the determination of species is necessary in many instances, but that disability—if it ranks as such—is shared by other cryptogams, and may possibly be considered an inducement rather than a deterrent to the study of lichens. For temporary examination of microscopic preparations, the normal condition is best observed by mounting them in water. If the plants are old and dry, the addition of a drop or two of potash —or ammonia—solution is often helpful in clearing the membranes of the cells and in restoring the shrivelled spores and paraphyses to their natural forms and dimensions.

If serial microtome sections are desired, more elaborate methods are required. For this purpose Peirce[1] has recommended that " when dealing with plants that are dry but still alive, the material should be thoroughly wetted and kept moist for two days, then killed and fixed in a saturated solution of corrosive sublimate in thirty-five per cent. alcohol." The solution should be used hot : the usual methods of dehydrating and embedding in paraffin are then employed with extra precautions on account of the extremely brittle nature of lichens.

Another method that also gave good results has been proposed by French[2]: " first the lichen is put into 95 per cent. alcohol for 24 hours, then into thin celloidin and thick celloidin 24 hours each. After this the specimens are embedded in thick celloidin which is hardened in 70 per cent. alcohol for 24 hours and then cut." French advises staining with borax carmine : it colours the fungal part pale carmine and the algal cells a greenish-red shade.

Modern research methods of work are generally described in full in the publications that are discussed in the following chapters. The student is referred to these original papers for information as to fixing, embedding, staining, etc.

Great use has been made of reagents in determining lichen species. They are extremely helpful and often give the clinching decision when morphological characters are obscure, especially if the plant has been much altered by the environment. It must be borne in mind, however, that a

[1] Peirce 1898.   [2] French 1898.

species is a morphological rather than a physiological unit, and it is not the structures but the cell-products that are affected by reagents. Those most commonly in use are saturated solutions of potash and of bleaching-powder (calcium hypochlorite). The former is cited in text-books as KOH or simply as K, the latter as CaCl or C. The C solution deteriorates quickly and must, therefore, be frequently renewed to produce the required reaction, *i.e.* some change of colour. These two reagents are used singly or, if conjointly, K followed by C. The significance of the colour changes has been considered in the discussion on lichen-acids.

Iodine is generally cited in connection with its staining effect on the hymenium of the fruit; the blue colour produced is, however, more general than was at one time supposed and is not peculiar to lichens; the asci of many fungi react similarly though to a less extent. The medullary hyphae in certain species also stain blue with iodine.

CHAPTER I

HISTORY OF LICHENOLOGY

A. INTRODUCTORY

THE term "lichen" is a word of Greek origin used by Theophrastus in his *History of Plants* to signify a superficial growth on the bark of olive-trees. The name was given in the early days of botanical study not to lichens, as we understand them, but to hepatics of the *Marchantia* type. Lichens themselves were generally described along with various other somewhat similar plants as "Muscus" (Moss) by the older writers, and more definitely as "Musco-fungus" by Morison[1]. In a botanical work published in 1700 by Tournefort[2] all the members of the vegetable kingdom then known were for the first time classified in genera, and the genus *Lichen* was reserved for the plants that have been so designated since that time, though Dillenius[3] in his works preferred the adjectival name *Lichenoïdes*.

A painstaking historical account of lichens up to the beginning of modern lichenology has been written by Krempelhuber[4], a German lichenologist. He has grouped the data compiled by him into a series of Periods, each one marked by some great advance in knowledge of the subject, though, as we shall see, the advance from period to period has been continuous and gradual. While following generally on the lines laid down by Krempelhuber, it will be possible to cite only the more prominent writers and it will be of much interest to British readers to note especially the work of our own botanists.

Krempelhuber's periods are as follows:

    I. From the earliest times to the end of the seventeenth century.

    II. Dating from the arrangement of plants into classes called genera by Tournefort in 1694 to 1729.

    III. From Micheli's division of lichens into different orders in 1729 to 1780.

    IV. The definite and reasoned establishment of lichen genera based on the structure of thallus and fruit by Weber in 1780 to 1803.

    V. The arrangement of all known lichens under their respective genera by Acharius in 1803 to 1846.

    VI. The recognition of spore characters in classification by De Notaris in 1846 to 1867.

---

[1] Morison 1699.   [2] Tournefort 1694 and 1700.   [3] Dillenius 1741.   [4] Krempelhuber 1867–1872.

A seventh period which includes modern lichenology, and which dates after the publication of Krempelhuber's *History*, was ushered in by Schwendener's announcement in 1867 of the hypothesis as to the dual nature of the lichen thallus. Schwendener's theory gave a new impulse to the study of lichens and strongly influenced all succeeding investigations.

B. Period I. Previous to 1694

Our examination of lichen literature takes us back to Theophrastus, the disciple of Plato and Aristotle, who lived from 371 to 284 B.C., and who wrote a *History of Plants*, one of the earliest known treatises on Botany. Among the plants described by Theophrastus, there are evidently two lichens, one of which is either an *Usnea* or an *Alectoria*, and the other certainly *Roccella tinctoria*, the last-named an important economic plant likely to be well known for its valuable dyeing properties. The same or somewhat similar lichens are also probably alluded to by the Greek physician Dioscorides, in his work on *Materia Medica*, A.D. 68. About the same time Pliny the elder, who was a soldier and traveller as well as a voluminous writer, mentions them in his *Natural History* which was completed in 77 A.D.

During the centuries that followed, there was little study of Natural History, and, in any case, lichens were then and for a long time after considered to be of too little economic value to receive much attention.

In the sixteenth century there was a great awakening of scientific interest all over Europe, and, after the printing-press had come into general use, a number of books bearing on Botany were published. It will be necessary to chronicle only those that made distinct contributions to the knowledge of lichens.

The study of plants was at first entirely from a medical standpoint and one of the first works, and the first book on Natural History, printed in England, was the *Grete Herball*[1]. It was translated from a French work, *Hortus sanitatis*, and published by Peter Treveris in Southwark. One of the herbs recommended for various ailments is "Muscus arborum," the tree-moss (*Usnea*). A somewhat crude figure accompanies the text.

Ruel[2] of Soissons in France, Dorstenius[3], Camerarius[4] and Tabernaemontanus[5] in Germany followed with works on medical or economic botany and they described, in addition to the tree-moss, several species of reputed value in the art of healing now known as *Sticta* (*Lobaria*) *pulmonaria*, *Lobaria laetevirens*, *Cladonia pyxidata*, *Evernia prunastri* and *Cetraria islandica*. Meanwhile L'Obel[6], a Fleming, who spent the latter part of his life in England and is said to have had charge of a physic garden at

---

[1] *Grete Herball* 1526. [2] Ruel 1536. [3] Dorstenius 1540.
[4] Camerarius 1586. [5] Tabernaemontanus 1590. [6] L'Obel 1576.

Hackney, was appointed botanist to James I. He published at Antwerp a large series of engravings of plants, and added a species of *Ramalina* to the growing list of recognized lichens. Dodoens[1], also a Fleming, records not only the *Usnea* of trees, but a smaller and more slender black form which is easily identifiable as *Alectoria jubata*. He also figures *Lichen pulmonaria* and gives the recipe for its use.

The best-known botanical book published at that time, however, is the *Herball* of John Gerard[2] of London, Master in Chirurgerie, who had a garden in Holborn. He recommends as medicinally valuable not only *Usnea*, but also *Cladonia pyxidata*, for which he coined the name "cuppe- or chalice-moss." About the same time Schwenckfeld[3] recorded, among plants discovered by him in Silesia, lichens now familiar as *Alectoria jubata*, *Cladonia rangiferina* and a species of *Peltigera*.

Among the more important botanical writers of the seventeenth century may be cited Colonna[4] and Bauhin[5]. The former, an Italian, contributes, in his *Ecphrasis*, descriptions and figures of three additional species easily recognized as *Physcia ciliaris*, *Xanthoria parietina* and *Ramalina calicaris*. Kaspar Bauhin, a professor in Basle, who was one of the most advanced of the older botanists, was the first to use a binomial nomenclature for some of his plants. He gives a list in his *Pinax* of the lichens with which he was acquainted, one of them, *Cladonia fimbriata*, being a new plant.

John Parkinson's[6] *Herball* is well known to English students; he adds one new species for England, *Lobaria pulmonaria*, already recorded on the Continent. Parkinson was an apothecary in London and held the office of the King's Herbarist; his garden was situated in Long Acre. How's[7] *Phytographia* is notable as being the first account of British plants compiled without reference to their healing properties. Five of the plants described by him are lichen species: "Lichen arborum sive pulmonaria" (*Lobaria pulmonaria*), "Lichen petraeus tinctorius" (*Roccella*), "Muscus arboreus" (*Usnea*), "Corallina montana" (*Cladonia rangiferina*) and "Muscus pixoides" (*Cladonia*). Several other British species were added by Merrett[8], who records in his *Pinax*, "Muscus arboreus umbilicatus" (*Physcia ciliaris*), "Muscus aureus tenuissimus" (*Teloschistes flavicans*), "Muscus caule rigido" (*Alectoria*) and "Lichen petraeus purpureus" (*Parmelia omphalodes*), the last-named, a rock lichen, being used, he tells us, for dyeing in Lancashire.

Merret or Merrett was librarian to the Royal College of Physicians. His *Pinax* was undertaken to replace How's *Phytographia* published sixteen years previously and then already out of print. Merrett's work was issued in 1666, but the first impression was destroyed in the great fire of London and most of the copies now extant are dated 1667. He arranged

[1] Dodoens 1583. [2] Gerard 1597. [3] Schwenckfeld 1600. [4] Colonna 1606.
[5] Bauhin 1623, pp. 360-2. [6] Parkinson 1640. [7] How 1650. [8] Merrett 1666.

the species of plants in alphabetical order, but as the work was not critical it fell into disuse, being superseded by John Ray's *Catalogus* and *Synopsis*. To Robert Plot[1] we owe the earliest record of *Cladonia coccifera* which had hitherto escaped notice; it was described and figured as a new and rare plant in the *Natural History of Staffordshire*[1]. Plot was the first Custos of Ashmole's Museum in Oxford and he was also the first to prepare a County Natural History.

The greatest advance during this first period was made by Robert Morison[2], a Scotsman from Aberdeen. He studied medicine at Angers in France, superintended the Duke of Orleans' garden at Blois, and finally, after his return to this country in 1669, became Keeper of the botanic garden at Oxford. In the third volume of his great work[2] on Oxford plants, which was not issued till after his death, the lichens are put in a separate group—"Musco-fungus"—and classified with some other plants under "Plantae Heteroclitae." The publication of the volume projects into the next historical period.

Long before this date John Ray had begun to study and publish books on Botany. His *Catalogue of English Plants*[3] is considered to have commenced a new era in the study of the science. The *Catalogue* was followed by the *History of Plants*[4], and later by a *Synopsis of British Plants*[5], and in all of these books lichens find a place. Two editions of the *Synopsis* appeared during Ray's lifetime, and to the second there is added an Appendix contributed by Samuel Doody which is entirely devoted to Cryptogamic plants, including not a few lichens—still called "Mosses"— discovered for the first time. Doody, himself an apothecary, took charge of the garden of the Apothecaries' Society at Chelsea, but his chief interest was Cryptogamic Botany, a branch of the subject but little regarded before his day. Pulteney wrote of him as the "Dillenius of his time."

Among Doody's associates were the Rev. Adam Buddle, James Petiver and William Sherard. Buddle was primarily a collector and his herbarium is incorporated in the Sloane Herbarium at the British Museum. It contains lichens from all parts of the world, many of them contributed by Doody, Sherard and Petiver. Only a few of them bear British localities: several are from Hampstead where Buddle had a church.

The Society of Apothecaries had been founded in 1617 and the members acquired land on the river-front at Chelsea, which was extended later and made into a Physick Garden. James Petiver[6] was one of the first Demonstrators of Plants to the Society in connection with the garden, and one of his duties was to conduct the annual herborizing tours of the apprentices in search of plants. He thus collected a large herbarium on the annual excursions, as well as on shorter visits to the more immediate

[1] Plot 1686.   [2] Morison 1699.   [3] Ray 1670.   [4] Ray 1686.   [5] Ray 1690.   [6] Petiver 1695.

neighbourhood of London. He wrote many tracts on Natural History subjects, and in these some lichens are included. He was one of the best known of Ray's correspondents, and owing to his connection with the Physic Garden received plants from naturalists in foreign countries.

Sherard, another of Doody's friends, had studied abroad under Tournefort and was full of enthusiasm for Natural Science. It was he who brought Dillenius to England and finally nominated him for the position of the first Sherardian Professor of Botany at Oxford. Another well-known contemporary botanist was Leonard Plukenet[1] who had a botanical garden at Old Palace Yard, Westminster. He wrote several botanical works in which lichens are included.

Morison is the only one of all the botanists of the time who recognized lichens as a group distinct from mosses, algae or liverworts, and even he had very vague ideas as to their development. Malpighi[2] had noted the presence of soredia on the thallus of some species, and regarded them as seeds. Porta[3], a Neapolitan, has been quoted by Krempelhuber as probably the first to discover and place on record the direct growth of lichen fronds from green matter on the trunks of trees.

C. PERIOD II. 1694–1729

The second Period is ushered in with the publication of a French work, *Les Élémens de Botanique* by Tournefort[4], who was one of the greatest botanists of the time. His object was—"to facilitate the knowledge of plants and to disentangle a science which had been neglected because it was found to be full of confusion and obscurity." Up to this date all plants were classified or listed as individual species. It was Tournefort who first arranged them in groups which he designated "genera" and he gave a careful diagnosis of each genus.

Les Élémens was successful enough to warrant the publication a few years later of a larger Latin edition entitled *Institutiones*[5] and thus fitted for a wider circulation. Under the genus *Lichen*, he included plants "lacking flowers but with a true cup-shaped shallow fruit, with very minute pollen or seed which appeared to be subrotund under the microscope." Not only the description but the figures prove that he was dealing with ascospores and not merely soredia, though under *Lichen* along with true members of the "genus" he has placed a *Marchantia*, the moss *Splachnum* and a fern. A few lichens were placed by him in another genus *Coralloides*.

Tournefort's system was of great service in promoting the study of Botany: his method of classification was at once adopted by the German writer Rupp[6] who published a Flora of plants from Jena. Among these

---

[1] Plukenet 1691–1696.   [2] Malpighi 1686.   [3] Porta 1688.
[4] Tournefort 1694.   [5] Tournefort 1700.   [6] Rupp 1718.

plants are included twenty-five species of lichens, several of which he considered new discoveries, no fewer than five being some form of *Lichen gelatinosus* (*Collema*). Buxbaum[1], in his enumeration of plants from Halle, finds place for forty-nine lichen species, with, in addition, eleven species of *Coralloides*; and Vaillant[2] in listing the plants that grew in the neighbourhood of Paris gives thirty-three species for the genus *Lichen* of which a large number are figured, among them species of *Ramalina*, *Parmelia*, *Cladonia*, etc.

In England, however, Dillenius[3], who at this time brought out a third edition of Ray's *Synopsis* and some years later his own *Historia Muscorum*, still described most of his lichens as "Lichenoides" or "Coralloides"; and no other work of note was published in our country until after the Linnaean system of classification and of nomenclature was introduced.

D. PERIOD III. 1729–1780

Lichens were henceforth regarded as a distinct genus or section of plants. Micheli[4], an Italian botanist, Keeper of the Grand Duke's Gardens in Florence, realized the desirability of still further delimitation, and he broke up Tournefort's large comprehensive genera into numerical Orders. In the genus *Lichen*, he found occasion for 38 of these Orders, determined mainly by the character of the thallus, and the position on it of apothecia and soredia. He enumerates the species, many of them new discoveries, though not all of them recognizable now. His great work on Plants is enriched by a series of beautiful figures. It was published in 1729 and marks the beginning of a new Period—a new outlook on botanical science. Micheli regarded the apothecia of lichens as "floral receptacles," and the soredia as the seed, because he had himself followed the development of lichen fronds from soredia.

The next writer of distinction is the afore-mentioned Dillen or Dillenius. He was a native of Darmstadt and began his scientific career in the University of Giessen. His first published work[5] was an account of plants that were to be found near Giessen in the different months of the year. Mosses and lichens he has assigned to December and January. Sherard induced him to come to England in 1721, and at first engaged his services in arranging the large collections of plants which he, Sherard, had brought from Smyrna or acquired from other sources.

Three years after his arrival Dillenius had prepared the third edition of Ray's *Synopsis* for the press, but without putting his name on the title-page[6]. Sherard explained, in a letter to Dr Richardson of Bierly in Yorkshire, that "our people can't agree about an editor, they are unwilling a foreigner should

[1] Buxbaum 1721.   [2] Vaillant 1727.   [3] Dillenius 1724 and 1741.
[4] Micheli 1729.   [5] Dillenius 1719.   [6] See Druce and Vines 1907.

put his name to it." Dillenius, who was quite aware of the prejudice against aliens, himself writes also to Dr Richardson: "there being some apprehension (me being a foreigner) of making natives uneasy if I should publicate it in my name." Lichens were already engaging his attention, and descriptions of 91 species were added to Ray's work. So well did this edition meet the requirements of the age, that the *Synopsis* remained the text-book of British Botany until the publication of Hudson's *Flora Anglica* in 1762.

William Sherard died in 1728. He left his books and plates to the University of Oxford with a sum of money to endow a Professorship of Botany. In his will he had nominated Dr Dillenius for the post. The great German botanist was accordingly appointed and became the first Sherardian Professor of Botany, though he did not remove to Oxford till 1734. The following years were devoted by him to the preparation of *Historia Muscorum*, which was finally published in 1741. It includes an account of the then known liverworts, mosses and lichens. The latter—still considered by Dillenius as belonging to mosses—were grouped under three genera, *Usnea, Coralloides* and *Lichenoides*. The descriptions and figures are excellent, and his notes on occasional lichen characteristics and on localities are full of interest. His lichen herbarium, which still exists at Oxford, mounted with the utmost care and neatness, has been critically examined by Nylander and Crombie[1] and many of the species identified.

Dillenius was ignorant of, or rejected, Micheli's method of classification, adopting instead the form of the thallus as a guide to relationship. He also differed from him in his views as to propagation, regarding the soredia as the pollen of the lichen, and the apothecia as the seed-vessels, or even in certain cases as young plants.

Shortly after the publication of Dillenius' *Historia*, appeared Haller's[2] *Systematic and Descriptive list of plants indigenous to Switzerland.* The lichens are described as without visible leaves or stamens but with "corpuscula" instead of flowers and leaves. He arranged his lichen species, 160 in all, under seven different Orders: 1. "Lichenes Corniculati and Pyxidati"; 2. "L. Coralloidei"; 3. "L. Fruticosi"; 4. "L. Pulmonarii"; 5. "L. Crustacei" (with flower-shields); 6. "L. Scutellis" (with shields but with little or no thallus); and 7. "L. Crustacei" (without shields).

This period extends till near the end of the eighteenth century, and thus includes within its scope the foundation of the binomial system of naming plants established by Linnaeus[3]. The renowned Swedish botanist rather scorned lichens as "rustici pauperrimi," happily translated by Schneider[4] as the "poor trash of vegetation," but he named and listed about 80 species. He divided his solitary genus *Lichen* into sections: 1. "Leprosi tuberculati"; 2. "Leprosi scutellati"; 3. "Imbricati"; 4. "Foliacei";

[1] Crombie 1880.   [2] Haller 1742.   [3] Linnaeus 1753.   [4] Schneider 1897.

5. "Coriacei"; 6. "Scyphiferi"; 7. "Filamentosi." By this ordered sequence Linnaeus showed his appreciation of development, beginning, as he does, with the leprose crustaceous thallus and continuing up to the most highly organized filamentous forms. He and his followers still included the genus *Lichen* among Algae.

A voluminous *History of Plants* had been published in 1751 by Sir John Hill[1], the first superintendent to be appointed to the Royal Gardens, Kew. In the *History* lichens are included under the Class "Mosses," and are divided into several vaguely limited "genera"—*Usnea*, tree mosses, consisting of filaments only; *Platysma*, flat branched tree mosses, such as lungwort; *Cladonia*, the orchil and coralline mosses, such as *Cladonia furcata*; *Pyxidium*, the cup-mosses; and *Placodium*, the crustaceous, friable or gelatinous forms. A number of plants are somewhat obscurely described under each genus. Not only were these new *Lichen* genera suggested by him, but among his plants are such binomials as *Usnea compressa*, *Platysma corniculatum*, *Cladonia furcata* and *Cladonia tophacea*; other lichens are trinomial or are indicated, in the way then customary, by a whole sentence. Hill's studies embraced a wide variety of subjects; he had flashes of insight, but not enough concentration to make an effective application of his ideas. In his *Flora Britannica*[2], which was compiled after the publication of Linnaeus's *Species Plantarum*, he abandoned his own arrangement in favour of the one introduced by Linnaeus and accepted again the single genus *Lichen*.

Sir William Watson[3], a London apothecary and physician of scientific repute at this period, proposed a rearrangement and some alteration of Linnaeus's sections. He had failed to grasp the principle of development, but he gives a good general account of the various groups. Watson was the progenitor of those who decry the makers and multipliers of species. So in regard to Micheli, who had increased the number to "298," he writes: "it is to be regretted, that so indefatigable an author, one whose genius particularly led him to scrutinize the minuter subjects of the science, should have been so solicitous to increase the number of species under all his genera: an error this, which tends to great confusion and embarassment, and must retard the progress and real improvement of the botanic science." Linnaeus however in redressing the balance earned his full approbation: "He has so far retrenched the genus (*Lichen*) that in his general enumeration of plants he recounts only 80 species belonging to it."

Linnaeus's binomial system was almost at once adopted by the whole botanical world and the discovery and tabulation of lichens as well as of other plants proceeded apace. Scopoli's[4] *Flora Carniolica*, for instance, published in 1760, still adhered to the old descriptive method of nomen-

[1] Hill 1751. Hill's genus *Collema* is *Nostoc*, etc.   [2] Hill 1760.   [3] Watson 1759.   [4] Scopoli 1760.

clature, but a second edition, issued twelve years later, is based on the new system: it includes 54 lichen species.

About this time Adanson[1] proposed a new classification of plants, dividing them into families, and these again into sections and genera. He transferred the lichens to the Family "Fungi," and one of his sections contains a number of lichen genera, the names of these being culled from previous workers, Dillenius, Hill, etc. A few new ones are added by himself, and one of them, *Graphis*, still ranks as a good genus.

In England, Hudson[2], who was an apothecary and became sub-librarian of the British Museum, followed Linnaeus both in the first and later editions of the *Flora Anglica*. He records 102 lichen species. Withering[3] was also engaged, about this time, in compiling his *Arrangement of Plants*. He translated Linnaeus's term "Algae" into the English word "Thongs," the lichens being designated as "Cupthongs." In later editions, he simply classifies lichens as such. Lightfoot[4], whose descriptive and economic notes are full of interest, records 103 lichens in the *Flora Scotica*, and Dickson[5] shortly after published a number of species from Scotland, some of them hitherto undescribed. Dickson was a nurseryman who settled in London, and his avocations kept him in touch with plant-lovers and with travellers in many lands.

E. PERIOD IV. 1780–1803

The inevitable next advance was made by Weber[6] who at the time was a Professor at Kiel. In a first work dealing with lichens he had followed Linnaeus; then he published a new method of classification in which the lichens are considered as an independent Order of Cryptogamia, and that Order, called "Aspidoferae," he subdivided into genera. His ideas had been partly anticipated by Hill and by Adanson, but the work of Weber indicates a more correct view of the nature of lichens. He established eight fairly well-marked genera, viz. *Verrucaria*, *Tubercularia*, *Sphaerocephalum* and *Placodium*, which were based on fruit-characters, the thallus being crustaceous and rather insignificant, and a second group *Lichen*, *Collema*, *Cladonia* and *Usnea*, in which the thallus ranked first in importance. Though Weber's scheme was published in 1780, it did not at first secure much attention. The great authority of Linnaeus dominated so strongly the botany of the period that for a long time no change was welcomed or even tolerated.

In our own country Relhan at Cambridge and Sibthorp[7] at Oxford were making extensive studies of plants. The latter was content to follow Linnaeus in his treatment of lichens. Relhan[8] also grouped his lichens under one genus though, in a second edition of his *Flora*, he broke away from the Linnaean tradition and adopted the classification of Acharius.

[1] Adanson 1763.　　　[2] Hudson 1762 and 1778.　　[3] Withering 1776.　　[4] Lightfoot 1777.
[5] Dickson 1785.　　　[6] Weber 1780.　　　　　　[7] Sibthorp 1794.　　[8] Relhan 1785 and 1820.

Extensive contributions to the knowledge of English plants generally were made by Sir James Edward Smith[1] who, in 1788, founded the Linnean Society of London of which he was President until his death in 1828. He began his great work, *English Botany*, in 1790 with James Sowerby as artist. Smith's and Sowerby's part of the work came to an end in 1814; but a supplement was begun in 1831 by Hooker who had the assistance of Sowerby's sons in preparing the drawings. Nearly all the lichens recorded by Smith are published simply as *Lichen*, and his *Botany* thus belongs to the period under discussion, though in time it stretches far beyond.

Continental lichenologists had been more receptive to new ideas, and other genera were gradually added to Weber's list, notably by Hoffmann[2] and Persoon[3].

For a long time little was known of the lichens of other than European countries. Buxbaum[4] in the East, Petiver[5] and Hans Sloane[6] in the West made the first exotic records. The latter notes how frequently lichens grew on the imported Jesuit's bark, and he quaintly suggests in regard to some of these species that they may be identical with the "hyssop that springeth out of the wall." It was not however till towards the end of the eighteenth century that much attention was given to foreign lichens, when Swartz[7] in the West Indies and Desfontaines[8] in N. Africa collected and recorded a fair number. Swartz describes about twenty species collected on his journey through the West Indian Islands (1783–87).

Interest was also growing in other aspects of lichenology. Georgi[9], a Russian Professor, was the first to make a chemical analysis of lichens. He experimented on some of the larger forms and extracted and examined the mucilaginous contents of *Ramalina farinacea*, *Platysma glaucum*, *Lobaria pulmonaria*, etc., which he collected from birch and pine trees. About this time also the French scientists Willomet[10], Amoreux and Hoffmann jointly published theses setting forth the economic value of such lichens as were used in the arts, as food, or as medicine.

F. Period V. 1803–1846

The fine constructive work of Acharius appropriately begins a new era in the history of lichenology. Previous writers had indeed included lichens in their survey of plants, but always as a somewhat side issue. Acharius made them a subject of special study, and by his scientific system of classification raised them to the rank of the other great classes of plants.

Acharius was a country doctor at Wadstena on Lake Mälar in Sweden, as he himself calls it, "the country of lichens." He was attracted to the

[1] Smith 1790. [2] Hoffmann 1798. [3] Persoon 1794. [4] Buxbaum 1728.
[5] Petiver 1712. [6] Sloane 1796 and 1807. [7] Swartz 1788 and 1791. [8] Desfontaines 1798–1800.
[9] Georgi 1797. [10] Willomet, etc. 1787.

study of them by their singular mode of growth and organization, both of thallus and reproductive organs, for which reason he finally judged that lichens should be considered as a distinct Order of Cryptogamia.

In his first tentative work[1] he had followed his great compatriot Linnaeus, classifying all the species known to him under the one genus *Lichen*, though he had progressed so far as to divide the unwieldy Genus into Families and these again into Tribes, these latter having each a tribal designation such as *Verrucaria, Opegrapha*, etc. He established in all twenty-eight tribes which, at a later stage, he transformed into genera after the example of Weber.

Acharius, from the beginning of his work, had allowed great importance to the structure of the apothecia as a diagnostic character though scarcely recognizing them as true fruits. He gave expression to his more mature views first in the *Methodus Lichenum*[2], then subsequently in the larger *Lichenographia Universalia*[3]. In the latter work there are forty-one genera arranged under different divisions; the species are given short and succinct descriptions, with habitat, locality and synonymy. No material alteration was made in the *Synopsis Lichenum*[4], a more condensed work which he published a few years later.

The Cryptogamia are divided by Acharius into six "Families," one of which, "Lichenes," is distinguished, he finds, by two methods of propagation: by propagula (soredia) and by spores produced in apothecia. He divides the family into classes characterized solely by fruit characters, and these again into orders, genera and species, of which diagnoses are given. With fuller knowledge many changes and rearrangements have been found necessary in the application and extension of the system, but that in no way detracts from the value of the work as a whole.

In addition to founding a scientific classification, Acharius invented a terminology for the structures peculiar to lichens. We owe to him the names and descriptions of "thallus," "podetium," "apothecium," "perithecium," "soredium," "cyphella" and "cephalodium," the last word however with a different meaning from the one now given to it. He proposed several others, some of which are redundant or have fallen into disuse, but many of his terms as we see have stood the test of time and have been found of service in allied branches of botany.

Lichens were studied with great zest by the men of that day. Hue[5] recalls a rather startling incident in this connection: Wahlberg, it is said, had informed Dufour that he had sent a large collection of lichens from Spain to Acharius who was so excited on receiving them, that he fell ill and died in a few days (Aug. 14th, 1819). Dufour, however, had added the comment that the illness and death might after all be merely a coincidence.

---

[1] Acharius 1798.   [2] Acharius 1803.   [3] Acharius 1810.   [4] Acharius 1814.   [5] Hue 1908.

Among contemporary botanists, we find that De Candolle[1] in the volume he contributed to Lamarck's *French Flora*, quotes only from the earlier work of Acharius. He had probably not then seen the *Methodus*, as he uses none of the new terms; the lichens of the volume are arranged under genera which are based more or less on the position of the apothecia on the thallus. Flörke[2], the next writer of consequence, frankly accepts the terminology and the new view of classification, though differing on some minor points.

Two lists of lichens, neither of particular note, were published at this time in our country: one by Hugh Davies[3] for Wales, which adheres to the Linnaean system, and the other by Forster[4] of lichens round Tonbridge. Though Forster adopts the genera of Acharius, he includes lichens among algae. A more important publication was S. F. Gray's[5] *Natural Arrangement of British Plants*. Gray, who was a druggist in Walsall and afterwards a lecturer on botany in London, was only nominally[6] the author, as it was mainly the work of his son John Edward Gray[7], sometime Keeper of Zoology in the British Museum. Gray was the first to apply the principles of the Natural System of classification to British plants, but the work was opposed by British botanists of his day. The years following the French Revolution and the Napoleonic wars were full of bitter feeling and of prejudice, and anything emanating, as did the Natural System, from France was rejected as unworthy of consideration.

In the *Natural Arrangement*, Gray followed Acharius in his treatment of lichens; but whereas Acharius, though here and there confusing fungus species with lichens, had been clear-sighted enough to avoid all intermixture of fungus genera, with the exception of one only, the sterile genus *Rhizomorpha*, Gray had allowed the interpolation of several, such as *Hysterium*, *Xylaria*, *Hypoxylon*, etc. He had also raised many of Acharius's subgenera and divisions to the rank of genera, thus largely increasing their number. This oversplitting of well-defined genera has somewhat weakened Gray's work and he has not received from later writers the attention he deserves.

The lichens of Hooker's[8] *Flora Scotica*, which is synchronous with Gray's work, number 195 species, an increase of about 90 for Scotland since the publication of Lightfoot's *Flora* more than 40 years before. Hooker also followed Acharius in his classification of lichens both in the *Flora Scotica* and in the *Supplement to English Botany*[9], which was undertaken by the younger Sowerbys and himself. To that work Borrer (1781–1862), a keen lichenologist, supplied many new and rare lichens collected mostly in Sussex.

It is a matter of regret that Greville should have so entirely ignored lichens in his great work on *Scottish Cryptogams*[10]. The two species of

---

[1] De Candolle 1805. [2] Flörke 1815–1819. [3] Davies 1813. [4] Forster 1816. [5] S. F. Gray 1821.
[6] Carrington 1870. [7] See *List of the Books*, etc. by John Edward Gray, p. 3, 1872.
[8] Hooker 1821. [9] Hooker 1831. [10] Greville 1823–1827.

Lichina are the only ones he figured, and these he took to be algae. He[1] was well acquainted with lichens, for in the *Flora Edinensis* he lists 128 species for the Edinburgh district, arranging the genera under "Lichenes" with the exception of *Opegrapha* and *Verrucaria* which are placed with the fungus genus *Poronia* in "Hypoxyla." Though he cites the publications of Acharius, he does not employ his scientific terms, possibly because he was writing his diagnoses in English. Two other British works of this time still remain to be chronicled: Hooker's[2] contributions to Smith's *English Flora* and Taylor's[3] work on lichens in Mackay's *Flora Hibernica*. Through these the knowledge of the subject was very largely extended in our country.

The classification of lichens and their place in the vegetable kingdom were now firmly established on the lines laid down by Acharius. Fries[4] in his important work *Lichenographia Europaea* more or less followed his distinguished countryman. The uncertainty as to the position and relationship of lichens had rendered the task of systematic arrangement one of peculiar difficulty and had unduly absorbed attention; but now that a satisfactory order had been established in the chaos of forms, the way was clear for other aspects of the study. Several writers expressed their views by suggesting somewhat different methods of classification, others wrote monographs of separate groups, or genera. Fée[5] published an Essay on the Cryptogams (mostly lichens) that grew on officinal exotic barks; Flörke[6] took up the difficult genus *Cladonia*; Wallroth[7] also wrote on *Cladonia*; Delise[8] on *Sticta*, and Chevalier[9] published a long and elaborate account of Graphideae.

Wallroth and Meyer at this time published, simultaneously, important studies on the general morphology and physiology of lichens. Wallroth[10] had contemplated an even larger work on the *Natural History of Lichens*, but only two of the volumes reached publication. In the first of these he devoted much attention to the "gonidia" or "brood-cells" and established the distinction between the heteromerous and homoiomerous distribution of green cells within the thallus; he also describes with great detail the "morphosis" and "metamorphosis" of the vegetative body. In the second volume he discusses their physiology—the contents and products of the thallus, colouring, nutrition, season of development, etc.—and finally the pathology of these organisms. He made no great use of the compound microscope, and his studies were confined to phenomena that could be observed with a single lens.

Meyer's[11] work contains a still more exact study of the anatomy and physiology of lichens; he also devotes many passages to an account of their metamorphoses, pointing out that species alter so much in varying conditions, that the same one at different stages may be placed even in different genera;

[1] Greville 1824.   [2] Hooker 1833.   [3] Taylor 1836.   [4] Fries 1831.   [5] Fée 1824.   [6] Flörke 1828.
[7] Wallroth 1829.   [8] Delise 1822.   [9] Chevalier 1824.   [10] Wallroth 1825.   [11] Meyer 1825.

he however carries his theory of metamorphosis too far and unites together widely separated plants. Meyer was the first to describe the growth of the lichen from spores, though his description is somewhat confused. Possibly the honour of having first observed their germination should be given to a later botanist, Holle[1]. The works of both Wallroth and Meyer enjoyed a great and well-merited reputation : they were standard books of consultation for many years. Koerber[2], who devoted a long treatise to the study of gonidia, confirmed Wallroth's theories: he considered at that time that the gonidia in the soredial condition were organs of propagation.

Mention should be made here of the many able and keen collectors who, in the latter half of the eighteenth century and the beginning of the nineteenth, did so much to further the knowledge of lichens in the British Isles. Among the earliest of these naturalists are Richard Pulteney (1730–1801), whose collection of plants, now in the herbarium of the British Museum, includes many lichens, and Hugh Davies (1739–1821), a clergyman whose Welsh plants also form part of the Museum collection. The Rev. John Harriman (1760–1831) sent many rare plants from Egglestone in Durham to the editors of *English Botany* and among them were not a few lichens. Edward Forster (1765–1849) lived in Essex and collected in that county, more especially in and near Epping Forest, and another East country botanist, Dawson Turner (1775–1858), though chiefly known as an algologist, gave considerable attention to lichens. In Scotland the two most active workers were Charles Lyell (1767–1849), of Kinnordy in Forfarshire, and George Don (1798–1856), also a Forfar man. Don was a gardener and became eventually a foreman at the Chelsea Physic Garden. Sir Thomas Gage of Hengrave Hall (1781–1823) botanized chiefly in his own county of Suffolk ; but most of his lichens were collected in South Ireland and are incorporated in the herbarium of the British Museum. Miss Hutchins also collected in Ireland and sent her plants for inclusion in *English Botany*. But in later years, the principal lichenologist connected with that great undertaking was W. Borrer, who spent his life in Sussex : he not only supplied a large number of specimens to the authors, but he himself discovered and described many new lichens.

American lichenologists were also extremely active all through this period. The comparatively few lichens of Michaux's[3] *Flora* grouped under " Lichenaceae " were collected in such widely separated regions as Carolina and Canada. A few years later Mühlenberg[4] included no fewer than 184 species in his *Catalogue of North American Plants*. Torrey[5] and Halsey[6] botanized over a limited area near New York, and the latter, who devoted himself more especially to lichens, succeeded in recording 176 different forms, old and new. These two botanists were both indebted for help in their work

[1] Holle 1849.   [2] Koerber 1839.   [3] Michaux 1803.
[4] Mühlenberg 1813.   [5] Torrey 1819.   [6] Halsey 1824.

to Schweinitz, a Moravian brother, who moved from one country to another, working and publishing, now in America and now in Europe. His name is however chiefly associated with fungi. Later American lichenology is nobly represented by Tuckerman[1] who issued his first work on lichens in 1839, and who continued for many years to devote himself to the subject. He followed at first the classification and nomenclature that had been adopted by Fée, but as time went on he associated himself with all that was best and most enlightened in the growing science.

Travellers and explorers in those days of high adventure were constantly sending their specimens to European botanists for examination and determination, and the knowledge of exotic lichens as of other classes of plants grew with opportunity. Among the principal home workers in foreign material, at this time, may be cited Fée[2] who described a very large series on officinal barks (*Cinchona*, etc.) so largely coming into use as medicines; he also took charge of the lichens in Martius's[3] *Flora of Brazil*. Montagne[4] named large collections, notably those of Leprieur collected in Guiana, and Hooker[5] and Walker Arnott determined the plants collected during Captain Beechey's voyage, which included lichens from many different regions.

G. PERIOD VI. 1846–1867

The last work of importance, in which microscopic characters were ignored, was the *Enumeratio critica Lichenum Europaeum* by Schaerer[6], a veteran lichenologist, who rather sadly realized at the end the limitations of that work, as he asks the reader to accept it " such as it is." Many years previously, Eschweiler[7] in his *Systema* and Fée[8] in his account of *Cryptogams on Officinal Bark*, had given particular attention to the internal structure as well as to the outward form of the lichen fructification. Fée, more especially, had described and figured a large number of spores; but neither writer had done more than suggest their value as a guide in the determination of genera and species.

It was an Italian botanist, Giuseppe de Notaris[9], a Professor in Florence, who took up the work where Fée had left it. His comparative studies of both vegetative and reproductive organs convinced him of the great importance of spore characters in classification, the spore being, as he rightly decided, the highest and ultimate product of the lichen plant. In his microscopic examination of the various recognized genera, he found that while, in some genera, the spores conformed to one distinct type, in others their diversities in form, septation or colour gave a decisive reason for the establishment of new genera, while minor differences in size, etc. of the spores proved to be of great value in distinguishing species. The spore standard thus marks a new

[1] Tuckerman 1839.   [2] Fée 1824.   [3] Martius 1833.   [4] Montagne 1851.   [5] Hooker 1841.
[6] Schaerer 1850.   [7] Eschweiler 1824.   [8] Fée 1824.   [9] De Notaris 1846.

departure in lichenology. De Notaris published the results of his researches
in a fragment of a projected larger work that was never completed. Though
his views were overlooked for a time, they were at length fully recognized
and further elaborated by Massalongo[1] in Italy, by Norman[2] in Norway, by
Koerber[3] in Germany and by Mudd[4] in our own country. Massalongo had
drawn up the scheme of a great *Scolia Lichenographica*, but like de Notaris,
he was only able to publish a part. After twelve years of ill-health, in which
he struggled to continue his work, he died at the early age of 36.

Lindsay[5], Mudd and Leighton[6] were at this time devoting great attention
to British lichens. Lauder Lindsay's *Popular History of British Lichens*,
with its coloured plates and its descriptive and economic account of these
plants has enabled many to acquire a wide knowledge of the group. Mudd's
Manual, a more complete and extremely valuable contribution to the subject,
followed entirely on the lines of Massalongo's work. From his large
experience in the examination of lichens he came to the conclusion that:
" Of all organs furnished by a given group of plants, none offer so many
real, constant and physiological characters as the spores of lichens, for the
formation of a simple and natural classification."

Meanwhile, a contemporary writer, William Nylander, was rising into
fame. He was born at Uleaborg in Finland[7] in 1822 and became interested
in lichens very early in his career. His first post was the professorship of
botany at Helsingfors; but in 1863 he gave up his chair and removed to
Paris where he remained, except for short absences, until his death. One
of his excursions brought him to London in 1857 to examine Hooker's
herbarium. He devoted his whole life to the study of lichens, and from
1852, the date of his first lichen publication, which is an account of the lichens
of Helsingfors, to the end of his life he poured out a constant succession of
books or papers, most of them in Latin. One of his earliest works was an
Essay on Classification[8] which he elaborated later, but which in its main
features he never altered. He relied, in his system, on the structure and form
of thallus, gonidia and fructifications, more especially on those of the
spermogonia (pycnidia), but he rejected ascospore characters except so far as
they were of use in the diagnosis of species. He failed by being too isolated
and by his unwillingness to recognize results obtained by other workers.
In 1866 he had discovered the staining reactions of potash and hypochlorite
of lime on certain thalli, and though these are at times unreliable owing to
growth conditions, etc., they have generally been of real service. Nylander,
however, never admitted any criticism of his methods; his opinions once
stated were never revised. He rejected absolutely the theory of the dual
nature of lichens propounded by Schwendener without seriously examining

---

[1] Massalongo 1852. [2] Norman 1852. [3] Koerber 1855. [4] Mudd 1861.
[5] Lindsay 1856. [6] Leighton 1851, etc. [7] See Hue 1899. [8] Nylander 1854 and 1855.

the question, and regarded as personal enemies those who dared to differ from him. The last years of his life were passed in complete solitude. He died in March 1899.

Owing to the very inadequate powers of magnification at the service of scientific workers, the study of lichens as of other plants was for long restricted to the collecting, examining and classifying of specimens according to their macroscopic characters; the microscopic details observed were isolated and unreliable except to some extent for spore characters. Special interest is therefore attached to the various schemes of classification, as each new one proposed reflects to a large extent the condition of scientific knowledge of the time, and generally marks an advance. It was the improvement of the microscope from a scientific toy to an instrument of research that opened up new fields of observation and gave a new impetus to the study of a group of plants that had proved a puzzle from the earliest times.

Tulasne was one of the pioneers in microscopic botany. He made a methodical study of a large series of lichens[1] and traced their development, so far as he was able, from the spore onwards. He gave special attention to the form and function of spermogonia and spermatia, and his work is enriched by beautiful figures of microscopic detail. Lauder Lindsay[2] also published an elaborate treatise on spermogonia, on their occurrence in the lichen kingdom and on their form and structure. The paper embodies the results of wide microscopic research and is a mine of information regarding these bodies.

Much interesting work was contributed at this time by Itzigsohn[3], Speerschneider[4], Sachs[5], Thwaites[6], and others. They devoted their researches to some particular aspect of lichen development and their several contributions are discussed elsewhere in this work.

Schwendener[7] followed with a systematic study of the minute anatomy of many of the larger lichen genera. His work is extremely important in itself and still more so as it gradually revealed to him the composite character of the thallus.

Several important monographs date from this period: Leighton[8] reviewed all the British "Angiocarpous" lichens with special reference to their "sporidia" though without treating these as of generic value. He followed up this monograph by two others, on the *Graphideae*[9] and the *Umbilicarieae*[10], and Mudd[11] published a careful study of the *British Cladoniae*. On the Continent Th. Fries[12] issued a revision of *Stereocaulon* and *Pilophoron* and other writers contributed work on smaller groups.

[1] Tulasne 1852.   [2] Lauder Lindsay 1859.   [3] Itzigsohn 1854–1855.   [4] Speerschneider 1853.
[5] Sachs 1855.   [6] Thwaites 1849.   [7] Schwendener 1863–1868.   [8] Leighton 1851.
[9] Leighton 1854.   [10] Leighton 1856.   [11] Mudd 1865.   [12] Th. Fries 1858.

H. Period VII. 1867 and after

Modern lichenology begins with the enunciation of Schwendener's[1] theory of the composite nature of the lichen plant. The puzzling resemblance of certain forms to algae, of others to fungi, had excited the interest of botanists from a very early date, and the similarity between the green cells in the thallus, and certain lower forms of algae had been again and again pointed out. Increasing observation concerning the life-histories of these algae and of the gonidia had eventually piled up so great a number of proofs of their identity that Schwendener's announcement must have seemed to many an inevitable conclusion, though no one before had hazarded the astounding statement that two organisms of independent origin were combined in the lichen.

The dual hypothesis, as it was termed, was not however universally accepted. It was indeed bitterly and scornfully rejected by some of the most prominent lichenologists of the time, including Nylander[2], J. Müller and Crombie[3]. Schwendener held that the lichen was a fungus parasitic on an alga, and his opponents judged, indeed quite rightly, that such a view was wholly inadequate to explain the biology of lichens. It was not till a later date that the truer conception of the "consortium" or "symbiosis" was proposed. The researches undertaken to prove or disprove the new theories come under review in Chapter II.

Stahl's work on the development of the carpogonium in lichens gave a new direction to study, and notable work has been done during the last forty years in that as in other branches of lichenology.

Exploration of old and new fields furnished the lichen-flora of the world with many new plants which have been described by various systematists—by Nylander, Babington, Arnold, Müller, Th. Fries, Stizenberger, Leighton, Crombie and many others, and their contributions are scattered through contemporary scientific journals. The number of recorded species is now somewhere about 40,000, though, in all probability, many of these will be found to be growth forms. Still, at the lowest computation, the number of different species is very large.

Systematic literature has been enriched by a series of important monographs, too numerous to mention here. While treating definite groups, they have helped to elucidate some of the peculiar biological problems of the symbiotic growth.

Morphology, since Schwendener's time, has been well represented by Zukal, Reinke, Lindau, Fünfstück, Darbishire, Hue, and by an increasing number of modern writers whose work is duly acknowledged under each

---

[1] Schwendener 1867.   [2] Nylander 1874.   [3] Crombie 1885.

subject of study. Hesse and Zopf, and more recently Lettau, have been engaged in the examination of those unique products, the lichen acids, while other workers have investigated lichen derivatives such as fats. Ecology of lichens has also been receiving increased attention. Problems of physiology, symbiosis, etc., are not yet considered to be solved and are being attacked from various sides.

British lichenologists since 1867 have been mainly engaged on field work, with the exception of Lauder Lindsay who published after that date a second great paper on the spermogonia of crustaceous lichens. Leighton in his *Lichen Flora* and Crombie in numerous publications gave the lead in systematic work, and with them were associated a band of indefatigable collectors. Among these may be recalled Alexander Croall (1809–85), a parish schoolmaster in Scotland whose *Plants of Braemar* include many of the rarer mountain lichens. Henry Buchanan Holl (1820–86), a surgeon in London, collected in the Scottish Highlands as well as in England and Wales. William Joshua (1828–98) worked mostly in the Western counties of Somerset and Gloucestershire. Charles Du Bois Larbalestier, who died in 1911, was a keen observer and collector during many years; he discovered a number of new species in his native Jersey, in Cambridgeshire and also in Connemara; his plants were generally sent to Nylander to be determined and described. He issued two sets of lichens, one of Channel Island plants, the other of more general British distribution, and he had begun the issue of Cambridgeshire lichens. Isaac Carroll (1828–80), an Irish botanist, issued a first fascicle of *Lichenes Hibernici* containing 40 numbers. More recently Lett[1] has reported 80 species and varieties from the Mourne Mountains in Ireland. Other more extensive sets were issued by Mudd and by Leighton, and later by Crombie and by Johnson. All these have been of great service to the study of lichenology in our country. Other collectors of note are Curnow (Cornwall), Martindale (Westmoreland), and E. M. Holmes whose valuable herbarium has been secured by University College, Nottingham.

The publication of the volume dealing with *Lichenes* in Engler and Prantl's *Pflanzenfamilien* has proved a boon to all who are interested in the study of lichens. Fünfstück[2] prepared the introduction, an admirable presentation of the morphological and physiological aspects of the subject, while Zahlbruckner[3], with equal success, took charge of the section dealing with classification.

---

[1] Lett 1890.   [2] Fünfstück 1898.   [3] Zahlbruckner 1903–1907.

CHAPTER II

CONSTITUENTS OF THE LICHEN THALLUS

I. LICHEN GONIDIA

THE thallus or vegetative bôdy of lichens differs from that of other green plants in the sharp distinction both of form and colour between the assimilative cells and the colourless tissues, and in the relative positions these occupy within the thallus: in the greater number of lichen species the green chlorophyll cells are confined to a narrow zone or band some way beneath and parallel with the surface (Fig. 1); in a minority of genera they are distributed through the entire thallus (Fig. 2); but in all cases the tissues

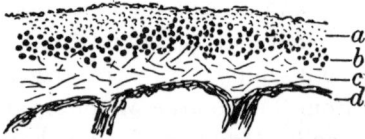

Fig. 1. *Physcia aipolia* Nyl. Vertical section of thallus. *a*, cortex; *b*, algal layer; *c*, medulla; *d*, lower cortex. × 100 (partly diagrammatic).

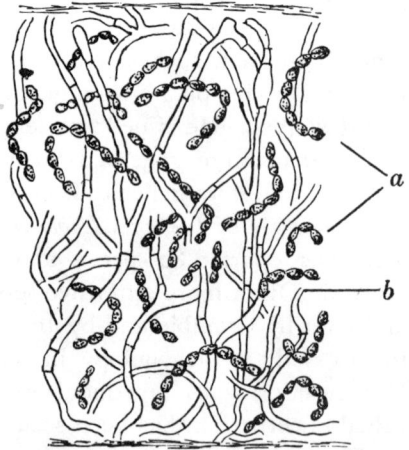

Fig. 2. *Collema nigrescens* Ach. Vertical section of thallus. *a*, chains of the alga *Nostoc*; *b*, fungal filaments. × 600.

remain distinct. The green zone can be easily demonstrated in any of the larger lichens by scaling off the outer surface cells, or by making a vertical section through the thallus. The colourless cells penetrate to some extent among the green cells; they also form the whole of the cortical and medullary tissues.

These two different elements we now know to consist of two distinct organisms, a fungus and an alga. The green algal cells were at one time considered to be reproductive bodies, and were called "gonidia," a term still in use though its significance has changed.

1. GONIDIA IN RELATION TO THE THALLUS

A. Historical account of Lichen Gonidia

There have been few subjects of botanical investigation that have roused so much speculation and such prolonged controversy as the question of these constituents of the lichen plant. The green cells and the colourless filaments which together form the vegetative structure are so markedly dissimilar, that constant attempts have been made to explain the problem of their origin and function, and thereby to establish satisfactorily the relationship of lichens to other members of the Plant Kingdom.

In gelatinous lichens, represented by *Collema*, of which several species are common in damp places and grow on trees or walls or on the ground, the chains of green cells interspersed through the thallus have long been recognized as comparable with the filaments of *Nostoc*, a blue-green gelatinous alga, conspicuous in wet weather in the same localities as those inhabited by *Collema*. So among early systematists, we find Ventenat[1] classifying the few lichens with which he was acquainted under algae and hazarding the statement that a gelatinous lichen such as *Collema* was only a *Nostoc* changed in form. Some years later Cassini[2] in an account of *Nostoc* expressed a somewhat similar view, though with a difference: he suggested that *Nostoc* was but a monstrous form of *Collema*, his argument being that, as the latter bore the fruit, it was the normal and perfect condition of the plant. A few years later Agardh[3] claimed to have observed the metamorphosis of *Nostoc* up to the fertile stage of a lichen, *Collema limosum*. But long before this date, Scopoli[4] had demonstrated a green colouring substance in non-gelatinous lichens by rubbing a crustaceous or leprose thallus between the fingers; and Persoon[5] made use of this green colour characteristic of lichen crusts to differentiate these plants from fungi. Sprengel[6] went a step further in exactly describing the green tissue as forming a definite layer below the upper cortex of foliaceous lichens.

The first clear description and delimitation of the different elements composing the lichen thallus was, however, given by Wallroth[7]. He drew attention to the great similarity between the colourless filaments of the lichen and the hyphae of fungi. The green globose cells in the chlorophyllaceous lichens he interpreted as brood-cells or gonidia, regarding them as organs of reproduction collected into a "stratum gonimon." To the same author we owe the terms "homoiomerous" and "heteromerous," which he coined to describe the arrangement of these green cells in the tissue of the thallus. In the former case the gonidia are distributed equally through the structure; in the latter they are confined to a distinct zone.

[1] Ventenat 1794, p. 36.   [2] Cassini 1817, p. 395.   [3] Agardh 1820.   [4] Scopoli 1760, p. 79.
[5] Persoon 1794, p. 17.   [6] Sprengel 1804, p. 325.   [7] Wallroth 1825, I.

Wallroth's terminology and his views of the function of the gonidia were accepted as the true explanation for many years, the opinion that they were solely reproductive bodies being entirely in accordance with the well-known part played by soredia in the propagation of lichens—and soredia always include one or more green cells.

B. Gonidia contrasted with Algae

In describing the gonidia of the Graphideae Wallroth[1] had pointed out their affinity with the filaments of *Chroolepus* (*Trentepohlia*) *umbrina*. He considered these and other green algae when growing loose on the trunks of trees to be but "unfortunate brood-cells" which had become free and, though capable of growth and increase, were unable to form again a lichen plant.

Further observations on gonidia were made by E. Fries[2]: he found that the green cells escaped from the lichen matrix and produced new individuals; and also that the whole thallus in moist localities might become dissolved into the alga known as *Protococcus viridis*; but, he continues, "though these *Protococcus* cells multiplied exceedingly, they never could rise again to the perfect lichen." Kützing[3], in a later account of *Protococcus viridis*, also recognized its affinity with lichens; he stated that he could testify from observation that, according to the amount of moisture present, it would develop, either in excessive moisture to a filamentous alga, or in drier conditions "to lichens such as *Lecanora subfusca* or *Xanthoria parietina*."

A British botanist, G. H. K. Thwaites[4], at one time superintendent of the botanical garden at Peradeniya in Ceylon, published a notable paper on lichen gonidia in which he pointed out that as in *Collema* the green constituents of the thallus resembled the chains of *Nostoc*, so in the non-gelatinous lichens, the green globose cells were comparable or identical with *Pleurococcus*, and Thwaites further observed that they increased by division within the lichen thallus. He insisted too that in no instance were gonidia reproductive organs: they were essential component parts of the vegetative body and necessary to the life of the plant. In a further paper on *Chroolepus ebeneus* Ag., a plant consisting of slender dark-coloured felted filaments, he described these filaments as being composed of a central strand which closely resembled the alga *Chroolepus*, and of a surrounding sheath of dark-coloured

Fig. 3. *Coenogonium ebeneum* A. L. Sm. Tip of lichen filament, the alga overgrown by dark fungal hyphae × 600.

---

[1] Wallroth 1825, I, p. 303.   [2] Fries 1831, pp. lvi and lvii.
[3] Kützing 1843.   [4] Thwaites 1849, pp. 219 and 241.

cells (Fig. 3): "occasionally," he writes, "the internal filament protrudes beyond the investing sheath, and may then be seen to consist of oblong cells containing the peculiar reddish oily-looking endochrome of *Chroolepus*." Thwaites placed this puzzling plant in a new genus, *Cystocoleus*, at the same time pointing out its affinity with the lichen genus *Coenogonium*. The plant is now known as *Coenogonium ebeneum*. Thwaites was on the threshold of the discovery as to the true nature of the relationship between the central filament and the investing sheath, but he failed to take the next forward step.

Very shortly after, Von Flotow[1] published his views on some other lichen gonidia. He had come to the conclusion that the various species of the alga, *Gloeocapsa*, so frequently found in damp places, among mosses and lichens, were merely growth stages of the gonidia of *Ephebe pubescens*, and bore the same relation to *Ephebe* as did *Lepra viridis* (*Protococcus*) to *Parmelia*. The gonidium of *Ephebe* is the gelatinous filamentous blue-green alga *Stigonema* (Fig. 4), and the separate cells are not unlike those of *Gloeocapsa*. Flotow had also demonstrated that the same type of gonidium was enclosed in the cephalodia of *Stereocaulon*. Sachs[2], too, gave evidence as to the close connection between *Nostoc* and *Collema*. He had observed numerous small clumps of the alga growing in proximity to equally abundant thalli of *Collema*, with every stage of development represented from one to the other. He found cases where the gelatinous coils of *Nostoc* chains were penetrated by fine colourless filaments "as if invaded by a parasitic fungus." Later these threads were seen to be attached

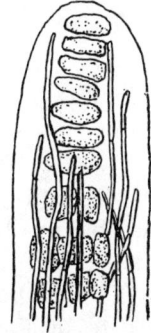

Fig. 4. *Ephebe pubescens* Nyl. Tip of lichen filament × 600.

to some cell of the *Nostoc* trichome. Sachs concluded, however, from very careful examination at the time, that the colourless filaments were produced by the green cells. As growth proceeded, the coloured *Nostoc* chains became massed towards the upper surface, while the colourless filaments tended to occupy the lower part of the thallus. He calculated that during the summer season the metamorphosis from *Nostoc* to a fertile *Collema* thallus took from three to four months. He judged that in favourable conditions the change would inevitably take place, though if there should be too great moisture no *Collema* would be formed. His study of *Cladonia* was less successful as he mistook some colonies of *Gloeocapsa* for a growth condition of *Cladonia* gonidia, an error corrected later by Itzigsohn[3].

But before this date Itzigsohn[4] had published a paper setting forth his views on thallus formation, which marked a distinct advance. He did not

[1] Flotow 1850.   [2] Sachs 1855.   [3] Itzigsohn 1855.   [4] Itzigsohn 1854.

hazard any theory as to the origin of gonidia, but he had observed spermatia growing, much as did the cells of *Oscillaria*: by increase in length, and, by subsequent branching, filaments were formed which surrounded the green cells; these latter had meanwhile multiplied by repeated division till finally a complete thallus was built up, the filamentous tissue being derived from the spermatia, while the green layer came from the original gonidium. In contrasting the development with that of *Collema*, he represents *Nostoc* as a sterile product of a lichen and, like the gonidia of other lichens, only able to form a lichen thallus when it encounters the fructifying spermatia.

Braxton Hicks[1], a London doctor, some time later, made experiments with *Chroococcus* algae which grew in plenty on the bark of trees, and followed their development into a lichen thallus. He further claimed to have observed a *Chlorococcus*, which was associated with a *Cladonia*, divide and form a *Palmella* stage.

C. CULTURE EXPERIMENTS WITH THE LICHEN THALLUS

It had been repeatedly stated that the gonidia might become independent of the thallus, but absolute proof was wanting until Speerschneider[2], who had turned his attention to the subject, made direct culture experiments and was able to follow the liberation of the green cells. He took a thinnish section of the thallus of *Hagenia* (*Physcia*) *ciliaris*, and, by keeping it moist, he was able to observe that the gonidial cells increased by division; the moist condition at the same time caused the colourless filaments to die away. This method of investigation was to lead to further results. It was resorted to by Famintzin and Baranetsky[3] who made cultures of gonidia extracted from three different lichens, *Physcia* (*Xanthoria*) *parietina*, *Evernia furfuracea* and *Cladonia* sp. They were able to observe the growth and division of the green cells and, in addition, the formation of zoospores. They recognized the development as entirely identical with that of the unicellular green alga, *Cystococcus humicola* Naeg. Baranetsky[4] continued the experiments and made cultures of the blue-green gonidia of *Peltigera canina* and of *Collema pulposum*. In both instances he succeeded in isolating them from the thallus and in growing them in moist air as separate organisms. He adds that "many forms reckoned as algae, may be considered as vegetating lichen gonidia such as *Cystococcus, Polycoccus, Nostoc*, etc." Meanwhile Itzigsohn[5] had further demonstrated by similar culture experiments that the gonidia of *Peltigera canina* corresponded with the algae known as *Gloeocapsa monococca* Kütz., and as *Polycoccus punctiformis* Kütz.

---

[1] Hicks 1860 and 1861.   [2] Speerschneider 1853.   [3] Famintzin and Baranetsky 1867.
[4] Baranetsky 1869.   [5] Itzigsohn 1867.

D. Theories as to the Origin of Gonidia

Though the relationship between the gonidia within the thallus and free-living algal organisms seemed to be proved beyond dispute, the manner in which gonidia first originated had not yet been discovered. Bayrhoffer[1] attacked this problem in a study of foliose and other lichens. According to his observations, certain colourless cells or filaments, belonging to the "gonimic" layer, grew in a downward direction and formed at their tips a faintly yellowish-green cell; it gradually enlarged and was at length thrown off as a free globose gonidium, which represented the female cell. Other filaments from the "lower fibrous layer" of the thallus at the same time grew upwards and from them were given off somewhat similar gonidia which functioned as male cells. His observations and deductions were fanciful, but it must be remembered that the attachment between hypha and alga in lichens is in many cases so close as to appear genetic, and also it often happens that as the gonidium multiplies it becomes free from the hypha.

In his *Mémoire sur les Lichens*, Tulasne[2] described the colourless filaments as being fungal in appearance. The green cells he recognized as organs of nutrition, and once and again in his paper he states that they arose directly by a sort of budding process from the medullary or cortical filaments, either laterally or at the apex. This apparently reasonable view of their origin was confirmed by other writers on the subject: by Speerschneider[3] in his account of the anatomy of *Usnea barbata*, by de Bary[4], and by Schwendener[5] in their earlier writings. But even while de Bary accepted the hyphal origin of the gonidia, he noted[6] that, accompanying *Opegrapha atra* and other Graphideae, on the bark were to be found free *Chroolepus* cells similar to the gonidia in the lichen thallus. He added that gonidia of certain other lichens in no way differed from *Protococcus* cells; and as for the gelatinous lichens he declared that "either they were the perfect fruiting form of Nostocaceae and Chroococcaceae—hitherto looked on as algae—or that these same Nostocaceae and Chroococcaceae are algae which take the form of *Collema*, *Ephebe*, etc., when attacked by an ascomycetous fungus."

All these investigators, and other lichenologists such as Nylander[7], still regarded the free-living organisms identified by them as similar to the green cells of the thallus, as only lichen gonidia escaped from the matrix and vegetating in an independent condition.

The old controversy has in recent years been unexpectedly reopened by Elfving[8] who has sought again to prove the genetic origin of the green cells. His method has been to examine a large series of lichens by making sections of the growing areas, and he claims to have observed in every case

---

[1] Bayrhoffer 1851.   [2] Tulasne 1852.   [3] Speerschneider 1854.   [4] de Bary 1866, p. 242.
[5] Schwendener 1860, p. 125.   [6] de Bary 1866, p. 291.   [7] Nylander 1870.   [8] Elfving 1903 and 1913.

the hyphal origin of the gonidia: not only of *Cystococcus* but also of *Trentepohlia*, *Stigonema* and *Nostoc*. In the case of *Cystococcus*, the gonidium, he says, arises by the swelling of the terminal cell of the hypha to a globose form, and by the gradual transformation of the contents to a chlrophyll-green colour, with power of assimilation. In the case of filamentous gonidia such as *Trentepohlia*, the hyphal cells destined to become gonidia are intercalary. In *Peltigera* the cells of the meristematic plectenchyma become transformed to blue-green *Nostoc* cells.

A study was also made by him of the formation of cephalodia[1], the gonidia of which differ from those of the "host" thallus. In *Peltigera aphthosa* he claims to have traced the development of these bodies to the branching and mingling of the external hairs which, in the end, form a ball of interwoven hyphae. The central cells of the ball are then gradually differentiated into *Nostoc* cells, which increase to form the familiar chains. Elfving allows that the gonidia mainly increase by division within the thallus, and that they also may escape and live as free organisms. His views are unsupported by direct culture experiments which are the real proof of the composite nature of the thallus.

E. MICROGONIDIA

Another attempt to establish a genetic origin for lichen gonidia was made by Minks[2]. He had found in his examination of *Leptogium myochroum* that the protoplasmic contents of the hyphae broke up into a regular series of globular corpuscles which had a greenish appearance. These minute bodies, called by him microgonidia, were, he states, at first few in number, but gradually they increased and were eventually set free by the mucilaginous degeneration of the cell wall. As free thalline gonidia, they increased in size and rapidly multiplied by division. Minks was at first enthusiastically supported by Müller[3] who had found from his own observations that microgonidia might be present in any of the lichen hyphae and in any part of the thallus, even in the germinating tube of the lichen spore, and was in that case most easily seen when the spores germinated within the ascus. He argued that as spores originated within the ascus, so microgonidia were developed within the hyphae. Minks's theories were however not generally accepted and were at last wholly discredited by Zukal[4] who was able to prove that the greenish bodies were contracted portions of protoplasm in hyphae that suffered from a lowered supply of moisture, the green colour not being due to any colouring substance, but to light effect on the proteins—an outcome of special conditions in the vegetative life of the plant. Darbishire[5] criticized Minks's whole work with great care and he has arrived at the conclusion that the microgonidium may be dismissed as a totally mistaken conception.

[1] See p. 133.   [2] Minks 1878 and 1879.   [3] Müller 1878 and 1884.   [4] Zukal 1884.   [5] Darbishire 1895[1].

F. Composite Nature of Thallus

Schwendener[1] meanwhile was engaged on his study of lichen anatomy. Though at first he adhered to the then accepted view of the genetic connection between hyphae and gonidia, his continued examination of the vegetative development led him to publish a short paper[2] in which he announced his opinion that the various blue-green and green gonidia were really algae and that the complete lichen in all cases represented a fungus living parasitically on an alga: in *Ephebe*, for example, the alga was a form of *Stigonema*, in the Collemaceae it was a species of *Nostoc*. In those lichens enclosing bright green cells, the gonidia were identical with *Cystococcus humicola*, while in *Graphideae* the brightly coloured filamentous cells were those of *Chroolepus* (*Trentepohlia*). This statement he repeated in an appendix to the larger work on lichens[3] and again in the following year[4] when he described more fully the different gonidial algae and the changes produced in their structure and habit by the action of the parasite: "though eventually the alga is destroyed," he writes, "it is at first excited to more vigorous growth by contact with the fungus, and in the course of generations may become changed beyond recognition both in size and form." In support of his theory of the composite constitution of the thallus, Schwendener pointed out the wide distribution and frequent occurrence in nature of the algae that become transformed to lichen gonidia. He claimed as further proof of the presence of two distinct organisms that, while the colourless filaments react in the same way as fungi on the application of iodine, the gonidia take the stain of algal membranes.

G. Synthetic Cultures

Schwendener's "dual hypothesis," as it was termed, excited great interest and no little controversy, the reasons for and against being debated with considerable heat. Rees[5] was the first who attempted to put the matter to the proof by making synthetic cultures. For this purpose he took spores from the apothecium of a *Collema* and sowed them on pure cultures of *Nostoc*, and as a result obtained the formation of a lichen thallus, though he did not succeed in producing any fructification. He observed further that the hyphal filaments from the germinating spore died off when no *Nostoc* was forthcoming.

Bornet[6] followed with his record of successful cultures. He selected for experiment the spores of *Physcia* (*Xanthoria*) *parietina* and was able to show that hyphae produced from the germinating spore adhered to the free-

---

[1] Schwendener 1860, etc.   [2] Schwendener 1867.   [3] Schwendener 1868, p. 195.

[4] Schwendener 1869.   [5] Rees 1871.   [6] Bornet 1872.

growing cells of *Protococcus*[1] *viridis* and formed the early stages of a lichen thallus. Woronin[2] contributed his observations on the gonidia of *Parmelia* (*Physcia*) *pulverulenta* which he isolated from the thallus and cultivated in pure water. He confirmed the occurrence of cell division in the gonidia and also the formation of zoospores, these again forming new colonies of algae identical in all respects with the thalline gonidia. He was able to see the germinating tube from a lichen spore attach itself to a gonidium, though he failed in his attempts to induce further growth. In our own country Archer[3] welcomed the new views on lichens, and attempted cultures but with very little success. Further synthetic cultures were made by Bornet[4], Treub[5] and Borzi[6] with a series of lichen spores. They also were able to observe the first stages of the thallus. Borzi observed spores of *Physcia* (*Xanthoria*) *parietina* scattered among *Protococcus* cells on the branch of a tree. The spores had germinated and the first branching hyphae had already begun to encircle the algae.

Additional evidence in favour of the theory of the independent origin of the colourless filaments and the green cells was furnished by Stahl's[7] research on hymenial gonidia in *Endocarpon* (Fig. 5). .By making synthetic

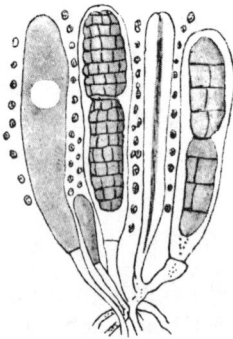

Fig. 5. *Endocarpon pusillum* Hedw. Asci and spores, with hymenial gonidia × 320 (after Stahl).

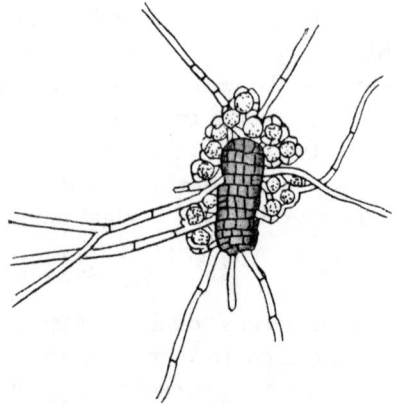

Fig. 6. *Endocarpon pusillum* Hedw. Spore germinating in contact with hymenial gonidia × 320 (after Stahl).

[1] The authors quoted have been followed in their designation of the various green algae that form lichen gonidia. It is however now recognized (Wille 1913) that either *Protococcus viridis* Ag., *Chlorella* or other Protococcaceae may form the universal green coating on trees, etc., and be incorporated as lichen gonidia. *Fleurococcus vulgaris* Naeg. and *Pleurococcus Naegeli* Chod. are synonyms of *Protococcus viridis*. In that alga there is no pyrenoid, and no zoospores are formed.

The genus *Cystococcus*, according to Chodat (1913), is characterized by the presence of a pyrenoid and by reproduction with zoospores and is identical with *Pleurococcus vulgaris* Menegh. (non Naeg.), though Wille regards Meneghini's species as of mixed content. Paulson and Hastings (1920) now find that Chodat's pyrenoid is the nucleus of the cell.

[2] Woronin 1872.   [3] Archer 1873, 1874, 1875.   [4] Bornet 1873 and 1874.
[5] Treub 1873.   [6] Borzi 1875.   [7] Stahl 1877.

cultures of the mature spores with these bodies, he was able to observe not only the germination of the spores and the attachment of the filaments to the gonidia (Fig. 6), but also the gradual building up of a complete lichen thallus to the formation of perithecia and spores.

Some years later Bonnier[1] made an interesting series of synthetic cultures between the spores of lichens germinated in carefully sterilized conditions, and algae taken from the open (Figs. 7 and 8). Separate control cultures of

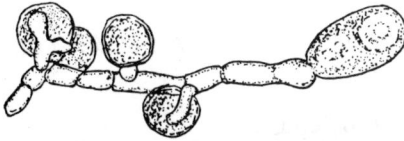

Fig. 7. Germination of spore of *Physcia parietina* De Not. in contact with *Protococcus viridis* Ag. × 950 (after Bornet).

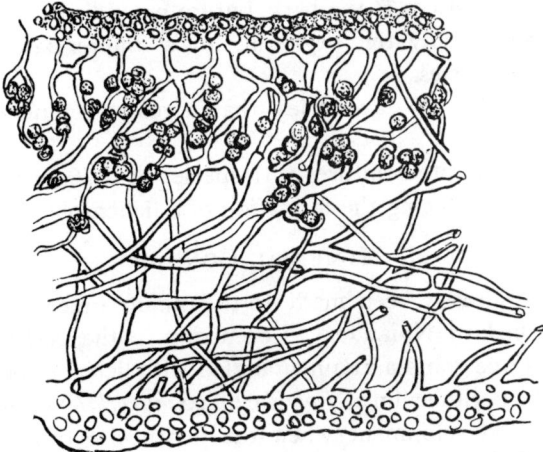

Fig. 8. *Physcia parietina* De Not. Vertical section of thallus obtained by synthetic culture × 130 (after Bonnier).

spores and algae were carried on at the same time, with the result that in one case lichen hyphae alone, in the other algae were produced. The various lichen spores with which he experimented were sown in association with the following algae:

(1) PROTOCOCCUS.

Pure synthetic cultures of *Physcia* (*Xanthoria*) *parietina* were begun in August 1884 on fragments of bark. In October 1886 the thallus was several centimetres in diameter, and some of the lobes were fruited.

Physcia stellaris was also grown on bark; in one case both thallus and apothecia were developed.

1 Bonnier 1886 and 1889.

Parmelia acetabulum, another corticolous species, formed only a minute thallus about 5 mm. in diameter, but entirely identical with normally growing specimens.

(2) PLEUROCOCCUS.

Lecanora (Rinodina) sophodes, sown on rock in 1883, reached in 1886 a diameter of 13 mm. with fully developed apothecia.

Lecanora ferruginea and *L. subfusca* after three years' culture formed sterile thalli only.

Lecanora coilocarpa in four years, and *L. caesio-rufa* in three years formed very small thalli without fructification.

(3) TRENTEPOHLIA (Chroolepus).

Opegrapha vulgata in two years had developed thallus and apothecia. The control culture of the spores formed, as in nature, a considerable felt of mycelium in the interstices of the bark, but no pycnidia or apothecia.

Graphis elegans. Only the beginning of a differentiated thallus was obtained with this species.

Verrucaria muralis (?)[1] gave in less than a year a completely developed thallus.

Bonnier also attempted cultures with species of *Collema* and *Ephebe,* but was unsuccessful in inducing the formation of a lichen plant.

H. HYMENIAL GONIDIA

Reference has already been made to the minute green cells which were originally described by Nylander[2] as occurring in the perithecia of a few Pyrenolichens as free gonidia, *i.e.* unentangled with lichen hyphae. Fuisting[3] found them in the perithecium of *Polyblastia (Staurothele) catalepta* at a very early stage of its development when the perithecial tissues were newly differentiated from those of the surrounding thallus. The gonidia enclosed in the perithecium differed in no wise from those of the thallus: they had become mechanically enclosed in the new tissue; and while those in the outer compact layers died off, those in the centre of the structure, where a hollow space arises, were subject to very active division, becoming smaller in the process and finally filling the cavity. Winter's[4] researches on similar lichens confirmed Fuisting's conclusions: he described them as similar to the thalline gonidia but lighter in colour and of smaller size, measuring frequently only 2·3 μ in diameter, though this size increased to about 7 μ when cultivated outside the perithecium.

Stahl[5] sufficiently demonstrated the importance of these gonidia in

---

[1] Bonnier was probably experimenting with an *Arthopyrenia*. *Verrucaria* species combine with *Protococcus* or according to Chodat with *Coccobotrys* gen. nov.

[2] Nylander 1858.   [3] Fuisting 1868, p. 674.   [4] Winter 1876, p. 264.   [5] Stahl 1877.

supplying the germinating spores with the necessary algae. They come to lie in vertical rows between the asci and, owing to pressure, assume an elongate form[1] (Figs. 5 and 6). They have been seen in very few lichens, in *Endocarpon* and *Staurothele*, both rather small genera of Pyrenolichens, and, so far as is known, in two Discolichens, *Lecidea phylliscocarpa* and *L. phyllocaris*, the latter recorded from Brazil by Wainio[2], and. on account of the inclusion of gonidia in the hymenium, placed by him in a section, *Gonothecium*.

I. NATURE OF ASSOCIATION BETWEEN ALGA AND FUNGUS

a. CONSORTIUM AND SYMBIOSIS. These cultures had established convincingly the composite nature of the lichen thallus, and Schwendener's opinion, that the relationship between the two organisms was some varying degree of parasitism, was at first unhesitatingly accepted by most botanists. Reinke[3] was the first to point out the insufficiency of this view to explain the long continued healthy life of both constituents, a condition so different from all known instances of the disturbing or fatal parasitism of one individual on another. He recognized in the association a state of mutual growth and interdependence, that had resulted in the production of an entirely new type of plant, and he suggested *Consortium* as a truer description of the connection between the fungus and the alga. This term had originally been coined by his friend Grisebach in a paper[3] describing the presence of actively growing *Nostoc* algae in healthy *Gunnera* stems; and Reinke compared that apparently harmless association with the similar phenomenon in the lichen thallus. The comparison was emphasized by him in a later paper[4] on the same subject, in which he ascribes to each "consort" its function in the composite plant, and declares that if such a mutual life of Alga and Ascomycete is to be regarded as one of parasitism, it must be considered as reciprocal parasitism; and he insists that "much more appropriate for this form of organic life is the conception and title of *Consortium*." In a special work on lichens, Reinke[5] further elaborated his theory of the physiological activity and mutual service of the two organisms forming the consortium.

Frank[6] suggested the term *Homobium* as appropriate, but it is faulty inasmuch as it expresses a relationship of complete interdependence, and it has been proved that the fungus partly, and the alga entirely, have the power of free growth.

A wider currency was given to this view of a mutually advantageous growth by de Bary[7]. He followed Reinke in refusing to accept as satisfactory the theory of simple parasitism, and adduced the evident healthy life of the algal cells—-the alleged victims of the fungus—as incompatible with the

---

[1] See p. 62.   [2] Wainio 1890, 2, p. 29.   [3] Reinke 1872, p. 108.
[4] Reinke 1873[1].   [5] Reinke 1873[2], p. 98.   [6] Frank 1876.   [7] de Bary 1879.

parasitic condition. He proposed the happily descriptive designation of a *Symbiosis* or conjoint life which was mostly though not always, nor in equal degree, beneficial to each of the partners or symbionts.

b. DIFFERENT FORMS OF ASSOCIATION. The type of association between the two symbionts varies in different lichens. Bornet[1], in describing the development of the thallus in certain members of the Collemaceae, found that though as a rule the two elements of the thallus, as in some species of *Collema* itself, persisted intact side by side, there was in other members of the genus an occasional parasitism: short branches from the main hyphae applied themselves by their tips to some cell of the *Nostoc* chain (Fig. 9). The cell thus seized upon began to increase in size, and the

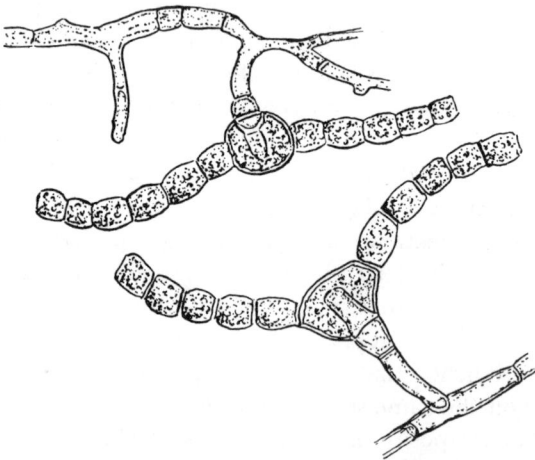

Fig. 9. *Physma chalazanum* Arn. Cells of *Nostoc* chains penetrated and enlarged by hyphae × 950 (after Bornet).

plasma became granular and gathered at the side furthest away from the point of attachment. Finally the contents were used up, and nothing was left but an empty membrane adhering to the fungus hypha. In another species the hypha penetrated the cell. These instances of parasitism are most readily seen towards the edge of the thallus where growth is more active; towards the centre the attached cells have become absorbed, and only the shortened broken chains attest their disappearance. The other cells of the chains remain uninjured.

In *Synalissa*, a small shrubby gelatinous genus, the hypha, as described by Bornet and by Hedlund[2], pierces the outer wall of the gelatinous alga (*Gloeocapsa*) and swells inside to a somewhat globose haustorium which rests in a depression of the plasma (Fig. 10). The alga, though evidently

---

[1] Bornet 1873.   [2] Hedlund 1892.

undamaged, is excited to a division which takes place on a plane that passes through the haustorium; the two daughter-cells then separate, and in so doing free themselves from the hypha.

Hedlund followed the process of association between the two organisms in the lichens *Micarea* (*Biatorina*) *prasina* and *M. denigrata* (*Biatorina synothea*), crustaceous species which inhabit trunks of trees or palings. In these the alga, one of the Chlorophyceae, has assumed the character of a *Gloeocapsa* but on cultivation it was found to belong to the genus *Gloeocystis*. The cells are globose and rather small; they increase by the division of the contents into two or at most four portions which become rounded off and covered with a membrane before they become free from the mother-cell. The lichen hypha, on contact with any one of the green cells, bores through the outer membrane and swells within to a haustorium, as in the gonidia of *Synalissa*.

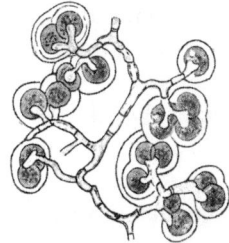

Fig. 10. *Synalissa symphorea* Nyl. Algae (*Gloeocapsa*) with hyphae from the internal thallus × 480 (after Bornet).

Penetrating haustoria were demonstrated by Peirce[1] in his study of the gonidia of *Ramalina reticulata*. In the first stage the tip of a hypha had pierced the outer wall of the alga, causing the protoplasm to contract away from the point of contact (Fig. 11). More advanced stages showed the extension of the haustorium into the centre of the cell, and, finally, the

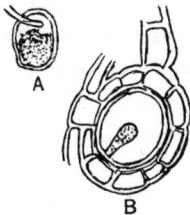

Fig. 11. Gonidia from *Ramalina reticulata* Nyl. A, gonidium pierced and cell contents shrinking × 560; B, older stage, the contents of gonidium exhausted × 900 (after Peirce).

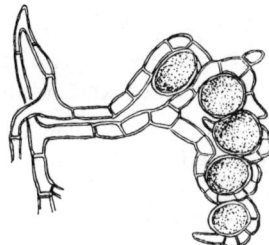

Fig. 12. *Pertusaria globulifera* Nyl. Fungus and gonidia from gonidial zone × 500 (after Darbishire).

complete disappearance of the contents. In many cases it was found that penetration equally with clasping of the alga by the filament sets up an irritation which induces cell-division, and the alga, as in *Synalissa*, thus becomes free from the fungus. Hue[2] has recorded instances of penetration in an Antarctic species, *Physcia puncticulata*. It is easy, he says, to see the tips of the hyphae pierce the sheath of the gonidium and penetrate to the nucleus.

[1] Peirce 1899.   [2] Hue 1915.

Lindau[1] has described the association between fungus and alga in *Pertusaria* and other crustaceous forms as one of contact only (Fig. 12). He found that the cell-membrane of the two adhering organisms was unbroken. Occasionally the algal cell showed a slight indentation, but was otherwise unchanged. The hyphal branch was somewhat swollen at the tip where it touched the alga, and the wall was slightly thinner. The attachment between the two cells was so close, however, that pressure on the cover-glass failed to separate them.

Generally the hypha simply surrounds the gonidium with clasping branches. Many algae also lie free in the gonidial zone, and Peirce[2] claims that these are larger, more deeply coloured and in every way healthier looking than those in the grasp of the fungus. He ignores, however, the case of the soredial algae which though very closely invested by the fungus are yet entirely healthy, since on their future increase depends in many cases the reproduction of new individual lichens.

In a recent study of a crustaceous sandstone lichen, "*Caloplaca pyracea*," Claassen[3] has sought to prove a case of pure parasitism. The rock was at first covered with the green cells of *Cystococcus* sp. Later there appeared greyish-white patches on the green, representing the invasion of the lichen fungus. These patches increased centrifugally, leaving in time a bare patch in the centre of growth which was again colonized by the green alga. The lichen fruited abundantly, but wherever it encroached the green cells were more or less destroyed. The true explanation seems to be that the green cells were absorbed into the lichen thallus, though enough of them persisted to start new colonies on any bare piece of the stone. In the same way large patches of *Trentepohlia aurea* have been observed to be gradually invaded by the dark coloured hyphae of *Coenogonium ebeneum*. In time the whole of the alga is absorbed and nothing is to be seen but the dark felted lichen. The free alga as such disappears, but it is hardly correct to describe the process as one of destruction.

This algal genus *Trentepohlia* (*Chroolepus*) forms the gonidia of the Graphideae, Roccelleae, etc. It is a filamentous aerial alga which increases by apical growth. In the Graphideae, many of which grow on trees beneath the outer bark (hypophloeodal), the association between the two symbionts may be of the simplest character, but was considered by Frank[4] to be of an advanced type. According to his observations and to those of Lindau[5], the fungal hyphae penetrate first between the cells of the periderm. The alga, frequently *Trentepohlia umbrina*, tends to grow down into any cracks of the surface. It goes more deeply in when preceded by the hyphae. In some species both organisms maintain their independent growth, though each shows increased vigour when it comes into contact with the other. In some

[1] Lindau 1895[1].   [2] Peirce 1899.   [3] Claassen 1914.   [4] Frank 1876.   [5] Lindau 1895.

instances the cells of the alga are clasped by the fungus which causes the disintegration of the filament. The cells lose their bright yellow or reddish colour and are changed in appearance to greenish lichen gonidia; but no penetration by haustoria has ever been observed in *Trentepohlia*.

Bachmann's[1] study of a similar gonidium in a calcicolous species of *Opegrapha* confirms Frank's results. The algae had pierced not only between the looser lime granules but also through a crystal of calcium carbonate, and occupied nests scooped out in the rock by means of acid formed and excreted by their filaments. When association took place with the fungus, the algal cells were more restricted to a gonidial zone; but some of the cells, having been pushed aside by the hyphae, had started new centres of gonidia. On contact with the hyphae there was a tendency to bud out in a yeast-like growth.

In the thallus of the Roccelleae, the algal filament, also a *Trentepohlia*, is broken up into separate cells, but in the Coenogoniaceae, whether the gonidium be a *Cladophora* as in *Racodium*, or a *Trentepohlia* as in *Coenogonium*, the filaments remain intact and are invested more or less closely by the hyphae.

A somewhat different type of association takes place between alga and fungus in *Strigula complanata*, an epiphyllous lichen more or less common in tropical regions. Cunningham[2], who found it near Calcutta, described the algal constituent and placed it in a new genus, *Mycoidea* (*Cephaleuros*). It forms small plate-like expansions on the surface of the leaf, and also penetrates below the cuticle, burrowing between that and the epidermal cells; occasionally, as observed by Cunningham, rhizoid-like growths pierce deeper into the tissue—into and below the epidermal layer. Very frequently, in the wet season, a fungus takes possession of the alga and slender colourless hyphae creep along its surface by the side of the cell rows, sending out branches which grow downwards. Marshall Ward[3] described the same lichen from Ceylon. He states that the alga may be attacked at any stage, and if it is in a very young condition it is killed by the fungus; at a more advanced period of growth it continues to develop as an integral part of

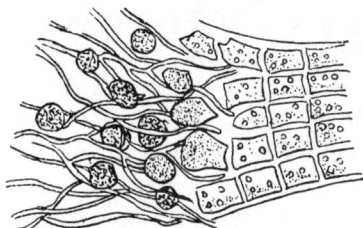

Fig. 13. Outer edge of *Phycopeltis expansa* Jenn., the alga attacked by hyphae and passing into separate gonidia × 500 (after Vaughan Jennings).

the lichen thallus, but with more frequently divided and smaller cells. Vaughan Jennings[4] observed *Strigula complanata* in New Zealand associated with a closely allied chroolepoid alga *Phycopeltis expansa*. He also noted the growth of the fungus over the alga breaking up the plates of tissue and

[1] Bachmann 1913.   [2] Cunningham 1879.   [3] Ward 1884.   [4] Jennings 1895.

separating the cells which, from yellow, change to a green colour and become rounded off (Fig. 13). The mature lichen, a white thallus dotted with black fruits, contrasts strikingly with the yellow membranous alga. Lichen formation usually begins near the edge of the leaf and the margin of the thallus itself is marked by a green zone showing where the fungus has recently come into contact with the alga.

More recently Hans Fitting[1] has described "*Mycoidea parasitica*" as it occurs on evergreen leaves in Java. The alga, a species of *Cephaleuros*, though at first an epiphyte, becomes partially parasitic at maturity. It penetrates below the cuticle to the outer epidermal cells and may even reach the tissue below. When it is joined by the lichen fungus, both constituents grow together to form the lichen. Fitting adds that the leaf is evidently but little injured. In this lichen the alga in the grip of the fungus loses its independence and may be killed off: it is an instance of something like intermittent parasitism.

J. Recent views on Symbiosis and Parasitism

No hyphal penetration of the bright-green algal cell by means of haustoria had been observed by the earlier workers, Bornet[2], Bonnier[3] and others, though they followed Schwendener[4] in regarding the relationship as one of host and parasite. Lindau, also, after long study accepted parasitism as the only adequate explanation of the associated growth, though he never found the fungus actually preying on the alga.

In recent years interest in the subject has been revived by the researches of Elenkin[5], a Russian botanist who claims to have established a case for parasitism or rather "endosaprophytism." He has demonstrated by means of staining reagents the presence in the thallus of large numbers of dead algal cells. A few empty membranes are to be found in the cortex and in the gonidial zone, but the larger proportion occur below the gonidial zone and partly in the medulla. He describes the lower layer as a "necral" or "hyponecral" zone, and he considers that the hyphae draw their nourishment chiefly from dead algal material. The fungus must therefore be regarded in this case as a saprophyte rather than a parasite. The algae, he considers, may have perished from want of sufficient light and air or they may have been destroyed by an enzyme produced by the fungus. The latter he thinks is the more probable, as dead cells are frequently present among the living algae of the gonidial zone. To the action of the enzyme he also attributes the angular deformed appearance of many gonidia and the paler colour and gradual disintegration of their contents which are finally used up as endosaprophytic nourishment by the fungus. Dead algal cells were more easily

---

[1] Fitting 1910.   [2] Bornet 1873.   [3] Bonnier 1889[2].   [4] Schwendener 1867.
[5] Elenkin 1902[1] and 1904[1], 1904[2].

seen, he tells us, in crustaceous lichens associated with "*Pleurococcus*" or "*Cystococcus*"; they were much less frequent in the larger foliose or fruticose lichens. Dead cells of *Trentepohlia* were also difficult to find.

In a second paper Elenkin records one clear instance of a haustorium entering an algal cell, and says he found some evidence of hyphal branches penetrating otherwise uninjured gonidia, round holes being visible in their outer wall, but he holds that it is the cell-wall of the alga that is mainly dissolved by the ferment and then used as food by the hyphae.

No allowance has been made by Elenkin for the normal wasting common to all organic beings: the lichen fungus is continually being renewed, especially in the cortical structures, and the alga must also be subject to change. He[1] claims, nevertheless, that his observations have proved that the one symbiont is always preying on the other, either as a parasite or as a saprophyte. He has likened the conception of symbiosis to that of a balance between two organisms, "a moveable equilibrium of the symbionts." If, he says, we could conceive a state where the conditions of life would be equally favourable for both partners there would be true mutualism, but in practice one only is favoured and gains the upper hand, using its advantage to prey on the other. Unless the balance is redressed, the complete destruction of the weaker is certain, and is followed in time by the death of the stronger. The fungus being the dominant partner, the balance, he considers, is tipped in its favour.

Elenkin's conclusions are not borne out by the long continued and healthy life of the lichen. There is no record of either symbiont having succumbed to the other, and the alga, when set free, is unchanged and able to resume its normal development. Without the alga the fungus cannot form the ascigerous fruit. Is that because as a parasite within the lichen it has degenerated past recovery, or has it become so adapted to symbiosis that in saprophytic conditions it fails to develop?

Another Russian lichenologist, U. N. Danilov[2], records results which would seem to support the theory of parasitism. He found that from the clasping hyphae minute haustoria were produced, which penetrate the algal cell-wall, and branch when within the outer membrane, thus forming a delicate network over the plasma; secondary haustoria arising from this network protrude into the interior and rob the cell-contents. He observed gonidia filled with well-developed hyphae and these, after having exhausted one cell, travel onwards to others. Some gonidia under the influence of the fungus had become deformed and were finally killed. As a proof of this latter statement he adduces the presence in the thallus of some gonidia containing shrivelled protoplasm, of others entirely empty. He considers, as further evidence in favour of parasitism, the finding of empty membranes as

[1] Elenkin 1906[2].   [2] Danilov 1910.

well as of colourless gonidia filled with the hyphal network. This description hardly tallies with the usual healthy appearance of the gonidial zone in the normal thallus, and it has been suggested that where the fungus filled the algal cell, it was as a saprophyte preying on dead material.

The gradual perishing of algal cells in time by natural decay and their subsequent absorption by the fungus is undisputed. It is open to question whether the varying results recorded by these workers have any further significance.

These observations of Elenkin and Danilov have been proved to be erroneous by Paulson and Somerville Hastings[1]. They examined the thalli of several lichens (*Xanthoria parietina, Cladonia* sp., etc.) collected in early spring when vegetative growth in these plants was found to be at its highest activity. They found an abundant increase of gonidia within the thallus, which they regarded as sporulation of the algae, and the most careful methods of staining failed to reveal any case of penetration of the gonidia by the hyphae.

Nienburg[2] has published some recent observations on the association of the symbionts. In the wide cortex of a *Pertusaria* he found not only the densely compact hyphae, but also isolated gonidia. In front of these latter there was a small hollow cavity and, behind, parallel hyphae rich in contents. These gonidia had originated from the normal gonidial zone. They were moved upward by special hyphae called by Nienburg "push-hyphae." After their transportation, the algae at once divide and the products of division pass to a resting stage and become the centre of a new thalline growth. A somewhat similar process was noted towards the apex of *Evernia furfuracea*. Radial hyphae pushed up the cortex, leaving a hollow space over the gonidial zone. Into the space isolated algae were thrust by "push-hyphae." In this lichen he also observed the penetration of the algal cell by haustoria of the fungus. He considers that the alga reaps advantage but also suffers harm, and he proposes the term *helotism* to express the relationship.

An instructive case of the true parasitism of a fungus on an alga has been described by Zukal[3] in the case of *Endomyces scytonemata* which he calls a "half-lichen." The mature fungus formed small swellings on the filaments of the *Scytonema* and, when examined, the hyphae were seen to have attacked the alga, penetrating the outer gelatinous sheath and then using up the contents of the green cells. It is only after the alga has been destroyed and absorbed, that asci are formed by the fungus. Zukal contrasts the development of this fungus with the symbiotic growth of the two constituents in *Ephebe* where both grow together for an indefinite time.

Mere associated growth however even between a fungus and an alga does not constitute a lichen. An instance of such growth is described by

[1] Paulson and Hastings 1920.   [2] Nienburg 1917.   [3] Zukal 1891.

Sutherland[1] in an account of marine microfungi. One of these, a species of *Mycosphaerella*, was found on *Pelvetia canaliculata*, and Sutherland claims that as no apparent injury was done to the alga, it was a case of symbiosis and that there was formed a new type of lichen. The mycelium, always intercellular, pervaded the whole host-plant, and the fungal fruits were invariably formed on the algal receptacles close to the oogonia. Their position there is, of course, due to the greater food supply at that region. Both fungus and alga fruited freely. A closer analogy could have been found by the writer in the smut fungus which grows with the host-cereal until fruiting time; or with the mycorrhiza of *Calluna* which also pervades every part of the host-plant without causing any injury. In the true lichen, the alga, though constituting an important part of the vegetative body, takes no part in reproduction, except by division and increase of the vegetative cells within the thallus. The fruiting bodies are always of a modified fungal nature.

2. PHYSIOLOGY OF THE SYMBIONTS

The occurrence of isolated cases of parasitism—the fungus preying on the alga—in any case leaves the general problem unsolved. The whole question turns on the physiological activity and requirements of the two component elements of the thallus. From what sources do they each procure the materials essential to them as living organisms? It is chiefly a question of nutrition.

A. NUTRITION OF ALGAE

a. CHARACTER OF ALGAL CELLS. Gonidia are chlorophyll-containing bodies and assimilate carbon-dioxide from the atmosphere by photo-synthesis as do the chlorophyll cells of other plants. They also require water and mineral salts which, in a free condition, they absorb from their immediate surroundings, but which, in the lichen thallus, they must obtain from the fungal hyphae. If the nutriment supplied to them in their inclosed position be greater or even equal to what the cells could procure as free-living algae, then they undoubtedly gain rather than lose by their association with the fungus, and are not to be considered merely as victims of parasitism.

b. SUPPLY OF NITROGEN. Important contributions on the subject of algal nutrition have been made by Beyerinck[2] and Artari[3]. The former conducted a series of culture experiments with green algae, including the gonidia of *Physcia* (*Xanthoria*) *parietina*. He successfully isolated the lichen gonidia and, at first, attempted to grow them on gelatine with an infusion of the Elm bark from which he had taken the lichen. Growth was

---

[1] Sutherland 1915.   [2] Beyerinck 1890.   [3] Artari 1902.

very slow and very feeble until he added to the culture-medium a solution of malt-extract which contains peptones and sugar. Very soon he obtained an active development of the gonidia, and they multiplied rapidly by division[1] as in the lichen thallus. This proved to him conclusively the great advantage to the algae of an abundant supply of nitrogen.

Artari in his work has demonstrated that there are two different physiological races of green algae: (1) those that absorb peptones—which he designates peptone-algae—and (2) those that do not so absorb peptones. He tested the cells of *Cystococcus humicola* taken from the thallus of *Physcia parietina*, and found that they belonged to the peptone group and were therefore dependent on a sufficiency of nitrogenous material to attain their normal vigorous growth. It was also discovered by Artari that the one race can be made by cultivation to pass over to the other: that ordinary algae can be educated to live on peptones, and peptone-algae to do without.

We learn further from Beyerinck's researches that Ascomycetes, the group of fungi from which the hyphae of most lichens are derived, are what he terms ammonia-sugar fungi; that is to say, the hyphae can abstract nitrogen from ammonia salts and, with the addition of sugar, can form peptones. The lichen peptone-algae are thus evidently, by their contact with such fungi, in a favourable position for securing the nitrogenous food supply most suited to their requirements. In their deep-seated layers, they are to a large extent deprived of light, but it has been proved by Artari[2] in a series of culture experiments extending over a long period, that the gonidia of *Xanthoria parietina* remain green in the dark under very varied conditions of nutriment, though the colour is distinctly fainter.

Recently Treboux[3] has revised the work done by Artari and Beyerinck in reference to *Cystococcus humicola*. He denies that two physiological races are represented in this alga, the lichen gonidia, in regard to the nitrogen that they absorb, behaving exactly as do the free-living forms of the species. He finds that the gonidium is not a peptone-carbohydrate organism in the sense that it requires nitrogen in the form of peptones, inorganic ammonia salts being a more acceptable food supply. Treboux concludes that his results favour the view that the gonidia are in an unfavourable situation for receiving the kind of nitrogenous compound most advantageous to them, that they are therefore in a sense "victims" of parasitism, though he qualifies the condition as being a lichen-parasitism or helotism. This view does not accord with Chodat's[4] results: in his cultures of gonidia he observed that with glycocoll or peptone, which are nearly equivalent, they developed four times better than with potassium nitrate as their nitrogenous food, and he concluded that they assimilated nitrogen better from bodies allied to peptides.

[1] See p. 56.   [2] Artari 1902.   [3] Treboux 1912.   [4] Chodat 1913.

c. EFFECT OF SYMBIOSIS ON THE ALGA. Treboux's observations how-ever convinced him that the alga leads but a meagre existence within the thallus. Cell-division—the expression of active vitality—was, he held, of rare occurrence in the slowly growing lichen-plant, and zoospore formation in entire abeyance. He contrasts this sluggish increase[1] with the rapid multi-plication of the free-living algal cells which cover whole tree-trunks with their descendants in a comparatively short time. These latter cells, he finds, are indeed rather smaller, being generally the products of recent division, but mixed with them are numbers of larger resting cells, com-parable in size with the lichen gonidia. He states further, that the gonidia are less brightly green and, as he judges, less healthy, though in soredial formation or in the open they at once regain both colour and power of division. Treboux had entirely failed to observe the sporulation which is so abundant at certain seasons.

Their quick recovery seems also a strong argument in favour of the absolutely normal condition of metabolism within the gonidial cell; and the paler appearance of the chlorophyll is doubtless associated with the acquisition of carbohydrates from other sources than by photosynthesis. There is a wide difference between any degree of unfavourable life-conditions and parasitism however slight, even though the balance of gain is on the side of the fungus. It is not too fanciful to conclude that the demand for nitrogen on the part of the alga has influenced its peculiar association with the fungus. In the thallus of hypophloeodal lichens it has been proved indeed that the alga *Trentepohlia* with apical growth is an active agent in the symbiotic union. *Cystococcus* and other green algal cells are stationary, but they are doubtless equally ready for—as many of them are equally benefited by—the association. Keeble[2] has pointed out in the case of *Convoluta roscoffensis* that nitrogen-hunger induces the green algae to combine forces with an animal organism, though the benefit to them is only temporary and though they are finally sacrificed. The lichen gonidia, on the contrary, persist for a long time, probably far beyond their normal period of existence as free algae.

Examples of algal association with other plants might be cited here: of *Nostoc* in the roots of *Cycas* and in the cells of *Anthoceros*, and of *Anabæna* in the leaf-cells of *Azolla*, but in these instances it is generally held that the alga secures only shelter. It was by comparing the lichen-association with the harmless invasion of *Gunnera* cells by *Nostoc* that Reinke[3] arrived at his conception of "consortism."

d. SUPPLY OF CARBON. Carbon, the essential constituent of all organic life, is partly drawn from the carbon-dioxide of the air, and assimilated by

---

[1] See Paulson and Hastings 1920.   [2] Keeble 1910.   [3] Reinke 1872.

the green cells; it is also partly contributed by the fungus as a product of its metabolism. A proof of this is afforded by Dufrenoy[1]: he found a *Parmelia* growing closely round pine needles and even sending suckers into the stomata. He covered the lichen with a black cloth and after seven weeks found that the gonidia had remained very green. That growth had not been checked was evidenced by an unusual development of soredia and of spermogonia. Dufrenoy describes the condition as a parasitism of the algae on the fungus which in turn was drawing nourishment from the pine needles.

Artari[2] has proved that lichen gonidia can obtain carbohydrates from the substratum as well as by photosynthesis. He cultivated the gonidia of *Xanthoria parietina* and *Placodium murorum* on media which contained organic substances as well as mineral salts, while depriving them of atmospheric carbon-dioxide and in some cases of light also. The gonidia not only grew well but, even in the dark, they remained normally green, a phenomenon coinciding with Etard and Bouilhac's[3] experience in growing *Nostoc* in the dark: with suitable culture media the alga retained its colour. *Nostoc* also grows in the dark in the rhizome of *Gunnera*. Radais'[4] experiments with *Chlorella vulgaris* confirmed these results. On certain organic media growth and cell-division were as rapid in the dark as in the light, and chlorophyll was formed. The colour was at first yellowish and the full green arrived slowly, especially on sugar media, but in ten days it was uniform and normal.

When making further experiments with the alga, *Stichococcus bacillaris*, Artari[5] found that it also grew well on an organic medium and that grape sugar was the most valuable carbonaceous food supply. Chodat[6] also found that sugar or glucose was a desirable ingredient of culture media.

Treboux[7], in his work on organic acids, has also proved by experimental cultures with a large series of algae, including the gonidia of *Peltigera*, that these green plants in the absence of light and in pure cultures would grow and form carbohydrates if the culture medium contained a small percentage of organic acids. The acids he employed were combined with potassium and were thus rendered neutral or slightly alkaline; acetate of potash proved to be the most advantageous compound of any that was tested. Amino-acids and ammonia salts were added to provide the necessary nitrogen. Oxalic acid and other organic acids of varying composition are peculiarly abundant in lichen tissues and may be a source of carbon supply. Marshall Ward[8] has found calcium carbonate crystals in the lower air-containing tissues of *Strigula complanata*.

Treboux finally concluded from his researches that just as fungi can

[1] Dufrenoy 1918.   [2] Artari 1899.   [3] Etard and Bouilhac 1898.   [4] Radais 1900.
[5] Artari 1901.   [6] Chodat 1913.   [7] Treboux 1905.   [8] Marshall Ward 1884.

extract carbohydrates from many sources, so algae can secure their carbon supply in a variety of ways. He affirms that the metabolic activity of the alga in these cultural conditions is entirely normal, and the various cell-contents are formed as in the light. Whether, in this case, starch is formed directly from the acids or through a series of combinations has not been determined. Uhlir[1], with electric lighting, made successful cultures of *Nostoc* isolated from Collemaceae on silicic acid, proving thereby that these gonidia do not require a rich nutriment. A certain definite humidity was however essential, and bacteria were never eliminated as they are associated with the gelatinous membranes of Nostocaceae.

e. NUTRITION WITHIN THE SYMBIOTIC PLANT. Culture experiments bearing more directly on the nutrition of lichens as a whole were carried out by F. Tobler[2]. He proved that the gonidia had undoubtedly drawn on the calcium oxalate secreted by the hyphae for their supply of carbon. In a culture medium of poplar-bark gelatine he grew hyphae of *Xanthoria parietina*, and noted an abundant deposit of oxalate crystals on their cell-walls. A piece of the lichen thallus including both symbionts and grown on a similar medium formed no crystals, and microscopic examination showed that crystals were likewise absent from the hyphae of the thallus that had grown normally on the tree, the inference being that the gonidia used them up as quickly as they were deposited. It must be remembered in this connection, however, that Zopf[3] has stated that where lichen acids are freely formed as, for instance, in *Xanthoria parietina*, there is always less formation and deposit of calcium oxalate crystals, which may partly account for their absence in the normal thallus so rich in parietin.

Tobler next introduced lichen gonidia into a culture medium in which the isolated hyphal constituent of a thallus had been previously cultivated, and placed the culture in the dark. In these circumstances he found that the gonidia were able to thrive but formed no colour: they were obtaining their carbohydrates, he decided, not from photosynthesis, but from the excretory products such as calcium oxalate that had been deposited in the culture medium by the lichen hyphae. We may conclude with more or less certainty that the loss of carbohydrates, due to the partial deprivation of light and air suffered by the alga owing to its position in the lichen thallus, is more than compensated by a physiological symbiosis with the fungus[4]. It has indeed been proved that in the absence of free carbon-dioxide, algae may utilize the half-bound CO_2 of carbonates, chiefly those of calcium and magnesium, dissolved in water.

f. AFFINITIES OF LICHEN GONIDIA. Chodat[5] has, in recent years, made cultures of lichen gonidia with a view to discovering their relation to

---

[1] Uhlir 1915.   [2] Tobler 1911.   [3] Zopf 1907.   [4] Chambers 1912.   [5] Chodat 1913.

free-living algae and to testing at the same time their source of carbon supply. He has come to the conclusion that lichen gonidia are probably in no instance the normal *Protococcus viridis*: they differ from that alga in the possession of a pyrenoid and in their reproduction by zoospores when free.

Careful cultures were made of different *Cladonia* gonidia which were morphologically indistinguishable, and which varied in size from 10 to 16 μ in diameter, though smaller ones were always present. He recognized them to be species of *Cystococcus*: they have a pyrenoid[1] in the centre and a disc-like chromatophore more or less starred at the edge. These gonidia grew well on agar, still better on agar-glucose, but best of all with an addition of peptone to the culture. There was invariably at first a slight difference in form and colour in the mass between the gonidia of one species and those of another, but as growth continued they became alike.

In testing for carbon supply, he found that gonidia grew slowly without sugar (glucose), and that, as sources of carbon, organic acids could not entirely replace glucose though, in the dark, the gonidia used them to some extent; the colony supplied with potassium nitrate, and grown in the dark, had reached a diameter of only 2 mm. in three months. With glucose, it measured 5 mm. in three weeks, while in three months it formed large culture patches.

A further experiment was made to test their absorption of peptones by artificial cultures carried out both in the light and the dark. The gonidia grew poorly in all combinations of organic nitrogen compounds. When combined with glucose, growth was at once more vigorous though only half as much in the dark as in the light, the difference in this respect being especially noticeable in the gonidia from *Cladonia pyxidata*. He concludes that as gonidia in these cultures are saprophytic, so in the lichen thallus also they are probably more or less saprophytic, obtaining not only their nitrogen in organic form but also, when possible, their carbon material as glucose or galactose from the hyphal symbiont which in turn is saprophytic on humus, etc.

B. Nutrition of Fungi

Fungi being without chlorophyll are always indebted to other organisms for their supply of carbohydrates. There has never therefore been any question as to the advantage accruing to the hyphal constituent in the composite thallus. The gonidia, as various workers have proved, have also a marked preference for organized nourishment, and, in addition, they obtain carbon by photosynthesis. Chodat[2] considers that probably they are thus able to assimilate carbon-dioxide in excess, a distinct advantage to the hyphae. In some instances the living gonidium is invaded and the contents

---

[1] See note Paulson and Hastings, p. 28.   [2] Chodat 1913.

used up by the fungus and any dead gonidia are likewise utilized for food supply. It is also taken for granted that the fungus takes advantage of the presence of humus whether in the substratum or in aerial dust. In such slow growing organisms, there is not any large demand for nourishment on the part of the hyphae: for many lichens it seems to be mere subsistence with a minimum of growth from year to year.

C. SYMBIOSIS OF OTHER PLANTS

The conception of an advantageous symbiosis of fungi with other plants has become familiar to us in Orchids and in the mycorhizal formation on the roots of trees, shrubs, etc. Fungal hyphae are also frequent inhabitants of the rhizoids of hepatics though, according to Gargeaune[1], the benefit to the hepatic host-plant is doubtful.

An association of fungus and green plant of great interest and bearing directly on the question of mutual advantage has been described by Servettaz[2]. In his study of mosses, he was able to confirm Bonnier's[3] account of lichen hyphae growing over such plants as *Vaucheria* and the protonema of mosses, which is undoubtedly hurtful; but he also found an association of a moss with one of the lower fungi, *Streptothrix* or *Oospora*, which was distinctly advantageous. In separate cultivation the fungus developed compact masses and grew well in peptone agar broth.

Cultures of the moss, *Phascum cuspidatum*, were also made from the spores on a glucose medium. The specimens in association with the fungus were fully grown in two months, while the control cultures, without any admixture of the fungus, had not developed beyond the protonema stage. Servettaz draws attention to the proved fact that, in certain instances, plants benefit when provided with substances similar to their own decay products, and he considers that the fungus, in addition to its normal gaseous products, has elaborated such substances, as acid products, from the glucose medium to the great advantage of the moss plant.

A symbiotic association of *Nostoc* with another alga, described by Wettstein[4], is also of interest. The blue-green cells were lodged in the pyriform outgrowths of the siphoneous alga, *Botrydium pyriforme* Kütz., which the author of the paper places in a new genus, *Geosiphon*. The sheltering *Nostoc symbioticum* fills all of the host left vacant by the plasma, and when the season of decay sets in, it forms resting spores which migrate into the rhizoids of the host, so that both plants regenerate together.

Wettstein has compared this symbiotic association with that of lichens, and finds the analogy all the more striking in that the membrane of his new alga had become chitinous, which he thinks may be due to organic nutrition.

---

[1] Gargeaune 1911.   [2] Servettaz 1913.   [3] See p. 65.   [4] Wettstein 1915.

II. LICHEN HYPHAE

A. Origin of Hyphae

Lichen hyphae form the ground tissue of the thallus apart from the gonidia or algal cells. They are septate branched filaments of single cell rows and are colourless or may be tinged by pigments or lichen acids to some shade of yellow, brown or black. They are of fungal nature, and are produced by the mature lichen spore.

The germination of the spore was probably first observed by Meyer[1]. His account of the actual process is somewhat vague, and he misinterpreted the subsequent development into thallus and fruit entirely for want of the necessary magnification; but that he did succeed in germinating the spores is unquestionable. He cultivated them on a smooth surface and they grew into a "dendritic formation"—a true hypothallus. Many years later the development of hyphae from lichen spores was observed by Holle[2] who saw and figured the process unmistakably in *Borrera* (*Physcia*) *ciliaris*.

A series of spore cultures was undertaken by Tulasne[3] with the twofold object of discovering the exact origin of hyphae and gonidia and of their relationship to each other. The results of his classical experiment with the spores of *Verrucaria muralis*—as interpreted by him—were accepted by the lichenologists of that time as conclusive evidence of the genetic origin of the gonidia within the thallus.

The spores of the lichen in large numbers had been sown by Tulasne in early spring on the smooth polished surface of a piece of limestone, and

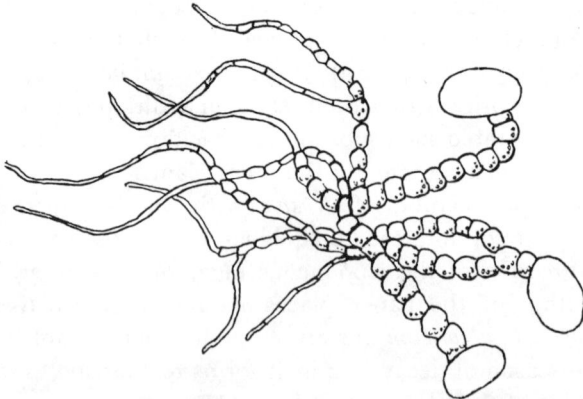

Fig. 14. Germinating spores of *Verrucaria muralis* Ach. after two months' culture × ca. 500 (after Tulasne).

were covered with a watch-glass to protect them from dust, etc. At irregular intervals they were moistened with water, and from time to time

[1] Meyer 1825.   [2] Holle 1849.   [3] Tulasne 1852.

a few spores were abstracted from the culture and examined microscopically. Tulasne observed that the spore did not increase or change in volume in the process of germination, but that gradually the contents passed out into the growing hyphae, till finally a thin membrane only was left and still persisted after two months (Fig. 14). For a considerable time there was no septation; at length cross-divisions were formed, at first close to the spore, and then later in the branches. The hyphae meanwhile increased in dimension, the cells becoming rounder and somewhat wider, though always more slender than the spore which had given rise to them. In time a felted tissue was formed with here and there certain cells, filled with green colouring matter, similar to the gonidia of the lichen and thus the early stages at least of a new thallus were observed. The green cells, we now know, must have gained entrance to the culture from the air, or they may have been introduced with the water.

B. Development of lichenoid Hyphae

Lichen hyphae are usually thick-walled, thus differing from those of fungi generally, in which the membranes, as a rule, remain comparatively thin. This character was adduced by the so-called "autonomous" school as a proof of the fundamental distinction between the hyphal elements of the two groups of plants. It can, however, easily be observed that, in the early stages of germination, the lichen hyphae, as they issue from the spore, are thin-walled and exactly comparable with those of fungi. Growth is apical, and septation and branching arise exactly as in fungi, and, in certain circumstances, anastomosis takes place between converging filaments. But if algae are present in the culture the peculiar lichen characteristics very soon appear.

Bonnier[1], who made a large series of synthetic cultures, distinguishes three types of growth in lichenoid hyphae (Fig. 15):

1. Clasping filaments, repeatedly branched, which attach and surround the algae.

2. Filaments with rather short swollen cells which ultimately form the hyphal tissues of cortex and medulla.

3. Searching filaments which elongate towards the periphery and go to the encounter of new algae.

In five days after germination of the spores, the clasping hyphae had laid hold of the algae which meanwhile had increased by division; the swollen cells had begun to branch out and ten days later a differentiation of tissue was already apparent. The searching filaments had increased in number and length, and anastomosis between them had taken place when

[1] Bonnier 1889[2].

no further algae were encountered. The cell-walls of the swollen hyphae and their branches had begun to thicken and to become united to form a kind of cellular tissue or "paraplectenchyma[1]." At a later date, about a month

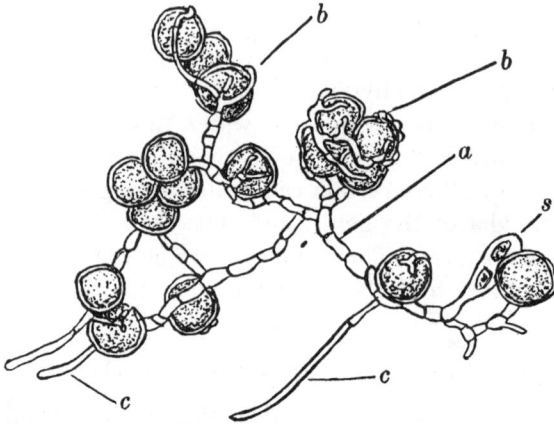

Fig. 15. Synthetic culture of *Physcia parietina* spores and *Protococcus viridis* five days after germination. *s*, lichen-spore; *a*, septate filaments; *b*, clasping filaments; *c*, searching filaments. × 500 (after Bonnier).

after the sowing of the spores, there was a definite cellular cortex formed over the thallus. The hyphal cells are uninucleate, though in the medulla they may be 1–2-nucleate.

The hyphae in close contact with the gonidia remain thin-walled, and have been termed by Wainio[2] "meristematic." They furnish the growing elements of the lichen either apical or intercalary. In most genera the organs of fructification take rise from them, or in their immediate neighbourhood, and isidia and soredia also originate from these gonidial hyphae.

As the filaments pass from the gonidial zone to other layers, the cell-walls become thicker with a consequent reduction of the cell-lumen, very noticeable in the pith, but carried to its furthest extent in the "decomposed" cortex where the cells in the degenerate tissue often become reduced to disconnected streaks indicating the cell-lumen, and the outer cortical layer is merely a continuous mass of mucilage.

All lichen tissues arise from the branching and septation of the hyphae, the septa always forming at right angles to the long axis of the filaments. There is no instance of longitudinal cell-division except in the spores of certain genera (*Collema, Urceolaria, Polyblastia*, etc.). The branching of the hypha is dichotomous or lateral, and very irregular. Frequent septation and coherent growth result in the formation of plectenchyma.

---

[1] Term coined by Lindau (1899) to describe the pseudo-cellular tissue of lichens and fungi now referred to as "plectenchyma."   [2] Wainio 1897.

C. Culture of Hyphae without Gonidia

Artificial cultures had demonstrated the germination of lichen spores, with the formation of hyphae, and from synthetic cultures of fungus and alga complete lichen plants had been produced. To Möller[1] we owe the first cultures of a thalline body from the fungus alone, both from spermatia and from ascospores. The germination of the spermatia has a direct bearing on their function as spores or as sexual organs and is described in a later chapter.

The ascospores of *Lecanora subfusca* were caught in a drop of water on a slide as they were ejaculated from the ascus, and, on the following day, a very fine germinating tube was seen to have pierced the exospore. The hypha became slightly thicker, and branching began on the third day. If in water alone the culture soon died off, but in a nutrient solution growth slowly continued. The hyphae branched out in all directions from the spore as a centre and formed an orbicular expansion which in fourteen days had reached a size of ·1 mm. in diameter. After three weeks' growth it was large enough to be visible without a lens; the mycelial threads were more crowded, and certain terminal hyphae had branched upwards in an aerial tuft, this development taking place from the centre outwards. Möller marked this stage as the transition from a mere protothallus to a thallus formation. In three months a diameter of 1·5–2 mm. was reached; a transverse section gave a thickness of ·86 mm. and from the under side loose hyphae branched downwards and attached the thallus, when it had been transferred to a solid substratum such as cork. Above these rhizoidal hyphae, a stratum of rather loose mycelium represented the medulla, and, surmounting that, a cortical layer in which the hyphae were very closely compacted. Delicate terminal branches rose into the air over the whole surface, very similar in character to hypothallic hyphae at the margin of the thallus.

Lecanora subfusca has a rather small simple spore; it emitted germinating tubes from each end, and a septum across the middle of the spore appeared after germination had taken place. Another experiment was with a much larger muriform spore measuring 80 μ in length and 20 μ in thickness. On germination about 20 tubes were formed, some of them rising into the air at once, the others encircling the spore, so that the thallus took form immediately; growth in this case also was centrifugal. In three months a diameter of 6 mm. was reached with a thickness of 1 to 2 mm. and showing a differentiation into medulla and cortex. The hyphae did not increase in width, but frequently globose or ovate swellings arose in or at the ends, a character which recurs in the natural growth of hyphae both of lichens and of Ascomycetes. These swellings depend on the nutrition.

[1] Möller 1887.

Pertusaria communis possesses a very large simple spore, but it is multi-nucleate and germinates with about 100 tubes which reach their ultimate width of 3 to 4 μ before they emerge from the exospore. The hyphae encircle the spore, and an opaque thalline growth is quickly formed from which rise terminal hyphal branches. In ten weeks the differentiation into medulla and cortex was reached, and in five months the hyphal thallus measured 4 mm. in diameter and 1 to 2 mm. in thickness.

Möller instituted a comparison between the thalli he obtained from the spores and those from the spermatia of another crustaceous lichen, *Buellia punctiformis* (*B. myriocarpa*). After germination had taken place the hyphae from the spermatia grew at first more quickly than those from the ascospores, but as soon as thallus formation began the latter caught up and, in eight weeks, both thalli were of equal size.

Another comparative culture with the spermatia and ascospores of *Opegrapha subsiderella* gave similar results: the spores of that species are elongate-fusiform and 6- to 8-septate; germination took place from the end cells in two to three days after sowing. The germinating hyphae corresponded exactly with those from the spermatia and growth was equally slow in both. The middle cells of the spores may also produce germinating tubes, but never more than about five were observed from any one spore. A browning of the cortical layer was especially apparent in the hyphal culture from another lichen, *Graphis scripta*: a clear brown colour gradually changing to black appeared about the same period in all the cultures.

The hyphae from the spores of *Arthonia* developed quickest of all: the hyphae were very slender, but in three to four months the growth had reached a diameter of 8 mm. In this plant there was the usual outgrowth of delicate hyphae from the surface; no definite cortical layer appeared, but only a very narrow line of more closely interwoven somewhat darker hyphae. Frequently, from the surface of the original thallus, excrescences arose which were the beginnings of further thalli.

Tobler[1] experimenting with *Xanthoria parietina* gained very similar results. The spores were grown in malt extract for ten days, then transferred to gelatine. In three to five weeks there was formed an orbicular mycelial felt about 3 mm. in diameter and 2 mm. thick. The mycelium was frequently brownish even in healthy cultures, but the aerial hyphae which, at first, rose above the surface were always colourless. After these latter disappeared a distinct brownish tinge of the thallus was visible. In seven months it had increased in size to 15 mm. in length, 7 mm. in width and 3 mm. thick with a differentiation into three layers: a lower rather dense tissue representing the pith, above that a layer of loose hyphae where the gonidial zone would

---

[1] Tobler 1909.

normally find place, and above that a second compact tissue, or outer cortex, from which arose the aerial hyphae. The culture could not be prolonged more than eight months.

D. Continuity of Protoplasm in Hyphal Cells

Wahrlich[1] demonstrated that continuity of protoplasm was as constant between the cells of fungi as it has been proved to be between the cells of the higher plants. His researches included the hyphae of the lichens, *Cladonia fimbriata* and *Physcia (Xanthoria) parietina*.

Baur[2] and Darbishire[3] found independently that an open connection existed between the cells of the carpogonial structures in the lichens they examined. The subject as regards the thalline hyphae was again taken up by Kienitz-Gerloff[4] who obtained his best results in the hypothecial tissue of *Peltigera canina* and *P. polydactyla*. Most of the cross septa showed one central protoplasmic strand traversing the wall from cell to cell, but in some instances there were as many as four to six pits in the walls. The thickening of the cell-walls is uneven and projects variously into the cavity of the cell. Meyer's[5] work was equally conclusive: all the cells of an individual hypha, he found, are in protoplasmic connection; and in plectenchymatous tissue the side walls are frequently perforated. Cell-fusions due to anastomosis are frequent in lichen hyphae, and the wall at or near the point of fusion is also traversed by a thread of protoplasm, though such connections are regarded as adventitious. Fusions with plasma connections are numerous in the matted hairs on the upper surface of *Peltigera canina* and they also occur between the hyphae forming the rhizoids of that lichen. The work of Salter[6] may also be noted. He claimed that his researches tended to show complete anatomical union between all the tissues of the lichen plant, not only between the hyphae of the various tissues but also between hyphae and gonidia.

III. LICHEN ALGAE

A. Types of Algae

The algal constituents of the lichen thallus belong to the two classes, Myxophyceae, generally termed blue-green algae, and Chlorophyceae which are coloured bright-green or yellow-green. Most of them are land forms, and, in a free condition, they inhabit moist or shady situations, tree-trunks, walls, etc. They multiply by division or by sporulation within the thallus; zoospores are never formed except in open cultivation. The determination of the genera and species to which the lichen algae severally belong is often uncertain, but their distribution within the lichen kingdom is as follows:

---

[1] Wahrlich 1893.   [2] Baur 1898.   [3] Darbishire 1899.
[4] Kienitz-Gerloff 1902.   [5] Meyer 1902.   [6] Salter 1902.

a. MYXOPHYCEAE ASSOCIATED WITH PHYCOLICHENS. The blue-green algae are characterized by the colour of their pigments which persists in the gonidial condition giving various tints to the component lichens, and by the gelatinous sheath in which most of them are enclosed. This sheath, both in the lichen gonidia[1] and in free-living forms, imbibes and retains moisture to a remarkable extent and the thallus containing blue-green algae profits by its power of storing moisture. Myxophyceae form the gonidia of the gelatinous lichens as well as of some other non-gelatinous genera. Several families are represented[2]:

Fam. CHROOCOCCACEAE. This family includes unicellular algae with thick gelatinous sheaths. They increase normally by division, and colonies arise by the cohesion of the cells. Several genera form gonidia:

1. CHROOCOCCUS Naeg. Solitary or forming small colonies of 2–4–8 cells (Fig. 16) generally surrounded by firm gelatinous colourless sheaths in definite layers (lamellate). *Chroococcus* is considered by some lichenologists to form the gonidium of *Cora*, a genus of Hymenolichens.

2. MICROCYSTIS Kütz. Globose or subglobose cells forming large colonies surrounded by a common gelatinous layer (gonidia of *Coriscium*).

3. GLOEOCAPSA Kütz. (including *Xanthocapsa*). Globose cells with a

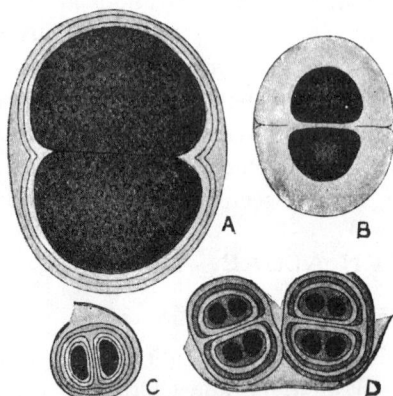

Fig. 17. *Gloeocapsa magma* Kütz. × 450 (after West).

Fig. 16. Examples of *Chroococcus*. A, *Ch. giganteus* West; B, *Ch. turgidus* Naeg.; C and D, *Ch. schizo-dermaticus* West × 450 (after West).

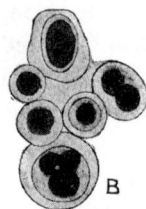

lamellate gelatinous wall, forming colonies enclosed in a common sheath (Fig. 17); the inner integument is often coloured red or orange. These

[1] Nylander (1866) gave the term "gonimia" to the blue-green algae of the Phycolichens, retaining the term "gonidia" for the bright-green algae of the Archilichens: the distinction is not now maintained.

[2] For further details see also the chapter on Classification.

two genera form the gonidia in the family Pyrenopsidaceae. *Gloeocapsa polydermatica* Kütz. has been identified as a lichen gonidium.

Fam. NOSTOCACEAE. Filamentous algae unbranched and without base or apex.

NOSTOC Vauch. Composed of flexuous trichomes, with intercalary heterocysts (colourless cells) (Fig. 18). Dense gelatinous colonies of definite

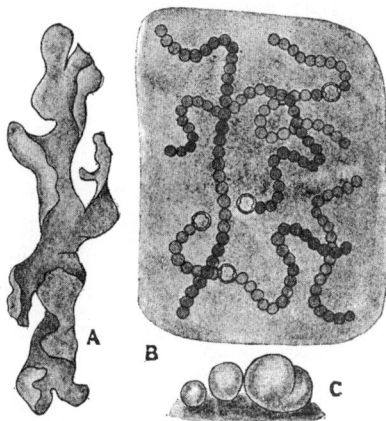

Fig. 18. Examples of *Nostoc*. *N. Linckia* Born. A, nat. size; B, small portion × 340; C, *N. coerulescens* Lyngbye, nat. size (after West).

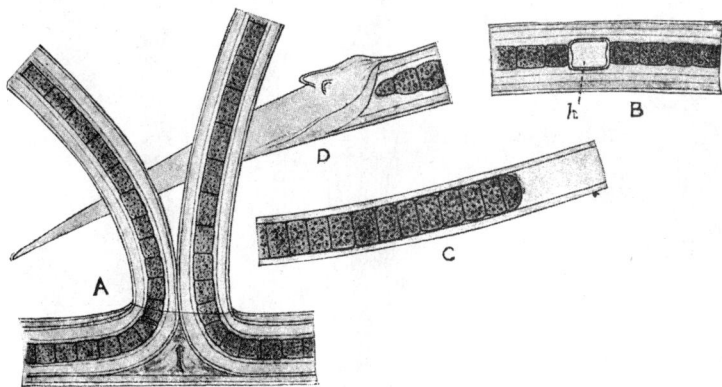

Fig. 19. Example of *Scytonema* alga. *S. mirabile* Thur. C, apex of a branch; D, organ of attachment at base of filament. × 440 (after West).

form are built up by cohesion. In some lichens the trichomes retain their chain-like appearance, in others they are more or less broken up and massed together, with disappearance of the gelatinous sheath (as in *Peltigera*); colour mostly dark blue-green.

Nostoc occurs in a few or all of the genera of Pyrenidiaceae, Collemaceae, Pannariaceae, Peltigeraceae and Stictaceae, and *N. sphaericum* Vauch

(*N. lichenoides* Kütz.) has been determined as the lichen gonidium. When the chains are broken up it has been wrongly classified as another alga, *Polycoccus punctiformis*.

Fam. SCYTONEMACEAE. Trichomes of single-cell rows, differentiated into base and apex. Pseudo-branching arises at right angles to the main filament.

SCYTONEMA Ag. Pseudo-branches piercing the sheath and passing out as twin filaments (Fig. 19); colour, golden-brown. This alga occurs in genera of Pyrenidiaceae, Ephebaceae, Pannariaceae, Heppiaceae, in *Petractis* a genus of Gyalectaceae, and in *Dictyonema* one of the Hymenolichens.

Fam. STIGONEMACEAE. Trichomes of several-cell rows with base and apex; colour, golden-brown.

STIGONEMA Ag. Stouter than *Scytonema*, with transverse and vertical division of the cells, and generally copious branching (Fig. 20). This alga occurs only in a few genera of Ephebaceae. *S. panniforme* Kirchn. (*Sirosiphon pulvinatus* Breb.) has been determined as forming the gonidium.

Fam. RIVULARIACEAE. Trichomes with a heterocyst at the base and tapering upwards, enclosed in mucilage (Fig. 21).

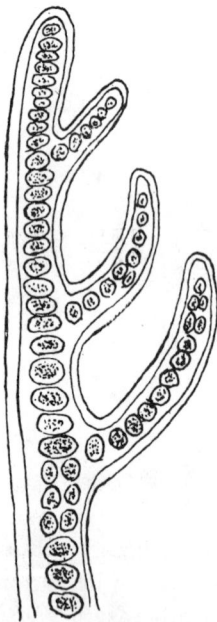

Fig. 20. *Stigonema* sp. × 200 (after Comère).

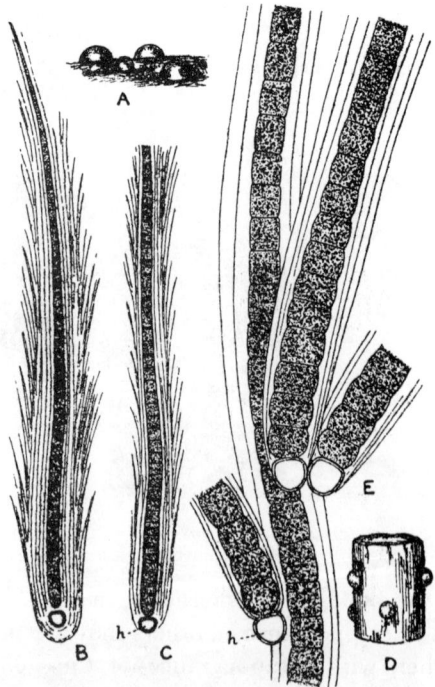

Fig. 21. Examples of *Rivularia*; A, B, C, *R. Biasolettiana* Menegh.; D and E, *R. minutula* Born. and Fl. A and D nat. size; B, C and E × 480 (after West).

RIVULARIA Thuret. In tufts fixed at the base and forming roundish gelatinous colonies; colour, blue-green. The gonidium of Lichinaceae has been identified as *R. nitida* Ag.

Algae belonging to one or other of these genera of Myxophyceae also combine with the hyphae of Archilichens to form cephalodia[1] and Krempelhuber[2] has recorded and figured a blue-green alga, probably *Gloeocapsa*, in *Baeomyces paeminosus* from the South Sea Islands. They also form the gonidia in a few species and genera of such families as Stictaceae and Peltigeraceae.

b. CHLOROPHYCEAE ASSOCIATED WITH ARCHILICHENS. The lichens of this group are by far the most numerous both in genera and species, though fewer algal families are represented.

Fam. PROTOCOCCACEAE. Consisting of globular single cells, aggregated in loose colonies, dividing variously.

I. PROTOCOCCUS VIRIDIS Ag. (*Pleurococcus vulgaris* Menegh., *Cystococcus humicola* Naeg.). Cells dividing into 2, 4 or 8 daughter-cells and not separating readily; in excessive moisture forming short filaments. The cells contain parietal chloroplasts, and, according to Chodat[3], are without a pyrenoid (Fig. 22). This alga, and allied species, forms the familiar green coating of tree-trunks, walls etc., and, in lichenological literature, are quoted as the gonidia of most of the crustaceous foliose and fruticose lichens. Chodat[3], who has

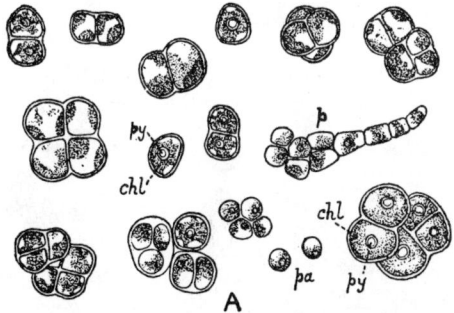

Fig. 22. *Pleurococcus vulgaris* Menegh. (*Protococcus viridis* Ag.). *chl.* chloroplast; *p.* protoderma stage; *pa*, palmelloid stage; *py*, pyrenoid. × 520 (after West).

recently made comparative artificial cultures of algae, throws doubt on the identity of many such gonidia. He lays great emphasis on the presence or absence of a pyrenoid in algal cells. West, on the contrary, considers the pyrenoid as an inconstant character. Chodat insists that the gonidia that contain pyrenoids belong to another genus, *Cystococcus* Chod. (*non* Naeg.), a pyrenoid-containing alga, which, in addition to multiplying by division of the cells, also forms spores and zoospores when cultivated. He further records the results of his cultures of gonidia, and finds that those taken from closely related lichens, such as different species of *Cladonia*, though they are alike morphologically, yet show constant variations in the culture colonies. These, he holds, are sufficient to indicate difference of race if not

[1] See p. 133.   [2] Krempelhuber 1873.   [3] Chodat 1913.

of species and he designates the algae, according to the lichen in which they occur, as *Cystococcus Cladoniae pyxidatae, C. Cladoniae fimbriatae*, etc.

Meanwhile Paulson and Somerville Hastings[1] by their careful research on the growing thallus have thrown considerable light on the identity of the Protococcaceous lichen gonidium. They selected such well-known lichens as *Xanthoria parietina, Cladonia* spp. and others, which they collected during the spring months, February to April, the period of most active growth. Many of the gonidia, they found, were in a stage of reproduction,

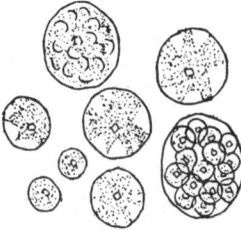

Fig. 23. *Cystococcus Cladoniae pyxidatae* Chod. from culture × 800 (after Chodat).

that showed a simultaneous rounding off of the gonidium contents into globose bodies varying in number up to 32. Chodat had figured this method of "sporulation" in his cultures of the lichen gonidium both in *Chlorella* Beij. and in *Cystococcus* Chod. (Fig. 23). It has now been abundantly proved that this form of increase is of frequent occurrence in the thallus itself. *Chlorella* has been suggested as probably the alga forming these gonidia and recently West has signified his acquiescence in this view[2].

2. CHLORELLA Beij. Occurring frequently on damp ground, bark of trees, etc., dividing into numerous daughter-cells, probably reduced zoogonidia (Fig. 23).

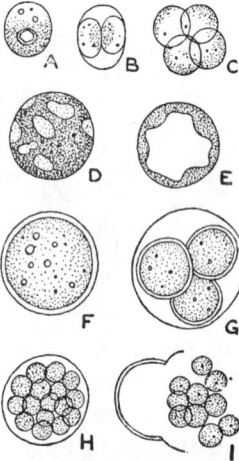

Fig. 23 A. A, C, *Chlorella vulgaris* Beyer. B and C, stages in division × about 800 (after Chodat); E, *Chl. faginea* Wille × 520 (after Gerneck); F—I *Chl. miniata*; F, vegetable cell; G—I, formation and escape of gonidia × 1000 (after Chodat).

Chodat distinguishes between *Cystococcus* and *Chlorella* in that *Cystococcus* may form zoospores (though rarely), *Chlorella* only aplanospores. He found three gonidial species, *Chlorella lichina* in *Cladonia rangiferina, Ch. viscosa* and *Ch. Cladoniae* in other *Cladonia* spp.

3. COCCOBOTRYS Chod. The cells of this new algal genus are smaller than those of *Cystococcus* or *Protococcus* and have no pyrenoid. They were isolated by Chodat from the thallus of *Verrucaria nigrescens* (Fig. 24), and, as they have thick membranes, they adhere in a continuous layer or thallus. Chodat also claims to have isolated a species of *Coccobotrys* from *Dermatocarpon miniatum*, a foliose Pyrenolichen.

4. COCCOMYXA Schmidle. Cells ellipsoid, also without a pyrenoid. Two species were obtained by Chodat from the thallus of *Solorinae* and are recorded as *Coccomyxa Solorinae croceae* and *C. Solorinae saccatae*.

---

[1] Paulson and Hastings 1920.   [2] Paulson in litt.

Coccomyxa subellipsoidea is given[1] as the gonidium of the primitive lichen *Botrydina vulgaris* (Fig. 25). The cells are surrounded by a common gelatinous sheath.

Fig. 24. *Coccobotrys Verrucariae* Chod. from culture × 800 (after Chodat).

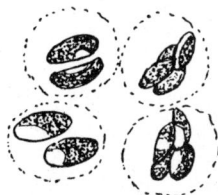

Fig. 25. *Coccomyxa subellipsoidea* Acton. Actively dividing cells, the dark portions indicating the chloroplasts × 1000 (after Acton).

5. DIPLOSPHAERA Bial.[2] *D. Chodati* was taken from the thallus of *Lecanora tartarea* and successfully cultivated. It resembles *Protococcus*, but has smaller cells and grows more rapidly; it is evidently closely allied to that genus, if not merely a form of it.

6. UROCOCCUS Kütz. Cells more or less globose, rather large, and coloured with a red-brown pigment, with the cell-wall thick and lamellate, forming elongate strands of cells (Fig. 26). Recorded by Hue[3] in the cephalodium of *Lepolichen coccophora*, a Chilian lichen.

Fam. TETRASPORACEAE. Cells in groups of 2 or 4 surrounded by a gelatinous sheath.

1. PALMELLA Lyngb. Cells globose, oblong or ellipsoid, grouped without order in a formless mucilage (Fig. 27). Among lichens associated with *Palmella* are the Epigloeaceae and Chrysothricaceae.

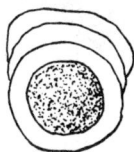

Fig. 26. *Urococcus* sp. Group of cells much magnified (after Hassall).

Fig. 27. *Palmella* sp. × 400 (after Comère).

2. GLOEOCYSTIS Naeg. Cells oblong or globose with a lamellate sheath forming small colonies; colour, red-brown (Fig. 28). This alga along with *Urococcus* was found by Hue in the cephalodia of *Lepolichen coccophora*, but whereas *Gloeocystis* frequently occupies the cephalodium alone, *Urococcus* is always accompanied by *Scytonema*, the normal gonidium of the cephalodium.

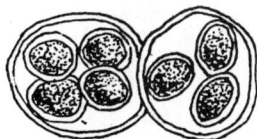

Fig. 28. *Gloeocystis* sp. × 400 (after Comère).

[1] Acton 1909.   [2] Bialosuknia 1909.   [3] Hue 1905.

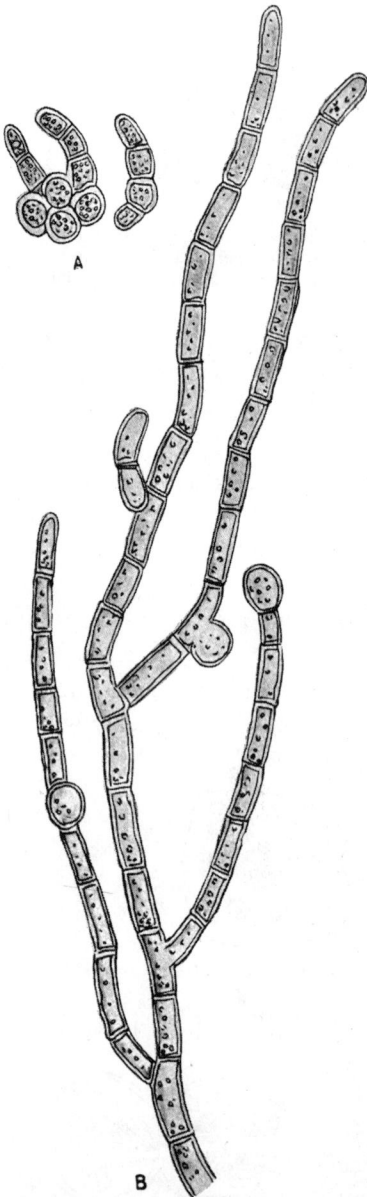

Fig. 29. A, *Trentepohlia umbrina* Born.;
B, *T. aurea* Mart. × 300 (after Kütz.).

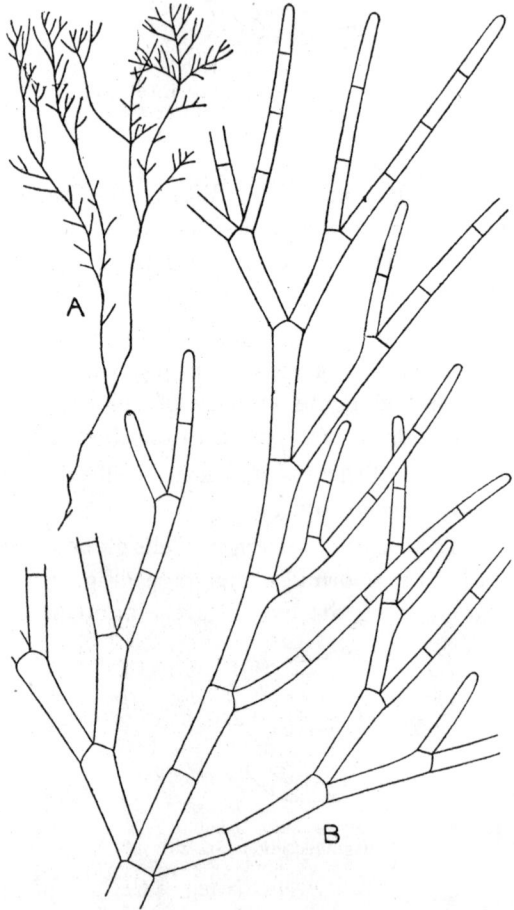

Fig. 30. Example of *Cladophora*. *Cl. glomerata* Kütz.
A, nat. size; B, × 85 (after West).

Fam. TRENTEPOHLIACEAE. Filamentous and branched, the filaments short and creeping or long and forming tufts and felts or cushions; colour, brownish-yellow or reddish-orange.

TRENTEPOHLIA Born. Branching alternate; cells filled with red or orange oil; no pyrenoids (Fig. 29). A large number of lichens are associated with this genus: Pyrenulaceae, Arthoniaceae, Graphidaceae, Roccellaceae, Thelotremaceae, Gyalectaceae and Coenogoniaceae, etc., in whole or in part. Two species have been determined, *T. umbrina* Born., the gonidium of the Graphidaceae, and *T. aurea* which is associated with the only European *Coenogonium, C. ebeneum* (Fig. 3). Deckenbach[1] claimed that he had proved by cultures that *T. umbrina* was a growth stage of *T. aurea*.

Fam. CLADOPHORACEAE. Filamentous, variously and copiously branched, the cells rather large and multinucleate.

CLADOPHORA Kütz. Filaments branching, of one-cell rows, attached at the base; colour, bright or dark green; mostly aquatic and marine (Fig. 30). Only one lichen, *Racodium rupestre*, a member of the Coenogoniaceae, is associated with *Cladophora*. It is a British lichen, and is always sterile.

Fam. MYCOIDEACEAE. Epiphytic algae consisting of thin discs which are composed of radiating filaments.

1. MYCOIDEA Cunningh. (Cephaleuros Kunze). In *Mycoidea parasitica* the filaments of the disc are partly erect and partly decumbent, reddish to green (Fig. 31). It forms the gonidium of the parasitic lichen, *Strigula complanata*, which was studied by Marshall Ward in Ceylon[2]. Zahlbruckner gives *Phyllactidium* as an alternative gonidium of Strigulaceae.

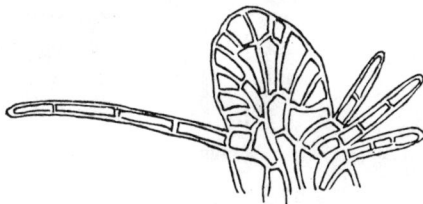

Fig. 31. *Mycoidea parasitica* Cunningh. much magnified (after Marshall Ward).

2. PHYCOPELTIS Millard. Disc a stratum one-cell thick, bearing seta, adnate to the lower surface of the leaf, yellow-green in colour. *Phycopeltis* (Fig. 32) has been identified as the gonidium of *Strigula complanata* in New Zealand and of *Mazosia* (Chiodectonaceae), a leaf lichen from tropical America.

[1] Deckenbach 1893.

[2] In a comparative study of leaf algae from Ceylon and Barbadoes, N. Thomas (1913) came to the conclusion that Marshall Ward's alga in its early stages is the same as *Phyllactidium tropicum* Moebius; and that the Barbadoes alga with which she was working represented the older stages, it being then subcuticular in habit, forming rhizoids, barren and sterile aerial hairs and subcuticular zoosporangia.

There is some confusion as to the genera of algae that form the gonidia of these epiphyllous lichens. *Phyllactidium* given by Zahlbruckner as the gonidium of all the Strigulaceae (except *Strigula* in part) is classified by de Toni[1] as probably synonymous with *Phycopeltis* Millard, and as differing from *Mycoidea parasitica* in the mode of growth.

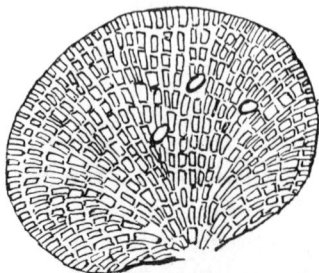

Fig. 32. *Phycopeltis expansa* Jenn. much magnified (after Vaughan Jennings).

Fam. PRASIOLACEAE. Thallus filamentous, often expanded into broad sheets by the fusion of the filaments in one plane.

PRASIOLA Ag. Thallus filamentous, of one- to many-cell rows, or widely expanded (Fig. 33). The gonidium of Mastoidiaceae (Pyrenocarpeae).

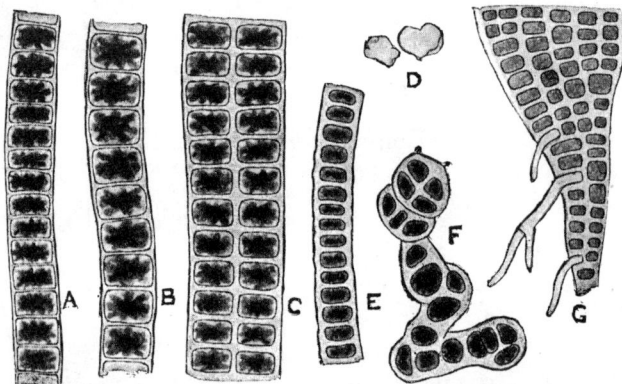

Fig. 33. *Prasiola parietina* Wille × 500 (after West).

B. CHANGES INDUCED IN THE ALGA

a. MYXOPHYCEAE. Though, as a general rule, the alga is less affected by its altered life-conditions than the fungus, yet in many instances it becomes considerably modified in appearance. In species of the genus *Pyrenopsis*—small gelatinous lichens—the alga is a *Gloeocapsa* very similar to *G. magma*. In the open it forms small colonies of blue-green cells surrounded by a gelatinous sheath which is coloured red with gloeocapsin. As a gonidium lying towards or on the outside of the granules composing the thallus, the red sheath of the cells is practically unchanged, so that the resemblance to *Gloeocapsa* is unmistakable. In the inner parts of the thallus, the colonies are somewhat broken up by the hyphae and the sheaths are not

[1] De Toni 1889.

only less evident but much more faintly coloured. In *Synalissa*, a minute shrubby lichen which has the same algal constituent, the tissue of the thallus is more highly evolved, and in it the red colour can barely be seen and then only towards the outside; at the centre it disappears entirely. The long chaplets of *Nostoc* cells persist almost unchanged in the thallus of the Collemaceae, but in heteromerous genera such as *Pannaria* and *Peltigera* they are broken up, or they are coiled together and packed into restricted areas or zones. The altered alga has been frequently described as *Polycoccus punctiformis*. A similar modification occurs in many cephalodia, so that the true affinity of the alga, in most instances, can only be ascertained after free cultivation.

Bornet[1] has described in *Coccocarpia molybdaea* the change that the alga *Scytonema* undergoes as the thallus develops: in very young fronds the filaments of *Scytonema* are unchanged and are merely enclosed between layers of hyphae. At a later stage, with increase of the thallus in thickness, the algal filaments are broken up, their covering sheath disappears, and the cells become rounded and isolated. *Petractis* (*Gyalecta*) *exanthematica* has also a *Scytonema* as gonidium, and equally exact observations have been made by Fünfstück[2] on the way it is transformed by symbiosis: with the exception of a very thin superficial layer, the thallus is immersed in the rock and is permeated by the alga to its lowest limits, 3 to 4 mm. below the surface, *Petractis* being a homoiomerous lichen. The *Scytonema* trichomes embedded in the rock become narrower, and the sheath, which in the epilithic part of the thallus is 4μ wide, disappears almost entirely. The green colour of the cells fades and septation is less frequent and less regular. The filaments in that condition are very like oil-hyphae and can only be distinguished as algal by staining reagents such as alkanna. They never seem to be in contact with the fungal elements: there is no visible appearance of parasitism nor even of consortism.

b. CHLOROPHYCEAE. As a rule the green-celled gonidium such as *Protococcus* is not changed in form though the colour may be less vivid, but in certain lichens there do occur modifications in its appearance. In *Micarea* (*Biatorina*) *prasina*, Hedlund[3] noted that the gonidium was a minute alga possessing a gelatinous sheath similar to that of a *Gloeocapsa*. He isolated the alga, made artificial cultures and found that, in the altered conditions, it gradually increased in size, threw off the gelatinous sheath and developed into normal *Protococcus* cells, measuring 7 to 10μ in diameter. The gelatinous sheath was thus proved to be merely a biological variation, probably of value to the lichen owing to its capacity to imbibe and retain moisture. Zukal[4] also made cultures of this alga, but wrongly concluded it was a *Gloeocystis*.

[1] Bornet 1873.   [2] Fünfstück 1899.   [3] Hedlund 1892.   [4] Zukal 1895, p. 19.

Moebius[1] has described the transformation from algae to lichen gonidia in a species epiphytic on Orchids in Porto Rico. He had observed that most of the leaves were inhabited by a membranaceous alga, *Phyllactidium*, and that constantly associated with it were small scraps of a lichen thallus containing isolated globose gonidia. The cells of the alga, under the influence of the invading fungus, were, in this case, formed into isolated round bodies which divided into four, each daughter-cell becoming surrounded by a membrane and being capable, in turn, of further division.

Frank[2] followed the change from a free alga to a gonidium in *Chroolepus* (*Trentepohlia*) *umbrinum*, as shown in the hypophloeodal thalli of the Graphideae. The alga itself is frequent on beech bark, where it forms wide-spreading brownish-red incrustations consisting of short chains occasionally branched. The individual cells have thick laminated membranes and vary in width from 20μ to 37μ. The free alga constantly tends to penetrate below the cortical layers of the tree on which it grows, and the immersed cells become not only longer and of a thinner texture, but the characteristic red colour so entirely disappears, that the growing penetrating apical cell may be light green or almost colourless. As a lichen gonidium the alga undergoes even more drastic changes: the red oily granules gradually vanish and the cells become chlorophyll-green or, if any retain a bright colour, they are orange or yellow. The branching of the chains is more regular, the cells more elongate and narrower; usually they are about 13 to 21μ long and 8μ wide, or even less. Deeper down in the periderm, the chains become disintegrated into separate units. Another notable alteration takes place in the cell-membrane which becomes thin and delicate. It has, however, been observed that if these algal cells reach the surface, owing to peeling of the bark, etc., they resume the appearance of a normal *Trentepohlia*.

In certain cases where two kinds of algae were supposed to be present in some lichens, it has been proved that one species only is represented, the difference in their form being caused by mechanical pressure of the surrounding hyphae, as in *Endocarpon* and *Staurothele* where the hymenial gonidia are cylindrical in form and much smaller than those of the thallus. They were on this account classified by Stahl[3] under a separate algal genus, *Stichococcus*, but they are now known to be growth forms of *Protococcus*, the alga that is normally present in the thallus. Similar variations were found by Neubner[4] in the gonidia of the Caliciaceae, but, by culture experiments with the gonidia apart from the hyphae, he succeeded in demonstrating transition forms in all stages between the "*Pleurococcus*" cells and those of "*Stichococcus*," though the characters acquired by the latter are transmitted to following generations. The transformation from spherical to cylindrical algal cells had been also noted by Krabbe[1] in the young podetia of some species of *Cladonia*, the change in form being due to the continued pressure in one direction of the parallel hyphae.

Isolated algal cells have been observed within the cortex of various lichens. They are carried thither by the hyphae from the gonidial zone in the process of cortical formation, but they soon die off as in that position they are deprived of a sufficiency of air and of moisture. Forssell[2] found *Xanthocapsa* cells embedded in the hymenium of *Omphalaria Heppii*. They were similar to those of the thallus, but they were not associated with hyphae and had undergone less change than the thalline algae.

C. Constancy of Algal Constituents

Lichen hyphae of one family or genus, as a rule, combine with the same species of alga, and the continuity of genera and species is maintained. There are, however, related lichens that differ chiefly or only in the characters of the gonidia. Among such closely allied genera or sections of genera may be cited *Sticta* with bright-green algae and the section *Stictina* with blue-green; *Peltidea* similarly related to *Peltigera* and *Nephroma* to *Nephromium*. In the genus *Solorina*, some of the species possess bright-green, others blue-green algae, while in one, *S. crocea*[3], there is an upper layer of small bright-green gonidia that project in irregular pyramids into the upper cortex; while below these there stretches a more or less interrupted band of blue-green *Nostoc* cells. The two layers are usually separated by strands of hyphae, but occasionally they come into close contact, and the hyphal filaments pass from one zone to the other. In this genus cephalodia containing blue-green *Nostoc* are characteristic of all the "bright-green" species. Harmand[4] has recorded the presence of two different types of gonidia in *Lecanora atra* f. *subgrumosa*; one of them, the normal *Protococcus* alga of the species, the other, pale-blue-green cells of *Nostoc* affinity.

Forssell[5] states that in *Lecanora* (*Psoroma*) *hypnorum*, the normal bright-green gonidia of some of the squamules may be replaced by *Nostoc*. In that case they are regarded as cephalodia, though in structure they exactly resemble the squamules of *Pannaria pezizoides*, and Forssell considers that there is sufficient evidence of the identity of the hyphal constituent in these two lichens, the alga alone being different.

It may be that in Archilichens with a marked capacity to form a second symbiotic union with blue-green algae, a tendency to revert to a primitive condition is evident—a condition which has persisted wholly in *Peltigera* with its *Nostoc* zone, but is manifested only by cephalodia formation in the

---

[1] Krabbe 1891.   [2] Forssell 1885.   [3] Hue 1910.   [4] Harmand 1913, p. 1050.
[5] Forssell 1886.

Peltidea section of the genus. In this connection, however, we must bear in mind Forssell's view that it is the Archilichens that are the more primitive[1].

The alien blue-green algae with their gelatinous sheaths are adapted to the absorption and retention of moisture, and, in this way, they doubtless render important service to the lichens that harbour them in cephalodia.

D. DISPLACEMENT OF ALGAE WITHIN THE THALLUS

a. NORMAL DISPLACEMENT. Lindau[2] has contrasted the advancing apical growth of the creeping alga *Trentepohlia* with the stationary condition of the unicellular species that multiply by repeated division or by sporulation, and thus form more or less dense zones and groups of gonidia in most lichens. The fungus in the latter case pushes its way among the algae and breaks up the compact masses by a shoving movement, thus letting in light and air. The growing hypha usually applies itself closely round an algal cell, and secondary branches arise which in time encircle it in a network of short cells. In the thallus of *Variolaria*[3] the hyphae from the lower tissues, termed push-hyphae by Nienburg[4], push their way into the algal groups and filaments composed of short cells come to lie closely round the individual gonidia. Continued growth is centrifugal, and the algae are carried outward with the extension of the hyphae (Fig. 12). Cell-division is more active at the periphery, that being the area of vigorous growth, and the algal cells are, in consequence, generally smaller in that region than those further back, the latter having entered more or less into a resting condition, or, as is more probable, these smaller cells are aplanospores not fully mature.

b. LOCAL DISPLACEMENT. Specimens of *Parmelia physodes* were found several times by Bitter, the grey-green surface of which was marbled with whitish lines, caused by the absence of gonidia under these lighter-coloured areas. The thallus was otherwise healthy as was manifested by the freely fruiting condition: no explanation of the phenomenon was forthcoming. Bitter compared the condition with the appearance of lighter areas on the thallus of *Parmelia obscurata*.

Something of the same nature was observed on the thallus of a *Peltigera* collected by F. T. Brooks near Cambridge. The marking took the form of a series of concentric circles, starting from several centres. The darker lines were found on examination to contain the normal blue-green algal zone, while the colour had faded from the lighter parts. The cause of the difference in colouration was not apparent.

---

[1] See Chap. VII.   [2] Lindau 1895.   [3] Darbishire 1897.   [4] Nienburg 1917.

E. Non-gonidial Organisms associated with Lichen Hyphae

Bonnier[1] made a series of cultures with lichen spores and green cells other than those that form lichen gonidia. In one instance he substituted *Protococcus botryoides* for the normal gonidia of *Parmelia* (*Xanthoria*) *parietina*; in another of his cultures he replaced *Protococcus viridis* by the filamentous alga *Trentepohlia abietina*. In both cases the hyphae attached themselves to the green cells and a certain stage of thallus formation was reached, though growth ceased fairly early. Another experiment made with the large filaments of *Vaucheria sessilis* met with the same amount of success (Fig. 34). The germinating hyphae attached themselves to the alga and grew all round it, but there was no advance to tissue formation.

Cultures were also made with the protonema of mosses. Either spores of mosses and lichens were germinated together, or lichen spores were sown in close proximity to fully formed protonemata. The developing hyphae seized on the moss cells and formed a network of branching anastomosing filaments along the whole length of the protonema without, however, penetrating the cells. If suitable algae were encountered, proper thallus formation commenced, and Bonnier considers that the hyphae receive stimulus and nourishment from the protonema sufficient to

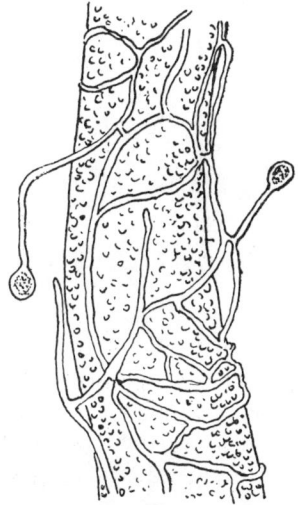

Fig. 34. Germinating hyphae of *Lecanora subfusca* Ach., growing over the alga *Vaucheria sessilis* DC., much magnified (after Bonnier).

tide them over a considerable period, perhaps until the algal symbiont is met. An interesting variation was noted in connection with the cultures of *Mnium hornum*[2]. If the protonema were of the usual vigorous type, the whole length was encased by the hyphal network; but if it were delicate and slender, the protoplasm collected in the cell that was touched by hyphae and formed a sort of swollen thick-walled bud (Fig. 35). This new body persisted when the rest of the filament and the hyphae had disappeared, and, in favourable conditions, grew again to form a moss plant.

F. Parasitism of Algae on Lichens

A curious instance of undoubted parasitism by an alga, not as in *Strigula* on one of the higher plants, but on a lichen thallus, is recorded by Forssell[3]. A group of *Protococcus*-like cells established on the thallus

---

[1] Bonnier 1888 and 1889[2]. [2] Bonnier 1889. [3] Forssell 1884, p. 34.

of *Peltigera* had found their way into the tissue, the underlying cortical cells having degenerated. The blue-green cells of the normal gonidial layer

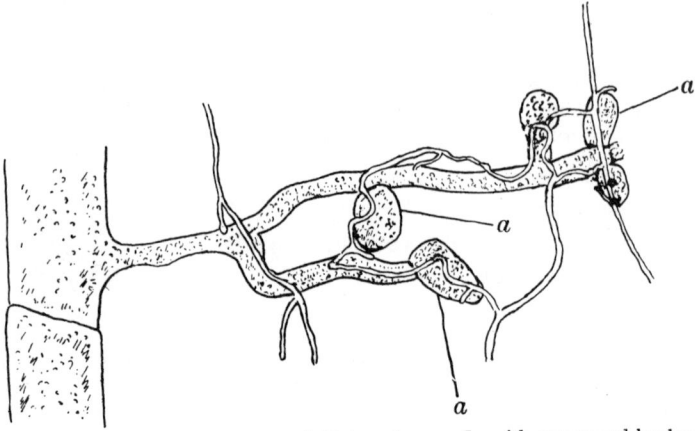

Fig. 35. Pure culture of protonema of *Mnium hornum* L. with spores and hyphae of *Lecidea vernalis* Ach. a,a,a, buds forming × 150 (after Bonnier).

had died off before their advance but no zone was formed by the invading algae; they simply withdrew nourishment and gave seemingly no return. The phenomenon is somewhat isolated and accidental but illustrates the capacity of the alga to absorb food supply from lichen hyphae.

An instance of epiphytic growth has also been recorded by Zahlbruckner[1]. He found an alga, *Trentepohlia abietina*, covering the thallus of a Brazilian lichen, *Parmelia isidiophora*, and growing so profusely as to obscure the isidiose character towards the centre of the thallus. There was no genetic connection of the alga with the lichen as the former was not that of the lichen gonidium. Lichen thalli are indeed very frequently the habitat of green algae, though their occurrence may be and probably is accidental.

[1] Zahlbruckner 1902.

CHAPTER III

MORPHOLOGY

GENERAL ACCOUNT OF LICHEN STRUCTURE

I. ORIGIN OF LICHEN STRUCTURES

THE two organisms, fungus and alga, that enter into the composition of the lichen plant are each characterized by the simplicity of their original structure in which there is little or no differentiation into tissues. The gonidia-forming algae are many of them unicellular, and increase mainly by division or by sporulation into daughter-cells which become rounded off and repeat the life of the mother-cell; others, belonging to different genera, are filaments, mostly of single cell-rows, with apical growth. The hyphal elements of the lichen are derived from fungi in which the vegetative body is composed of branching filaments, a character which persists in the lichen thallus.

The union of the two symbionts has stimulated both, but more especially the fungus, to new developments of vegetative form, in which the fungus, as the predominant partner, provides the framework of the lichen plant-body. Varied structures have been evolved in order to secure life conditions favourable to both constituents, though more especially to the alga; and as the close association of the assimilating and growing tissues is maintained, the thallus thus formed is capable of indefinite increase.

A. Forms of Cell-Structure

There is no true parenchyma or cellular structure in the lichen thallus such as forms the ground tissue of the higher plants. The fungal hyphae are persistently filamentous and either simple or branched. By frequent and regular cell-division—always at right angles to the long axis—and by coherent growth, a pseudoparenchyma may however be built up which functions either as a protective or strengthening tissue (Fig. 36).

Lindau[1] proposed the name "plectenchyma" for the tangled weft of hyphae that is the principal tissue system in fungi as well as lichens. The more elaborated pseudoparenchyma he designates as "paraplectenchyma," while the term "prosoplectenchyma" he reserved for the fibrous

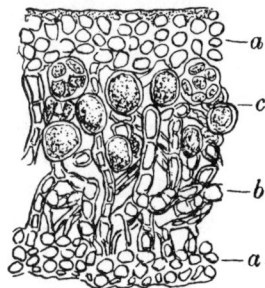

Fig. 36. Vertical section of young stage of stratose thallus (*Xanthoria parietina* Th. Fr.). *a*, plectenchyma of cortex; *b*, medullary hyphae; *c*, gonidial zone. × 500 (after Schwendener).

[1] Lindau 1899.

or chondroid strands of compact filaments that occur frequently in the thallus of the larger fruticose lichens, and are of service in strengthening the fronds. The term plectenchyma is now generally used for pseudo-parenchyma.

B. TYPES OF THALLUS

Three factors, according to Reinke[1], have been of influence in determining the thalline development. The first, and most important, is the necessity to provide for the work of photosynthesis on the part of the alga. There is also the building up of a tissue that should serve as a storage of reserve material, essential in a plant the existence of which is prolonged far beyond the natural duration of either of the component organisms; and, finally, there is the need of protecting the long-lived plant as a whole though more particularly the alga.

Wallroth was the first to make a comparative study of the different lichen thalli. He distinguished those lichens in which the green cells and the colourless filaments are interspersed equally through the entire thallus as "homoiomerous" (Fig. 2), and those in which there are distinct layers of cortex, gonidia, and medulla, as "heteromerous" (Fig. 1), terms which, though now considered of less importance in classification, still persist and are of service in describing the position of the alga with regard to the general structure. A less evident definition of the different types of thallus has been proposed by Zukal[2] who divides them into "endogenous" and "exogenous."

a. ENDOGENOUS THALLUS. The term has been applied to a comparatively small number of homoiomerous lichens in which the alga predominates in the development, and determines the form of the thallus. These algae, members of the Myxophyceae, are extremely gelatinous, and the hyphae grow alongside or within the gelatinous sheath. In the simpler forms the vegetative structure is of the most primitive type: the alga retains its original character almost unchanged, and the ascomycetous fungus grows along with and beside it (Fig. 4). Such are the minutely tufted thalli of *Thermutis* and *Spilonema* and the longer strands of *Ephebe*, in which the associated *Scytonema* or *Stigonema*, filamentous blue-green algae, though excited to excessive growth, scarcely lose their normal appearance, making it difficult at times to recognize the lichenoid character unless the fruits also are present.

Equally primitive in most cases is the structure of the thallus associated with *Gloeocapsa*. The resulting lichens, *Pyrenopsis*, *Psorotichia*, etc. are simply gelatinous crusts of the alga with a more or less scanty intermingling of fungal hyphae.

[1] Reinke 1895.   [2] Zukal 1895, p. 562.

In the Collemaceae, the gonidial cells of which are species of *Nostoc* (Fig. 2), there appears a more developed thallus; but in general, symbiosis in *Collema* has wrought the minimum of change in the habit of the alga, hence the indecision of the earlier botanists as to the identification and classification of *Nostoc* and *Collema*. Though in many of the species of the genus *Collema* no definite tissue is formed, yet, under the influence of symbiosis, the plants become moulded into variously shaped lobes which are specifically constant. In some species there is an advance towards more elaboration of form in the protective tissues of the apothecia, a layer of thin-walled plectenchyma being occasionally formed beneath or around the fruit as in *Collema granuliferum*.

In all these lichens, it is only the thallus that can be considered as primitive: the fruit is a more or less open apothecium—more rarely a perithecium—with a fully developed hymenium. Frequently it is provided with a protective thalline margin.

b. EXOGENOUS THALLUS. In this group, composed almost exclusively of heteromerous lichens, Zukal includes all those in which the fungus takes the lead in thalline development. He counts as such *Leptogium*, a genus closely allied to *Collema* but with more membranous lobes, in which the short terminal cells of the hyphae have united to form a continuous cortex. A higher development, therefore, becomes at once apparent, though in some genera, as in *Coenogonium*, the alga still predominates, while the simplest forms may be merely a scanty weft of filaments associated with groups of algal cells. Such a thallus is characteristic of the Ectolechiaceae, and some Gyalectaceae, etc., which have, indeed, been described by Zahlbruckner[1] as homoiomerous though their gonidia belong to the non-gelatinous Chlorophyceae.

Heteromerous lichens have been arranged by Hue[2] according to their general structure in three great series:

1. *Stratosae*. Crustaceous, squamulose and foliose lichens with a dorsiventral thallus.

2. *Radiatae*. Fruticose, shrubby or filamentous lichens with a strap-shaped or cylindrical thallus of radiate structure.

3. *Stratosae-Radiatae*. Primary dorsiventral thallus, either crustaceous or squamulose, with a secondary upright thallus of radiate structure called the podetium (Cladoniaceae).

---

[1] Zahlbruckner 1907.　　　　　[2] Hue 1899.

II. STRATOSE THALLUS

1. CRUSTACEOUS LICHENS

A. General Structure

In the series "Stratosae," the plant is dorsiventral, the tissues forming the thallus being arranged more or less regularly in strata one above the other (Fig. 37). On the upper surface there is a hyphal layer constituting

Fig. 37. Vertical section of crustaceous lichen (*Lecanora subfusca* var. *chlarona* Hue) on bark. *a*, lichen cortex; *b*, gonidia; *c*, cells of the periderm. × 100.

a cortex, either rudimentary or highly elaborated; beneath the cortex is situated the gonidial zone composed of algae and hyphae in close association; and deeper down the medulla, generally a loose tissue of branching hyphae. The lower cortex which abuts on the medulla may be as fully developed as the upper or it may be absent.

The growing tissue is chiefly marginal; the hyphae on the outer edge remain "meristematic"[1] and provide for horizontal as well as vertical extension; and there is also continual increase of the algal cells. There is in addition a certain amount of intercalary growth due to the activity of the gonidial tissue, both algal and fungal, providing for the renewal of the cortex, and even interposing new tissue.

B. Saxicolous Lichens

a. Epilithic Lichens. The crustaceous lichens forming this group spread over the rock surfaces. The support must be stable to allow the necessary time for the slowly developing organism, and therefore rocks that are friable or subject to continual weathering are bare of lichens.

aa. **Hypothallus or Prothallus.** The first stage of growth in the lichen thallus can be most easily traced in epilithic crustaceous species, especially in those that inhabit a smooth rock surface. The spore, on germination, produces a delicate branching septate mycelium which radiates on all sides, as was so well observed and recorded by Tulasne[2] in *Verrucaria muralis* (Fig. 14). Zukal[3] has called this first beginning the prothallus. In time the

---

[1] Wainio has adopted this term for growing hyphae 1897, p. 33.

[2] Tulasne 1852. [3] Zukal 1895.

cell-walls of the filaments become much thicker and though, in some species, they remain colourless, in others they become dark-coloured, all except the extreme tips, owing to the presence of lichen pigments—a provision, Zukal[1] considers, to protect them against the ravages of insects, etc. The pro-thallic filaments adhere closely to the substratum and the branching becomes gradually more dendroid in form, though sometimes hyphae are united into strands, or even form a kind of plectenchymatous tissue. This purely hyphal stage may persist for long periods without much change. In time there may be a fortuitous encounter with the algae (Fig. 38 A) which become the gonidia of the plant. Either these have been already established on the substra-tum as free-growing organisms, or, as accidentally conveyed, they alight on the prothallus. The contact between alga and hypha excites both to active growth and to cell-division; and the rapidly multiplying gonidia are as speedily sur-rounded by the vigorously growing hyphal filaments.

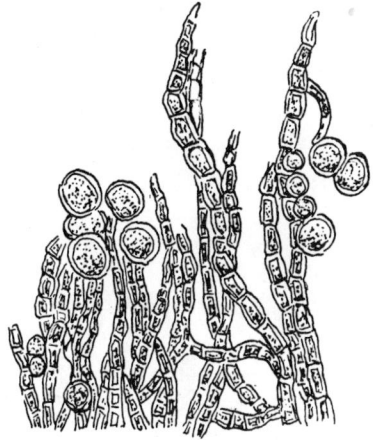

Fig. 38 A. Hypothallus of *Rhizocarpon confervoides* DC., from the extreme edge, with loose gonidia × 600.

Schwendener[2] has thus described the origin and further development of pro-thallus and gonidia: on the dark-coloured proto- or prothallus, he noted small nestling groups of green cells which he, at that time, regarded as direct outgrowths from the lichen hyphae. These gonidial cells, increasing by division, multiplied gradually and gathered into a connected zone. He also observed that the hyphae in contact with the gonidia became more thin-walled and produced many new branches. Some of these newly formed branches grow upwards and form the cortex, others grow downwards and build up the medulla or pith; the filaments at the circumference continue to advance and may start new centres of gonidial activity (Fig. 38 B). In many species, however, this prothallus or, as it is usually termed at this stage, the hypothallus, be-comes very soon overgrown and obscured by the vigorous increase of the first formed symbiotic tissue and can barely be seen as a white or dark line bordering the thallus (Fig. 39). Schwendener[3] has stated that probably only lichens that develop from the spore are distinguished by a proto-thallus, and that those arising from soredia do not form these first creeping filaments.

---

[1] Zukal 1895. [2] Schwendener 1866. [3] Schwendener 1863.

bb. **Formation of crustaceous tissues.** Some crustaceous lichens have a persistently scanty furfuraceous crust, the vegetative development never advancing much beyond the first rather loose association of gonidia and

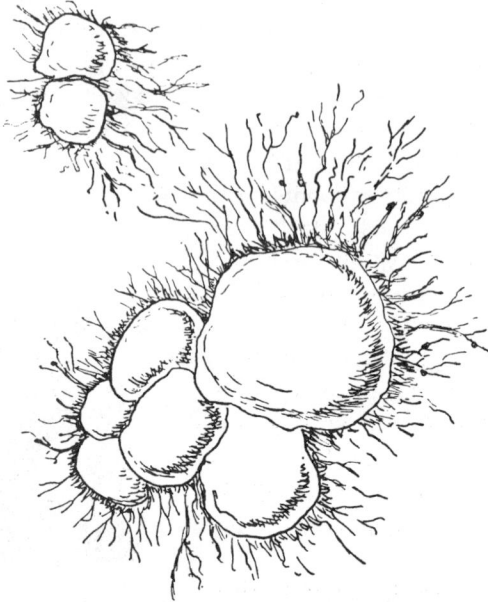

Fig. 38 B. Young thallus of *Rhizocarpon confervoides* DC., with various centres of gonidial growth on the hypothallus × 30.

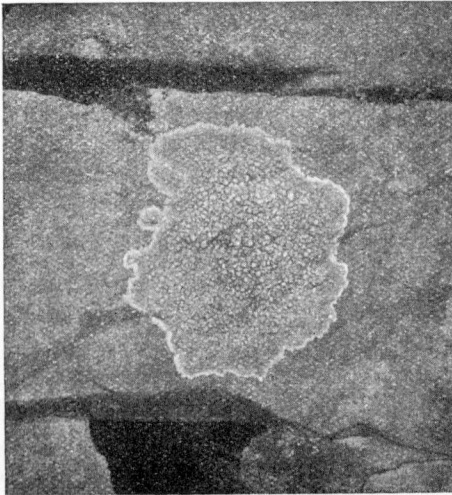

Fig. 39. *Lecanora parella* Ach. Determinate thallus with white bordering hypothallus, reduced (M. P., *Photo.*).

hyphae; but in those in which a distinct crust or granules are formed, three different strata of tissue are discernible:

1st. An upper cortical tissue of interlaced hyphae with frequent septation and with swollen gelatinous walls, closely compacted and with the lumen of the cells almost obliterated, not unfrequently a layer of mucilage serving as an outer cuticle. This type of cortex has been called by Hue[1] "decomposed." It is subject to constant surface weathering, thin layers being continually peeled off, but it is as continually being renewed endogenously by the upward growth of hyphae from the active gonidial zone. Exceptions to this type of cortex in crustaceous lichens are found in some *Pertusariae* where a secondary plectenchymatous cortex is formed, and in *Dirina* where it is fastigiate[2] as in *Roccella*.

2nd. The gonidial zone—a somewhat irregular layer of algae and hyphae below the cortex—which varies in thickness according to the species.

3rd. The medullary tissue of somewhat loosely intermingled branching hyphae, with generally rather swollen walls and narrow lumen. It rests directly on the substratum and follows every inequality and crack so closely, even where it does not penetrate, that the thallus cannot be detached without breaking it away.

In *Verrucaria mucosa*, a smooth brown maritime lichen found on rocks between tide-levels, the thallus is composed of tightly packed vertical rows of hyphae, slender, rather thin-walled, and divided into short cells. The gonidia are chiefly massed towards the upper surface, but they also occur in vertical rows in the medulla. One or two of the upper cells are brown and form an even cortex. The same formation occurs in some other sea-washed species; the arrangement of the tissue elements recalls that of crustaceous Florideae such as *Hildenbrandtia, Cruoria*, etc.

cc. **Formation of areolae.** An "areolate" thallus is seamed and scored by cracks of varying width and depth which divide it into minute compartments. These cracks or fissures or chinks originate in two ways depending on the presence or absence of hypothallic hyphae. Where the hypothallus is active, new areolae arise when the filaments encounter new groups of algae. More vigorous growth starts at once and proceeds on all sides from these algal centres, until similarly formed areolae are met, a more or less pronounced fissure marking the limits of each. This primary areolation, termed rimose or rimulose, is well seen in the thin smooth thallus of *Rhizocarpon geographicum* (Fig. 40); but the first-formed areolae are also very frequently slightly

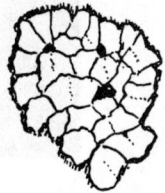

Fig. 40. Young thallus of *Rhizocarpon geographicum* DC., with primary and subsequent (dotted lines) areolation × 5.

[1] Hue 1906.   [2] See p. 83.

marked by subsequent cracks due to unequal growth. The areolation caused by primary growth conditions tends to become gradually less obvious or to disappear altogether.

Secondary areolation is due to unequal intercalary growth of the otherwise continuous thallus[1]. A more active increase of any minute portions provokes a tension or straining of the cortex between the swollen areas and the surrounding more sluggish tissues; the surface layers give way and chinks arise, a condition described by older lichenologists as "rimose-diffract" or sometimes as "rhagadiose." The thallus is generally thicker, more broken and granular in the older central parts of the lichen. Towards the circumference, where the tissue is thinner and growth more equal, the chinks are less evident. Sometimes the more vigorously growing areolae may extend over those immediately adjoining, in which case the covered portions become brown and their gonidia gradually disappear.

Strongly marked intersecting lines, similar to those round the margin of the thallus, are formed when hypothalli that have themselves started from different centres touch each other. A large continuous patch of crustaceous thallus may thus be composed of many individuals (Fig. 41).

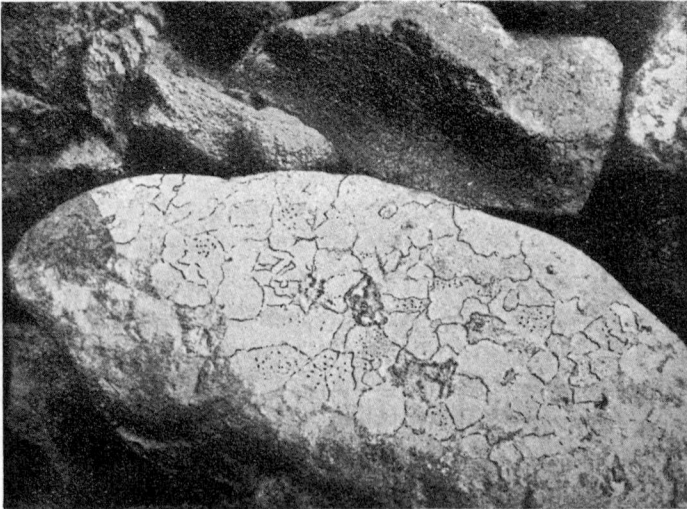

Fig. 41. *Rhizocarpon geographicum* DC. on boulder, reduced (M. P., *Photo.*).

b. ENDOLITHIC LICHENS. In many species, only the lower hyphae penetrate the substratum either of rock or soil. In a few, more especially those growing on limestone, the greater part or even the whole of the vegetative thallus and sometimes also the fruits are, to some extent, immersed

---

[1] Malinowski 1911.

in the rock. It has now been demonstrated that a number of lichens, formerly described as athalline, possess a considerable vegetative body which cannot be examined until the limestone in which they are embedded is dissolved by acids. One such species, *Petractis (Gyalecta) exanthematica*, studied by Steiner[1] and later by Fünfstück[2], is associated with the blue-green filamentous alga, *Scytonema*, and is homoiomerous in structure, the alga growing through and permeating the whole of the embedded thallus. A partly homoiomerous thallus, associated with *Trentepohlia*, has been described by Bachmann[3]. He found the bright-yellow filaments of the alga covering the surface of a calcareous rock. By reason of their apical growth, they pierced the rock and dissolved a way for themselves, not only among the loose particles, but right through a clear calcium crystal reaching generally to a depth of about 200μ, though isolated threads had gone 350μ below the surface. Near the outside the tendency was for the algae to become stouter and to increase by intercalary growth and by budded yeast-like outgrowths; lower down they were somewhat smaller. The hyphae that became united with the algae were unusually slender and were characterized by frequent anastomoses. They closely surrounded the gonidia and also filled the loose spaces of the limestone with their fine thread-like strands. Though oil was undoubtedly present in the lower hyphae there were no swollen nor sphaeroid cells[4]. Some interesting experiments with moisture proved that the part of the rock permeated with the lichen absorbed much more water and retained it longer than the part that was lichen-free.

Generally the embedded tissues follow the same order as in other crustaceous lichens: an upper layer of cortical hyphae, next a gonidial zone, and beneath that an interlaced tissue of medullary or rhizoidal hyphae which often form fat-cells[4]. Friedrich[5] has given measurements of the immersed thallus of *Lecanora (Biatorella) simplex*: under a cortical layer of hyphae there was a gonidial zone $600–700\mu$ thick, while the lower hyphae reached a depth of 12 mm.; he has also recorded an instance of a thallus reaching a depth of 30 mm.

On siliceous rocks such as granite, rhizoidal hyphae penetrate the rock chiefly between the thin separable flakes of mica. Bachmann[6] has recognized in these conditions three distinct series of cell-formations: (1) slender long-celled sparsely branched hyphae which form a network by frequent anastomoses; (2) further down, though only occasionally, hyphae with short thick-walled bead-like cells; and (3) beneath these, but only in or near mica crystals, spherical cells containing oil or some albuminous substance.

---

[1] Steiner 1881.   [2] Fünfstück 1899.   [3] Bachmann 1913.

[4] See p. 215.   [5] Friedrich 1906.   [6] Bachmann 1907.

c. CHEMICAL NATURE OF THE SUBSTRATUM. Lichens growing on calcareous rocks or soils are more or less endolithic, those on siliceous rocks are largely epilithic, but Bachmann[1] found that the mica crystals in granite were penetrated, much in the same way as limestone, by the lichen hyphae. These travel through the mica in all directions, though they tend to follow the line of cleavage, thus taking the direction of least cohesion. He found that oil-hyphae were formed, and also certain peculiar bristle-like terminal branches; in other cases there were thin layers of plectenchyma, and gonidia were also present. If however felspar or quartz crystals, no matter how thin, blocked the way, further growth was arrested, the hyphae being unable to pierce through or even to leave any trace on the quartz[2]. On granite containing no mica constituents the hyphae can only follow the cracks between the different impenetrable crystals.

Stahlecker[3] has confirmed Bachmann's observations, but he considers that the difference in habit and structure between the endolithic and epilithic series of lichens is due rather to the chemical than to the physical nature of the substratum. Thus in a rock of mixed composition such as granite, the more basic constituents are preferred by the hyphae, and are the first to be surrounded: mica, when present, is at once penetrated; particles of hornblende, which contain 40 to 50 per cent. only of silicic acid, are laid hold of by the filaments of the lichen before the felspar, of which the acid content is about 60 per cent.; quartz grains which are pure silica are attacked last of all, though in the course of time they also become corroded.

The character of the substratum also affects to a great extent the comparative development of the different thalline layers: the hyphal tissues in silicicolous lichens are much thinner than in lichens on limestone, and the gonidial zone is correspondingly wider. In a species of *Staurothele* on granite, Stahlecker[3] estimated the gonidial zone to be about 600 μ thick, while the lower medullary hyphae, partly burrowing into the rock, measured about 6 mm. Other measurements at different parts of the thallus gave a rhizoidal depth of 3 mm., while on a more finely granular substratum, with a gonidial zone of 350 μ, the rhizoidal hyphae measured only $1\frac{1}{2}$ mm. On calcareous rocks, on the contrary, with a gonidial zone that is certainly no larger, the hyphal elements penetrate the rock to varying depths down to 15 mm. or even more.

Lang[4] has recorded equally interesting measurements for *Sarcogyne* (*Biatorella*) *latericola*: on slaty rock which contained no mixture of lime, the gonidial zone had a thickness of 80 μ, a considerable proportion of the very thin thallus. Fünfstück[5] has indeed suggested that this lichen on acid

[1] Bachmann 1904.   [2] Bachmann 1904.   [3] Stahlecker 1906.
[4] Lang 1903.   [5] Fünfstück 1899.

rocks is only a starved condition of *Sarcogyne* (*Biatorella*) *simplex*, which on calcareous rocks, though with a broader gonidial zone, has, as noted above, a correspondingly much larger hyphal tissue.

Stahlecker's theory is that the hyphae require more energy to grow in the acid conditions that prevail in siliceous rocks, and therefore they make larger demands on the algal symbionts. It follows that the latter must be stimulated to more abundant growth than in circumstances favourable to the fungus, such as are found in basic (calcareous) rocks; he concludes that on the acid (siliceous) rocks, the epilithic or superficial condition is not only a physical but a biological necessity, to enable the algae to grow and multiply in a zone well exposed to light with full opportunity for active photosynthesis and healthy increase.

C. Corticolous Lichens

The crustaceous lichens occurring on bark or on dead wood, like those on rocks, are either partly or wholly immersed in the substratum (hypophloeodal), or they grow on the surface (epiphloeodal); but even those with a superficial crust are anchored by the lower hyphae which enter any crack or crevice of wood or bark and so securely attach the thallus, that it can only be removed by cutting away the underlying substance.

a. Epiphloeodal Lichens. These lichens originate in the same way as the corresponding epilithic series from soredia or from germinating spores, and follow the same stages of growth; first a hypothallus with subsequent colonization of gonidia, the formation of granules, areolae, etc. The small compartments are formed as primary or secondary areolae; the larger spaces are marked out by the encounter of hypothalli starting from different centres.

The thickness of the thallus varies considerably according to the species. In some *Pertusariae* with a stoutish irregular crust there is a narrow amorphous cortical layer of almost obliterated cells, a thin gonidial zone about $35\,\mu$ in width and a massive rather dense medulla of colourless hyphae. Darbishire[1] has described and figured in *Varicellaria microsticta*, one of the Pertusariaceae, single hyphae that extend like beams across the wide medulla and connect the two cortices. In some *Lecanorae* and *Lecideae* there is, on the contrary, an extremely thin thallus consisting of groups of algae and loose fungal filaments, which grow over and between the dead cork cells of the outer bark. On palings, there is often a fairly substantial granular crust present, with a gonidial zone up to about $80\,\mu$ thick, while the underlying or medullary hyphae burrow among the dead wood fibres.

[1] Darbishire 1897.

b. HYPOPHLOEODAL LICHENS. These immersed lichens are comparable with the endolithic species of the rock formations, as their thallus is almost entirely developed under the outer bark of the tree. They are recognizable, even in the absence of any fructification, by the somewhat shining brownish, white or olive-green patches that indicate the underlying lichen. This type of thallus occurs in widely separated families and genera, *Lecidea*, *Lecanora*, etc., but it is most constant in Graphideae and in those Pyreno-lichens of which the algal symbiont belongs to the genus *Trentepohlia*. The development of these lichens is of peculiar interest as it has been proved that though both symbionts are embedded in the corky tissues, the hyphae arrive there first, and, at some later stage, are followed by the gonidia. There is therefore no question of the alga being a "captured slave" or "unwilling mate."

Frank[1] made a thorough study of several subcortical forms. He found that in *Arthonia radiata*, the first outwardly visible indication of the presence of the lichen on ash bark was a greenish spot quite distinct from the normal dull-grey colour of the periderm. Usually the spots are round in outline, but they tend to become ellipsoid in a horizontal direction, being influenced by the growth in thickness of the tree. At this early stage only hyphae are present; Bornet[2] as well as Frank described the outer periderm cells as penetrated and crammed with the colourless slender filaments. Lindau[3], in a more recent work, disputes that statement: he found that the hyphae invariably grew between the dead cork cells, splitting them up and disintegrating the bark, but never piercing the membranes. The purely prothallic condition, as a weft of closely entangled hyphae, may last, Frank considers, for a long period in an almost quiescent condition—possibly for several years—before the gonidia arrive.

It is always difficult to observe the entrance of the gonidia but they seem to spread first under the second or third layers of the periderm. With care it is possible to trace a filament of *Trentepohlia* from the surface downwards, and to see that the foremost cell is really the growing and advancing apex of the creeping alga. Both symbionts show increased vigour when they encounter each other: the thallus at once develops in extent and in depth, and, ultimately, reproductive bodies are formed. In some species the apothecia or perithecia alone emerge above the bark, in others the outer peridermal cells are thrown off, and the thallus thus becomes superficial to some extent as a white scurfy or furfuraceous crust.

The change from a hypophloeodal to a partly epiphloeodal condition depends largely on the nature of the bark. Frank[1] found that *Lecanora pallida* remained for a long time immersed when growing on the thick rugged bark of oak trunks. When well lighted, or on trees with a thin

[1] Frank 1876.   [2] Bornet 1873, p. 81.   [3] Lindau 1895.

periderm, such as the ash, the lichen emerges much earlier and becomes superficial.

Black (or occasionally white) lines intersect the thallus and mark, as in saxicolous lichens (Fig. 41), the boundary lines between different individuals or different species. The pioneer hyphae of certain lichens very frequently become dark-coloured, and Bitter[1] has suggested as the reason for this that in damp weather the hypothallic growth is exceptionally vigorous. When dry weather supervenes, with high winds or strong sunshine, the outlying hyphae, unprotected by the thallus, become dark-coloured. On the return of more normal conditions the blackened tips are thrown off. Bitter further states that species of Graphideae do not form a permanent black limiting line when they grow in an isolated position: it is only when their advance is checked by some other thallus that the dark persistent edge appears, a characteristic also to be seen in the crust of other lichens. The dark boundary is always more marked in sunny exposed situations: in the shade, the line is reduced to a mere thread.

Bitter's restriction of black boundary lines to cases of encountering thalli only, would exclude the comparison one is tempted to make between the advancing hyphae of lichens and those of many woody fungi where the extreme edge of the white invaded woody tissue is marked by a dark line. In the latter case however it is the cells of the host that are stained black by the fungus pigment.

2. SQUAMULOSE LICHENS

A. Development of the Squamule

The crustaceous thallus is more or less firmly adherent to, or confused with, the substratum. Further advance to a new type of thallus is made when certain hyphal cells of soredium or granule take the lead in an ascending direction both upwards and outwards. As growth becomes definitely apical or one-sided, the structure rises free from the substratum, and small lobules or leaflet-like squamules are formed. Each squamule in this type of thallus is distinct in origin and not merely the branch of a larger whole.

In a few lichens the advance from the crustaceous to the squamulose structure is very slight. The granules seem but to have been flattened out at one side, and raised into minute rounded projections such as those that compose the thallus of *Lecanora badia* generally described as "subsquamulose." The squamulose formation is more pronounced in *Lecidea ostreata*, and in some species of *Pannaria*; and the whole thallus may finally consist of small separate lobes as in *Lecidea lurida*, *Lecanora crassa*, *L. saxicola*,

[1] Bitter 1899.

species of *Dermatocarpon* and the primary thallus of the *Cladoniae*. Most of these squamules are of a firm texture and more or less round in outline; in some species of *Cladonia*, etc., they are variously crenate, or cut into pinnate-like leaflets. Squamulose lichens grow mostly on rocks or soil, occasionally on dead wood, and are generally attached by single rhizoidal hyphae, either produced at all points of the under surface, or from the base only, growth in the latter case being one-sided. In a few instances, as in *Heppia Guepini*, there is a central hold-fast.

A frequent type of squamulose thallus is that termed "placodioid," or "effigurate," in which the squamulose character is chiefly apparent at the circumference. The thallus is more or less orbicular in outline; the centre may be squamulose or granular and cracked into areolae; the outer edge is composed of radiating lobules closely appressed to the substratum (Fig. 42).

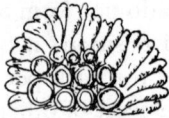

Fig. 42. *Placodium murorum* DC. Part of placodioid thallus with apothecia × 2.

All lichens with this type of thallus were at one time included in the genus *Placodium*, now restricted by some lichenologists to squamulose or crustaceous species with polarilocular spores. Many of them rival *Xanthoria parietina* in their brilliant yellow colouring.

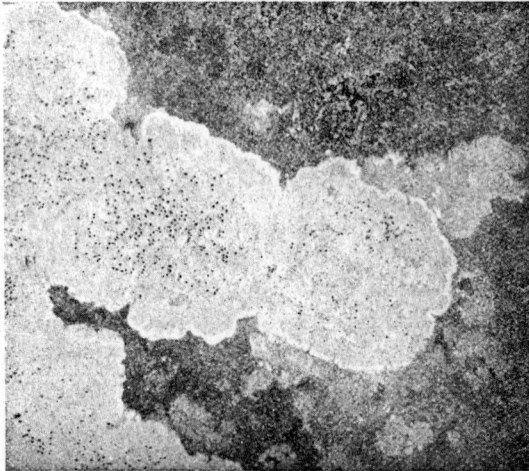

Fig. 43. *Lecania candicans* A. Zahlbr., with placodioid thallus, reduced (S. H., *Photo.*).

There are also greyish-white effigurate lichens such as *Lecanora saxicola*, *Lecania candicans* (Fig. 43) and *Buellia canescens*, well-known British species.

B. Tissues of Squamulose Thallus

The anatomical structure of the squamules is in general somewhat similar to that of the crustaceous thallus: an upper cortex, a gonidial zone, and below that a medullary layer of loose hyphae with sometimes a lower cortex.

1. The upper cortex, as in crustaceous lichens, is generally of the "decomposed"[1] or amorphous type: interlaced hyphae with thick gelatinous walls. A more highly developed form is apparent in *Parmeliella* and *Pannaria* where the upper cortex is formed of plectenchyma, while in the squamules of *Heppia* the whole structure is built up of plectenchyma, with the exception of a narrow band of loose hyphae in the central pith.

2. The gonidia are Myxophyceae or Chlorophyceae; the squamules in some instances may be homoiomerous as in *Lepidocollema*, but generally they belong to the heteromerous series, with the gonidia in a circumscribed zone, and either continuous or in groups. Friedrich[2] held that, as in crustaceous lichens the development of the gonidial as compared with the other tissues depended on the substratum. The squamules of *Pannaria micro-phylla* on sandstone were 100 μ thick, and the gonidial layer occupied 80 or 90 μ of the whole[3]. With that may be compared *Placodium Garovagli* on lime-containing rock: the gonidial layer measured only 50 μ across, the pith hyphae 280 μ and the rhizoidal hyphae that penetrated the rock 500 μ.

3. The medullary layer, as a rule, is of closely compacted hyphae which give solidity to the squamules; in those of *Heppia* it is almost entirely formed of plectenchyma.

4. The lower cortex is frequently little developed or absent, especially when the squamules are closely applied to the support as in some species of *Dermatocarpon*. In some of the squamulose *Lecanorae* (*L. crassa* and *L. saxicola*) the lowest hyphae are somewhat more closely interwoven; they become brown in colour, and the lichen is attached to the substratum by rhizoid-like branches. In *Lecanora lentigera* there is a layer of parallel hyphae along the under surface. Further development is reached when a plectenchyma of thick-walled cells is formed both above and below, as in *Psoroma hypnorum*, though on the under surface the continuity is often broken. The squamules of *Cladoniae* are described under the radiate-stratose series.

---

[1] See p. 83.   [2] Friedrich 1906.   [3] See p. 76.

3. FOLIOSE LICHENS

A. Development of Foliose Thallus

The larger leafy lichens are occasionally monophyllous and attached at
a central point as in *Umbilicaria*, but mostly they are broken up into lobes
which are either imbricate and crowded, or represent the dividing and
branching of the expanding thallus at the circumference. They are horizontal spreading structures, with marginal and apical growth. The several
tissues of the squamule are repeated in the foliose thallus, but further provision is made to meet the requirements of the larger organism. There is the
greater development of cortical tissue, especially on the lower surface, and
the more abundant formation of rhizoidal organs to attach the large flat
fronds to the support. There are also various adaptations to secure the aeration of the internal tissues[1].

B. Cortical Tissues

Schwendener[2] was the first who, with the improved microscope, made
a systematic study of the minute structure of lichens. He examined typical
species in genera of widely different groups and described their anatomy in
detail. The most variable and perhaps the most important of the tissues
of lichens is the cortex, which is most fully developed in the larger thalli, and
as the same type of cortical structures recurs in lichens widely different in
affinity as well as in form, it seems well to group together here the ascertained
facts about these covering layers.

a. Types of Cortical Structure. Zukal[3], and more recently
Hue[4], have made independent studies in the comparative morphology of
the thallus and have given particular attention to the different varieties
of cortex. They each find that the variations come under a definite series
of types. Zukal recognized five of these:

1. **Pseudoparenchymatous** (plectenchyma): by frequent septation of
regularly arranged hyphae and by coalescence a kind of continuous cell-
structure is formed.

2. **Palisade cells**: the outer elongate ends of the hyphae lie close
together in a direction at right angles to the surface of the thallus and form
a coherent row of parallel cells.

3. **Fibrous**: the cortical hyphae lie in strands of fine filaments parallel
with the surface of the thallus.

4. **Intricate**: hyphae confusedly interwoven and becoming dark in
colour form the lower cortex of some foliose lichens.

[1] See p. 126.   [2] Schwendener 1860, 1863 and 1868.   [3] Zukal 1895, p. 1305.   [4] Hue 1906.

These four types, Zukal finds, are practically without interstices in the tissue and form a perfect protection against excessive transpiration. He adds yet another form:

5. **A cortex formed of hyphae with dark-coloured swollen cells,** which is not a protection against transpiration. It occurs among lower crustaceous forms.

Hue has summed up the different varieties under four types, but as he has omitted the "fibrous" cortex, we arrive again at five different kinds of cortical formation, though they do not exactly correspond to those of Zukal. A definite name is given to each type:

1. **Intricate:** an intricate dense layer of gelatinous-walled hyphae, branching in all directions, but not coalescent (Fig. 44). This rather unusual type of cortex occurs in *Sphaerophorus* and *Stereocaulon*, both of which have an upright rigid thallus (fruticose).

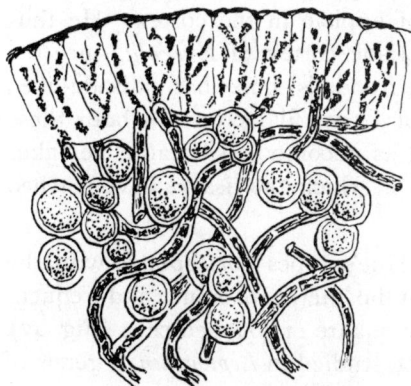

Fig. 44. *Sphaerophorus coralloides* Pers. Transverse section of cortex and gonidial layer near the growing point of a frond × 600.

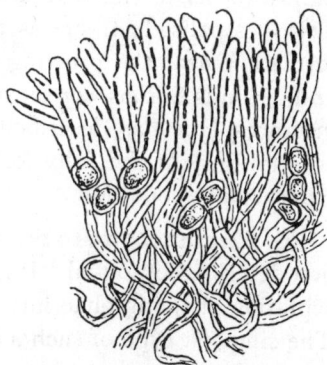

Fig. 45. *Roccella fuciformis* DC. Transverse section of cortex near the growing point of a frond × 600.

2. **Fastigiate:** the hyphae bend outwards or upwards to form the cortex. A primary filament can be distinguished with abundant branches, all tending in the same direction; anastomosis may take place between the hyphae. The end branches are densely packed, though there are occasional interstices (Fig. 45). Such a cortex occurs in *Thamnolia*; in several genera of Roccellaceae—*Roccellographa, Roccellina, Reinkella, Pentagenella, Combea, Schizopelte* and *Roccella*—and also in the crustaceous genus *Dirina*. The fastigiate cortex corresponds with Zukal's palisade cells.

3. **Decomposed:** in this, the most frequent type of cortex, the hyphae that travel up from the gonidial layer become irregularly branched and frequently septate. The cell-walls of the terminal branches become swollen into a gelatinous mass, the transformation being brought about by a change

in the molecular constituents of the cell-walls which permits the imbibition and storage of water. The tissue, owing to the enormous increase of the wall, is so closely pressed together that the individual hyphae become indistinct; the cell-lumen finally disappears altogether, or, at most, is only to be detected in section as a narrow disconnected dark streak. The decomposed cortex is characteristic of many lichens, crustaceous (Fig. 46) and squamulose, as well as of such highly developed genera as *Usnea, Letharia, Ramalina, Cetraria, Evernia* and certain *Parmeliae.*

Fig. 46. *Lecanora glaucoma* var. *corrugata* Nyl. Vertical section of cortex × 500 (after Hue).

Zukal took no note of the decomposed cortex, but the omission is intentional and is due to his regarding the structure of the youngest stages of the thallus near the growing point as the most typical and as giving the best indication as to the true arrangement of hyphae in the cortex. He thus describes palisade tissue as the characteristic cortex of *Evernia,* since the formation near the growing point of the fronds is somewhat palisade-like; and he finds fibrous cortex at the tips of *Usnea* filaments. In both these instances Hue has described the cortex as decomposed because he takes account only of the fully formed thallus in which the tissues have reached a permanent condition.

4. **Plectenchymatous**: the last of Hue's types corresponds with the first described by Zukal. It is the result of the lateral coherence and frequent septation of the hyphae into short almost square or rounded cells (Fig. 47). The simplest type of such a cortex can be studied in *Leptogium,* a genus of

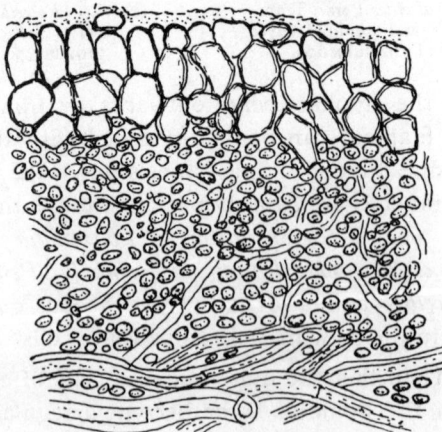

Fig. 47. *Peltigera canina* DC. Vertical section of cortex and gonidial zone × 600.

gelatinous lichens in which the tips of the hyphae are cut off at the surface by one or more septa. The resulting cells are wider than the hyphae and they cohere together to form, in some species, disconnected patches of cells; in others, a continuous cortical covering one or more cells thick, while in the margin of the apothecium they form a deep cellular layer. The cellular type of cortex is found also, as already stated, in some crustaceous *Pertusariae*, and in a few squamulose genera or species. It forms the uppermost layer of the *Peltigera* thallus and both cortices of many of the larger foliose lichens such as *Sticta*, *Parmelia*, etc.

5. The "fibrous" cortex must be added to this series, as was pointed out by Heber Howe[1] who gave the less appropriate designation of "simple" to the type. It consists of long rather sparingly branched slender hyphae that grow in a direction parallel with the surface of the thallus (Fig. 48). It is characteristic of several fruticose and foliose lichens with more or less upright growth, such as we find in several of the *Physciae*, and in the allied genus *Teloschistes*, in *Alectoria*, several genera of Roccellaceae, in *Usnea longissima* and in *Parmelia pubescens*, etc. Zukal would have included all the *Usneae* as the tips are fibrous.

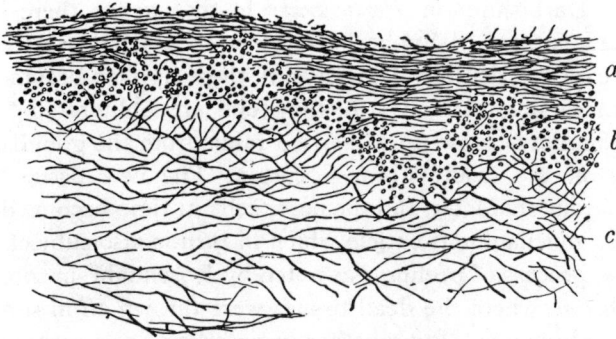

Fig. 48. *Physcia ciliaris* DC. Vertical section of thallus. *a*, cortex; *b*, gonidial zone; *c*, medulla. × 100.

More than one type of cortex, as already stated, may appear in a genus; a striking instance of variability occurs in *Solorina* where, as Hue[2] has pointed out, the cortex of *S. octospora* is fastigiate, that of all the other species being plectenchymatous. Cortical development is a specific rather than a generic characteristic.

b. ORIGIN OF VARIATION IN CORTICAL STRUCTURE. The immediate causes making for differentiation in cortical development are: the prevailing direction of growth of the hyphae as they rise from the gonidial zone; the amount of branching and the crowding of the filaments; the frequency of septation; and the thickening or degeneration of the cell-walls which may

[1] Heber Howe 1912.   Hue 1911.

become almost or entirely mucilaginous. In the plectenchymatous cortex, the walls may remain quite thin and the cells small as in *Xanthoria parietina*, or the walls may be much thickened as in both cortices of *Sticta*. As a result of stretching the cell may increase enormously in size: in some instances where the internal hyphae are about 3μ to 4μ in width, the cortical cells formed from these hyphae may have a cell cavity 15μ to 16μ in diameter.

c. LOSS AND RENEWAL OF CORTEX. Very frequently the cortex is covered over by a layer of homogeneous mucilage which forms an outer cuticle. It arises from the continual degeneration of the outer cell-walls and it is liable to friction and removal by atmospheric agency as was first described by Schwendener[1] in the weather-beaten cortex of *Umbilicaria pustulata*. He had noted the irregular jagged outline of the cross section of the thallus, and he then suggested, as the probable reason, the decay of the outer rind with the constant renewal of it by the hyphae from the underlying gonidial zone, though he was unable definitely to prove his theory. The peeling of the dead outer layer (with its replacement by new tissue) has however been observed many times since his day. It has been described by Darbishire[2] in *Pertusaria*: in that genus there is at first a primary cortex formed of hyphae that grow in a radial direction, parallel to the surface of the thallus. The walls of these hyphae become gradually more and more mucilaginous till the cells are obliterated. Meanwhile short-celled filaments grow up in serried ranks from the gonidial layer and finally push off the dead "fibrous" cortex. The new tissue takes on a plectenchymatous character, and the outer cells in time become decomposed and provide a mucilaginous cuticle which in turn is also subject to wasting.

The same process of peeling was noted by Rosendahl[3] in some species of brown *Parmeliae*, where the dead tissues were thrown off in shreds, though only in isolated patches. But whether in patches or as a continuous sheath, there is constant degeneration, with continual renewal of the dead material from the internal tissues.

The cortex is the most highly developed of all the lichen structures and is of immense importance to the plant as may be judged from the various adaptations to different needs[4]. The cortical cell-walls are frequently impregnated with some dark-coloured substance which, in exposed situations, must counteract the influence of too direct sunlight and be of service in sheltering the gonidia. Lichen acids—sometimes very brightly coloured—and oxalic acid are deposited in the cortical tissues in great abundance and aid in retaining moisture; but the two chief functions to

[1] Schwendener 1863, p. 180.   [2] Darbishire 1897.   [3] Rosendahl 1907.
[4] See p. 96.

which the cortex is specially adapted are the checking of transpiration and the strengthening of the thallus against external strains.

d. CORTICAL HAIRS OR TRICHOMES. Though somewhat rare, cortical hairs are present on the upper surface of several foliose lichens. They take rise, in all the instances noted, as a prolongation of one of the cell-rows forming a plectenchymatous cortex.

In *Peltidea* (*Peltigera*) *aphthosa* they are especially evident near the growing edges of the thallus; and they take part in the development of the superficial cephalodia[1] which are a constant feature of the lichen. They tend to disappear with age and leave the central older parts of the thallus smooth and shining. In several other species of *Peltigera* (*P. canina*, etc.) they are present and persist during the life of the cortex. In these lichens the cells of the cortical tissue are thin-walled, all except the outer layer, the membranes of which are much thicker. The hairs rising from them are also thick-walled and septate. Generally they branch in all directions and anastomose with neighbouring hairs so that a confused felted tangle is formed; they vary in size but are, as a rule, about double the width of the medullary hyphae as are the cortical cells from which they rise. They disappear from the thallus, frequently in patches, probably by weathering, but over large surfaces, and especially where any inequality affords a shelter, they persist as a soft down.

Hairs are also present on the upper surface of some *Parmeliae*. Rosendahl[2] has described and figured them in *P. glabra* and *P. verruculifera*—short pointed unbranched hyphae, two or more septate and with thickened walls. They are most easily seen near the edge of the thallus, though they persist more or less over the surface; they also grow on the margins of the apothecia. In *P. verruculifera* they arise from the soredia; in *P. glabra* a few isolated hairs are present on the under surface.

In *Nephromium tomentosum* there is a scanty formation of hairs on the upper surface. They are abundant on the lower surface, and function as attaching organs. A thick tomentum of hairs is similarly present on the lower surface of many of the Stictaceae either as an almost unbroken covering or in scattered patches. In several species of *Leptogium* they grow out from the lower cortical cells and attach the thin horizontal fronds; and very occasionally they are present in *Collema*.

C. GONIDIAL TISSUES

With the exception of some species of *Collema* and *Leptogium* lichens included under the term foliose, are heteromerous in structure, and the algae that form the gonidial zone are situated below the upper cortex and, there-

---

[1] See p. 133.　　　　　　　　　　　　[2] Rosendahl 1907.

fore, in the most favourable position for photosynthesis. Whether belonging
to the Myxophyceae or the Chlorophyceae, they form a green band, straight
and continuous in some forms, in others somewhat broken up into groups.
In certain species they push up at intervals among the cortical cells, as in
Gyrophora and in *Parmelia tristis*. In *Solorina crocea* a regular series of
gonidial pyramids rises towards the upper surface. The green cells are
frequently more dense at some points than at others, and they may penetrate in groups well into the medulla.

The fungal tissue of the gonidial zone is composed of hyphae which
have thinner walls, and are generally somewhat loosely interlacing. In
Peltigera[1] the gonidial hyphae are so connected by frequent branching and
by anastomosis that a net-like structure is formed, in the meshes of which
the algae—a species of *Nostoc*—are massed more or less in groups. In
lichens with a plectenchymatous cortex, the cellular tissue may extend
downwards into the gonidial zone and the gonidia thus become enmeshed
among the cells, a type of formation well seen in the squamulose species,
Dermatocarpon lachneum and *Heppia Guepini*, where the massive plectenchyma of both the upper and lower cortices encroaches on the pith. In
Endocarpon and in *Psoroma* the gonidia are also surrounded by short cells.

A similar type of structure occurs in *Cora Pavonia*, one of the Hymeno-
lichenes: the gonidial hyphae in that species form a cellular tissue in which
are embedded the blue-green *Chroococcus* cells[2].

D. MEDULLA AND LOWER CORTEX

a. MEDULLA. The hyphal tissue of the dorsiventral thallus that lies
between the gonidial zone and the lower cortex or base of the plant is
always referred to as the medulla or pith. It is, as a rule, by far the most
considerable portion of the thallus. In *Parmelia caperata* (Fig. 49), for
instance, the lobes of which are about 300 μ thick, over 200 μ of the space
is occupied by this layer. It varies however very largely in extent in
different lichens according to species, and also according to the substratum.
In another *Parmelia* with a very thin thallus, *P. alpicola* growing on quartzite, the medulla measures scarcely twice the width of the gonidial zone.
It forms a fairly massive tissue in some of the crustaceous lichens—in some
Pertusariae and *Lecanorae*—attaining a width of about 600 μ.

Nylander[3] distinguished three types of medullary tissue in lichens:

(1) *felted*, which includes all those of a purely filamentous structure;

(2) *cretaceous* or *tartareous*, more compact than the felted, and containing
granular or crystalline substances as in some *Pertusariae*; and lastly

(3) the *cellular* medulla in which the closely packed hyphae are divided

---

[1] Meyer 1902.					[2] See p. 52.					[3] Nylander 1858.

into short cells and a kind of plectenchyma is formed, as in *Lecanora* (*Psoroma*) *hypnorum*, in *Endocarpon*, etc.

Fig. 49. *Parmelia caperata* Ach. (S. H., *Photo.*).

The felted medulla is characteristic of most lichens and is formed of loose slender branching septate hyphae with thickish walls. This interwoven hyphal texture provides abundant air-spaces.

Hue[1] has noted that the walls of the medullary hyphae in *Parmeliae* are smooth, unless they have been exposed to great extremes of heat or cold, when they become wrinkled or scaly. They are very thick-walled in *Peltigera* (Fig. 50).

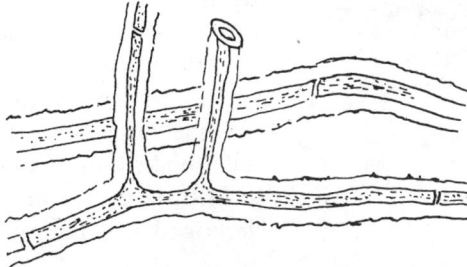

Fig. 50. Hyphae from lower medulla of *Peltigera canina* DC. × 600.

[1] Hue 1898.

b. LOWER CORTEX. In some foliose lichens such as *Peltigera* there is no special tissue developed on the under surface. In *Lobaria pulmonaria* large patches of the under surface are bare, and the medulla is exposed to the outer atmosphere, sheltered only by its position. In some other lichens the lowermost hyphae lie closer together and a kind of felt of almost parallel filaments is formed, generally darker in colour, as in *Lecanora lentigera*, and in some species of *Physcia.*

Most frequently however the tissues of the upper cortex are repeated on the lower surface, though differing somewhat in detail. In all of the brown *Parmeliae*, according to Rosendahl[1], the structure is identical for both cortices, though the upper develops now hairs, now isidia, breathing pores, etc., while the lower produces rhizinae. The amorphous mucilaginous cuticle so often present on the upper surface is absent from the lower, the walls of the latter being often charged instead with dark-brown pigments.

c. HYPOTHALLIC STRUCTURES. An unusual development of hyphae from the lower cortex occurs in the genera *Anzia* and *Pannoparmelia*—both closely related to *Parmelia*—whereby a loose sponge-like hypothallus of anastomosing reticulate strands is formed. In one of the simpler types, *Anzia colpodes,* a North American species, the hyphae passing out from the lower medulla become abruptly dark-brown in colour, and are divided into short thick-walled cells. Frequent branching and anastomosis of these hyphae result in the formation of a cushion-like structure about twice the bulk of the thallus. In another species from Australia (*A. Japonica*) there is a lower cortex, distinct from the medulla, consisting of septate colourless hyphae with thick walls. From these branch out free filaments, similar in structure but dark in colour, which branch and anastomose as in the previous species.

In *Pannoparmelia* the lower cortex and the outgrowths from it are several cells thick; they may be thick-walled as in *Anzia*, or they may be thin-walled as described and figured by Darbishire[2] in

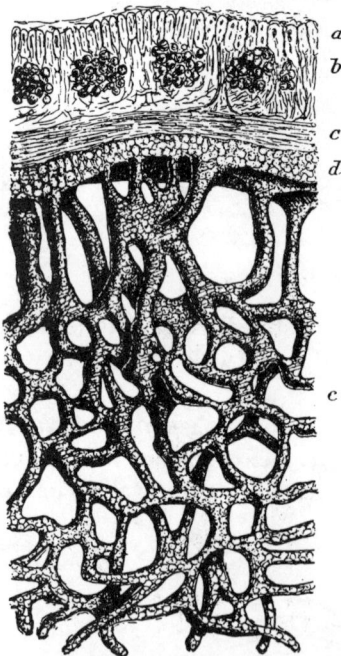

Fig. 51. *Pannoparmelia anzioides* Darb. Vertical section of thallus and hypothallus. *a,* cortex; *b,* gonidial zone; *c,* medulla; *d,* lower cortex; *e,* hypothallus. × ca. 450 (after Darbishire).

[1] Rosendahl 1907.

[2] Darbishire 1912.

Pannoparmelia anzioides, a species from Tierra del Fuego (Fig. 51). A somewhat dense interwoven felt of hyphae occurs also in certain parts of the
under surface of *Parmelia physodes*[1].

This peculiar structure, regarded as a hypothallus, is probably of service
in the retention of moisture. The thick cell-walls in most of the forms
suggest some such function.

E. STRUCTURES FOR PROTECTION AND ATTACHMENT

Such structures are almost wholly confined to the larger foliose and
fruticose lichens and are all of the same simple type; they are fungal
in origin and very rarely are gonidia associated with them.

a. CILIA. In a few widely separated lichens stoutish cilia are borne,
mostly on the margins of the thallus lobes, or on the margins of the apo-

Fig. 52. *Usnea florida* Web. Ciliate apothecia (S. H., *Photo.*).

thecia (Fig. 52). They arise from the cortical cells or hyphae, several of
which grow out in a compact strand which tapers gradually to a point.
Cilia vary in length up to about 1 cm. or even longer. In some lichens they

[1] Porter 1919.

retain the colour of the cortex and are greyish or whitish-grey, as in *Physcia ciliaris* or in *Physcia hispida* (Fig. 110). They provide a yellow fringe to the apothecia of *Physcia chrysophthalma* and a green fringe to those of *Usnea florida*. They are dark-brown or almost black in *Parmelia perlata* var. *ciliata* and in *P. cetrata*, etc. as also in *Gyrophora cylindrica*. The fronds of *Cetraria islandica* and other species of the genus are bordered with short spinulose brown hairs whose main function seems to be the bearing of "pycnidia" though in many cases they are barren (Fig. 128).

Superficial cilia are more rarely formed than marginal ones, but they are characteristic of one not uncommon British species, *Parmelia proboscidea* (*P. pilosella* Hue). Scattered over the surface of that lichen are numerous crowded groups of isidia which, frequently, are prolonged upwards as dark-brown or blackish cilia. Nearly every isidium bears a small brown spot on the apex at an early stage of growth. Similar cilia are sparsely scattered over the thallus, but their base is always a rather stouter grey structure, which suggests an isidial origin. Cilia also occur on the margin of the lobes.

As lichens are a favourite food of snails, insects, etc., it is considered that these structures are protective in function, and that they impede, if they do not entirely prevent, the larger marauders in their work of destruction.

b. RHIZINAE. Lichen rootlets are mainly for the purpose of attachment and have little significance as organs of absorption. They have been noted in only one crustaceous lichen, *Varicellaria microsticta*[1], an alpine species that spreads over bark or soil, and which is further distinguished by being

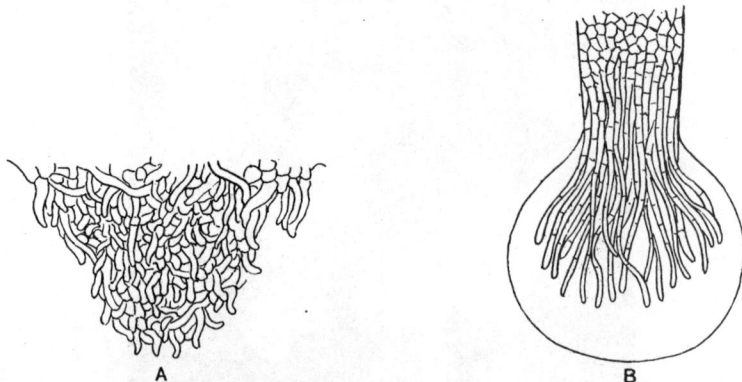

Fig. 53. Rhizoid of *Parmelia exasperata* Carroll (*P. aspidota* Rosend.). A, hyphae growing out from lower cortex × 450. B, tip of rhizoid with gelatinous sheath × 335 (after Rosendahl).

provided with a lower cortex of plectenchyma. In foliose lichens they are frequently abundant, though by no means universal, and attach the spreading fronds to the support. They originate, as Schwendener[2] pointed out, from the outer cortical cells, exactly as do the cilia, and are scattered over the

[1] Darbishire 1897.   [2] Schwendener 1860.

under surface or are confined to special areas. Rosendahl[1] has described their development in the brown species of *Parmeliae*: the under cortex in these lichens is formed of a cellular plectenchyma with thickish walls; the rootlets arise by the outgrowth of several neighbouring cells from some slight elevation near the edge of the thallus. Branching and interlacing of these growing rhizinal hyphae follow, the outermost frequently spreading outwards at right angles to the axis, and forming a cellular cortex. The apex of the rhizoid is generally an enlarged tuft of loose hyphae involved in mucilage (Fig. 53), a provision for securing firmer cohesion to the support; or the tips spread out as a kind of sucker. Not unfrequently neighbouring "rootlets" are connected by mucilage at the tips, or by outgrowths of their hyphae, and a rather large hold-fast sheath is formed.

In species of *Peltigera* (Fig. 54) the rhizinae are confined to the veins or ridges (Fig. 55); they are thickish at the base, and are generally rather

Fig. 54. *Peltigera canina* DC. (S. H., *Photo*).

Fig. 55. *Peltigera canina* DC. Under surface with veins and rhizoids (after Reinke).

long and straggling. Meyer[2] states that the central hyphae are stoutish and much entangled owing to the branching and frequent anastomosis of one hypha with another; the peripheral terminal branches are thinner-walled and free. These rhizinae vary in colour from white in *Peltigera canina* to brown or black in other species. Most species of *Peltigera* spread over grass or mosses, to which they cling by these long loose "rootlets."

Lichen rhizinae, distinguished by Reinke[3] as "aerial rhizinae," are more

[1] Rosendahl 1907.   [2] Meyer 1902.   [3] Reinke 1895, p. 186.

or less characteristic of all the species of *Parmelia* with the exception of
those belonging to the subgenus *Hypogymnia* in which they are of very rare
occurrence, arising, according to Bitter[1], only in response to some external
friction. They are invariably dark-coloured, rather short, about one to a
few millimetres in length, and are simple or branched. The branches may
go off at any angle and are sometimes curved back at the ends in anchor-
like fashion. The *Parmeliae* grow on firm substances, trees, rocks, etc., and
the irregularities of their attaching structures are conditioned by the obstacles
encountered on the substratum. Not unfrequently the lobes are attached
by the rhizinae to underlying portions of the thallus.

In the genus *Gyrophora*, the rhizinae are simple strands of hyphae
(*G. polyrhiza*) or they are corticate structures (*G. murina*, *G. spodochroa*
and *G. vellea*). They are also present in species of *Solorina*, *Ricasolia*,
Sticta and *Physcia* and very sparingly in *Cetraria* (*Platysma*).

c. HAPTERA. Sernander[2] has grouped all the more distinctively aerial
organs of attachment, apart from rhizinae, under the term "hapteron" and he
has described a number of instances in which cilia and even the growing
points of the thallus may become transformed to haptera or sucker-like
sheaths.

The long cilia of *Physcia ciliaris* occasionally form haptera at their tips
where the hyphae are loose and in active growing condition. Contact with
some substance induces branching by which a spreading sheath arises; a
plug-like process may also be developed which pierces the substance encountered—not unfrequently another lobe of its own thallus. The long
flaccid fronds of *Evernia furfuracea* are frequently connected together by
bridge-like haptera which rise at any angle of the thallus or from any part
of the surface.

The spinous hairs that border the thalline margins in *Cetraria* may also,
in contact with some body—often another frond of the lichen—form a
hapteron, either while the spermogonium, which occupies the tip of the
spine, is still in a rudimentary stage, or after it has discharged its spermatia.
The small sucker sheath may in that case arise either from the apex of the
cilium, from the wall of the spermogonium or from its base. By means of
these haptera, not only different individuals become united together, but
instances are given by Sernander in which *Cetraria islandica*, normally a
ground lichen, had become epiphytic by attaching itself in this way to the
trunk of a tree (*Pinus sylvestris*).

In *Alectoria*, haptera are formed at the tip of the thallus filament as an
apical cone-like growth from which hyphae may branch out and penetrate
any convenient object. A species of this genus was thus found clinging to

---

[1] Bitter 1901.   [2] Sernander 1901.

stems of *Betula nana*. Apical haptera are very frequent in *Cladonia rangi-ferina* and *Cl. sylvatica*, induced here also by contact. These two plants, as well as several species of *Cetraria*, tend, indeed, to become entirely epiphytic on the heaths of the *Calluna* formations. Haptera similar to those of *Alectoria* occur in *Usnea, Evernia, Ramalina* and *Cornicularia* (*Cetraria*). In *Evernia prunastri* var. *stictoceros*, a heath form, the fronds become attached to the stems and branches of *Erica tetralix* by hapteroid strands of slender glutinous hyphae which persist on the frond of the lichen after it is detached as small very dark tubercles surmounted, as Parfitt[1] pointed out, by a dark-brown grumous mass of cells. Plug-like haptera may be formed at the base of *Cladoniae* which attach them to each other and to the substratum. The brightly coloured fronds of *Letharia vulpina* are attached to each other in somewhat tangled fashion by lateral bridges or by fascicles of hyphae dark-brown at the base but colourless at the apices, exactly like aerial adventitious rhizinae. They grow out from the fronds generally at or near the tips and lay hold of a neighbouring frond by means of mucilage. These haptera are evidently formed in response to friction. Haptera along with other lichen attachments have received considerable attention from Galløe[2]. He finds them arising on various positions of the lichen fronds and has classified them accordingly.

After the haptera have become attached, they increase in size and strength and supply a strong anchorage for the plant; the point of contact frequently forms a basis for renewed growth while the part beneath the hapteron may gradually die off. Haptera are more especially characteristic of fruticose lichens, but Sernander considers that the rhizinae of foliose species may function as haptera. They are important organs of tundra and heath formations as they enable the lichens to get a foothold in well-lighted positions, and by their aid the fronds are more able to resist the extreme tearing strains to which they are subjected in high and unsheltered moor-lands.

F. Strengthening Tissues of Stratose Lichens

Squamulose and foliose lichens grow mostly in close relation with the support, and the flat expanding thallus, as in the *Parmeliae*, is attached at many points to the substance—tree, rock, etc.—over which the plants spread. Special provision for support is therefore not required, and the lobes remain thin and flaccid. Yet, in a number of widely different genera the attachment to the substratum is very slight, and in these we find an adaptation of existing tissues fitted to resist tearing strains, resistance being almost invariably secured by the strengthening of the cortical layers.

[1] Parfitt in Leighton 1871, p. 470.   [2] Galløe 1915.

a. BY DEVELOPMENT OF THE CORTEX.   Such a transformation of tissue is well illustrated in *Heppia Guepini.* The thallus consists of rigid squamules which are attached at one point only; the cortex of both surfaces is plectenchymatous and very thick and even the medulla is largely cellular.

The much larger but equally rigid coriaceous thallus of *Dermatocarpon miniatum* (Fig. 56) has also a single central attachment or umbilicus, and

Fig. 56. *Dermatocarpon miniatum* Th. Fr. (S. H., *Photo.*).

both cortices consist of a compact many-layered plectenchyma.   The same structure occurs in *Umbilicaria pustulata* and in some species of *Gyrophora,* which, having only a single central hold-fast, gain the necessary stiffening through the increase of the cortical layers.

In the Stictaceae there are a large number of widely-expanded forms, and as the attachment depends mostly on a somewhat short tomentum, strength is obtained here also by the thick plectenchymatous cortex of both surfaces.   When areas denuded of tomentum and cortex occur, as in *Lobaria pulmonaria,* the under surface is not sensibly weakened, since the cortical tissue remains connected in a stout and firm reticulation.

b. BY DEVELOPMENT OF VEINS OR NERVES.   Certain ground lichens belonging to the Peltigeraceae have a wide spreading thallus often with very large lobes.   The upper cortex is a many-layered plectenchyma, but the under surface is covered only by a loose felt of hyphae which branch out into a more or less dense tomentum.   As the firm upper cortex continues to increase by intercalary growth from the branching upwards of hyphae from the meristematic gonidial zone, there occurs an extension of the upper thallus with which the lower cannot keep pace[1]. A little way back from the edge, the result of the stretching is seen in the splitting asunder of the felted hyphae of the under surface, and in the consequent formation of a reticulate series of ridges known as the veins or nerves ; they represent the original tomentose covering, and are white, black or brown, according to the colour of the tomentum itself. The naked ellipsoid interstices show the white medulla, and, if the veins are wide, the colourless areas are correspondingly small. Rhizinae are formed on the nerves in several of the species, and anchor the thallus to the support. In *Peltigera canina*, the under surface is almost wholly colourless, the veins are very prominent (Fig. 55), and are further strengthened by the growth and branching of the parallel hyphae of which they are composed. They serve to strengthen the large and flabby thallus and form a rigid base for the long rhizinae by which the lichen clings to the grass or moss over which it grows.

The most perfect development of strengthening nerves is to be found in *Hydrothyria venosa*[2], a rather rare water lichen that occurs in the streams of North America. It consists of fan-like lobes of thin structure, the cortex being only about one cell thick. The fronds are about 3 cm. wide and they are contracted below into a stalk which serves to attach the plant to the substratum. Several fronds may grow together in a dense tuft, the expanded upper portion floating freely in the water. Frequently the plants form a dense growth over the rocky beds of the stream.

At the point where the stalk expands into the free erect frond, there arise a series of stout veins which spread upwards and outwards. They are definitely formed structures and not adaptations of pre-existing tissues : certain hyphae arise from the medulla at the contracted base of the frond, take a radial direction and, by increase, become developed into firm strands. The individual hyphae also increase in size, and the swelling of the nerve gives rise to a ridge prominent on both surfaces. They seldom anastomose at first but towards the tips they become smaller and spread out in delicate ramifications which unite at various points. There is no doubt, as Bitter[1] points out, that the nerves function as strengthening tissues and preserve the frond from the strain of the water currents which would, otherwise, tear apart the delicate texture.

[1] Bitter 1899.   [2] Sturgis 1890.

III. RADIATE THALLUS

1. CHARACTERS OF RADIATE THALLUS

In the stratose dorsiventral thallus, there is a widely extended growing area situated round the free margins of the thallus. In the radiate thallus of the fruticose or filamentous lichens, growth is confined to an apical region. Attachment to the substratum is at one point only—the base of the plant— thus securing the exposure of all sides equally to light. The cortex surrounds the fronds, and the gonidia (mostly Protococcaceae) lie in a zone or in groups between the cortex and the medulla. It is the highest type of vegetative development in the lichen kingdom, since it secures the widest room for the gonidial layer, and the largest opportunity for photosynthesis.

Shrubby upright lichens consist mostly of strap-shaped fronds, either simple or branched, which may be broadened to thin bands (Fig. 57) or may be narrowed and thickened till they are almost cylindrical. The fronds vary in length according to the species from a few millimetres upwards:

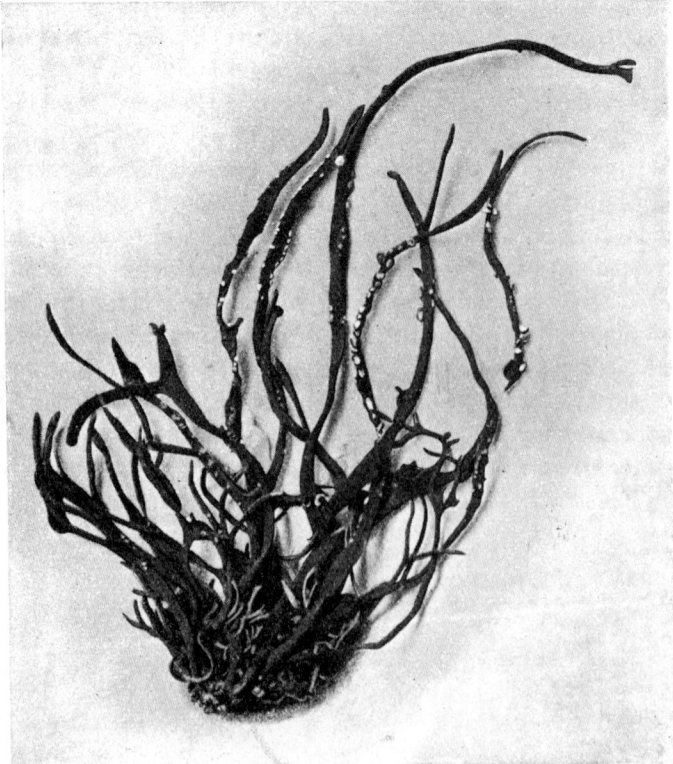

Fig. 57. *Roccella fuciformis* DC.

those of *Roccella* have been found measuring 30 cm. in length; those of *Ramalina reticulata*, the largest of all the American lichens, extend to considerably more.

Lichens of filamentous growth are more or less cylindrical (Fig. 58). They are in some species upright and of moderate length, but in a few

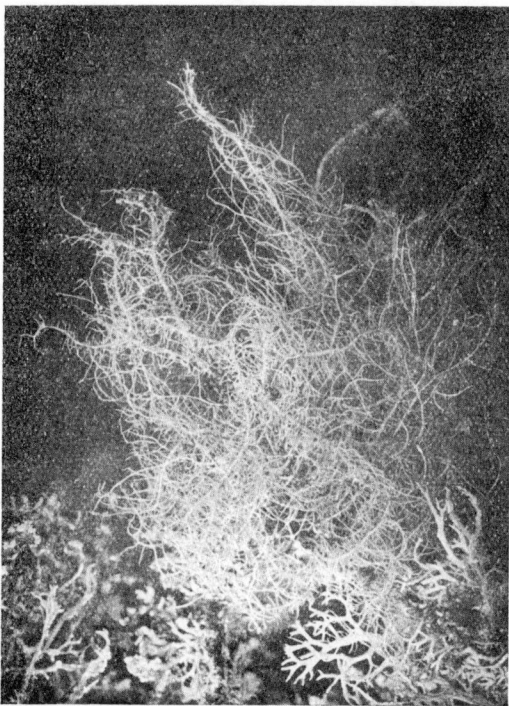

Fig. 58. *Usnea barbata* Web. (S. H., *Photo.*).

pendulous forms they grow to a great length: specimens of *Usnea longissima* have been recorded that measured 6 to 8 metres from base to tip.

The radiate type of thallus occurs in most of the lichen groups but most frequently in the Gymnocarpeae. In gelatinous Discolichens it is represented in the Lichinaceae. It is rare among Pyrenocarpeae: there is one very minute British lichen in that series, *Pyrenidium actinellum*, and one from N. America, *Pyrenothamnia*, that are of fruticose habit.

2. INTERMEDIATE TYPES OF THALLUS

Between the foliose and the fruticose types, there are intermediate forms that might be, and often are, classified now in one group and now in the other. These are chiefly: *Physcia (Anaptychia) ciliaris*, *Ph. leucomelas* and the species of *Evernia*.

In the two former the habit is more or less fruticose as the plants are affixed to the substratum at a basal point, but the fronds are decumbent and the internal structure is of the dorsiventral type : there is an upper "fibrous" cortex of closely compacted parallel hyphae, a gonidial zone—the gonidia lying partly in the cortex and partly among the loose hyphae of the medulla—and a lower cortex formed of a weft of hyphae which also run somewhat parallel to the surface. Both species are distinguished by the numerous marginal cilia, either pale or dark in colour. These two lichens are greyish-coloured on the upper surface and greyish or whitish below.

Evernia furfuracea with a basal attachment[1], and with a partly horizontal and partly upright growth, has a dorsiventral thallus, dark greyish-green above and black beneath, with occasional rhizinae towards the base. The cortex of both surfaces belongs to the "decomposed" type ; the gonidial zone lies below the upper surface, and the medullary tissue is of loose hyphae. In certain forms of the species isidia are abundant on the upper surface, a character of foliose rather than of fruticose lichens. *E. furfuracea* grows on trees and very frequently on palings.

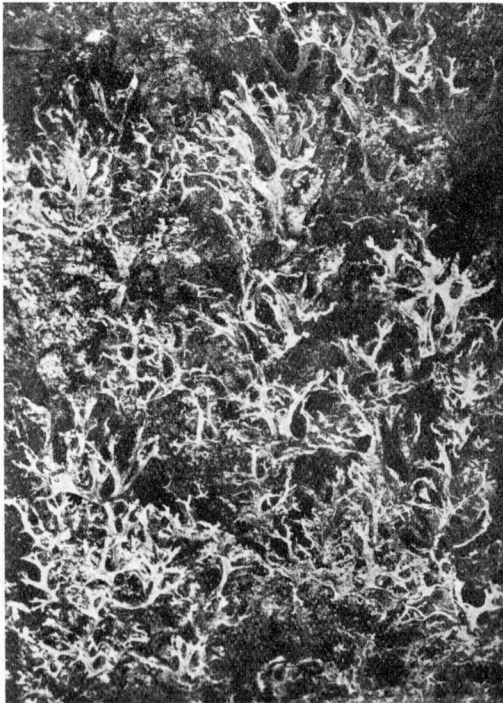

Fig. 59. *Evernia prunastri* Ach. (M. P., *Photo.*).

[1] See p. 108.

E. prunastri, the second species of the genus, is more distinctly upright in habit, with a penetrating basal hold-fast and upright strap-shaped branching fronds, light-greyish green on the "upper" surface and white on the other (Fig. 59). The internal structure is sub-radiate; both cortices are "decomposed"; the gonidial zone consists of somewhat loose groups of algae, very constant below the "upper" surface, with an occasional group in the pith near to the lower cortex in positions that are more exposed to light. There is also a tendency for the gonidial zone to pass round the margin and spread some way along the under side. The medulla is of loose arachnoid texture and the whole plant is very limp when moist. It grows on trees, often in dense clusters.

3. FRUTICOSE AND FILAMENTOUS THALLUS

A. General Structure of Thallus

The conditions of strain and tension in the upright plant are entirely different from those in the decumbent thallus, and to meet the new requirements, new adaptations of structure are provided either in the cortex or in the medulla.

Cortical Structures. With the exception of the distinctly plectenchymatous cortex, all the other types already described recur in fruticose lichens; in various ways they have been modified to provide not only covering but support to the fronds.

a. **The fastigiate cortex.** This reaches its highest development in *Roccella* in which the branched hyphal tips, slightly clavate and thick-walled, lie closely packed in palisade formation at right angles to the main axis (Fig. 45). They afford not only bending power, but give great consistency to the fronds. The cortex is further strengthened in *R. fuciformis*[1] by the compact arrangement of the medullary hyphae that run parallel with the surface, and among which occur single thick-walled filaments. The plant grows on maritime rocks in very exposed situations; and the narrow strap-shaped fronds, as stated above, may attain a length of 30 cm., though usually they are from 10 to 18 cm. in height. The same type of cortex, but less highly differentiated, affords a certain amount of stiffness to the cylindrical much weaker fronds of *Thamnolia*.

b. **The fibrous cortex.** This type is found in a number of lichens with long filamentous hanging fronds. It consists of parallel hyphae, rarely septate and rarely branched, but frequently anastomosing and with strongly thickened "sclerotic" walls. Such a cortex is the only strengthening element in *Alectoria*, and it affords great toughness and flexibility to the thong-like

[1] Darbishire 1898.

thallus. It is also present in *Ramalina* (*Alectoria*) *thrausta*, a species with slender fronds (Fig. 60).

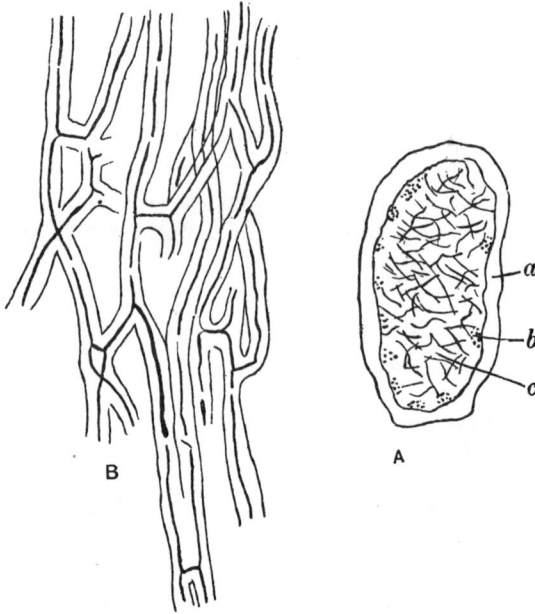

Fig. 60. *Alectoria thrausta* Ach. A, transverse section of frond; *a*, cortex; *b*, gonidia; *c*, arachnoid medulla × 37. B, fibrous hyphae from longitudinal section of cortex. × 430 (after Brandt).

In *Usnea longissima* the cortex both of the fibrillose branchlets and of the main axis is fibrous, and is composed of narrow thick-walled hyphae which grow in a long spiral round the central strand. The hyphae become more frequently septate further back from the apex (Fig. 61). Such a type of cortex provides an exceedingly elastic and efficient protection for the long slender thallus.

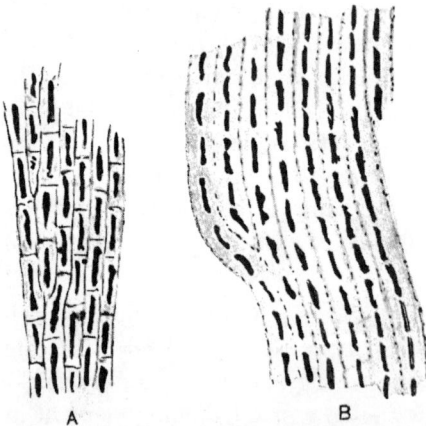

Fig. 61. *Usnea longissima* Ach. Longitudinal sections of outer cortex. A, near the apex; B, the middle portion of a fibril. × 525 (after Schulte).

The same type of cortex forms the strengthening element in the fruticose or partly fruticose members of the family Physciaceae. One of these, *Teloschistes flavicans*, is a bright yellow filamentous lichen with a somewhat straggling habit. The fronds are very slender and are either cylindrical or slightly flattened. The hyphae of the outer cortex are compactly fibrous; added toughness is given by the presence of some longitudinal strands of hyphae in the central pith.

Another still more familiar grey lichen, *Physcia ciliaris*, has long flat branching fronds which, though dorsiventral in structure, are partly upright in habit. Strength is secured as in *Teloschistes* by the fibrous upper cortex. Other species of *Physciae* are somewhat similar in habit and in structure.

In *Dendrographa leucophaea*, a slender strap-shaped rock lichen, Darbishire[1] has described the outer cortex as composed of closely compacted parallel hyphae resembling the strengthening cortex of *Alectoria* and very different from the fastigiate cortex of the *Roccellae* with which it is usually classified.

B. Special strengthening Structures

a. Sclerotic strands. This form of strengthening tissue is characteristic of *Ramalina*. With the exception of *R. thrausta* (more truly an *Alectoria*) all the species have a rather weak cortical layer of branching intricate thick-walled hyphae, regarded by Brandt[2] as plectenchymatous, but more correctly by Hue[3] as "decomposed" on account of the gelatinous walls and diminishing lumen of the irregularly arranged cells.

In *R. evernioides*, a plant with very wide flat almost decumbent fronds of soft texture, in *R. ceruchis* and in *R. homalea* there is a somewhat compact medulla which gives a slight stiffness to the thallus. The other species of the genus are provided with strengthening mechanical tissue within the cortex formed of closely united sclerotic hyphae that run parallel to the surface (Fig. 62). In a transverse section of the thallus, this tissue appears

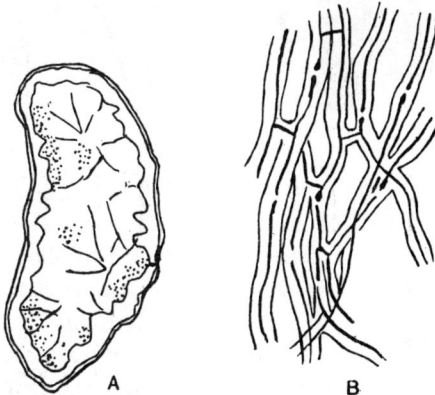

Fig. 62. *Ramalina minuscula* Nyl. A, transverse section of frond × 37; B, longitudinal strengthening hyphae of inner cortex × 430 (after Brandt).

[1] Darbishire 1895.   [2] Brandt 1906.   [3] Hue 1906.

sometimes as a continuous ring which may project irregularly into the pith (*R. calicaris*); more frequently it is in the form of strands or bundles which alternate with the groups of gonidia (*R. siliquosa, R. Curnowii*, etc.). In *R. fraxinea* these strands may be scarcely discernible in young fronds, though sometimes already well developed near the tips. Occasionally isolated strands of fibres appear in the pith (*R. Curnowii*), or the sclerotic projections may even stretch across the pith to the other side (*R. strepsilis*) (Fig. 75 B).

In the *Cladoniae* support along with flexibility is secured to the upright podetium by the parallel closely packed hyphae that form round the hollow cylinder a band called the "chondroid" layer from its cartilage-like consistency.

b. CHONDROID AXIS. The central medullary tissue in *Ramalina* is, with few exceptions, a loose arachnoid structure; often the fronds are almost hollow. In one species of *Usnea, U. Taylori*, found in polar regions, there is a similar loose though very circumscribed medullary and gonidial tissue in the centre of the somewhat cylindrical thallus, and a wide band of sclerotic fibres towards the cortex.

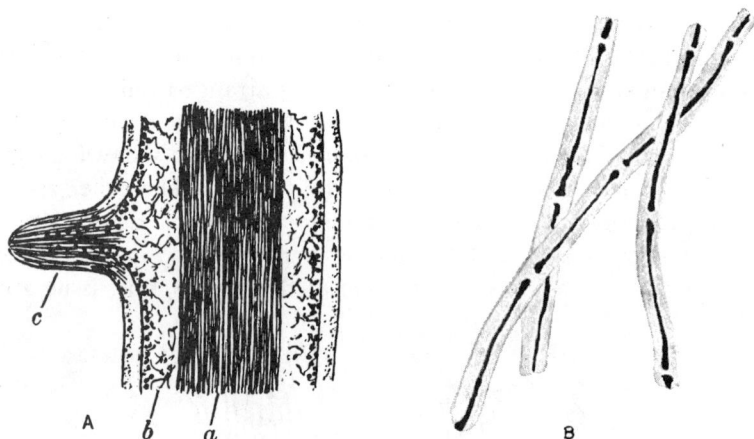

Fig. 63 A. A, *Usnea barbata* Web. Longitudinal section of filament with young adventitious branch. *a*, chondroid axis; *b*, gonidial tissue; *c*, cortex. × 100 (after Schwendener). B, *U. longissima* Ach. Hyphae from central axis × 525 (after Schulte).

In all other species of *Usnea* the medulla itself is transformed into a strong central strand of long-celled thick-walled hyphae closely knit together by frequent anastomoses (Fig. 63 A). This central strand of the Usneas is known as the "chondroid axis." A narrow band of loose air-containing hyphae and a gonidial zone lie round the central axis between it and the outer cortex (Fig. 63 A, *b*). At the extreme apex, the external cortical hyphae grow in a direction parallel with the long axis of the plant, but further back, they branch out at right angles and become swollen and mostly "decomposed" as in the cortex of *Ramalina*.

In *Letharia* (*L. vulpina*, etc.) the structure is midway between *Ramalina* and *Usnea* : the central axis is either a solid strand of chondroid hyphae or several separate strands.

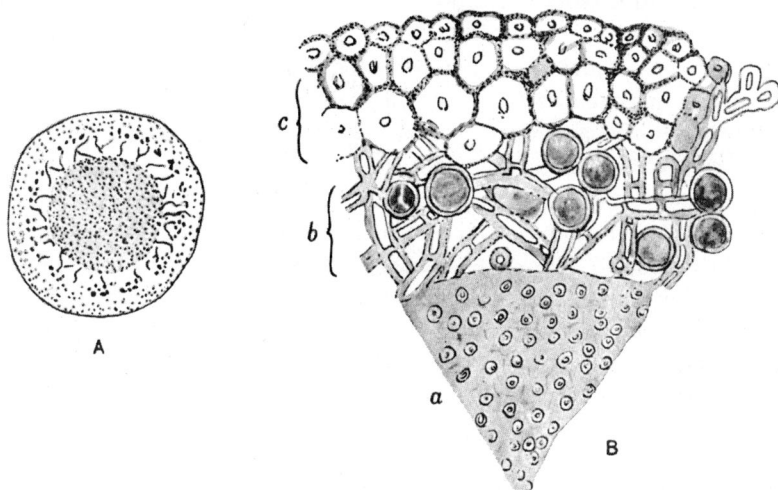

Fig. 63 B. *Usnea longissima* Ach. A, transverse section of fibril × 85. B, *a*, chondroid axis; *b*, gonidial tissue; *c*, cortex × 525 (after Schulte).

In three other genera with upright fruticose thalli, *Sphaerophorus, Argopsis* and *Stereocaulon*, rigidity is maintained by a medulla approaching the chondroid type. In *Sphaerophorus* the species may have either flattened or cylindrical branching stalks, but in all of them, the centre is occupied by longitudinal strands of hyphae. *Argopsis*, a monotypic genus from Kerguelen, has a cylindrical branching thallus with a strong solid axis; it is closely allied to *Stereocaulon*, a genus of familiar moorland lichens. The central tissue of the stalks in *Stereocaulon* is also composed of elongate, thick-walled conglutinate hyphae, formed into a strand which is, however, not entirely solid.

C. SURVEY OF MECHANICAL TISSUES

Mechanical tissues scarcely appear among fungi, except perhaps as stoutish cartilaginous hyphae in the stalks of some Agarics (*Collybiae*, etc.), or as a ring of more compact consistency round the central hyphae of rhizomorphic strands. It is practically a new adaptation of hyphal structure confined to lichens of the fruticose group, where there is the same requirement as in the higher plants for rigidity, flexure and tenacity.

Rigidity is attained as in other plants by groups or strands of mechanical tissue situated close to the periphery, as they are so arranged in *Ramalina* and *Cladonia*; or the same end is achieved by a strongly developed fastigiate cortex as in *Roccella*. Bending strains to which the same lichens are subjected, are equally well met by the peripheral disposition of the mechanical elements.

Tenacity and elasticity are provided for in the pendulous forms either by a fibrous cortex as in *Alectoria,* or by the chondroid axis in *Usnea.* Haberlandt[1] has recorded some interesting results of tests made by him as to the stretching capacity of a freshly gathered pendulous species in which the central strand was from ·5 to 1 mm. thick. He found he could draw it out 100 to 110 per cent. of its normal length before it gave way. In an upright species the frond broke when stretched 60 to 70 per cent. In both of the plants tested, the central strand retained its elasticity up to 20 per cent. of stretching. The outer cortical tissue was cracked and broken in the experiments. Schulte[2] calculated somewhat roughly the tenacity of *Usnea longissima* and found that a piece of the main axis 8 cm. long carried up to 300 grms. without breaking.

D. RETICULATE FRONDS

In the upright radiate thallus, more especially among the *Ramalinae,* though also among *Cladoniae*[3], there has appeared a reticulate thallus resulting from the elongate splitting of the tissues, and due to unequal growth tension and straining of the gelatinous cortex when swollen with moisture. In several species of *Ramalina,* the strap-shaped frond is hollow in the centre; and strands of strengthening fibres give rise to a series of cortical ridges. The thinner tissue between is frequently torn apart and ellipsoid openings appear which do not however pierce beyond the central hollow. Such breaks are irregular and accidental though occurring constantly in *Ramalina fraxinea, R. dilacerata,* etc.

A more complete type of reticulation is always present in a Californian lichen, *Ramalina reticulata,* in which the large flat frond is a delicate open network from tip to base (Fig. 64). It grows on the branches of deciduous trees and hangs in crowded tufts up to 30 cm. or more in length. Usually it is so torn, that the real size attainable can only be guessed at. It is attached at the base by a spreading discoid hold-fast, and, in mature plants, consists of a stoutish main axis from which side branches are irregularly given off. These latter are firm at the base like the parent stalk, but soon they broaden out into very wide fronds. Splitting begins at the tips of the branches while still young ; they are then spathulate in form with a slightly. narrower recurved tip, below which the first perforations are visible, small at first, but gradually enlarging with the growth of the frond.

Ramalina reticulata is an extremely gelatinous lichen and the formation

---

[1] Haberlandt 1896.   [2] Schulte 1904.   [3] See p. 120.

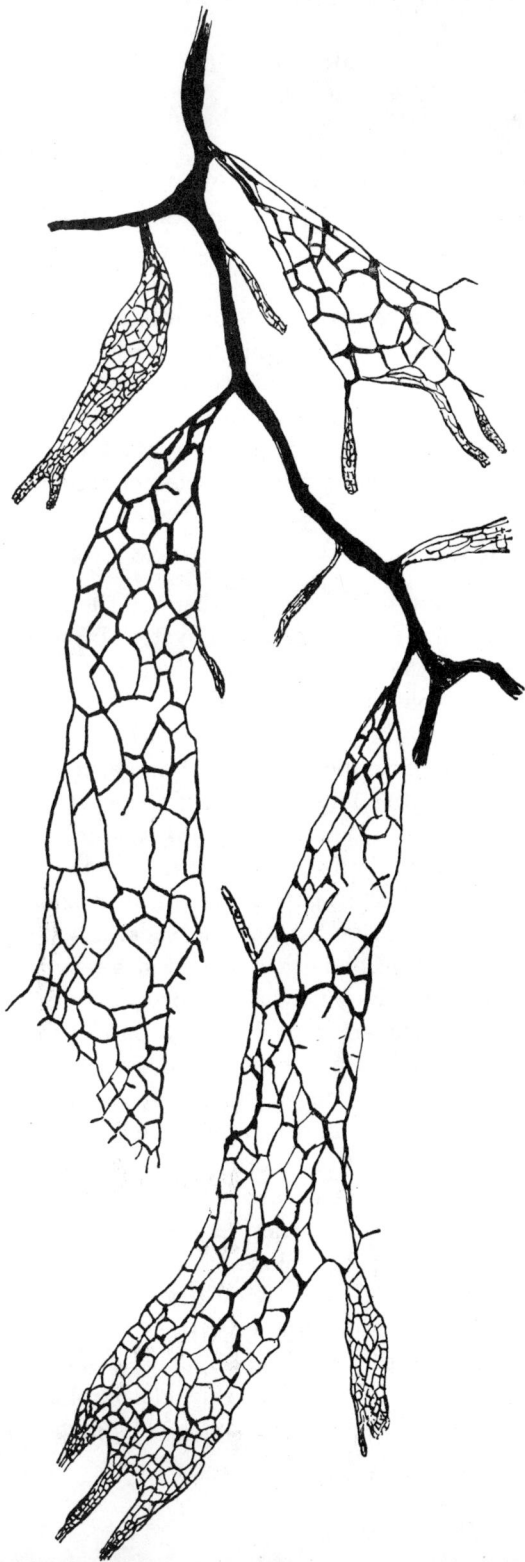

Fig. 64. *Ramalina reticulata* Krempelh. Portion of frond (after Cramer).

of the network was supposed by Lutz[1] to be entirely due to the swelling of the tissues, or the imbibition of water, causing tension and splitting. A more exact explanation of the phenomenon is given by Peirce[2]: he found that it was due to the thickened incurved tip, which, on the addition of moisture, swells in length, breadth and thickness, causing it to bend slightly upwards and then curve backwards over the thallus, thus straining the part immediately behind. These various movements result in the splitting of the frond while it is young and the cortices are thin and weak.

Peirce made a series of experiments to test the capacity of the tissues to support tensile strains. In a dry state, a piece of the lichen held a weight up to 150 grms.; when wet it broke with a weight of 30 grms. It was also observed that the thickness of the frond doubled on wetting.

E. Rooting Base in Fruticose Lichens

Fruticose and filamentous lichens are distinguished by their mode of attachment to the substratum : instead of a system of rhizinae or of hairs spread over a large area, there is usually one definite rooting base by which the plant maintains its hold on the support.

Intermediate between the foliose and fruticose types of thallus are several species which are decumbent in habit, but which are attached at one (or sometimes more) definite points, with but little penetration of the underlying substance. One such lichen, *Evernia furfuracea*, has been classified now as foliose, and again as fruticose. The earliest stage of the thallus is in the form of a rosette-like sheath which bears rhizinae on the under surface, very numerous at the centre of the sheath, but entirely wanting towards the periphery. A secondary thallus of strap-shaped rather narrow ,fronds rises from the sheath and increases by irregular dichotomous branching. These branches, which are considered by Zopf[3] as adventitious, may also come into contact with the substratum and produce a few rhizinae at that point; or if the frond is more closely applied, the irritation thus produced causes a still greater outgrowth of rhizinae and the formation of a new base from which other fronds originate. These renewed centres of growth are not of very frequent occurrence; they were first observed and described by Lindau[4] in another species, *Evernia prunastri*, and were aptly compared by him to the creeping stolons of flowering plants.

Evernia furfuracea grows frequently on dead wood, palings, etc., as well as on trees. *E. prunastri* grows invariably on trees, and has a more constantly upright fruticose habit; in this species also, a basal sheath is present, and the attachment is secured by means of rhizoidal hyphae which penetrate deeply into the periderm of the tree, taking advantage of the openings

[1] Lutz 1894.   [2] Peirce 1898.   [3] Zopf 1903.   [4] Lindau 1895.

afforded by the lenticels. The sheath hyphae are continuous with the medullary hyphae of the frond, and gonidia are frequently enclosed in the tissues; the sheath spreads to some extent over the surface of the bark, and round the base of the fronds, thus rendering the attachment of the lichen to the tree doubly secure.

Among *Ramalinae*, the development of the base was followed by Brandt[1] in one species, *R. Landroensis*, an arboreal lichen from S. Tyrol. A rosette-like sheath was formed consisting solely of strands of thick-walled hyphae which spread over the bark. There were no gonidia included in the tissue.

A different type of attachment was found by Lilian Porter[2] in corticolous *Ramalinae—R. fraxinea, R. fastigiata*, and *R. pollinaria*. The lichens were anchored to the tree by strands of closely compacted hyphae longitudinally arranged and continuous with the cortical hyphae. These enter the periderm of the tree by cracks or lenticels, and by wedge action cause extensive splitting. The strands may also spread horizontally and give rise to new plants. The living tissues of the tree were thus penetrated and injured, and there was evidence that hypertrophied tissue was formed and caused erosion of the wood.

Several *Ramalinae—R. siliquosa, R. Curnowii*, etc.—grow on rocks, often in extremely exposed situations, in isolated tufts or in crowded swards (Fig. 65). The separate tufts are not unfrequently connected at the base by

Fig. 65. *Ramalina siliquosa* A. L. Sm., on rocks, reduced (M. P., *Photo.*)

[1] Brandt 1906.　　　　[2] Porter 1916.

a crustaceous thallus. It is possible also to see on the rock, here and there, small areas of compact thalline granules that have scarcely begun to put out the upright fronds. These granules are corticate on the upper surface and contain gonidia; from the lower surface, slender branching hyphae in rhizoid-like strands penetrate down between the inequalities and separable particles of the rock, if the formation is granitic. They frequently have groups of gonidia associated with them, and they continue to ramify and spread, the pure white filaments often enough enclosing morsels of the rock. The upright fronds are continuous with the base and are thus securely anchored to the substratum.

On a smooth rock surface such as quartzite a continuous sward of *Ramalina* growth is impossible. The basal hyphae being unable to penetrate the even surface of the rock, the attachment is slight and the plants are easily dislodged. They do however succeed, sometimes, in taking hold, and small groups of fronds arise from a crustaceous base which varies in depth from ·5 to 1 mm. The tissues of this base are very irregularly arranged: towards the upper surface loose hyphae with scattered groups of algae are traversed by strands of gelatinized sclerotic hyphae similar to the strengthening tissues of the upright fronds, while down below there are to be found not only slender hyphae, but a layer of gonidia visible as a white and green film on the rock when the overlying particles are scaled off.

Darbishire[1] found that attachment to the substratum by means of a basal sheath was characteristic of all the genera of Roccellaceae. He looks on this sheath, which is the first stage in the development of the plant, as a primary or proto-thallus, analogous to the primary squamules of the *Cladoniae*, and he carries the analogy still further by treating the upright fronds as podetia. The sheath of the Roccellaceae varies in size but it is always of very limited extent; it is mainly composed of medullary hyphae, and gonidia may or may not be present. The whole structure is permanent and important, and is generally protected by a well-developed upper cortex similar in structure to that of the upright thallus, *i.e.* of a fastigiate type. There is no lower cortex.

The two British species of *Roccella*—*R. fuciformis* and *R. phycopsis*—grow on maritime rocks, the latter also occasionally on trees. In *R. fuciformis*, the attaching sheath is a flat structure which slopes up a little round the base of the upright frond. It is about 2 mm. thick, the cortex occupying about 40 μ of that space; a few scattered gonidia are present immediately below. The remaining tissue of the sheath is composed of firmly wefted slender filaments. Towards the lower surface, there is a more closely compacted dark brown layer from which pass out the hyphae that penetrate the rock.

[1] Darbishire 1898.

The sheath of *R. phycopsis* is a small structure about 3 to 4 mm. in width and 1·5 mm. thick. A few gonidia may be found below the dense cortical layer, but they tend to disappear as the upright fronds become larger and the shade, in consequence, more dense. Lower down the hyphae take an intensely yellow hue; mixed with them are also some brown filaments. A somewhat larger sheath 7 to 8 mm. wide forms the base of *R. tinctoria*. In structure it corresponds—as do those of the other species—with the ones already described.

In purely filamentous species such as *Usnea* there is also primary sheath formation: the medullary hyphae spread out in radiating strands which force their way wherever possible into the underlying substance; on trees they enter into any chink or crevice of the outer bark like wedges; or they ramify between the cork cells which are split up by the mere growth pressure. By the vertical increase of the base, the fronds may be hoisted up and an intercalary basal portion may arise lacking both gonidia and cortical layer. Very frequently several bases are united and the lichen appears to be of tufted habit.

A basal sheath provides a similar firm attachment for *Alectoria jubata* and allied species: these are slender mostly dark brown lichens which hang in tangled filaments from the branches of trees, rocks, etc.

These attaching sheaths differ in function as well as in structure from the horizontal thallus of the Cladoniaceae. They may be more truly compared with the primary thallus of the red algae *Dumontia* and *Phyllophora* which are similarly affixed to the substratum, while upright fronds of subsequent formation bear the fructifications.

IV. STRATOSE-RADIATE THALLUS

1. STRATOSE OR PRIMARY THALLUS

A. GENERAL CHARACTERISTICS

This series includes the lichens of one family only, the Cladoniaceae, the genera of which are characterized by the twofold thallus, one portion being primary, horizontal and stratose, the other secondary and radiate, the latter an upright simple or branching structure termed a "podetium" which narrows above, or widens to form a trumpet-shaped cup or "scyphus" (Fig. 66). The apothecia are terminal on the podetium or on the margins of the scyphi; in a few species they are developed on the primary thallus. Some degree of primary thallus-formation has been demonstrated in all the genera, if not in all the species of the family. The genus *Cladina* was established to include those species of *Cladonia* in which, it was believed, only a secondary

Fig. 66.   *Cladonia pyxidata* Hoffm. Basal squamule and podetium. *a*, apothecia; *s*, spermogonia (after Krabbe).

podetial thallus was present, but Wainio[1] found in *Cladonia sylvatica* a granular basal crust and, in *Cladonia uncialis*, minute round scales with crenate margins measuring from ·5 to 1 mm. in width. In some species (subgenus *Cladina*) the primary thallus is quickly evanescent, in others it is granular or squamulose and persistent. Where the basal thallus is so much reduced as to be practically non-existent, apothecia are rarely developed and soredia are absent. Renewal of growth in these lichens is secured by the dispersal of fragments of the podetial thallus; they are torn off and scattered by the wind or by animals, and, if suitable conditions are met, a new plant arises.

Cladonia squamules vary in size from very small scales as in *Cl. uncialis* to the fairly large foliose fronds of *Cl. foliacea* which extend to 5 cm. in length and about 1 cm. or more in width. It is interesting to note that when the primary thallus is well developed, the podetia are relatively unimportant and frequently are not formed. As a rule the squamules are rounded or somewhat elongate in form with entire or variously cut and crenate margins. They may be very insignificant and sparsely scattered over the substratum, or massed in crowded swards of leaflets which are frequently almost upright. In colour they are bluish-grey, yellowish or brownish above, and white beneath (red in *Cl. miniata*), frequently becoming very dark-coloured towards the rooting base. These several characteristics are specific and are often of considerable value in diagnosis. In certain conditions of shade or moisture, squamules are formed on the podetium ; they repeat the characters of the basal squamules of the species.

B. TISSUES OF THE PRIMARY THALLUS

The stratose layers of tissue in the squamules of *Cladonia* are arranged as in other horizontal thalli.

a. CORTICAL TISSUE. In nearly all these squamules the cortex is of the "decomposed" type. In a few species there is a plectenchymatous formation—in *Cl. nana*, a Brazilian ground species, and in two New Zealand species, *Cl. enantia* f. *dilatata* and *Cl. Neo-Zelandica*. The principal growing area is situated all round the margins though generally there is more activity at the apex. Frequently there is a gradual perishing of the squamule at the base which counterbalances the forward increase.

The upper surface in some species is cracked into minute areolae; the cracks, seen in section, penetrate almost to the base of the decomposed gelatinous cortex. They are largely due to alternate swelling and contraction of the gelatinous surface, or to extension caused, though rarely, by intercalary growth from the hyphae below. The surface is subject to weathering and peeling as in other lichens; but the loss is constantly repaired by the upward growth of the meristematic hyphae from the gonidial zone ; they push up

[1] Wainio 1880.

between the older cortical filaments and so provide for the expansion as well as for the renewal of the cortical tissue.

b. GONIDIAL TISSUE. The gonidia consisting of Protococcaceous algae form a layer immediately below the cortex. Isolated green cells are not unfrequently carried up by the growing hyphae into the cortical region, but they do not long survive in this compact non-aerated tissue. Their empty membranes can however be picked out by the blue stain they take with iodine and sulphuric acid.

Krabbe[1] has described the phases of development in the growing region: he finds that differentiation into pith, gonidial zone and cortex takes place some little way back from the edge. At the extreme apex the hyphae lie fairly parallel to each other; further back, they branch upwards to form the cortex, and to separate the masses of multiplying gonidia, by pushing between them and so spreading them through the whole apical tissue. The gonidia immediately below the upper cortex, where they are well-lighted, continue to increase and gradually form into the gonidial zone; those that lie deeper among the medullary hyphae remain quiescent, and before long disappear altogether.

Where the squamules assume the upright position (as in *Cladonia cervicornis*), there is a tendency for the gonidia to pass round to the lower surface, and soredia are occasionally formed.

c. MEDULLARY TISSUE. The hyphae of the medulla are described by Wainio as having long cells with narrow lumen, and as being encrusted with granulations that may coalesce into more or less detachable granules; in colour they are mostly white, but pale-yellow in *Cl. foliacea* and blood-red in *Cl. miniata*, a subtropical species. They are connected at the base of the squamules with a filamentous hypothallus which penetrates the substratum and attaches the plant. In a few species rhizinae are formed, while in others the hyphae of the podetium grow downwards, towards and into the substratum as a short stout rhizoid.

d. SOREDIA. Though frequent on the podetia, soredia are rare on the squamules, and, according to Wainio[2], always originate at the growing region, from which they spread over the under surface—rather sparsely in *Cl. cariosa*, *Cl. squamosa*, etc., but abundantly in *Cl. digitata* and a few others. In some instances, they develop further into small corticate areolae on the under surface (*Cl. coccifera*, *Cl. pyxidata* and *Cl. squamosa*).

---

[1] Krabbe 1891. [2] Wainio 1897.

2. RADIATE OR SECONDARY THALLUS

A. Origin of the Podetium

The upright podetium, as described by Wainio[1] and by Krabbe[2], is a secondary product of the basal granule or squamule. It is developed from the hyphae of the gonidial zone, generally where a crack has occurred in the cortex and rather close to the base or more rarely on or near the edge of the squamule (*Cl. verticillata*, etc.). At these areas, certain meristematic gonidial hyphae increase and unite to form a strand of filaments below the upper cortex but above the gonidial layer, the latter remaining for a time undisturbed as to the arrangement of the algal cells.

This initial tissue—the primordium of the podetium—continues to grow not only in width but in length: the basal portion grows downwards and at length displaces the gonidial zone, while the upper part as a compact cylinder forces its way through the cortex above, the cortical tissue, however, taking no part in its formation; as it advances, the edges of the gonidial and cortical zones bend upwards and form a sheath distinguishable for some time round the base of the emerging podetium.

Even when the primary horizontal thallus is merely crustaceous, the podetia take origin similarly from a subcortical weft of hyphae in an areola or granule.

B. Structure of the Podetium

a. GENERAL STRUCTURE. In the early stages of development the podetium is solid throughout, two layers of tissue being discernible—the hyphae forming the centre of the cylinder being thick-walled and closely compacted, and the hyphae on the exterior loosely branching with numerous air-spaces between the filaments.

In all species, with the exception of *Cl. solida*, which remains solid during the life of the plant, a central cavity arises while the podetium is still quite short (about 1 to 1·5 mm. in *Cl. pyxidata* and *Cl. degenerans*). The first indication of the opening is a narrow split in the internal cylinder, due to the difference in growth tension between the more free and rapid increase of the external medullary layer and the slower elongation of the chondroid tissue at the centre. The cavity gradually widens and becomes more completely tubular with the upward growth of the podetium; it is lined by the chondroid sclerotic band which supports the whole structure (Fig. 67).

b. GONIDIAL TISSUE. In most species of Cladoniaceae, a layer of gonidial tissue forms a more or less continuous outer covering of the podetium,

---

[1] Wainio 1880.   [2] Krabbe 1891.

thus distinguishing it from the purely hyphal stalks of the apothecia in
Caliciaceae. Even in the genus *Baeomyces*,
while the podetia of some of the species
are without gonidia, neighbouring species
are provided with green cells on the upright stalks clearly showing their true
affinity with the *Cladoniae*. In one British
species of *Cladonia* (*Cl. caespiticia*) the
short podetium consists only of the fibrous
chondroid cylinder, and thus resembles the
apothecial stalk of *Baeomyces rufus*, but
in that species also there are occasional
surface gonidia that may give rise to
squamules.

Krabbe[1] concluded from his observations that the podetial gonidia of *Cladonia*
arrived from the open, conveyed by wind,
water or insects from the loose soredia that
are generally so plentiful in any *Cladonia*

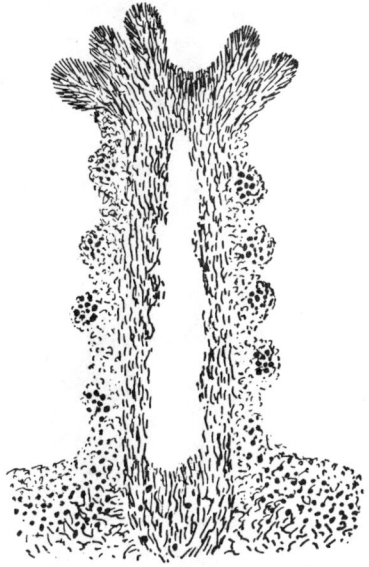

Fig. 67. *Cladonia squamosa* Hoffm. Vertical section of podetium with early
stage of central tube and of podetial
squamules × 100 (after Krabbe).

colony. They alighted, he held, on the
growing stalks and, being secured by the
free-growing ends of the exterior hyphae,
they increased and became an integral part of the podetium. In more
recent times Baur[2] has recalled and supported Krabbe's view, but Wainio[3],
on the contrary, claims to have proved that in the earliest stages of the
podetium the gonidia were already present, having been carried up from
the gonidial zone of the primary thallus by the primordial hyphae. Increase
of these green cells follows normally by cell-division or sporulation.

Algal cells have been found to be common to different lichens, but in
Cladoniae Chodat[4] claims to have proved by cultures that each species
tested has a special gonidium, determined by him as a species of *Cystococcus*,
which would render colonization by algae from the open much less probable.
In addition, the fungal hyphae are specific, and any soredia (with their
combined symbionts) that alighted on the podetium could only be utilized
if they originated from the same species; or, if they were incorporated, the
hyphae belonging to any other species would of necessity die off and be
replaced by those of the podetium.

c. CORTICAL TISSUE. In some species a cortex of the decomposed type
of thick-walled conglutinate hyphae is present, either continuous over the
whole surface of the podetium, as in *Cl. gracilis* (Fig. 68), or in interrupted

[1] Krabbe 1891.   [2] Baur 1904.   [3] Wainio 1880.   [4] Chodat 1913.

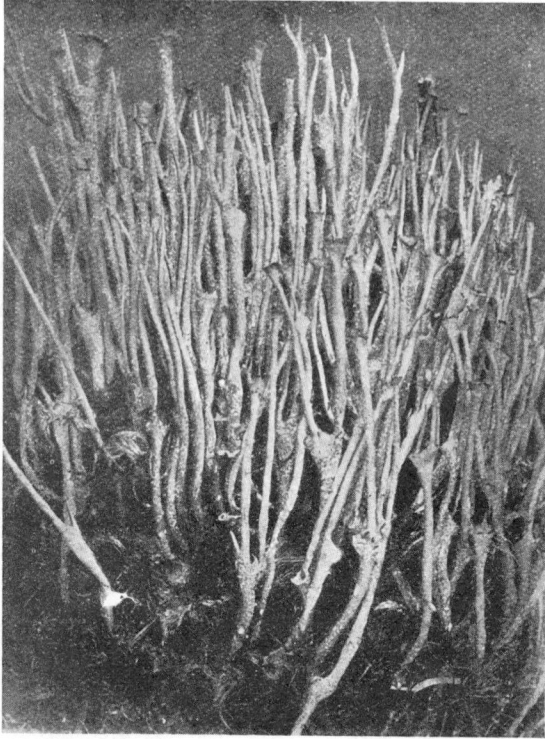

Fig. 68. *Cladonia gracilis* Hoffm. (S. H., *Photo*.).

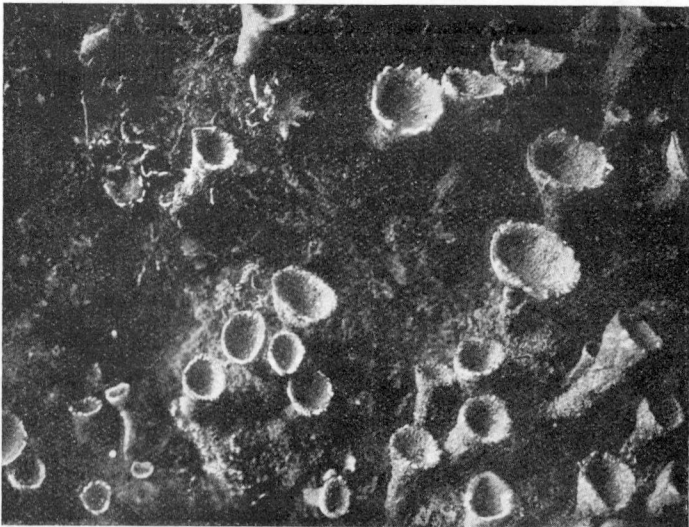

Fig. 69. *Cladonia pyxidata* Hoffm. (S. H., *Photo*.).

areas or granules as in *Cl. pyxidata* (Fig. 69) and others. In *Cl. degenerans*, the spaces between the corticated areolae are filled in by loose filaments without any green cells. *Cl. rangiferina, Cl. sylvatica*, etc. are non-corticate, being covered all over with a loose felt of intricate hyphae.

In the section *Clathrinae* (*Cl. retepora*, etc.) the cortex is formed of longitudinal hyphae with thick gelatinous walls.

d. SOREDIA. Frequently the podetium is coated in whole or in part by granules of a sorediate character—coarsely granular in *Cl. pyxidata*, finely pulverulent in *Cl. fimbriata*. Though fairly constant to type in the different species, they are subject to climatic influences, and, when there is abundant moisture, both soredia and areolae develop into squamules on the podetium. A considerable number of species have thus a more or less densely squamulose "form" or "variety."

C. DEVELOPMENT OF THE SCYPHUS

Two types of podetia occur in *Cladonia*: those that end abruptly and are crowned when fertile by the apothecia or spermogonia (pycnidia), or if sterile grow indefinitely tapering gradually to a point (Fig. 70); and those

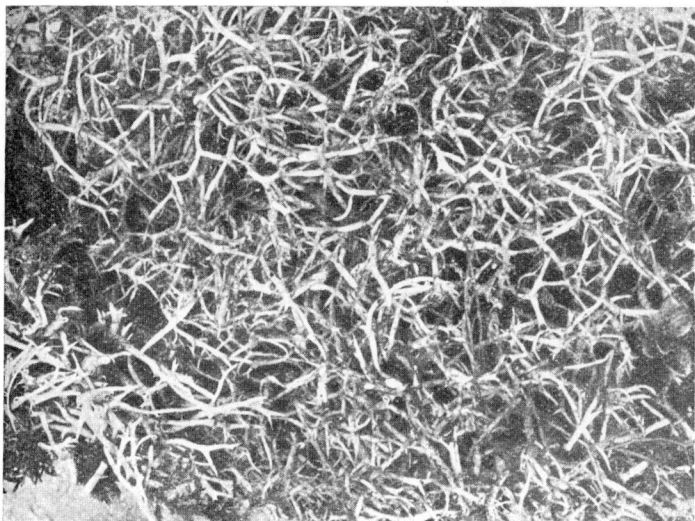

Fig. 70. *Cladonia furcata* Schrad. Sterile thallus (S.H., *Photo.*).

that widen out into the trumpet-shaped or cup-like expansion called the scyphus (Fig. 69). Species may be constantly scyphiferous or as constantly ascyphous; in a few species, and even in individual tufts, both types of podetium may be present.

Wainio[1], who has studied every stage of development in the *Cladoniae*, has described the scyphus as originating in several different ways:

a. FROM ABORTIVE APOTHECIA. In certain species the apothecium appears at a very early stage in the development of the podetium of which it occupies the apical region. Owing to the subsequent formation of the tubular cavity in the centre of the stalk, the base of the apothecium may eventually lie directly over the hollow space and, therefore, out of touch with the growing assimilating tissues; or even before the appearance of the tube, the wide separation between the primordium of the apothecium and the gonidia, entailing deficient nutrition, may have produced a similar effect. In either case central degeneration of the apothecium sets in, and the hypothecial filaments, having begun to grow radially, continue to travel in the same direction both outwards and upwards so that gradually a cup-shaped structure is evolved—the amphithecium of the fruit without the thecium.

The whole or only a part of the apothecium may be abortive, and the scyphus may therefore be entirely sterile or the fruits may survive at the edges. The apothecia may even be entirely abortive after a fertile commencement, but in that case also the primordial hyphae retain the primitive impulse not only to radial direction, but also to the more copious branching, and a scyphus is formed as in the previous case. It must also be borne in mind that the tendency in many *Cladonia* species to scyphiform has become hereditary.

Baur[2], in his study of *Cl. pyxidata*, has taken the view that the origin of the scyphus was due to a stronger apical growth of the hyphae at the circumference than over the central tubular portion of the podetium, and that considerable intercalary growth added to the expanding sides of the cup.

Scyphi originating from an abortive apothecium are characteristic of species in which the base is closed (Wainio's Section *Clausae*), the tissue in that case being continuous over the inside of the cup as in *Cl. pyxidata*, *Cl. coccifera* and many others.

b. FROM POLYTOMOUS BRANCHING. Another method of scyphus formation occurs in *Cl. amaurocrea* and a few other species in which the branching is polytomous (several members rising from about the same level). Concrescence of the tissues at the base of these branches produces a scyphus; it is normally closed by a diaphragm that has spread out from the different bases, but frequently there is a perforation due to stretching. These species belong to the Section *Perviae*.

c. FROM ARRESTED GROWTH. In most cases however where the scyphus is open as in *Cl. furcata*, *Cl. squamosa*, etc., development of the cup

---

[1] Wainio 1897.   [2] Baur 1904.

follows on cessation of growth, or on perforation at the summit of the podetium. Round this quiescent portion there rises a circle of minute prominences which carry on the apical development. As they increase in size, the spaces between them are bridged over by lateral growth, and the scyphus thus formed is large or small according to the number of these outgrowths. Apothecia or spermogonia may be produced at their tips, or the vegetative development may continue. Scyphi formed in this manner are also open or "pervious."

d. GONIDIA OF THE SCYPHUS. Gonidia are absent in the early stages of scyphus formation when it arises from degeneration of the apical tissues, either fertile or vegetative; but gradually they migrate from the podetium, from the base of young outgrowths, or by furrows at the edge, and so spread over the surface of the cup. Soredia may possibly alight, as Krabbe insists that they do, and may aid in colonizing the naked area. Their presence, however, would only be accidental; they are not essential, and scyphi are formed in many non-sorediate species such as *Cl. verticillata.* The cortex of the scyphus becomes in the end continuous with that of the podetium and is always similar in type.

e. SPECIES WITHOUT SCYPHI. In species where the whole summit of the podetium is occupied by an apothecium, as in *Cl. bellidiflora,* no scyphus is formed. There is also an absence of scyphi in podetia that taper to a point. In those podetia the hyphae are parallel to the long axis and remain in connection with the external gonidial layer so that they are unaffected by the central cavity. Instances of tapering growth are also to be found in species that are normally scyphiferous such as *Cl. fimbriata* subsp. *fibula,* and *Cl. cornuta,* as well as in species like *Cl. rangiferina* that are constantly ascyphous.

The scyphus is considered by Wainio[1] to represent an advanced stage of development in the species or in the individual, and any conditions that act unfavourably on growth, such as excessive dryness, would also hinder the formation of this peculiar lichen structure.

D. BRANCHING OF THE PODETIUM

Though branching is a constant feature in many species, regular dichotomy is rare; more often there is an irregular form of polytomy in which one of the members grows more vigorously than the others and branches again, so that a kind of sympodium arises, as in *Cl. rangiferina, Cl. sylvatica,* etc.

Adventitious branches may also arise from the podetium, owing to some disturbance of the normal growth, some undue exposure to wind or to too

[1] Wainio 1897.

great light, or owing to some external injury. They originate from the gonidial tissue in the same way as does the podetium from the primary thallus; the parallel hyphae of the main axis take no part in their development.

In a number of species secondary podetia arise from the centre of the scyphus—constantly in *Cl. verticillata* and *Cl. cervicornis*, etc., accidentally or rarely in *Cl. foliacea, Cl. pyxidata, Cl. fimbriata*, etc. Wainio[1] has stated that they arise when the scyphus is already at an advanced stage of growth and that they are to be regarded as adventitious branches.

The proliferations from the borders of the scyphus are in a different category. They represent the continuity of apical growth, as the edges of the scyphus are but an enlarged apex. These marginal proliferations thus correspond to polytomous branching. In many instances their advance is soon stopped by the formation of an apothecium and they figure more as fruit stalks than as podetial branches.

E. Perforations and Reticulation of the Podetium

Perforations in the podetial wall at the axils of the branches are constant in certain species such as *Cl. rangiferina, Cl. uncialis*, etc. They are caused by the tension of the branches as they emerge from the main stalk. A tearing of the tissue may also arise in the base of the scyphus, due to its increase in size, which causes the splitting of the diaphragm at the bottom of the cup.

Among the *Cladoniae* the reticulate condition recurs now and again. In our native *Cladonia cariosa* the splitting of the podetial wall is a constant character of the species, the carious condition being caused by unequal growth which tears apart the longitudinal fibres that surround the central hollow.

A more advanced type of reticulation arises in the group of the *Clathrinae* in which there is no inner chondroid cylinder. In *Cladonia aggregata*, in which the perforations are somewhat irregular, two types of podetia have been described by Lindsay[2] from Falkland Island specimens: those bearing apothecia are short and broad, fastigiately branched upwards and with reticulate perforations, while podetia bearing spermogonia are slender, elongate and branched, with fewer reticulations. An imperfect network is also characteristic of *Cl. Sullivani*, a Brazilian species. But the most marvellous and regular form of reticulation occurs in *Cl. retepora*, an Australian lichen (Fig. 71): towards the tips of the podetia the ellipsoid meshes are small, but they gradually become larger towards the base. In this species the outer tissue, though of parallel hyphae, is closely interwoven and forms

---

[1] Wainio 1897. [2] Lindsay 1859, p. 171.

a continuous growth at the edges of the perforations, giving an unbroken smooth surface and checking any irregular tearing. The enlargement of the walls is solely due to intercalary growth. The origin of the reticulate structure in the *Clathrinae* is unknown, though it is doubtless associated

Fig. 71. *Cladonia retepora* Fr. From Tasmania.

with wide podetia and rendered possible by the absence of an internal chondroid layer. The reticulate structure is marvellously adapted for the absorption of water: *Cl. retepora*, more especially, imbibes and holds moisture like a sponge.

F. Rooting Structures of Cladoniae

The squamules of the primary thallus are attached, as are most squamules, to the supporting substance by strands of hyphae which may be combined into simple or branching rhizinae and penetrate the soil or the wood on which the lichen grows. There is frequently but one of these rooting structures and it branches repeatedly until the ultimate branchlets end in delicate mycelium. Generally they are grey or brown and are not easily traced, but when they are orange-coloured, as according to Wainio[1] they frequently are in *Cladonia miniata* and *Cl. digitata*, they are more readily observed, especially if the habitat be a mossy one.

In *Cl. alpicola* it has been found that the rooting structure is frequently as thick as the podetium itself. If the podetium originates from the basal portion of the squamule, the hyphae from the chondroid layer, surrounding the hollow centre, take a downward direction and become continuous with the rhizoid. Should the point of insertion be near the apex of the squamule, these hyphae form a nerve within the squamule or along the under surface, and finally also unite with the rhizoid at the base, a form of rooting characteristic of *Cl. cartilaginea*, *Cl. digitata* and several other species.

Mycelium may spread from the rhizinae along the surface of the substratum and give rise to new squamules and new tufts of podetia, a method of reproduction that is of considerable importance in species that are generally sterile and that form no soredia.

Many species, especially those of the section *Cladina*, soon lose all connection with the substratum, there being a continual decay of the lower part of the podetia. As apical growth may continue for centuries, the perishing of the base is not to be wondered at.

G. Haptera

The presence of haptera in *Cladoniae* has already been alluded to. They occur usually in the form of cilia or rhizinae[2], but differ from the latter in their more simple regular growth being composed of conglutinate parallel hyphae. They arise on the edges of the squamules or of the scyphus, but in *Cl. foliacea* and *Cl. ceratophylla* they are formed at the points of the podetial branches (more rarely in *Cl. cervicornis* and *Cl. gracilis*). By the aid of these rhizinose haptera the squamule or branch becomes attached to any substance within reach. They also aid in the production of new individuals by anchoring some fragment of the thallus to a support until it has grown to independent existence and has produced new rhizinae or holdfasts. They are a very prominent feature of *Cl. verticillaris* f. *penicillata* in which they form a thick fringe on the edges of the squamules, or frequently grow out as branched cilia from the proliferations on the margins of the scyphus.

H. Morphology of the Podetium

In the above account, the podetia have been treated as part of the vegetative thallus, seeing that, partly or entirely, they are assimilative and absorptive organs. This view does not, however, take into account their origin and development, in consideration of which Wainio[3] and later Krabbe[4]

---

[1] Wainio 1897.   [2] Wainio 1897, p. 9.   [3] Wainio 1880.   [4] Krabbe 1891.

considered them as part of the sporiferous organ. This view was also held by some of the earliest lichenologists: Necker[1], for instance, constantly referred to the upright structure as "stipes"; Persoon[2] included it, under the term "pedunculus," as part of the "inflorescence" of the lichen, and Acharius[3] established the name "podetium" to describe the stalk of the apothecium in *Baeomyces*.

Later lichenologists, such as Wallroth[4], looked on the podetia as advanced stages of the thallus, or as forming a supplementary thallus. Tulasne[5] described them as branching upright processes from the horizontal form, and Koerber[6] considered them as the true thallus, the primary squamule being merely a protothallus. By them and by succeeding students of lichens the twofold character of the thallus was accepted until Wainio and Krabbe by their more exact researches discovered the endogenous origin of the podetium, which they considered was conclusive evidence of its apothecial character: they claimed that the primordium of the podetium was homologous with the primordium of the apothecium. Reinke[7] and Wainio are in accord with Krabbe as to the probable morphological significance of the podetium, but they both insist on its modified thalline character. Wainio sums up that: "the podetium is an apothecial stalk, that is to say an elongation of the conceptacle most frequently transformed by metamorphosis to a vertical thallus, though visibly retaining its stalk character." Sättler[8], one of the most recent students of *Cladonia*, regards the podetium as evolved with reference to spore-dissemination, and therefore of apothecial character. His views are described and discussed in the chapter on phylogeny.

Reinke and others sought for a solution of the problem in *Baeomyces*, one of the more primitive genera of the Cladoniaceae. The thallus, except in a few mostly exotic species, scarcely advances beyond the crustaceous condition; the podetia are short and so varied in character that species have been assigned by systematists to several different genera. In one of them, *Baeomyces roseus*, the podetium or stalk originates according to Nienburg[9] deep down in the medulla of a fertile granule as a specialized weft of tissue; there is no carpogonium nor trichogyne formed; the hyphae that grow upward and form the podetium are generative filaments and give rise to asci and paraphyses. In a second species, *B. rufus (Sphyridium)*, the gonidial zone and outer cortex of a thalline granule swell out to form a thalline protuberance; the carpogonium arises close to the apex, and from it branch the generative filaments. Nienburg regards the stalk of *B. roseus* as apothecial and as representing an extension of the proper margin[10] (*excipulum proprium*), that of *B. rufus* as a typical vegetative podetium.

[1] Necker 1871. [2] Persoon 1794. [3] Acharius 1803. [4] Wallroth 1829, p. 61.
[5] Tulasne 1852. [6] Koerber 1855. [7] Reinke 1894. [8] Sättler 1914.
[9] Nienburg 1908. [10] See p. 183.

In the genus *Cladonia*, differentiation of the generative hyphae may take place at a very early stage. Wainio[1] observed, in *Cl. caespiticia*, a trichogyne in a still solid podetium only 90μ in height; usually they appear later, and, where scyphi are formed, the carpogonium often arises at the edge of the scyphus. Baur[2] and Wolff[3] have furnished conclusive evidence of the late appearance of the carpogonium in *Cl. pyxidata*, *Cl. degenerans*, *Cl. furcata* and *Cl. gracilis*: in all of these species carpogonia with trichogynes were observed on the edge of well-developed scyphi. Baur draws the conclusion that the podetium is merely a vertical thallus, citing as additional evidence that it also bears the spermogonia (or pycnidia), though at the same time he allows that the apothecium may have played an important part in its phylogenetic development. He agrees also with the account of the first appearance of the podetium as described by Krabbe, who found that it began with the hyphae of the gonidial zone branching upwards in a quite normal manner, only that there were more of them, and that they finally pierced the cortex. Krabbe also asserted that in the early stages the podetia were without gonidia and that these arrived later from the open as colonists, in this contradicting Wainio's statement that gonidia were carried up from the primary thallus.

It seems probable that the podetium—as Wainio and Baur both have stated—is homologous with the apothecial stalk, though in most cases it is completely transformed into a vertical thallus. If the view of their formation from the gonidial zone is accepted, then they differ widely in origin from normal branches in which the tissues of the main axis are repeated in the secondary structures, whereas in this vertical thallus, hyphae from the gonidial zone alone take part in the development. It must be admitted that Baur's view of the podetium as essentially thalline seems to be strengthened by the formation of podetia at the centre of the scyphus, as in *Cl. verticillata*, which are new structures and are not an elongation of the original conceptacular tissue. It can however equally be argued that the acquired thalline character is complete and, therefore, includes the possibility of giving rise to new podetia.

The relegation of the carpogonium to a position far removed from the base or primordium of the apothecium need not necessarily interfere with the conception of the primordial tissue as homologous with the conceptacle; but more research is needed, as Baur dealt only with one species, *Cl. pyxidata*, and Gertrude Wolff confined her attention to the carpogonial stages at the edge of the scyphus.

The *Cladoniae* require light, and inhabit by preference open moorlands, naked clay walls, borders of ditches, exposed sand-dunes, etc. Those with large and persistent squamules can live in arid situations, probably because

---

[1] Wainio 1897.   [2] Baur 1904.   [3] Wolff 1905.

the primary thallus is able to retain moisture for a long time[1]. When the primary thallus is small and feeble the podetia are generally much branched and live in close colonies which retain moisture. Sterile podetia are long-lived and grow indefinitely at the apex though the base as continually perishes and changes into humus. Wainio[2] cites an instance in which the bases of a tuft of *Cl. alpestris* had formed a gelatinous mass more than a decimetre in thickness.

I. Pilophorus and Stereocaulon

These two genera are usually included in Cladoniaceae on account of their twofold thallus and their somewhat similar fruit formation. They differ from *Cladonia* in the development of the podetia which are not endogenous in origin as in that genus, but are formed by the growth upwards of a primary granule or squamule and correspond more nearly to Tulasne's conception of the podetium as a process from the horizontal thallus. In *Pilophorus* the primary granular thallus persists during the life of the plants; the short podetium is unbranched, and consists of a some-what compact medulla of parallel hyphae surrounded by a looser cortical tissue, such as that of the basal granule, in which are embedded the algal cells. The black colour of the apothecium is due to the thick dark hypo-thecium.

Stereocaulon is also a direct growth from a short-lived primary squamule[3]. The podetia, called "pseudopodetia" by Wainio, are usually very much branched. They possess a central strand of hyphae not entirely solid, and an outer layer of loose felted hyphae in which the gonidia find place. A coating of mucilage on the outside gives a glabrous shiny surface, or, if that is absent, the surface is tomentose as in *St. tomentosum*. In all the species the podetia are more or less thickly beset with small variously divided squamules similar in form to the primary evanescent thallus. Gall-like cephalodia are associated with most of the species and aid in the work of assimilation.

Stereocaulon cannot depend on the evanescent primary thallus for attach-ment to the soil. The podetia of the different species have developed various rooting bases: in *St. ramulosum* there is a basal sheath formed, in *St. coral-loides* a well-developed system of rhizoids[4].

---

[1] Aigret 1901.   [2] Wainio 1897.   [3] Wainio 1890, p. 67.   [4] Reinke 1895.

V. STRUCTURES PECULIAR TO LICHENS

I. AERATION STRUCTURES

A. Cyphellae and Pseudocyphellae

The thallus of Stictaceae has been regarded by Nylander[1] and others as one of the most highly organized, not only on account of the size attained by the spreading lobes, but also because in that family are chiefly found those very definite cup-like structures which were named "cyphellae" by Acharius[2]. They are small hollow depressions about ½ mm. or more in width scattered irregularly over the under surface of the thallus.

a. HISTORICAL. Cyphellae were first pointed out by the Swiss botanist, Haller[3]. In his description of a lichen referable to *Sticta fuliginosa* he describes certain white circular depressions "to be found among the short brown hairs of the under surface." At a later date Schreber[4] made these "white excavated points" the leading character of his lichen genus *Sticta*.

In urceolate or proper cyphellae, the base of the depression rests on the medulla; the margin is formed from the ruptured cortex and projects slightly inwards over the edge of the cup. Contrasted with these are the pseudocyphellae, somewhat roundish openings of a simpler structure which replace the others in many of the species. They have no definite margin; the internal hyphae have forced their way to the exterior and form a protruding tuft slightly above the surface. Meyer[5] reckoned them all among soredia; but he distinguished between those in which the medullary hyphae became conglutinated to form a margin (true cyphellae) and those in which there was a granular outburst of filaments (pseudocyphellae). He also included a third type, represented in *Lobaria pulmonaria* on the under surface of which there are numerous non-corticate, angular patches where the pith is laid bare (Fig. 72). Delise[6], writing about the same time on the *Sticteae*, gives due attention to their occurrence, classifying the various species of *Sticta* as cyphellate or non-cyphellate.

Acharius had limited the name "cyphella" to the hollow urceolate bodies that had a well-defined margin. Nylander[7] at first included under that term both types of structure, but later[8] he classified the pulverulent "soredia-like" forms in another group, the pseudocyphellae. As a rule they bear no relation to soredia, and algae are rarely associated with the protruding filaments. Schwendener[9], and later Wainio[10], in describing *Sticta aurata* from Brazil, state, as exceptional, that the citrine-yellow pseudocyphellae of that species are sparingly sorediate.

[1] Nylander 1858, p. 63.   [2] Acharius 1810, p. 12.   [3] Haller 1768, p. 85.
[4] Schreber 1791, p. 768.   [5] Meyer 1825, p. 148.   [6] Delise 1822.   [7] Nylander 1858, p. 14.
[8] Nylander 1860, p. 333.   [9] Schwendener 1863, p. 169.   [10] Wainio 1890, I. p. 183.

b. DEVELOPMENT OF CYPHELLAE. The cortex of both surfaces in the thallus of *Sticta* is a several-layered plectenchyma of thick-walled closely

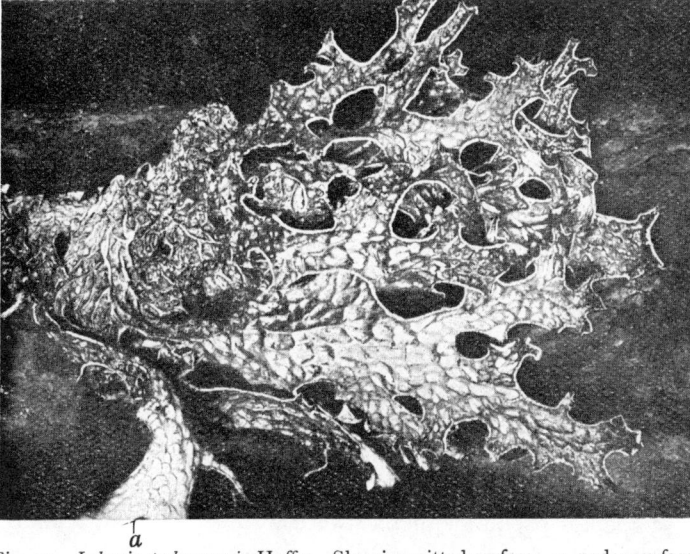

Fig. 72. *Lobaria pulmonaria* Hoffm. Showing pitted surface. *a*, under surface. Reduced (S. H., *Photo.*).

packed cells, the outer layer growing out into hairs on the under surface of most of the species. Where either cyphellae or pseudocyphellae occur, a more or less open channel is formed between the exterior and the internal tissues of the lichen. In the case of the cyphellae, the medullary hyphae which line the cup are divided into short roundish cells with comparatively thin walls (Fig. 73). They form a tissue sharply differentiated from the

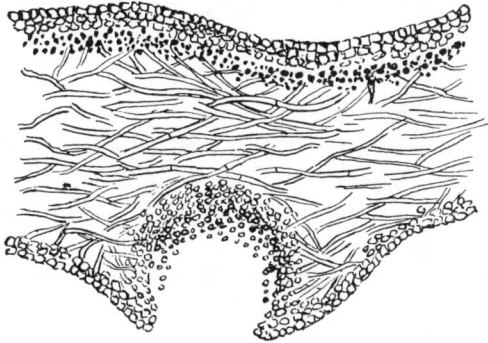

Fig. 73. *Sticta damaecornis* Nyl. Transverse section of thallus with cyphella × 100.

loose hyphae that occupy the medulla. The rounded cells tend to lie in vertical rows, though the arrangement in fully formed cyphellae is generally somewhat irregular. The terminal empty cells are loosely attached and as they are eventually abstricted and strewn over the inside of the cup they give to it the characteristic white powdery appearance.

According to Schwendener[1] development begins by an exuberant growth of the medulla which raises and finally bursts the cortex; prominent cyphellae have been thus formed in *Sticta damaecornis* (Fig. 73). In other species the swelling is less noticeable or entirely absent. The opening of the cup measures usually about $\frac{1}{2}$ mm. across, but it may stretch to a greater width.

c. PSEUDOCYPHELLAE. In these no margin is formed, the cortex is simply burst by the protruding filaments which are of the same colour—yellow or white—as the medullary hyphae. They vary in size, from a minute point up to 4 mm. in diameter.

d. OCCURRENCE AND DISTRIBUTION. The genus *Sticta* is divided into two sections : (1) *Eusticta* in which the gonidia are bright-green algae, and (2) *Stictina* in which they are blue-green. Cyphellae and pseudocyphellae are fairly evenly distributed between the sections; they never occur together. Stizenberger[2] found that 36 species of the section *Eusticta* were cyphellate, while in 43 species pseudocyphellae were formed. In the section *Stictina* there were 38 of the former and only 31 of the latter type. Both sections of the genus are widely distributed in all countries, but they are most abundant south of the equator, reaching their highest development in Australia and New Zealand.

In the British Isles *Sticta* is rather poorly represented as follows:

§*Eusticta* (with bright-green gonidia).
Cyphellate: *S. damaecornis.*
Pseudocyphellate: *S. aurata.*
§*Stictina* (with blue-green gonidia).
Cyphellate: *S. fuliginosa, S. limbata, S. sylvatica, S. Dufourei.*
Pseudocyphellate: *S. intricata* var. *Thouarsii, S. crocata.*

Structures resembling cyphellae, with an overarching rim, are sprinkled over the brown under surface of the Australian lichen, *Heterodea Mülleri*; the thallus is without a lower cortex, the medulla being protected by thickly woven hyphae. *Heterodea* was at one time included among Stictaceae, though now it is classified under Parmeliaceae. Pseudocyphellae are also present on the non-corticate under surface of *Nephromium tomentosum*, where they occur as little white pustules among the brown hairs; and the white impressed spots on the under surface of *Cetraria Islandica* and allied species, first determined as air pores by Zukal[3], have also been described by Wainio[4] as pseudocyphellae.

---

[1] Schwendener 1863, p. 169. [2] Stizenberger 1895. [3] Zukal 1895, p. 1355. [4] Wainio 1909.

There seems no doubt that the chief function of these various structures is, as Schwendener[1] suggested, to allow a free passage of air to the assimilating gonidial zone. Jatta[2] considers them to be analogous to the lenticels of higher plants and of service in the interchange of gases—expelling carbonic acid and receiving oxygen from the outer atmosphere. It is remarkable that such serviceable organs should have been evolved in so few lichens.

B. BREATHING-PORES

a. DEFINITE BREATHING-PORES. The cyphellae and pseudocyphellae described above are confined to the under surface of the thallus in those lichens where they occur. Distinct breathing-pores of a totally different structure are present on the upper surface of the tree-lichen, *Parmelia aspidota* (*P. exasperata*), one of the brown-coloured species. They are somewhat thickly scattered as isidia- or cone-like warts over the lichen thallus (Fig. 74) and give it the characteristically rough or "exasperate" character. They are direct outgrowths from the thallus, and Zukal[3], who discovered their peculiar nature and function,

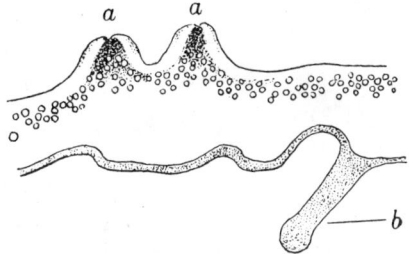

Fig. 74. *Parmelia exasperata* Carroll. Vertical section of thallus. *a*, breathing-pores; *b*, rhizoid. × 60 (after Rosendahl).

describes them as being filled with a hyphal tissue, with abundant air-spaces, and in direct communication with the medulla; gonidia, if present, are confined to the basal part. The cortex covering these minute cones, he further states, is very thin on the top, or often wanting, so that a true pore is formed which, however, is only opened after the cortex elsewhere has become thick and horny. Rosendahl[4], who has re-examined these "breathing-pores," finds that in the early stage of their growth, near the margin or younger portion of the thallus, they are entirely covered by the cortex. Later, the hyphae at the top become looser and more frequently septate, and a fine net-work of anastomosing and intricate filaments takes the place of the closely cohering cortical cells. These hyphae are divided into shorter cells, but do not otherwise differ from those of the medulla. Rosendahl was unable to detect an open pore at any stage, though he entirely agrees with Zukal as to the breathing function of these structures. The gonidia of the immediately underlying zone are sparsely arranged and a few of them are found in the lower half of the cone; the hyphae of the medulla can be traced up to the apex.

[1] Schwendener 1863, p. 169.   [2] Jatta 1889, p. 48.   [3] Zukal 1895, p. 1357.
[4] Rosendahl 1907.

Zukal[1] claims to have found breathing-pores in *Cornicularia* (*Parmelia*) *tristis* and in several other *Parmeliae*, notably in *Parmelia stygia*. The thallus of the latter species has minute holes or openings in the upper cortex, but they are without any definite form and may be only fortuitous.

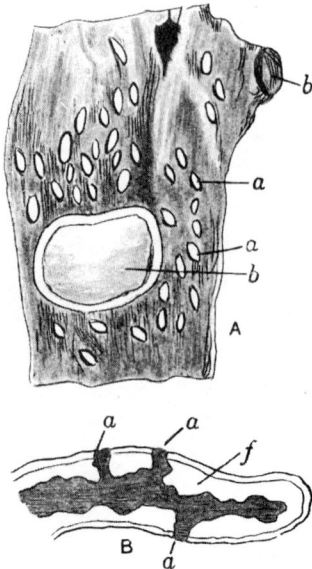

Fig. 75 A. *Ramalina fraxinea* Ach. A, surface view of frond. *a*, air-pores; *b*, young apothecia. × 12. B, transverse section of part of frond. *a*, breathing-pore; *f*, strengthening fibres. × 37 (after Brandt).

Zukal[1] published drawings of channels of looser tissue between the exterior and the pith in *Oropogon Loxensis* and in *Usnea barbata*. He considered them to be of definite service in aeration. The fronds of *Ramalina dilacerata* by stretching develop a series of elongate holes. Reinke[2] found openings in *Ramalina Eckloni* which pierced to the centre of the thallus, and Darbishire[3] has figured a break in the frond of another species, *R. fraxinea* (Fig. 75 A), which he has designated as a breathing-pore. Finally Brandt[4], in his careful study of the anatomy of *Ramalinae*, has described as breathing-pores certain open areas usually of ellipsoid form in the compact cortex of several species: in *R. strepsilis* (Fig. 75 B) and *R. Landroensis*, and in the British species, *R. siliquosa* and *R. fraxinea*. These openings are however mostly rare and difficult to find or to distinguish from holes that may be due to any accident in the life of the lichen. It is noteworthy that

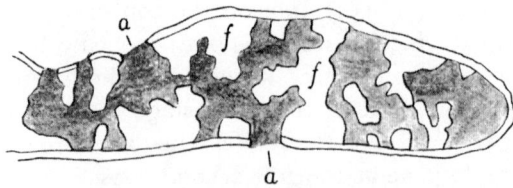

Fig. 75 B. *Ramalina strepsilis* Zahlbr. Transverse section of part of frond showing distribution of: *a*, air-pores, and *f*, strengthening fibres. × 37 (after Brandt).

Rosendahl found no further examples of breathing-pores in the brown *Parmeliae* that he examined in such detail. No other organs specially adapted for aeration of the thallus have been discovered.

b. OTHER OPENINGS IN THE THALLUS. *Lobaria* is the only genus of Stictaceae in which neither cyphellae nor pseudocyphellae are formed; but in two species, *L. scrobiculata* and *L. pulmonaria*, the lower surface is marked

[1] Zukal 1895.   [2] Reinke 1895, p. 183.   [3] Darbishire 1901.   [4] Brandt 1906.

with oblong or angular bare convex patches, much larger than cyphellae. They are exposed portions of the medulla, which at these spots has been denuded of the covering cortex. Corresponding with these bare spots there is a pitting of the upper surface.

A somewhat similar but reversed structure characterizes *Umbilicaria pustulata*, which as the name implies is distinguished by the presence of pustules, ellipsoid swellings above, with a reticulation of cavities below. Bitter[1] in this instance has proved that they are due to disconnected centres of intercalary growth which are more vigorous on the upper surface and give rise to cracks in the less active tissue beneath. These cracks gradually become enlarged; they are, as it were, accidental in origin but are doubtless of considerable service in aeration.

In some *Parmeliae* there are constantly formed minute round holes, either right through the apothecia (*P. cetrata*, etc.), or through the thallus (*P. pertusa*). Minute holes are also present in the under cortex of *Parmelia vittata* and of *P. enteromorpha*, species of the subgenus *Hypogymnia*. Nylander[2], who first drew attention to these holes of the lower cortex, described them as arising at the forking of two lobes; but though they do occur in that position, they as frequently bear no relation to the branching. Bitter's[3] opinion is that they arise by the decay of the cortical tissues in very limited areas, from some unknown cause, and that the holes that pierce right through the thallus in other species may be similarly explained.

Still other minute openings into the thallus occur in *Parmelia vittata*, *P. obscurata* and *P. farinacea* var. *obscurascens*. In the two latter the openings like pin-holes are terminal on the lobes and are situated exactly on the apex, between the pith and the gonidial zone; sometimes several holes can be detected on the end of one lobe. Further growth in length is checked by these holes. They appear more frequently on the darker, better illuminated plants. In *Parmelia vittata* the terminal holes are at the end of excessively minute adventitious branches which arise below the gonidial zone on the margin of the primary lobes. All these terminal holes are directed upwards and are visible from above.

Bitter does not attribute any physiological significance to these very definite openings in the thallus. It has been generally assumed that they aid in the aeration of the thallus; it is also possible that they may be of service in absorption, and they might even be regarded as open water conductors.

[1] Bitter 1899.   [2] Nylander 1874[2].   [3] Bitter 1901[2].

C. General Aeration of the Thallus

Definite structures adapted to secure the aeration of the thallus in a limited number of lichens have been described above. These are the breathing-pores of *Parmelia exasperata* and the cyphellae and pseudocyphellae of the Stictaceae, with which also may be perhaps included the circumscribed breaks in the under cortex in some members of that family.

Though lichens are composed of two actively growing organisms, the symbiotic plant increases very slowly. The absorption of water and mineral salts must in many instances be of the scantiest and the formation of carbo-hydrates by the deep-seated chlorophyll cells of correspondingly small amount. Active aeration seems therefore uncalled for though by no means excluded, and there are many indirect channels by which air can penetrate to the deeper tissues.

In crustaceous forms, whether corticate or not, the thallus is often deeply seamed and cracked into areolae, and thus is easily pervious to water and air. The growing edges and growing points are also everywhere more or less loose and open to the atmosphere. In the larger foliose and fruticose lichens, the soredia that burst an opening in the thallus, and the cracks that are so frequent a feature of the upper cortex, all permit of gaseous interchange. The apical growing point of fruticose lichens is thin and porous, and in many of them the ribs and veins of their channelled surfaces entail a straining of the cortical tissue that results in the formation of thinner permeable areas. Zukal[1] devoted special attention to the question of aeration, and he finds evidence of air-passages through empty spermogonia and through the small round holes that are constant in the upper surface of certain foliose species. He claims also to have proved a system of air-canals right through the thallus of the gelatinous Collemaceae. Though his proof in this instance is somewhat unconvincing, he establishes the abundant presence of air in the massively developed hypothecium of *Collema* fruits. He found that the carpogonial complex of hyphae was always well supplied with air, and that caused him to view with favour the suggestion that the function of the trichogyne is to provide an air-passage. In foliose lichens, the under surface is frequently non-corticate, in whole or in part; or the cortex becomes seamed and scarred with increasing expansion, the growth in the lower layers failing to keep pace with that of the overlying tissues, as in *Umbili-caria pustulata*.

It is unquestionable that the interior of the thallus of most lichens con-tains abundant empty spaces between the loose-lying hyphae, and that these spaces are filled with air.

[1] Zukal 1895, p. 1348.

2. CEPHALODIA

A. HISTORICAL AND DESCRIPTIVE

The term "cephalodium" was first used by Acharius[1] to designate certain globose apothecia (pycnidia). At a later date he applied it to the peculiar outgrowths that grow on the thallus of *Peltigera aphthosa*, already described by earlier writers, along with other similar structures, as "corpuscula," "maculae," etc. The term is now restricted to those purely vegetative gall-like growths which are in organic connection with the thallus of the lichen, but which contain one or more algae of a different type from the one present in the gonidial zone. They are mostly rather small structures, and they take various forms according to the lichen species on which they occur. They are only found on thalli in which the gonidia are bright-green algae (Chlorophyceae) and, with a few exceptions, they contain only blue-green (Myxophyceae). Cephalodia with bright-green algae were found by Hue[2] on two *Parmeliae* from Chili, in addition to the usual blue-green forms; the one contained *Urococcus*, the other *Gloeocystis*. Several with both types of algae were detected also by Hue[2] within the thallus of *Aspicilia* spp.

Flörke[3] in his account of German lichens described the cephalodia that grow on the podetia of *Stereocaulon* as fungoid bodies, "corpuscula fungosa." Wallroth[4], who had made a special study of lichen gonidia, finally established that the distinguishing feature of the cephalodia was their gonidia which differed in colour from those of the normal gonidial zone. He considered that the outgrowths were a result of changes that had arisen in the epidermal tissues of the lichens, and, to avoid using a name of mixed import such as "cephalodia," he proposed a new designation, calling them "phymata" or warts.

Further descriptions of cephalodia were given by Th. M. Fries[5] in his *Monograph of Stereocaulon and Pilophorus*; but the greatest advance in the exact knowledge of these bodies is due to Forssell[6] who made a comprehensive examination of the various types, examples of which occurred, he found, in connection with about 100 different lichens. Though fairly constant for the different species, they are not universally so, and are sometimes very rare even when present, and then difficult to find. A striking instance of variability in their occurrence is recorded for *Ricasolia amplissima* (*Lobaria laciniata*) (Fig. 76). The cephalodia of that species are prominent upright branching structures which grow in crowded tufts irregularly scattered over the surface. They are an unfailing and conspicuous specific character of the lichens in Europe, but are entirely wanting in North American specimens.

[1] Acharius 1803.
[2] Hue 1904 and 1910.
[3] Flörke 1815, IV. p. 15.
[4] Wallroth 1825, p. 678.
[5] Th. M. Fries 1858.
[6] Forssell 1884.

As cephalodia contain rather dark-coloured, blue-green algae, they are nearly always noticeably darker than the thalli on which they grow, varying from yellowish-red or brown in those of *Lecanora gelida* to pale-coloured in

Fig. 76. *Ricasolia amplissima* de Not. (*Lobaria laciniata* Wain.) on oak, reduced. The dark patches are tufts of branching cephalodia (A. Wilson, *Photo.*).

Lecidea consentiens[1], a darker red in *Lecidea panaeola* and various shades of green, grey or brown in *Stereocaulon, Lobaria (Ricasolia)*, etc. They form either flat expansions of varying size on the upper surface of the thallus, rounded or wrinkled wart-like growths, or upright branching structures. On the lower surface, where they are not unfrequent, they take the form of small brown nodules or swellings. In a number of species packets of blue-green algae surrounded by hyphae are found embedded in the thallus, either in the pith or immediately under the cortex. They are of the same nature as the superficial excrescences and are also regarded as cephalodia.

[1] Leighton 1869.

B. Classification

Forssell has drawn up a classification of these structures, as follows :

I. Cephalodia vera.

1. **Cephalodia epigena** (including **perigena**) developed on the upper outer surface of the thallus, which are tuberculose, lobulate, clavate or branched in form. These are generally corticate structures.

2. **Cephalodia hypogena** which are developed on the under surface of the thallus; they are termed "thalloid" if they are entirely superficial, and "immersed" when they are enclosed within the tissues. They are non-corticate though surrounded by a weft of hyphae. Forssell further includes here certain placodioid (lobate), granuliform and fruticose forms which develop on the hypothallus of the lichen, and gradually push their way up either through the host thallus, or, as in *Lecidea panaeola*, between the thalline granules.

Nylander[1] arranged the cephalodia known to him in three groups: (1) Ceph. epigena, (2) Ceph. hypogena and (3) Ceph. endogena. Schneider[2] still more simply and practically describes them as Ectotrophic (external), and Endotrophic (internal).

II. Pseudocephalodia.

These are a small and doubtful group of cephalodia which are apparently in very slight connection with the host thallus, and show a tendency to independent growth. They occur as small scales on *Solorina bispora*[3] and *S. spongiosa* and also on *Lecidea pallida*. Forssell has suggested that the cephalodia of *Psoroma hypnorum* and of *Lecidea panaeola* might also be included under this head.

Forssell and others have found and described cephalodia in the following families and genera:

Sphaerophoraceae.
Sphaerophorus (*S. stereocauloides*).
Lecideaceae.
Lecidea (*L. panaeola, L. consentiens, L. pelobotrya*, etc.).
Cladoniaceae.
Stereocaulon, Pilophorus and *Argopsis*.
Pannariaceae.
Psoroma (*P. hypnorum*).
Peltigeraceae.
Peltigera (*Peltidea*), *Nephroma* and *Solorina*.

---

[1] Nylander 1878.   [2] Schneider 1897.   [3] Hue 1910.

Stictaceae.
  Lobaria, Sticta.

Lecanoraceae.
  Lecania (*L. lecanorina*), *Aspicilia*[1].

Physciaceae.
  Placodium bicolor[2].

C. Algae that form Cephalodia

The algae of the cephalodia belong mostly to genera that form the normal gonidia of other lichens. They are:

Stigonema,—in *Lecanora gelida, Stereocaulon, Pilophorus robustus,* and *Lecidea pelobotrya.*

Scytonema,—a rare constituent of cephalodia.

Nostoc,—the most frequent gonidium of cephalodia. It occurs in those of the genera *Sticta, Lobaria, Peltigera, Nephroma, Solorina* and *Psoroma*; occasionally in *Stereocaulon* and in *Lecidea pallida.*

Lyngbya and *Rivularia,*—rarely present, the latter in *Sticta oregana*[3].

Chroococcus and *Gloeocapsa,*—also very rare.

Scytonema, Chroococcus, Gloeocapsa and *Lyngbya* are generally found in combination with some other cephalodia-building alga, though Nylander[4] found *Scytonema* alone in the lobulate cephalodia of *Sphaerophorus stereocauloides,* a New Zealand lichen, and the only species of that genus in which cephalodia are developed; and Hue[1] records *Gloeocapsa* as forming internal cephalodia in two species of *Aspicilia.* Bornet[5] found *Lyngbya* associated with *Scytonema* in the cephalodia of *Stereocaulon ramulosum,* and, in the same lichen, Forssell[6] found, in the several cephalodia of one specimen, *Nostoc, Scytonema,* and *Lyngbya,* while, in those of another, *Scytonema* and *Stigonema* were present. In the latter instance these algae were living free on the podetium. Forssell[6] also determined two different algae, *Gloeocapsa magma* and *Chroococcus turgidus,* present in a cephalodium on *Lecidea panaeola* var. *elegans.*

As a general rule only one kind of alga enters into the formation of the cephalodia of any species or genus. A form of *Nostoc,* for instance, is invariably the gonidial constituent of these bodies in the genera, *Lobaria, Sticta,* etc. In other lichens different blue-green algae, as noted above, may occupy the cephalodia even on the same specimen. Forssell finds alternative algae occurring in the cephalodia of:

Lecanora gelida and *Lecidea illita* contain either *Stigonema* or *Nostoc*;
Lecidea panaeola, with *Gloeocapsa, Stigonema* or *Chroococcus*;

---

[1] Hue 1910.   [2] Tuckerman 1875.   [3] Schneider 1897, p. 58.   [4] Nylander 1869.
[5] Bornet 1873, p. 72.   [6] Forssell 1885, p. 24.

Lecidea pelobotrya, with *Stigonema* or *Nostoc*;
Pilophorus robustus, with *Gloeocapsa*, *Stigonema*, or *Nostoc*.

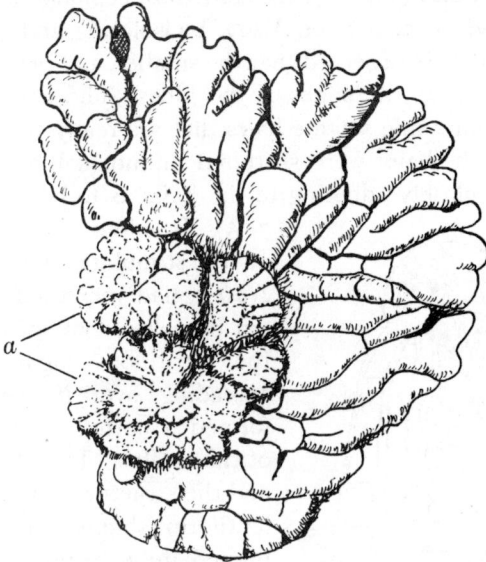

Fig. 77. *Lecanora gelida* Ach. *a*, lobate cephalodia
× 12 (after Zopf).

Riddle[1] has employed cephalodia with their enclosed algae as diagnostic characters in the genus *Stereocaulon*. When the alga is *Stigonema*, as in *S. paschale*, etc., the cephalodia are generally very conspicuous, grey in colour, spherical, wrinkled or folded, though sometimes black and fibrillose (*S. denudatum*). Those containing *Nostoc* are, on the contrary, minute and are coloured verdigris-green (*S. tomentosum* and *S. alpinum*).

Instances are recorded of algal colonies adhering to, and even penetrating, the thallus of lichens, but as they never enter into relationship with the lichen hyphae, they are antagonistic rather than symbiotic and have no relation to cephalodia.

D. DEVELOPMENT OF CEPHALODIA

a. ECTOTROPHIC. Among the most familiar examples of external cephalodia are the small rather dark-coloured warts or swellings that are scattered irregularly over the surface of *Peltigera* (*Peltidea*) *aphthosa*. This lichen has a grey foliose thallus of rather large sparingly divided lobes; it spreads about a hand-breadth or more over the surface of the ground in moist upland localities. The specific name "aphthosa" was given by Linnaeus to

[1] Riddle 1910.

the plant on account of the supposed resemblance of the dotted thallus to the infantile ailment of "thrush." Babikoff[1] has published an account of the formation and development of these *Peltidea* cephalodia. He determined the algae contained in them to be *Nostoc* by isolating and growing them on moist sterilized soil. He observed that the smaller, and presumably younger, excrescences were near the edges of the lobes. The cortical cells in that position grow out into fine septate hairs that are really the ends of growing hyphae. Among the hairs were scattered minute colonies of *Nostoc* cells lying loose or so closely adhering to the hairs as to be undetachable (Fig.

Fig. 78 A. Hairs of *Peltigera aphthosa* Willd. associated with *Nostoc* colony much magnified (after Babikoff).

78A). In older stages the hairs, evidently stimulated by contact with the *Nostoc*, had increased in size and sent out branches, some of which penetrated the gelatinous algal colony; others, spreading over its surface, gradually formed a cortex continuous with that of the thallus. The alga also increased, and the structure assumed a rounded or lentiform shape. The thalline cortex immediately below broke down, and the underlying gonidial zone almost wholly died off and became absorbed. The hyphae of the cephalodium had meanwhile penetrated downwards as root-like filaments, those of the thallus growing upwards into the new overlying tissue (Fig. 78 B). The foreign alga has been described as parasitic, as it draws from the lichen hyphae the necessary inorganic food material; but it might equally well be considered as a captive pressed into the service of the lichen to aid in the work of assimilation or as a willing associate giving and receiving mutual benefit.

Th. M. Fries[2] had previously described the development of the cephalodia in *Stereocaulon* but failed to find the earliest stages. He concluded from his observations that parasitic algae were common in the cortical layer of the lichens, but only rarely formed the "monstrous growths" called cephalodia.

b. ENDOTROPHIC. Winter[3] examined the later stages of internal cephalodine formation in a species of *Sticta*. The alga, probably a species of *Rivularia*, which gives origin to the cephalodia, may be situated immediately below the upper cortex, in the medullary layer close to the gonidial zone, or between the pith and the under cortex. The protuberance caused by the increasing tissue, which also contains the invading alga, arises accordingly either on the upper or the lower surface. In some cases it was found that the normal gonidial layer had been pushed up by the protruding cephalodium

[1] Babikoff 1878.   [2] Th. M. Fries 1866.   [3] Winter 1877.

and lay like a cap over the top. The cephalodia described by Winter are endogenous in origin, though the mature body finally emerges from the interior and becomes either epigenous or hypogenous. Schneider[1] has followed the development of a somewhat similar endotrophic or endogenous type

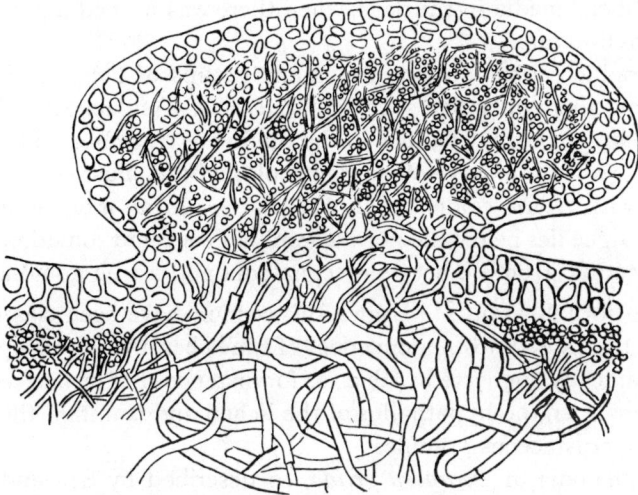

Fig. 78 B. *Peltigera aphthosa* Willd. Vertical section of thallus and cephalodium × 480 (after Babikoff).

in *Sticta oregana* due also to the presence of a species of *Rivularia*. How the alga attained its position in the medulla of the thallus was not observed.

Both the algal cells of internal cephalodia and the hyphae in contact with them increase vigorously, and the newly formed tissue curving upwards or downwards appears on the outside as a swelling or nodule varying in size from that of a pin-head to a pea. On the upper surface the gonidial zone partly encroaches on the nodule, but the foreign alga remains in the centre of the structure well separated from the thalline gonidia by a layer of hyphae. The group is internally divided into small nests of dark-green algae surrounded by strands of hyphae (Fig. 79). The swellings, when they

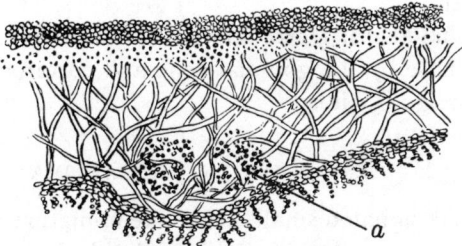

Fig. 79. *Nephroma expallidum* Nyl. Vertical section of thallus. *a*, endotrophic cephalodium × 100 (after Forssell).

[1] Schneider 1897.

occur on the lower surface of the lichen, correspond to those of the upper in general structure, but there is no intermixture of thalline gonidia. That *Nostoc* cells can grow and retain the power to form chlorophyll in adverse conditions was proved by Etard and Bouilhac[1] who made a culture of the alga on artificial media in the dark, when there was formed a green pigment of chlorophyll nature.

Endotrophic cephalodia occur in many groups of lichens. Hue[2] states that he found them in twelve species of *Aspicilia*. As packets of blue-green algae they are a constant feature in the thallus of *Solorinae*. The species of that genus grow on mossy soil in damp places, and must come frequently in contact with *Nostoc* colonies. In *Solorina crocea* an interrupted band of blue-green algae lies below the normal gonidial zone and sometimes replaces it—a connecting structure between cephalodia and a true gonidial zone.

c. PSEUDOCEPHALODIA. Under this section have been classified those cephalodia that are almost independent of the lichen thallus though to some extent organically connected with it, as for instance that of *Lecidea panaeola* which originate on the hypothallus of the lichen and maintain their position between the crustaceous granules.

The cephalodia of *Lecanora gelida*, as described by Sernander[3], might also be included here. He watched their development in their native habitat, an exposed rock-surface which was richly covered with the lichen in all stages of growth. Two kinds of thallus, the one containing blue-green algae (*Chroococcus*), the other bright-green, were observed on the rock in close proximity. At the point of contact, growth ceased, but the thallus with bright-green algae, being the more vigorous, was able to spread round and underneath the other and so gradually to transform it to a superficial flat cephalodium. All such thalli encountered by the dominant lichen were successively surrounded in the same way. The cephalodium, growing more slowly, sent root-like hyphae into the tissue of the underlying lichen, and the two organisms thus became organically connected. Sernander considers that the two algae are antagonistic to each other, but that the hyphae can combine with either.

The pseudocephalodia of *Usnea* species are abortive apothecia; they are surrounded at the base by the gonidial zone and cortex of the thallus, and they contain no foreign gonidia.

E. AUTOSYMBIOTIC CEPHALODIA

Bitter[4] has thus designated small scales, like miniature thalli, that develop constantly on the upper cortex of *Peltigera lepidophora*, a small lichen not uncommon in Finland, and first recorded by Wainio as a variety of *Peltigera*

[1] Etard and Bouilhac 1898.   [2] Hue 1910.   [3] Sernander 1907.   [4] Bitter 1904.

canina. The alga contained in the scales is a blue-green *Nostoc* similar to the gonidia of the thallus. Bitter[1] described the development as similar to that of the cephalodia of *Peltigera aphthosa*, but the outgrowths, being lobate in form, are less firmly attached and thus easily become separated and dispersed; as the gonidia are identical with those of the parent thallus they act as vegetative organs of reproduction.

Bitter's work has been criticized by Linkola[2] who claims to have discovered by means of very thin microtome sections that there is a genetic connection between the scales and the underlying thallus, not only with the hyphae, as in true cephalodia, but with the algae as well, so that these outgrowths should be regarded as.isidia.

In the earliest stages, according to Linkola, a small group of algae may be observed in the cortical tissue of the *Peltigera* apart from the gonidial zone and near the upper surface. Gradually a protruding head is formed which is at first covered over with a brown cortical layer one cell thick. The head increases and becomes more lobate in form, being attached to the thallus at the base by a very narrow neck and more loosely at other parts of the scale. In older scales, the gonidia are entirely separated from those of the thallus, and a dark-brown cortex several cells in thickness covers over the top and sides; there is a colourless layer of plectenchyma beneath. At this advanced stage the scales are almost completely superficial and correspond with the cephaloidal rather than with the isidial type of formation. The algae even in the very early stages are distinct from the gonidial zone and the whole development, if isidial, must be considered as somewhat abnormal.

3. SOREDIA

A. Structure and Origin of Soredia

Soredia are minute separable parts of the lichen thallus, and are composed of one or more gonidia which are clasped and surrounded by the lichen hyphae (Fig. 80). They occur on the surface or margins of the thallus of a fairly large number of lichens either in a powdery excrescence or in a pustule-like body comprehensively termed a "soralium" (Fig. 81). The soralia vary in form and dimensions according to the species. Each individual soredium is capable of developing into a new plant; it is a form of vegetative reproduction characteristic of lichens.

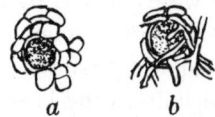

Fig. 80. Soredia. *a*, of *Physcia pulverulenta* Nyl.; *b*, of *Ramalina farinacea* Ach. × 600.

Acharius[3] gave the name " soredia " to the powdery bodies with reference to their propagating function; he also interpreted the soredium as an " apothecium of the second order." But long before his time they had been

---

[1] Bitter 1904.   [2] Linkola 1913.   [3] Acharius, 1798, p. xix, and 1810, pp. 8 and 10.

observed and commented on by succeeding botanists: first by Malpighi[1] who judged them to be seeds, he having seen them develop new plants; by

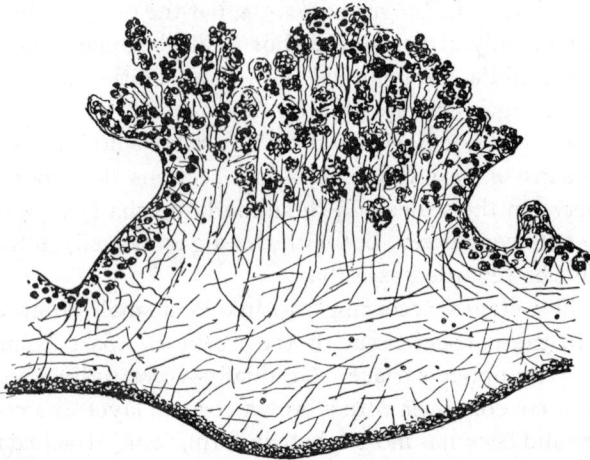

Fig. 81. Vertical section of young soralium of *Evernia furfuracea* var. *soralifera* Bitter × 60 (after Bitter).

Micheli[2] who however distinguished between the true fruit and those seeds; and by Linnaeus[3] who considered them to be the female organs of the plant, the apothecia being, as he then thought, the male organs. Hedwig[4], on the other hand, regarded the apothecia as the seed receptacles and the soredia as male bodies. Sprengel's[5] statement that they were "a subtile germinating powder mixed with delicate hair-like threads which take the place of seeds" established finally their true function. Wallroth[6], who was the first really to investigate their structure and their relation to the parent plant, recognized them as of the same type as the "brood-cells" or gonidia; and as the latter, he found, could become free from the thallus and form a green layer on trees, walls, etc., in shady situations, so the soredia also could become free, though for a time they remained attached to the lichen and were covered by a veil, *i.e.* by the surrounding hyphal filaments. Koerber[7] also gave much careful study to soredia, their nature and function. As propagating organs he found they were of more importance than spores, especially in the larger lichens.

According to Schwendener[8], the formation of soredia is due to increased and almost abnormal activity of division in the gonidial cell; the hyphal filament attached to it also becomes active and sends out branches from the cell immediately below the point of contact which force their way between the newly divided gonidia and finally surround them. A soredial "head"

---

[1] Malpighi, 1686, p. 50, pl. 27, fig. 106.   [2] Micheli 1729, pp. 73, 74.   [3] Linnaeus 1737, p. 325.
[4] Hedwig 1798.   [5] Sprengel 1807, Letter XXIII.   [6] Wallroth 1825, I. p. 595.
[7] Koerber 1841.   [8] Schwendener 1860.

of smaller or larger size is thus gradually built up on the stalk filament or filaments, and is ultimately detached by the breaking down of the slender support.

a. SCATTERED SOREDIA. The simplest example of soredial formation may be seen on the bark of trees or on palings when the green coating of algal cells is gradually assuming a greyish hue caused by the invasion of hyphal lichenoid growth. This condition is generally referred to as " leprose " and has even been classified as a distinct genus, *Lepra* or *Lepraria*. Somewhat similar soredial growth is also associated with many species of *Cladonia*, the turfy soil in the neighbourhood of the upright podetia being often powdered with white granules. Such soredia are especially abundant in that genus, so much so, that Meyer[1], Krabbe[2] and others have maintained that the spores take little part in the propagation of species. The under side of the primary thallus, but more frequently the upright podetia, are often covered with a coating of soredia, either finely furfuraceous, or of larger growth and coarsely granular, the size of the soredia depending on the number of gonidia enclosed in each " head."

Soredia are only occasionally present on the apothecial margins: the rather swollen rims in *Lobaria scrobiculata* are sometimes powdery-grey, and Bitter[3] has observed soredia, or rather soralia, on the apothecial margins of *Parmelia vittata*; they are very rare, however, and are probably to be explained by excess of moisture in the surroundings.

b. ISIDIAL SOREDIA. In a few lichens soredia arise by the breaking down of the cortex at the tips of the thalline outgrowths termed "isidia." In *Parmelia verruculifera*, for instance, where the coralloid isidia grow in closely packed groups or warts, the upper part of the isidium frequently becomes soredial. In that lichen the younger parts of the upper cortex bear hairs or trichomes, and the individual soredia are also adorned with hairs. The somewhat short warted isidia of *P. subaurifera* may become entirely sorediose, and in *P. farinacea* the whole thallus is covered with isidia transformed into soralia. The transformation is constant and is a distinct specific character. Bitter[3] considers that it proves that no sharp distinction exists between isidia and soralia, at least in their initial stages.

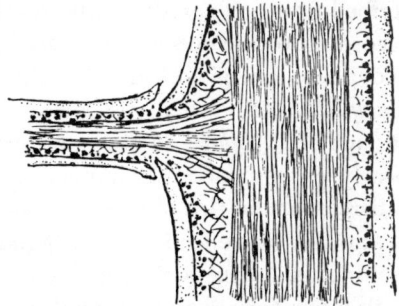

Fig. 82. *Usnea barbata* Web. Longitudinal section of filament and base of "soredial" branch × 40 (after Schwendener).

c. SOREDIA AS BUDS. Schwendener[4] has described soredia in the

[1] Meyer 1825, p. 170. [2] Krabbe 1891. [3] Bitter 1901. [4] Schwendener 1860, p. 137.

genus *Usnea* which give rise to new branches. Many of the species in that genus are plentifully sprinkled with the white powdery bodies. A short way back from the apex of the filament the separate soredia show a tendency to apical growth and might be regarded as groups of young plants still attached to the parent branch. One of these developing more quickly pushes the others aside and by continued growth fills up the soredial opening in the cortex with a plug of tissue; finally it forms a complete lateral branch. Schwendener calls them "soredial" branches (Fig. 82) to distinguish them from the others formed in the course of the normal development.

B. SORALIA

In lichens of foliose and fruticose structure, and in a few crustaceous forms, the soredia are massed together into the compact bodies called soralia, and thus are confined to certain areas of the plant surface. The simpler soralia arise from the gonidial zone below the cortex by the active division of some of the algal cells. The hyphae, interlaced with the green cells, are thin-walled and are, as stated by Wainio[1], still in a meristematic condition; they are thus able readily to branch and to form new filaments which clasp the continually multiplying gonidia. This growth is in an upward or outward direction away from the medulla, and strong mechanical pressure is exerted by the increasing tissue on the overlying cortical layers. Finally the soredia force their way through to the surface at definite points. The cortex is thrown back and forms a margin round the soralium, though shreds of epidermal tissue remain for a time mixed with the powdery granules.

a. FORM AND OCCURRENCE OF SORALIA. The term "soralium" was first applied only to the highly developed soredial structures considered by Acharius to be secondary apothecia; it is now employed for any circumscribed group of soredia. The soralia vary in size and form and in position, according to the species on which they occur; these characters are constant enough to be of considerable diagnostic value. Within the single genus *Parmelia*, they are to be found as small round dots sprinkled over the surface of *P. dubia*; as elongate furrows irregularly placed on *P. sulcata*; as pearly excrescences at or near the margins of *P. perlata*, and as swollen tubercles at the tips of the lobes of *P. physodes* (Fig. 83). Their development is strongly influenced and furthered by shade and moisture, and, given such conditions in excess, they may coalesce and cover large patches of the thallus with a powdery coating, though only in those species that would have borne soredia in fairly normal conditions.

Soralia of definite form are of rather rare occurrence in crustaceous lichens,

---

[1] Wainio 1897, p. 32.　　　　　　[2] Reinke 1895, p. 380.

with the exception of the Pertusariaceae, where they are frequent, and some species of *Lecanora* and *Placodium*. They are known in only two hypo-

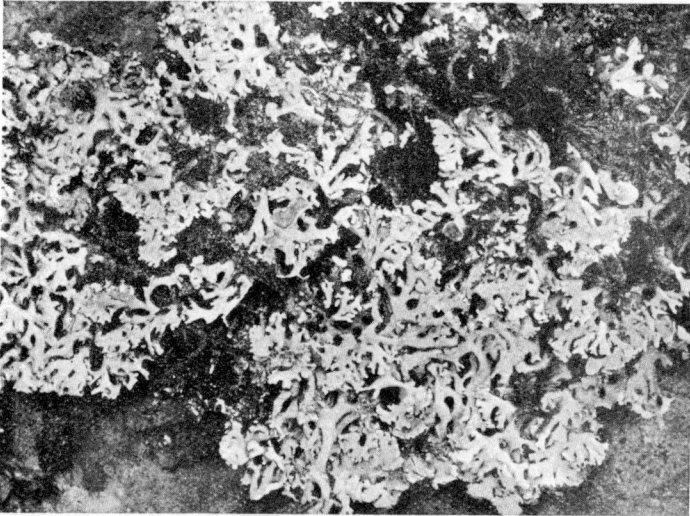

Fig. 83. *Parmelia physodes* Ach. Thallus growing horizontally; soredia on the ends of the lobes (S. H., *Photo.*).

phloeodal (subcortical) lichens, *Arthonia pruinosa* and *Xylographa spilomatica*. Among squamulose thalli they are typical of some *Cladoniae*, and also of *Lecidea* (*Psora*) *ostreata*, where they are produced on the upper surface towards the apex of the squamule.

    b. POSITION OF SORALIFEROUS LOBES. According to observations made by Bitter[1], the occurrence of soralia on one lobe or another may depend to a considerable extent on the orientation of the thallus. He cites the variability in habit of the familiar lichen, *Parmelia physodes* and its various forms, which grow on trees or on soil. In the horizontal thalli there is much less tendency to soredial formation, and the soredia that arise are generally confined to branching lobes on the older parts of the thallus.

    That type of growth is in marked contrast with the thallus obliged to take a vertical direction as on a tree. In such a case the lobes, growing downward from the point of origin, form soralia at their tips at an early stage (Fig. 84). The lateral lobes, and especially those that lie close to the substratum, are the next to become soraliate. Similar observations have been made on the soraliferous lobes of *Cetraria pinastri*. The cause is probably due to the greater excess of moisture draining downwards to the lower parts of the thallus. The lobes that bear the soralia are generally

---

[1] Bitter 1901.

narrower than the others and are very frequently raised from contact with the substratum. They tend to grow out from the thallus in an upright

Fig. 84. *Parmelia physodes* Ach. Thallus growing vertically; soredia chiefly on the lobes directed downwards, reduced (M. P., *Photo.*).

direction and then to turn backwards at the tip, so that the opening of the soralium is directed downwards. Bitter says that the cause of this change in direction is not clear, though possibly on teleological reasoning it is of advantage that the opening of the soralium should be protected from direct rainfall. The opening lies midway between the upper and lower cortex, and the upper tissue in these capitate soralia continues to grow and to form an arched helmet or hood-covering which serves further to protect the soralium.

Similar soralia are characteristic of *Physcia hispida* (*Ph. stellaris* subsp. *tenella*), the apical helmet being a specially pronounced feature of that species, though, as Lesdain[1] has pointed out, the hooded structures are primarily the work of insects. In vertical substrata they occur on the lower lobes of the plant.

Apical soralia are rare in fruticose lichens, but in an Alpine variety of

[1] Lesdain 1910.

Ramalina minuscula they are formed at the tips of the fronds and are protected by an extension of the upper cortical tissues. Another instance occurs
in a *Ramalina* from New Granada referred by Nylander to *R. calicaris* var.
farinacea; it presents a striking example of the helmet tip.

   c. DEEP-SEATED SORALIA. In the cases already described Schwendener[1]
and Nilson[2] held that the algae gave the first impulse to the formation of
the soredia; but in the Pertusariaceae[3], a family of crustaceous lichens, there
has been evolved a type of endogenous soralium which originates with the
medullary hyphae. In these, special hyphae rise from a weft of filaments
situated just above the lowest layer of the thallus at the base of the medulla,
the weft being distinguished from the surrounding tissue by staining blue
with iodine. A loose strand of hyphae staining the usual yellow colour rises
from the surface of the "blue" weft and, traversing the medullary tissue,
surrounds the gonidia on the under side of the gonidial zone. The hyphae
continue to grow upward, pushing aside both the upper gonidial zone and
the cortex, and carrying with them the algal cells first encountered. When
the summit is reached, there follows a very active growth of both gonidia
and hyphae. Each separate soredium so produced consists finally of five to
ten algal cells surrounded by hyphae and measures 8μ to 13μ in diameter.
The cortex forms a well-defined wall or margin round the mass of soredia.

   A slightly different development is found in *Lecanora tartarea*, one of
the "crottle" lichens, which has been placed by Darbishire in Pertusariaceae. The hyphae destined to form soredia also start from the weft of
tissue at the base of the thallus, but they simply grow through the gonidial
zone instead of pushing it aside.

   In his examination of Pertusariaceae Darbishire found that the apothecia
also originated from a similar deeply seated blue-staining tissue, and he concluded that the soralia represented abortive apothecia and really corresponded
to Acharius's "apothecia of the second order." His conclusion as to the
homology of these two organs is disputed by Bitter[4], who considers that
the common point of origin is explained by the equal demand of the hyphae
in both cases for special nutrition, and by the need of mechanical support
at the base to enable the hyphae to reach the surface and to thrust back the
cortex without deviating from their upward course through the tissues.

C. DISPERSAL AND GERMINATION OF SOREDIA

   Soredia become free by the breaking down of the hyphal stalks at the
septa or otherwise. They are widely dispersed by wind or water and soon
make their appearance on any suitable exposed soil. Krabbe[5] has stated

[1] Schwendener 1860.   [2] Nilson 1903.   [3] Darbishire 1897.   [4] Bitter 1901, p. 191.
[5] Krabbe 1891.

that, in many cases, the loosely attached soredia coating some of the *Cladonia* podetia are of external origin, carried thither by the air-currents. Insects too aid in the work of dissemination: Darbishire[1] has told us how he watched small mites and other insects moving about over the soralia of *Pertusaria amara* and becoming completely powdered by the white granules.

Darbishire[1] also gives an account of his experiments in the culture of soredia. He sowed them on poplar wood about the beginning of February in suitable conditions of moisture, etc. Long hyphal threads were at once produced from the filaments surrounding the gonidia, and gonidia that had become free were seen to divide repeatedly. Towards the end of August of the same year a few soredia had increased in size to about 450μ in diameter, and were transferred to elm bark. By September they had further increased to a diameter of 520μ, and the gonidia showed a tendency towards aggregation. No further differentiation or growth was noted.

More success attended Tobler's[2] attempt to cultivate the soredia of *Cladonia* sp. He sowed them on soil kept suitably moist in a pot and after about nine months he obtained fully formed squamules, at first only an isolated one or two, but later a plentiful crop all over the surface of the soil. Tobler also adds that soredia taken from a *Cladonia*, that had been kept for about half a year in a dry room, grew when sown on a damp substratum. The algae however had suffered more or less from the prolonged desiccation, and some of them failed to develop.

A suggestion has been made by Bitter[3] that a hybrid plant might result from the intermingling of soredia from the thallus of allied lichens. He proposed the theory to explain the great similarity between plants of *Parmelia physodes* and *P. tubulosa* growing in close proximity. There is no proof that such mingling of the fungal elements ever takes place.

D. EVOLUTION OF SOREDIA

Soredia have been compared to the gemmae of the Bryophytes and also to the slips and cuttings of the higher plants. There is a certain analogy between all forms of vegetative reproduction, but soredia are peculiar in that they include two dissimilar organisms. In the lichen kingdom there has been evolved this new form of propagation in order to secure the continuance of the composite life, and, in a number of species, it has almost entirely superseded the somewhat uncertain method of spore germination inherited from the fungal ancestor, but which leaves more or less to chance the encounter with the algal symbiont.

From a phylogenetic point of view we should regard the sorediate lichens as the more highly evolved, and those which have no soredia as phylo-

[1] Darbishire 1907.   [2] Tobler 1911[2], II.   [3] Bitter 1901[2].

genetically young, though, as Lindau[1] has pointed out, soredia are all comparatively recent. They probably did not appear until lichens had reached
a more or less advanced stage of development, and, considering the polyphyletic origin of lichens, they must have arisen at more than one point,
and probably at first in circumstances where the formation of apothecia was
hindered by prolonged conditions of shade and moisture.

That soredia are ontogenetic in character, and not, as Nilson[2] has asserted,
accidental products of excessively moist conditions is further proved by the
non-sorediate character of those species of crustaceous lichens belonging to
Lecanora, Verrucaria, etc. that are frequently immersed in water. Bitter[3]
found that the soredia occurring on *Peltigera spuria* were not formed on the
lobes which were more constantly moist, nor at the edges where the cortex
was thinnest: they always emerged on young parts of the thallus a short
way back from the edge.

Bitter[3] points out that in extremely unfavourable circumstances—in the
polluted atmosphere near towns, or in persistent shade—lichens, that would
otherwise form a normal thallus, remain in a backward sorediose state. He
considers, however, that many of these formless crusts are autonomous growths
with specific morphological and chemical peculiarities. They hold these
outposts of lichen vegetation and are not found growing in any other localities.
The proof would be to transport them to more favourable conditions, and
watch development.

4. ISIDIA

A. Form and Structure of Isidia

Many lichens are rough and scabrous on the surface, with minute simple
or divided coral-like outgrowths of the same texture as the underlying thallus,
though sometimes they are darker in colour as in *Evernia furfuracea*. They
always contain gonidia and are covered by a cortex continuous with that
of the thallus.

This very marked condition was considered by Acharius[4] as of generic
importance and the genus, *Isidium*, was established by him, with the diagnostic
characters: "branchlets produced on the surface, or coralloid, simple and
branched." In the genus were included the more densely isidioid states of
various crustaceous species such as *Isidium corallinum* and *I. Westringii*,
both of which are varieties of *Pertusariae*. Fries[5], with his accustomed insight,
recognized them as only growth forms. The genus was however still accepted
in English Floras[6] as late as 1833, though we find it dropped by Taylor[7] in
the *Flora Hibernica* a few years later.

---

[1] Lindau 1895.   [2] Nilson 1903.   [3] Bitter 1904.   [4] Acharius 1798, pp. 2, 87.
[5] Fries 1825.   [6] Hooker 1833.   [7] Taylor 1836.

The development of the isidial outgrowth has been described by Rosen-dahl[1] in several species of *Parmelia*. In one of them, *P. papulosa*, which has a cortical layer one cell thick, the isidium begins as a small swelling or wart on the upper surface of the thallus. At that stage the cells of the cortex have already lost their normal arrangement and show irregular division. They divide still further, as gonidia and hyphae push their way up. The full-grown isidia in this species are cylindrical or clavate, simple or branched.

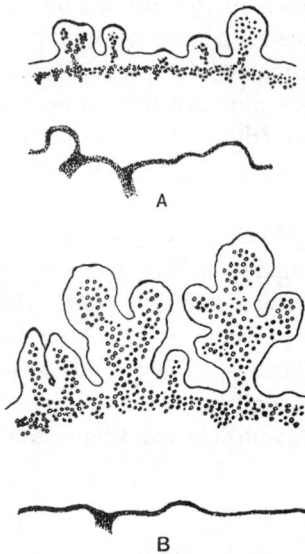

Fig. 85. Vertical section of isidia of *Parmelia scortea* Ach. A, early stage; B. later stage. × 60 (after Rosendahl).

They are peculiar in that they bear laterally here and there minute rhizoids, a development not recorded in any other isidia. The inner tissue accords with that of the normal thallus and there is a clearly marked cortex, gonidial zone and pith. A somewhat analogous development takes place in the isidia of *Parmelia proboscidea*; in that lichen they are mostly prolonged into a dark-coloured cilium.

In *Parmelia scortea* the cortex is several cells thick, and the outermost rows are compressed and dead in the older parts of the thallus; but here also the first appearance of the isidium is in the form of a minute wart. The lower layers (4 to 6) of living cortical cells divide actively; the gonidia also share in the new growth, and the protuberance thus formed pushes off the outer dead cortex and emerges as an isidium (Fig. 85). They are always rather stouter in form than those of *P. papulosa* and may be simple or branched. The gonidia in this case do not form a definite zone, but are scattered through the pith of the isidium.

Here also should be included the coralloid branching isidia that adorn the upper surface and margins of the thallus of *Umbilicaria pustulata*. They begin as small tufts of somewhat cylindrical bodies, but they sometimes broaden out to almost leafy expansions with crisp edges. Most frequently they are situated on the bulging pustules where intercalary growth is active. Owing to their continued development on these areas, the tissue becomes slack, and the centre of the isidial tuft may fall out, leaving a hole in the thallus which becomes still more open by the tension of thalline expansion. New isidia sprout from the edges of the wound and the process may again be repeated. It has been asserted that these structures are only formed on injured parts of the thallus—something like gall-formations—but Bitter[2] has proved that the wound is first occasioned by the isidial growth weakening the thallus.

[1] Rosendahl 1907.   [2] Bitter 1899.

B. Origin and Function of Isidia

Nilson[1] (later Kajanus[2]) insists that isidia and soredia are both products of excessive moisture. He argues that lichen species, in the course of their development, have become adapted to a certain degree of humidity, and, if the optimum is passed, the new conditions entail a change in the growth of the plant. The gonidia are stimulated to increased growth, and the mechanical pressure exerted by the multiplying cells either results in the emergence of isidial structures where the cortex is unbroken, or, if the cortex is weaker and easily bursts, in the formation of soralia.

This view can hardly be accepted; isidia as well as soredia are typical of certain species and are produced regularly and normally in ordinary conditions; both of them are often present on the same thallus. It is not denied, however, that their development in certain instances is furthered by increased shade or moisture. In *Evernia furfuracea* isidia are more freely produced on the older more shaded parts of the thallus. Zopf[3] has described such an instance in *Evernia olivetorina* (*E. furfuracea*), which grew in the high Alps on pine trees, and which was much more isidiose when it grew on the outer ends of the branches, where dew, rain or snow had more direct influence. He[4] quotes other examples occurring in forms of *E. furfuracea* which grew on the branches of pines, larches, etc. in a damp locality in S. Tyrol. The thalli hung in great abundance on each side of the branches, and were invariably more isidiose near the tips, because evidently the water or snow trickled down and was retained longer there than at the base.

Bitter[5] has given a striking instance of shade influence in *Umbilicaria*. He found that some boulders on which the lichen grew freely had become covered over with fallen pine needles. The result was at first an enormous increase of the coralline isidia, though finally the lichen was killed by the want of light.

Isidia are primarily of service to the plant in increasing the assimilating surface. Occasionally they grow out into new thallus lobes. The more slender are easily rubbed off, and, when scattered, become efficient organs of propagation. This view of their function is emphasized by Bitter who points out that both in *Evernia furfuracea* and in *Umbilicaria pustulata* other organs of reproduction are rare or absent. Zopf[3] found new plants of *Evernia furfuracea* beginning to grow on the trunk of a tree lower down than an old isidiose specimen. They had developed from isidia which had been detached and washed down by rain.

[1] Nilson 1903.   [2] Kajanus (Nilson) 1911.   [3] Zopf 1903.   [4] Zopf 1905[2].
[5] Bitter 1899.

VI. HYMENOLICHENS

A. Supposed Affinity with other Plants

Lichens in which the fungal elements belong to the Hymenomycetes are confined to three tropical genera. They are associated with blue-green algae and are most nearly related to the Thelephoraceae among fungi. The spores are borne, as in that family, on basidia.

The best known Hymenolichen, *Cora Pavonia* (Fig. 86), was discovered by Swartz[1] during his travels in the W. Indies (1785–87) growing on trees

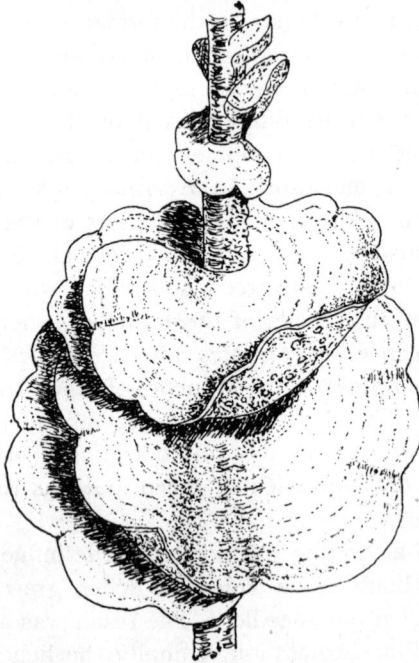

Fig. 86. *Cora Pavonia* Fr. (after Mattirolo).

in the mountains of Jamaica, and the new plant was recorded by him as *Ulva montana*. Gmelin[2] also included it in *Ulva* in close association with *Ulva* (*Padina*) *Pavonia*, but that classification was shortly after disputed by Woodward[3] who thought its affinity was more nearly with the fungi and suggested that it should be made the type of a new genus near to *Boletus* (*Polystictus*) *versicolor*. Fries[4] in due time made the new genus *Cora*, though he included it among algae; finally Nylander[5] established the lichenoid character of the thallus and transferred it to the Lecanorei.

It was made the subject of more exact investigation by Mattirolo[6] who

[1] Swartz 1788.   [2] Gmelin 1791.   [3] Woodward 1797.   [4] Fries 1825.
[5] Nylander 1855.   [6] Mattirolo 1881.

recognized its affinity with *Thelephora*, a genus of Hymenomycetes. Later Johow[1] went to the West Indies and studied the Hymenolichens in their native home. The genera and species described by Johow have been reduced to *Cora* and *Dictyonema*; a new genus *Corella* has since been added by Wainio[2].

Johow found that *Cora* grew on the mountains usually from 1000 to 2000 ft. above sea-level. As it requires for its development a cool damp climate with strong though indirect illumination, it is found neither in sunny situations nor in the depths of dark woods. It grows most freely in diffuse light, on the lower trunks and branches of trees in open situations, but high up on the stem where the vegetation is more dense. It stands out from the tree like a small thin bracket fungus, one specimen placed above another, with a dimidiate growth similar to that of *Polystictus versicolor*. Both surfaces are marked by concentric zones which give it an appearance somewhat like *Padina Pavonia*. These zones indicate unequal intercalary growth both above and below. The whole plant is blue-green when wet, greyish-white when dry, and of a thin membranaceous consistency.

B. STRUCTURE OF THALLUS

There is no proper cortex in any of the genera, but in *Cora* there is a fastigiate branching of the hyphae in parallel lines towards the upper surface; just at the outside they turn and lie in a horizontal direction, and, as the branching becomes more profuse, a rather compact cover is formed. The gonidia, which consist of blue-green *Chroococcus* cells, lie at the base of the upward branches

Fig. 87. *Cora Pavonia* Fr. Vertical section of thallus. *a*, upper cortex; *b*, gonidial layer; *c*, medulla and lower cortex of crenate cells; *d*, tuft of fertile hyphae. × 160. *e*, basidia and spores × 1000 (after Johow).

and they are surrounded with thin-walled short-celled hyphae closely interwoven into a kind of cellular tissue. The medulla of loose hyphae passes over to the lower cortex, also of more or less loose filaments. The outermost cells of the latter very frequently grow out into short jagged or crenate processes (Fig. 87).

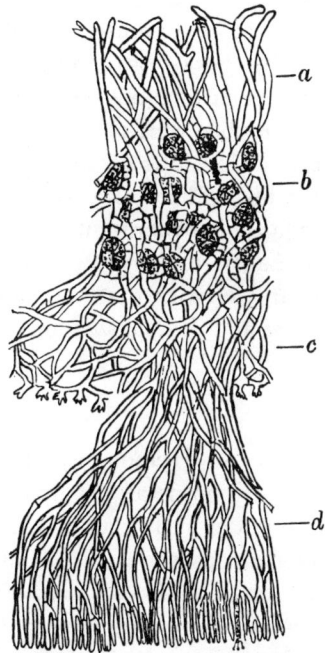

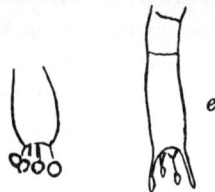

[1] Johow 1884.   [2] Wainio 1890.

In *Corella*, the mature lichen is squamulose or consists of small lobes; in *Dictyonema* there is a rather flat dimidiate expansion; in both the alga is *Scytonema*, the trichomes of which largely retain their form and are surrounded by parallel growths of branching hyphae. The whole tissue is loose and spongy.

Corella spreads over soil on a white hypothallus without rhizinae. In the other two genera which live on soil, or more frequently on trees, there is a rather extensive formation of hold-fast tissue. When the dimidiate thallus grows on a rough bark, rhizoidal strands of hyphae travel over it and penetrate between the cracks; if the bark is smooth, there is a more continuous weft of hyphae. In both cases a spongy cushion of filamentous tissue develops at the base of the lichen between the tree and the bracket thallus. There is also in both genera an encrusting form which Johow regarded as representing a distinct genus *Laudatea*, but which Möller found to be merely a growth stage. Möller[1] judged from that and from other characteristics that the same fungus enters into the composition of both *Cora* and *Dictyonema* and that only the algal constituents are different.

C. Sporiferous Tissues

As in Hymenomycetes, the spores of Hymenolichens are exogenous, and are borne at the tips of basidia which in these lichens are produced on the under surface of the thallus. In *Cora* the fertile filaments may form a continuous series of basidia over the surface, but generally they grow out in separate though crowded tufts. As these tufts broaden outwards, they tend to unite at the free edges, and may finally present a continuous hymenial layer. Each basidium bears four sterigmata and spores (Fig. 87 e); paraphyses exactly similar to the basidia are abundant in the hymenium. In *Dictyonema* the hymenium is less regular, but otherwise it resembles that of *Cora*. No hymenium has as yet been observed in *Corella*; it includes, so far as known, one species, *C. brasiliensis*, which spreads over soil or rocks.

[1] Möller 1893.

CHAPTER IV

REPRODUCTION

I. REPRODUCTION BY ASCOSPORES

A. Historical Survey

The earliest observations as to the propagation of lichens were made by Malpighi[1] who recorded the presence of soredia on the lichen plant and noted their function as reproductive bodies. He was followed after a considerable interval by Tournefort[2] who placed lichens in a class apart owing to the form of the fruit: "This fruit," he writes, "is a species of bason or cup which seems to take the place of seeds in these kinds of plants." He figures *Ramalina fraxinea* and *Physcia ciliaris*, both well fruited specimens, and he represents the "minute dust" contained in the fruits as subrotund in form. The spores of *Physcia ciliaris* are of a large size and dark in colour and were undoubtedly seen by Tournefort. Morison[3], in his *History of Oxford Plants*, published very shortly after, dismissed Tournefort's "seeds" as being too minute to be of any practical interest.

Micheli[4], with truer scientific insight, made the fruiting organs the subject of special study. He decided that the apothecia were floral receptacles, *receptacula florum*, and that the spores were the "flowers" of the lichen. He has figured them in a vertical series *in situ*, in a section of the disc of *Solorina saccata*[5] and also in a species of *Pertusaria*[5], in both of which plants the ascospores are unusually large. He adds that he had not so far seen the "semina."

Micheli's views were not shared by his immediate successors. Dillenius[6] scarcely believed that the spores could be "flowers" and, in any case, he concluded that they were too minute to be of any real significance in the life of the plant.

Linnaeus[7], and after him Necker[8], Scopoli[9] and others describe the apothecia as the male, the soredia as the female organs of lichens. These old time botanists worked with very low powers of magnification, and easily went astray in the interpretation of imperfectly seen phenomena.

Koelreuter[10], a Professor of Natural History in Carlsruhe, who published a work on *The discovered Secret of Cryptogams*, next hazarded the opinion that the seeds of lichens originated from the substance of the pith, and that the overlying cortical layer supplied the fertilizing sap. Hoffmann[11]

---

[1] Malpighi 1686.   [2] Tournefort 1694.   [3] Morison 1699.   [4] Micheli 1729.
[5] Micheli, Pls. 52 and 56.   [6] Dillenius 1741.   [7] Linnaeus 1737.   [8] Necker 1771, p. 257.
[9] Scopoli 1772.   [10] Koelreuter 1777.   [11] Hoffmann 1784.

devoted a great deal of attention to lichen fructification and he also thought that fertilization must take place within the tissue of the lichens. He regarded the soredia as the true seeds, while allowing that a second series of seeds might be contained in the scutellae (apothecia).

A distinct advance was made by Hedwig[1], a Professor of Botany in Leipzig, towards the end of the eighteenth century. He followed Tournefort in selecting *Physcia ciliaris* for research, and in that plant he describes and figures not only the apothecia with the dark-coloured septate spores, but also the pycnidia or spermogonia which he regarded as male organs. The soredia, typically represented and figured by him on *Parmelia physodes*, he judged to be " male flowers of a different type."

Acharius[2] did not add much to the knowledge of reproduction in lichens, though he takes ample note of the various fruiting structures for which he invented the terms *apothecia, perithecia* and *soredia.* Under still another term *gongyli* he included not only spores, but the spore guttulae as well as the gonidia or cells forming the soredia.

Hornschuch[3] of Greifswald described the propagation of the lower lichens as being solely by means of a germinating " powder "; the more highly organized forms were provided with receptacles or apothecia containing spores which he considered as analogous to flowers rather than to fruits. The important contributions to Lichenology of Wallroth[4] and Meyer[5] close this period of uncertainty: the former deals almost exclusively with the form and character of the vegetative thallus and the function of the " reproductive gonidia." Meyer, a less prolix writer, very clearly states that the method of reproduction is twofold: by spores produced in fruits, or by the germinating granules of the soredia.

B. Forms of Reproductive Organs

From the time of Tournefort, considerable attention had been given to the various forms of *scutellae, tuberculae*, etc., as characters of diagnostic importance. Sprengel[6] grouped these bodies finally into nine different types with appropriate names which have now been mostly superseded by the comprehensive terms, apothecia and perithecia. A general classification on the lines of fruit development was established by Luyken[7], who, following Persoon's[8] classification of fungi, and thus recognizing their affinity, summed up all known lichens as *Gymnocarpeae* with open fruits, and *Angiocarpeae* with closed fruits.

a. APOTHECIA. As in discomycetous fungi, the lichen apothecium is in the form of an open concave or convex disc, but generally of rather small

[1] Hedwig 1784.   [2] Acharius 1810.   [3] Hornschuch 1821.   [4] Wallroth 1825.
[5] Meyer 1825.   [6] Sprengel 1804.   [7] Luyken 1809.   [8] Persoon 1801.

size, rarely more than 1 cm. in diameter (Fig. 88); there is no development in lichen fruits equal to the cup-like ascomata of the larger *Pezizae*. In

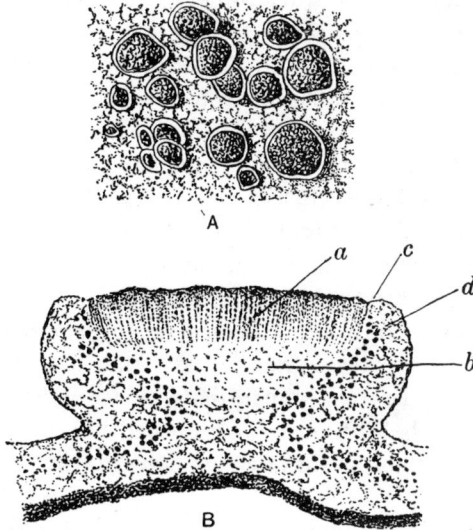

Fig. 88. *Lecanora subfusca* Ach. A, thallus and apothecia × 3; B, vertical section of apothecium. *a*, hymenium; *b*, hypothecium; *c*, thalline margin or amphithecium; *d*, gonidia. × 60 (after Reinke).

most cases the lichen apothecium retains its vitality as a spore-bearing organ for a considerable period, sometimes for several years, and it is strengthened and protected by one or more external margins of sterile tissue. Immediately surrounding the fertile disc there is a compact wall of interwoven hyphae. In some of the shorter-lived soft fruits, as in *Biatora*, this hyphal margin may be thin, and may gradually be pushed aside as the disc develops and becomes convex, but generally it forms a prominent rim round the disc and may be tough or even horny, and often hard and carbonaceous. This wall, which is present, to some extent, in nearly all lichens, is described as the "proper margin." A second "thalline margin" containing gonidia is present in many genera[1]: it is a structure peculiar to the lichen apothecium and forms the *amphithecium*.

At the base of the apothecium there is a weft of light- or dark-coloured hyphae called the *hypothecium*, which is continued up and round the sides as the *parathecium* merging into the "proper margin." It forms the lining of a cup-shaped hollow which is filled by the paraphyses, which are upright closely packed thread-like hyphae, and by the spore-containing asci or *thecae*, these together constituting the thecium or hymenium. The paraphyses are very numerous as compared with the asci; they are simple or branched,

[1] See also p. 166.

frequently septate, especially towards the apex, and mostly slender, varying in width from 1–4µ, though Hue describes paraphyses in *Aspicilia atroviolacea* as 8–12µ thick. They may be thread-like throughout their length, or they may widen towards the tips which are not infrequently coloured. Small apical cells are often abstricted and lie loose on the epithecium, giving at times a pruinose or powdered character to the disc. In some genera there is a profuse branching of the paraphyses to form a dense protective epithecium over the surface of the hymenium as in the genus *Arthonia*.

The apothecia may be sessile and closely adnate to or even sunk in the thallus, or they may be shortly stalked. The thalline margin shares generally the characters of the thallus; the disc is mostly of a firm consistency and is light or dark in colour according to genus or species; most frequently it is some shade of brown. Marginate apothecia, *i.e.* those with a thalline margin, are often referred to as "lecanorine," that being a distinctive feature of the genus *Lecanora*. In the immarginate series, with a proper margin only, the texture may be soft and waxy, termed "biatorine" as in *Biatora*; or hard and carbonaceous as in the genus *Lecidea*, and is then described as "lecideine."

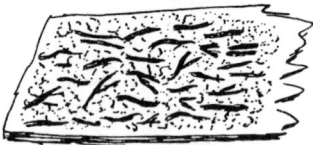

In the subseries Graphidineae, the apothecium has the form of a very flat, roundish or irregular body entirely without a margin, called an "ardella" as in *Arthonia*; or more generally it is an elongate narrow "lirella," in which the disc is a mere slit between two dark-coloured proper margins. The hypothecium of the lirellae is sometimes much reduced and in that case the hymenium rests directly on a thin layer above the thalline tissue as in *Graphis elegans* (Fig. 89).

Fig. 89. *Graphis elegans* Ach. A, thallus and lirellae; B, vertical section of furrowed lirella. × ca. 50.

Lichen fruits require abundant light, and plants growing in the shade are mostly sterile. Naturally, therefore, the reproductive bodies are to be found on the best illuminated parts of the thallus. In crustaceous and in most foliose forms, they are variously situated on the upper surface, wherever the light falls most directly. In the genera *Nephromium* and *Nephromopsis*, on the contrary, they arise on the under surface, though at the extreme margin, but as the fertile lobes eventually turn upwards the apothecia as they mature become fully exposed. In shrubby or fruticose lichens their position is lateral on the fronds, or more frequently at or near the tips.

b. PERITHECIA. The small closed perithecium is characteristic of the Pyrenocarpeae which correspond with the Pyrenomycetes among fungi. It is partially or entirely immersed in the thallus or in the substratum on which the lichen grows, and is either a globose or conical body wholly surrounded by a hyphal wall, when it is described as "entire" (Fig. 90), or it is somewhat hemispherical in form and the outer wall is developed only on the upper exposed part: a type of perithecium usually designated by the term "dimidiate." As the perithecial wall gives sufficient protection to the asci, the paraphyses are of less importance and are frequently very sparingly produced, or they may even be dissolved and used up at an early stage. The thallus of the Pyrenocarpeae is often extremely reduced, and the perithecia are then the only visible portion of the lichen.

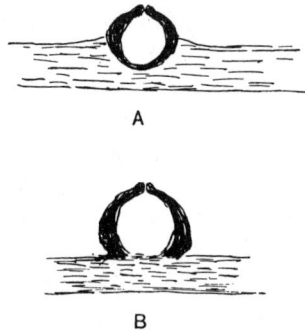

Fig. 90. A, entire perithecium of *Porina olivacea* A. L. Sm. × ca. 40; B, dimidiate perithecium of *Acrocordia gemmata* Koerb. × ca. 20.

A few lichens among Graphidineae and Pyrenocarpeae grow in a united body generally looked on as a stroma; but Wainio[1] has demonstrated that as the fruiting bodies give rise to this structure by agglomeration—by the cohesion of their margins—it can only be regarded as a pseudostroma. Two British genera of Pyrenolichens, *Mycoporum* and *Mycoporellum*, exhibit this pseudo-stromatoid formation.

C. DEVELOPMENT OF REPRODUCTIVE ORGANS

As most known lichens belong to the Ascolichens, the study of development has been concentrated on that group. Tulasne[2] was the first to make a microscopic study of lichen tissues and he described in considerable detail the general anatomical structure of apothecia and perithecia. Later, Fuisting[3] traced the development of a number of perithecia through their different stages of growth, but his most interesting discovery was made in *Lecidea fumosa*, a crustaceous Discolichen with an areolate thallus in which the apothecia are seated on the fungal hyphae between the areolae. In the very early stages represented by a complex of slender hyphae, he observed an unbranched septate filament with short cuboid cells, richer in contents than the surrounding filaments and somewhat similar to the structure known to mycologists as "Woronin's hypha," which is an ascogonial structure. These specialized cells disappeared as the hymenium began to form.

[1] Wainio 1890.   [2] Tulasne 1852.   [3] Fuisting 1868.

I. DISCOLICHENS

a. CARPOGONIA OF GELATINOUS LICHENS. Stahl's[1] work on various Collemaceae followed on the same lines as that of Fuisting. The first species selected by him for examination, *Collema* (*Leptogium*) *microphyllum*, is a gelatinous lichen which grows on old trunks of poplars and willows. It has a small olive-green thallus which, in autumn, is crowded with apothecia; the spermogones or pycnidia appear as minute reddish points on the edge of the thallus. Within the thallus, and midway between the upper and lower surface, there arises, as a branch from a vegetative hypha, a many-septate filament coiled in spiral form at the base, with the free end growing upwards and projecting a short distance above the surface and occasionally forked (Fig. 91). The tip-cell is slightly swollen and covered with a mucilaginous

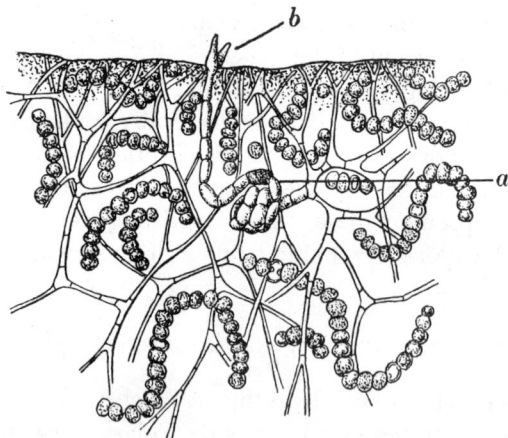

Fig. 91. *Collema microphyllum* Ach. Vertical section of thallus. *a*, carpogonium; *b*, trichogyne. × 350 (after Stahl).

coat continuous with the mucilage of the thallus. The whole structure, characterized by the larger size and by the richer contents of its cells, was regarded by Stahl as a carpogonium, the coiled base representing the asco-gonium, the upright hypha functioning as the receptive organ or trichogyne, comparable to that of the Florideae. The spermatia, which mature at this early stage of carpogonial development, are expelled from a neighbouring spermogonium on the addition of moisture and easily reach the protruding trichogyne. They adhere to the mucilaginous wall of the end-cell, and, in two or three instances, Stahl found that copulation had taken place. As the affixed spermatium was empty, he concluded that the contents had passed over into the trichogyne, and that the nucleus had travelled down to the ascogonium. Certain degenerative changes that followed seemed to confirm

[1] Stahl 1877.

the view that there had been fertilization: the cells of the trichogyne had
lost their turgidity and at the same time the cross-walls had swollen considerably and stood out like knots in the
hypha (Fig. 92). The ascogonial cells had
also increased not only in size but in number
by intercalary division, so that the spiral
arrangement became obscured. Ascogenous
hyphae arose from the ascogonial cells, and
asci cut off by a basal septum were finally
formed from these hyphae. Lateral branches
from below the septum also formed asci.

Stahl's observations were repeated and
extended by Borzi[1] on another of the Collemaceae, *Collema nigrescens*. In that plant the
foliaceous thallus is of thin texture and has
a distinct cellular cortex. The carpogonia
were found at varying depths near to the cortical region; the ascogonium, of two and a
half to four spirals, consisted of ten to fifteen
cells with very thin walls, the trichogyne of
five to ten cells, the terminal cell projecting
above the thallus. Borzi also found spermatia
fused with the tip-cell.

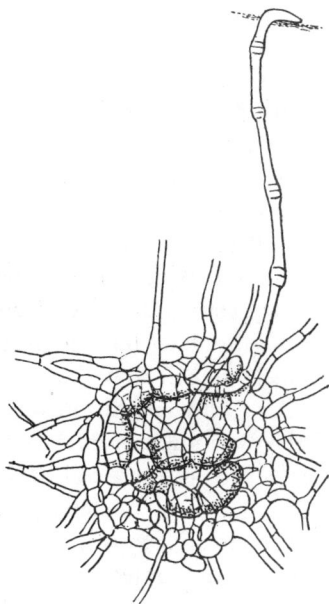

Fig. 92. *Collema microphyllum* Ach.
Carpogonium and trichogyne after
copulation × 500 (after Stahl).

A further important contribution was made by Baur[2] in his study of
Collema crispum[3]. There occur in nature two forms of this lichen, one of
them crowded with apothecia and spermogonia, the other with a more
luxuriant thallus, but with few apothecia and no spermogonia. On the latter
almost sterile form Baur found in spring and again in autumn immense
numbers of carpogonia—about one thousand in a medium sized thallus—
which nearly all gradually lost the characteristics of reproductive organs,
and, anastomising with other hyphae, became part of the vegetative system.
In a few cases in which, presumably, a spermatium had fused with a trichogyne, very large apothecia had developed.

As the first-mentioned form was always crowded with apothecia in every
stage of development, as well as with carpogonia and spermogonia, it seemed
natural to conclude that the difference was entirely due to the presence or
absence of spermatia in sufficient numbers to ensure fertilization. The
period during which copulation is possible passes very rapidly, though
subsequent development is slow, occupying about half-a-year from the time
of fertilization to the formation of the first ascus.

[1] Borzi 1878. [2] Baur 1898.
[3] Fünfstück (1902) suggests that the lichen worked at by Baur is *Collema cheileum* Ach.

Baur confirmed Stahl's observations on the various developmental changes. In several instances he found a spermatium fused with the trichogyne, though he could not see continuity between the lumina of the fusing cells. After copulation with the spermatium the trichogyne nucleus, which occupied the lower third of the terminal cell, had disappeared, and the plasma contents had acquired a deeper tint; the other trichogyne cells, which had also lost their nuclei, were partly collapsed owing to the pressure of the surrounding tissue, and openings were plainly visible through some of the swollen septa, especially of the lower cells. In addition the ascogonial cells, all of which were uninucleate, had increased in number by intercalary division. Plasma connections were opened from cell to cell, but only in the primary septa, the later formed cell-membranes being continuous. Ascogenous hyphae had branched out from the ascogonium as a series of uninucleate cell rows from which the asci finally arose.

Baur's interpretation was that the first cell of the ascogonium reached by the male nucleus after its passage down through the cells of the trichogyne represented the egg-cell, and that, after fusion, the resultant nucleus divided, and a daughter nucleus passed on to the other auxiliary-cells. No male nucleus nor fusion of nuclei was, however, observed by him, and his deductions rest on conjecture.

Krabbe[1] and after him Mäule[2] found in *Collema pulposum* reproductive organs similar to those described by Stahl, but in a recent paper on an American form of that species a peculiar condition has been described by Freda Bachmann[3]. She[4] found that the spermatia originated, not in spermogonia, but as groups of cells budded off from vegetative hyphae within the tissue of the lichen and occupying the same position as spermogonia, *i.e.* the region close below the upper surface. The trichogynes, therefore, never emerged into the open, but travelled towards these internal spermatia, and fusion with them was effected. The changes that afterwards took place in the carpogonial cells were similar to those that had been recognized by Stahl and Baur as consequent on fertilization.

Additional cytological details have been published in a subsequent paper[5]: after fusion with the spermatium the terminal cell of the trichogyne collapsed, its nucleus became disintegrated and the cross septa of the lower trichogyne cells became perforated, these perforations being closed again at a later stage by a gelatinous plug. The nuclear history is more doubtful: the disappearance of the nuclei from the spermatium and from the terminal cell of the trichogyne was noted; two nuclei were seen to be present in the penultimate cell, and these the author interpreted as division products of the

---

[1] Krabbe 1883.   [2] Mäule 1891.   [3] F. Bachmann 1912.
[4] This species of *Collema* has been described as *Collemodes Bachmannianum* by Bruce Fink 1918.
[5] F. Bachmann 1913.

original cell nucleus. In the same cell, lying close against the lower septum and partly within the opening, there was a mass of chromatin material which might be the male nucleus migrating downwards. The next point of interest was observed in the twelfth cell from the tip in which there were two nuclei, a larger and a smaller, the latter judged to be the male cell, the small size being due to probable division of the spermatium nucleus either before or after leaving the spermatium. It is stated however that the spermatium was always uninucleate. Meanwhile the cells of the ascogonium had increased in size, the perforations of the septa between the cells became more evident, and their nucleï persisted. In one cell at this stage two nuclei were present, one of the two presumably a male nucleus; no fusion of nuclei was observed in the ascogonial cells. Later the cross walls between the cells were seen to have disappeared more completely and migration of nuclei had taken place, so that some of the cells appeared to be empty while others were multinucleate. Considerable multiplication of the nuclei occurred before the ascogenous hyphae were formed: twelve nuclei were observed in a part of the ascogonium which was just beginning to give off a branch. Several branches might arise from one cell, and their cells were either uni- or binucleate, the nuclei being larger than those of the vegetative hyphae. The formation of the asci was not distinctly seen, but young binucleate asci were not uncommon. The fusion of the two nuclei was followed by the enlargement of the ascus and the subsequent nuclear division for spore formation. In the first heterotypic division twelve chromosomes, double the number observed in the vegetative nucleus, were counted on the equatorial plate. In the third division they were reduced to the normal number of six, from which F. Bachmann concludes that a twofold fusion must have taken place—in the ascogonium and again in the ascus.

Spiral or coiled ascogonia were observed by Wainio[1] in the gelatinous crustaceous genus *Pyrenopsis*, but the trichogynes did not reach the surface. In *Lichina*[2], a maritime gelatinous lichen where the carpogonia occur in groups, trichogynes have not been demonstrated.

A peculiarity of some gelatinous lichens noted by Stahl[3] and others in species of *Physma*, and by Forssell[4] in *Pyrenopsis* and *Psorotichia*, is the development of carpogonia at the base of, and within the perithecial walls of old spermogonia. No special significance is however attached to this phenomenon, and it is interesting to note that a similar growth was observed by Zukal[5] in a pyrenomycetous fungus, *Pleospora collematum*, a harmless parasite on *Physma compactum* and other Collemaceae. The structures invaded were true pycnidia of the fungus as the minute spores were seen to germinate. A "Woronin's hypha" at the base of several of these pycnidia developed asci which pushed up among the spent sporophores.

[1] Wainio 1. 1890.   [2] Wolff 1905.   [3] Stahl 1877.   [4] Forssell 1885².   [5] Zukal 1887, p. 42.

b. CARPOGONIA OF NON-GELATINOUS LICHENS. The soft loose tissue of the gelatinous lichens is more favourable for the minute study of apothecial development than the closely interwoven hyphae of non-gelatinous forms, but Borzi[1] had already extended the study to species of *Parmelia, Anaptychia, Sticta, Ricasolia* and *Lecanora*, and in all of them he succeeded in establishing the presence of ascogonia and trichogynes. After him a constant succession of students have worked at the problem of reproduction in lichens.

Lindau[2] published results of the examination of a considerable series of lichens. In *Anaptychia (Physcia) ciliaris, Physcia stellaris, Ph. pulverulenta, Ramalina fraxinea, Placodium (Lecanora) saxicolum, Lecanora subfusca* and *Lecidea enteroleuca* he demonstrated the presence of ascogonia with trichogynes. In *Parmelia tiliacea* and in *Xanthoria parietina* he found ascogonia but failed to see trichogynes. In none of the species examined by him did he observe any fusion between the trichogyne and a spermatium.

In *Anaptychia ciliaris* he was able to pick out extremely early stages by staining with a solution of chlor-zinc-iodine. Mäule[3] applied the same test to *Physcia pulverulenta*, but found that to be successful the reaction required some time. Certain cells of the hyphae—mostly terminal cells—in the lower area of the gonidial zone and even occasionally in the pith (according to Lindau) coloured a deep brown, while the ordinary thalline hyphae were tinted yellow. He assumed that these were initial ascogonial cells on account of the richer plasma contents, and also because of the somewhat larger size of the cells. In the same region of the thallus young carpogonia were observed as outgrowths from vegetative hyphae, though the trichogynes had not yet reached the surface.

At a more advanced stage the carpogonia were seen to be embedded in the gonidial zone and occurred in groups. The cells of the ascogonium, easily recognized by the darker stain, were short and stout, measuring about 6–8 μ in length and 4·4 μ in width. They were arranged in somewhat indistinct spirals; but the crowding of the groups resulted in a confused intermingling of the various generative filaments. The trichogynes composed of longer narrower cells rose above the hyphae of the cortex; they also stained a deep brown and the projecting cell was always thin-walled. Lindau frequently observed spermatia very

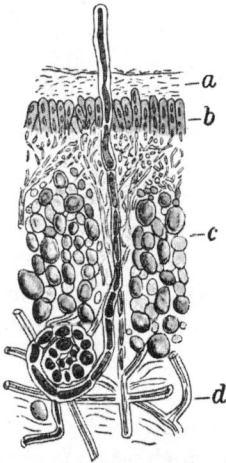

Fig. 93. *Physcia pulverulenta* Nyl. Vertical section of thallus and carpogonium before fertilization. *a*, outer cortex; *b*, inner cortex; *c*, gonidial layer; *d*, medulla. × ca. 540 (after Darbishire).

[1] Borzi 1878. [2] Lindau 1888. [3] Mäule 1891.

firmly attached to the trichogyne cell but without any plasma connection between the two. The changes in the trichogyne described by Stahl and Baur in Collemaceae were not seen in *Anaptychia*; the peculiar swelling of the septa seems to be a phenomenon confined to gelatinous lichens. During the trichogyne stage in this lichen the vegetative hyphae from the medulla grow up and surround the young carpogonia, and, at the same time, very slender hyphae begin to branch upwards to form the paraphyses. Darbishire's[1] examination of *Physcia pulverulenta* demonstrated the presence of the coiled ascogonium and the trichogyne in that species (Fig. 93).

Baur[1] has also given the, results of an examination of *Anaptychia*. He frequently observed copulation between the spermatium and the tip of the trichogyne, but not any passage of nucleus or contents. After copulation the ascogonial cells increased in size and became irregular in form, and open communication was established between them (Fig. 94). There was no increase in their number by intercalary division as in *Collema*. After

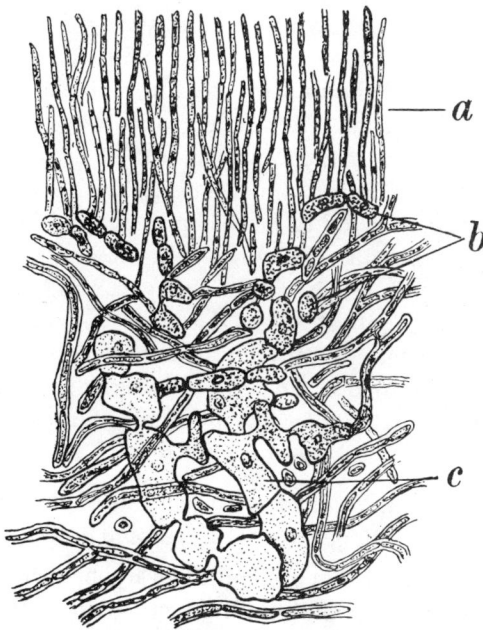

Fig. 94. *Physcia* (*Anaptychia*) *ciliaris* DC. Vertical section of developing ascogonium. *a*, paraphyses; *b*, ascogonial hyphae; *c*, ascogonial cells. × 800 (after Baur).

producing ascogenous hyphae the cells were seen to have lost their contents and then to have gradually disappeared. The fertile hyphae, which now took a blue colouration with chlor-zinc-iodine, gradually spread out and

[1] Darbishire 1900.   [2] Baur 1904.

formed a wide-stretching hymenium   Several carpogonia took part in the formation of one apothecium.

The tissue below the ascogonium meanwhile developed vigorously, forming a weft of encircling hyphae, while the upper branches grew vertically towards the cortex. Gonidia in contact with the developing fruit also increased, and, with the hyphae, formed the exciple or thalline margin. The growth upward of the paraphyses raises the overlying cortex which in *Anaptychia* is "fibrous"; it gradually dies off and allows the exposure of the disc, though small shreds of dead tissue are frequently left. In species such as those of *Xanthoria* where the cortex is of vertical cell-rows, the apothecial hyphae simply push their way between the cell-rows and so through to the open.

Baur found the development of the apothecium somewhat similar in the crustaceous corticolous lichen, *Lecanora subfusca.* After a long period of sterile growth, spermogonia appeared in great abundance, and, a little later, carpogonia in groups of five to ten; the trichogynes emerged very slightly above the cortex; they were now branched. The ascogonia were frequently a confused clump of cells, though sometimes they showed distinct spirals. The surrounding hyphae had taken a vertical direction towards the cortex at a still earlier stage, and the brown tips were visible on the exterior before the trichogynes were formed. The whole growth was extremely slow.

In *Physcia stellaris* the carpogonia occurred in groups also, though Lindau[1] thinks that, unlike *Anaptychia* (*Physcia*) *ciliaris*, only one is left to form the fruit. Only one, according to Darbishire[2], entered into the apothecium in the allied species, *Physcia pulverulenta.* In the latter plasma connections were visible from cell to cell of the trichogyne, and, after copulation with the spermatium, the ascogonial cells increased in size—though not in number—and the plasma connections between them became so wide that the ascogonium had the appearance of an almost continuous multinucleate cell or coenogamete[3]. As in gelatinous lichens, each of these cells gave rise to ascogenous hyphae.

c. GENERAL SUMMARY. The main features of development described above recur in most of the species that have been examined.

(1) The carpogonia arise in a complex of hyphae situated on the under side of, or immediately below the gonidial zone. Usually they vary in number from five to twenty for each apothecium, though as many as seventy-two have been computed for *Icmadophila ericetorum*[4], and Wainio[5] describes them as so numerous in *Coccocarpia pellita* var., that their trichogynes covered some of the young apothecia with a hairy pile perceptible with a hand lens, though at the same time other apothecia on the same specimens were absolutely smooth.

---

[1] Lindau 1888.   [2] Darbishire 1900.   [3] See also p. 180.   [4] Nienburg 1908.   [5] Wainio 1. 1890.

(2) The trichogynes, when present, travel up through the gonidial and cortical regions of the thallus; Darbishire[1] observes that in *Physcia pulverulenta*, they may diverge to the side to secure an easier course between the groups of algae. They emerge above the surface to a distance of about 15μ or less; after an interval they collapse and disappear. Their cells, which are longer and narrower than those of the ascogonium, are uninucleate and vary in number according to species or to individual lichens. Baur[2] thought that possibly several trichogynes in succession might arise from one ascogonium.

(3) How many carpogonia share in the development of the apothecium is still a debated question. In *Collema* only one is functional. Baur[3] was unable to decide if one or more were fertilized in *Parmelia acetabulum*, and in *Usnea* Nienburg[4] found that, out of several, one alone survived (Fig. 95). But in *Anaptychia ciliaris* and in *Lecanora subfusca* Baur[3] considers it proved that several share in the formation of the apothecium. In this connection it is interesting to note that, according to Harper[5] and others, several ascogonia enter into one *Pyronema* fruit.

Fig. 95. *Usnea barbata* Web. Carpogonium with trichogyne × 1100 (after Nienburg).

(4) The ascogonial cells, before and after fertilization, are distinguished from the surrounding hyphae by a reaction to various stains, which is different from that of the vegetative hyphae, and also by the shortness and width of their cells. The whole of the apothecial primordium is generally recognizable by the clear shining appearance of the cells.

(5) The ascogonia do not always form a distinct spiral; frequently they lie in irregular groups. Each cell is uninucleate and may ultimately produce ascogenous hyphae, though in *Anaptychia* · Baur[3] noted that some of the cells failed to develop.

(6) The hyphae from the ascogonial cells spread out in a complex layer at the base of the hymenium, and send up branches which form the asci, either, as in most Ascomycetes, from the penultimate cell of the fertile branch, or from the last cell, as in *Sphyridium* (*Baeomyces rufus*)[4] and in *Baeomyces roseus*. The same variation has been observed in fungi—in a species of *Peziza*[6], in which it is the end-cell of the branch that becomes the mother-cell of the ascus; but this deviation from the normal is evidently of rare occurrence either in lichens or fungi.

d. HYPOTHECIUM AND PARAPHYSES. The hypothecium is the layer of hyphae that subtends the hymenium, and is formed from the complex of

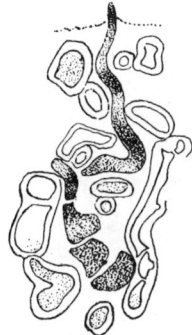

---

[1] Darbishire 1900.   [2] Baur 1901.   [3] Baur 1904.   [4] Nienburg 1908.
[5] Harper 1900.   [6] Guilliermond 1904, p. 60.

hyphae that envelope the first stages of the carpogonia. It is vegetative in origin and distinct from the generative system.

In lichens belonging to the Collemaceae, the paraphyses rise from the branching of the carpogonial stalk-cell immediately below the ascogonium[1], but have no plasma connection with it. They are thus comparable in origin with the paraphyses of many Discomycetes.

In several genera in which the algal constituents are blue-green, such as *Stictina, Pannaria, Nephroma, Ricasolia* and *Peltigera*, Sturgis[2] found that reproduction was apogamous and also that asci and paraphyses originated from the same cell-system: a tuft of paraphyses arose from the basal cell of the ascus, or an ascus from the basal cell of a paraphysis. These results are at variance with those of most other workers, but the figures drawn by Sturgis seem to be clear and convincing.

Again in *Usnea barbata*, as described by Nienburg[3], the ascogonial cells, after the disappearance of the trichogyne, branch profusely not only upwards towards the cortex but also downwards and to each side. The upward branches give rise normally to the asci, the lower branches produce the subhymenium and later the paraphyses, and the two systems are thus genetically connected, though they remain distinct from each other, and asci are never formed from the lower cells.

In most heteromerous lichens, however, the origin of the paraphyses is exclusively vegetative: they arise as branches from the primordial complex that forms the covering hyphae of the ascogonium both above and below. Schwendener[4] had already pointed out the difference in origin between the two constituents of the hymenium in one of his earlier studies on the development of the apothecium, and this view has been repeatedly confirmed by recent workers, except by Wahlberg[5] who has insisted that they rise from the same cells as the asci, a statement disproved by Baur[6]. The paraphyses originate not only from the covering hyphae, but from vegetative cells in close connection with the primordium. In this mode of development, lichens diverge from fungi, but even in these a vegetative origin for the paraphyses has been pointed out in *Lachnea scutellata*[7] where they branch from the hyphae lying round the ascogonium.

There is no general rule for the order of development. In *Lecanora subfusca* Baur[6] found that vertical filaments had reached the surface by the time the trichogyne was formed, and their pointed brown tips gave a ready clue to the position of the carpogonia. In *Lecidea enteroleuca*[8] they show their characteristic form and arrangement before there is any trace of ascus formation. In *Solorina*[8] they are well formed before the ascogenous hyphae appear. In other lichens such as *Placodium saxicolum*[9], *Peltigera*

[1] Baur 1899.   [2] Sturgis 1890.   [3] Nienburg 1908.   [4] Schwendener 1864.   [5] Wahlberg 1902.
[6] Baur 1904.   [7] Brown 1911.   [8] Moreau 1916.   [9] Lindau 1888.

rufescens[1] and *P. malacea*[1] the two systems—paraphyses and ascogonium—grow simultaneously, though in *P. horizontalis* the ascogonium has disappeared by the time the paraphyses are formed. In the genus *Nephroma*, in *Physcia stellaris* and in *Xanthorina parietina* the paraphyses are also late in making their appearance.

In most instances, the paraphyses push their way up between the cortical cells which gradually become absorbed, or they may stop short of the surface as in *Nephromium tomentosum*[1]. The overlying layer of cortical cells in that case dies off gradually and in time disappears. Such an apothecium is said to be "at first veiled." Later formed paraphyses at the circumference of the apothecium form the parathecium, which is thus continuous with the hypothecium.

e. VARIATIONS IN APOTHECIAL DEVELOPMENT. Lichens are among the least stereotyped of plants: instances of variation have been noted in several genera.

aa. PARMELIAE. A somewhat complicated course of development has been traced by Baur[2] in *Parmelia acetabulum*. In that lichen the group of three to six carpogonia do not lie free in the gonidial tissue, but originate nearer the surface (Fig. 96) and are surrounded from the first by a tissue connected with, and resembling the tissue of the cortex. In the several ascogonia, there are more cells and more spirals than in *Collema* or in *Physcia*, and all of them are somewhat confusedly intertwined. The trichogynes are composed of three to five cells and project 10 to 15 μ above the surface. When further development begins, the ascogonial cells branch out and form a primary darker layer or hypo-

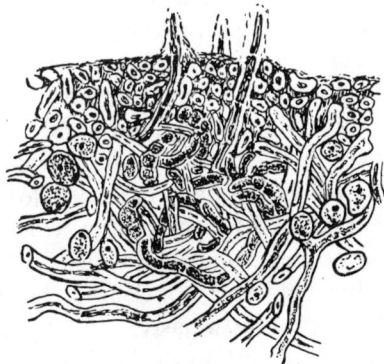

Fig. 96. *Parmelia acetabulum* Dub. Vertical section of thallus and carpogonial group × 550 (after Baur).

thecium above which extends the subhymenium, a light-coloured band of loosely woven hyphae. Branches from the ascogonial hyphae at a later stage push their way up through this tissue and form above it a second plexus of hyphae—the base of the hymenium. Baur considers this a very advanced type of apothecium; he found it also present in *Parmelia saxatilis*, though, in that species, the further growth of the first ascogonial layer was more rapid and the secondary plexus and hymenium were formed earlier in the life of the apothecium. He has also stated that a similar development occurs in other genera such as *Usnea*, though Nienburg's[3] work scarcely confirms that view.

[1] Fünfstück 1884.   [2] Baur 1904.   [3] Nienburg 1908.

In the brown *Parmeliae*, Rosendahl[1] found the same series of apothecial tissues, but he interprets the course of development somewhat differently: the basal dark layer or hypothecium he found to be of purely vegetative origin; above it extended the lighter-coloured subhymenium; the ascogenous hyphae were present only in the second layer of dark tissue immediately under the hymenium.

In most lichens the primordium of the apothecium arises towards the lower side of the gonidial zone, the hyphae of which retain the meristematic character. In *Parmeliae*, as was noted by Lindau[2] in *P. tiliacea*, and by Baur[3] and Rosendahl[1] in other species, the carpogonial groups are formed above the gonidial zone, either immediately below the cortex as in *P. glabratula*, or in a swelling of the cortex itself as in *P. aspidota*, in which species the external enlargement is visible by the time the trichogynes reach the surface. In *P. glabra*, with a development entirely similar to that of *P. aspidota*, no trichogynes were seen at any stage. The position of the primordium close under the cortex is also a feature of *Ramalina fraxinea* as described by G. Wolff[4]. The trichogynes in that species are fairly numerous.

A further peculiarity in *Parmelia acetabulum* attracted Baur's[3] attention. Carpogonia with trichogynes are extremely numerous in that species as are the spermogonia, the open pores of which are to be found everywhere between the trichogynes, and yet fertilization can occur but rarely, as disintegrating carpogonia are abundant and very few apothecia are formed. Baur makes the suggestion that possibly cross-fertilization may be necessary, or that the spermatia, in this instance, do not fertilize and that development must therefore be apogamous, in which case the small number of fruits formed is due to some unknown cause. Fünfstück[5] thought that degeneration of the carpogonia had not gone so far, but that a few had acquired the power to develop apogamously. In *Parmelia saxatilis* only a small percentage of carpogonia attain to apothecia, although spermogonia are abundant and in close proximity, but in that species, unlike *P. acetabulum*, a large number reach the earlier stages of fruit formation; the more vigorous apothecia seem to inhibit the growth of those that lag behind.

bb. PERTUSARIAE. In *Pertusaria*, the apothecial primordium is situated immediately below the gonidial zone; the cells have a somewhat larger lumen and thinner walls than those of the vegetative hyphae. In the ascogonium there are more cells than in *Parmelia acetabulum*; the trichogynes are short-lived, and several carpogonia probably enter into the formation of each apothecium; the paraphyses arise from the covering hyphae. So far the course of development presents nothing unusual. The peculiar pertusarian feature as described by Krabbe[6], and after him by Baur[7], does not appear

---

[1] Rosendahl 1907.   [2] Lindau 1888.   [3] Baur 1904.   [4] Wolff 1905.
[5] Fünfstück 1902.   [6] Krabbe 1882.   [7] Baur 1901.

till a later stage. By continual growth in thickness of the overlying thallus, the apothecia gradually become submerged and tend to degenerate; meanwhile, however, a branch from the ascogonial hyphae at the base of the hymenium pushes up along one side and forms a secondary ascogonial cell-plexus over the top of the first-formed disc. A new apothecium thus arises and remains sporiferous until it also comes to lie in too deep a position, when the process is repeated. Sometimes the regenerating hypha travels to the right or left away from the original apothecium, it may be to a distance of 2 mm. or according to Fünfstück even considerably farther. Fünfstück[1] has gathered indeed from his own investigations that such cases of regeneration are by no means rare: ascogenous hyphae, several centimetres long, destined to give rise to new apothecia are not unusual, and their activity can be recog-

Fig. 97. *Rhizocarpon petraeum* Massal. Concentrically arranged apothecia, reduced (J. Adams, *Photo.*).

nized macroscopically by the linear arrangement of the apothecia in such lichens as *Rhizocarpon* (*petraeum*) *concentricum* (Fig. 97).

In *Variolaria*, a genus closely allied to or generally included in *Pertusaria*, Darbishire[2] has described the primordial tissue as taking rise almost at the base of the crustaceous thallus: strands of delicate hyphae, staining

---

[1] Fünfstück 1902.   [2] Darbishire 1897.

blue with iodine, mount upwards from that region through the medulla and gonidial zone[1]. The ascogonium does not appear till the surface is almost reached.

cc. Graphideae. Several members of the Graphidaceae were studied by G. Wolff[2]: she demonstrated the presence of carpogonia with emerging trichogynes in *Graphis elegans*, a species which is distinguished by the deeply furrowed margins of the lirellae (Fig. 89). Before the carpogonia appeared it was possible to distinguish the cushion-like primordial tissue of the apothecium in the thallus which is almost wholly immersed in the periderm layers of the bark on which it grows. The trichogynes were very sparingly septate, and a rather large nucleus occupied a position near the tip of the terminal cell. The dark carbonaceous outer wall makes its appearance in this species at an early stage of development along the sides of the lirellae, but never below, as there is always a layer of living cells at the base. After the first-formed hymenium is exhausted, these basal cells develop a new apothecium with a new carbonaceous wall that pushes back the first-formed, leaving a cleft between the old and the new. This regenerating process, somewhat analogous to the formation of new apothecia in *Pertusaria*, may be repeated in *Graphis elegans* as many as five times, the traces of the older discs being clearly seen in the channelled margins of the lirellae.

dd. Cladoniae. The chief points of interest in the *Cladoniae* are the position of the apothecial primordia and the function of the podetium,

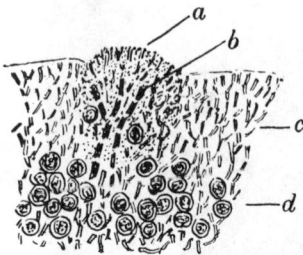

Fig. 98. *Cladonia decorticata* Spreng. Vertical section of squamule and primordium of podetium. *a*, developing podetium; *b*, probably fertile hyphae; *c*, cortical tissue; *d*, gonidial cells. ɟ × 600 (after Krabbe).

which are discussed later[3]. Krabbe[4] determined not only the endogenous origin of the podetium but also the appearance of fertile cells in the primordium (Fig. 98). Both frequently take rise where a crack occurs in the cortex of the primary squamule, the cells of the gonidial tissue being especially active at these somewhat exposed places. The fertile hyphae elongate and branch within the stalk of the developing podetium, sometimes very early, or not until there is a pause in growth, when carpogonia are formed. As a rule trichogynes emerge in great numbers[2], generally close to, or rather below, the spermogonia. In *Cl. pyxidata*[5] the carpogonia are characterized by the large diameter of the cells—three to five times that of the vegetative hyphae. Though most of the trichogynes disappear at an early stage, some of them may persist for a considerable period. As development proceeds, the vegetative hyphae interspersed among the ascogonial cells grow upwards, slender

[1] See also p.147.   [2] Wolff 1905.   [3] See Chap. VII.   [4] Krabbe 1883 and 1891.   [5] Baur 1904.

branches push up between them and gradually a compact sheath of para-physes is built up. The ascogenous hyphae meanwhile spread radially at the base of the paraphyses and the asci begin to form. The apothecia may be further enlarged by intercalary growth, and this vigorous development of vegetative tissue immediately underneath raises the whole fruit structure well above the surface level.

Sättler[1] in his paper on *Cladoniae*[2] cites as an argument in favour of fertilization the relative positions of carpogonia and spermogonia on the podetia. The carpogonia with their emerging trichogynes being situated rather below the spermogonia. Both organs, he states, have been demon-strated in eleven species; he himself observed them in the primordial podetia of *Cladonia botrytes* and of *Cl. Floerkeana*.

2. PYRENOLICHENS

a. DEVELOPMENT OF THE PERITHECIUM. It is to Fuisting[3] that we owe the first account of development in the lichen perithecium. Though he failed to see the earlier stages (in *Verrucaria Dufourii*), he recognized the primordial complex of hyphae in the gonidial zone of the thallus, from which originated a vertical strand of hyphae destined to form the tubular neck of the perithecium. Growth in the lower part is in abeyance for a time, and it is only after the neck is formed, and the fruiting body is widened by the ingrowth of external hyphae, that the asci begin to branch up from the tissue at the base.

b. FORMATION OF CARPOGONIA. Stahl[4] had indicated that not only in gymnocarpous but also in angiocarpous lichens, it would be found that carpo-gonia were formed as in *Collema*. Baur[5] justified this surmise, and demonstrated the presence of ascogonia in groups of three to eight, with trichogynes that reached the surface in *Endocarpon* (*Dermatocarpon*) *mi-niatum* (Fig. 99). It is one of the few foliaceous Pyrenolichens, and the leathery thallus is attached to the substratum by a central point, thus allowing in the thallus not only peripheral but also intercalary growth, the latter specially active round the point of basal attachment; carpogonia may be found in any region where the tissue is newly formed, and at any season. The upper cortex is composed of short-celled thick-

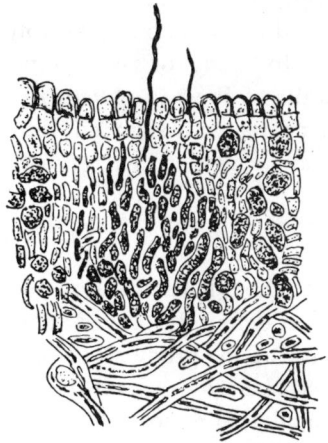

Fig. 99. *Dermatocarpon miniatum* Th. Fr. Vertical section of thallus and carpogonial group × 600 (after Baur).

[1] Sättler 1914. [2] See Chap. VII. [3] Fuisting 1868. [4] Stahl 1877. [5] Baur 1904.

walled hyphae, with branching vertical to the surface, and so closely packed that there is an appearance of plectenchyma ; the medullary hyphae are also thick-walled but with longer cells. The carpogonia of this species arise as a branch from the vegetative hyphae and are without special covering hyphae, so frequent a feature in other lichens. The trichogynes bore their way through the compact cortex and rise well above the surface. After they have disappeared—presumably after fertilization—the vegetative hyphae round and between the ascogonia become active and travel upwards slightly converging to a central point. The asci begin to grow out from the asco-genous hyphae of the base before the vertical filaments have quite pierced the cortex.

Pyrenula nitida has also been studied by Baur[1]. It is a very common species on smooth bark, with a thin crustaceous thallus immersed among the outer periderm cells. Unlike most other lichens, it forms carpogonia in spring only, from February to April. A primordial coil of.hyphae lies at the base of the gonidial layer, and, before there is any appearance of carpo-gonia, a thick strand of hyphae is seen to be directed upwards, so that a definite form and direction is given to the perithecium at a very early stage. The ascogonial cells which are differentiated are extremely small, and, like those of all other species examined, are uninucleate. There are five to ten carpogonia in each primordium ; the trichogynes grow up through the hyphal strand and emerge 5–10 μ above the surface. After their disappearance, a weft of ascogenous tissue is formed at the base, and, at the same time, the surrounding vegetative tissue takes part in the building up of a plecten-chymatous wall of minute dark-coloured cells. Further development is rapid and occupies probably only a few weeks.

In many of the pyrenocarpous lichens—*Verrucariae* and others—the walls of the paraphyses dissolve in mucilage as the spores become mature, a character associated with spore ejection and dispersal. In some genera and species, as in *Pyrenula*, they remain intact.

D. APOGAMOUS REPRODUCTION

Though fertilization by an externally produced male nucleus has not been definitely proved there is probability that, in some instances, the fruit may be the product of sexual fusion. There are however a number of genera and species in which the development is apogamous so far as any external copulation is possible and the sporiferous tissue seems to be a purely vege-tative product up to the stage of ascus formation.

In *Phlyctis agelaea* Krabbe[2] found abundant apothecia developing nor-mally and not accompanied by spermogonia; in *Phialopsis rubra* studied

---

[1] Baur 1901.   [2] Krabbe 1882.

also by him the primordium arises among the cells of the periderm on which the lichen grows, and he failed to find any trace of a sexual act. In his elaborate study of Gloeolichens Forssell[1] established the presence of carpogonia with trichogynes in two species—*Pyrenopsis phaeococca* and *P. impolita*, but without any appearance of fertilization; in all the others examined, the origin of the fruit was vegetative. Wainio[2] records a similar observation in a species of *Pyrenopsis* in which there was formed a spiral ascogonium and a trichogyne, but the latter never reached the surface.

Neubner[3] claimed to have proved a vegetative origin for the asci in the Caliciaceae; but he overlooked the presence of spermogonia and his conclusions are doubtful.

Fünfstück[4] found apogamous development in *Peltigera* (including *Peltidea*) and his results have never been disputed. The ascogonial cells are surrounded at an early stage by a weft of vegetative hyphae. No trichogynes are formed and spermogonia are absent or very rare in the genus, though pycnidia with macrospores occur occasionally.

Some recent work by Darbishire[5] on the genus supplies additional details. The apothecial primordium always originated near the growing margin of the thallus, where certain medullary hyphae were seen to swell up and stain more deeply than others. These at first were uninucleate, but the nuclei increased by division as the cells became larger, and in time there was formed a mass of closely interwoven cells full of cytoplasm. "No coiled carpogonia can be made out, but these darkly stained cells form part of a connected system of branching hyphae coming from the medulla further back." Long unbranched multiseptate hyphae—evidently functionless trichogynes—travelled towards the cortex but gradually died off. Certain of the larger cells—the "ascogonia"—grew out as ascogenous hyphae into which the nuclei passed in pairs and finally gave rise to the asci.

These results tally well with those obtained by M. and Mme Moreau[6], though they make no mention of any trichogyne. They found that the terminal cells of the ascogenous hyphae were transformed into asci, and the two nuclei in these cells fused—the only fusion that took place. In *Nephromium*, one of the same family, the case for apogamy is not so clear; but Fünfstück found no trichogynes, and though spermogonia were present on the thallus, they were always somewhat imperfectly developed.

Sturgis[7] supplemented these results in his study of other lichens containing blue-green algae. In species of *Heppia*, *Pannaria*, *Hydrothyria*, *Stictina* and *Ricasolia*, he failed to find any evidence of fertilization by spermatia.

Solorina, also a member of Peltigeraceae, was added to the list of

---

[1] Forssell 1885. [2] Wainio 1890, p. x. [3] Neubner 1893. [4] Fünfstück 1884.
[5] Darbishire 1913. [6] Moreau 1915. [7] Sturgis 1890.

apogamous genera by Metzger[1] and his work was confirmed and amplified by Baur[2]: certain hyphae of the gonidial zone branch out into larger ascogonial cells which increase by active intercalary growth, by division and by branching, and so gradually give rise to the ascogenous hyphae and finally to the asci. Baur looked on this and other similar formations as instances of degeneration from the normal carpogonial type of development. Moreau[3] (Fernand and Mme) have also examined *Solorina* with much the same results: the paraphyses rise first from cells that have been produced by the gonidial hyphae; later, ascogenous hyphae are formed and spread horizontally at the base of the paraphyses, finally giving rise at their tips to the asci. Metzger[1] had further discovered that spermogonia were absent and trichogynes undeveloped in two very different crustaceous lichens, *Acarospora* (*Lecanora*) *glaucocarpa* and *Verrucaria calciseda*, the latter a pyrenocarpous species and, as the name implies, found only on limestone.

Krabbe[4] had noted the absence of any fertilization process in *Gyrophora vellea*. At a later date, *Gyrophora cylindrica* was made the subject of exact research by Lindau[5]. In that species the spermogonia (or pycnidia) are situated on the outer edge of the thallus lobes; a few millimetres nearer the centre appear the primordia of the apothecia, at first without any external indication of their presence. The initial coil which arises on the lower side of the gonidial zone consists of thickly wefted hyphae with short cells, slightly thicker than those of the thallus. It was difficult to establish their connection with the underlying medullary hyphae since these very soon change to a brown plectenchyma. From about the middle of the ascogonial coil there rises a bundle of parallel stoutish hyphae which traverse the gonidial zone and the cortex and slightly overtop the surface. They are genetically connected at the base with the more or less spirally coiled hyphae, and are similar to the trichogynes described in other lichens. Lindau did not find that they had any sexual significance, and ascribed to them the mechanical function of terebrators or borers. The correctness of his deductions has been disputed by various workers: Baur[2] looks on these "trichogynes" as the first paraphyses. The reproductive organs in *Stereocaulon* were examined by G. Wolff[6], and the absence of trichogynes was proved, though spermogonia were not wanting. She also failed to find any evidence of fertilization in *Xanthoria parietina*, in which lichen the ascogenous hyphae branch out from an ascogonium that does not form a trichogyne.

Rosendahl[7], as already stated, could find no trichogynes in *Parmelia glabra*. In *Parmelia obscurata*, on the contrary, Bitter[8] found that carpogonia with trichogynes were abundant and spermogonia very rare. In other species of the subgenus, *Hypogymnia*, he has pointed out that apothecia are either

[1] Metzger 1903. [2] Baur 1904. [3] Moreau 1916. [4] Krabbe 1882. [5] Lindau 1899.
[6] Wolff 1905. [7] Rosendahl 1907. [8] Bitter 1901².

absent or occur but seldom, while spermogonia are numerous, and he concludes that the spermatia must function as spores or conidia. Baur[1] however does not accept that conclusion; he suggests as probable that the male organs persist longer in a functionless condition than do the apothecia.

Still more recently Nienburg[2] has described the ascogonium of *Baeomyces* sp. and also of *Sphyridium byssoides* (*Baeomyces rufus*) as reduced and probably degenerate. His results do not disprove those obtained by Krabbe[3] on the same lichen (*Sphyridium fungiforme*). The apothecia are terminal on short stalks in that species. When the stalk is about ·5 mm. in height, sections through the tip show numerous primordia (12 to 15) ranged below the outer cortex, though only one, or at most three, develop further. These ascogonial groups are connected with each other by delicate filaments, and Nienburg concluded that they were secondary products from a primary group lower down in the tissue. Spirals were occasionally seen in what he considered to be the secondary ascogonia, but usually the fertile cells lie in loose uncoiled masses; isolated hyphae were observed to travel upwards from these cells, but they never emerged above the surface.

Usnea macrocarpa—if Schulte's[4] work may be accepted—is also apogamous, though in *Usnea barbata* Nienburg[2] found trichogynes (Fig. 95) and the various developments that are taken as evidence of fertilization. Wainio[5] had demonstrated emergent straight trichogynes in *Usnea laevis* but without any sign of fertilization.

E. DISCUSSION OF LICHEN REPRODUCTION

In Ascolichens fertilization by the fusion of nuclei in the ascogonium is still a debated question. The female organ or carpogonium, as outlined above, comprises a twisted or spirally coiled multiseptate hypha, with a terminal branch regarded as a trichogyne which is also multiseptate, and through which the nucleus of the spermatium must travel to reach the female cell. It is instructive to compare the lichen carpogonium with that of other plants.

a. THE TRICHOGYNE. In the Florideae, or red seaweeds, in which the trichogyne was first described, that organ is merely a hair-like prolongation of the egg-cell and acts as a receptive tube. It contains granular protoplasm but no nucleus and terminates in a shiny tip covered with mucilage. The spermatium, unlike that of lichens, is a naked cell, and being non-motile is conveyed by water to the tip of the trichogyne to which it adheres; the intervening wall then breaks down and the male nucleus passes over. After this process of fertilization a plug of mucilage cuts off the trichogyne, and it withers away.

---

[1] Baur 1904.   [2] Nienburg 1908.   [3] Krabbe 1882.   [4] Schulte 1904.   [5] Wainio 1890.

REPRODUCTION

In *Coleochaete*, a genus of small fresh-water green algae, a trichogyne is also present in some of the species: it is again a prolongation of an oogonial cell.

In the Ascomycetes, certain cells or cell-processes associated with the ascogonium have been described as trichogynes or receptive cells. In one of the simpler types, Monascus[1], the " trichogyne " is a cell cut off from the ascogonial cell. When fertilization takes place, the wall between the two cells breaks down to allow the passage of the male nucleus, but closes up when the process is effected. In *Pyronema confluens*[2] it is represented by a process from the ascogonial cell which fuses directly with the male cell. A more elaborate "trichogyne" has been evolved in *Lachnea stercorea*[3], another Discomycete: in that fungus it takes the form of a 3–5-septate hypha with a longer terminal cell; it rises from some part of the ascogonial cell but has no connection with any process of fertilization, so that the greater elaboration of form is in this case concomitant with loss of function.

In the Laboulbeniaceae, a numerous and very peculiar series of Asco-mycetes that live on insects, there are, in nearly all of the reproductive bodies, a carpogonial cell, a trichophoric cell and a trichogyne. The last-named organ is in some gener.. a simple continuous cell, in others it is septate and branched, occasionally it is absent[4]. The male cells are spermatia of two kinds, exogenous or endogenous, and the plants are monoecious or dioecious. Laboulbeniaceae have no connection with lichens. Faull[5], a recent worker on the group, states that though he observed spermatia attached to the tri-chogynes, he was not able to demonstrate copulation (possibly owing to over-staining), nor could he trace any migration of the nucleus through the trichophoric cell down to the carpogonial cell. In two species of *Laboulbenia* that he examined there were no antheridia, and the egg-cell acquired its second nucleus from the neighbouring trichophoric cell. These conjugate nuclei divided simultaneously and the two daughter nuclei passed on to the ascus and fused, as in other Ascomycetes, to form the definitive nucleus.

Convincing evidence as to the importance of the trichogyne in fungi was supposed, until lately, to be afforded by the presence and functional activity of that organ associated with spermogonia in a few Pyrenomycetes—in *Poronia*, *Gnomonia* and *Polystigma*. *Poronia* was examined by M. Dawson[6] who found that a trichogyne-like filament distinct from the vegetative hyphae rose from the neighbourhood of the ascogonial cells. It took an upward course towards the exterior, but there was no indication that it was ever receptive. In *Gnomonia erythrostoma* and in *Polystigma rubrum* spermogonia with spermatia—presumably male organs—are produced in abundance shortly before the ascosporous fruit is developed. The spermatia in both cases exhibit

---

[1] Schikorra 1909.   [2] Harper 1900.   [3] Fraser 1907.   [4] Thaxter 1912.
[5] Faull 1911.   [6] Dawson 1900.

the characters of male cells, *i.e.* very little cytoplasm and a comparatively large nucleus that occupies most of the cell cavity, along with complete incapacity to germinate. Brooks[1] found in *Gnomonia* that tufts of the so-called trichogynes originated near the ascogonial cells, but they were " mere continuations of ordinary vegetative hyphae belonging to the coil." They are septate and reach the surface, and the tip-cell is longer than the others as in the lichen trichogyne.

A somewhat similar arrangement is present in *Polystigma*, in which Blackman and Welsford[2] have proved that the filaments, considered as trichogynes by previous workers, are merely vegetative hyphae. A trichogyne-like structure is also present in *Capnodium*, one of the more primitive Pyrenomycetes, but it has no sexual significance.

Lindau[3] in his paper on *Gyrophora* suggested that the trichogyne in lichens acted as a " terebrator " or boring apparatus, of service to the deeply immersed carpogonium in enabling it to reach the surface. Van Tieghem[4] explained its presence on physiological grounds as necessary for respiration, a view also favoured by Zukal[5], while Wainio[6] and Steiner[7] see in it only an "end-hypha," the vigorous growth of which is due to its connection with the well-nourished cells of the ascogonium.

Lindau's view has been rejected by succeeding writers: as has been already stated, it is the paraphyses that usually open the way outward for the apothecium. Van Tieghem's theory has been considered more worthy of attention and both Dawson and Brooks incline to think that the projecting filaments described above may perform some service in respiration, even though primarily they may have functioned as sexual receptive organs.

There is very little support to be drawn from fungi for the theory that the presence of a trichogyne necessarily entails fertilization by spermatia. Lichens in this connection must be judged as a class apart.

It has perhaps been too lightly assumed that the trichogyne in lichens indicates some relationship with the Florideae[8]. Such a view might be possible if we could regard lichens and Florideae as derived from some common remote ancestor, though even then the difference in spore production—in one case exogenous, and in the other in asci and therefore endogenous—would be a strong argument against their affinity. But all the evidence goes to prove that lichens are late derivatives of fungi and have originated from them at different points. Fungi are interposed between lichens and any other ancestors, and inherited characters must have been transmitted through them. F. Bachmann's suggestion[9] that *Collema pulposum* should be regarded " as a link between aquatic red algae and terrestrial ascomycetes such as *Pyronema* and the mildews " cannot therefore be accepted. It seems more

[1] Brooks 1910.   [2] Blackman and Welsford 1912.   [3] Lindau 1899.   [4] Van Tieghem 1891.
[5] Zukal 1895.   [6] Wainio 1890.   [7] Steiner 1901.   [8] See also Chap. VII.   [9] F. Bachmann 1913.

probable that the lichen trichogyne is a new structure evolved in response to some physiological requirement—either sexual or metabolic—of the deeply embedded fruit primordium.

b. THE ASCOGONIUM. In fungi there is usually one cell forming the ascogonium, a coenogamete, which after fertilization produces ascogenous hyphae. There are exceptions, such as Cutting[1] found in *Ascophanus carneus*, in which it is composed of several cells in open contact by the formation of wide secondary pores in the cell-walls. In lichens the ascogonium is divided into a varying number of uninucleate cells. Darbishire[2] (in *Physcia*) and Baur[3] (in *Anaptychia*) have described an opening between the different cells, after presumed fertilization, that might perhaps constitute a coenogamete. Ascogenous hyphae arise from all, or nearly all the cells, whether fertilized by spermatia or not, and asci continue to be formed over a long period of time. There may even be regeneration of the entire fruiting body as described in *Graphis elegans* and in *Pertusaria*, apparently without renewed fertilization.

Spermogonia (or pycnidia) and the ascosporous fruits generally grow on the same thallus, though not unfrequently only one of the two kinds is present. As the spermogonia appear first, while the apothecia or perithecia are still in the initial stages, that sequence of development seems to add support to the view that their function is primarily sexual; but it is equally valid as a proof of their pycnidial nature since the corresponding bodies in fungi precede the more perfect ascosporous fruits in the life-cycle.

The differences in fertility between the two kinds of thallus in *Collema crispum* may be recalled[4]. Baur considered that development of the carpogonia was dependant on the presence of spermatia: a strong argument for the necessity of fertilization by these. The conditions in *Parmelia acetabulum*, also recorded by Baur, lend themselves less easily to any conclusion. On the thallus of that species the spermogonia and carpogonia present are out of all proportion to the very few apothecia that are ultimately formed. Though Baur suggested that cross-fertilization might be necessary, he admits that the development may be vegetative and so uninfluenced by the presence or absence of spermatia.

It is the very frequent occurrence of the trichogyne as an integral part of the carpogonium that constitutes the strongest argument for fertilization by spermatia. There is a possibility that such an organ may have been universal at one time both in fungi and in lichens, and that it has mostly degenerated through loss of function in the former, as it has disappeared in many instances in lichens. Again, there is but a scanty and vestigial record of spermogonia in Ascomycetes. They may have died out, or they may have developed into the asexual pycnidia which are associated with so many species. If we take that view we may trace the same tendency in lichens, as

[1] Cutting 1909.   [2] Darbishire 1900.   [3] Baur 1904.   [4] See p. 161.

for instance in the capacity of various spermatia to germinate, though in lichen spermogonia there has been apparently less change from the more primitive condition. It is also possible that some process of nuclear fusion, or more probably of conjugation, takes place in the ascogonial cells, and that in the latter case the only fusion, as in some (or most) fungi, is between the two nuclei in the ascus.

If it be conceded that fully developed carpogonia with emergent trichogynes, accompanied by spermogonia and spermatia, represent fertilization, or the probability of fertilization, then the process may be assumed to take place in a fairly large and widely distributed series of lichens. Copulation between the spermatium and the trichogyne has been seen by Stahl[1], Baur[2] and by F. Bachmann[3] in *Collema*. In *Physcia pulverulenta* Darbishire[4] could not prove copulation in the earlier stages, but he found what he took to be the remains of emptied spermatia adhering to the tips of old trichogynes. Changes in the trichogyne following on presumed copulation have been demonstrated by several workers in the Collemaceae, and open communication as a result of fertilization between the cells of the ascogonium has been described in two species. This coenocytic condition of the ascogonium (or archicarp), considered by Darbishire and others as an evidence of fertilization, has been demonstrated by Fitzpatrick[5] in the fungus *Rhizina undulata*. The walls between the cells of the archicarp in that Ascomycete became more or less open, so that the ascogenous hyphae growing from the central cells were able easily to draw nutrition from the whole coenocyte, but no process of fertilization in *Rhizina* preceded the breaking down of the septa and no fusion of nuclei was observed until the stage of ascus formation.

The real distinction between fertile and vegetative hyphae lies, according to Harper[6], in the relative size of the nuclei. F. Bachmann speaks of one large nucleus in the spermatium of *Collema pulposum* which would indicate sexual function. There is however very little nuclear history of lichens known at any stage until the beginning of ascus formation, when fusion of two nuclei certainly take place as in fungi to form the definitive nucleus of the ascus.

The whole matter may be summed up in Fünfstück's[7] statement that: "though research has proved as very probable that fertilization takes place, it is an undoubted fact that no one has observed any such process."

F. Final Stages of Apothecial Development

The emergence of the lichen apothecium from the thallus, and the form it takes, are of special interest, as, though it is essentially fungal in structure, it is subject to various modifications entailed by symbiosis.

[1] Stahl 1877.   [2] Baur 1898.   [3] F. Bachmann 1912 and 1913.   [4] Darbishire 1900.
[5] Fitzpatrick 1918.   [6] Harper 1900.   [7] Fünfstück 1902.

a. OPEN OR CLOSED APOTHECIA. Schwendener[1] drew attention to two types of apothecia directly influenced by the thallus: those that are closed at first and only open gradually, and those which are, as he says, open from the first. The former occur in genera and species in which the thallus has a stoutish cortex, as, for instance, in *Lobaria* where the young fructification has all the appearance of an opening perithecium. The open apothecia (*primitus aperta*) are found in non-corticate lichens, in which case the pioneer paraphyses arrive at the surface easily and without any converging growth. Similar apothecia are borne directly on the hypothallus at the periphery, or between the thalline areolae, and they are also characteristic of thin or slender thalli as in *Coenogonium*.

In both types of apothecium, the paraphyses pierce the cortex (Fig. 100) and secure the emergence of the developing ascomata.

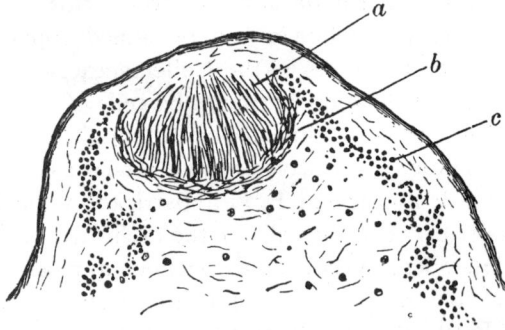

Fig. 100. *Physcia ciliaris* DC. Vertical section of apothecium still covered by the cortex. *a*, paraphyses; *b*, hypothecium; *c*, gonidia of thallus and amphithecium. × 150 (after Baur).

b. EMERGENCE OF THE ASCOCARP. Hue[2] has taken up this subject in recent years and has described the process by which the vegetative hyphae surrounding the fruit primordium, excited to active growth by contact with the generative system, take part in the later stages of fruit formation. The primordium generally occupies a position near to, or just within, the upper medulla, and the hyphae in contact with it soon begin to branch freely in a vertical direction, surrounding the developing fruit and carrying it upwards generally to a superficial position. The different methods of the final emergence give two very distinct types of mature apothecium: the *lecideine* in which the gonidial zone takes no part in the upward growth, and the *lecanorine* into which the gonidia enter as an integral part.

In the lecideine series (Fig. 101) the encircling hyphae from the upper medulla rise as a compact column through the gonidial zone to the surface of the thallus; they then spread radially before curving up to form the outer

[1] Schwendener 1864.   [2] Hue 1906.

wall or "proper margin" round the spore-bearing disc. The branching of the hyphae is fastigiate with compact shorter branches at the exterior. In such an apothecium gonidia are absent both below the hypothecium and in the margins.

In lecanorine development the ascending hyphae from the medulla, in some cases, carry with them algal

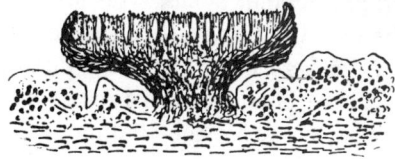

Fig. 101. *Lecidea parasema* Ach. Vertical section of thallus and apothecium with proper margin only × ca. 50.

cells which multiply and spread as a second gonidial layer under the hypothecium (Fig. 102). These hyphae may also spread in a radial direction while still within the thallus and give rise to an "immersed" apothecium which is lecanorine as it encloses gonidia within its special tissues, for example, in *Acarospora* and *Solorina*. But in most cases the lecanorine fruit is superficial and not unfrequently it is raised on a short stalk (*Usnea*, etc.);

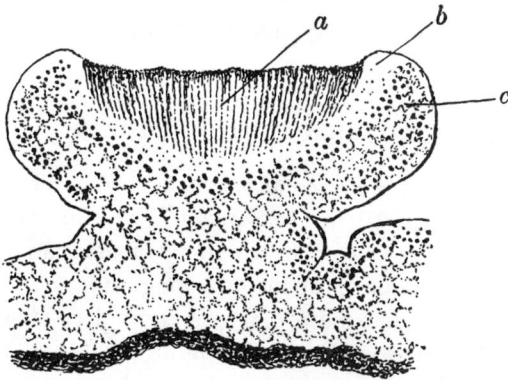

Fig. 102. *Lecanora tartarea* Ach. Vertical section of apothecium. *a*, hymenium; *b*, proper margin or parathecium; *c*, thalline margin or amphithecium. × 30 (after Reinke).

both the primary gonidial zone of the thallus and the outer cortex are associated with the medullary column of hyphae from the first and grow up along with it, thus providing the outer part of the apothecium, an additional "thalline margin" continuous with the thallus itself. It is an advanced type of development peculiar to lichens, and it provides for fertility of long continuance which is in striking contrast with the fugitive ascocarps of the Discomycetes.

The distinction between lecideine and lecanorine apothecia is of great value in classification, but it is not always easily demonstrable; it is occasionally necessary to examine the early stages, as in the more advanced the thalline margin may be pushed aside by the turgid disc and become practically obliterated.

The "proper margin" reaches its highest development in the lecideine and graphideine types. It is less prominent or often almost entirely replaced when the thalline margin is superadded, except in genera such as *Thelotrema* and *Diploschistes* which have distinct "double margins."

There is an unusual type of apothecium in the genus *Gyrophora*. The fruit is lecideine, the thalline gonidia taking no part in the development.

Fig. 103. Apothecial gyrose discs of *Gyrophora cylindrica* Ach. × 12 (after Lindau).

The growth of the initial ascogenous tissue, according to Lindau[1], is constantly towards the periphery of the disc so that a weak spot arises in the centre which is promptly filled by a vigorous sterile growth of paraphyses. This process is repeated from new centres again and again, resulting in the irregularly concentric lines of sterile and fertile areas of the "gyrose" fruit (Fig. 103). The paraphyses soon become black at the tips. Asci are not formed until the ascogenous layer has acquired a certain degree of stability, and spores are accordingly present only in advanced stages of growth.

G. LICHEN ASCI AND SPORES

a. HISTORICAL. The presence of spores, as such, in the lichen fruit was first established by Hedwig[2] in *Anaptychia* (*Physcia*) *ciliaris*. He rightly judged the minute bodies to be the "semina" of the plant. In that species they are fairly large, measuring about $50\,\mu$ long and $24\,\mu$ thick, and as they are very dark in colour when mature, they stand out conspicuously from the surrounding colourless tissue of the hymenium. Acharius[3] also took note of these "semina" and happily replaced the term by that of "spores." They may be produced, he states, in a compact nucleus (*Sphaerophoron*), in a naked disc (*Calicium*), or they may be embedded in the disc (*Opegrapha* and *Lecidea*). Sprengel[4] opined that the spores—which he figures—were true seeds, though he allows that there had been no record of their development into new plants. Luyken[5] made a further contribution to the subject by dividing lichens into gymnocarpous and angiocarpous forms, according as the spores, enclosed in cells or vesicles (thecae), were borne in an open disc or in a closed perithecium.

In his *Systema* of lichen genera Eschweiler[6], some years later, described and figured the spores as "thecae" enclosed in cylindrical asci. Fée[7] in contemporary works gave special prominence to the colour and form of the spores in all the lichens dealt with.

---

[1] Lindau 1899. [2] Hedwig 1784. [3] Acharius 1803. [4] Sprengel 1807.
[5] Luyken 1809. [6] Eschweiler 1824. [7] Fée 1824.

b. DEVELOPMENT OF THE ASCUS. The first attempt to trace the origin and development of lichen asci and spores was made by Mohl[1]. He describes the mother-cell (the ascus) as filled at first with a clouded granular substance changing later into a definite number—usually eight—of simple or septate spores. Dangeard[2] included the lichens *Borrera* (*Physcia*) *ciliaris* and *Endocarpon* (*Dermatocarpon*) *miniatum* among the plants that he studied for ascus and spore development. He found that in lichens, as in fungi, the ascus arose usually from the penultimate cell of a crooked hypha (Fig. 104) and that it contained at first two nuclei derived from adjoining cells. These nuclei are similar in size to those of the vegetative hyphae, and in each there is a large nucleolus with chromatin material massed on one side. Fusion takes place, as in fungi, between the two nuclei, and the secondary or definitive nucleus thus formed divides successively to form the eight spore-nuclei. Baur[3] and Nienburg[4] have confirmed Dangeard's results as regards lichens, and René Maire[5] has also contributed important cytological details on the development of the spores. In *Anaptychia* (*Physcia*) *ciliaris* he found that the fused nucleus became larger and that a synapsis stage supervened during which the long slender chromatin filaments

Fig. 104. Developing asci of *Physcia ciliaris* DC. × 800 (after Baur).

became paired, and at the same time shorter and thicker. The nuclear membrane disappeared as the chromatin filaments were united in masses joined together by linin threads which also disappeared later. At the most advanced stage observed by Maire there was visible a nucleolus embedded in a condensed plasma and surrounded by eight medianly constricted filaments destined to form the equatorial plate. A few isolated observations were also made on the cytology of the ascus in *Peltigera canina*, in which lichen the preceding ascogonial development is wholly vegetative. The secondary nucleus was seen to contain a chromatin mass and a large nucleolus; in addition two angular bodies of uncertain signification were associated with the nucleolus, each with a central vacuole. The nucleolus disappeared in the prophase of the first division and four double chromosomes were then plainly visible. The succeeding phases of the first and the second nuclear division were not seen, but in the prophase of the third it was possible to distinguish four chromatin masses outside the nucleolus. The slow growth of the lichen plant renders continuous observation extremely difficult.

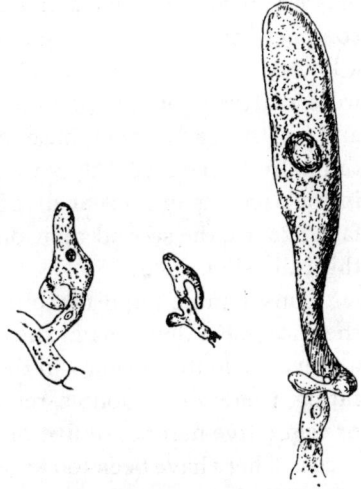

[1] Mohl 1833.   [2] Dangeard 1894.   [3] Baur 1904.   [4] Nienburg 1908.   [5] Maire 1905.

F. Bachmann[1] was able to make important cytological observations in her study of *Collema pulposum*. As regards the vegetative and ascogonial nuclei, five or perhaps six chromosomes appeared on the spindle when the nucleus divided. In the asci, the usual paired nuclei were present in the early stages and did not fuse until the ascus had elongated considerably. After fusion the definitive nucleus enlarged with the growth of the ascus and did not divide until the ascus had attained full size. The nucleolus was large, and usually excentric, and there were at first a number of chromatin masses on an irregular spirem. In synapsis the spirem was drawn into a compact mass, but after synapsis, "the chromatin is again in the form of a knotty spirem." In late prophases the chromosomes, small ovoid bodies, were scattered on the spindle; later they were aggregated in the centre, and, in the early metaphase, about twelve were counted now split longitudinally. There were thus twice as many chromosomes in the first division in the ascus as in nuclear divisions of the vegetative hyphae. F. Bachmann failed to see the second division; there were at least five chromosomes in the third division.

Considerable importance is given to the number of the chromosomes in the successive divisions in the ascus since they are considered to be proof of a previous double fusion—in the ascogonium and again in the ascus—necessitating, therefore, a double reduction division to arrive at the gametophytic or vegetative number of five or six chromosomes in the third division in the ascus. There have been too few observations to draw any general conclusions.

c. DEVELOPMENT OF SPORES. The spore wall begins to form, as in Ascomycetes, at the apex of the nucleus with the curving over of the astral threads, the nucleus at that stage presenting the figure of a flask the neck of which is occupied by the centrosome. The final spore-nucleus, as observed by Maire, divides once again in *Anaptychia* and division is followed by the formation of a median septum, the mature spore being two-celled. In *Peltigera* the spore is at first ovoid, but both nucleus and spore gradually elongate. The fully formed spore is narrowly fusiform and by repeated nuclear division and subsequent cross-septation it becomes 4- or even 5–6-celled.

The spores of lichens are wholly fungoid, and, in many cases, form a parallel series with the spores of the Ascomycetes. Markings of the epispore, such as reticulations, spines, etc., are rarely present (*Solorina spongiosa*), though thickening of the wall occurs in many species (*Pertusariae*, etc.), a peculiarity which was first pointed out by Mohl[2] who contrasted the spore walls with the delicate membranes of other lichen cells. Some spores, described as "halonate," have an outer gelatinous covering which probably prevents the spore from drying up and thus prolongs the period of possible germination. Both asci and spores are, as a rule, more sparingly produced

---

[1] Bachmann 1913.   [2] Mohl 1833.

than in fungi; in many instances some or all of the spores in the ascus
are imperfectly formed, and the full complement is frequently lacking,
possibly owing to some occurrence of adverse conditions during the long
slow development of the apothecium. In the larger number of genera and
species the spores are small bodies, but in some, as for instance in the
Pertusariae and in some *Pyrenocarpeae*, they exceed in size all known fungus
spores. In *Varicellaria microsticta*, a rare crustaceous lichen of high mountains, the solitary 1-septate spore measures up to 350 μ in length and 115 μ in
width. Most spores contain reserve material in the form of fat, etc., many are
dark-coloured; Zukal[1] has suggested that the colour may be protective.

Their ejection from the ascus at maturity is caused by the twofold
pressure of the paraphyses and the marginal hyphae on the addition of
moisture. The spores may be shot up at least 1 cm. from the disc[2].

d. SPORE GERMINATION. Meyer[3] was the first who cultivated lichen
spores and the dendritic formation which he obtained by growing them on
a smooth surface was undoubtedly the prothallus (or hypothallus) of the
lichen. Actual germination was however not observed till Holle[4] in 1846
watched and figured the process as it occurs in *Physcia ciliaris*.

Spores divided by transverse septa into two or more cells, as well as
those that have become "muriform" by transverse and longitudinal septation,
may germinate from each cell.

e. MULTINUCLEATE SPORES. These spores, which are all very large,
occur in several genera or subgenera: in *Lecidea* subg. *Mycoblastus* (Fig. 105),
Lecanora subg. *Ochrolechia* and in Pertusariaceae. Tulasne[5] in his experi-

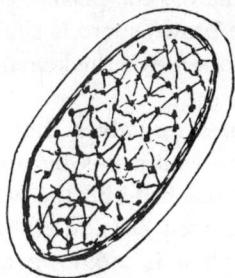

Fig. 105. Multinucleate spore of *Lecidea*
(*Mycoblastus*) *sanguinaria* Ach. × 540
(after Zopf).

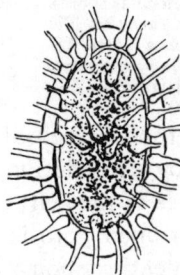

Fig. 106. Germination of multinucleate
spore of *Ochrolechia pallescens* Koerb.
× 390 (after de Bary).

ments with germinating spores found that in *Lecanora parella* (*Ochrolechia
pallescens?*) germinating tubes were produced all over the surface of the
spore (Fig. 106). De Bary[6] verified his observations in that and other species
and added considerable detail: about twenty-four hours after sowing spores
of *Ochrolechia pallescens*, numerous little warts arose on the surface of the

[1] Zukal 1895.　　　[2] Fée 1824.　　　[3] Meyer 1825.　　　[4] Holle 1849.
[5] Tulasne 1852.　　　　　[6] De Bary 1866–1867.

spore which gradually grew out into delicate hyphae. All these spores contain fat globules and finely granular protoplasm with a very large number of minute nuclei; the presence of the latter has been demonstrated by Haberlandt[1] and later by Zopf[2] who reckoned about 200 to 300 in the spore of *Mycoblastus sanguinarius.* These nuclei had continued to multiply during the ripening of the spore while it was still contained in the ascus[2]. Owing to the presence of the large fat globules the plasma is confined to an external layer close to the spore wall; the nuclei are embedded in the plasma and are connected by strands of protoplasm. The epispore in some of these large spores is extremely developed: in some *Pertusariae* it measures 4–5 μ in thickness.

f. POLARIBILOCULAR SPORES. The most peculiar of all lichen spores are those termed *polaribilocular*—signifying a two-celled spore of which the median septum has become so thickened that the cell-cavities with their contents are relegated to the two poles of the spore, an open canal frequently connecting the two cell-spaces (Fig. 107). Other terms have been suggested and used by various writers to describe this unusual character such as blasteniospore[3], orculiform[4] and placodiomorph[5] or more simply polarilocular.

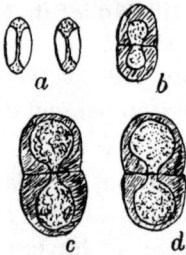

Fig. 107. Polarilocular spores. *a, Xanthoria parietina* Th. Fr.; *b, Rinodina roboris* Th. Fr.; *c, Physcia pulverulenta* Nyl.; *d, Physcia ciliaris* DC. × 600.

The polarilocular colourless spore is found in a connected series of lichens—crustaceous, foliose and fruticose (*Placodium, Xanthoria, Teloschistes*). In another series with a darker thallus (*Rinodina* and *Physcia*) the spore is brown-coloured, and the median septum cuts across the plasma-connection. In other respects the brown spore is similar to the colourless one and possesses a thickened wall with reduced cell-cavities.

The method of cell-division in these spores resembles that known as "cleavage by constriction," in which the cross wall arises by an ingrowth from all sides of the cell; in time the centre is reached and the wall is complete, or an open pore is left between the divided cells. Cell "cleavage" occurs frequently among Thallophytes, though it is unknown among the higher plants. Among Algae it is the normal form of cell-division in *Cladophora* and also in *Spirogyra*, though in the latter the wall passes right across and cuts through the connecting plasma threads. Harper[6] found "cleavage by constriction" in two instances among fungi: the conidia of *Erysiphe* and the gametes of *Sporodinia* are cut off by a septum which originates as a circular ingrowth of the outer wall, comparable, he considers, with the cell-division of *Cladophora*.

[1] Haberlandt 1887.   [2] Zopf 1905.   [3] Massalongo 1852.   [4] Koerber 1855.
[5] Wainio 1. 1890, p. 113.   [6] Harper 1899.

The development of the thickened wall of polarilocular spores has been studied by Hue[1], who contends however that there is no true septation in the colourless spores so long as the central canal remains open. According to his observations the wall of the young spore is formed of a thin tegument, everywhere equal in thickness, and consisting of concentric layers. This tegument becomes continually thicker at the equator of the spore by the addition of new layers from the interior, and the protoplasmic contents are compressed into a gradually diminishing space. In the end the wall almost touches at the centre, and the spore consists of two polar cell-cavities with a narrow open passage between. A median line pierced by the canal is frequently seen. In a few species there is a second constriction cleavage and the spore becomes quadrilocular.

Hue insists that this spore should be regarded as only one-celled; for though the walls may touch at the centre, he says they never coalesce. He has unfortunately given no cytological observations as to whether the spore is uni- or binucleate.

In *Xanthoria parietina*, one of the species with characteristic polari-bilocular spores, germination, it would seem, takes place mostly at one end only of the spore, though a germinating tube issues at both ends frequently enough to suggest that the spore is binucleate and two-celled. The absence of germination from one or other of the cells only may probably be due to the drain on their small resources. Hue has cited the rarity of such instances of double germination in support of his view of the one-celled nature of the spore. He instances that out of fifteen spores, Tulasne[2] has figured only three that have germinated at each end; Bornet[3] figures one in seven with the double germination and Bonnier[4] one in sixteen spores.

Further evidence is wanted as to the nuclear history of these hyaline spores. In the case of the brown spores, which show the same thickening of the wall and restricted cell-cavity, though with a distinct median septum, nuclear division was observed by René Maire[5] before septation in one such species, *Anaptychia ciliaris*.

II. SECONDARY SPORES

A. REPRODUCTION BY OIDIA

In certain conditions of nutrition, fungal hyphae break up into separate cells, each of which functions as a reproductive *conidium* or *oidium*, which on germination forms new hyphae. Neubner[6] has demonstrated a similar process in the hyphae of the Caliciaceae and compares it with the oidial formation described by Brefeld[7] in the Basidiomycetes.

---

[1] Hue 1911[2].   [2] Tulasne 1852.   [3] Bornet 1873.   [4] Bonnier 1889[2].
[5] Maire 1905.   [6] Neubner 1893.   [7] Brefeld 1889.

The thallus of this family of lichens is granular or furfuraceous; it never goes beyond the *Lepra* stage of development[1]. In some species it is scanty, in others it is abundant and spreads over large areas of the trunks of old trees. It is only when growth is especially luxuriant that oidia are formed. Neubner was able to recognize the oidial condition by the more opaque appearance of the granules, and under the microscope he observed the hyphae surrounding the gonidia gradually fall away and break up into minute cylindrical cells somewhat like spermatia in size and form. There was no question of abnormal or unhealthy conditions, as the oidia were formed in a freely fruiting thallus.

The gonidia associated with the oidial hyphae also showed unusual vitality and active division took place as they were set free by the breaking up of the encircling hyphae. The germination of the oidia provides an abundance of hyphal filaments for the rapidly increasing algal cells, and there follows a widespread development of the lichen thallus.

Oidial formation has not been observed in any other family of lichens.

B. REPRODUCTION BY CONIDIA

a. INSTANCES OF CONIDIAL FORMATION. It is remarkable that the type of asexual reproduction so abundantly represented in fungi by the large

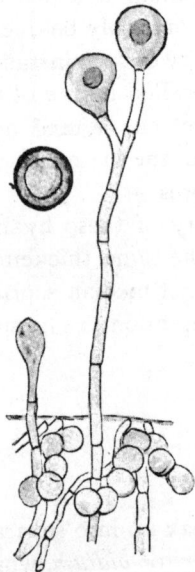

Fig. 108. Conidia developed from thallus of *Arnoldia minutula* Born. × 950 (after Bornet).

and varied group of the Hyphomycetes is practically absent in lichens. An exception is to be found in a minute gelatinous lichen that grows on soil. It was discovered by Bornet[2] and called by him *Arnoldia (Physma) minutula*. From the thallus rise up simple or sparingly branched colourless conidiophores which bear at the tips globose brown conidia (Fig. 108). Bornet[3] obtained these conidia by keeping very thin sections of the thallus in a drop of water[2].

Yet another instance of conidial growth is given by Steiner[4]. He had observed that the apothecia on plants of *Caloplaca aurantia* var. *callopisma* Stein. differed from those of normal appearance in the warted unevenness of the disc and also in being more swollen and convex, the thalline margin being almost obliterated. He found, on microscopical examination, that the hymenium was occupied by paraphyses and by occasional asci, the latter seldom containing spores, and being

[1] See p. 143. [2] Bornet 1873.
[3] Bornet's observations have not been repeated, and it is possible that he may have been dealing with a parasitic hyphomycetous fungus. [4] Steiner 1901.

usually more or less collapsed. The component parts of the apothecium were entirely normal and healthy, but the paraphyses and the few asci were crushed aside by the intrusion of numerous slender unbranched septate conidiophores. Several of these might spring from one base and the hypha from which they originated could be traced some distance into the ascogenous layer, though a connection with that cell-system could not be demonstrated. While still embedded in the hymenium, an ellipsoid or obovate swelling began to form at the apex of the conidiophore; it became separated from the stalk by a septum and later divided into a two-celled conidium. The conidiophore increased in length by intercalary growth and finally emerged above the disc; the mature conidium was pyriform and measured 15–20 μ × 9–11 μ.

Steiner regarded these conidia as entirely abnormal; pycnidia with stylospores are unknown in the genus and they were not, he alleges, the product of any parasitic growth.

b. COMPARISON WITH HYPHOMYCETES. The conidial form of fructification in fungi, known as a Hyphomycete, is generally a stage in the life-cycle of some Ascomycete; it represents the rapid summer form of asexual reproduction. The ascospore of the resting fruit-form in many species germinates on any suitable matrix and may at once produce conidiophores and conidia, which in turn germinate, and either continue the conidial generation or proceed to the formation of the perfect fruiting form with asci and ascospores.

Such a form of transient reproduction is almost impossible in lichens, as the hypha produced by the germinating lichen ascospore has little vitality without the algal symbiont. In natural conditions development practically ceases in the absence of symbiosis. When union between the symbionts takes place, and growth becomes active, thallus construction at once commences. But in certain conditions of shade and moisture, only the rudiments of a lichen thallus are formed, known as a leprose or sorediose condition. Soredia also arise in the normal life of many lichens. As the individual granules or soredia may each give rise to a complete lichen plant, they may well be considered as replacing the lost conidial fructification.

C. CAMPYLIDIUM AND ORTHIDIUM

Müller[1] has described under the name *Campylidium* a supposed new type of asexual fructification which he found on the thallus of tropical species of *Gyalecta, Lopadium*, etc., and which he considered analogous to pycnidia and spermogonia. Wainio[2] has however recognized the cup-like structure as a fungus, *Cyphella aeruginascens* Karst., which grows on the bark of trees and occasionally is parasitic on the crustaceous thallus of lichens. Wainio has

---

[1] Müller 1881.   [2] Wainio 1890, II. p. 27.

also identified the plant, *Lecidea irregularis*, first described by Fée[1], as also synonymous with the fungus.

Another name *Orthidium* was proposed by Müller[2] for a type of fructification he found in Brazil which he contrasts or associates with *Campylidium*. It has an open marginate disc with sporophores bearing acrogenous spores. He found it growing in connection with a thin lichen thallus on leaves and considered it to be a form of lichen reproduction. Possibly *Orthidium* is also a *Cyphella*.

III. SPERMOGONIA OR PYCNIDIA

A. HISTORICAL ACCOUNT OF SPERMOGONIA

The name spermogonium was given by Tulasne[3] to the "punctiform conceptacles" that are so plentifully produced on many lichen thalli, on the assumption that they were the male organs of the plant, and that the spore-like bodies borne in them were non-motile male cells or spermatia.

The first record of their association with lichens was made by Dillenius[4], who indicates the presence of black tubercles on the thallus of *Physcia ciliaris*. He figures them also on several species of *Cladonia*, on *Ramalina* and on *Dermatocarpon*, but without any suggestion as to their function. Hedwig's[5] study of the reproductive organs of the Linnaean Cryptogams included lichens. He examined *Physcia ciliaris*, a species that not only is quite common but is generally found in a fruiting condition and with very prominent spermogonia, and has been therefore a favourite lichen for purposes of examination and study. Hedwig describes and figures not only the apothecia but also those other bodies which he designates as "punctula mascula," or again as "puncta floris masculi." In his later work he gives a drawing of *Lichen* (*Gyrophora*) *proboscideus*, with two of the spermogonia in section.

Acharius[6] included them among the lichen structures which he called "cephalodia": he described them as very minute tubercles rising up from the substance of the thallus and projecting somewhat above it. He also figures a section through two "cephalodia" of *Physcia ciliaris*. Fries[7] looked on them as being mostly "anamorphoses of apothecia, the presence of abortive fruits transforming the angiocarpous lichen to the appearance of a gymnocarpous form." Wallroth[8] assigned the small black fruits to the comprehensive fungus genus *Sphaeria* or classified lichens bearing spermogonia only as distinct genera and species (*Pyrenothea* and *Thrombium*). Later students of lichens—Schaerer[9], Flotow[10], and others—accepted Wallroth's interpretation of their relation to the thallus, or they ignored them altogether in their descriptions of species.

[1] Fée 1873.   [2] Müller 1890.   [3] Tulasne 1851.   [4] Dillenius 1741.   [5] Hedwig 1784 and 1789.
[6] Acharius 1810.   [7] Fries 1831.   [8] Wallroth 1825.   [9] Schaerer 1823–1842.   [10] Flotow 1850.

B. Spermogonia as Male Organs

Interest in these minute "tubercles" and their enclosed "corpuscles" was revived by Itzigsohn[1] who examined them with an improved microscope. He macerated in water during a few days that part of the thallus on which they were developed, and, at the end of the time, discovered that the solution contained large numbers of motile bodies which he naturally took to be the corpuscles from the broken down tubercles. He claimed to have established their function as male motile cells or spermatozoa. The discovery seemed not only to prove their sexual nature, but to link up the reproduction of lichens with that of the higher cryptogams. The tubercles in which the "spermatozoa" were produced he designated as antheridia. More prolonged maceration of the tissue to the very verge of decay yielded still larger numbers of the "spermatozoa" which we now recognize to have been motile bacilli.

Tulasne[2] next took up the subject, and failing to find the motile cells, he wrongly insisted that Itzigsohn had been misled by mere Brownian movement, but at the same time he accepted the theory that the minute conceptacles were spermogonia or male organs of lichens. He also pointed out that their constant occurrence on the thallus of practically every species of lichen, and their definite form, though with considerable variation, rendered it impossible to regard them as accidental or of no importance to the life of the plant. He compared them with fungal pycnidia such as *Phyllosticta* or *Septoria* which outwardly they resembled, but whereas the pycnidial spores germinated freely, the spermatia of the spermogonia, as far as his experience went, were incapable of germination.

C. Occurrence and Distribution

a. Relation to Thallus and Apothecia. We owe to Tulasne[3] the first comparative study of lichen spermogonia. He described not only their outward form, but their minute structure, in a considerable number of representative species. A few years later Lindsay[4] published a memoir dealing with the spermogonia of the larger foliose and fruticose lichens, and, in a second paper, he embodied the results of his study of an equally extensive selection of crustaceous species. Lindsay's work is unfortunately somewhat damaged by faulty determination of the lichens he examined, and by lack of the necessary discrimination between one thallus and another of associated and intermingled species. Both memoirs contain, however, much valuable information as to the forms of spermogonia, with their spermatiophores and spermatia, and as to their distribution over the lichen thallus.

Though spermogonia are mostly found associated with apothecia, yet

[1] Itzigsohn 1850.   [2] Tulasne 1851.   [3] Tulasne 1852.   [4] Lindsay 1859 and 1872.

in some lichens, such as *Cerania* (*Thamnolia*) *vermicularis*, they are the only sporiferous organs known. Not unfrequently crustaceous thalli bear spermogonia only, and in some *Cladoniae*, more especially in ascyphous species, spermogonia are produced abundantly at the tips of the podetial branches (Fig. 109), while apothecia are exceedingly rare. Usually they occur in scattered or crowded groups, more rarely they are solitary. Very often they are developed and the contents dispersed before the apothecia reach the surface of the thallus; hence the difficulty in relating these organisms, since the mature apothecium is mostly of extreme importance in determining the species.

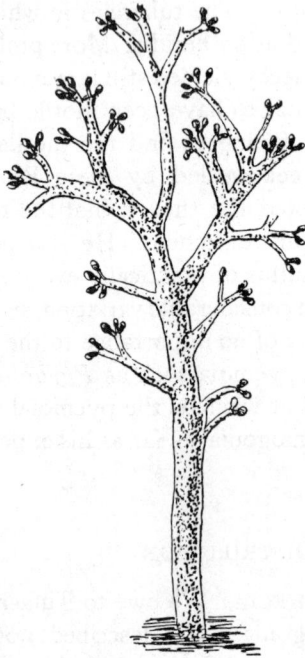

Fig. 109. *Cladonia furcata* Schrad. Branched podetium with spermogonia at the tips (after Krabbe).

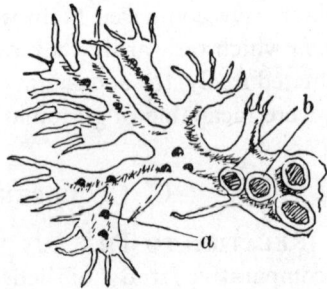

Fig. 110. *Physcia hispida* Tuckerm. Ciliate frond. *a*, spermogonia; *b*, apothecia. × ca. 5 (after Lindsay).

In a very large number of lichens, both crustaceous and foliose, the spermogonia are scattered over the entire thallus (Fig. 110), covering it more or less thickly with minute black dots, as in *Parmelia conspersa*. In other instances, they are to some extent confined to the peripheral areas as in *Parmelia physodes*; or they occur on the extreme edge of the thallus as in the crustaceous species *Lecanora glaucoma* (*sordida*). In *Pyrenula nitida* they grow on the marginal hypothallus, usually on the dark line of demarcation between two thalli.

They tend to congregate on, and indeed are practically restricted to the better lighted portions of the thallus. On the fronds of foliose forms, they appear, for instance, on the swollen pustules of *Umbilicaria pustulata*, while in *Lobaria pulmonaria*, they are mostly lodged in the ridges that surround the depressions in the thallus. In *Parmelia conspersa, Urceolaria (Diploschistes) scruposa* and some others, they occasionally invade the margins of the apothecium or even the apothecial disc as in *Lichina*. Forssell[1] found that a spermogonium had developed among cells of *Gloeocapsa* that covered the disc of a spent apothecium of *Pyrenopsis haematopis*.

In fruticose lichens such as *Usnea, Ramalina*, etc. they occur near the apex of the fronds, and in *Cladonia* they occupy the tips of the ascyphous podetia or the margins of the scyphi. In some *Cladoniae*, however, spermogonia are produced on the basal squamules, more rarely on the squamules that clothe the podetia.

b. FORM AND SIZE. Spermogonia are specifically constant in form, the same type being found on the same lichen species all over the globe. The larger number are entirely immersed and are ovoid or roundish (Fig. 111 A) or occasionally somewhat flattened bodies(*Nephromium laevigatum*),or again, but more rarely, they are irregular in outline with an infolding of the walls that gives the interior a chambered form (Fig. 111 B) (*Lichina pygmaea*); but all of these are only visible as minute points on the thallus.

Fig. 111. Immersed spermogonia. A, globose in *Parmelia acetabulum* Dub. × 600; B, with infolded walls in *Lecidea (Psora) testacea* Ach. × 144 (after Glück).

A second series, also immersed, are borne in small protuberances of the thallus. These very prominent forms are rarely found in crustaceous lichens, but they are characteristic of such well-known species as *Ramalina fraxinea, Xanthoria parietina, Ricasolia amplissima, Baeomyces roseus*, etc. Other spermogonia project slightly above the level of the thallus, as in *Cladonia papillaria* and *Lecidea lurida*; while in a few instances they are practically free, these last strikingly exemplified in *Cetraria islandica* where they occupy the small projections or cilia (Fig. 112) that fringe the margins of the lobes; they are free also in most species of *Cladonia*.

[1] Forssell 1885.

In size they vary from such minute bodies as those in *Parmelia exasperata* which measure 25–35 μ in diam., up to nearly 1 mm. in *Lobaria laetevirens*.

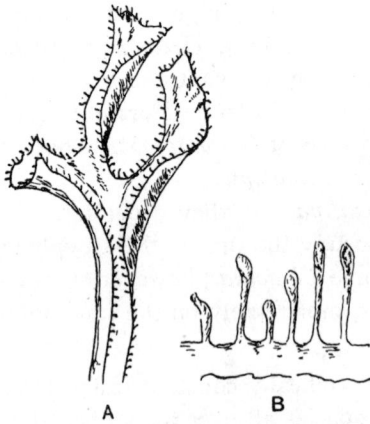

As a rule, they range from about 150 μ to 400 μ across the widest part, and are generally rather longer than broad. They open above by a small slit or pore called the ostiole about 20 μ to 100 μ wide which is frequently dark in colour. In one instance, in *Icmadophila aeruginosa*, Nienburg[1] has described a spermogonium with a wide opening, the spermatiophores being massed in palisade formation along the bottom of a cup-like structure.

c. COLOUR OF SPERMOGONIA. Though usually the ostiole is visible as a darker point than the surrounding tissue, sper-

Fig. 112. Free spermogonia in spinous cilia of *Cetraria islandica* Ach. A, part of frond; B, cilia. × 10.

mogonia are often difficult to locate unless the thallus is first wetted, when they become visible to slight magnification. They appear as black points in many *Parmeliae*, *Physciae*, *Roccellae*, etc., though even in these cases they are often brown when moistened. They are distinctly brown in some *Cladoniae*, in *Nephromium*, and in some *Physciae*; orange-red or yellow in *Placodium* and concolorous with the thallus in *Usnea*, *Ramalina*, *Stereocaulon*, etc.

D. STRUCTURE

a. ORIGIN AND GROWTH. The spermogonia (or pycnidia) of lichens when mature are more or less hollow structures provided with a distinct wall or " perithecium," sometimes only one cell thick and then not easily demonstrable, as in *Physcia speciosa*, *Opegrapha vulgata*, *Pyrenula nitida*, etc. More generally the " perithecium " is composed of a layer of several cells with stoutish walls which are sometimes colourless, but usually some shade of yellow to dark-brown, with a darker ostiole. The latter, a small slit or pore, arises by the breaking down of some of the cells at the apex. After the expulsion of the spermatia, a new tissue is formed which completely blocks up the empty spermogonium. In filamentous lichens such as *Usnea* a dangerous local weakening of the thallus is thus avoided.

Spermogonia originate from hyphae in or near the gonidial zone. The earliest stages have not been seen, but Möller[2] noted as the first recognizable appearance or primordium of the "pycnidia" in cultures of *Calicium trachelinum* a ball or coil of delicate yellowish-coloured hyphae. At a more

[1] Nienburg 1908. [2] Möller 1887.

advanced stage the sporophores (or spermatiophores) could be traced as outgrowths from the peripheral hyphae, directed in palisade formation towards the centre of the hyphal coil about 20–30 μ long and very slender and colourless. They begin to bud off spermatia almost immediately, as it has been found that these are present in abundance while the developing spermogonium is still wholly immersed in the thallus. Meanwhile there is gradually formed on the outside a layer of plectenchyma which forms the wall. Additional spermatiophores arise from the wall tissue and push their way inwards between the ranks of the first formed series. The spermogonium slowly enlarges and stretches and as the spermatiophores do not grow any longer a central hollow arises which becomes packed with spermatia (or spores) before the ostiole is open.

A somewhat similar process of development is described by Sturgis[1] in the spermogonia of *Ricasolia amplissima*, in which species the primordium arises by a profuse branching of the medullary hyphae in certain areas close to the gonidial zone. The cells of these branching hyphae are filled with oily matter and gradually they build up a dense, somewhat cylindrical body which narrows above to a neck-like form. The growth is upwards through the gonidial layer, and the structure widens to a more spherical outline. It finally reaches the outer cortex when some of the apical cell membranes are absorbed and a minute pore is formed. The central part becomes hollow, also by absorption, and the space thus left is lined and almost filled with multicellular branches of the hyphae forming the wall; from the cells of this new tissue the spermatia are abstricted.

b. FORMS AND TYPES OF SPERMATIOPHORES. The variations in form of the fertile hyphae in the spermogonium were first pointed out by Nylander[2] who described them as sterigmata[3]. He considered the differences in branching, etc. as of high diagnostic value, dividing them into two groups: simple "sterigmata" (or spermatiophores), with non-septate hyphae, and arthrosterigmata, with jointed or septate hyphae.

Simple "sterigmata" comprise those in which the spore or spermatium is borne at the end of a secondary branch or sterigma, the latter having arisen from a cell of the upright spermatiophore or from a simple basal cell. The arthrosterigmata consist of "short cells almost as broad as they are long, much pressed together, and appearing almost agglutinate especially toward the base; they fill almost the whole cavity of the spermogonium." The arthrosterigmata may grow out into the centre of the cavity as a single cell-row, as a loose branching network, or, as in *Endocarpon*, they may form

---

[1] Sturgis 1890.   [2] Nylander 1858, pp. 34, 35.

[3] Nylander, Crombie and others apply the term "sterigma" to the whole spermatiophore. In the more usual restricted sense, it refers only to the short process from which the spermatium is abstricted.

a tissue filling the whole interior. Each cell of this tissue that borders on a cavity may bud off a spermatium either directly or from the end of a short process.

The most important contributions on the subject of spermogonia in recent years are those of Glück[1] and Steiner[2]. Glück, who insisted on the

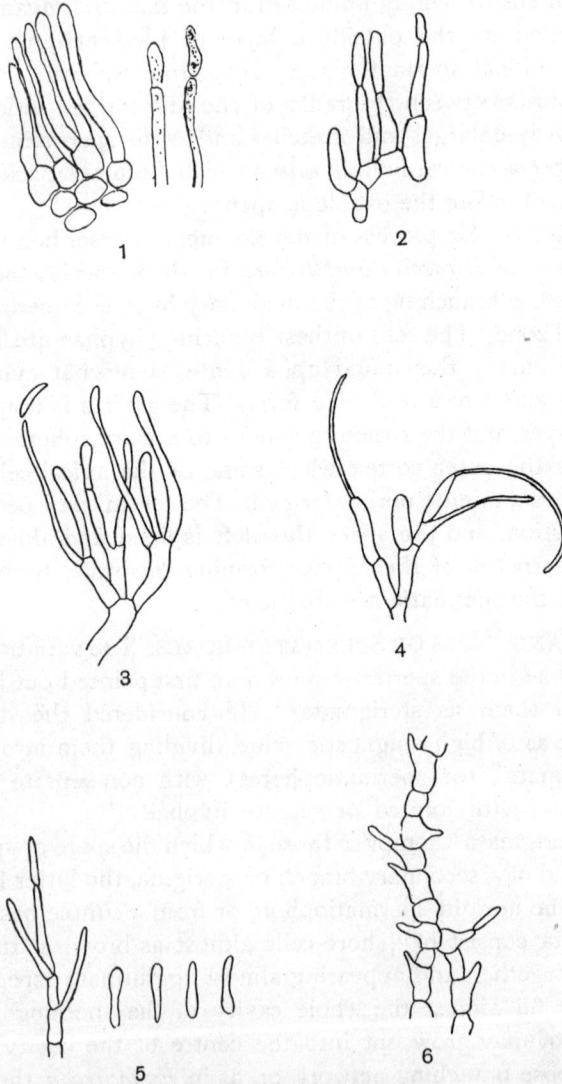

Fig. 113 A. Types of lichen "sporophores" and pycnidiospores. 1, *Peltigera rufescens* Hoffm. × 910; 2, *Lecidea (Psora) testacea* Ach. × 1200; 3, *Cladonia cariosa* Spreng. × 1000; 4, *Pyrenula nitida* Ach. × 1130; 5, *Parmelia tristis* Nyl. × 700; 6, *Lobaria pulmonaria* Hoffm. × 1000 (after Glück).

[1] Glück 1899.   [2] Steiner 1901.

"pycnidial" non-sexual character of the organs, recognized eight types of "sporophores" differing in the complexity of their branching or in the form of the "spores" (Fig. 113 A):

1. The *Peltigera* type: the sporophores consist of a basal cell bearing one or more long sterigmata and rather stoutish ellipsoid spores. (These are true pycnidia.)

2. The *Psora* type: a more elongate simple sporophore with sterigmata and oblong spores.

3. The *Cladonia* type: a branching sporophore, each branch with sterigmata and oblong spores.

4. The *Squamaria* type ('called by Glück *Placodium*): also a branching sporophore but with long sickle-like bent spores.

5. The *Parmelia* type: a more complicated system of branching and anastomosing of the sporophores, with oblong spores.

6, and 7. The *Sticta* and *Physcia* types: in both of these the sporophores are multiseptate; they consist of a series of radiately arranged hyphae rising from a basal tissue all round the pycnidium. They anastomose to form a network and bud off "spermatia" from the free cells or rather from minute sterigmata. In the *Physcia* type there is more general anastomosis of the sporophores and frequently masses of sterile cells along with the fertile members occupy the centre of the pycnidium. The spermatia of these and the following *Endocarpon* type are short cylindrical bodies (Fig. 113 B).

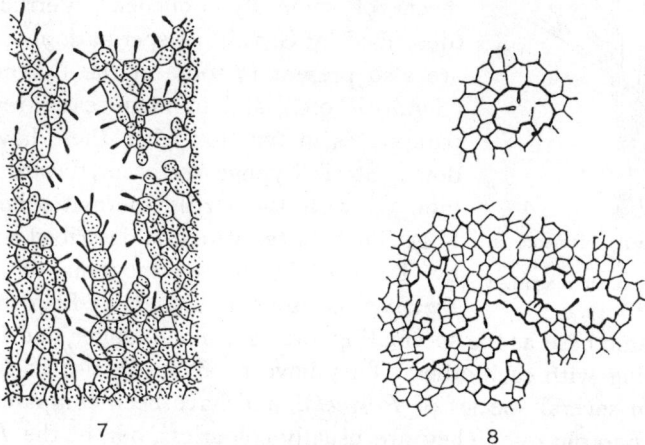

Fig. 113 B. 7, *Physcia ciliaris* DC. × 600; 8, *Endocarpon* sp. × 600 (after Glück).

8. *Endocarpon* type: the pycnidium is filled by a tissue of short broad cells, with irregular hollow spaces lined by fertile cells similar to those of the *Sticta* and *Physcia* types.

The three last named types of sporophores represent Nylander's section of arthrosterigmata. Steiner has followed Nylander in also arranging the various forms into two leading groups. The first, characterized by the secondary branch or "sterigma," he designates "exobasidial"; the second, comprising the three last types in which the spores are borne directly on the cells of the sporophore or on very short processes, he describes as " endobasidial." Steiner also introduces a new term, *fulcrum*, for the sporophore.

The pycnidia in which these different sporophores occur are not, as a rule, characteristic of one family. *Peltigera* type is found only in one family and the *Cladonia* type is fairly constant in *Cladoniae*, but " *Psora* " pycnidia are found on very varying lichens among the Lecideaceae, Verrucariaceae and others. The *Squamaria* type with long bent spores is found not only in *Squamaria* (Glück's *Placodium*) but also in *Lecidea, Roccella, Pyrenula*, etc. *Parmelia* type is characteristic of many *Parmeliae* and also of species of *Evernia, Alectoria, Platysma* and *Cetraria*. The *Sticta* type occurs in *Gyrophora, Umbilicaria, Nephromium* and *Lecanora* as well as in *Sticta* and in one species at least of *Collema*. To the *Physcia* type belong the pycnidia of most *Physciaceae* and of various *Parmeliae*, and to the closely related *Endocarpon* type the pycnidia of *Endocarpon* and of *Xanthoria parietina*.

c. PERIPHYSES AND STERILE FILAMENTS. In a few species, *Roccella tinctoria,Pertusaria globulifera*,etc.,short one-celled sterile hyphae are formed within the spermogonium near the ostiole, towards which they converge.

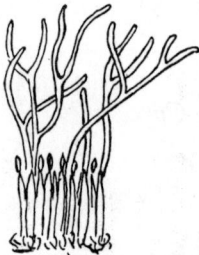

Fig. 114. Sterile filaments in spermogonia of *Lecidea fuscoatra* Ach. much magnified (after Lindsay).

They correspond to the periphyses in the perithecia of some Pyrenolichens, Verrucaria, etc. (described by Gibelli[1] as spermatiophores); they are also present in some of the Pyrenomycetes (*Sordaria*, etc.), and in many cases replace the paraphyses in function when these have broken down. Sterile hyphae also occur, towards the base, mingled with the fertile spermatiophores (Fig. 114). These latter were first described and figured by Tulasne[2] in the spermogonia of *Ramalina fraxinea* as stoutish branching filaments, rising from the same base as the spermatiophores but much longer, and frequently anastomosing with each other. They have been noted also in *Usnea barbata* and in several species of *Parmelia*, and have been compared by Nylander[3] to paraphyses. They are usually colourless, but, in the *Parmeliae*, are often brownish and thus easily distinguished from the spermatiophores. It has been stated that these filaments are sometimes fertile. Similar sterile hyphae have been recorded in the pycnidia of fungi, in *Sporocladus* (*Hendersonia*) *lichenicola* (Sphaeropsideae) by Corda[4] who described them as

¹ Gibelli 1866.   ² Tulasne 1852.   ³ Nylander 1858.   ⁴ Corda 1839.

paraphyses, and also in *Steganosporium cellulosum* (Melanconieae). These observations have been confirmed by Allescher[1] in his recent work on *Fungi Imperfecti.* Keiszler[2] has described a *Phoma*-like pycnidium parasitic on the leprose thallus of *Haematomma elatinum.* It contains short slender sporophores and, mixed with these, long branched sterile hyphae which reach to the ostiole and evidently function as paraphyses, though Keiszler suggests that they may be a second form of sporophore that has become sterile. On account of their presence he placed the fungus in a new genus *Lichenophoma.*

E. SPERMATIA OR PYCNIDIOSPORES

a. ORIGIN AND FORM OF SPERMATIA. Lichen spermatia arise at the tips of the sterigmata either through simple abstriction or by budding. In the former case—as in the *Squamaria* type—a delicate cross-wall is formed by which the spermatium is separated off. When they arise by budding, there is first a small clavate sac-like swelling of the end of the short process or sterigma which gradually grows out into a spermatium on a very narrow base. This latter formation occurs in the *Sticta, Physcia* and *Endocarpon* types.

Nylander[3] has distinguished the following forms of spermatia:

1. Ob-clavate, the broad end attached to the sterigma as in *Usneae, Cetraria glauca* and *C. juniperina.*

2. Acicular and minute but slightly swollen at each end, somewhat dumb-bell like, in *Cetraria nivalis, C. cucullata, Alectoria, Evernia* and some *Parmeliae,* frequently borne on "arthrosterigmata."

3. Acicular, cylindrical and straight, the most common form; these occur in most of the *Lecanorae, Cladoniae, Lecideae,* Graphideae, Pyrenocarpeae and occasionally they are budded off from arthrosterigmata.

4. Acicular, cylindrical, bent; sometimes these are very long, measuring up to 40 μ; they are found in various *Lecideae, Lecanorae,* Graphideae, Pyrenocarpeae, and also in *Roccella, Pilophorus* and species of *Stereocaulon.*

5. Ellipsoid or oblong and generally very minute; they are borne on simple sterigmata and are characteristic of the genera *Calicium, Chaenotheca, Lichina,Ephebe,*of the small genus *Glypholecia* and of a few species of *Lecanora* and *Lecidea.*

In many instances there is more or less variation of form and of size in the species or even in the individual. There are no spherical spermatia.

b. SIZE AND STRUCTURE. The shortest spermatia in any of our British lichens are those of *Lichina pygmaea* which are about 1·4 μ in length and the longest are those of *Lecanora crassa* which measure up to 39 μ. In width they vary from about 0·5 μ to 2 μ. The mature spermogonium is filled with

---

[1] Allescher 1901–3.   [2] Keiszler 1911.   [3] Nylander 1858, p. 37.

spermatia and, generally, with a mass of mucilage that swells with moisture and secures their expulsion.

The spermatia of lichens are colourless and are provided with a cell-wall and a nucleus. The presence of a nucleus was demonstrated by Möller[1] in the spermatia of *Calicium parietinum, Opegrapha atra, Collema microphyllum, C. pulposum* and *C. Hildenbrandii,* and by Istvanffi[2] in those of *Buellia puncti-formis (B. myriocarpa), Opegrapha subsiderella, Collema Hildenbrandii, Cali-cium trachelinum, Pertusaria communis* and *Arthonia communis (A. astroidea).* Istvanffi made use of fresh material, fixing the spermatia with osmic acid, and in all of these very minute bodies he demonstrated the presence of a nucleus which stained readily with haematoxylin and which he has figured in the spermatia of *Buellia punctiformis* as an extremely small dot-like structure in the centre of the cell. On germination, as in the cell-multi-plication of other plants, the nucleus leads the way. Germination is preceded by nuclear division, and each new hyphal cell of the growing mycelium receives a nucleus.

c. GERMINATION OF SPERMATIA (pycnidiospores). The strongest argu-ment in favour of regarding the spermatia of lichens as male cells had always been the impossibility of inducing their germination. That difficulty had at length been overcome by Möller[1] who cultivated them in artificial solutions, and by that means obtained germination in nine different lichen species. He therefore rejected the commonly employed terms spermatia and spermo-gonia and substituted pycnoconidium and pycnidia. Pycnidiospore has been however preferred as more in accordance with modern fungal termi-nology. His first experiment was with the "spermatia" of *Buellia punctiformis (B. myriocarpa)* which measure about 8–10 μ in length and about 3 μ in width, and are borne directly on the septate spermatiophores (arthrosterig-mata). In a culture drop, the spore had swelled to about double its size by the second or third day, and germination had taken place at both ends, the membrane of the spore being continuous with that of the germinating tube. In a short time cross septa were formed in the hyphae which at first were very close to each other. While apical growth advanced these first formed cells increased in width to twice the original size and, in consequence, became slightly constricted at the septa. In fourteen days a circular patch of my-celium had been formed about 280 μ in diameter. The development exactly resembled that obtained from the ascospores of the same species grown in the absence of gonidia. The largest thallus obtained in either case was about 2 mm. in diameter after three months' growth. The older hyphae had a tendency to become brownish in colour; those at the periphery remained colourless. In *Opegrapha subsiderella* the development, though equally

---

[1] Möller 1887.   [2] Istvanffi 1895.

successful, was very much slower. The pycnidiospores (or spermatia) have the form of minute bent rods measuring $5·7 \mu \times 1·5 \mu$. Each end of the spore produced slender hyphae about the fifth or sixth day after sowing. In four weeks, the whole length of the filament with the spore in the middle was 300μ. In four months a patch of mycelium was formed 2 mm. in diameter. Growth was even more sluggish with the pycnidiospores of *Opegrapha atra*. In that species they are rod-shaped and $5-6 \mu$ long. Germination took place on the fifth or sixth day and in fourteen days a germination tube was produced about five times the length of the spore. In four weeks the first branching was noticed and was followed by a second branching in the seventh week. In three months the mycelial growth measured $200-300 \mu$ across.

Germination was also observed in a species of *Arthonia*, the spores of which had begun to grow while still in the pycnidium. The most complete results were obtained in species of *Calicium*: in *C. parietinum* the spores, which are ovoid, slightly bent, and brownish in colour, swelled to an almost globose shape and then germinated by a minute point at the junction of spore and sterigma, and also at the opposite end; very rarely a third germinating tube was formed. Growth was fairly rapid, so that in four weeks there was a loose felt of mycelium measuring about 2 cm. × 1 cm. and 1 mm. in depth. Parallel cultures were carried out with the ascospores and the results in both cases were the same; in five or six weeks small black points appeared, which gradually developed to pycnidia with mature pycnidiospores from which further cultures were obtained.

On *C. trachelinum*, which has a thin greyish-white thallus spreading over old trunks of trees, the pycnidia are usually abundant. Lindsay had noted two different kinds and his observation was confirmed by Möller. The spores in one pycnidium are ovoid, measuring $2·5-3 \mu \times 1·5-2 \mu$; in the other rarer form, they are rod-shaped and $5-7 \mu$ long. In the artificial cultures they both swelled, the rod-like spores to double their width before germination, and sometimes several tubes were put forth. Growth was slow, but of exactly the same kind from these two types of spores as from the ascospores. At the end of the second month pycnidia appeared on all the cultures, in each case producing the ovoid type of spore.

In a second paper Möller[1] recorded the partially successful germination of the "spermatia" of *Collema* (*Leptogium*) *microphyllum*, the species in which Stahl had demonstrated sexual reproduction. Growth was extraordinarily slow: after a month in the culture solution the first swelling of the spermatium prior to germination took place, and some time later small processes were formed in two or three directions. In the fourth month a branched filament was formed.

Möller's experiments with ascospores and pycnidiospores were primarily

[1] Möller 1888.

undertaken to prove that the lichen hyphae were purely fungal and parasitic on the algae. A series of cultures were made by Hedlund[1] in order to demonstrate that the pycnidiospores were asexual reproductive bodies; they were grown in association with the lichen alga and their germination was followed up to the subsequent formation of a lichen thallus.

d. VARIATION IN PYCNIDIA. On the thallus of *Catillaria denigrata* (*Biatorina synothea*) Hedlund found that there were constantly present two types of pycnidia: the one with short slightly bent spores 4–8 μ × 1·5 μ, the other with much longer bent spores 10–20 μ × 1·5 μ; there were numerous transition forms between the two kinds of spores. Germination took place by the prolongation of the spore; the hypha produced became septate and branches were soon formed. Hedlund found that frequently germination had already begun in the spores expelled from the spermogonium. In newly formed thalline areolae it was possible to trace back the mycelium to innumerable germinating spores of both types, long and short.

Lindsay had recorded more than one form of spermogonium on the same lichen thallus, the spermatia varying considerably in size; but he was most probably dealing with the mixed growth of more than one species. The observations of Möller and Hedlund on this point are more exact, but the limits of variation would very well include the two forms found by Möller in *Calicium trachelinum*; and in the different pycnidia of *Catillaria denigrata* Hedlund not only observed transition stages between the two kinds of spores, but the longer pycnidiospores, as he himself allows, indicated the elongation prior to germination : there is no good evidence of more than one form in any species.

F. PYCNIDIA WITH MACROSPORES

Tulasne[2] records the presence on the lichen thallus of "pycnidia" as well as of "spermogonia"; the former producing stylospores, larger bodies than spermatia, occasionally septate and containing oil-drops or guttulae. These spores are pyriform or ovoid in shape and are always borne at the tips of simple sporophores. He compared the pycnidia with the fungus genera *Cytospora*, *Septoria*, etc. As a rule they occur on lichens with a poorly developed thallus, on some species of *Lecanora*, *Lecanactis*, *Calicium*, *Porina*, in the family Strigulaceae and in *Peltigera*.

There is no morphological difference between pycnidia and spermogonia except that the spermatia of the latter are narrower; but the difference is so slight that, as Steiner has pointed out, these organs found on *Lecanora piniperda*, *L. Sambuci* and *L. effusa* have been described at one time as containing microconidia (spermatia), at another macroconidia (stylospores).

[1] Hedlund 1892.   [2] Tulasne 1852.

He also regards as macrospores those of the pycnidia of *Calicium trachelinum* which Möller was able to germinate so successfully, and all the more so as they were brownish in colour, true microspores or spermatia being colourless.

Müller[1] has recorded some observations on the pycnidia and stylospores of the Strigulaceae, a family of tropical lichens inhabiting the leaves of the higher plants. On the thallus of *Strigula elegans* var. *tremula* from Madagascar and from India, he found pycnidia with stylospores of abnormal dimensions measuring 18–26μ in length and 3μ in width, and with 1 to 7 cross septa. In *Strigula complanata* var. *genuina* the stylospores were 2–8-septate and varied from 7–65μ in length, some of the spores being thus ten times longer than others, while the width remained the same. Müller considers that in these cases the stylospore has already grown to a septate hypha while in the pycnidium. As in the pycnidiospores, described later by Hedlund, the spores had germinated by increase in length followed by septation.

The spermogonia of *Strigula*, which are exactly similar to the pycnidia in size and structure, produce spermatia, measuring about 3μ × 2μ, and it is suggested by Müller that the stylospores may represent merely an advanced stage of development of these spermatia. Both organs were constantly associated on the same thallus; but whereas the spermogonia were abundant on the younger part of the thallus at the periphery, they were almost entirely replaced by pycnidia on the older portions near the centre, only a very few spermogonia (presumably younger pycnidial stages) being found in that region.

Lindsay[2] has described a great many different lichen pycnidia, but in many instances he must have been dealing with species of the "Fungi imperfecti" that were growing in association with the scattered granules of crustaceous lichens. There are many fungi—Discomycetes and Pyrenomycetes—parasitic on lichen thalli, and he has, in some cases, undoubtedly been describing their secondary pycnidial form of fruit, which indeed may appear far more frequently than the more perfect ascigerous form, and might easily be mistaken for the pycnidial fructification of the lichen.

G. General Survey

a. Sexual or Asexual. It has been necessary to give the preceding detailed account of these various structures—pycnidia or spermogonia—in view of the extreme importance attached to them as the possible male organs of the lichen plant, and, in giving the results obtained by different workers, the terminology employed by each one has been adopted as far as

<hr/>

[1] Müller 1885.   [2] Lindsay 1859 and 1872.

possible: those who consider them to be sexual structures call them spermo-gonia; those who refuse to accept that view write of them as pycnidia.

Tulasne, Nylander and others unhesitatingly accepted them as male organs without any knowledge of the female cell or of any method of ferti-lization. Stahl's discovery of the trichogyne seemed to settle the whole question; but though he had evidence of copulation between the spermatium and the receptive cell or trichogyne he had no real record of any sexual process.

Many modern lichenologists reject the view that they are sexual; they regard them as secondary organs of fructification analogous to the pycnidia so abundant in the related groups of fungi. One would naturally expect these pycnidia to reappear in lichens, and it might be considered somewhat arbitrary to classify pycnidia in Sphaeropsideae as asexual reproductive organs, and then to regard the very similar structures in lichens as sexual spermogonia. It has also been pointed out that when undoubted pycnidia do occur on the lichen thallus, as in *Calicium, Strigula, Peltigera*, etc., they in no way differ from structures regarded as spermogonia except in the size of the pycnidiospores—and, even among these, there are transition forms. The different types of spermatia can be paralleled among the fungal pyc-nidiospores and the same is also true as regards the sporophores generally. Those described as arthrosterigmata by Nylander—as endosporous by Steiner—were supposed to be peculiar to lichens; but recently Laubert[1] has described a fungal pycnidium which grew on the trunk of an apple tree and in which the spores are not borne on upright sporophores but are budded off from the cells of the plectenchyma lining the pycnidium. It may be that future research will discover other such instances, though that type of sporo-phore is evidently of very rare occurrence among fungi.

b. Comparison with Fungi. The most obvious spermogonia among fungi with which to compare those of lichens occur in the Uredineae where they are associated with the life-cycle of a large number of rust species. They are small flask-shaped structures very much like the simpler forms of pycnidia and they produce innumerable spermatia which are budded off from the tips of simple spermatiophores. The mature spermatium has a delicate cell-wall and contains a thin layer of cytoplasm with a dense nucleus which occupies almost the whole cavity, cytological characters which, as Blackman[2] has pointed out, are characteristic of male cells and are not found in any asexual reproductive spores. If we accept Istvanffi's[3] description and figures of the lichen spermatia as correct, their structure is wholly different: there being a very small nucleus in the centre of the cell comparable in size with those of the vegetative hyphae (Fig. 115).

---

[1] Laubert 1911.   [2] Blackman 1904.   [3] Istvanffi 1895.

Lichen "spermatia" also differ very strikingly from the male cells of any given group of plants in their very great diversity of form and size; but the

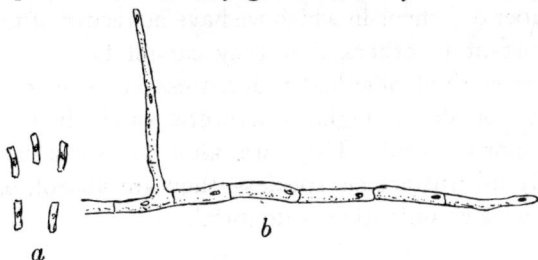

Fig. 115. *a*, spermatia; *b*, hypha produced from spermatium of *Buellia punctiformis* Th. Fr. × 950 (after Istvanffi).

chief argument adduced by the opponents of the sexual theory is the capacity of germination that has been proved to exist in a fair number of species. It is true that germination has been induced in the spermatia of the Uredines by several research workers—by Plowright[1], Sappin-Trouffy[2] and by Brefeld[3]— who employed artificial nutritive solutions (sugar or honey), but the results obtained were not much more than the budding process of yeast cells. Brefeld also succeeded in germinating the "spermatia" of a pyrenomycetous fungus, *Polystigma rubrum*, one of the germinating tubes reaching a length four times that of the spore; but it is now known that all of these fungal spermatia are non-functional, either sexually or asexually, and degenerate soon after their expulsion, or even while still in the spermogonium.

c. INFLUENCE OF SYMBIOSIS. In any consideration of lichens it is constantly necessary to hark back to their origin as symbiotic organisms, and to bear in mind the influence of the composite life on their development. After germination from the spore, the lichen hypha is so dependant on its association with the alga, that, in natural conditions,. though it persists without the gonidia for a time, it attains to only a rather feeble growth of mycelial filaments. In nutritive cultures, as Möller has proved, the absence of the alga is partly compensated by the artificial food supply, and a scanty thalline growth is formed up to the stage of pycnidial fruits. Not only in pycnidia but in all the fruiting bodies of lichens, symbiosis has entailed a distinct retrogression in the reproductive importance of the spores, as compared with fungi.

In Ascomycetes, the asci constitute the overwhelming bulk of the hymenium ; in most lichens, there are serried ranks of paraphyses with comparatively few asci, and the spores are often imperfectly developed. It would not therefore be surprising if the bodies claimed by Möller and others as pycnidiospores had also lost even to a considerable extent their reproductive capacity.

[1] Plowright 1889.   [2] Sappin-Trouffy 1896.   [3] Brefeld 1891.

d. VALUE IN DIAGNOSIS. Lichen spermogonia have once and again been found of value in deciding the affinity of related plants, and though there are a number of lichens in which we have no record of their occurrence, they are so constant in others, that they cannot be ignored in any true estimation of species. Nylander laid undue stress on spermogonial characters, considering them of almost higher diagnostic value than the much more important ascosporous fruit. They are, after all, subsidiary organs, and often—especially in crustaceous species—they are absent, or their relation to the species under examination is doubtful.

CHAPTER V

PHYSIOLOGY

I. CELLS AND CELL PRODUCTS

ANY study of cells or cell-membranes in lichens should naturally include those of both symbionts, but the algae though modified have not been profoundly changed, and their response to the influences of the symbiotic environment has been already described in the discussion of lichen gonidia. The description of cells and their contents refers therefore mainly to the fungal tissues which form the framework of the plant; they have been transformed by symbiosis to lichenoid hyphae in some respects differing from, in others resembling, the fungal hyphae from which they are derived.

A. CELL-MEMBRANES

a. CHITIN. It was recognized by workers in the early years of the nineteenth century that the substance forming the cell-walls of fungal hyphae differed very markedly from the cellulose of the membranes in other groups of plants, the blue colouration with iodine and sulphuric acid so characteristic of cellulose being absent in most fungi. Various explanations were suggested; but it was always held that the doubtful substance was a cellulose containing something peculiar to fungi, this view being strengthened by the fact that, after long treatment with potash, a blue reaction was obtained. It was called fungus-cellulose by De Bary[1] in order to distinguish it from true cellulose.

It was not till a much later date that any exact work was done on the fungal cell, and that Gilson[2] by his researches was able to prove that the membranes of fungi contained probably no cellulose, or, "if cellulose were present, it was in a different condition from the cellulose of other plants." Winterstein[3] followed with the results of his examination of fungus-cellulose: he found that it contained nitrogen and therefore differed very considerably from typical plant cellulose. Gilson[4] published a second paper dealing entirely with fungal tissues in which he also established the presence of nitrogen, and added that this nitrogenous compound resembled in various ways the chitin[5] of animal cells. He further discovered that by heating it with potash a substance was obtained that took a reddish-violet stain when treated with iodine and weak sulphuric acid. This substance, called by him mycosin, was proved later to be similar to chitosan[5], a product of chitin.

---

[1] De Bary 1866, p. 7.　　[2] Gilson 1893.　　[3] Winterstein 1893.　　[4] Gilson 1894.
[5] The chemical formula of chitin is given as $C_{60}H_{100}N_8O_{38}$, that of chitosan as $C_{14}H_{26}N_2O_{10}$.

Escombe[1] analysed the hyphal membranes of *Cetraria* and found that they consisted mainly of a body called by him lichenin and of a para-galactan. From *Peltigera* he extracted a substance with physical properties agreeing fairly well with those of chitosan, though analysis did not give percentages reconcilable with that substance; the yield however was very small. No lichenin was detected.

Van Wisselingh[2] examined the hyphae of lichens as well as of fungi and experimented with a considerable number of both types of plants. He succeeded in proving the presence of chitin in the higher fungi (Basidio-mycetes and Ascomycetes) and in lichens with one or two exceptions (*Cladonia* and *Cetraria*). Though in some the quantity found was exceed-ingly small, in others, such as *Peltigera*, the walls of the hyphae were extremely chitinous. More recently Wester[3] has gone into the question as regards lichens, and he has practically confirmed all the results previously obtained by Wisselingh. In some species, as for instance in *Cladonia rangi-ferina*, *Cl. squamosa*, *Cl. gracilis*, *Ramalina calicaris*, *Solorina crocea* and others, he found that chitin existed in large quantities, while in *Evernia prunastri*, *Usnea florida*, *U. articulata*, *Sticta damaecornis* and *Parmelia saxatilis* very little was present. The variation in the amount present may be very great even in the species of one genus: none for instance has been detected in *Cetraria islandica* nor in *C. nivalis* while it is abundant in other *Cetrariae*. There is also considerable variation in quantity in different individuals of the same species, and even in different parts of the thallus of one lichen. Factors such as habitat, age of the plant, etc., may, however, account to a considerable extent for the differences in the results obtained.

b. LICHENIN AND ALLIED CARBOHYDRATES. It has been proved, as already stated, that chitin is present in the hyphal cell-walls of all the lichens examined except in those of *Cetraria islandica* (Iceland Moss), *C. nivalis* and, according to Wester[3], in those of *Bryopogon* (*Alectoriae*). In these lichens another substance of purely carbohydrate nature is the chief consti-tuent of the cell-walls which swell up when soaked in water to a colourless gelatinous substance.

Berzelius[4] first drew attention to the peculiar qualities of this lichen product, and, recognizing its resemblance in many respects to ordinary starch, he called it "lichen-starch" or "moss-starch." More exact observations were made later by Guérin-Varry[5] who described its properties and showed by his experiments that it contained no admixture of either starch or gum. He adopted the name lichenin for this organic soluble part of Iceland Moss. An analysis of lichenin was made by Mulder[6] who detected in addition to lichenin, which coloured yellow with iodine, small quantities of a blue-

---

[1] Escombe 1896.   [2] Wisselingh 1898.   [3] Wester 1909.   [4] Berzelius 1813.
[5] Guérin-Varry 1834.   [6] Mulder 1838.

colouring substance which could be dissolved out from the lichenin and which he considered to be true starch. Berg[1] also demonstrated the compound nature of lichenin: he isolated two isomerous substances with the formula $C_6 H_{10} O_5$. The name "isolichenin" was given to the second blue-colouring substance by Beilstein[2] in 1881.

More recently Escombe[3] has chemically analysed the cell-wall of *Cetraria islandica*: after the elimination of fat, oil, colouring matter and bitter constituents he found that there remained the compound lichenin, an anhydride of galactose with the formula $C_6 H_{10} O_5$, which, as stated above, consists of two substances lichenin and isolichenin[4]; the latter is soluble in cold water and gives a blue reaction with iodine, lichenin is only soluble in hot water and is not coloured blue. Both are derivatives of galactose, a sugar found in a great number of organic tissues and substances, among others in gums.

Lichenin has also been obtained by Lacour[5] from *Lecanora esculenta*, an edible desert lichen supposed to be the manna of the Israelites. Wisselingh[6] tested the hymenium of thirteen different lichens for lichenin. He found it in the walls of the ascus of all those he examined except *Graphis*. Everniin, a constituent of *Evernia prunastri*, was isolated and described by Stüde[7]. It is soluble in water and, though considered by Czapek[8] to be identical with lichenin, it differs, according to Ulander[9], in being dextro-rotatory to polarized light; lichenin on the contrary is optically inactive. Escombe[3] also obtained a substance from *Evernia* which he considered to be comparable with chitosan. Usnein which has been extracted[6] from *Usnea barbata* may also be identical with lichenin, but that has not yet been established. Ulander[9] examined chemically the cell-walls of a fairly large number of lichens. *Cetraria islandica, C. aculeata* and *Usnea barbata*, designated as the "Cetraria group," contained soluble mucilage-forming substances similar to lichenin. A second "Cladonia group" which included *Cl. rangiferina* with the variety *alpestris, Stereocaulon paschale* and *Peltigera aphthosa* yielded almost none. After the soluble carbohydrates were removed by hot water, the insoluble substances were hydrolysed and the "Cetraria group" was found to contain abundant d-glucose with small quantities of d-mannose and d-galactose; the "Cladonia group," abundant d-mannose and d-galactose with but little d-glucose. Hydrolysis was easier and quicker with the former group than with the latter.

Besides these, which rank as hexosans, Ulander found small quantities of pentosans and methyl pentosans. All these substances which are such important constituents of the hyphal membranes of lichens are classed by Ulander as hemicelluloses of the same nature as mannan, galactan and dextran, or as substances between hemicellulose and the glucoses represented

[1] Berg 1873.   [2] Beilstein ex Errera 1882, p. 16 (note).   [3] Escombe 1896.   [4] Wiesner 1900.
[5] Lacour 1880.   [6] Wisselingh 1898.   [7] Stüde 1864.   [8] Czapek 1905, I. p. 515.   [9] Ulander 1905.

212 PHYSIOLOGY

by lichenin, everniin, etc. They are doubtless reserve stores of food material, and they are chiefly located in the cell-walls of the medullary hyphae which are often so thick as almost to obliterate the lumen of the cells. Ulander made no test for chitin in his researches.

Ulander's results have been confirmed by those obtained by K. Müller[1]. In *Cladonia rangiferina*, Müller found that the cell-membranes of the hyphae contained, as hemicelluloses, pentosans in small quantities and galactan, but no lichenin and very little chitin. In *Evernia prunastri* hemicelluloses formed the chief constituents of the thallus, and from it he was able to isolate galactan soluble in weak hot acid, and everniin soluble in hot water, the latter with the formula $C_7H_{15}O_6$, a result differing from that obtained by Stüde[2] who has given it as $C_9H_{14}O_7$; chitin was also present in small quantities. In *Ramalina fraxinea*, the soluble part of the thallus (in hot water) differed from everniin and might probably be lichenin. *Cetraria islandica* was also analysed and yielded various hemicelluloses, chiefly dextran and galactan, with less pentosan. No chitin has ever been found in this lichen. In testing minute quantities of material for chitin, Wisselingh[3] heated the tissue in potash to 160° C. The potash was then gradually replaced by glycerine and distilled water; the precipitate was placed on a slide and the preparation stained under the microscope by potassium-iodide-iodine and weak sulphuric acid. Chitin, if present, would have been changed by the potash to mycosin which gives a violet colour with the staining solution.

It has been stated by Schellenberg[4] that these lichen membranes may become lignified. He obtained a red reaction with phloroglucine test for lignin in *Cetraria islandica* and *Cladonia furcata*. Further research is required.

c. CELLULOSE. Several workers claim to have found true cellulose in the cell-walls of the hyphal tissues of a few lichens; but the more careful analyses of Escombe[5] Wisselingh[3] and Wester[6] have disproved their results. The cell-walls of all the gonidia, however, are formed of cellulose, or according to Escombe of glauco-cellulose, except those of *Peltigera* in which Wester found neither cellulose nor chitin. Czapek[7] suggests that the blue reaction with iodine characteristic of the cell-walls in some apothecia, of the asci and of the hyphae in cortex or medulla in a few instances, may be due to the presence of carbohydrates of the nature of galactose. Moreau[8] in a recent paper terms the substance that gives a blue reaction with iodine at the tips of the asci "amyloid." In *Peltigera* the ascus tip is occupied by such a plug of amyloid which at maturity is projected like a cork from the ascus and may be found on the surface of the hymenium.

[1] Müller 1905. [2] Stüde 1864. [3] Wisselingh 1898. [4] Schellenberg 1896.
[5] Escombe 1896. [6] Wester 1909. [7] Czapek 1905, 1. p. 515. [8] Moreau 1916.

B. Contents and Products of the Fungal Cells

a. Cell-substances. The cells of lichen hyphae contain protoplasm and nucleus with glucoses. It is doubtful if starch has been found in fungal hyphae; it is replaced, in some of the tissues at least, by glycogen, a carbohydrate ($C_6 H_{10} O_5$) very close to, if not identical with, animal glycogen, a substance which is soluble in water and colours reddish-brown (wine-red) with iodine. Errera[1] first detected its presence in Ascomycetes where it is associated with the epiplasm of the cells, more especially of the asci, and he considered it to be physiologically homologous with starch. He included lichens, as Ascomycetes, in his survey of fungi and quotes, in support of his view that lichen hyphae also contain glycogen, a statement made by Schwendener[2] that "the contents of the ascogenous hyphae of *Coenogonium Linkii* stain a deep-brown with iodine." Errera also instances the red-brown reaction with iodine, described by de Bary[3], as characteristic of the large spores of *Ochrolechia (Lecanora) pallescens*, while the germinating tubes of these spores become yellow with iodine like ordinary protoplasm. Glycogen has been, so far, found only in the cells of the reproductive system.

Iodine was found by Gautier[4] in the gonidia of *Parmelia* and *Peltigera*, *i.e.* both in bright-green and blue-green algae. The amount was scarcely calculable.

Herissey[5] claims to have established the presence of emulsin in a large series of lichens belonging to such widely separated genera as *Cladonia*, *Cetraria*, *Evernia*, *Peltigera*, *Pertusaria*, *Parmelia*, *Ramalina*, and *Usnea*. It is a ferment which acts upon amygdalin, though its presence has been proved in plants such as lichens where no amygdalin has been found[6]. Diastase was demonstrated in the cells of *Roccella tinctoria*, *R. Montagnei* and of *Dendrographa leucophaea* by Ronceray[7] who states that, in conjunction with air and ammonia, it forms orchil, the well-known colouring substance of these lichens. Diastatic ferments have also been determined[8] in *Usnea florida*, *Physcia parietina*, *Parmelia perlata* and *Peltigera canina*.

b. Calcium Oxalate. Oxalic acid ($C_2H_2O_4$) is an oxidation product of alcohol and of most carbohydrates and in combination is a frequent constituent of plant cells. Knop[9] held that it was formed in lichens by the reduction and splitting of lichen acids, though, as Zopf[10] has pointed out, these are generally insoluble. Hamlet and Plowright[11] demonstrated the presence of free oxalic acid in many families of fungi including *Pezizae* and *Sphaeriae*. The acid combines with calcium to form the oxalate (CaC_2O_4), which in the crystalline form is very common in lichens. In the higher

---

[1] Errera 1882. [2] Schwendener 1862, p. 231. [3] De Bary 1866–1867, p. 211. [4] Gautier 1899.
[5] Herissey 1898. [6] Czapek 1905, II. p. 257. [7] Ronceray 1904. [8] Zopf in Schenk 1890, p. 448.
[9] Knop 1872. [10] Zopf 1907. [11] Hamlet and Plowright 1877.

plants the crystals are formed within the cell, but in lichens they are always deposited on the outer surface of the hyphal membranes, mainly of the medulla and the cortex.

Calcium oxalate was first detected in lichens by Henri Braconnot[1], who extracted it by treating the powdered thallus of a number of species (*Pertusaria communis, Diploschistes scruposus*, etc.) with different reagents. The quantity present varies greatly in lichens: Zopf[2] found that it was abundant in all the species inhabiting limestone, and states that in such plants the more purely lichenic acids are relatively scarce. Errera[3] has calculated the amount of calcium oxalate in *Lecanora esculenta*, a desert lime-loving lichen, to be about 60 per cent. of the whole substance of the thallus. Euler[4] gives for the same lichen even a larger proportion, 66 per cent. of the dry weight. In *Pertusaria communis*, a corticolous species, the oxalate occurs as irregular crystalline masses in the medulla (Fig. 116) and has

been calculated as 47 per cent. of the whole substance. Other crustaceous species such as *Diploschistes scruposus, Haematomma coccineum, H. ventosum, Lecanora saxicola, Lecanora tartarea*, etc., contain large amounts either in the form of octahedral crystals or as small granules.

Fig. 116. *Pertusaria communis* DC. Vertical section of thallus. *a*, cortex; *b*, gonidia; *c*, medulla; *d*, crystal of calcium oxalate. × ca. 100.

Rosendahl[5] has recently made observations as to the presence of the oxalate in the thallus of the brown *Parmeliae*. Of the fourteen species examined by him, eleven contained calcium oxalate as octahedral crystals or as small prisms, often piled up in thick irregular masses. Usually the crystals were located in the medullary part of the thallus, but in two species, *Parmelia verruculifera* and *P. papulosa*, they were abundant on the surface cells of the upper cortex.

c. IMPORTANCE OF CALCIUM OXALATE TO THE LICHEN PLANT. It is natural to conclude that a substance of frequent occurrence in any group of plants is of some biological significance, and suggestions have not been lacking as to the value of oxalic acid or of calcium oxalate in the economy of the lichen thallus. Oxalic acid is known to be one of the most efficient solvents of argillaceous earth and of iron oxides likely to be in the soil. These materials are also conveyed to the thallus as air-borne dust, and would thus, with the aid of the acid, be easily dissolved and absorbed. As a direct proof of this, Knop[6] has stated that lichen-ash always contains argillaceous earth. According to Kratzmann[7], aluminium, a product of clay, is stored up in various lichens. He proved the amount in the ash of *Umbilicaria*

[1] Braconnot 1825.   [2] Zopf 1907.   [3] Errera 1893.   [4] Euler 1908, p. 7.
[5] Rosendahl 1907.   [6] Knop 1872.   [7] Kratzmann 1913.

pustulata to be 4·46 per cent., in *Usnea barbata* 1·79 per cent., in *U. longissima* considerable quantities while in *Roccella tinctoria* it occurred in great abundance. It was also abundant in *Diploschistes scruposus*, 28·17 per cent.; it declined in *Variolaria (Pertusaria) dealbata* to 7·77 per cent., in *Cladonia rangiferina* to 1·76–2·12 per cent. and in *Ramalina fraxinea* to 1·8 per cent.

Calcium oxalate is directly advantageous to the thallus by virtue of the capacity of the crystals to reduce or prevent evaporation, as has been pointed out by Zukal[1]. A like service afforded by crystals to the leaves of the higher plants in desert lands has been described by Kerner[2]. These are frequently encrusted with lime crystals which allow the copious night dews to soak underneath them to the underlying cells, while during the day they impede, if they do not altogether check, evaporation.

Calcium oxalate crystals are insoluble in acetic acid, soluble in hydrochloric acid without evolution of gas; they deposit gypsum crystals in a solution of sulphuric acid.

C. Oil-Cells

a. Oil-Cells of Endolithic Lichens. Calcicolous immersed lichens are able to dissolve the lime of the substratum, and their hyphae penetrate more or less deeply into the rock. In some forms the entire thallus may thus be immersed, the fruits alone being visible on the surface of the stone. In two such species, *Verrucaria calciseda* and *Petractis (Gyalecta) exanthematica*, Steiner[3] detected peculiar sphaeroid or barrel-shaped cells that differed from the other hyphal cells of the thallus, not only in their form, but in their greenish-coloured contents. Similar cells were found by Zukal[4] in another immersed (endolithic) lichen, *Verrucaria rupestris* f. *rosea*. He describes them as roundish organs crowded on the hyphae and filled with a greenish shimmering protoplasm. He[5] found the same types of sphaeroid and other swollen cells in the immersed thallus of several calcicolous lichens and he finally determined the contents as fat in the form of oil. He found also that these fat-cells, though very frequent, were not constantly present even in the same species. His observations were confirmed by Hulth[6] for a number of allied crustaceous lichens that grow not only on limestone but on volcanic rocks. In them he found a like variety of fat-cells—intercalary or torulose cells, terminal sphaeroid cells and hyphae containing scattered oil-drops. Bachmann[7] followed with a study of the thallus of purely calcicolous lichens. The specialized oil-cells were fairly constant in the species he examined, and, as a rule, they were formed either in the tissues immediately below, or at some distance from, the gonidial zone. Fünfstück[8] has also

---

[1] Zukal 1895, p. 1311. [2] Kerner and Oliver 1894, p. 235. [3] Steiner 1881. [4] Zukal 1884.
[5] Zukal 1886. [6] Hulth 1891. [7] Bachmann 1892. [8] Fünfstück 1895.

published an account of various oil-cells in a large series of calcicolous lichens (Fig. 117).

The occurrence of oil- (or fat-) cells is not dependent on the presence of any particular alga as the gonidium of the lichen. Fünfstück[1] has described the immersed thallus of *Opegrapha saxicola* as one of those richest in fat-cells. The gonidia belong to the filamentous alga *Trentepohlia umbrina* and form a comparatively thin layer about 160μ thick near the upper surface; isolated algal branches may grow down to 350 μ into the rock, while the fungal elements descend to 11·5 mm., and though the very lowest hyphae were without oil—as were those immediately beneath the gonidia—the interlying filaments, he found, were crowded with oil-cells. Sphaeroid terminal cells were not present.

Fünfstück[1] has re-examined the thallus of *Petractis exanthematica*, an almost wholly immersed lichen with a gelatinous gonidium, a species of *Scytonema*. The thallus is homoiomerous: the alga forms no special zone, it intermingles with the hyphae down to the very base of the thallus; the hyphae are extremely slender and at the base they measure only about 1μ in width. Oil-cells are abundant in the form of intercalary cells about 3–5μ in thickness. Nearer the surface sphaeroid cells are formed on short lateral outgrowths; they measure 14–16μ in diameter and occur in groups of 15 to 20. The superficial part of the thallus is a mere film; the hyphae composing it are slightly stouter and more thickly interwoven.

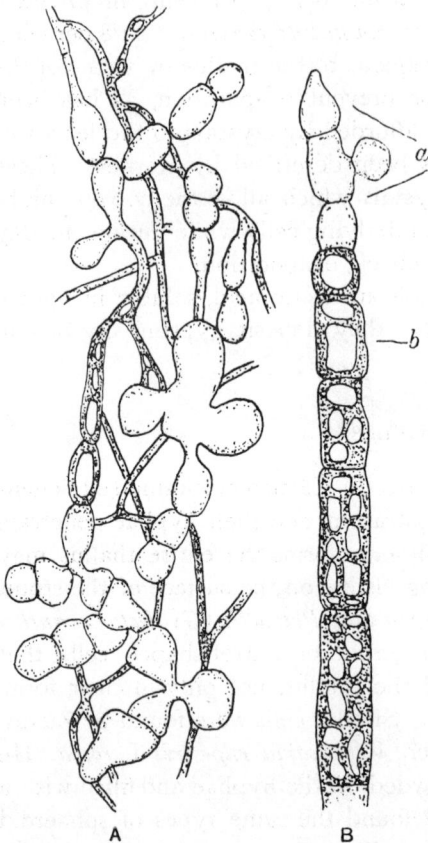

Fig. 117. *Lecidea immersa* Ach. A, sphaeroid fat-cells from about 8 mm. below the surface × 550. B, oil-hyphae in process of emptying: *a*, sphaeroid cells containing oil; *b*, cells with oil-globules × 600 (after Fünfstück).

Bachmann[2] and Lang[3] have further described the anatomy of endolithic thalli especially with reference to oil-cells, and have supplemented the researches of previous workers. New methods of cutting the rock in thin

[1] Fünfstück 1899.   [2] Bachmann 1904[1].   [3] Lang 1906.

slices and of dissolving away the lime enabled them to see the tissues in their relative positions. In these immersed lichens, as described by them and by previous writers, and more especially in calcicolous species, the gonidial zone of Protococcaceous algae lies near the surface of the rock, and is mingled with delicate, thin-walled hyphae which usually do not contain oil. The more deeply immersed layer is formed of a weft of equally thin-walled hyphae, some of the cells of which are swollen and filled with fat globules. These oil-cells may occur at intervals along the hyphae or they may form an almost continuous row. In addition, strands or bundles of hyphae (Fig. 118) containing few or many oil globules traverse the tissue, and true

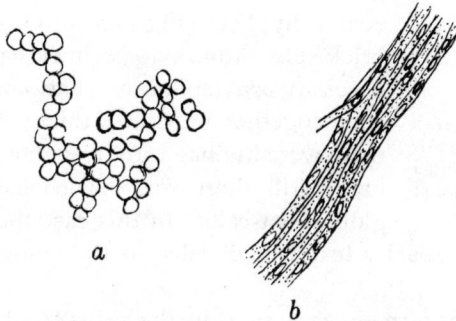

Fig. 118. *Biatorella* (*Sarcogyne*) *simplex* Br. and Rostr.
a, sphaeroid oil-cells; *b*, strand of oil-hyphae from
10–15 mm. below the surface. × 585 (after Lang).

sphaeroid cells are generally present. These latter arise in great numbers on short lateral branchlets, usually near the tip of a filament and the groups of cells are not unlike bunches of grapes. Sometimes the oil-cells are massed together into a complex tissue. Hyphae from this layer pierce still deeper into the rock and constitute the rhizoidal portion of the thallus. They also produce sphaeroid oil-cells in great abundance (Fig. 119). In the immersed

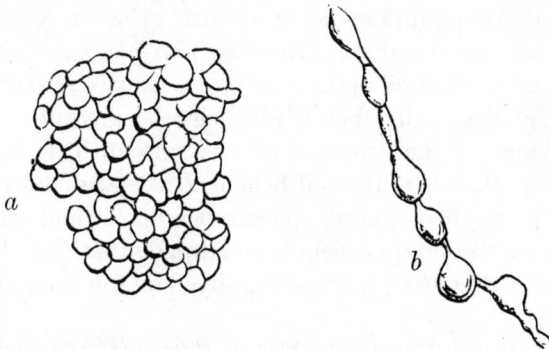

Fig. 119. *Biatorella pruinosa* Mudd. *a*, complex of sphaeroid
oil-cells from 10 mm. below the surface; *b*, hypha of sphaeroid
cells also from inner part of the thallus. × 585 (after Lang).

thallus of *Sarcogyne* (*Biatorella*) *pruinosa* Lang[1] estimated the gonidial zone as $175-200\mu$ in thickness, while the colourless hyphae penetrated the rock to a depth of quite 15 mm.

b. OIL-CELLS OF EPILITHIC LICHENS. The general arrangement of the tissues and the occurrence and form of the oil-cells vary in the different species according to the nature of the substratum. This has been clearly demonstrated by Bachmann[2] in *Aspicilia* (*Lecanora*) *calcarea*, an almost exclusively calcareous lichen as the name implies. On limestone, he found sphaeroid cells formed in great abundance on the deeply penetrating rhizoidal hyphae (Fig. 120). On a non-calcareous brick substratum[3], a specimen had grown which of necessity was epilithic. The cortex and gonidial zone together were 40μ thick; immediately below there were hyphae with irregular cells free from oil; lower still there was formed a compact tissue of globose fat-cells. In this case the calcareous lichen still retained the capacity to form oil-cells on the non-calcareous impenetrable substance.

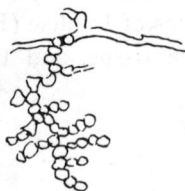

Fig. 120. *Lecanora* (*Aspicilia*) *calcarea* Sommerf. Early stage of sphaeroid cell formation × 175 (after Bachmann).

Very little oil is formed, as a rule, in the cells of siliceous crustaceous lichens which are almost wholly epilithic, but Bachmann found a tissue of oil-cells in the thallus of *Lecanora caesiocinerea*, from Labrador, on a granite composed of quartz, orthoclase and traces of mica. A thallus of the same species collected in the Tyrol, though of a thicker texture, contained no oil. Bachmann[3] suggests no explanation of the variation.

On granite, rhizoidal hyphae penetrate the rock to a slight extent between the different crystals, but only in connection with the mica[4] are typical sphaeroid cells formed.

More or less specialized oil-cells have been demonstrated by Fünfstück[5] in several superficial (epilithic) lichens which grow on a calcareous substratum, as for instance *Lecanora* (*Placodium*) *decipiens*, *Lecanora crassa* and other similar species. The oil in these lichens is usually restricted to more or less swollen or globose cells; but it may also be present in the ordinary hyphae as globules. Zukal[6] found that the smooth little round granules sprinkled over the thallus of the soil-lichens, *Baeomyces roseus* and *B. rufus*, contained in the hyphae typical sphaeroid oil-cells and that they were specially well developed in specimens from Alpine situations. In still another soil-lichen, *Lecidea granulosa*, shimmering green oil was found in short-celled torulose hyphae.

Rosendahl's[7] researches on the brown *Parmeliae* resulted in the unex-

[1] Lang 1906, p. 171.   [2] Bachmann 1892.   [3] Bachmann 1904[1].   [4] Bachmann 1904[2].
[5] Fünfstück 1895.   [6] Zukal 1895, p. 1372.   [7] Rosendahl 1907.

pected discovery of specialized oil-cells situated in the cortices—upper and lower—of five species out of fourteen which he examined. In one of the species, *P. papulosa*, they also occurred in the cortex of the rhizoids. The oil-cells were thinner-walled and larger than the neighbouring cortical cells; they were clavate or ovate in form and sometimes formed irregular external processes. They were more or less completely filled with oil which coloured brown with osmic acid, left a fat stain on paper and, when extracted, burned with a shining reddish flame. These oil-cells were never formed in the medulla nor in the gonidial region.

c. SIGNIFICANCE OF OIL-FORMATION. Zukal[1] regarded the oil stored in these specialized cells as a reserve product of service to the plant in the strain of fruit-formation, or in times of prolonged drought or deprivation of light. According to his observations fat was most freely formed in lichens when periods of luxuriant growth alternated with periods of starvation. He cites, as proof of his view, the frequent presence of empty sphaeroid cells, and the varying production of oil affected by the condition, habitat, etc. of the plant. Fünfstück[2], on the other hand, considers the oil of the sphaeroid and swollen cells as an excretion, representing the waste products of metabolism in the active tissue, but due chiefly to the presence of an excess of carbonic acid which, being set free by the action of the lichen acids on the carbonate of lime, forms the basis of fat-formation. He points out that the development of fat-cells is always greater in endolithic species in which the gonidial layer—the assimilating tissue—is extremely reduced. In epilithic lichens with a wide gonidial zone, the formation of oil is insignificant. He states further that if the oil were a direct product of assimilation, the cells in which it is stored would be found in contact with the gonidia, and that is rarely the case, the maximum of fat production being always at some distance.

Fünfstück tested the correctness of his views by a prolonged series of growth experiments; he removed the gonidial layer in an endolithic lichen, and found that fat storage continued for some time afterwards, its production being apparently independent of assimilative activity. The correctness of his deductions was further proved by observations on lichens from glacier stones. In such unfavourable conditions the gonidia were scanty or absent, having died off, but the hyphae persisted and formed oil. He[3] also placed in the dark two quick-growing calcicolous lichens, *Verrucaria calciseda* and *Opegrapha saxicola*. At the end of the experiment, he found that they had increased in size without using up the fat. Lang[4] also is inclined to reject Zukal's theory, seeing that the fat is formed at a distance from the tissues —reproductive and others—in need of food supply. He agrees with Fünfstück that the oil is an excretion and represents a waste-product of the plant.

[1] Zukal 1895.　　[2] Fünfstück 1896.　　[3] Fünfstück 1899.　　[4] Lang 1906.

Considerable light is thrown on the subject of oil-formation by the results of recent researches on the nutrition of algae and fungi. Beijerinck[1] made comparative cultures of diatoms taken from the soil, and he found that so long as culture conditions were favourable, any fat that might be formed was at once assimilated. If, however, some adverse influence checked the growth of the organism while carbonic acid assimilation was in full vigour, fat was at once accumulated. The adverse influence in this case was the lack of nitrogen, and Beijerinck considers it an almost universal rule in plants and animals, that where there is absence of nitrogen, in a culture otherwise suitable, fat-oils will be massed in those cells which are capable of forming oil. He observed that in two of the cultures of diatoms the one which alone was supplied with nitrogen grew normally, while the other, deprived of nitrogen, formed quantities of oil-drops. Wehmer[2] records the same experience in his cultural study of *Aspergillus*. Sphaeroid fat-cells, similar to those described by Zukal in calcicolous lichens, were formed in the hyphae of a culture containing an overplus of calcium carbonate, and he judged, entirely on morphological grounds, that these were not of the nature of reserve-storage cells.

Stahel[3] has definitely established the same results in cultures of other filamentous fungi. In an artificial culture medium in which nitrogen was almost wholly absent, the cells of the mycelium seemed to be entirely occupied by oil-drops, and this fatty condition he considered to be a symptom of degeneration due to the lack of nitrogen. These experiments enable us to understand how the hyphae of calcicolous lichens, buried deep in the substratum, deprived of nitrogen and overweighted with carbonic acid, may suffer from fatty degeneration as shown by the formation of " sphaeroid-cells." The connection between cause and effect is more obscure in the case of lichens growing on the surface of the soil, such as *Baeomyces roseus*, or of tree lichens such as the brown *Parmeliae*, but the same influence—lack of sufficient nitrogenous food—may be at work in those as well as in the endolithic species, though to a less marked extent.

It seems probable that the capacity to form oil- or fat-cells has become part of the inherited development of certain lichen species and persists through changes of habitat as exemplified in *Lecanora calcarea*[4].

In considering the question of the formation and the function of fat in plant cells, it must be remembered that the service rendered to the life of the organism by this substance is a very variable one. In the higher plants (in seeds, etc.) fat undoubtedly functions in the same way as starch and other carbohydrates as a reserve food. It is evidently not so in lichens, and in one of his early researches, Pfeffer[5] proved that similarly oil was only

---

[1] Beijerinck 1904.   [2] Wehmer 1891.   [3] Stahel 1911.   [4] See p. 218.
[5] Pfeffer 1877.

an excretion in the cells of hepatics. He grew various species in which oil-cells occurred in the dark and then tested the cell contents. He found that after three months of conditions in which the formation of new carbohydrates was excluded, the oil in the cells, instead of having served as reserve material, was entirely unchanged and must in that instance be regarded as an excretion.

D. LICHEN-ACIDS

a. HISTORICAL. The most distinctive and most universal of lichen products are the so-called lichen-acids, peculiar substances found so far only in lichens. They occur in the form of crystals or minute granules deposited in greater or less abundance as excretory bodies on the outer surface of the hyphal cells. Though usually so minute as scarcely to be recognized as crystals, yet in a fairly large series their form can be clearly seen with a high magnification. Many of them are colourless; others are a bright yellow, orange or red, and give the clear pure tone of colour characteristic of some of our most familiar lichens.

The first definite discovery of a lichen-acid was made towards the beginning of the nineteenth century and is due to the researches of C. H. Pfaff[1]. He was engaged in an examination of *Cetraria islandica*, the Iceland Moss, which in his time was held in high repute, not only as a food but as a tonic. He wished to determine the chemical properties of the bitter principle contained in it, which was so much prized by the Medical Faculty of the period, though the bitterness had to be removed to render palatable the nutritious substance of the thallus. He succeeded in isolating an acid which he tested and compared with other organic acids and found that it was a new substance, nearest in chemical properties to succinic acid. In a final note, he states that the new " lichen-acid," as he named it, approached still nearer to boletic acid, a constituent of a fungus, though it was distinct from that substance also in several particulars. The name " cetrarin " was proposed, at a later date, by Herberger[2] who described it as a " subalkaloidal substance, slightly soluble in cold water to which it gives a bitter taste; soluble in hot water, but, on continued boiling, throwing down a brown powder which is slightly soluble in alcohol and readily soluble in ether." Knop and Schnederman[3] found that Herberger's "cetrarin" was a compound substance and contained besides other substances " cetraric acid " and lichesterinic acid. It has now been determined by Hesse[4] as fumarprotocetraric acid ($C_{62}H_{50}O_{35}$), a derivative of which is cetraric acid or triaethylprotocetraric acid with the formula $C_{54}H_{39}O_{24}(OC_2H_5)_3$ and not $C_{20}H_{18}O_9$ as had been supposed. Cetraric acid has not yet been isolated with certainty from any lichen[5].

[1] Pfaff 1826.   [2] Herberger 1830.   [3] Knop and Schnederman 1846.   [4] Hesse 1904.
[5] Zopf 1907, p. 179.

After this first isolation of a definite chemical substance, further research was undertaken, and gradually a number of these peculiar acids were recognized, the lichens examined being chiefly those that were of real or supposed economic value either in medicine or in the arts. In late years a wider chemical study of lichen products has been vigorously carried on, and the results gained have been recently arranged and published in book form by Zopf[1]. Many of the statements on the subject included here are taken from that work. Zopf gives a description of all the acids that had been discovered up to the date of publication, and the methods employed for extracting each substance. The structural formulae, the various affinities, derivatives and properties of the acids, with their crystalline form, are set forth along with a list of the lichens examined and the acids peculiar to each species. In many instances outline figures of the crystals obtained by extraction are given. For a fuller treatment of the subject, the student is referred to the book itself, as only a general account can be attempted here.

b. OCCURRENCE AND EXAMINATION OF LICHEN-ACIDS. Acids have been found, with few exceptions, in all the lichens examined. They are sometimes brightly coloured and are then easily visible under the microscope. Generally their presence can only be determined by reagents. Over 140 different kinds have been recognized and their formulae determined, though many are still imperfectly known. As a rule related lichen species contain the same acids, though in not a few cases one species may contain several different kinds. In growing lichens, they form 1 to 8 per cent. of the dry weight, and as they are practically, while unchanged, insoluble in water, they are not liable to be washed out by rain, snow or floods. Their production seems to depend largely on the presence of oxygen, as they are always found in greatest abundance on the more freely aerated parts of the thallus, such as the soredial hyphae, the outer rind or the loose medullary filaments. They are also often deposited on the exposed disc of the apothecium, on the tips of the paraphyses, and on the wall lining the pycnidia. They are absent from the thallus of the Collemaceae, these being extremely gelatinous lichens in which there can be little contact of the hyphae with the atmosphere. No free acids, so far as is known, are contained in *Sticta fuliginosa*, but a compound substance, trimethylamin, is present in the thallus of that lichen. It has also been affirmed that acids do not occur in any *Peltigera* nor in two species of *Nephromium*, but Zopf[1] has extracted a substance peltigerin both from species of *Peltigera* and from the section *Peltidea*.

For purposes of careful examination freshly gathered lichens are most serviceable, as the acids alter in herbarium or stored specimens. It is well, when possible, to use a fairly large bulk of material, as the acids are often present in small quantities. The lichens should be dried at a temperature

[1] Zopf 1907.

not above 40° C. for fear of changing the character of the contained substances, and they should then be finely powdered. When only a small
quantity of material is available, it has been recommended that reagents
should be applied and the effect watched under the microscope with a low
power magnification. This method is also of great service in determining
the exact position of the acids in the thallus.

In microchemical examination, Senft[1] deprecates the use of chloroform,
ether, etc., seeing that their too rapid evaporation leaves either an amorphous
or crystalline mass of material which does not lend itself to further examination. He recommends as more serviceable some oil solution, preferably
"bone oil" (neat's-foot oil), in which a section of the thallus should be broken
up under a cover-glass and subjected to a process of slow heating; some
days must elapse before the extraction is complete. The surplus oil is then
to be drained off, the section further bruised and the substance examined.

Acids in bulk should be extracted by ether, acetone, chloroform,
benzole, petrol-ether and lignoin or by carbon bisulphide. Such solvents as
alcohols, acetates and alkali solutions should not be used as they tend to
split up or to alter the constitution of the acids. For the same reason, the
use of chloroform is to a certain extent undesirable as it contains a percentage
of alcohol. Ether and acetone, or a mixture of both, are the most efficient
solvents, and all acids can be extracted by their use, if the material is left
to soak a sufficient length of time, either in the cold or warmed. It is
however advisable to follow with a second solvent in case any other acid
should be present in the tissues. Concentrated sulphuric acid dissolves out
all acids but often induces colour changes in the process.

All known lichen-acids form crystals, though the crystalline form may
alter with the solution used. After filtering and distilling, the residue will
be found to contain a mixture of these crystals along with other substances,
which may be removed by washing, etc.

c. CHARACTER OF ACIDS. Many lichen-acids are more or less bitter to
the taste; they are usually of an acid nature though certain of the substances
are neutral, such as zeorin, a constituent of various Lecanoraceae, Physciaceae
and Cladoniaceae, stictaurin, originally obtained from *Sticta aurata*, lei-
phemin, from *Haematomma coccineum*, and others.

A large proportion are esters or alkyl salts formed by the union of an
alcohol and an acid; these are insoluble in alkaline carbonates. It is considered probable that the fungus generates the acid, while the alcohol arises
in the metabolic processes in the alga. It has indeed been proved that the
alcohol, erythrit, is formed in at least two algae, *Protococcus vulgaris* and
Trentepohlia jolithus; and the lichen-acid, erythrin ($C_{20}H_{22}O_{10}$), obtained
from species of *Roccella* in which the alga is *Trentepohlia*, is, according to

[1] Senft 1907.

Hesse, the erythrit ester of lecanoric acid ($C_{16} H_{14} O_7$), a very frequent constituent of lichen thalli. It is certain that the interaction of both symbionts is necessary for acid production. This was strikingly demonstrated by Tobler[1] in his cultural study of the lichen thallus. He succeeded in growing, to a limited extent, the hyphal part of the thallus of *Xanthoria parietina* on artificial media; but the filaments remained persistently colourless until he added green algal cells to the culture. Almost immediately thereafter the characteristic yellow colour appeared, proving the presence of parietin, formerly known as chrysophanic acid. Tobler's observation may easily be verified in plants from natural habitats. A depauperate form of *Placodium citrinum* consisting mainly of a hypothallus of felted hyphae, with minute scattered granules containing algae, was tested with potash, and only the hyphae immediately covering the algal granules took the stain; the hypothallus gave no reaction.

It has been suggested[2] that when a decrease of albumenoids takes place, the quantity of lichen-acid increases, so that the excreted substance should be regarded as a sort of waste product of the living plant, "rather than as a product of deassimilation." The subject is not yet wholly understood.

d. Causes of Variation in Quantity and Quality of Lichen-Acids. Though it has been proved that lichen-acids are formed freely all the year round on any soil or in any region, it happens occasionally that they are almost or entirely lacking in growing plants. Schwarz[3] found this to be the case in certain plants of *Lecanora tartarea*, and he suggests that the gyrophoric acid contained in the outer cortex of that lichen had been broken up by the ammonia of the atmosphere into carbonic acid and orcin which is soluble in water, and would thus be washed away by rain. It has also been shown by Schwendener[4] and others that the outer layers of the older thallus in many lichens slowly perish, first breaking up and then peeling off; the denuded areas would therefore have lost, for some time at least, their particular acids. Fünfstück[5] considers that the difference in the presence and amount of acid in the same species of lichen may be due very often to variation in the chemical character of the substratum, and this view tallies with the results noted by Heber Howe[6] in his study of American *Ramalinae.* He observed that, though all showed a pale-yellow reaction with potash, those growing on mineral substrata gave a more pronouncedly yellow colour.

M. C. Knowles[7] found that in *Ramalina scopulorum* the colour reaction to potash varied extremely, being more rapid and more intense, the more the plants were subject to the influence of the sea-spray.

Lichen-acids are peculiarly abundant in soredia, and as, in some species,

---

[1] Tobler 1909.   [2] Keegan 1907.   [3] Schwarz 1880, p. 264.   [4] Schwendener 1863, p. 180.
[5] Fünfstück 1902.   [6] Heber Howe 1913.   [7] Knowles 1913.

the thallus forms these outgrowths, or even becomes leprose more freely in damp weather, the amount of acids produced may depend on the amount of moisture in the atmosphere.

Their formation is also strongly influenced by light, as is well shown by the varying intensity of colour in some yellow thalli. *Placodium elegans*, always a brightly coloured lichen, changes from yellow to sealing-wax red in situations exposed to the full blaze of the sun. *Haematomma ventosum*, though greenish-yellow in lowland situations is intensely yellow in the high Alps. The same variation of colour is characteristic of *Rhizocarpon geographicum* which is a bright citron-yellow at high altitudes, and becomes more greenish in hue as it nears the plains. The familiar foliose lichen *Xanthoria parietina* is a brilliant orange-yellow in sunny situations, but grey-green in the shade, and then yielding only minute quantities of parietin. West[1] and others have noted its more luxuriant growth and brighter colour when it grows in positions where nitrogenous food is plentiful, such as the roofs of farm-buildings, which are supplied with manure-laden dust, and boulders by the sea-shore frequented by birds.

e. DISTRIBUTION OF ACIDS. Some acids, so far as is known, are only to be found in one or at most in very few lichens, as for instance cuspidatic acid which is present in *Ramalina cuspidata*, and scopuloric acid, a constituent of *Ramalina scopulorum*, the acids having been held to distinguish by their reactions the one plant from the other.

Others of these peculiar products are abundant and widely distributed. Usninic acid, one of the commonest, has been determined in some 70 species belonging to widely diverse genera, and atranorin, a substance first discovered in *Lecanora atra*, has been found again many times; Zopf gives a list of about 73 species or varieties from which it has been extracted. Another widely distributed acid is salazinic acid which has been found by Lettau[2] in a very large number of lichens.

E. CHEMICAL GROUPING OF LICHEN-ACIDS

Most of these acids have been provisionally arranged by Zopf in groups under the two great organic series: I. The Fat series; and II. The Benzole or Aromatic series.

I. LICHEN-ACIDS OF THE FAT SERIES

Group 1. Colourless substances soluble in alkali, the solution not coloured by iron chloride. *Exs.* protolichesterinic acid $(C_{19}H_{34}O_4)$ obtained from species of *Cetraria*, and roccellic acid $(C_{17}H_{32}O_4)$ from species of *Roccella*, from *Lecanora tartarea*, etc.

[1] West, W. 1905.   [2] Lettau 1914.

Group 2. Neutral colourless substances insoluble in alkalies, but soluble in alcohol, the solution not coloured by iron chloride. *Exs.* zeorin ($C_{52}H_{88}O_4$), a product of widely diverse lichens, such as *Lecanora* (*Zeora*) *sulphurea, Haematomma coccineum, Physcia caesia, Cladonia deformis,* etc. and barbatin ($C_9H_{14}O$), a product of *Usnea barbata.*

Group 3. Brightly coloured acids, yellow, orange or red, all derivatives of pulvinic acid ($C_{18}H_{12}O_5$), a laboratory compound which has not been found in nature. The group includes among others vulpinic acid ($C_{19}H_{14}O_5$) from the brilliant yellow *Evernia* (*Letharia*) *vulpina,* stictaurin ($C_{36}H_{22}O_9$) deposited in orange-red crystals on the hyphae of *Sticta aurata,* and rhizocarpic acid ($C_{26}H_{20}O_6$) chiefly obtained from *Rhizocarpon geographicum*: it crystallizes out in slender citron-yellow prisms.

Group 4. Only one acid, usninic ($C_{18}H_{16}O_7$), a derivative of acetylacetic acid, is placed in this group. It is of very wide-spread occurrence, having been found in at least 70 species belonging to very different genera and families of crustaceous shrubby and leafy lichens. Zopf himself isolated it from 48 species.

Group 5. The thiophaninic acid ($C_{12}H_6O_9$) group representing only a small number. They are all sulphur-yellow in colour and soluble in alcohol, the solution becoming blackish-green or dirty blue on the addition of iron chloride, with one exception, that of subauriferin obtained from the yellow-coloured medulla of *Parmelia subaurifera* which stains faintly wine-red in an iron solution. Thiophaninic acid, which gives its name to this group, occurs in *Pertusaria lutescens* and *P. Wulfenii,* both of which are yellowish crustaceous lichens growing mostly on the trunks of trees.

II. LICHEN-ACIDS OF THE BENZOLE SERIES

The larger number of lichen-acids belong to this series, of which 94 at least are already known. They are divided into two subseries: I. Orcine derivatives, and II. Anthracene derivatives.

SUBSERIES I. ORCINE DERIVATIVES

Zopf specially insists that the grouping of this series must be regarded as only a provisional arrangement of the many lichen-acids that are included therein. All of them are split up into orcine and carbonic acid by ammonia and other alkalies. On exposure to air, the ammoniacal or alkaline solution changes gradually into orceine, the colouring principle and chief constituent of commercial orchil. Orcine is not found free in nature. The orcine sub-series includes five groups:

Group 1. The substances in this group form, with hypochlorite of lime ("CaCl"), red-coloured compounds which yield, on splitting, orsellinic acid. Zopf enumerates seven acids as belonging to this group, among which is lecanoric acid ($C_{16}H_{14}O_7$), found in many different lichens, *e.g. Roccella tinctoria, Lecanora tartarea*, etc.: whenever there is a differentiated pith and cortex it occurs in the pith alone. Erythrin ($C_{20}H_{22}O_{10}$), a constituent of the British marine lichen *Roccella fuciformis*, also belongs to this orsellinic group.

Group 2. Substances which also form red products with CaCl, but do not break up into orsellinic acid. Among the most noteworthy are olivetoric acid ($C_{21}H_{26}O_7$), a constituent of *Evernia furfuracea*, perlatic acid ($C_{28}H_{30}O_{10}$) and glabratic acid ($C_{24}H_{26}O_{11}$), which are obtained from species of *Parmelia*.

Group 3. Contains three acids of somewhat restricted occurrence. They do not form red products with CaCl, and they yield on splitting everninic acid. They are: evernic acid ($C_{17}H_{16}O_7$), found in *Evernia prunastri* var. *vulgaris*, ramalic acid ($C_{17}H_{16}O_7$) in *Ramalina pollinaria*, and umbilicaric acid ($C_{25}H_{22}O_{11}$) in species of *Gyrophora*.

Group 4. The numerous acids of this group are not easily soluble and have a very bitter taste. They are not coloured by CaCl; when extracted with concentrated sulphuric acid, the solution obtained is reddish-yellow or deep red. Among the most frequent are fumarprotocetraric acid ($C_{62}H_{50}O_{35}$), the bitter principle of *Cetraria islandica, Cladonia rangiferina*, etc., psoromic acid ($C_{20}H_{14}O_9$), obtained from *Alectoria implexa, Lecanora varia, Cladonia pyxidata* and many other lichens, and salazinic acid ($C_{19}H_{14}O_{10}$), recorded by Zopf as occurring in *Stereocaulon salazinum* and in several *Parmeliae*, but now found by Lettau[1] to be very wide-spread. He used micro-chemical methods and detected its presence in 72 species from twelve different families. The distribution of the acid in the thallus varies considerably.

Group 5. This is called the atranorin group from one of the most important members. They are colourless substances and, like the preceding group, are not affected by CaCl, but when split they form bodies that colour a more or less deep red with that reagent. Atranorin ($C_{19}H_{18}O_8$) is one of the most widely spread of all lichen-acids; it occurs in Lecanoraceae, Parmeliaceae, Physciaceae and Lecideaceae. Barbatinic acid ($C_{19}H_{20}O_7$), another member, is found in *Usnea ceratina, Alectoria ochroleuca* and in a variety of *Rhizocarpon geographicum*. A very large number of acids more or less fully studied belong to this group.

SUBSERIES II. ANTHRACENE DERIVATIVES

The constituents of this subseries are derived from the carbohydrate anthracene, and are characterized by their brilliant colours, yellow, red, brown, red-brown or violet-brown. So far, only ten different kinds have been isolated and studied. Parietin[2] ($C_{16}H_{12}O_5$), one of the best known, has been extracted from *Xanthoria parietina, Placodium murorum* and several other bright-yellow

[1] Lettau 1914.

[2] Parietin differs chemically from chrysophanic acid of *Rheum*, etc.

lichens; solorinic acid ($C_{15}H_{14}O_5$) occurs in orange-red crystals on the hyphae of the pith and under surface of *Solorina crocea*; nephromin ($C_{16}H_{12}O_6$) is found in the yellow medulla of *Nephromium lusitanicum*; rhodocladonic acid ($C_{12}H_8O_6$ or $C_{14}H_{10}O_7$) is the red substance in the apothecia of the red-fruited *Cladoniae*.

There are, in addition, a short series of coloured substances which are of uncertain position. They are imperfectly known and are of rare occurrence. An acid containing nitrogen has been extracted from *Roccella fuciformis*, and named picroroccellin[1] ($C_{27}H_{29}N_3O_5$). It crystallizes in comparatively large prisms, has an exceedingly bitter taste, and is very sparingly soluble. It is the only lichen-acid in which nitrogen has been detected.

One acid at least, belonging to the Fat series, vulpinic acid, which gives the greenish-yellow colour to *Letharia vulpina*, has been prepared synthetically by Volkard[2].

F. CHEMICAL REAGENTS AS TESTS FOR LICHENS

The employment of chemical reagents as colour tests in the determination of lichen species was recommended by Nylander[3] in a paper published by him in 1866. Many acids had already been extracted and examined, and as they were proved to be constant in the different species where they occurred, he perceived their systematic importance. As an example of the new tests, he cited the use of hypochlorite of lime, a solution of which, applied directly to the thallus of species of *Roccella*, produced a bright-red "erythrinic" reaction. Caustic potash was also found to be of service in demonstrating the presence of parietin in lichens by a beautiful purple stain. Many lichenologists eagerly adopted the new method, as a sure and ready means of distinguishing doubtful species; but others have rejected the tests as unnecessary and not always to be relied on, seeing that the acids are not always produced in sufficient abundance to give the desired reaction, and that they tend to alter in time.

The reagents most commonly in use are caustic potash, generally indicated by K; hypochlorite of calcium or bleaching powder by CaCl; and a solution of iodine by I. The sign + signifies a colour reaction, while − indicates that no change has followed the application of the test solution. Double signs ‡ or any similar variation indicate the upper or lower parts of the thallus affected by the reagent. In some instances the reaction only follows after the employment of two reagents represented thus: K (CaCl) +. In such a case the potash breaks up the particular acid and compounds are formed which become red, orange, etc., on the subsequent application of hypochlorite of lime.

---

[1] Stenhouse and Groves 1877. [2] Volkard 1804. [3] Nylander 1866.

As an instance of the value of chemical tests, Zopf cites the reaction of hypochlorite of lime on the thallus of four different species of *Gyrophora*, the "tripe de roche":—

Gyrophora torrefacta CaCl ⊤.
        „   polyrhiza CaCl ‡.
        „   proboscidea CaCl ±.
        „   erosa CaCl ⁻.

It must however be borne in mind that these species are well differentiated and can be recognized, without difficulty, by their morphological characters. Experienced systematists like Weddell refuse to accept the tests unless they are supported by true morphological distinctions, as the reactions are not sufficiently constant.

G. Chemical Reactions in Nature

Similar colour changes may often be observed in nature. The acids of the exposed thallus cortex are not unfrequently split up by the gradual action of the ammonia in the atmosphere, one of the compounds thus set free being at the same time coloured by the alkali. Thus salazinic acid, a constituent of several of our native *Parmeliae*, is broken up into carbonic acid and salazininic acid, the latter taking a red colour. Fumarprotocetraric acid is acted on somewhat similarly, and the red colour may be seen in *Cetraria* at the base of the thallus where contact with soil containing ammonia has affected the outer cortex of the plant. The same results are produced still more effectively when the lichen comes into contact with animal excrement.

Gummy exudations from trees which are more or less ammoniacal may also act on the thallus and form red-coloured products on contact with the acids present. *Lecanora* (*Aspicilia*) *cinerea* is so easily affected by alkalies that a thin section left exposed may become red in time owing to the ammonia in the atmosphere.

II. GENERAL NUTRITION

A. Absorption of Water

Lichens are capable of enduring almost complete desiccation, but though they can exist with little injury through long periods of drought, water is essential to active metabolism. They possess no special organs for water conduction, but absorb moisture over their whole surface. Several inter-dependent factors must therefore be taken into account in considering the question of absorption: the type of thallus, whether gelatinous or non-gelatinous, crustaceous, foliose or fruticose, as also the nature of the substratum and the prevailing condition of the atmosphere.

a. Gelatinous Lichens. The algal constituent of these lichens is some member of the Myxophyceae and is provided with thick gelatinous walls which have great power of imbibition and swell up enormously in damp surroundings, becoming reservoirs of water. Species of *Collema*, for instance, when thoroughly wet, weigh thirty-five times more than when dry[1]. There are no interstices in the thallus and frequently no cortex in these lichens, but the gelatinous substance itself forms on drying an outer skin that checks evaporation so that water is retained within the thallus for a longer period than in non-gelatinous forms. They probably always retain some amount of moisture, as they share with gelatinous algae the power of revival after long desiccation.

Gelatinous lichens are entirely dependent on a surface supply of water: their hyphae—or rhizinae when present—rarely penetrate the substratum.

b. Crustaceous non-gelatinous Lichens. The lichens with this type of thallus are in intimate contact with the substratum whether it be soil, rock, tree or dead wood. The hyphae on the under surface of the thallus function primarily as hold-fasts, but if water be retained in the substratum, the lichen will undoubtedly benefit, and water, to some extent, will be absorbed by the walls of the hyphae or will be drawn up by capillary attraction. In any case, it could only be surface water that would be available, as lichens have no means of tapping any deeper sources of supply.

Lichens are, however, largely independent of the substratum for their supply of water. Sievers[2], who gave attention to the subject, found that though some few crustaceous lichens took up water from below, most of them absorbed the necessary moisture on the surface or at the edges of the thallus or areolae, where the tissue is looser and more permeable. The swollen gelatinous walls of the hyphae forming the upper layers of such lichens are admirably adapted for the reception and storage of water, though, according to Zukal[3], less hygroscopic generally than in the larger forms. Beckmann[4] proved this power of absorption, possessed by the upper cortex, by placing a crustaceous lichen, *Haematomma* sp., in a damp chamber: he found after a while that water had been taken up by the cortex and by the gonidial zone, while the lower medullary hyphae had remained dry.

Herre[5] has recorded an astonishing abundance of lichens from the desert of Reno, Nevada, and these are mostly crustaceous forms, belonging to a limited number of species. The yearly rainfall of the region is only about eight or ten inches, and occurs during the winter months, chiefly as snow. It is during that period that active vegetation goes on; but the plants still manage to exist during the long arid summer, when their only possible water supply is that obtained from the moisture of the atmosphere during the night, or from the surface deposit of dews.

[1] Jumelle 1892.   [2] Sievers 1908.   [3] Zukal 1895.   [4] Beckmann 1907.   [5] Herre 1911[2].

c. FOLIOSE LICHENS. Though many of the leafy lichens are provided with a tomentum of single hyphae, or with rhizinae on the under surface, the principal function of these structures is that of attaching the thallus. Sievers[1] tested the areas of absorption by placing pieces of the thallus of *Parmeliae*, of *Evernia furfuracea*, and of *Cetraria glauca* in a staining solution. After washing and cutting sections, it was seen that the coloured fluid had penetrated by the upper surface and by the edge of the thallus, as in crustaceous forms, but not through the lower cortex.

By the same methods of testing, he proved that water penetrates not only by capillarity between the closely packed hyphae, but also within the cells. A considerable number of lichens were used for experiment, and great variations were found to exist in the way in which water was taken up. It has been proved that in some species of *Gyrophora* water is absorbed from below: in those in which rhizinae are abundant, water is held by them and so gradually drawn up into the thallus; the upper cortex in this genus is very thick and checks transpiration. Certain other northern lichens such as *Cetraria islandica*, *Cladonia rangiferina*, etc., imbibe water very slowly, and they, as well as *Gyrophora*, are able to endure prolonged wet periods.

That foliose lichens do not normally contain much water was proved by Jumelle[2] who compared the weight of seven different species when freshly gathered, and after being dried; he found that the proportion of fresh weight to dry weight showed least variation in *Parmelia acetabulum*, as 1·14 to 1; in *Xanthoria parietina* it was as 1·21 to 1.

d. FRUTICOSE LICHENS. There is no water-conducting tissue in the elongate thallus of the shrubby or filamentous lichens, as can easily be tested by placing the base in water: it will then be seen that the submerged parts alone are affected. Many lichens are hygroscopic and become water-logged when placed simply in damp surroundings. The thrallus of *Usnea*, for instance, can absorb many times its weight of water: a mass of *Usnea* filaments that weighed 3·8 grms. when dry increased to 13·3 grms. after having been soaked in water for twelve hours. Schrenk[3], who made the experiment, records in a second instance an increase in weight from 3·97 grms. to 11·18 grms. The *Cladoniae* retain large quantities of water in their upright hollow podetia. The Australian species, *Cladonia retepora*, the podetium of which is a regular network of holes, competes with the *Sphagnum* moss in its capacity to take up water.

To conclude: as a rule, heteromerous, non-gelatinous lichens do not contain large quantities of water, the weight of fresh plants being generally about three times only that of the dry weight. Their ordinary water content is indeed smaller than that of most other plants, though it varies at once with a change in external conditions. It is noteworthy that a number of

---

[1] Sievers 1908.   [2] Jumelle 1892.   [3] Schrenk 1898.

lichens have their habitat on the sea-shore, constantly subject to spray from the waves, but scarcely any can exist within the spray of a waterfall, possibly because the latter is never-ceasing.

B. Storage of Water

The gonidial algae *Gloeocapsa*, *Scytonema*, *Nostoc*, etc. among Myxophyceae, *Palmella* and occasionally *Trentepohlia* among Chlorophyceae, have more or less gelatinous walls which act as a natural reservoir of water for the lichens with which they are associated. In these lichens the hyphae for the most part have thin walls, and the plectenchyma when formed—as below the apothecium in *Collema granuliferum*, or as a cortical layer in *Leptogium*—is a thin-walled tissue. In lichens where, on the contrary, the alga is non-gelatinous—as generally in Chlorophyceae—or where the gelatinous sheath is not formed as in the altered *Nostoc* of the *Peltigera* thallus, the fungal hyphae have swollen gelatinous walls both in the pith and the cortex, and not only imbibe but store up water.

Bonnier[1] had his attention directed to this thickening of the cell-walls as he followed the development of the lichen thallus. He made cultures from the ascospore of *Physcia* (*Xanthoria*) *parietina* and obtained a fair amount of hyphal tissue, the cell-walls of which became thickened, but more slowly and to a much less extent than when associated with the gonidia.

He noted also that when his cultures were kept in a continuously moist atmosphere there was much less thickening, scarcely more than in fungi ordinarily; it was only when they were grown under drier conditions with necessity for storage, that any considerable swelling of the walls took place. Further he found that the thallus of forms cultivated in an abundance of moisture could not resist desiccation as could those with the thicker membranes. These latter survived drying up and resumed activity when moisture was supplied.

C. Supply of Inorganic Food

As in the higher plants, mineral substances can only be taken up when they are in a state of solution. Lichens are therefore dependent on the substances that are contained in the water of absorption : they must receive their inorganic nutriment by the same channels that water is conveyed to them.

a. Foliose and Fruticose Lichens. These larger lichens are provided with rhizinae or with hold-fasts, which are only absorptive to a very limited extent; the main source of water supply is from the atmosphere and the salts required in the metabolism of the cell must be obtained there also—

---

[1] Bonnier 1889[2].

from atmospheric dust dissolved in rain, or from wind-borne particles deposited on the surface of the thallus which may be gradually dissolved and absorbed by the cortical and growing hyphae. That substances received from the atmospheric environment may be all important is shown by the exclusive habitat of some marine lichens; the *Roccellae*, *Lichinae*, some species of *Ramalina* and others which grow only on rocky shores are almost as dependent on sea-water as are the submerged algae. Other lichens, such as *Hydrothyria venosa* and *Lecanora lacustris*, grow in streams, or on boulders that are subject to constant inundation, and they obtain their inorganic food mainly, if not entirely, from an aqueous medium.

Though lichens cannot live in an atmosphere polluted by smoke, they thrive on trees and walls by the road-side where they are liable to be almost smothered by soil-dust. West[1] has observed that they flourish in valleys that are swept by moisture laden winds more especially if near to a highway, where animal excreta are mingled with the dust. The favourite habitats of *Xanthoria parietina* are the walls and roofs of farm-buildings where the dust must contain a large percentage of nitrogenous material; or stones by the sea-shore that are the haunts of sea-birds. Sandstede[2] found on the island of Rügen that while the perpendicular faces of the cliffs were quite bare, the tops bore a plentiful crop of *Lecanora saxicola*, *Xanthoria lychnea* and *Candellariella vitellina*. He attributed their selection of habitat to the presence of the excreta of sea-birds. As already stated the connection of foliose and fruticose lichens with the substratum is mainly mechanical but occasionally a kind of semiparasitism may arise. Friedrich[3] gives an instance in a species of *Usnea* of unusually vigorous development. It grew on bark and the strands of hyphae, branching from the root-base of the lichen, had reached down to the living tissue of the tree-trunk and had penetrated between the cells by dissolving the middle lamella. It was possible to find holes pierced in the cell-walls of the host, but it was difficult to decide if the hyphae had attacked living cells or were merely preying on dead material. Lindau[4] held very strongly that lichen hyphae were non-parasitic, and merely split apart the tissues already dead, and the instance recorded by Friedrich is of rare occurrence[5].

That the substratum does have some indirect influence on these larger lichens has been proved once and again. Uloth[6], a chemist as well as a botanist, made analyses of plants of *Evernia prunastri* taken from birch bark and from sandstone. Qualitatively the composition of the lichen substances was the same, but the quantities varied considerably. Zopf[7] has, more recently, compared the acid content of a form of *Evernia furfuracea* on rock with that of the same species growing on the bark of a tree. In the case of

[1] West 1905.   [2] Sandstede 1904.   [3] Friedrich 1906.   [4] Lindau 1895².
[5] See p. 109.   [6] Uloth 1861.   [7] Zopf 1903.

the latter, the thallus produced 4 per cent. of physodic acid and 2·2 per cent. of atranorin. In the rock specimen, which, he adds, was a more graceful plant than the other, the quantities were 6 per cent. of physodic acid, and 2 75 per cent. of atranorin. In both cases there was a slight formation of furfuracinnic acid. He found also that specimens of *Evernia prunastri* on dead wood contained 8·4 per cent. of lichen-acids, while in those from living trees there was only 4·4 per cent. or even less. Other conditions, however, might have contributed to this result, as Zopf[1] found later that this lichen when very sorediate yielded an increased supply of atranoric acid.

Ohlert[2], who made a study of lichens in relation to their habitat, found that though a certain number grew more or less freely on either tree, rock or soil, none of them was entirely unaffected. *Usnea barbata, Evernia prunastri* and *Parmelia physodes* were the most indifferent to habitat; normally they are corticolous species, but *Usnea* on soil formed more slender filaments, and *Evernia* on the same substratum showed a tendency to horizontal growth, and became attached at various points instead of by the usual single base.

b. CRUSTACEOUS LICHENS. The crustaceous forms on rocks are in a more favourable position for obtaining inorganic salts, the lower medullary hyphae being in direct contact with mineral substances and able to act directly on them. Many species are largely or even exclusively calcicolous, and there must be something in the lime that is especially conducive to their growth. The hyphae have been traced into the limestone to a depth of 15 mm.[3] and small depressions are frequently scooped out of the rock by the action of the lichen, thus giving a lodgement to the foveolate fruit.

On rocks mainly composed of silica, the lichen has a much harder substance to deal with, and one less easily affected by acids, though even silica may be dissolved in time. Uloth[4] concluded from his observations that the relation of plants to the substratum was chemical even more than physical, so far as crustaceous species were concerned. He found that the surface of the area of rock inhabited was distinctly marked: even such a hard substance as chalcedony was corroded by a very luxuriant lichen flora, the border of growth being quite clearly outlined. The corrosive action is due he considered to the carbon dioxide liberated by the plant, though oxalic acid, so frequent a constituent of lichens, may also share in the corrosion. Egeling[5] made similar observations in regard to the effect of lichen growth on granite rocks; and he further noticed that pieces of glass, over which lichens had spread, had become clouded, the dulness of the surface being due to a multitude of small cracks eaten out by the hyphae. Buchet[6] also gives an instance of glass which had been corroded by the action of lichen hyphae. It formed

---

[1] Zopf 1907.   [2] Ohlert 1871.   [3] See p. 75.   [4] Uloth 1861.
[5] Egeling 1881.   [6] Buchet 1890.

part of an old stained window in a chapel that was obscured by a lichen growth which adhered tenaciously. When the window was taken down and cleaned, it was found that the surface of the glass was covered with small, more or less hemispherical pits which were often confluent. The different colours in the picture were unequally attacked, some of the figures or draperies being covered with the minute excavations, while other parts were intact. It happened also, occasionally, that a colour while slightly corroded in one pane would be uninjured in another, but the suggestion is made that there might in that case have been a difference in the length of attack by the lichen. The selection of colours by the lichens might also be influenced by some chemical or physical characters.

Bachmann[1] found that on granite there is equally a selection of material by the hyphae: as a rule they avoid the acid silica constituents, while they penetrate and traverse the grains of mica which are dissolved by them exactly as are lime granules.

On another rock consisting mainly of muscovite and quartz he[2] found that crystals of garnet embedded in the rock were reduced to a powder by the action of the lichen. He concludes that the destroying action of the hyphae is accelerated by the presence of carbon dioxide given off by the lichen, and dissolved in the surrounding moisture. Lang[3] and Stahlecker[4] have both come to the conclusion that even the quartz grains are corroded by the lichen hyphae. Stahlecker finds that they change the quartz into amorphous silicic acid, and thus bring it into the cycle of organic life. Chalk and magnesia are extracted from the silicates where no other plant could procure them. Lichens are generally rare on pure quartz rocks, chiefly, however, for the mechanical reason that the structure is of too close a grain to afford a foothold.

D. Supply of Organic Food

a. From the Substratum. The Ascomycetous fungi, from which so many of the lichens are descended, are mainly saprophytes, obtaining their carbohydrates from dead plant material, and lichen hyphae have in some instances undoubtedly retained their saprophytic capacity. It has been proved that lichen hyphae, which naturally could not exist without the algal symbiont, may be artificially cultivated on nutrient media without the presence of gonidia, though the chief and often the only source of carbon supply is normally through the alga with which the hyphae are associated in symbiotic union.

A large number of crustaceous lichens grow on the bark of trees, and their hyphae burrow among the dead cells of the outer bark using up the

---

[1] Bachmann 1904.   [2] Bachmann 1911.   [3] Lang 1903.   [4] Stahlecker 1906.

material with which they come in contact. Others live on dead wood, palings, etc. where the supply of disintegrated organic substance is even greater; or they spread over withered mosses and soil rich in humus.

b. FROM OTHER LICHENS. Bitter[1] has recorded several instances observed by him of lichens growing over other lichens and using up their substance as food material. Some lichens are naturally more vigorous than others, and the weaker or more slow growing succumb when an encounter takes place. *Pertusaria globulifera* is one of these marauding species; its habitat is among mosses on the bark of trees, and, being a quick grower, it easily overspreads its more sluggish neighbours. It can scarcely be considered a parasite, as the thallus of the victim is first killed, probably by the action of an enzyme.

Lecanora subfusca and allied species which have a thin thallus are frequently overgrown by this *Pertusaria* and a dark line generally precedes the invading lichen; the hyphae and the gonidia of the *Lecanorae* are first killed and changed to a brown structureless mass which is then split up by the advancing hyphae of the *Pertusaria* into small portions. A little way back from the edge of the predatory thallus the dead particles are no longer visible, having been dissolved and completely used up. *Pertusaria amara* also may overgrow *Lecanorae*, though, generally, its onward course is checked and deflected towards a lateral direction; if however it is in a young and vigorous condition, it attacks the thallus in its path, and ahead of it appears the rather broad blackish line marking the fatal effect of the enzyme, the rest of the host thallus being unaffected. Neither *Pertusaria* seems to profit much, and does not grow either faster or thicker; the thallus appears indeed to be hindered rather than helped by the encounter. *Biatora* (*Lecidea*) *quernea* with a looser, more furfuraceous thallus is also killed and dissolved by *Pertusariae*; but if the *Biatora* is growing near to a withering or dead lichen it, also, profits by the food material at hand, grows over it and uses it up. Bitter has also observed lichens overgrown by *Haematomma* sp.; the growth of that lichen is indeed so rapid that few others can withstand its approach.

Another common rock species, *Lecanora sordida* (*L. glaucoma*), has a vigorous thallus that easily ousts its neighbours. *Rhizocarpon geographicum*, a slow-growing species, is especially liable to be attacked; from the thallus of *L. sordida* the hyphae in strands push directly into the other lichen in a horizontal direction and split up the tissues, the algae persist unharmed for some time, but eventually they succumb and are used up; the apothecia, though more resistant than the thallus, are also gradually undermined and hoisted up by the new growth, till finally no trace of the original lichen is left. *Lecanora sordida* is however in turn invaded by *Lecidea insularis* (*L. intumescens*) which is found forming small orbicular areas on the

[1] Bitter 1899.

Lecanora thallus. It kills its host in patches and the dead material mostly drifts away. On any strands that are left *Candellariella vitellina* generally settles and evidently profits by the dead nutriment. It does not spread to the living thallus. *Lecanora polytropa* also forms colonies on these vacant patches, with advantage to its growth.

Even the larger lichens are attacked by these quick-growing crusts. *Pertusaria globulifera* spreads over *Parmelia perlata* and *P. physodes*, gradually dissolving and consuming the different thalline layers; the lower cortex of the victim holds out longest and can be seen as an undigested black substance within the *Pertusaria* thallus for some time. As a rule, however, the lichens with large lobes grow over the smaller thalli in a purely mechanical fashion.

c. FROM OTHER VEGETATION. Zukal[1] has given instances of association between mosses and lichens in which the latter seemed to play the part of parasite. The terricolous species *Baeomyces rufus* (*Sphyridium*) and *Biatora decolorans*, as well as forms of *Lepraria* and *Variolaria*, he found growing over mosses and killing them. Stems and leaves of the moss *Plagiothecium sylvaticum* were grown through and through by the hyphae of a *Pertusaria*, and he observed a leaf of *Polytrichum commune* pierced by the rhizinae of a minute *Cladonia* squamule. The cells had been invaded and the neighbouring tissue was brown and dead.

Perhaps the most voracious consumer of organic remains is *Lecanora tartarea*, more especially the northern form *frigida*. It is the well-known cud-bear lichen of West Scotland, and is normally a rock species. It has an extremely vigorous thickly crustaceous and quick-growing thallus, and spreads over everything that lies in its path—decaying mosses, dead leaves, other lichens, etc. Kihlman[2] has furnished a graphic description of the way it covers up the vegetation on the high altitudes of Russian Lapland. More than any other plant it is able to withstand the effect of the cold winds that sweep across these inhospitable plains. Other plant groups at certain seasons or in certain stages of growth are weakened or killed by the extreme cold of the wind, and, immediately, a growth of the more hardy grey crust of *Lecanora tartarea* begins to spread over and take possession of the area affected—very frequently a bank of mosses, of which the tips have been destroyed, is thus covered up. In the same way the moorland *Cladoniae*, *C. rangiferina* (the reindeer moss) and some allied species, are attacked. They have no continuous cortex, the outer covering of the long branching podetia being a loose felt of hyphae; they are thus sensitive to cold and liable to be destroyed by a high wind, and their stems, which are blackened as decay advances, become very soon dotted with the whitish-grey crust of the more vigorous and resistant *Lecanora*.

[1] Zukal 1879.   [2] Kihlman 1890.

III. ASSIMILATION AND RESPIRATION

A. Influence of Temperature

a. High Temperature. It has been proved that plants without chlorophyll are less affected by great heat than those that contain chlorophyll. Lichens in which both types are present are more capable of enduring high temperatures than the higher plants, but with undue heat the alga succumbs first. In consequence, respiration, by the fungus alone, can go on after assimilation (photosynthesis) and respiration in the alga have ceased.

Most Phanerogams cease assimilation and respiration after being subjected for ten minutes to a temperature of 50° C. Jumelle[1] made a series of experiments with lichens, chiefly of the larger fruticose or foliaceous types, with species of *Ramalina, Physcia* and *Parmelia,* also with *Evernia prunastri* and *Cladonia rangiferina.* He found that as regards respiration, plants which had been kept for three days at 45° C., fifteen hours at 50°, then five hours at 60°, showed an intensity of respiration almost equal to untreated specimens, gaseous interchange being manifested by an absorption of oxygen and a giving up of carbon dioxide.

The power of assimilation was more quickly destroyed: as a rule it failed after the plants had been subjected successively to a temperature of one day at 45° C., then three hours at 50° and half-an-hour at 60°. The assimilating green alga, being less able to resist extreme heat, as already stated, succumbed more quickly than the fungus. Jumelle also gives the record of an experiment with a crustaceous lichen, *Lecidea (Lecanora) sulphurea,* a rock species. It was kept in a chamber heated to 50° for three hours and when subsequently placed in the sunlight respiration took place but no assimilation.

Very high temperatures may be endured by lichen plants in quite natural conditions, when the rock or stone on which they grow becomes heated by the sun. Zopf[2] tested the thalli of crustaceous lichens in a hot June, under direct sunlight, and found that the thermometer registered 55° C.

b. Low Temperature. Lichens support extreme cold even better than extreme heat. In both cases it is the power of drying up and entering at any season into a condition of lowered or latent vitality that enables them to do so. In winter during a spell of severe cold they are generally in a state of desiccation, though that is not always the case, and resistance to cold is not due to their dry condition. The water of imbibition is stored in the cell-walls and it has been found that lichens when thus charged with moisture are able to resist low temperatures, even down to − 40° C. or − 50° as well as when they are dry. Respiration in that case was proved by

[1] Jumelle 1892.   [2] Zopf 1890, p. 489.

Jumelle[1] to continue to − 10°, but assimilation was still possible at a temperature of − 40°: *Evernia prunastri* exposed to that extreme degree of cold, but in the presence of light, decomposed carbon dioxide and gave off oxygen.

B. INFLUENCE OF MOISTURE

a. ON VITAL FUNCTIONS. Gaseous interchange has been found to vary according to the degree of humidity present[1]. In lichens growing in sheltered positions, or on soil, there is less complete desiccation, and assimilation and respiration may be only enfeebled. Lichens more exposed to the air—those growing on trees, etc.—dry almost completely and gaseous interchange may be no longer appreciable. In severe cold any water present would become frozen and the same effect of desiccation would be produced. At normal temperatures, on the addition of even a small amount of moisture the respiratory and assimilative functions at once become active, and to an increasing degree as the plant is further supplied with water until a certain optimum is reached, after which the vital processes begin somewhat to diminish.

Though able to exist with very little moisture, lichens do not endure desiccation indefinitely, and both assimilation and respiration probably cease entirely during very dry seasons. A specimen of *Cladonia rangiferina* was kept dry for three months, and then moistened: respiration followed but it was very feeble and assimilation had almost entirely ceased. Somewhat similar results were obtained with *Ramalina farinacea* and *Usnea barbata*.

In normal conditions of moisture, and with normal illumination, assimilation in lichens predominates over respiration, more carbon dioxide being decomposed than is given forth; and Jumelle has argued from that fact, that the alga is well able to secure from the atmosphere all the carbon required for the nutrition of the whole plant. The intensity of assimilation, however, varies enormously in different lichens and is generally more powerful in the larger forms than in the crustaceous: the latter have often an extremely scanty thallus and they are also more in contact with the substratum—rock, humus or wood—on which they may be partly saprophytic, thus obtaining carbohydrates already formed, and demanding less from the alga.

An interesting comparison might be made with fungi in regard to which many records have been taken as to their possible duration in a dry state, more especially on the viability of spores, *i.e.* their persistent capacity of germination. A striking instance is reported by Weir[2] of the regeneration of the sporophores of *Polystictus sanguineus*, a common fungus of warm countries. The plant was collected in Brazil and sent to Munich. After about two years in the mycological collection of the University, the branch on which it grew

---

[1] Jumelle 1892.   [2] Weir 1919.

was exposed in the open among other branches in a wood while snow still lay on the ground. In a short time the fungus revived and before the end of spring not only had produced a new hymenium, but enlarged its hymenial surface to about one-fourth of its original size and had also formed one entirely new, though small, sporophore.

b. ON GENERAL DEVELOPMENT. Lichens are very strongly influenced by abundance or by lack of moisture. The contour of the large majority of species is concentric, but they become excentric owing to a more vigorous development towards the side of damper exposure, hence the frequent one-sided increase of monophyllous species such as *Umbilicaria pustulata*. Wainio[1] observed that species of *Cladonia* growing in dry places, and exposed to full sunlight, showed a tendency not to develop scyphi, the dry conditions hindering the full formation of the secondary thallus. As an instance may be cited *Cl. foliacea*, in which the primary thallus is much the most abundantly developed, its favourite habitat being the exposed sandy soil of sea-dunes.

Too great moisture is however harmful: Nienburg[2] has recorded his observations on *Sphyridium* (*Baeomyces rufus*): on clay soil the thallus was pulverulent, while on stones or other dryer substratum it was granular—warted or even somewhat squamulose.

Parmelia physodes rarely forms fruits, but when growing in an atmosphere constantly charged with moisture[3], apothecia are more readily developed, and the same observation has been made in connection with other usually barren lichens. It has been suggested that, in these lichens, the abrupt change from moist to dry conditions may have a harmful effect on the developing ascogonium.

The perithecia of *Pyrenula nitida* are smaller on smooth bark[4] such as that of *Corylus*, *Carpinus*, etc., probably because the even surface does not retain water.

IV. ILLUMINATION OF LICHENS

A. EFFECT OF LIGHT ON THE THALLUS

As fungi possess no chlorophyll, their vegetative body has little or no use for light and often develops in partial or total darkness. In lichens the alga requires more or less direct illumination; the lichen fungus, therefore, in response to that requirement has come out into the open: it is an adaptation to the symbiotic life, though some lichens, such as those immersed in the substratum, grow with very little light. Like other plants they are sensitive to changes of illumination: some species are shade plants, while others are as truly sun plants, and others again are able to adapt themselves to varying degrees of light.

[1] Wainio 1897, p. 16.   [2] Nienburg 1908.   [3] Metzger 1903.   [4] Bitter 1899.

Wiesner[1] made a series of exact observations on what he has termed the "light-use" of various plants. He took as his standard of unity for the higher plants the amount of light required to darken photographic paper in one second. When dealing with lichens he adopted a more arbitrary standard, calculating as the unit the average amount of light that lichens would receive in entirely unshaded positions. He does not take account of the strength or duration of the light, and the conclusions he draws, though interesting and instructive, are only comparative.

a. SUN LICHENS. The illumination of the Tundra lichens is reckoned by Wiesner as representing his unit of standard illumination. In the same category as these are included many of our most familiar lichens, which grow on rocks subject to the direct incidence of the sun's rays, such as, for instance, *Parmelia conspersa, P. prolixa,* etc. *Physcia tenella (hispida)* is also extremely dependent on light, and was never found by Wiesner under $\frac{1}{4}$ of full illumination. *Dermatocarpon miniatum,* a rock lichen with a peltate foliose thallus, is at its best from $\frac{1}{3}$ to $\frac{1}{8}$ of illumination, but it grows well in situations where the light varies in amount from 1 to $\frac{1}{24}$. *Psora (Lecidea) lurida,* with dark-coloured crowded squamules, grows on calcareous soil among rocks well exposed to the sun and has an illumination from 1 to $\frac{1}{30}$, but with a poorer development at the lower figure. Many crustaceous rock lichens are also by preference sun-plants as, for instance, *Verrucaria calciseda* which grows immersed in calcareous rocks but with an illumination of 1 to $\frac{1}{3}$; in more shady situations, where the light had declined to $\frac{1}{29}$, it was found to be less luxuriant and less healthy.

Sun lichens continue to grow in the shade, but the thallus is then reduced and the plant is sterile. Zukal has made a list of those which grow best with a light-use of 1 to $\frac{1}{10}$, though they are also found not unfrequently in habitats where the light cannot be more than $\frac{1}{50}$. Among these light-loving plants are the Northern Tundra species of *Cladonia, Stereocaulon, Cetraria, Parmelia, Umbilicaria,* and *Gyrophora,* as also *Xanthoria parietina, Placodium elegans, P. murorum,* etc., with some crustaceous species such as *Lecanora atra, Haematomma ventosum, Diploschistes scruposus,* many species of Lecideaceae, some Collemaceae and some Pyrenolichens.

Wiesner's conclusion is that the need of light increases with the lowering of the temperature, and that full illumination is of still more importance in the life of the plants when they grow in cold regions and are deprived of warmth: sun lichens are, therefore, to be looked for in northern or Alpine regions rather than in the tropics.

b. COLOUR-CHANGES DUE TO LIGHT. Lichens growing in full sunlight frequently take on a darker hue. *Cetraria islandica* for instance in an open situation is darker than when growing in woods; *C. aculeata* on bare sand-

[1] Wiesner 1895.

dunes is a deeper shade of brown than when growing entangled among heath plants. *Parmelia saxatilis* when growing on exposed rocks is frequently a deep brown colour, while on shaded trees it is normally a light bluish-grey.

An example of colour-change due directly to light influences is given by Bitter[1]. He noted that the thallus of *Parmelia obscurata* on pine trees, and therefore subject only to diffuse light, grew to a large size and was of a light greyish-green colour marked by lighter-coloured lines, the more exposed lobes being always the most deeply tinted. In a less shaded habitat or in full sunlight the lichen was distinguished by a much darker colour, and the lobes were seamed and marked by blackish lines and spots. Bruce Fink[2] noted a similar development of dark lines on the thallus of certain rock lichens growing in the desert, more especially on *Parmelia conspersa, Acarospora xanthophana* and *Lecanora muralis*. He attributes a protective function to the dark colour and observes that it seemingly spreads from centres of continued exposure, and is thus more abundant in older parts of the thallus. He contrasts this colouration with the browning of the tips of the fronds of fruticose lichens by which the delicate growing hyphae are protected from intense light.

Galløe[3] finds that protection against too strong illumination is afforded both by white and dark colourations, the latter because the pigments catch the light rays, the former because it throws them back. The white colour is also often due to interspaces filled with air which prevent the penetration of the heat rays.

A deepening of colour due to light effect often visible on exposed rock lichens such as *Parmelia saxatilis* is more pronounced still in Alpine and tropical species: the cortex becomes thicker and more opaque through the cuticularizing and browning of the hyphal membranes, and the massing of crystals on the lighted areas. The gonidial layer becomes, in consequence, more reduced, and may disappear altogether. Zukal[4] found instances of this in species of *Cladonia, Parmelia, Roccella*, etc. The thickened cortex acts also as a check to transpiration and is characteristic of desert species exposed to strong light and a dry atmosphere.

Bitter[5] remarked the same difference of development in plants of *Parmelia physodes*: he found that the better lighted had a thicker cortex, about 20–30 μ in depth, as compared with 15–22 μ or even only 12 μ in the greener shade-plants, and also that there was a greater deposit of acids in the more highly illuminated cortices, thus giving rise to the deeper shades of colour.

Many lichens owe their bright tints to the presence of coloured lichen-acids, the production of which is strongly influenced by light and by clear air. *Xanthoria parietina* becomes a brilliant yellow in the sunlight: in the

[1] Bitter 1901, p. 465.   [2] Fink 1909.   [3] Galløe 1908.   [4] Zukal 1896.   [5] Bitter 1901.

shade it assumes a grey-green hue and yields only small quantities of parietin. *Placodium elegans*, normally a brightly coloured yellow lichen, becomes, in the strong light of the high Alps, a deep orange-red. *Rhizocarpon geographicum* is a vivid citrine-yellow on high mountains, but is almost green at lesser elevations.

c. SHADE LICHENS. Many species grow where the light is abundant though diffuse. Those on tree-trunks rarely receive direct illumination and may be generally included among shade-plants. Wiesner found that corticolous forms of *Parmelia saxatilis* grew best with an illumination between $\frac{1}{8}$ and $\frac{1}{17}$ of full light, and *Pertusaria amara* from $\frac{1}{12}$ to $\frac{1}{21}$; both of them could thrive from $\frac{1}{8}$ to $\frac{1}{56}$, but were never observed on trees in direct light. *Physcia ciliaris*, which inhabits the trunks of old trees, is also a plant that prefers diffuse light. In warm tropical regions, lichens are mostly shade-plants: Wiesner records an instance of a species found on the aerial roots of a tree with an illumination of only $\frac{1}{250}$.

In a study of subterranean plants, Maheu[1] takes note of the lichens that he found growing in limestone caves, in hollows and clefts of the rocks, etc. A fair number grew well just within the opening of the caves; but species such as *Cl. cervicornis*, *Placodium murorum* and *Xanthoria parietina* ceased abruptly where the solar rays failed. Only a few individuals of one or two species were found to remain normal in semi-darkness: *Opegrapha hapalea* and *Verrucaria muralis* were found at the bottom of a cave with the thallus only slightly reduced. The nature of the substratum in these cases must however also be taken into account, as well as the light influences: limestone for instance is a more favourable habitat than gypsum; the latter, being more readily soluble, provides a less permanent support.

Maheu has recorded observations on growth in its relation to light in the case of a number of lichens growing in caves.

Physcia obscura grew in almost total darkness; *Placodium murorum* within the cave had lost nearly all colour; *Placodium variabile* var. deep within the cave, sterile; *Opegrapha endoleuca* in partial obscurity; *Verrucaria rupestris* f. in total obscurity, the thallus much reduced and sterile; *Verrucaria rupestris* in partial obscurity, the asci empty; *Homodium* (*Collema*) *granuliferum* in the inmost recess of the cave, sterile, and the hyphae more spongy than in the open.

Siliceous rocks in darkness were still more barren, but a few odd lichens were collected from sandstone in various caves: *Cladonia squamosa*, *Parmelia perlata* var. *ciliata*, *Diploschistes scruposus*, *Lecidea grisella*, *Collema nigrescens* and *Leptogium lacerum*.

d. VARYING SHADE CONDITIONS. It has been frequently observed that on the trees of open park lands lichens are more abundant on the side

[1] Maheu 1906.

of the trunk that faces the prevailing winds. Wiesner[1] remarks that spores and soredia would more naturally be conveyed to that side; but there are other factors that would come into play: the tree and the branches frequently lean away from the wind, giving more light and also an inclined surface that would retain water for a longer period on the windward side[2]. Spores and soredia would also develop more readily in those favourable conditions.

In forests there are other and different conditions: on the outskirts, whether northern or southern, the plants requiring more light are to be found on the side of the trunk towards the outside; in the depths of the forest, light may be reduced from $\frac{1}{200}$ to $\frac{1}{300}$, and any lichens present tend to become mere leprose crusts. Krempelhuber[3] has recorded among his Bavarian lichens those species that he found constantly growing in the shade: they are in general species of Collemaceae and Caliciaceae, several species of *Peltigera* (*P. venosa*, *P. horizontalis* and *P. polydactyla*); *Solorina saccata*; *Gyalecta Flotovii*, *G. cupularis*; *Pannaria microphylla*, *P. triptophylla*, *P. brunnea*; *Icmadophila aeruginosa*, etc.

B. EFFECT ON REPRODUCTIVE ORGANS

In the higher plants, it is recognized that a certain light-intensity is necessary for the production of flowers and fruit. In the lower plants, such as lichens, light is also necessary for reproduction; it is a common observation that well-lighted individuals are the most abundantly fruited. In the higher fungi also, the fruiting body is more or less formed in the light.

a. POSITION AND ORIENTATION OF FRUITS WITH REGARD TO LIGHT. There is an optimum of light for the fruits as well as for the thallus in each species of lichen: in most cases it is the fullest light that can be secured.

Zukal[4] finds an exception to that rule in species of *Peltigera*: when exposed to strong sunlight, the lobes, fertile at the tips, curve over so that to some extent the back of the apothecium is turned to the light; with diffuse light, the horizontal position is retained and the apothecia face upwards. In the closely allied genera *Nephroma*, *Nephromium* and *Nephromopsis*, the apothecia are produced on the back of the lobe at the extreme tip, but as they approach maturity the fertile lobes turn right back and they become exposed to direct illumination. In a well-developed specimen the full-grown fruits may thus become so prominent all over the thallus, that it is difficult to realize they are on reversed lobes. In one species of *Cetraria* (*C. cucullata*) the rarely formed apothecia are adnate to the back of the lobe; but in that case the margins of the strap-shaped fronds are incurved and connivent, and the back is more exposed than the front.

In *Ramalina* the frond frequently turns at a sharp angle at the point of

---

[1] Wiesner 1895.   [2] R. Paulson, ined.   [3] Krempelhuber 1861.   [4] Zukal 1896, p. 111.

insertion of the apothecium which is thus well exposed and prominent; but Zukal[1] sees in this formation an adaptation to enable the frond to avoid the shade cast by the apothecium which may exceed it in width. In most lichens, however, and especially in shade or semi-shade species, the reproductive organs are to be found in the best-lighted positions.

b. INFLUENCE OF LIGHT ON COLOUR OF FRUITS. Lichen-acids' are secreted freely in the apothecium from the tips of the paraphyses which give the colour to the disc, and as acid-formation is furthered by the sun's rays, the well-lighted fruits are always deeper in hue. The most familiar examples are the bright-yellow species that are rich in chrysophanic acid (parietin). Hedlund[2] has recorded several instances of varying colour in species of *Micarea* (*Biatorina*, etc.) in which very dark apothecia became paler in the shade. He also cites the case of two crustaceous species, *Lecidea helvola* and *L. sulphurella*, which have white apothecia in the shade, but are darker in colour when strongly lighted.

V. COLOUR OF LICHENS

The thalli of many lichens, more especially of those associated with blue-green gonidia, are hygroscopic, and it frequently happens that any addition of moisture affects the colour by causing the gelatinous cell-walls to swell, thus rendering the tissues more transparent and the green colour of the gonidia more evident. As a general rule it is the dry state of the plant that is referred to in any discussion of colour.

In the large majority of species the colouring is of a subdued tone—soft bluish-grey or ash-grey predominating. There are, however, striking exceptions, and brilliant yellow and white thalli frequently form a conspicuous feature of vegetation. Black lichens are rare, but occasionally the very dark brown of foliaceous species such as *Gyrophora* or of crustaceous species such as *Verrucaria maura* or *Buellia atrata* deepens to the more sombre hue.

A. ORIGIN OF LICHEN-COLOURING

The colours of lichens may be traced to several different causes.

a. COLOUR GIVEN BY THE ALGAL CONSTITUENT. As examples may be cited most of the gelatinous lichens, Ephebaceae, Collemaceae, etc. which owe, as in *Collema*, their dark olivaceous-green appearance, when somewhat moist, to the enclosed dark-green gonidia, and their black colour, when dry, to the loss of transparency. When the thallus is of a thin texture as in *Collema nigrescens*, the olivaceous hue may remain constant. *Leptogium Burgessii*, another thin plant of the same family, is frequently of a purplish

[1] Zukal 1896.   [2] Hedlund 1892, p. 22.

hue owing to the purple colour of the gonidial *Nostoc* cells. The dull-grey crustaceous thallus of the Pannariaceae becomes more or less blue-green when moistened, and the same change has been observed in the Hymeno-lichens, *Cora*, etc.

In *Coenogonium*, the alga is some species of *Trentepohlia*, a filamentous genus mostly yellow, which often gives its colour to the slender lichen filaments, the covering hyphae being very scanty. Other filamentous species, such as *Usnea barbata*, etc., are persistently greenish from the bright-green Protococcaceous cells lying near the surface of the thalline strands. Many of the furfuraceous lichens are greenish from the same cause, especially when moist, as are also the larger lichens, *Physcia ciliaris*, Stereocaulons, Cladonias and others.

b. COLOUR DUE TO LICHEN-ACIDS. These substances, so characteristic of lichens, are excreted from the hyphae, and lie in crystals on the outer walls; they are generally most plentiful on exposed tissues such as the cortex of the upper surface or the discs of the apothecia. Many of these crystals are colourless and are without visible effect, except in sometimes whitening the surface, strikingly exemplified in *Thamnolia vermicularis*[1]; but others are very brightly coloured. These latter belong to two chemical groups and are found in widely separated lichens[2]:

1. Derivatives of pulvinic acid which are usually of a bright-yellow colour. They are the colouring substance of *Letharia vulpina*, a northern species, not found in our islands, of *Cetraria pinastri* and *C. juniperina*[3] which inhabit mountainous or hilly regions. The crustaceous species, *Lecidea lucida* and *Rhizocarpon geographicum*, owe their colour to rhizocarpic acid.

The brilliant yellow of the crusts of some species of Caliciaceae is due to the presence of the substance calycin, while coniocybic acid gives the greenish sulphur-yellow hue to *Coniocybe furfuracea*. Epanorin colours the hyphae and soredia of *Lecanora epanora* a citrine-yellow and stictaurin is the deep-yellow substance found in the medulla and under surface of *Sticta aurata* and *S. crocata*.

2. The second series of yellow acids are derivatives of anthracene. They include parietin, formerly described as chrysophanic acid, which gives the conspicuous colour to *Xanthoriae* and to various wall lichens; solorinic acid, the crystals of which cover the medullary hyphae and give a reddish-grey tone to the upper cortex of *Solorina crocea*, and nephromin which similarly colours the medulla of *Nephromium lusitanicum* a deep yellow, the colour of the general thallus being, however, scarcely affected. In this group must also be included the acids that cause the yellow colouring of the medulla in *Parmelia subaurifera* and the yellowish thallus of some *Pertusariae*.

[1] Zopf 1893.   [2] Zopf 1907.   [3] Zopf 1892.

In many cases, changes in the normal colouring[1] are caused by the breaking up of the acids on contact with atmospheric or soil ammonia. Alkaline salts are thus formed which may be oxidized by the oxygen in the air to yellow, red, brown, violet-brown or even to entirely black humus-like products which are insoluble in water. These latter substances are frequently to be found at the base of shrubby lichens or on the under surface of leafy forms that are closely appressed to the substratum.

c. COLOUR DUE TO AMORPHOUS SUBSTANCES. These are the various pigments which are deposited in the cell-walls of the hyphae. The only instance, so far as is known, of· colours within the cell occurs in *Baeomyces roseus*, in which species the apothecia owe their rose-colour to oil-drops in the cells of the paraphyses, and in *Lecidea coarctata* where the spores are rose-coloured when young. In a few instances the colouring matter is excreted (*Arthonia gregaria* and *Diploschistes ocellatus*); but Bachmann[2], who has made an extended study of this subject and has examined 120 widely diversified lichens, found that with few exceptions the pigment was in the membranes.

Bachmann was unable to determine whether the pigments were laid down by the protoplasm or were due to changes in the cell-wall. The middle layer, he found, was generally more deeply coloured than the inner one, though that was not universal. In other cases the outer sheath was the darkest, especially in cortices one to two cells thick such as those of *Parmelia olivacea*, *P. fuliginosa* and *P. revoluta*, and in the brown thick-walled spores of *Physcia stellaris* and of *Rhizocarpon geographicum*. Still another variation occurs in *Parmelia tristis* in which the dark cortical cells show an outer colourless membrane over the inner dark wall.

The coloured pigments are mainly to be found in the superficial tissues, but if the thallus is split by areolation, as in crustaceous lichens, the internal hyphae may be coloured like those of the outer cortex wherever they are exposed. The hyphae of the gonidial layer are persistently colourless, but the lower surface and the rhizoids of many foliose lichens are frequently very deeply stained, as are the hypothalli of crustaceous species.

The fruiting bodies in many different families of lichens have dark coloured discs owing to the abundance of dark-brown pigment in the paraphyses. In these the walls, as determined by Bachmann, are composed generally of an inner wall, a second outer wall, and the outermost sheath which forms the middle lamella between adjacent cells. In some species the second wall is pigmented, in others the middle lamella is the one deeply coloured. The hymenium of many apothecia and the hyphae forming the amphithecium are often deeply impregnated with colour. The wall hyphae

[1] Knop 1872.   [2] Bachmann 1890.

of the pycnidia are also coloured in some forms; more frequently the cells round the opening pore are more or less brown.

The presence of these coloured substances enables the cell-wall to resist chemical reactions induced by the harmful influences of the atmosphere or of the substratum. The darker the cell-wall and the more abundant the pigment, the less easily is the plant injured either by acids or alkalies. The coloured tips of the paraphyses thus give much needed protection to the long lived sporiferous asci, and the dark thalline tissues prevent premature rotting and decay.

d. ENUMERATION OF AMORPHOUS PIGMENTS:

1. **Green.** Bachmann found several different green pigments: "Lecidea-green," colouring red with nitric acid, is the dark blue-green or olive-green (smaragdine) of the paraphyses of many apothecia in the Lecideaceae, and may vary to a lighter blue; it appears almost black in thalline cells[1]. "Aspicilia-green" occurs in the thalline margin and sometimes in the epithecium of the fruits of species of *Aspicilia*; it becomes a brighter green on the application of nitric acid. "Bacidia-green," also a rare pigment, becomes violet with the same acid; it is found in the epithecium of *Bacidia muscorum* and *Bacidia acclinis* (Lecideaceae). "Thalloidima-green" in the apothecia of some species of *Biatorina* is changed to a dirty-red by nitric acid and to violet by potash. Still another termed "rhizoid-green" gives the dark greenish colour to the rhizoids of *Physcia pulverulenta* and *P. aipolia* and to the spores of some species of *Physcia* and *Rhizocarpon*. It becomes more olive-green with potash.

2. **Blue.** A very rare colour in lichens, so far found in only a few species, *Biatora* (*Lecidea*) *atrofusca, Lecidea sanguinaria* and *Aspicilia flavida* f. *coerulescens*. It forms a layer of amorphous granules embedded in the outer wall of the paraphyses, becoming more dense towards the epithecium. A few granules are also present in the hymenium.

3. **Violet.** "Arthonia-violet" as it is called by Bachmann is a constituent of the tissues of *Arthonia gregaria*, occurring in minute masses always near the cortical cells; it is distinct from the bright cinnabarine granules present in every part of the thallus.

4. **Red.** Several different kinds of red have been distinguished: "Urceolaria-red," visible as an interrupted layer on the upper side of the medulla in the thallus of *Diploschistes ocellatus*, a continental species with a massive, crustaceous, whitish thallus that shows a faint rose tinge when wetted. "Phialopsis-red" is confined to the epithecium of the brightly coloured

---

[1] A similar reaction with nitric acid is produced on the blue hypothalline hyphae of *Placynthium nigrum*.

apothecia of *Phialopsis rubra*. "Lecanora-red," by which Bachmann designates the purplish colour of the hymenium, is an unfailing character of
Lecanora atra; the colouring substance is lodged in the middle lamella of
the paraphysis cells; it occurs also in *Rhizocarpon geographicum* and in *Rh.
viridiatrum*; it becomes more deeply violet with potash. M. C. Knowles[1]
noted the blue colouring of *Rh. geographicum* growing in W. Ireland near
the sea and she ascribed it to an alkaline reaction. Two more rare pigments,
"Sagedia-red" and "Verrucaria-red," are found in species of Verrucariaceae. These tinge the calcareous rocks in which the lichens are embedded
a beautiful rose-pink. They are scarcely represented in our country.

5. **Brown.** A frequent colouring substance, but also presenting several
different kinds of pigment which may be arranged in two groups:

(1) **Substances with some characteristic chemical reaction.** These
are of somewhat rare occurrence: "Bacidia-brown" in the middle lamella
of the paraphyses of *Bacidia fuscorubella* stains a clear yellow with acids
or a violet colour with potash; "Sphaeromphale-brown," which occurs
in the perithecia and in the cortex of *Staurothele clopismoides*, becomes
deep olive-green with potash, changing to yellow-brown on the application
of sulphuric acid; "Segestria-brown" in *Porina lectissima* changes to a
beautiful violet colour with sulphuric acid, while "Glomellifera-brown,"
which is confined to the outer cortical cells of the upper surface of *Parmelia
glomellifera*, becomes blue with nitric and sulphuric acids, but gives no reaction with potash. Rosendahl[2] confirmed Bachmann's discovery of this
colour and further located it in corresponding cells of *Parmelia prolixa* and
P. locarensis.

(2) **Substances with little or no chemical reaction.** There is only
one such to be noted: "Parmelia-brown," usually a very dark pigment, which
is lodged in the outer membranes of the cells. It becomes a clearer colour
with nitric acid, and if the reagent be sufficiently concentrated, some of the
pigment is dissolved out. Some tissues, such as the lower cortex of some
Parmeliae, may be so impregnated and hardened, that nothing short of boiling
acid has any effect on the cells; membranes less deeply coloured and changed,
such as the cortex of the *Gyrophorae*, become disintegrated with such drastic
treatment. With potash the colour becomes darker, changing from a clear
brown to olivaceous-brown or -green, or in some cases, as in a more faintly
coloured epithecium, to a dirty-yellow, but the lighter colour produced there
is largely due to the swelling up of the underlying tissues to which the potash
penetrates readily between the paraphyses.

"Parmelia-brown" is a colouring substance present in the dark epithecium and hypothecium of the fruits of many widely diverse lichens, and

[1] Knowles 1915.   [2] Rosendahl 1907.

in the cortical cells and rhizoids of many thalli. In some plants the thallus is brown both above and below, in others, as in *Parmelia revoluta*, etc. only the under surface is dark-coloured.

   e. COLOUR DUE TO INFILTRATION. There are several crustaceous lichens that are rusty-red, the colour being due to the presence of iron. These lichens occur on siliceous rocks of gneiss, granite, etc., and more especially on rocks rich in iron. Iron as a constituent of lichens was first demonstrated by John[1] in *Ramalina fraxinea* and *R. calicaris*. Grimbel[2] proved that the colour of rust lichens was due to an iron salt, and Molisch[3] by microscopic examination located minute granules of ferrous oxide as incrustations on the hyphae of the upper surface of the thallus. Molisch held that the rhizoids or penetrating hyphae dissolved the iron from the rocks by acid secretions. Rust lichens however grow on rocks that are frequently under water in which the iron is already present.

   Among "rusty" lichens are the British forms, *Lecanora lacustris*, the thallus of which is normally white, though generally more or less tinged with iron; it inhabits rocks liable to inundation. *L. Dicksonii* owes its ferruginous colour to the same influences. *Lecidea contigua* var. *flavicunda* and *L. confluens* f. *oxydata* are rusty conditions of whitish-grey lichens.

   Nilson[4] found rusty lichens occurring frequently in the Sarak-Gebirge, more especially on glacier moraines where they were liable, even when uncovered by snow, to be flooded by water from the higher reaches. It is the thallus that is affected by the iron, rarely if ever are apothecia altered in colour.

[1] John 1819.   [2] Grimbel 1856.   [3] Molisch 1892.   [4] Nilson 1907.

BACHMANN'S PIGMENT REACTIONS

Name of Pigment or Lichen	Colour	KOH	NH₃	Ba(OH)₂	HNO₃	H₂SO₄	Special Reactions
Lecidea-green	green				copper or brick-red		KOH then HCl: blue
Aspicilia-green	green						HNO₃: brighter green
Bacidia-green	green					violet	HCl: violet
Thalloidima-green	green	violet			violet		HCL: indistinctly purple-red
Rhizoid-green	bluish-green	olive-green to brown			indistinctly purple-red olive-green		
Biatora atrofusca	blue	dissolves with greenish-blue colour			violet, then yellow, then decolourized	dissolves	H₂O insoluble
Phialopsis rubra	brick-red		dirty purple-red		violet		
Lecanora-red	purple-red		deep violet				
Sagedia decipivum	bluish-red	blue (green)	greenish-blue, then grey-black	blue			
Verrucaria Hoffmanni f. purpurascens	rose-red	dark-green		dark-green			KOH, then HNO₃, then H₂SO₄: violet crystals
Bacidia fuscorubella	yellowish-brown	violet	violet	violet			KOH, then H₂SO₄, then HNO₃: blackish
Sphaeromphale clopismoides	leather-brown	deep olive-green	violet				
Segestria lectissima—perithecia	yellow-brown	rose-red			bright yellow		dilute H₂SO₄: bright yellow
Segestria lectissima—entire tissue	brown and colourless						Strong H₂SO₄: deep violet, then grey
Parmelia glomellifera	leather-brown				blue, then violet, at last grey		CaCl₂O₂: blue, then grey; finally decolourized
Parmelia-brown	yellow to blackish-brown	dirty- to olive-brown			bright red-brown		

CHAPTER VI

BIONOMICS

A. Growth and Duration

LICHENS are perennial plants mostly of slow growth and of long continuance; there can therefore only be approximate calculations either as to their rate of increase in dimensions or as to their duration in time. A series of somewhat disconnected observations have however been made that bear directly on the question, and they are of considerable interest.

Meyer[1] was among the first to be attracted by this aspect of lichen life, and after long study he came to the conclusion that growth varied in rapidity according to the prevailing conditions of the atmosphere and the nature of the substratum; but that nearly all species were very slow growers. He enumerates several,—*Lichen (Xanthoria) parietinus, L. (Parmelia) tiliaceus, L. (Rhizocarpon) geographicus, L. (Haematomma) ventosus*, and *L. (Lecanora) saxicolus*,—all species with a well-defined outline, which, after having attained some considerable size, remained practically unchanged for six and a half years, though, in some small specimens of foliose lichens, he noted, during the same period, an increase of one-fourth to one-third of their size in diameter. In one of the above crustaceous species, *L. ventosus*, the specimen had not perceptibly enlarged in sixteen years, though during that time the centre of the thallus had been broken up by weathering and had again been regenerated.

Meyer also records the results of culture experiments made in the open, possibly with soredia or with thalline scraps: he obtained a growth of *Xanthoria parietina* (on wrought iron kept well moistened), which fruited in the second year, and in five years had attained a width of 5–6 lines (about 1 cm.); *Lecanora saxicola* growing on a moist rock facing south grew 4–7 lines in six and a half years, and bore very minute apothecia.

Lindsay[2] quotes a statement that a specimen of *Lobaria pulmonaria* had been observed to occupy the same area of a tree after the lapse of half a century. Berkeley[3] records that a plant of *Rhizocarpon geographicum* remained in much the same condition of development during a period of twenty-five years. The latter is a slow grower and, in ordinary circumstances, it does not fruit till about fifteen years after the thallus has begun to form. Weddell[4], also commenting on the long continuance of lichens, says there are crustaceous species occupying on the rock a space that might be covered by a five-franc piece, that have taken a century to attain that size.

Phillips[5] on the other hand argues against the very great age of lichens,

[1] Meyer 1825, p. 44.   [2] Lindsay 1856.   [3] Berkeley 1857.   [4] Weddell 1869.   [5] Phillips 1878.

and suggests 20 years as a sufficient time for small plants to establish themselves on hard rocks and attain full development. He had observed a small
vigorous plant of *Xanthoria parietina* that in the course of five years had
extended outwards to double its original size. The centre then began to
break up and the whole plant finally disappeared.

Exact measurements of growth have been made by several observers.
Scott Elliot[1] found that a *Pertusaria* had increased about half a millimetre
from the 1st February to the end of September. Vallot[2] kept under observation at first three then five different plants of *Parmelia saxatilis* during a
period of eight years: the yearly increase of the thallus was half a centimetre,
so that specimens of twenty centimetres in breadth must have been growing
from forty to fifty years.

Bitter's[3] observations on *Parmelia physodes* agree in the main with those
of Vallot: the increase of the upper lobes during the year was 3–4 mm. In
a more favourable climate Heere found that *Parmelia caperata* (Fig. 49) on
a trunk of *Aesculus* in California had grown longitudinally 1·5 cm. and trans-
versely 1 cm. The measurements extended over a period of seven winter
months, five of them being wet and therefore the most favourable season of
growth. In warm regions lichens attain a much greater size than in temperate or northern countries, and growth must be more rapid.

A series of measurements was also made by Heere[4] on *Ramalina reticulata* (Fig. 64), a rapid growing tree-lichen, and one of the largest American
species. The shorter lobes were selected for observation, and were tested
during a period of seven months from September to May, five of the months
being in the wet season. There was great variation between the different
lobes but the average increase during that period was 41 per cent.

Krabbe[5] took notes of the colonization of *Cladonia rangiferina* (Fig. 127)
on burnt soil: in ten years the podetia had reached a height of 3 to 5 cm.,
giving an annual growth of about 3–5 mm. It is not unusual to find specimens in northern latitudes 18 inches long (50 cm.), which, on that computation, must have been 100 to 160 years old; but while increase goes on at the
apex of the podetia, there is constant perishing at the base of at least as
much as half the added length and these plants would therefore be 200 or
300 years old. Reinke[6] indeed has declared that apical growth in these
Cladina species may go on for centuries, given the necessary conditions of
good light and undisturbed habitat.

Other data as to rate of growth are furnished by Bonnier[7] in the account
of his synthetic cultures which developed apothecia only after two to three
years. The culture experiments of Darbishire[8] and Tobler[9] with *Cladonia*
soredia are also instructive, the former with synthetic spore- and alga-cultures

[1] Scott Elliot 1907.   [2] Vallot 1896.   [3] Bitter 1901.   [4] Heere 1904.   [5] Krabbe 1891, p. 131.
[6] Reinke 1894, p. 18.   [7] Bonnier, see p. 29.   [8] Darbishire, see p. 148.   [9] Tobler, see p. 148.

having obtained a growth of soredia in about seven months; the latter, starting with soredia, had a growth of well-formed squamules in nine months.

It has been frequently observed that abundance of moisture facilitates growth, and this is nowhere better exemplified than in crustaceous soil-lichens. Meyer found that on lime-clay soil which had been thrown up from a ditch in autumn, lichens such as *Gyalecta geoica* were fully developed the following summer. He gives an account also of another soil species, *Verrucaria* (*Thrombium*) *epigaea*, which attained maturity during the winter half of the year. Stahl[1] tells us that *Thelidium minutulum*, a pyrenocarpous soil-lichen, with a primitive and scanty thallus, was cultivated by him from spore to spore in the space of three months. Such lichens retain more of the characteristics of fungi than do those with a better developed thallus. Rapid colonization by a soil-lichen was also observed in Epping Forest by Paulson[2]. In autumn an extensive growth of *Lecidea uliginosa* covered as if with a dark stain patches of soil that had been worn bare during the previous spring. The lichen had reached full development and was well fruited.

These facts are quite in harmony with other observations on growth made on Epping Forest lichens. The writers[3] of the report record the finding of "fruiting lichens overspreading decaying leaves which can scarcely have lain on the ground more than two or three years; others growing on old boots or on dung and fruiting freely; others overspreading growing mosses." They also cite a definite instance of a mass of concrete laid down in 1903 round a surface-water drain which in 1910—seven years later—was covered with *Lecanora galactina* in abundant fruit; and of another case of a Portland stone garden-ornament, new in 1904, and, in 1910, covered with patches of a fruiting *Verrucaria* (probably *V. nigrescens*). Both these species, they add, have a scanty thallus and generally fruit very freely.

A series of observations referring to growth and "ecesis" or the spreading of lichens have been made by Bruce Fink[4] over a period of eight years. His aim was mainly to determine the time required for a lichen to re-establish itself on areas from which it had been previously removed. Thus a quadrat of limestone was scraped bare of moss and of *Leptogium lacerum*, except for bits of the moss and particles of the lichen which adhered to the rock, especially in depressions of the surface. After four years, the moss was colonizing many small areas on which grew patches of the lichen 2 to 10 mm. across. Very little change occurred during the next four years.

Numerous results are also recorded as to the rate of growth, the average being 1 cm. per year or somewhat under. The greatest rate seems to have been recorded for a plant of *Peltigera canina* growing on "a mossy rock along a brook in a low moist wood, well-shaded." A plant, measuring 10 by 14 cm., was deprived of several large apothecia. The lobes all pointed

[1] Stahl 1877, p. 34.   [2] Paulson 1918.   [3] Paulson and Thompson 1913.   [4] Fink 1917.

in the same direction, and the plant increased 1·75 cm. in one year. Two other plants, deprived of their lobes, regenerated and increased from 2 and 5 cm. respectively to 3·5 and 6 cm. No other measurements are quite so high as these, though a plant of *Parmelia caperata* (sterile), measuring from 1 to 2 cm. across, reached in eight years a dimension of 10 by 13 cm. Other plants of the same species gave much slower rates of increase. A section of railing was marked bearing minute scattered squamules of *Cladonia pityrea*. After two years the squamules had attained normal size and podetia were formed 2 to 4 mm. long.

Several areas of *Verrucaria muralis* were marked and after ten months were again measured; the largest plants, measuring 2·12 by 2·4 cm. across, had somewhat altered in dimensions and gave the measurements 2·2 by 3 cm. Some crustose species became established and produced thalli and apothecia in two to eight years. Foliose lichens increased in diameter from 0·3 to 3·5 cm. per year. So far as external appearance goes, apothecia are produced in one to eight years; it is concluded that they require four to eight years to attain maturity in their natural habitats.

B. SEASON OF FRUIT FORMATION

The presence of apothecia (or perithecia) in lichens does not always imply the presence of spores. In many instances they are barren, the spores having been scattered or not yet matured; the disc in these cases is composed of paraphyses only, with possible traces of asci. In any month of the year, however, some lichens may be found in fruit.

Baur[1] found, for instance, that *Parmelia acetabulum* developed carpogonia the whole year round, though somewhat more abundantly in spring and autumn. *Pertusaria communis* similarly has a maximum period of fruit-formation at these two seasons. This is probably true of tree-lichens generally: in summer the shade of the foliage would inhibit the formation of fruits, as would the extreme cold of winter; but were these conditions relaxed spore-bearing fruits might be expected at any season though perhaps not continuously on the same specimen.

An exception has been noted by Baur in *Pyrenula nitida*, a crustaceous tree Pyrenolichen. He found carpogonia only in February and April, and the perithecia matured in a few weeks, presumably at a date before the trees were in full leaf; but even specimens of *Pyrenula* are not unusual in full spore-bearing conditions in the autumn of the year.

To arrive at any true knowledge as to the date and duration of spore production, it would be necessary to keep under observation a series of one species, examining them microscopically at intervals of a few weeks or months

[1] Baur 1901.

and noting any conditions that might affect favourably or unfavourably the reproductive organs. A comparison between corticolous and saxicolous species would also be of great interest to determine the influence of the substratum as well as of light and shade. But in any case it is profitable to collect and examine lichens at all seasons of the year, as even when the bulk of the spores is shed, there may remain belated apothecia with a few asci still intact.

C. Dispersal and Increase

The natural increase of lichen plants may primarily be sought for in the dispersal of the spores produced in the fruiting-bodies. These are ejected, as in fungi, by the pressure of the paraphyses on the mature ascus. The spores are then carried away by wind, water, insects, etc. In a few lichens gonidia are enclosed in the hymenium and are ejected along with the spores, but, in most, the necessary encounter with the alga is as fortuitous, and generally as certain, as the pollination of anemophilous flowers. A case of dispersal in *Sagedia microspora* has been described by Miyoshi[1] in which entire fruits, small round perithecia, were dislodged and carried away by the wind. The addition of water caused them to swell enormously and brought about the ejection of the spores. Areas covered by the thallus are also being continually enlarged by the spreading growth of the hypo-thallus.

a. Dispersal of Crustaceous Lichens. These lichens are distributed fairly equally on trees or wood (corticolous) and on rocks (saxicolous). Some species inhabit both substrata. As regards corticolous lichens that live on smooth bark such as hazel or mountain-ash, the vegetative body or thallus is generally embedded beneath the epidermis of the host. Soredia are absent and the thallus is protected from dispersal. In these lichens there is rather an abundant and constant formation of apothecia or perithecia.

Other species that affect rugged bark and are more superficial are less dependent on spore production. The thallus is either loosely granular, or is broken up into areolae. The areolae are each a centre of growth, and with an accession of moisture they swell up and exert pressure on each other. Parts of the thallus thus become loosened and are dislodged and carried away. If anchored on a suitable substratum they grow again to a complete lichen plant. Sorediate lichens are dependent almost wholly on these bud-like portions for increase in number; soredia are easily separated from the parent plant, and easily scattered. Darbishire[2] noted frequently that small *Poduridae* in moving over the surface of *Pertusaria amara* became powdered with soredia and very evidently took a considerable part in the dissemination of the species.

[1] Miyoshi 1901. [2] Darbishire 1897, p. 657.

Crustaceous rock lichens are rarely sorediate, but they secure vegetative propagation[1] by the dispersal of small portions of the thallus. The thalli most securely attached are cracked into small areolae which, by unequal growth, become very soon lop-sided, or, by intercalary increase, form little warts and excrescences on their surface. These irregularities of development give rise to more or less tension which induces a loosening of the thallus from the substratum. Weather changes act similarly and gradually the areolae are broken off. Loosening influence is also exercised by the developing fruits, the expanding growth of which pushes aside the neighbouring tissues. Wind or water then carries away the thalline particles which become new centres of growth if a suitable substratum is reached.

b. DISPERSAL OF FOLIOSE LICHENS. It is a matter of common observation that, in foliose lichens where fruits are abundant, there are few or no soredia and *vice versa*. In either case propagation is ensured. In addition to these obvious methods of increase many lichens form isidia, outgrowths from the thallus which are easily detached. Bitter[2] considers for instance that the coralloid branchlets, which occur in compact tufts on the thallus of *Umbilicaria pustulata*, are of immense service as organs of propagation. Apothecia and pycnidia are rarely present in that species, and the plant thus falls back on vegetative production. Slender crisp thalline outgrowths, easily separable, occur also on the edges of lobes, as in species of *Peltigera*, *Platysma*, etc.

Owing to the gelatinous character of lichen hyphae, the thallus quickly becomes soft with moisture and is then easily torn and distributed by wind, animals, etc. The action of lichens on rocks has been shown to be of a constantly disintegrating character, and the destruction of the supporting rock finally entails the scattering of the plant. This cause of dispersal is common to both crustaceous and foliose species. The older central parts of a lichen may thus have disappeared while the areolae on lobes of the circumference are still intact and in full vigour.

As in crustaceous lichens the increase in the area of growth may take place by means of the lichen mycelium which, originating from the rhizinae in contact with the substratum, spreads as a hypothallus under the shelter of the lobes and far beyond them. When algae are encountered a new lobe begins to form. The process can be seen perhaps most favourably in lichens on decaying wood which harbours moisture and thus enables the wandering hyphae to retain life.

c. DISPERSAL OF FRUTICOSE LICHENS. Many of these lichens are abundantly fruited; in others soralia are as constantly developed. Species of *Usnea*, *Alectoria*, *Ramalina* and many *Cladoniae* are mainly propagated

---

[1] Beckmann 1907.   [2] Bitter 1899.

by soredia. They are all peculiarly liable to be broken and portions of the thallus scattered by the combined action of wind and rain.

Peirce[1] found that *Ramalina reticulata* (Fig. 65), of which the fronds are an open network, was mainly distributed by the tearing of the lichen in high wind. This takes place during the winter rains, when not only the lichen is wet and soft in texture, but when the deciduous trees are bare of leaves, at a season, therefore, when the drifting thalline scraps can again catch on to branch or stem. A series of observations on the dispersal of forms of long pendulous Usneas was made by Schrenk[2]. In the Middle and North Atlantic States of America these filamentous species rarely bear apothecia. The high winds break and disperse them when they are in a wet condition. They generally grow on Spruces and Firs, because the drifting filaments are more easily caught and entangled on short needles. The successive wetting and drying causes them to coil and uncoil, resulting in a tangle impossible to unravel, which holds them securely anchored to the support.

D. ERRATIC LICHENS

In certain lichens, there is a tendency for the thallus to develop excrescences of nodular form which easily become free and drift about in the wind while still living and growing. They are carried sometimes very long distances, and fall in thick deposits over localities far from their place of origin. The most famous instance is the "manna lichen," *Lecanora esculenta*, which has been scientifically examined and described by Elenkin[3]. He distinguishes seven different forms of the species: f. *esculenta*, f. *affinis*, f. *alpina*, and f. *fruticulosa-foliacea* which are Alpine lichens, the remainder, f. *desertoides*, f. *foliacea* and f. *esculenta-tarquina*, grow on the steppes or in the desert[4].

Elenkin[3] adds to the list of erratic lichens a variety of *Parmelia molliuscula* along with *P. ryssolea* from S. Russia, from the Asiatic steppes and from Alpine regions. Mereschkovsky[5] has also recorded from the Crimea *Parmelia vagans*, probably derived from *P. conspersa* f. *vaga* (f. nov.). It drifts about in small rather flattened bits, and, like other erratics, it never fruits.

Meyer[6] long ago described the development of wandering lichens: scraps that were torn from the parent thallus continued to grow if there were sufficient moisture, but at the same time undergoing considerable change in appearance. The dark colour of the under surface disappears in the frequently altered position, as the lobes grow out into narrow intermingling fronds forming a more or less compact spherical mass; the rhizoids also become modified and, if near the edge, grow out into threadlike structures which

---

[1] Peirce 1898.   [2] Schrenk 1898.   [3] Elenkin 1901.   [4] See Chap. X.
          [5] Mereschkovsky 1918.   [6] Meyer 1825, p. 44.

bind the mass together. Meyer says that "wanderers" have been noted as belonging to *Parmelia acetabulum, Platysma glaucum* and *Anaptychia ciliaris*.

The most notable instance in Britain of the "erratic" habit is that of *Parmelia revoluta* var. *concentrica* (Fig. 121), first found on Melbury Hill

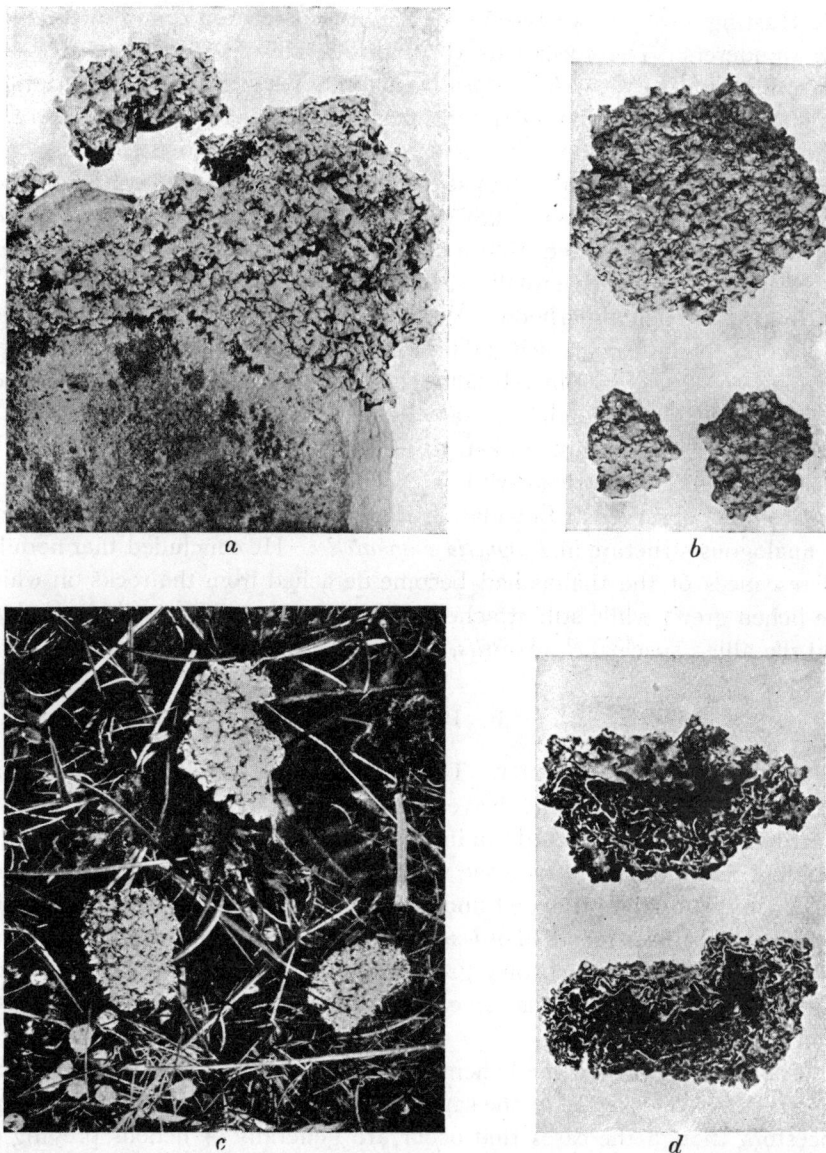

Fig. 121. *Parmelia revoluta* var. *concentrica* Cromb. *a*, plant on flint with detached fragment; *b*, upper surface of three specimens; *c*, three specimens as found on chalk downs; *d*, specimens in section showing central cavity (S. H., *Photo.*).

near Shaftesbury, Dorset, and described as " a spherical unattached lichen which rolls on the exposed downs." It has recently been observed on the downs near Seaford in Sussex, where, however, it seems to be confined to a small area about eight acres in extent which is exposed to south-west winds. The lichen is freely distributed over this locality. To R. Paulson and Somerville Hastings[1] we owe an account of the occurrence and origin of the *revoluta* wanderers. The specimens vary considerably in shape and size, and measure from 1 to 7 cm. in longest diameter. Very few are truly spherical, some are more or less flattened and many are quite irregular. The revolute edges of the overlapping lobes give a rough exterior to the balls, which thereby become entangled amongst the grass, etc., and movement is impeded or prevented, except in very high winds. Crombie[2] had suggested that the concentric plant originated from a corticolous habitat, but no trees are near the Seaford locality. Eventually specimens were found growing on flints in the immediate neighbourhood. While still on the stone the lichen tends to become panniform, a felt of intermingling imbricate lobes is formed, portions of which, in time, become crowded out and dislodged. When scattered over the ground, these are liable to be trampled on by sheep or other animals and so are broken up; each separate piece then forms the nucleus of new concentric growth.

Crombie[2] observed at Braemar, drifting about on the detritus of Morrone, an analogous structure in *Parmelia omphalodes*. He concluded that nodular excrescences of the thallus had become detached from the rocks on which the lichen grew; while still attached to the substratum *Parmelia omphalodes* and the allied species, *P. saxatilis*, form dense cushion-like masses.

E. PARASITISM

a. GENERAL STATEMENT. The parasitism of *Strigula complanata*, an exotic lichen found on the leaves of evergreen trees, has been already described[3]; Dufrenoy[4] records an instance of hyphae from a *Parmelia* thallus piercing pine-needles through the stomata and causing considerable injury. Lichen hyphae have attacked and destroyed the protonemata of mosses. Cases have also been recorded of *Usnea* and *Ramalina* penetrating to the living tissue of the tree on which they grew, and there may be other similar parasitisms; but these exceptions serve to emphasize the independent symbiotic growth of lichens.

There are however some lichens belonging to widely diverse genera that have retained, or reverted to, the saprophytic or parasitic habit of their fungal ancestors, though the cases that occur are generally of lichens preying on

---

[1] Paulson and Somerville Hastings 1914.	[2] Crombie 1872.	[3] See p. 35.
[4] Dufrenoy 1918.

other lichens. The conditions have been described as those of " antagonistic symbiosis " when one lichen is hurtful or fatal in its action on the other, and as " parasymbiosis " when the association does little or no injury to the host. The parasitism of fungi on lichens, though falling under a different category, in many instances exhibits features akin to parasymbiosis.

The parasitism of fungus on fungus is not unusual; there are instances of its occurrence in all the different classes. In the Phycomycetes there are genera wholly parasitic on other fungi such as *Woronina* and other Chytridiaceae; *Piptocephalus*, one of the Mucorini, is another instance. *Cicinnobolus*, one of the Sphaeropsideae, preys on *Perisporiae*; a species of *Cordyceps* is found on *Elaphomyces*, and *Orbilia coccinella* on *Polyporus*; while among Basidiomycetes, *Nyctalis*, an agaric, grows always on *Russula*.

There are few instances of lichens finding a foothold on fungi, for the simple reason that the latter are too short lived. On the perennial *Polyporeae* a few have been recorded by Arnold[1], but these are not described as doing damage to the host. They are mostly species of *Lecidea* or of allied genera. Kupfer[2] has also listed some 15 different lichens that he found on *Lenzites* sp.

b. ANTAGONISTIC SYMBIOSIS. In discussing the nutrition of lichens[3] note has been taken of the extent to which some species by means of enzymes destroy the thallus of other lichens in their vicinity and then prey on the dead tissues. A constantly cited[4] example is that of *Lecanora atriseda* which in its early stages lives on the thallus of *Rhizocarpon geographicum* inhabiting mountain rocks. A detailed examination of the relationship between these two plants was made by Malme and later by Bitter[5]. Both writers found that the *Lecanora* thallus as it advanced caused a blackening of the *Rhizocarpon* areolae, the tissues of which were killed by the burrowing slender filaments of the *Lecanora*, easily recognized by their longer cells. The invader thereafter gradually formed its own medulla, gonidial layer and cortex right over the surface of the destroyed thallus. *Lecidea insularis* (*L. intumescens*) similarly takes possession of and destroys the thallus of *Lecanora glaucoma* and Malme[4] strongly suspects that *Buellia verruculosa* and *B. aethalea* may be living on the thallus of *Rhizocarpon distinctum* with which they are constantly associated.

Other cases of facultative parasitism have been studied by Hofmann[6], more especially three different species, *Lecanora dispersa*, *Lecanora* sp. and *Parmelia hyperopta*, which were found growing on the thick foliose thallus of *Dermatocarpon miniatum*. These grew, at first independently, on a wall along with many examples of *Endocarpon* on to which they spread as opportunity offered. The thallus of the latter was in all cases distorted, the area occupied by the invaders being finally killed. The attacking lichens had

[1] Arnold 1874. [2] Kupfer 1894. [3] See p. 236. [4] Malme 1895.
[5] Bitter 1899. [6] Hofmann 1906.

benefited materially by the more nutritive substratum: their apothecia were more abundant and their thallus more luxuriant. The gonidia especially had profited; they were larger, more brightly coloured, and they increased more freely. Hoffmann offers the explanation that the strain on the algae of providing organic food for the hyphal symbiont was relaxed for the time, hence their more vigorous appearance.

Arthonia subvarians is always parasitic on the apothecia of *Lecanora galactina*, and Almquist[1] discovered that the hymenium of the host alone is injured, the hypothecium and excipulum being left intact.

The "parasitism" of *Pertusaria globulifera* on *Parmelia perlata* and *P. physodes*, as described by Bitter[2], may also be included under antagonistic symbiosis. The hyphae pierce the *Parmelia* thallus, break it up and gradually absorb it. Chemical as well as mechanical influences are concerned in the work of destruction as both the fungus and the alga of the victim are dissolved. *Lecanora tartarea* already dealt with as a marauding lichen[3] over decaying vegetation may spread also to living lichens. Fruticose soil species, such as *Cetraria aculeata* and others, die from the base and the *Lecanora* gains entrance to their tissues at the decaying end which is open.

Arnold[4] speaks of these facultative parasites that have merely changed their substratum as pseudo-parasites, and he gives a list of instances of such change. In many cases it is rather the older thalli that are taken possession of, and, in nearly every case, the invader is some crustaceous species. The plants attacked are generally ground lichens or more particularly those that inhabit damp localities, such as *Peltigera* or *Cladonia* or certain bark lichens. Drifting soredia or particles of a lichen would easily take hold of the host thallus and develop in suitable conditions. To give a few of the instances observed, there have been found, by Arnold, Crombie and others:

on *Peltigera canina*: *Callopisma cerina*, *Rinodina turfacea* var., *Bilimbia obscurata* and *Lecanora aurella*;

on *Peltigera aphthosa*: *Lecidea decolorans*;

on *Cladoniae*: *Bilimbia microcarpa*, *Bacidia Beckhausii* and *Urceolaria scruposa*, etc.

Urceolaria (*Diploschistes*) has a somewhat bulky crustaceous thallus which may be almost evanescent in its semi-parasitic condition, the only gonidia retained being in the margin of the apothecia. Nylander[5] found isolated apothecia growing vigorously on *Cladonia* squamules.

Hue[6] describes *Lecanora aspidophora* f. *errabunda*, an Antarctic lichen, as not only a wanderer but as a "shameless robber." It is to be seen everywhere on and about other lichens, settling small glomeruli of apothecia here and

---

[1] Almquist 1880.   [2] Bitter 1899.   [3] See p. 237.   [4] Arnold 1874.
          [5] Nylander 1852.   [6] Hue 1915.

there on the thallus of *Umbilicariae* or between the areolae of *Buelliae*, and always too vigorous to be ousted from its position.

Bacidia flavovirescens has been regarded by some lichenologists[1] as a parasite on *Baeomyces*, but recent work by Tobler[2] seems to have proved that the bright green thallus is that of the *Bacidia*.

c. PARASYMBIOSIS. There are certain lichens that are obligative parasites and pass their whole existence on an alien thallus. They may possibly have degenerated from the condition of facultative parasitism as the universal history of parasitism is one of increased dependence on the host, and of growing atrophy of the parasite, but, in the case of lichens, there is always the peculiar symbiotic condition to be considered : the parasite produces its own vigorous hyphae and normal healthy fruits, it often claims only a share of the carbohydrates manufactured by the gonidia. The host lichen is not destroyed by this parasymbiosis though the tissues are very often excited to abnormal growth by the presence of the invading organism.

Lauder Lindsay[3] was one of the first to study these "microlichens" as he called them, and he published descriptions of those he had himself observed on various hosts. He failed however to discriminate between lichens and parasitic fungi. It is only by careful research in each case that the affinity to fungi or to lichens can be determined; very frequently the whole of them, as possessing no visible thallus, have been classified with fungi, but that view ignores the symbiosis that exists between the hyphae of the parasite and the gonidia of the host.

Parasitic lichens are rather rare on gelatinous thalli; but even among these, a few instances have been recorded. Winter[4] has described a species of *Leptoraphis*, the perithecia of which are immersed in the thallus of *Physma franconicum*. The host is wholly unaffected by the presence of the parasite except for a swelling where it is situated. The foreign hyphae are easily distinguishable; they wander through the thallus of the host with their free ends in the mucilage of the gonidial groups from which they evidently extract nourishment. Species of the lichen genus *Obryzum* are also parasitic on gelatinous lichens.

The parasitic genus *Abrothallus*[5] has been the subject of frequent study. There are a number of species which occur as little black discs on various thalli of the large foliose lichens. They were first of all described as parasitic fungi, later Tulasne[6] affirmed their lichenoid nature as proved by the structure, consistence and long duration of the apothecia. Lindsay[7] wrote a monograph of the genus dealing chiefly with *Abrothallus Smithii* (*Buellia Parmeliarum*) and *A. oxysporus*, with their varieties and forms that occur on

---

[1] Th. Fries 1874, p. 343.   [2] Tobler 1911[2].   [3] Lindsay 1869[2].   [4] Winter 1877.
[5] *Abrothallus* has been included in the lichen genus *Buellia*.   [6] Tulasne 1852.
[7] Lindsay 1856.

several different hosts. In some instances the thallus is apparently quite unaffected by the presence of *Abrothallus*, in others, as in *Cetraria glauca*, there is considerable hypertrophy produced, the portion of the thallus on which the parasites are situated showing abnormal growth in the form of swellings or pustules which may be regarded as gall-formations. Crombie[1] points this out in a note on *C. glauca* var. *ampullacea*, figured first by Dillenius, which is merely a swollen condition due to the presence of *Abrothallus*.

The internal structure and behaviour of *Abrothallus* has more recently been followed in detail by Kotte[2]. He recognized a number of different species growing on various thalli of *Parmelia* and *Cetraria*, but *Abrothallus Cetrariae* was the only one that produced gall-formation. The mycelium of the parasite in this instance penetrates to the medulla of the host lichen as a loose weft of hyphae which are divided into more or less elongate cells. These send out side branches, which grow towards the algal cells, and by their short-celled filaments clasp them exactly in the same way as do the normal lichen hyphae. Thus in the neighbourhood of the parasite an algal cell may be surrounded by the hyphae not only of the host, but also by those of *Abrothallus*. The two different hyphae can generally be distinguished by their reaction to iodine: in some cases *Abrothallus* hyphae take the stain, in others the host hyphae. In addition to apothecia, spermogonia or pycnidia are produced, but in one of the species examined by Kotte, *Abrothallus Peyritschii* on *Cetraria caperata*, there was no spermogonial wall formed. The hyphae also penetrate the host soredia or isidia, so that on the dispersal of these vegetative bodies the perpetuation of both organisms is secured in the new growth.

Abrothallus draws its organic food from the gonidia in the same way as the host species, and possibly the parasitic hyphae obtain also water and inorganic food along with the host hyphae. They have been traced down to the rhizinae and may even reach the hypothallus, but no injury to the host has been detected. It is a case of joint symbiosis and not of parasitism. Microscopic research has therefore justified the inclusion of these and other forms among lichens.

d. PARASYMBIOSIS OF FUNGI. There occur on lichens, certain parasites classed as fungi which at an early stage are more or less parasymbionts of the host; as growth advances they may become parasitic and cause serious damage, killing the tissues on which they have settled.

Zopf[3] found several instances of such parasymbiosis in his study of fungal parasites, such as *Rhymbocarpus punctiformis*, a minute Discomycete which inhabits the thallus of *Rhizocarpon geographicum*. By means of staining reagents he was able to trace the course of the parasitic hyphae,

[1] Crombie 1894. [2] Kotte 1910. [3] Zopf 1896.

and found that they travelled towards the gonidia and clasped them lichen-wise without damaging them, since these remained green and capable of division. At no stage was any harm caused to the host by the alien organism. Another instance he observed was that of *Conida rubescens* on the thallus of *Rhizocarpon epipolium*. By means of fine sections through the apothecia of *Conida* and the thallus of the host, he proved the presence of numerous gonidia in the subhymenial tissue, these being closely surrounded by the hyphae of the parasite, and entirely undamaged : they retained their green colour, and in size and form were unchanged. Zopf[1] at first described these parasites as fungi though later[1] he allows that they may represent lower forms of lichens.

Tobler[2] has added two more of these parasymbiotic species on the border line between lichens and fungi, similar to those described by Zopf. One of these, *Phacopsis vulpina*, belonging to the fungus family Celidiaceae, is parasitic on *Letharia vulpina*. The fronds of the host plant are considerably altered in form by its presence, being more branched and curly. Where the parasite settles a swelling arises filled with its hyphae, and the host gonidia almost disappear from the immediate neighbourhood, only a few "nests" being found and these very mucilaginous. These nests as well as single gonidia are surrounded by *Phacopsis* hyphae which have gradually displaced those of the *Letharia* thallus. The gonidia are excited to division and increase in number on contact with either lichen or fungus hyphae, but in the latter case the increase is more abundant owing doubtless to a more powerful chemical irritant in the fungus. As development advances, the *Phacopsis* hyphae multiply to the exclusion of both lichen hyphae and gonidia from the area of invasion. Finally the host cortex is split, the fungus bursts through, and the tissue beneath the parasite becomes brown and dead. *Phacopsis* begins as a "parasymbiont," then becomes parasitic, and is at last saprophytic on the dead cells. The hyphae travel down into the medulla of the host and also into the soredial outgrowths, and are dispersed along with the host. The effect of *Verrucula* on the host thallus may also be cited[3].

Tobler gives the results of his examination of still another fungus, *Karschia destructans*. It becomes established on the thallus of *Chaenotheca chrysocephala* and its hyphae gradually penetrate down to the underlying bark (larch). The lichen thallus beneath the fungus is killed, but gonidia in the vicinity are sometimes clasped : *Karschia* also is thus a parasymbiont, then a parasite, and finally a saprophyte.

Elenkin[4] describes certain fungi which to some extent are parasymbionts. One of these, *Conidella urceolata* n.sp., grew on forms of *Lecanora esculenta*. The other, a stroma-forming species, had invaded the thallus of *Parmelia*

---

[1] Zopf 1898, p. 249.   [2] Tobler 1911[2].   [3] See p. 276.   [4] Elenkin 1901[2].

molliuscula, where it caused gall-formation. As the growth of the gall was due to the co-operation of the lichen gonidia, the fungus must at first have been a parasymbiont. Only dead gonidia were present in the stroma; probably they had been digested by the parasite. Because of the stroma Elenkin placed the fungus in a new genus, *Trematosphaeriopsis.*

e. FUNGI PARASITIC ON LICHENS. A solution or extract of lichen thallus is a very advantageous medium in which to grow fungi. It is therefore not surprising that lichens are a favourite habitat for parasitic fungi. Stahl[1] has noted that the lichens themselves flourish best where there is frequent moistening by rain or dew with equally frequent drying which effectively prevents the growth of fungi. Species of *Peltigera* are however able to live in damp conditions: without being injured, they have been observed to maintain their vigour when cultivated in a very moist hot-house while all the other forms experimented with were attacked and finally destroyed by various fungi.

Lindsay[2] devoted a great deal of attention to the microscopic study of the minute fruiting bodies so frequently present on lichen thalli and published descriptions of microlichens, microfungi and spermogonia. He and others naturally considered these parasitic organisms to be in many cases either the spermogonia or pycnidia of the lichen itself. It is often not easy to determine their relationship or their exact systematic position; many of them are still doubtful forms.

There exists however a very large number of fully recognized parasitic microfungi belonging to various genera. Lindsay discovered many of them. Zopf[3] has given exact descriptions of a series of forms, with special reference to their effect on the host thallus. In an early paper he described a species, *Pleospora collematum,* that he found on *Physma compactum* and other Collemaceae. The hyphae of the parasite differed from those of the host in being of a yellow colour; they did not penetrate or spread far, being restricted to rhizoid-like filaments at the base of their fruiting bodies (perithecia and pycnidia). Their presence caused a slight protuberance but otherwise did no harm to the host; the *Nostoc* cells in their immediate vicinity were even more brightly coloured than in other parts of the thallus. In another paper[4] he gives an instance of gall-formation in *Collema pulposum* induced by the presence of the fungus *Didymosphaeria pulposi.* Small protuberances were formed on the margins of the apothecia, more rarely on the lobes of the thallus, each one the seat of a perithecium of the fungus. No damage was done to either constituent of the thallus.

Agyrium flavescens grows parasitically on the under surface of *Peltigera polydactyla.* M. and Mme Moreau[5] found that the hyphae of the fungus spread between the medullary filaments of the lichen; no haustoria were

[1] Stahl 1904.   [2] Lindsay 1859, 1869, 1871.   [3] Zopf 1896.   [4] Zopf 1898.   [5] Moreau 1916[3].

observed. The mature fruiting body had no distinct excipulum, but was surrounded by a layer of dead lichen cells.

It is not easy to determine the difference between parasites that are of fungal nature and those that are lichenoid; but as a general rule the fungi may be recognized by their more transient character, very frequently by their effect on the host thallus, which is more harmful than that produced by lichens, and generally by their affinity to fungi rather than to lichens. Opinions differ and will continue to differ on this very difficult question.

The number of such fungi determined and classified has gradually increased, and now extends to a very long list. Even as far back as 1896 Zopf reckoned up 800 instances of parasitism of 400 species of fungi on about 350 different lichens and many more have been added. Abbé Vouaux[1] is the latest writer on the subject, but his work is mostly a compilation of species already known. He finds representatives of these parasites in nine families of Pyrenomycetes and six of Discomycetes. He leaves out of account the much debated Coniocarps, but he includes with fungi all those that have been proved to be parasymbiotic, such as *Abrothallus*.

A number of fungus genera, such as *Conida*, etc., are parasitic only on lichens. Most of them have one host only; others, such as *Tichothecium pygmaeum*, live on a number of different thalli. Crustaceous species are often selected by the parasites, and no great damage, if any, is caused to these hosts, except when the fungus is seated on the disc of the apothecium, so that the spore-bearing capacity is lessened or destroyed.

In some of the larger lichens, however, harmful effects are more visible. In *Lobaria pulmonaria*, the fruits of which are attacked by the Discomycete, *Celidium Stictarum*[2], there is at first induced an increased and unusual formation of lichen apothecia. These apothecia are normally seated for the most part on the margins of the lobes or pustules, but when they are invaded by the fungus, they appear also in the hollows between the pustules and even on the under surface of the thallus. In the large majority of cases the fungus is partly or entirely embedded in the thallus; the gonidia in the vicinity may remain green and healthy, or all the tissues in the immediate neighbourhood of the parasite may be killed.

f. MYCETOZOA PARASITIC ON LICHENS. Mycetozoa live mostly on decayed wood, leaves, humus, etc. One minute species, *Listerella paradoxa*, always inhabits the podetia of *Cladonia rangiferina*. Another species, *Hymenobolina parasitica*, was first detected and described by Zukal[3] as a true parasite on the thallus of Physciaceae; it has since been recorded in the British Islands on *Parmeliae*[4]. This peculiar organism differs from other mycetozoa in that the spores on germination produce amoebae. These unite to form a rose-red plasmodium which slowly burrows into the lichen thallus

---

[1] Vouaux 1912, etc.   [2] Bitter 1904.   [3] Zukal 1893.   [4] Lister 1911.

and feeds on the living hyphae. It is a minute species, but when abundant the plasmodia can just be detected with the naked eye as rosy specks scattered over the surface of the lichen. Later the grey sporangia are produced on the same areas.

F. Diseases of Lichens

a. Caused by Parasitism. Zopf[1] has stated that of all plants, lichens are the most subject to disease, reckoning as diseases all the instances of parasitism by fungi or by other lichens. There are however only rare instances in which total destruction or indeed any permanent harm to the host is the result of such parasitism. At worst the trouble is localized and does not affect the organism as a whole. Some of these cases have been already noted under antagonistic symbiosis or parasymbiosis. Several instances have however been recorded where real injury has been caused by the penetration of some undetermined fungus mycelium. Zukal[2] records two such observed by him in *Parmelia encausta* and *Physcia villosa*: the thallus of the former was dwarfed and deformed by the presence of the alien mycelium, the latter was excited to abnormal proliferation.

b. Caused by crowding. Lichens suffer frequently from being overgrown by other lichens; they may also be crowded out by other plants. My attention was called by Mr P. Thompson to a burnt plot of ground in Epping Forest, which, after the fire, had been colonized by *Peltigera spuria*. In the course of a few years, other vegetation had followed, depriving the lichen of space and light and gradually driving it out. When last examined only a few miserable specimens remained, and these were reduced in vitality by an attack of the lichen parasite *Illosporium carneum*.

c. Caused by adverse conditions. Zukal considers as pathological, at least in origin, the cracking of the thallus so frequent in crustaceous lichens as well as in the more highly developed forms. As the cracks are beneficial in the aeration of the plant, they can hardly be regarded as symptoms of a diseased condition. The more evident ringed breaks in the cortex of *Usneae*, due probably to wind action, have more reason to be so regarded; they are most pronounced in *Usnea articulata*, where the portions bounded by the rings are contracted and swollen, and a hollow space is formed between the cortex and the central axis. The swellings that are produced on lichen thalli, such as those of *Umbilicaria* and some species of *Gyrophora*, due to intercalary growth are normal to the plant, though occasionally the swollen weaker portions may become ruptured and the cortex be thrown off. As pathological also must be regarded the loss of cortex sometimes occasioned by excessive soredial formation at the margins of the lobes:

[1] Zopf 1897.   [2] Zukal 1896, p. 258.

the upper cortex may be rolled back and eventually torn away; the gonidial layer is exposed and transformed into soredia which are swept away by the wind and rain, till finally only traces of the lower cortex are left.

Zukal[1] has instanced, as a case of diseased condition observed by him, the undue thickening of the cortex in *Pertusaria communis* whereby the formation of the fruiting bodies is inhibited and even vegetative development is rendered impossible. There arrives finally a stage when splitting takes place and the whole thallus breaks down and disappears. As a rule however there need be no limit to the age of the lichen plant. There is no vital point or area in the thallus; injury of one part leaves the rest unhurt, and any fragment in growing condition, if it combines both symbionts, can carry on the life of the plant, the constant renewal of gonidia preventing either decay or death. Barring accidents many lichens might exist as long as the world endures.

G. Harmful Effect of Lichens

One lichen only, *Strigula complanata,* a tropical species, has been proved to be truly and constantly parasitic. It grows on the surface of thick leathery leaves such as those of *Camellia*[2], etc. and the alga and fungus both penetrate the epidermis and burrow beneath the cuticle and outer cells, causing them to become brown. It undoubtedly injures the leaves.

Friedrich[3] has given an isolated instance of the hold-fast hyphae of *Usnea* piercing through the cortex to the living tissue of the host, and not only destroying the middle lamella by absorption, but entering the cells. The *Usnea* plant was characterized by exceptionally vigorous growth. Practically all corticolous lichens are epiphytic and the injury they cause is of an accidental nature Crustaceous species on the outer bark occupy the dead cortical layers and seem to be entirely harmless[4]. The larger foliose and fruticose forms are not so innocuous: by their abundant enveloping growth they hinder the entrance of air and moisture, and thus impede the life of the higher plant. Gleditsch[5], one of the earliest writers on Forestry, first indicated the possibly harmful effect of lichens especially on young trees and "in addition," he says, "they serve as cover for large numbers of small insects which are hurtful in many ways to the trees." Lindau[6] pointed out the damage done to pine-needles by *Xanthoria parietina* which grew round them like a cuff and probably choked the stomata, the leaves so clothed being mostly withered. Dufrenoy[7] states that he found the hyphae of a *Parmelia* entering a pine-needle by the stomata, and that the starch disappeared from the neighbouring parenchyma the cells of which tended to disintegrate.

It is no uncommon sight to see neglected fruit trees with their branches crowded with various lichens, *Evernia prunastri, Ramalina farinacea,* etc. Such lichens often find the lenticels a convenient opening for their hold-fasts

[1] Zukal 1896, p. 255.   [2] Cunningham 1879.   [3] Friedrich 1906, p. 401.   [4] See p. 78.
[5] Gleditsch 1775, p. 31.   [6] Lindau 1895, p. 53.   [7] Dufrenoy 1881.

and excercise a smothering effect on the trees. Lilian Porter[1] distinctly states that *Ramalinae* by their penetrating bases damage the tissues of the trees. The presence of lichens is however generally due to unhealthy conditions already at work. Friedrich[2] reported of a forest which he examined, in which the atmospheric moisture was very high, with the soil water scarce, that those trees that were best supplied with soil water were free from lichens, while those with little water at the base bore dead branches which gave foothold to a rich growth of the epiphytes.

Experiments to free fruit trees from their coating of lichens were made by Waite[3]. With a whitewash brush he painted over the infested branches with solutions of Bordeaux mixture of varying strength, and found that this solution, commonly in use as a fungicide, was entirely successful. The trees were washed down about the middle of March, and some three weeks later the lichens were all dead, the fruticose and foliose forms had changed in colour to a yellowish or brownish tint and were drooping and shrivelled.

Waite was of opinion that the lichens did considerable damage to the trees, but it has been held by others that in very cold climates they may provide protection against severe frost. Instances of damage are however asserted by Bouly de Lesdain[4]. The bark of willows he found was a favourite habitat of numerous lichens: certain species, such as *Xanthoria parietina*, completely surrounded the branches, closing the stomata; others, such as *Physcia ascendens*, by the mechanical strain of the rhizoids, first wet and then dry, gradually loosened the outer bark and gave entry to fungi which completed the work of destruction.

H. GALL-FORMATION

Several instances of gall-formation to a limited extent have been already noted as caused by parasitic fungi or lichens. Greater abnormality of development is induced in a few species by the presence of minute animals, mites, wood-lice, etc. Zopf[5] noted these deformations of the thallus in specimens of *Ramalina Kullensis* collected on the coasts of Sweden. The fronds were frequently swollen in a sausage-like manner, and branching was hindered or altogether prevented; apothecia were rarely formed, though pycnidia were abundant. Here and there, on the swollen portions of the thallus, small holes could be detected and other larger openings of elliptical outline, about $1-1\frac{1}{2}$ mm. in diameter, the margins of which had a nibbled appearance. Three types of small articulated animals were found within the openings: species of mites, spiders and wood-lice. Mites were the most constant and were more or less abundant in all the deformations; frequently a minute Diplopodon belonging to the genus *Polyxenus* was also met with.

Zopf came to the conclusion that the gall-formation was mainly due to the mites: they eat out the medulla and possibly through some chemical

[1] Porter 1917.　　[2] Friedrich 1906.　　[3] Waite 1893.　　[4] Lesdain 1912.　　[5] Zopf 1907.

irritation excite the algal zone and cortex to more active growth, so that an extensive tangential development takes place. The small spiders may exercise the same power; evidently the larger holes were formed by them.

Later Zopf added to gall-deformed plants *Ramalina scopulorum* var. *incrassata* and *R. cuspidata* var. *crassa*. He found in the hollow swollen fronds abundant evidence of mites, but whether identical with those that attacked *R. Kullensis* could not be determined. These two *Ramalinae* are maritime species; they are morphologically identical, as are also the deformed varieties, and the presence of mites, excreta, etc., are plainly visible in our British specimens.

Bouly de Lesdain[1] found evidence of mite action in *Ramalina farinacea* collected from *Pinus sylvestris* on the dunes near Dunkirk. The cortex had been eaten off either by mites or by a small mollusc (*Pupa muscorum*) and the fronds had collapsed to a more or less convex compact mass. Somewhat similar deformations, though less pronounced, were observed in other *Ramalinae*.

In *Cladonia sylvatica* and also in *Cl. rangiformis* Lesdain has indicated ff. *abortiva* Harm. as evidently the result of insect attack. In both cases the tips of the podetia are swollen, brown, bent and shrivelled.

One of the most curious and constant effects, also worked out by Lesdain, occurs in *Physcia hispida* (*Ph. stellaris* var. *tenella*). In that lichen the gonidia at the tips of the fronds are scooped out and eaten by mites, so that the upper cortex becomes separated from the lower part of the thallus. As the hyphae of the cortex continue to develop, an arched hood is formed of a whitish shell-like appearance and powdery inside. Sometimes the mites penetrate at one point only, at other times the attack is at several places which may ultimately coalesce into one large cavity. In a crustaceous species, *Caloplaca* (*Placodium*) *citrina* he found constant evidence of the disturbing effect of the small creatures, which by their action caused the areolae of the thallus to grow into minute adherent squamules. A pathological variety, which he calls var. *sorediosa*, is distinguished by the presence of cup-like hollows which are scooped out by Acarinae and are filled by yellowish soredia. In another form, var. *maritima*, the margins of the areolae, occasionally the whole surface, become powdery with a citrine yellow efflorescence as a result of their nibbling.

Zukal[2] adds to the deformations due to organic agents, the hypertrophies and abnormalities caused by climatic conditions. He finds such irregularities of structure more especially developed in countries with a very limited rainfall, as in certain districts of Chili, Australia and Africa, where changes in cortex and rhizoids and proliferations of the thallus testify to the disturbance of normal development.

---

[1] Lesdain 1910.   [2] Zukal 1896, p. 258.

CHAPTER VII

PHYLOGENY

I. GENERAL STATEMENT

A. ORIGIN OF LICHENS

THOUGH lichens are very old members of the vegetable kingdom, as symbiotic plants they yet date necessarily from a time subsequent to the evolution of their component symbionts. Phylogeny of lichens begins with symbiosis.

The algae, which belong to those families of Chlorophyceae and Myxophyceae that live on dry land, had become aerial before their association with fungi to form lichens. They must have been as fully developed then as now, since it is possible to refer them to the genus or sometimes even to the species of free-living forms. The fungus hyphae have combined with a considerable number of different algae, so that, even as regards the algal symbiont, lichens are truly polyphyletic in origin.

The fungus is, however, the dominant partner, and the principal line of development must be traced through it, as it provides the reproductive organs of the plant. Representatives of two great groups of fungi are associated with lichens: Basidiomycetes, found in only a few genera, and Ascomycetes which form with the various algae the great bulk of lichen families. In respect of their fungal constituents lichens are also polyphyletic, and more especially in the Ascolichens which can be traced back to several starting points. But though lichens have no common origin, the manner of life is common to them all and has influenced them all in certain directions: they are fitted for a much longer existence than that of the fungi from which they started; and both the thallus and the fruiting bodies—at least in the sub-class Ascolichens—can persist through great climatic changes, and can pass unharmed through prolonged periods of latent or suspended vitality.

Another striking note of similarity that runs through the members of this sub-class, with perhaps the exception of the gelatinous lichens, is the formation of lichen-acids which are excreted by the fungus. These substances are peculiar to lichens and go far to mark their autonomy. The production of the acids and the many changes evolved in the vegetative thallus suggest the great antiquity of lichens.

B. Algal Ancestors

It is unnecessary to look far for the algae as they have persisted through the ages in the same form both without and within the lichen thallus. By many early lichenologists the free-living algae, similar in type to lichen algae, were even supposed to be lichen gonidia in a depauperate condition and were, for that reason, termed by Wallroth "unfortunate brood-cells." In the condition of symbiosis they may be considerably modified, but they revert to their normal form, and resume their normal life-history of spore production, etc., under suitable and free culture. The different algae taking part in lichen-formation have been treated in an earlier chapter[1].

C. Fungal Ancestors

a. Hymenolichens. The problem of the fungal origin in this sub-class is comparatively simple. It contains but three genera of tropical lichens which are all associated with Myxophyceae, and the fungus in them, to judge from the form and habit of the plants, is a member of the Thelephoraceae. It may be that Hymenolichens are of comparatively recent origin and that the fungi belonging to the Basidiomycetes had, in the course of time, become less labile and less capable of originating a new method of existence. Whatever the reason, they lag immeasurably behind Ascomycetes in the formation of lichens.

b. Ascolichens. Lichens are again polyphyletic within this sub-class. The main groups from which they are derived are evident. Whether there has been a series of origins within the different groups or a development from one starting point in each it would be difficult to determine. In any case great changes have taken place after symbiosis became established.

The main divisions within the Ascolichens are related to fungi thus:

Series 1. Pyrenocarpineae⎫
       2. Coniocarpineae ⎬ to Pyrenomycetes.
       3. Graphidineae   to Hysteriaceae.
       4. Cyclocarpineae to Discomycetes.

II. THE REPRODUCTIVE ORGANS

A. Theories of Descent in Ascolichens

It has been suggested that ascomycetous fungi, from which Ascolichens are directly derived, are allied to the Florideae, owing to the appearance of a trichogyne in the carpogonium of both groups. That organ in the red seaweeds is a long delicate cell in direct communication with the egg-cell of the carpogonium. It is a structure adapted to totally submerged conditions, and fitted to attach the floating spermatia.

[1] See p. 51.

In fungi there is also a structure considered as a trichogyne[1], which, in the Laboulbeniales, is a free, simple or branching organ. There is no other instance of any similar emergent cell or cells connected with the ascogonium of the Ascomycetes, though the term has been applied in these fungi to certain short hyphal branches from the ascogonium which remain embedded in the tissue. In the Ascomycetes examined all traces of emergent receptive organs, if they ever existed, have now disappeared; in some few there are possible internal survivals which never reach the surface.

In Ascolichens, on the contrary, the "trichogyne," a septate hyphal branch extending upwards from the ascogonium, and generally reaching the open, has been demonstrated in all the different groups except, as yet, in the Coniocarpineae which have not been investigated. Its presence is a strong point in the argument of those who believe in the Floridean ancestry of the Ascomycetes. It should be clearly borne in mind that Ascolichens are evolved from the Ascomycetes: these latter stand between them and any more remote ancestry.

In the Ascomycetes, there is a recognized progression of development in the form of the sporophore from the closed perithecium of the Pyrenomycetes and possibly through the Hysteriaceae, which are partially closed, to the open ascocarp of the Discomycetes. If the fungal and lichenoid "trichogyne" is homologous with the carpogonial organ in the Florideae, then it must have been retained in all the groups of Ascomycetes as an emergent structure, and as such passed on from them to their lichen derivatives. Has that organ then disappeared from fungi since symbiosis began? There is no trace of it now, except as already stated in Laboulbeniales with which lichens are unconnected.

Were Ascolichens monophyletic in origin, one could more easily suppose that both the fungal and lichen series might have started at some early stage from a common fungal ancestor possessing a well-developed trichogyne which has persisted in lichens, but has been reduced to insignificance in fungi, while fruit development proceeded on parallel lines in both. There is no evidence that such progression has taken place among lichens; the theory of a polyphyletic origin for the different series seems to be unassailable. At the same time, there is no evidence to show in which series symbiosis started first.

It is more reasonable to accept the polyphyletic origin, as outlined above, from forms that had already lost the trichogyne, if they ever really possessed it, and to regard the lichen trichogyne as a new organ developing in lichens in response to some requirement of the deep-seated ascogonium. Its sexual function still awaits satisfactory proof, and it is wiser to withhold judgment as to the service it renders to the developing fruit.

[1] See p. 177 et seq.

B. Relation of Lichens to Fungi

a. Pyrenocarpineae. In Phycolichens (containing blue-green gonidia) and especially in the gelatinous forms, fructification is nearly always a more or less open apothecium. The general absence of the perithecial type is doubtless due to the gelatinous consistency of the vegetative structure; it is by the aid of moisture that the hymenial elements become turgid enough to secure the ejection of the spores through the narrow ostiole of the perithecium, and this process would be frustrated were the surrounding and enveloping thallus also gelatinous. There is only one minutely foliose or fruticose gelatinous family, the Pyrenidiaceae, in which Pyrenomycetes are established, and the gonidia, even though blue-green, have lost the gelatinous sheath and do not swell up.

In Archilichens (with bright-green gonidia), perithecial fruits occur frequently; they are nearly always simple and solitary; in only a few families with a few representatives, is there any approach to the stroma formation so marked among fungi. The single perithecium is generally semi-immersed in the thallus. It may be completely surrounded by a hyphal "entire" wall, either soft and waxy or dark coloured and somewhat carbonaceous. In numerous species the outer protective wall covers only the upper portion that projects beyond the thallus, and such a perithecium is described as "dimidiate," a type of fruit occurring in several genera, though rare among fungi.

As to internal structure, there is a dissolution and disappearance of the paraphyses in some genera, their protective function not being so necessary in closed fruits, a character paralleled in fungi. There is a great variety of spore changes, from being minute, simple and colourless, to varied septation, general increase in size, and brown colouration. The different types may be traced to fungal ancestors with somewhat similar spores, but more generally they have developed within the lichen series. From the life of the individual it is possible to follow the course of evolution, and the spores of all species begin as simple, colourless bodies; in some genera they remain so, in others they undergo more or less change before reaching the final stage of colour or septation that marks the mature condition.

As regards direct fungal ancestors, the Pyrenocarpineae, with solitary perithecia, are nearest in fruit structure to the Mycosphaerellaceae, in which family are included several fungus genera that are parasitic on lichens such as *Ticothecium, Müllerella*, etc. In that family occurs also the genus *Stigmatea*, in which the perithecia in form and structure are very similar to dimidiate *Verrucariae*.

Zahlbruckner[1] has suggested as the starting point for the Verrucariaceae

---

[1] Zahlbruckner 1903.

the fungus genus *Verrucula*. It was established by Steiner[1] to include two species, *V. cahirensis* and *V. aegyptica*, their perithecia being exactly similar to those of *Verrucaria*[2] in which genus they were originally placed. Both are parasitic on species of *Caloplaca* (*Placodium*). The former, on *C. gilvella*, transforms the host thallus to the appearance of a minutely lobed *Placodium*; the latter occupies an island-like area in the centre of the thallus of *Caloplaca interveniens*, and gives it, with its accompanying parasite, the character of an *Endopyrenium* (*Dermatocarpon*), while the rest of the thallus is normal and fertile.

Zahlbruckner may have argued rightly, but it is also possible to regard these rare desert species as reversions from an originally symbiotic to a purely parasitic condition. Reinke came to the conclusion that if a parasitic species were derived directly from a lichen type, then it must still rank as a lichen, a view that has a direct bearing on the question. The parallel family of Pyrenulaceae which have *Trentepohlia* gonidia is considered by Zahlbruckner to have originated from the fungus genus *Didymella*.

Compound or stromatoid fructifications occur once and again in lichen families; but, according to Wainio[3], there is no true stroma formation, only a pseudostroma resulting from adhesions and agglomerations of the thalline envelopes or from cohesions of the margins of developing fruit bodies. These pseudostromata are present in the genera *Chiodecton* and *Glyphis* (Graphidineae) and in *Trypethelium*, *Mycoporium*, etc. (Pyrenocarpineae). This view of the nature of the compound fruits is strengthened, as Wainio points out, by the presence in certain species of single apothecia or perithecia on the same specimen as the stromatoid fruits.

b. CONIOCARPINEAE. This subseries is entirely isolated. Its peculiarity lies in the character of the mature fruit in which the spores, owing to the early breaking down of the asci, lie as a loose mass in the hymenium, while dispersal is delayed for an indefinite time. This type of fruit, termed a *mazaedium* by Acharius, is in the form of a stalked or sessile roundish head —the capitulum—closed at first and only half-open at maturity rarely, as in *Cyphelium*, an exposed disc. There is a suggestion, but only a suggestion, of a similar fructification in the tropical fungus *Camillea* in which there is sometimes a stalk with one or more perithecia at the tip, and in some species early disintegration of the asci, leaving spore masses[4]. But neither in fungi nor in other lichens is there any obvious connection with Coniocarpineae. In some of the genera the fungus alone forms the stalk and the wall of the capitulum; in others the thallus shares in the fruit-formation growing around it as an amphithecium.

The semi-closed fruits point to their affinity with Pyrenolichens, though

---

[1] Steiner 1896.   [2] Müller-Argau 1880.   [3] Wainio 1890, p. xxiii.   [4] Lloyd 1917.

they are more advanced than these judging from the thalline wall that is present in some genera and also from the half-open disc at maturity. The latter feature has influenced some systematists to classify the whole subseries among Cyclocarpineae. The thallus, as in *Sphaerophorus*, reaches a high degree of fruticose development; in other genera it is crustaceous without any formation of cortex, while in several genera or species it is non-existent, the fruits being parasites on the thalli of other lichens or saprophytes on dead wood, humus, etc. These latter—both parasites and saprophytes— are included by Rehm[1] and others among fungi, which has involved the breaking up of this very distinctive series. Rehm has thus published as Discomycetes the lichen genera *Sphinctrina, Cyphelium, Coniocybe, Ascolium,* *Calicium* and *Stenocybe*, since some or all of their species are regarded by him as fungi.

Reinke[2] in his lichen studies states that it might not be impossible for a saprophytic fungus to be derived from a crustaceous lichen—a case of reversion—but that no such instance was then known. More exact studies[3] of parasymbiosis and antagonistic symbiosis have shown the wide range of possible life-conditions, and such a reversion does not seem improbable. We must also bear in mind that in suitable cultures, lichen hyphae can be grown without gonidia: they develop in that case as saprophytes.

On Reinke's[2] view, however, that these saprophytic species, belonging to different genera in the Coniocarpineae, are true fungi, they would represent the direct and closely related ancestors of the corresponding lichen genera, giving a polyphyletic origin within this group. As fungus genera he has united them in Protocaliciaceae, and the representatives among fungi he distinguishes, as does Wainio[4], under such names as *Mycocalicium* and *Mycoconiocybe*.

If we might consider the saprophytic forms as also retrogressive lichens, a monophyletic origin from some remote fungal ancestor would prove a more satisfactory solution of the inheritance problem. This view is even supported by a comparison Reinke himself has drawn between the development of the fructification in *Mycocalicium parietinum*, a saprophyte, and in his view a fungus, and *Chaenotheca chrysocephala,* a closely allied lichen. Both grow on old timber. In the former (the fungus), the mycelium pervades the outer weathered wood-cells, and the fruit stalk rises from a clump of brownish hyphae; there is no trace of gonidia. *Chaenotheca chrysocephala* differs in the presence of gonidia which are associated with the mycelium in scattered granular warts; but the fruit stalk here also rises directly from the mycelium between the granules. The presence of a lichen thallus chiefly differentiates between the two plants, and this thallus is not a casual or recent association: it is constant and of great antiquity as it is richly provided with lichen-acids.

[1] Rehm 1890.   [2] Reinke 1894.   [3] See p. 260.   [4] Wainio 1890.

Reinke has indicated the course of evolution within the series but that is on the lines of thalline development and will be considered later.

c. GRAPHIDINEAE. This series contains a considerable variety of lichen forms, but all possess to a more or less marked degree the linear form of fructification termed a " lirella " which has only a slit-like opening. There is a tendency to round discoid fruits in the *Roccellae* and also in the *Arthoniae*; the apothecia of the latter, called by early lichenologists "ardellae," are without margins. In nearly all there is a formation of carbonaceous black tissue either in the hypothecium or in the proper margins. In some of them the paraphyses are branched and dark at the tips, the branches interlocking to form a strong protective epithecium. There are, however, constant exceptions, in some particular, to any generalization in genera and in species. Müller-Argau's[1] pronouncement might be held to have special reference to Graphidineae: " that in any genus, species or groups of species are to be found which outwardly shew something that is peculiar, though of slight importance." The most constant type of gonidium is *Trentepohlia*, but *Palmella* and *Phycopeltis* occasionally occur. The spores are various in colour and form; they are rarely simple.

The genus *Arthonia* is derived from a member of the Patellariaceae, from which family many of the Discomycetes have arisen. The course of development does not follow from a closed to an open fruit; the apothecium is open from the first, and growth proceeds from the centre outwards, the fertile cells gradually pushing aside the sterile tissue of the exterior. The affinity of *Xylographa* (with *Palmella* gonidia) is to be found in *Stictis* in the fungal family Stictidaceae, the apothecia of *Stictis* being at first closed, then open, and with a thick margin; *Xylographa* has a more elongate lirella fruit, though otherwise very similar, and has a very reduced thallus. Rehm[2] has classified *Xylographa* as a fungus.

The genera with linear apothecia are closely connected with Hysteriaceae, and evidently inherit their fruit form severally from that family. There is thus ample evidence of polyphyletic descent in the series. Stromatoid fruits occur in Chiodectonaceae, with deeply sunk, almost closed disc, but they have evidently evolved within the series, possibly from a dividing up of the lirellae.

In Graphidineae there are also forms, more especially in Arthoniaceae, on the border line between lichens and fungi: those with gonidia being classified as lichens, those without gonidia having been placed in corresponding genera of fungi. These latter athalline species live as parasites or saprophytes.

The larger number of genera have a poorly developed thallus; in many of them it is embedded within the outer periderm-cells of trees, and is known

[1] Müller-Argau 1862.   [2] Rehm 1890.

as "hypophloeodal." But in some families, such as Roccellaceae, the thallus attains a very advanced form and a very high production of acids.

The conception of Graphidineae as a whole is puzzling, but one or other characteristic has brought the various members within the series. It is in this respect an epitome of the lichen class of which the different groups, with all their various origins and affinities, yet form a distinct and well-defined section of the vegetable kingdom.

d. CYCLOCARPINEAE. This is by far the largest series of lichens. The genera are associated with algae belonging both to the Myxophyceae and the Chlorophyceae, and from the many different combinations are produced great variations in the form of the vegetative body. The fruit is an emergent, round or roundish disc or open apothecium in all the members of the series except Pertusariaceae, where it is partially immersed in thalline "warts." In its most primitive form, described as "biatorine" or "lecideine," it may be soft and waxy (*Biatora*) or hard and carbonaceous (*Lecidea*), in the latter the paraphyses being mostly coloured at the tips; these are either simple or but sparingly branched, so that the epithecium is a comparatively slight structure. The outer sterile tissue forms a protective wall or "proper margin" which may be entirely pushed aside, but generally persists as a distinct rim round the disc.

A great advance within the series arose when the gonidial elements of the thallus took part in fruit-formation. In that case not only is the hymenium generally subtended by a layer of algae, but thalline tissue containing algae grows up around the fruit, and forms a second wall or thalline margin. This type of apothecium, termed "lecanorine," is thus intimately associated with the assimilating tissue and food supply, and it gains in capacity of ascus renewal and of long duration. This development from non-marginate to marginate ascomata is necessarily an accompaniment of symbiosis.

There is no doubt that the Cyclocarpineae derive from some simple form or forms of Discomycete in the Patellariaceae. The relationship between that family and the lower *Lecideae* is very close. Rehm[1] finds the direct ancestors of *Lecidea* itself in the fungus genus, *Patinella*, in which the apothecia are truly lecideine in character—open, flat and slightly margined, the hypothecium nearly always dark-coloured and the paraphyses branched, septate, clavate and coloured at the tips, forming a dark epithecium. More definitely still he describes *Patinella atroviridis*, a new species he discovered, as in all respects a *Lecidea*, but without gonidia.

In the crustaceous Lecideaceae, a number of genera have been delimited on spore characters—colourless or brown, and simple or variously septate. In Patellariaceae as described by Rehm are included a number of fungus

[1] Rehm 1890.

genera which correspond to these lichen genera. Only two of them—
Patinella and *Patellaria*—are saprophytic; in all the other genera of the
family, the species with very few exceptions are parasitic on lichens : they
are parasymbionts sharing the algal food supply; in any case, they thrive
on a symbiotic thallus.

Rehm unhesitatingly derives the corresponding lichen genera from these
fungi. He takes no account of the difficulty that if these parasitic (or saprophytic) fungi are primitive, they have yet appeared either later in time than
the lichens on which they exist, or else in the course of ages they have
entirely changed their substratum.

He has traced, for instance, the lichen, *Buellia*, to a saprophytic fungus
species, *Karschia lignyota*, to a genus therefore in which most of the species
are parasitic on lichens and have generally been classified as parasitic lichens.
There is no advance in apothecial characters from the fungus, *Karschia*, to
Buellia, merely the change to symbiosis. It therefore seems more in accordance with facts to regard *Buellia* as a genus evolved within the lichen series
from *Patinella* through *Lecidea*, and to accept these species of *Karschia* on
the border line as parasitic, or even as saprophytic, reversions from the
lichen status. We may add that while these brown-spored lichens are fairly
abundant, the corresponding athalline or fungus forms are comparatively
few in number, which is exactly what might be expected from plants with
a reversionary history.

Occasionally in biatorine or lecideine species with a slight thalline
development all traces of the thallus disappear after the fructification has
reached maturity. The apothecia, if on wood or humus, appear to be
saprophytic and would at first sight be classified as fungi. They have undoubtedly retained the capacity to live at certain stages, or in certain conditions, as saprophytes.

The thallus disappears also in some species of the crustaceous genera
that possess apothecia with a thalline margin, and the fruits may be left
stranded and solitary on the normal substratum, or on some neighbouring
lichen thallus where they are more or less parasitic; but as the thalline
margin persists, there has been no question as to their nature and affinity.

Rehm suggests that many species now included among lichens may be
ultimately proved to be fungi; but it is equally possible that the reverse may
be the case, as for instance *Bacidia flavovirescens*, held by Rehm and others to
be a parasitic fungus species, but since proved by Tobler[1] to be a true lichen.

A note by Lightfoot[2], one of our old-time botanists who gave lichens a
considerable place in his Flora, foreshadows the theory of evolution by
gradual advance, and his views offer a suggestive commentary on the subject
under discussion. He was debating the systematic position of the maritime

---

[1] Tobler 1911[2], p. 407.   [2] Lightfoot 1777, p. 965.

lichen genus *Lichina*, considered then a kind of *Fucus*, and had observed its similarity with true lichens. "The cavity," he writes, "at the top of the fructification (in *Lichina*) is a proof how nearly this species of *Fucus* is related to the scutellated lichens. Nature disdains to be limited to the systematic rules of human invention. She never makes any sudden starts from one class or genus to another, but is regularly progressive in all her works, uniting the various links in the chain of beings by insensible connexions."

III. THE THALLUS

A. General Outline of Development

a. Preliminary Considerations. The evolution of lichens, as such, has reference mainly to the thallus. Certain developments of the fructification are evident, but the changes in the reproductive organs have not kept pace with those of the vegetative structures: the highest type of fruit, for instance, the apothecium with a thalline margin, occurs in genera and species with a very primitive vegetative structure as well as in those that have attained higher development.

Lichens are polyphyletic as regards their algal, as well as their fungal, ancestors, so that it is impossible to indicate a straight line of progression, but there is a general process of thalline development which appears once and again in the different phyla. That process, from simpler to more complicated forms, follows on two lines: on the one there is the endeavour to increase the assimilating surface, on the other the tendency to free the plant from the substratum. In both, the aim has been the same, to secure more favourable conditions for assimilation and aeration. Changes in structure have been already described[1], and it is only needful to indicate here the main lines of evolution.

b. Course of Evolution in Hymenolichens. There is but little trace of development in these lichens. The fungus has retained more or less the form of the ancestral *Thelephora* which has a wide-spreading superficial basidiosporous hymenium. Three genera have been recognized, the differences between them being due to the position within the thallus, and the form of the *Scytonema* that constitutes the gonidium. The highest stage of development and of outward form is reached in *Cora*, in which the gonidial zone is central in the tissue and is bounded above and below by strata of hyphae.

c. Course of Evolution in Ascolichens. It is in the association with Ascomycetes that evolution and adaptation have had full scope. In that subclass there are four constantly recurring and well-marked stages of thalline development. (1) The earliest, most primitive stage, is the

[1] See Chap. III.

crustaceous: at first an accretion of separate granules which may finally be united into a continuous crust with a protective covering of thick-walled amorphous hyphae forming a "decomposed" cortex. The extension of a granule by growth in one direction upwards and outwards gives detachment from the substratum, and originates (2) the squamule which is, however, often of primitive structure and attached to the support, like the granule, by the medullary hyphae. Further growth of the squamule results in (3) the foliose thallus with all the adaptations of structure peculiar to that form. In all of these, the principal area of growth is round the free edges of the thallus. A greater change takes place in the advance to (4) the fruticose type in which the more active growing tissue is restricted to the apex, and in which the frond or filament adheres at one point only to the support, a new series of strengthening and other structures being evolved at the same time.

The lichen fungi associate, as has been already stated, with two different types of algae: those combined with the Myxophyceae have been designated *Phycolichenes*, those with Chlorophyceae as *Archilichenes*. The latter predominate, not only in the number of lichens, but also in the more varied advance of the thallus, although, in many instances, genera and species of both series may be closely related.

B. COMPARATIVE ANTIQUITY OF ALGAL SYMBIONTS

One of the first questions of inheritance concerns the comparative antiquity of the two gonidial series: with which kind of alga did the fungus first form the symbiotic relationship? No assistance in solving the problem is afforded by the type of fructification. The fungus in Archilichens is frequently one of the more primitive Pyrenomycetes, though more often a Discomycete, while in Phycolichens Pyrenomycetes are very rare. There is, as already stated, no corelation of advance between the fruit and the thallus, as the most highly evolved apothecia with well-formed thalline margins are constantly combined with thalli of low type.

Forssell[1] gave considerable attention to the question of antiquity in his study of gelatinous crustaceous lichens in the family Pyrenopsidaceae, termed by him Gloeolichens, and he came to the conclusion that Archilichens represented the older combination, Phycolichens being comparatively young.

His view is based on a study of the development of certain lichen fungi that seem able to adapt themselves to either kind of algal symbiont. He found[1] in *Euopsis (Pyrenopsis) granatina*, one of the Pyrenopsidaceae, that certain portions of the thallus contained blue-green algae, while others contained *Palmella*, and that these latter, though retrograde in development,

[1] Forssell 1885.

might become fertile. The granules with blue-green gonidia were stronger, more healthy and capable of displacing those with *Palmella*, but not of bearing apothecia, though spermogonia were embedded in them—a first step, according to Forssell, towards the formation of apothecia. These granules, not having reached a fruiting stage, were reckoned to be of a more recent type than those associated with *Palmella*. In other instances, however, the line of evolution has been undoubtedly from blue-green to more highly evolved bright-green thalli.

The striking case of similarity between *Psoroma hypnorum* (bright-green) and *Pannaria rubiginosa* (blue-green) may also be adduced. Forssell considers that *Psoroma* is the more ancient form, but as the fungus is adapted to associate with either kind of alga, the type of squamules forming the thallus may be gradually transformed by the substitution of blue-green for the earlier bright-green—the *Pannaria* superseding the *Psoroma*. There is a close resemblance in the fructification—that is of the fungus—in these two different lichens.

Hue[1] shares Forssell's opinion as to the greater antiquity of the bright-green gonidia and cites the case of *Solorina crocea*. In that lichen there is a layer of bright-green gonidia in the usual dorsiventral position, below the upper cortex. Below this zone there is a second formed entirely of blue-green cells. Hue proved by his study of development in *Solorina* that the bright-green were the normal gonidia of the thallus, and were the only ones present in the growing peripheral areas; the blue-green were a later addition, and appeared first in small groups at some distance from the edge of the lobes.

The whole subject of cephalodia-development[2] has a bearing on this question. These bodies always contain blue-green algae, and are always associated with Archilichens. Mostly they occur as excrescences, as in *Stereocaulon* and in *Peltigera*. The fungus of the host-lichen though normally adapted to bright-green algae has the added capacity of forming later a symbiosis with the blue-green. This tendency generally pervades a whole genus or family, the members of which, as in Peltigeraceae, are too closely related to allow as a rule of separate classification even when the algae are totally distinct.

C. Evolution of Phycolichens

The association of lichen-forming fungi with blue-green algae may have taken place later in time, or may have been less successful than with the bright-green: they are fewer in number, and the blue-green type of thallus is less highly evolved, though examples of very considerable development are to be found in such genera as *Peltigera*, *Sticta* or *Nephromium*.

[1] Hue 1911[1]. [2] See p. 133.

a. GLOEOLICHENS. Among crustaceous forms the thallus is generally elementary, more especially in the Gloeolichens (Pyrenopsidaceae). The algae of that family, *Gloeocapsa*, *Xanthocapsa* or *Chroococcus*, are furnished with broad gelatinous sheaths which, in the lichenoid state, are penetrated and traversed by the fungal filaments, a branch hypha generally touching with its tip the algal cell-wall. Under the influence of symbiosis, the algal masses become firmer and more compact, without much alteration in form; algae entirely free from hyphae are often intermingled with the others. Even among Gloeolichens there are signs of advancing development both in the internal structure and in outward form. Lobes free from the substratum, though very minute, appear in the genus *Paulia*, the single species of which comes from Polynesia. Much larger lobes are characteristic of *Thyrea*, a Mediterranean and American genus. The fruticose type, with upright fronds of minute size, also appears in our native genus *Synalissa*. It is still more marked in the coralloid thalli of *Peccania* and *Phleopeccania*. In most of these genera there is also a distinct tendency to differentiation of tissues, with the gonidia congregating towards the better lighted surfaces. The only cortex formation occurs in the crustaceous genus *Forssellia* in which, according to Zahlbruckner[1], it is plectenchymatous above, the thallus being attached below by hyphae penetrating the substratum. In another genus, *Anema*[2], which is minutely lobate-crustaceous, the internal hyphae form a cellular network in which the algae are immeshed. As regards algal symbionts, the members of this family are polyphyletic in origin.

b. EPHEBACEAE AND COLLEMACEAE. In Ephebaceae the algae are tufted and filamentous, *Scytonema*, *Stigonema* or *Rivularia*, the trichomes of which are surrounded by a common gelatinous sheath. The hyphae travel in the sheath alongside the cell-rows, and the symbiotic plant retains the tufted form of the alga as in *Lichina* with *Rivularia*, *Leptogidium* with *Scytonema*, and *Ephebe* with *Stigonema*. The last named lichen forms a tangle of intricate branching filaments about an inch or more in length. The fruticose habit in these plants is an algal characteristic; it has not been acquired as a result of symbiosis, and does not signify any advance in evolution.

A plectenchymatous cortex marks some progress here also in *Leptodendriscum*, *Leptogidium* and *Polychidium*, all of which are associated with *Scytonema*. These genera may well be derived from an elementary form such as *Thermutis*. They differ from each other in spore characters, etc., *Polychidium* being the most highly developed with its cortex of two cell-rows and with two-celled spores.

Nostoc forms the gonidium of Collemaceae. In its free state it is extremely gelatinous and transmits that character more or less to the lichen. In the crustaceous genus *Physma*, which forms the base of the *Collema* group or

---

[1] Zahlbruckner 1907.   [2] Reinke 1895.

phylum, there is but little difference in form between the thalline warts of the lichen crust and the original small *Nostoc* colonies such as are to be found on damp mosses, etc.

In *Collema* itself, the less advanced species are scarcely more than crusts, though the more developed show considerable diversity of lobes, either short and pulpy, or spreading out in a thin membrane. The *Nostoc* chains pervade the homoiomerous thallus, but in some species they lie more towards the upper surface. There is no cortex, though once and again plectenchyma appears in the apothecial margin, both in this genus and in *Leprocollema* which is purely crustaceous.

Leptogium is a higher type than *Collema*, the thallus being distinguished by its cellular cortex. The tips of the hyphae, lying close together at the surface, are cut off by one or more septa, giving a one- or several-celled cortical layer. The species though generally homoiomerous are of thinner texture and are less gelatinous than those of *Collema*.

c. PYRENIDIACEAE. This small family of pyrenocarpous Phycolichens may be considered here though its affinity, through the form of the fruiting body, is with Archilichens. The gonidia are species of *Nostoc*, *Scytonema* and *Stigonema*. There are only five genera; one of these, *Eolichen*, contains three species, the others are monotypic.

The crustaceous genera have a non-corticate thallus, but an advance to lobate form takes place in *Placothelium*, an African genus. The two genera that show most development are both British: *Coriscium* (*Normandina*), which is lobate, heteromerous and corticate—though always sterile—and *Pyrenidium* which is fruticose in habit; the latter is associated with *Nostoc* and forms a minute sward of upright fronds, corticate all round; the perithecium is provided with an entire wall and is immersed in the thallus.

If the thallus alone were under consideration these lichens would rank with Pannariaceae.

d. HEPPIACEAE AND PANNARIACEAE. The next stage in the development of Phycolichens takes place through the algae, *Scytonema* and *Nostoc*, losing not only their gelatinous sheaths, but also, to a large extent, their characteristic forms. Chains of cells can frequently be observed, but accurate and certain identification of the algal genus is only possible by making separate cultures of the gonidia.

Scytonema forms the gonidium of the squamulose Heppiaceae consisting of the single genus *Heppia*. The ground tissue of the species is either wholly of plectenchyma with algae in the interstices, or the centre is occupied by a narrow medulla of loose filaments.

In the allied family Pannariaceae, a number of genera contain *Scytonema* or *Nostoc*, while two, *Psoroma* and *Psoromaria*, have bright-green gonidia.

The thallus varies from crustaceous or minutely squamulose, to lobes of fair dimension in *Parmeliella* and in *Hydrothyria venosa*, an aquatic lichen. Plectenchyma appears in the upper cortex of both of these, and in the proper margin of the apothecia, while the under surface is frequently provided with rhizoidal filaments.

These two families form a transition between the gelatinous, and mostly homoiomerous thallus, and the more developed entirely heteromerous thallus of much more advanced structure. The fructification in all of them, gelatinous and non-gelatinous, is a more or less open apothecium, sometimes immarginate, and biatorine or lecideine, but often, even in species nearly related to these, it is lecanorine with a thalline amphithecium. Rarely are the sporiferous bodies sunk in the tissue, with a pseudo-perithecium, as in *Phylliscum*. It would be difficult to trace advance in all this group on the lines of fruit development. The two genera with bright-green gonidia, *Psoroma* and *Psoromaria*, have been included in Pannariaceae owing to the very close affinity of *Psoroma hypnorum* with *Pannaria rubiginosa*; they are alike in every respect except in their gonidia. *Psoromaria* is exactly like *Psoroma*, but with immarginate biatorine apothecia, representing therefore a lower development in that respect.

These lichens not only mark the transition from gelatinous to nongelatinous forms, but in some of them there is an interchange of gonidia. The progression in the phylum or phyla has evidently been from blue-green up to some highly evolved forms with bright-green algae, though there may have been, at the beginning, a substitution of blue-green in place of earlier bright-green algae, Phycolichens usurping as it were the Archilichen condition.

e. PELTIGERACEAE AND STICTACEAE. The two families just examined marked a great advance which culminated in the lobate aquatic lichen *Hydrothyria*. This lichen, as Sturgis pointed out, shows affinity with other Pannariaceae in the structure of the single large-celled cortical layer as well as with species of *Nephroma* (Peltigeraceae). A still closer affinity may be traced with *Peltigera* in the presence in both plants of veins on the under surface. The capacity of *Peltigera* species to grow in damp situations may also be inherited from a form like the submerged *Hydrothyria*. In both families there are transitions from blue-green to bright-green gonidia, or *vice versa*, in related species. Thus in Peltigeraceae we find *Peltigera* containing *Nostoc* in the gonidial zone, with *Peltidea* which may be regarded as a separate genus, or more naturally as a section of *Peltigera*; it contains bright-green gonidia, but has cephalodia containing *Nostoc* associated with its thallus.

The genus *Nephroma* is similarly divided into species with a bright-green gonidial zone, chiefly Arctic or Antarctic in distribution, and species with *Nostoc* (subgenus *Nephromium*) more numerous and more widely distributed.

Peltigera and *Nephroma* are also closely related in the character of the fructification. It is a flat non-marginate disc borne on the edge of the thallus: in *Peltigera* on the upper surface, in *Nephroma* on the under surface. The remaining genus *Solorina* contains normally a layer of bright-green algae, but, along with these, there are always present more or fewer *Nostoc* cells, either in a thin layer as in *S. crocea* or as cephalodia in others, while, in three species the algae are altogether blue-green.

The members of the Peltigeraceae have a thick upper cortex of plecten-chyma and in some cases strengthening veins, and long rhizinae on the lower side. Some of the species attain a large size, and, in some, soredia are formed, an evidence of advance, this being a peculiarly lichenoid form of reproduction.

The Stictaceae form a parallel but more highly organized family, which also includes closely related bright-green and blue-green series. They are all dorsiventral, but they are mostly attached by a single hold-fast and the lobes in some species suggest the fruticose type in their long narrow form. A wide cortex of plectenchyma protects both the upper and the lower surface and a felt of hairs replaces the rhizinae of other foliose lichens. In the genus *Sticta* (including the section *Stictina*) special aeration organs, cyphellae or pseudocyphellae, are provided; in *Lobaria* these are replaced by naked areas which serve the same purpose.

Nylander[1] regarded the Stictaceae as the most highly developed of all lichens, and they easily take a high place among dorsiventral forms, but it is generally conceded that the fruticose type is the more highly organized. In any case they are the highest reach of the phylum or phyla that started with Pyrenopsidaceae and Collemaceae; the lowly gelatinous thalli changing to more elaborate structures with the abandonment of the gelatinous algal sheath, as in the Pannariaceae, and with the replacement of blue-green by bright-green gonidia. Reinke[2], considers the Stictaceae as evolved from the Pannariaceae more directly from the genus *Massalongia*. Their relationship is certainly with Pannariaceae and Peltigeraceae rather than with Par-meliaceae; these latter, as we shall see, belong to a wholly different series.

D. EVOLUTION OF ARCHILICHENS

The study of Archilichens as of Phycolichens is complicated by the many different kinds of fungi and algae that have entered into combination; but the two principal types of algae are the single-celled *Protococcus* group and the filamentous *Trentepohlia*: as before only the broad lines of thalline development will be traced.

The elementary forms in the different series are of the simplest type—a somewhat fortuitous association of alga and fungus, which in time bears the

---

[1] See p. 126.　　　　[2] Reinke 1895.

lichen fructification. It has been stated that the greatest advance of all took place with the formation of a cortex over the primitive granule, followed by a restricted area of growth outward or upward which resulted finally in the foliose and fruticose thalli. Guidance in following the course of evolution is afforded by the character of the fructification, which generally shows some great similarity of type throughout the different phyla, and remains fairly constant during the many changes of thalline evolution. Development starting from one or many origins advances point by point in a series of parallel lines.

a. THALLUS OF PYRENOCARPINEAE. In this series there are two families of algae that function as gonidia: Protococcaceae, consisting of single cells, and Trentepohliaceae, filamentous. *Phyllactidium* (*Cephaleuros*) appears in a single genus, *Strigula*, a tropical epiphytic lichen.

Associated with these types of algae are a large number of genera and species of an elementary character, without any differentiation of tissue. In many instances the thallus is partly or wholly embedded in the substratum.

Squamulose or foliose forms make their appearance in Dermatocarpaceae: in *Normandina* the delicate shell-like squamules are non-corticate, but in other genera, *Endocarpon*, *Placidiopsis*, etc., the squamules are corticate and of firmer texture, while in *Dermatocarpon*, foliose fronds of considerable size are formed. The perithecial fruits are embedded in the upper surface.

In only one extremely rare lichen, *Pyrenothamnia Spraguei* (N. America), is there fruticose development: the thallus, round and stalk-like at the base, branches above into broader more leaf-like expansions.

b. THALLUS OF CONIOCARPINEAE. At the base of this series are genera and species that are extremely elementary as regards thalline formation, with others that are saprophytic and parasitic. The simplest type of thallus occurs in Caliciaceae, a spreading mycelium with associated algae (Protococcaceae) collected in small scattered granules, resembling somewhat a collection of loose soredia. The species grow mostly on old wood, trunks of trees, etc. In *Calicium* (*Chaenotheca*) *chrysocephalum* as described by Neubner[1] the first thallus formation begins with these scattered minute granules; gradually they increase in size and number till a thick granular coating of the substratum arises, but no cortex is formed and there is no differentiation of tissue.

The genus *Cyphelium* (Cypheliaceae) is considered by Reinke to be more highly developed, inasmuch as the thalline granules, though non-corticate, are more extended horizontally, and, in vertical section, show a distinct differentiation into gonidial zone and medulla. The sessile fruit also takes origin from the thallus, and is surrounded by a thalline amphithecium, or rather it remains embedded in the thalline granule. A closely allied tropical

[1] Neubner 1893.

genus *Pyrgillus* has reached a somewhat similar stage of development, but with a more coherent homogeneous thallus, while in *Tylophoron*, also tropical or subtropical, the fruit is raised above the crustaceous thallus but is thickly surrounded by a thalline margin. The alga of that genus is *Trentepohlia*, a rare constituent of Coniocarpineae.

A much more advanced formation appears in the remaining family Sphaerophoraceae. In *Calycidium*, a monotypic New Zealand genus, the thallus consists of minute squamules, dorsiventral in structure but with a tendency to vertical growth, the upper surface is corticate and the mazaedial apothecia—always open—are situated on the margins. *Tholurna dissimilis*, (Scandinavian) still more highly developed, has two kinds of rather small fronds corticate on both surfaces, the one horizontal in growth, crenulate in outline, and sterile, the other vertical, about 2 mm. in height, hollow and terminating in a papilla in which is seated the apothecium.

Two other monotypic subtropical genera form a connecting link with the more highly evolved forms. In the first, *Acroscyphus sphaerophoroides*, the fronds are somewhat similar to the fertile ones of *Tholurna*, but they possess a solid central strand and the apical mazaedium is less enveloped by the thallus. The other, *Pleurocybe madagascarea*, has narrow flattish branching fronds about 3 cm. in height, hollow in the centre and corticate with marginal or surface fruits.

The third genus, *Sphaerophorus*, is cosmopolitan; three of the species are British and are fairly common on moorlands, etc. They are fruticose in habit, being composed of congregate upright branching stalks, either round or slightly compressed and varying in height from about 1 to 8 cm. The structure is radiate with a well-developed outer cortex, and a central strand which gives strength to the somewhat slender stalks. The fruits are lodged in the swollen tips and are at first enclosed; later, the covering thallus splits irregularly and exposes the hymenium.

Coniocarpineae comprise only a comparatively small number of genera and species, but the series is of unusual interest as being extremely well defined by the fruit-formation and as representing all the various stages of thalline development from the primitive crustaceous to the highly evolved fruticose type. With the primitive thallus is associated a wholly fungal fruit, both stalk and capitulum, which in the higher forms is surrounded and protected by the thallus. Lichen-acids are freely produced even in crustaceous forms, and they, along with the high stage of development reached, testify to the great antiquity of the series.

c. THALLUS OF GRAPHIDINEAE. As formerly understood, this series included only crustaceous forms with an extremely simple development of thallus, fungi and algae—whether Palmellaceae, etc., or more frequently Trentepohliaceae—growing side by side either superficially or embedded in tree or rock, the presence of the vegetative body being often signalled only by a deeper colouration of the substratum. The researches of Almquist, and more recently of Reinke and Darbishire, have enlarged our conception of the series, and the families Dirinaceae and Roccellaceae are now classified in Graphidineae.

Arthoniaceae, Graphidaceae and Chiodectonaceae are all wholly crustaceous. The first thalline advance takes place in Dirinaceae with two allied genera, *Dirina* and *Dirinastrum*. Though the thallus is still crustaceous, it is of considerable thickness, with differentiation of tissues: on the lower side there is a loosely filamentous medulla from which hyphae pierce the substratum and secure attachment. *Trentepohlia* gonidia lie in a zone above the medulla, and the upper cortex is formed of regular palisade hyphae forming a "fastigiate cortex." It is the constant presence of *Trentepohlia* algae as well as the tendency to ellipsoid or lirellate fruits that have influenced the inclusion of Dirinaceae and Roccellaceae in the series.

The thallus of Dirinaceae is crustaceous, while the genera of Roccellaceae are mostly of an advanced fruticose type, though in one, *Roccellina*, there is a crustaceous thallus with an upright portion consisting of short swollen podetia-like structures with apothecia at the tips; and in another, *Roccellographa*, the fronds broaden to leafy expansions. They are nearly all rock-dwellers, often inhabiting wind-swept maritime coasts, and a strong basal sheath has been evolved to strengthen their foothold. In some genera the sheath contains gonidia; in others the tissue is wholly of hyphae—in nearly every case it is protected by a cortex.

In the upright fronds the structure is radiate: generally a rather loose strand of hyphae more or less parallel with the long axis of the plant forms a central medulla. The gonidia lie outside the medulla and just within the outer cortex. The latter, in a few genera, is fibrous, the parallel hyphae being very closely compacted; but in most members of the family the fastigiate type prevails, as in the allied family Dirinaceae.

d. THALLUS OF CYCLOCARPINEAE. This is by far the largest and most varied series of Archilichens. It is derived, as regards the fungal constituent, from the Discomycetes, but in these fungi, the vegetative or mycelial body gives no aid to the classification which depends wholly on apothecial characters. In the symbiotic condition, on the contrary, the thallus becomes of extreme importance in the determination of families, genera and species. There has been within the series a great development both of apothecial and of thalline characters in parallel lines or phyla.

AA. LECIDEALES. The type of fruit nearest to fungi in form and origin occurs in the Lecideales. It is an open disc developed from the fungal symbiont alone, the alga taking no part. There are several phyla to be considered.

aa. Coenogoniaceae. There are two types of gonidial algae in this family, and both are filamentous forms, *Trentepohlia* in *Coenogonium* and *Cladophora* in *Racodium*. The resulting lichens retain the slender thread-like form of the algae, their cells being thinly invested by the hyphae and both symbionts growing apically. The thalline filaments are generally very sparingly branched and grow radially side by side in a loose flat expansion attached at one side by a sheath, or the strands spread irregularly over the substratum. Plectenchyma appears in the apothecial margin in *Coenogonium*. Fruiting bodies are unknown in *Racodium*.

Coenogoniaceae are a group apart and of slight development, only the one kind of thallus appearing; the form is moulded on that of the gonidium, and is, as Reinke[1] remarks, perfectly adapted to receive the maximum of illumination and aeration.

bb. Lecideaceae and Gyrophoraceae. The origin of this thalline phylum is distinct from that of the previous family, being associated with a different type of gonidium, the single-celled alga of the Protococcaceae.

The more elementary species are of extremely simple structure as exemplified in such species as *Lecidea* (*Biatora*) *uliginosa* or *Lecidea granulosa*. These lichens grow on humus-soil and the thallus consists of a spreading mycelium or hypothallus with more or less scattered thalline granules containing gonidia, but without any defined structure. The first advance takes place in the aggregation and consolidation of such thalline granules and the massing of the gonidia towards the light, thus substituting the heteromerous for the homoiomerous arrangement of the tissues. The various characters of thickness, areolation, colour, etc. of the thallus are constant and are expressed in specific diagnoses. Frequently an amorphous cortex of swollen hyphae provides a smooth upper surface and forms a protective covering for such long-lived species as *Rhizocarpon geographicum*, etc.

The squamulose thallus is well represented in this phylum. The squamules vary in size and texture but are mostly rather thick and stiff. In *Lecidea ostreata* they rise from the substratum in serried rows forming a dense sward; in *L. decipiens*, also a British species, the squamules are still larger, and more horizontal in direction; they are thick and firm and the upper cortex is a plectenchyma of cells with swollen walls. Solitary hyphae from the medulla pass downwards into the support.

Changes in spore characters also arise in these different thalline series, as for instance in genera such as *Biatorina* and *Buellia*, the one with colourless, the other with brown, two-celled spores. These variations, along with changes in the thallus, are of specific or generic importance following the significance accorded to the various characters.

In one lichen of the series, the monotypic Brazilian genus *Sphaerophoropsis*

[1] Reinke 1895, p. 110.

stereocauloides, the thallus is described by Wainio[1] as consisting of minute clavate stalks of interwoven thick-walled hyphae, with gelatinous algae, like *Gloeocapsa*, interspersed in groups, though with a tendency to congregate towards the outer surface.

The highest development along this line of advance is to be found in the Gyrophoraceae, a family of lichens with a varied foliose character and dark lecideine apothecia. The thallus may be monophyllous and of fairly large dimensions or polyphyllous; it is mostly anchored by a central stout hold-fast and both surfaces are thickly corticate with a layer of plectenchyma; the under surface is mostly bare, but may be densely covered with rhizina-like strands of dark hyphae. They are all northern species and rock-dwellers exposed to severe extremes of illumination and temperature, but well protected by the thick cortex and the dark colouration common to them all.

cc. CLADONIACEAE. This last phylum of Lecideales is the most interesting as it is the most complicated. It possesses a primary, generally sterile, thallus which is dorsiventral and crustaceous, squamulose or in some in-stances almost foliaceous, along with a secondary thallus of upright radiate structure and of very varied form, known as the podetium which bears at the summit the fertile organs.

A double thallus has been suggested in the spreading base, containing gonidia, of some radiate lichens such as *Roccella*, but the upright portion of such lichens, though analogous, is not homologous with that of Cladoniaceae.

The algal cells of the family belong to the Protococcaceae. Blue-green algae are associated in the cephalodia of *Pilophorus* and *Stereocaulon*. The primary thallus is a feature of all the members, though sometimes very slight and very short-lived, as in *Stereocaulon* or in the section *Cladina* of the genus *Cladonia*. Where the primary thallus is most largely developed, the secondary (the podetium) is less prominent.

This secondary thallus originates in two different ways: (1) the primary granule may grow upward, the whole of the tissues taking part in the new development; or (2) the origin may be endogenous and proceed from the hyphae only of the gonidial zone: these push upwards in a compact fascicle, as in the apothecial development of *Lecidea*, but instead of spreading outward on reaching the surface, they continue to grow in a vertical direction and form the podetium. In origin this is an apothecial stalk, but generally it is clothed with gonidial tissue. The gonidia may travel upwards from the base or they may possibly be wind borne from the open. The podetium thus takes on an assimilative function and is a secondary thallus.

The same type of apothecium is common to all the genera; the spores

[1] Wainio 1890.

are colourless and mostly simple, but there are also changes in form and septation not commensurate with thalline advance, as has been already noted. Thus in *Gomphillus*, with primitive thallus and podetium, the spores are long and narrow with about 100 divisions.

1. ORIGIN OF CLADONIA. There is no difficulty in deriving Cladoniaceae from *Lecidea*, or, more exactly, from some crustaceous species of the section *Biatora* in which the apothecia—as in Cladoniaceae—are waxy and more or less light-coloured and without a thalline margin. In only a very few isolated instances has a thalline margin grown round the *Cladonia* fruit.

There are ten genera included in the Cladoniaceae, of which five are British. Considerable study has been devoted to the elucidation of developmental problems within the family by various workers, more especially in the large and varied genus *Cladonia* which is complicated by the presence of the two thalli. The family is monophyletic in origin, though many subordinate phyla appear later.

2. EVOLUTION OF THE PRIMARY THALLUS. At the base of the series we find here also an elementary granular thallus which appears in some species of most of the genera. In *Gomphillus*, a monospecific British genus, the granules have coalesced into a continuous mucilaginous membrane. In *Baeomyces*, though mostly crustaceous, there is an advance to the squamulose type in *B. placophyllus*, and in two Brazilian species described by Wainio, one of which, owing to the form of the fronds, has been placed in a separate genus *Heteromyces*. The primary thallus becomes almost foliose also in *Gymnoderma coccocarpum* from the Himalayas, with dorsiventral stratose arrangement of the tissues, but without rhizinae. The greatest diversity is however to be found in *Cladonia* where granular, squamulose and almost foliose thalli occur. The various tissue formations have already been described[1].

3. EVOLUTION OF THE SECONDARY THALLUS. Most of the interest centres round the development and function of the podetium. In several genera the primordium is homologous with that of an apothecium; its elongation to an apothecial stalk is associated with delayed fructification, and though it has taken on the function of the vegetative thallus, the purpose of elongation has doubtless been to secure good light conditions for the fruit, and to facilitate a wide distribution of spores: therefore, not only in development but in function, its chief importance though now assimilative was originally reproductive. The vegetative development of the podetium is correlated with the reduction of the primary thallus which in many species bears little relation in size or persistence to the structure produced from it, as, for instance, in *Cladonia rangiferina* where the ground thallus is of the

[1] See Chap. III.

scantiest and very soon disappears, while the podetial thallus continues to grow indefinitely and to considerable size.

4. COURSE OF PODETIAL DEVELOPMENT. In *Baeomyces* the podetial primordium is wholly endogenous in some species, but in others the outer cortical layer of the primary thallus as well as the gonidial hyphae take part in the formation of the new structure which, in that case, is simply a vertical extension of the primary granule. This type of podetium—called by Wainio[1] a pseudopodetium—also recurs in *Pilophorus* and in *Stereocaulon*. To emphasize the distinction of origin it has been proposed to classify these two latter genera in a separate family, but in that case it would be necessary to break up the genus *Baeomyces*. We may assume that the endogenous origin of the "apothecial stalk" is the more primitive, as it occurs in the most primitive lecideine lichens, whereas a vertical thallus is always an advanced stage of vegetative development.

Podetia are essentially secondary structures, and they are associated both with crustaceous and squamulose primary thalli. If monophyletic in origin their development must have taken place while the primary thallus was still in the crustaceous stage, and the inherited tendency to form podetia must then have persisted through the change to the squamulose type. In species such as *Cl. caespiticia* the presence of rudimentary podetia along with large squamules suggests a polyphyletic origin, but Wainio's[1] opinion is that such instances may show retrogression from an advanced podetial form, and that the evidence inclines to the monophyletic view of their origin.

The hollow centre of the podetium arises in the course of development and is common to nearly all advanced stages of growth. There are however some exceptions : in *Glossodium aversum*, a soil lichen from New Granada, and the only representative of the genus, a simple or rarely forked stalk about 2 cm. in height rises from a granular or minutely squamulose thallus. The apothecium occupies one side of the flattened and somewhat wider apex. There is no external cortex and the central tissue is of loose hyphae. In *Thysanothecium Hookeri*, also a monotypic genus from Australia, the podetia are about the same height, but, though round at the base, they broaden upwards into a leaf-like expansion. The central tissue below is of loose hyphae, but compact strands occur above, where the apothecium spreads over the upper side. The under surface is sterile and is traversed by nerve-like strands of hyphae.

5. VARIATION IN CLADONIA. It is in this genus that most variation is to be found. Characters of importance and persistence have arisen by which secondary phyla may be traced within the genus: these are mainly (1) the relative development of the horizontal and vertical structures, (2) formation

---

[1] Wainio 1897.

of the scyphus and branching of the podetium, with (3) differences in colour both in the vegetative thallus and in the apothecia

Wainio has indicated the course of evolution on the following lines: (1) the crustaceous thallus is monophyletic in origin and here as elsewhere precedes the squamulose. The latter he considers to be also monophyletic, though at more than one point the more advanced and larger foliose forms have appeared: (2) the primitive podetium was subulate and unbranched, and the apex was occupied by the apothecium. Both scyphus and branching are later developments indicating progress. They are in both cases associated with fruit-formation—scyphi generally arising from abortive apothecia[1], branching from aggregate apothecia. In forms such as *Cl. fimbriata*, where both scyphiferous and subulate sterile podetia are frequent, the latter (sub-species *fibula*) are retrogressive, and reproduce the ancestral pointed pode-tium. (3) In subgen. *Cenomyce*, with a squamulose primary thallus, there is a sharp division into two main phyla characterized by the colour of the apothecia, brown in *Ochrophaeae*—the colour being due to a pigment—and red in *Cocciferae* where the colouring substance is a lichen-acid, rhodocladonic acid. In the brown-fruited *Ochrophaeae* there are again several secondary phyla. Two of these are distinguished primarily by the character of the branching: (a) the *Chasmariae* in which two or several branches arise from the same level, entailing perforation of the axils (*Cl. furcata, Cl. rangi-formis, Cl. squamosa*, etc.), the scyphi also are perforated. They are further characterized by peltate aggregate apothecia, this grouping of the apothecia according to Wainio being the primary cause of the complex branching, the several fruit stalks growing out as branches. The second group (b), the *Clausae*, are not perforated and the apothecia are simple and broad-based on the edge of the scyphus (*Cl. pyxidata, Cl. fimbriata*, etc.), or on the tips of the podetia (*Cl. cariosa, Cl. leptophylla*, etc.). A third very small group also of *Clausae* called (c) *Foliosae* has very large primary squamules and reduced podetia (*Cl. foliacea*, etc.), while finally (d) the *Ochroleucae*, none of which is British, have poorly developed squamules and variously formed yellowish podetia with pale-coloured apothecia.

The *Cocciferae* represent a phylum parallel in development with the *Ochrophaeae*. The species have perhaps most affinity with the *Clausae*, the vegetative thallus—both the squamules and the podetia—being very much alike in several species. Wainio distinguishes two groups based on a differ-ence of colour in the squamules, glaucous green in one case, yellowish in the other.

6. CAUSES OF VARIATION. External causes of variation in *Cladonia* are chiefly humidity and light, excess or lack of either effecting changes which may have become fixed and hereditary. Minor changes directly traceable

[1] See Chap. III.

to these influences are also frequent, viz. size of podetia, proliferation and the production more or less of soredia or of squamules on the podetia, though only in connection with species in which these variations are already an acquired character. The squamules on the podetium more or less repeat the form of the basal squamules.

7. PODETIAL DEVELOPMENT AND SPORE-DISSEMINATION. In a recent paper by Hans Sättler[1] the problem of podetial development in *Cladonia* is viewed from a different standpoint. He holds that as the podetia are apothecial stalks, their service to the plant consists in the raising of the mature fruit in order to secure a wide distribution of the spores, and that changes in the form of the podetium are therefore but new adaptations for the more efficient discharge of this function.

Following out this idea he regards as the more primitive forms those in which both the spermogonia, as male reproductive bodies, and the carpogonia occur on the primary thallus, ascogonia and trichogynes being formed before the podetium emerges from the thallus. Fertilization thus must take place at a very early period, though the ultimate fruiting stage may be long delayed. Sättler considers that any doubt as to actual fertilization is without bearing on the question, as sexuality he holds must have originally existed and must have directed the course of evolution in the reproductive bodies. In this primitive group, called by him the "Floerkeana" group, the podetia are always short and simple, they are terminated by the apothecium and no scyphi are formed (*Cl. Floerkeana, Cl. leptophylla, Cl. cariosa, Cl. caespiticia, Cl. papillaria*, etc.).

In his second or "pyxidata" group, he places those species in which the apothecia are borne at the edge of a scyphus. That structure he follows Wainio in regarding as a morphological reaction on the failure of the first formed apical apothecium: it is, he adds, a new thallus in the form of a spreading cup and bears, as did the primary thallus, both the female primordia and the spermogonia. In some species, such as *Cl. foliacea*, there may be either scyphous or ascyphous podetia, and spermogonia normally accompany the carpogonium appearing accordingly along with it either on the squamule or on the scyphus.

As the pointed podetia are the more primitive, Sättler points out that they may reappear as retrogressive structures, and have so appeared in the "pyxidata" group in such species as *Cl. fimbriata*. He refers to Wainio's statement that the abortion of the apothecium being a retrogressive anomaly, while scyphus formation is an evolutionary advance, the scyphiferous species present the singular case, "that a progressive transmutation induced by a retrogressive anomaly has become constant."

[1] Sättler 1914.

His third group includes those forms that grow in crowded tufts or swards such as *Cl. rangiferina*, *Cl. furcata*, *Cl. gracilis*, etc. They originate, as did the pyxidata group, in some *Floerkeana*-like form, but in the "rangiferina" group instead of cup-formation there is extensive branching. In the closely packed phalanx of branches water is retained as in similar growths of mosses, and moist conditions necessary for fertilization are thus secured as efficiently as by the water-holding scyphus.

Sättler in his argument has passed over many important points. Above all he ignores the fact that whatever may have been the original nature and function of the podetium, it has now become a thalline structure and provides for the vegetative life of the plant, and that it is in its thalline condition that the many variations have been formed; the scyphus is not, as he contends, a new thallus, it is only an extension of thalline characters already acquired.

8. PILOPHORUS, STEREOCAULON AND ARGOPSIS. These closely related genera are classified with *Cladonia* as they share with it the twofold thallus and the lecideine apothecia. The origin of the podetium being different they may be held to constitute a phylum apart, which has however taken origin also from some *Biatora* form.

The primary thallus is crustaceous or minutely squamulose and the podetia of *Pilophorus*, which are short and unbranched (or very sparingly branched), are beset with thalline granules. The podetia of *Stereocaulon* and *Argopsis* are copiously branched and are more or less thickly covered with minute variously divided leaflets. Cephalodia containing blue-green algae occur on the podetia of these latter genera; in *Pilophorus* they are intermixed with the primary thallus.

The tissue systems are less advanced in these genera than in *Cladonia*: there is no cortex present either in *Pilophorus* or in *Argopsis* or in some species of *Stereocaulon*, though in others a gelatinous amorphous layer covers the podetia and also the stalk leaflets. The stalks are filled with loose hyphae in the centre.

BB. LECANORALES. This second group of Cyclocarpineae is distinguished by the marginate apothecium, a thalline layer providing a protecting amphithecium. The lecanorine apothecium is of a more or less soft and waxy consistency, and though the disc is sometimes almost black, neither hypothecium nor parathecium is carbonaceous as in *Lecidea*. The affinity of *Lecanora* is with sect. *Biatora*, and development must have been from a biatorine form with a persistent thallus. The margin or amphithecium varies in thickness: in some species it is but scanty and soon excluded by the over-topping growth of the disc, so that a zone of gonidia underlying the hypothecium is often the only evidence of gonidial intrusion left in fully formed fruits.

The marginate apothecium has appeared once and again as we have seen. It is probable however that its first development was in this group of lichens, and even here there may have been more than one origin as there' is certainly more than one phylum.

aa. COURSE OF DEVELOPMENT. At the base of the series, the thallus is of the crustaceous type somewhat similar to that of *Lecidea*, but there are none of the very simple primitive forms. *Lecanora* must have originated when the crustaceous lecideine thallus was already well established. Its affinity is with *Lecidea* and not with any fungus: where the thallus is evanescent or scanty, its lack is due to retrogressive rather than to primitive characters.

bb. LECANORACEAE. A number of genera have arisen in this large family, but they are distinguished mainly if not entirely by spore characters, and by some systematists have all been included in the one genus *Lecanora*, since the changes have taken place within the developing apothecium.

There is one genus, *Harpidium*, which is based on thalline characters, represented by one species, *H. rutilans*, common enough on the Continent, but not yet found in our country. It has a thin crustaceous homoiomerous thallus, the component hyphae of which are divided into short cells closely packed together and forming a kind of cellular tissue in which the algae are interspersed. The dorsiventral stratose arrangement prevails however in the other genera and a more or less amorphous "decomposed" cortex is frequently present. The medulla rests on the substratum.

With the stouter thallus, there is slightly more variety of crustaceous form than in Lecideaceae: there occurs occasionally an outgrowth of the thalline granules as in *Haematomma ventosum* which marks the beginning of fruticulose structure. Of a more advanced structure is the thallus of *Lecanora esculenta*, a desert lichen which becomes detached and erratic, and which in some of its forms is almost coralline, owing to the apical growth of the original granules or branches: a more or less radiate arrangement of the tissues is thus acquired.

The squamulose type is well represented in *Lecanora*, and the species with that form of thallus have frequently been placed in a separate genus, *Squamaria*. These squamules are never very large; they possess an upper, somewhat amorphous, cortex; the medulla rests on the substratum, except in such a species as *Lecanora lentigera*, where they are free, a sort of fibrous cortex being formed of hyphae which grow in a direction parallel with the surface. In none of them are rhizinae developed.

cc. PARMELIACEAE. The chief advance, apart from size, of the squamulose to the foliose type is the acquirement of a lower cortex along with definite organs of attachment which in Parmeliaceae are invariably rhizoidal and are composed of compact strands of hyphae extending from the cells of the lower cortex.

In the genus *Parmelia* rhizinae are almost a constant character, though in a few species, such as *Parmelia physodes*, they are scanty or practically absent. It is not possible, however, to consider that these species form a lower group, as in other respects they are highly evolved, and rhizinae may be found at points on the lower surface where there is irritation by friction. Soredia and isidia occur frequently and, in several species, almost entirely replace reproduction by spores. In one or two northern or Alpine species, *P. stygia* and *P. pubescens*, the lobes are linear or almost filamentous. They are retained in *Parmelia* because the apothecia are superficial on the fronds which are partly dorsiventral, and because rhizinae have occasionally been found. Some of the *Parmeliae* attain to a considerable size; growth is centrifugal and long continued.

Two monotypic genera classified under Parmeliaceae, *Physcidia* and *Heterodea*, are of considerable interest as they indicate the bases of parallel development in *Parmelia* and *Cetraria*. The former, a small lichen, is corticate only on the upper surface, and without rhizinae; and from the description, the cortex is of a fastigiate character. The solitary species grows on bark in Cuba; it is related to *Parmelia*, as the apothecia are superficial on the lobes. The second, *Heterodea Mülleri*, a soil-lichen from Australasia, is more akin to *Cetraria* in that the apothecia are terminal. The upper surface is corticate with marginal cilia, the lower surface naked or only protected by a weft of brownish hyphae amongst which cyphellae are formed; pseudocyphellae appear in *Cetraria*.

The genus *Cetraria* contains very highly developed thalline forms, either horizontal (subgenus *Platysma*), or upright (*Eucetraria*). Rhizinae are scanty or absent, but marginal cilia in some upright species act as haptera. *Cetraria aculeata* is truly fruticose with a radiate structure.

An extraordinary development of the under cortex characterizes the genera *Anzia*[1] and *Pannoparmelia*: rhizinae-like strands formed from the cortical cells branch and anastomose with others till a wide mesh of a spongy nature is formed. They are mostly tropical or subtropical or Australasian, and possibly the spongy mass may be of service in retaining moisture. A species of *Anzia* has been recorded by Darbishire[2] from Tierra del Fuego.

dd. Usneaceae. As we have seen, the change to fruticose structure has arisen as an ultimate development in a number of groups; it reaches however its highest and most varied form in this family. Not only are there strap-shaped thalli, but a new form, the filamentous and pendulous, appears; it attains to a great length, and is fitted to withstand severe strain. The

---

[1] See p. 90.   [2] Darbishire 1912.

various adaptations of structure in these two types of thallus have already been described[1].

In *Parmelia* itself there are indications of this line of development in *P. stygia*, with short stiff upright branching fronds, and in *P. pubescens*, with its tufts of filaments, but these two species are more or less dorsiventral in structure and do not rise from the substratum. In *Cetraria* also there is a tendency towards upright growth and in *C. aculeata* even to radiate structure. But advance in these directions has stopped short, the true line of evolution passing through species like *Parmelia physodes* with raised, and in some varieties, tubular fronds, and the somewhat similar species *P. Kamtschadalis* with straggling strap-like lobes, to *Evernia*. That genus is a true link between foliose and fruticose forms and has been classified now with one series, now with the other.

In *Evernia furfuracea*, the lobes are free from the substratum except when friction causes the development of a hold-fast and the branching out of new lobes from that point. It is however dorsiventral in structure, the under surface is black and the gonidial zone lies under the upper cortex. *Evernia prunastri* is white below and is more fruticose in habit, the long fronds all rising from one base. They are thin and limp, no strengthening tissue has been evolved, and they tend to lie over on one side; both surfaces are corticate and gonidia sometimes travel round the edge, becoming frequently lodged here and there along the under side.

The extreme of strap-shaped fruticose development is reached in the genus *Ramalina*. In less advanced species such as *R. evernioides* there is a thin flat expansion anchored to the substratum at one point and alike on both surfaces. In *R. fraxinea* the fronds may reach considerable width (var. *ampliata*), but in that and in most species there is a provision of sclerotic strands to support and strengthen the fronds. One of those best fitted to resist bending strains is *R. scopulorum* (*siliquosa*) which grows by preference on sea-cliffs and safely withstands the maximum of exposure to wind or weather.

The filamentous structure appears abruptly, unless we consider it as foreshadowed by *Parmelia pubescens*. The base is secured by strong sheaths of enduring character; tensile strains are provided for either by a chondroid axis, as in *Usnea*, or by cortical development, as in *Alectoria*; the former method of securing strength seems to be the most advantageous to the plant as a whole, since it leaves the outer structures more free to develop, and there is therefore in *Usnea* a greater variety of branching and greater growth in length, which are less possible with the thickened cortex of *Alectoria*.

ee. PHYSCIACEAE. There remains still an important phylum of Lecanorales well defined by the polarilocular spores[2]. It also arises from a *Biatora*

[1] See p. 101.   [2] See p. 188.

species and forms a parallel development. Even in this phylum there are two series : one with colourless spores and mostly yellow or reddish either in thallus or apothecium, and the other with brown spores and with cinereous-grey or brown thalli. The dark spores are in many of the species typically polarilocular, though in some the median septum is not very wide and no canal is visible. Practically all of the lighter coloured forms contain parietin either in thallus or apothecia or in both; it is absent in the dark-spored series.

Among the lighter coloured forms it is difficult to decide which of these two striking characteristics developed first, the acid or the peculiar spore. Probably the acid has the priority: there is one common rock lichen in this country, *Placodium rupestre* (*Lecanora irrubata*), which gives a strong red acid reaction with potash, but in which the spores are still simple, and the fruit structure in the biatorine stage. Another species, *Pl. luteoalbum*, with a purplish reaction in the fruit only, shows septate spores but with only a rather narrow septum. The development continues through biatorine forms to lecanorine with a fully formed thalline margin. Among these latter we encounter *Pl. nivale* which is well provided with acid but in which the spores have become long and fusiform with little trace of the polar cells or central canal. We must allow here also for reversions, and wanderings from the straight road.

From crustaceous the advance is normal and simple to squamulose forms which in this phylum maintain a stiff regularity of thalline outline termed "effigurate"; the squamules, developing from the centre, extend outwards in a radiate-stellate manner. There are also foliose thalli in the genus *Xanthoria* and fruticose in *Teloschistes*. The cortex in the former horizontal genus is of plectenchyma, and no peculiar structures have emerged. In *Teloschistes* the cortex is of compact parallel hyphae (fibrous) which form the strengthening structure of the narrow compressed fronds (*T. flavicans*).

In the brown-spored series there is a considerable number of species that are crustaceous united in the genus *Rinodina*, all of which have marginate apothecia. One of them, *Rinodina oreina*, approaches in thalline structure the effigurate forms of *Placodium*; while in *R. isidioides*, a rare British species, there is an isidioid squamulose development.

Among foliose genera, the tropical genus *Pyxine* is peculiar in its almost lecideine fruit, a few gonidia occurring only in the early stages; its affinity with *Physcia* holds, however, through the one-septate brown spores with very thick walls and the reduced lumen of the cells. The more simple type of fruit may be merely retrogressive.

Physcia, the remaining genus, is mainly foliose and with dorsiventral thallus. A few species have straggling semi-upright fronds and these have sometimes been placed in a separate genus *Anaptychia*. Only one "*Anaptychia*," *Ph. intricata*, has a radiate structure with fibrous cortex all round; in the others the upper cortex alone is fibrous—of long parallel hyphae—

but that character appears in nearly every one of the horizontal species as well, sometimes in the upper, sometimes in the lower cortex.

In *Physcia* the horizontal thallus is of smaller dimensions than in *Parmelia*, and never becomes so free from the substratum: it is attached by rhizinae and soredia appear frequently. Very often the circular effigurate type of development prevails.

It is difficult to trace with any certainty the origin of this series of the phylum. Some workers have associated it with the purely lecideine genus, *Buellia*, but the brown septate spores of the latter are of simple structure, though occasionally approaching the *Rinodina* type. There are also differences in the thallus, that of *Buellia*, especially when it is saxicolous, inclining to *Rhizocarpon* in form. It is more consistent with the outer and inner structure to derive *Rinodina* from some crustaceous *Placodium* form with a marginate apothecium, therefore from a form of fairly advanced development. As the parietin content disappeared—perhaps from the preponderance of other acids—the colouration changed and the spores became dark-coloured.

Many genera and even families, such as Thelotremaceae, etc., have necessarily been omitted from this survey of phylogeny in lichens, but the tracing of the main lines of development has indicated the course of evolution, and has demonstrated not only the close affinity between the members of this polyphyletic class of plants, as shown in the constantly recurring thalline types, but it has proved the extraordinary vigour gained by both the component organisms through the symbiotic association.

The principal phyla[1], developing on somewhat parallel lines, are given in the appended table:

ARCHILICHENS

Phyla	Crustose	Squamulose	Foliose	Fruticose
Pyrenolichens	Verrucariaceae	Dermatocarpaceae		
Coniocarpineae	Caliciaceae	Sphaerophoraceae		Sphaerophoraceae
Graphidineae	{ Arthoniaceae, Graphidaceae, Dirinaceae			Roccellaceae
Cyclocarpineae				
Lecideales	{ Lecideaceae, Coenogoniaceae (filamentous gonidia), Cladoniaceae (primary and secondary thalli)	Gyrophoraceae		
Lecanorales	Lecanoraceae		Parmeliaceae	Usneaceae
Polariloculares				
{ Colourless spores	Placodium		Xanthoria	Teloschistes
{ Brown spores	Rinodina, Pyxine		Physcia	Physcia (Anaptychia)

[1] Dr Church (1920) has published a new conception of the origin of lichens. See postscript at the end of the volume, p. 421.

SCHEME OF SUGGESTED PROGRESSION IN LICHEN STRUCTURE

PYRENOCARPINEAE

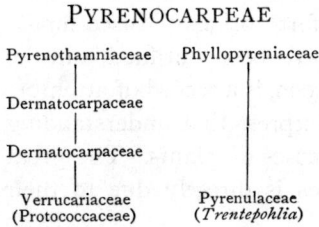

PYRENOCARPEAE

Pyrenothamniaceae   Phyllopyreniaceae
|
Dermatocarpaceae
|
Dermatocarpaceae
|
Verrucariaceae   Pyrenulaceae
(Protococcaceae)   (*Trentepohlia*)

CONIOCARPINEAE

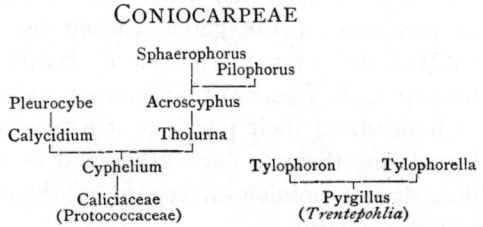

CONIOCARPEAE

Sphaerophorus
| Pilophorus
|
Pleurocybe   Acroscyphus
Calycidium   Tholurna
|
Cyphelium   Tylophoron   Tylophorella
|
Caliciaceae   Pyrgillus
(Protococcaceae)   (*Trentepohlia*)

CYCLOCARPINEAE

PHYCOLICHENS (CYANOPHILI)

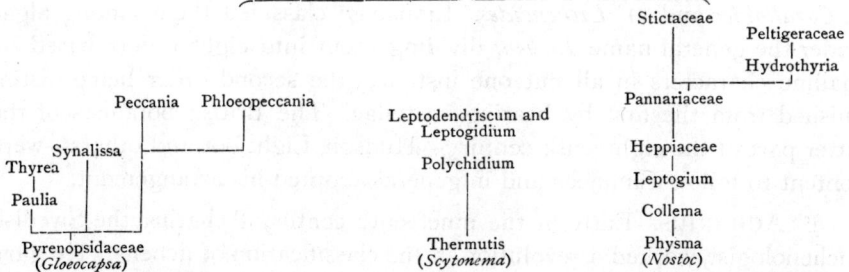

Stictaceae
| Peltigeraceae
| Hydrothyria
|
Pannariaceae

Peccania   Phloeopeccania   Leptodendriscum and
| Leptogidium   Heppiaceae
Synalissa   Polychidium   Leptogium
Thyrea   Collema
Paulia   Physma
Pyrenopsidaceae   Thermutis   (*Nostoc*)
(*Gloeocapsa*)   (*Scytonema*)

LECIDEALES   LECANORALES   POLARILOCULARES

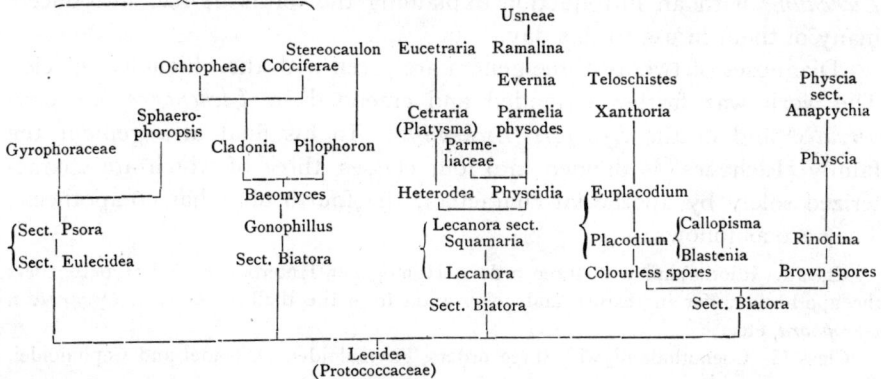

Usneae
|
Stereocaulon   Eucetraria   Ramalina
Ochropheae   Cocciferae   Evernia   Teloschistes   Physcia
| Cetraria   Parmelia   Xanthoria   sect.
Sphaero-   (Platysma)   physodes   Anaptychia
phoropsis   Cladonia   Pilophoron   Parme-
Gyrophoraceae   liaceae   Physcia
| Baeomyces   Heterodea   Physcidia   Euplacodium
| Sect. Psora   Gonophillus   Lecanora sect.   Callopisma
| Sect. Eulecidea   Sect. Biatora   Squamaria   Placodium   Rinodina
                                        Lecanora   Colourless spores   Blastenia   Brown spores
                                        Sect. Biatora   Sect. Biatora

Lecidea
(Protococcaceae)

CHAPTER VIII

SYSTEMATIC

I. CLASSIFICATION

A. WORK OF SUCCESSIVE SYSTEMATISTS

SINCE the time when lichens were first recognized as a separate class—as members of the genus Lichen by Tournefort[1] or as "Musco-fungi" by Morison[2],—many schemes of classification have been outlined, and the history of the science of lichenology, as we have seen, is a record of attempts to understand their puzzling structure, and to express that understanding by relating them to each other and to allied classes of plants. The great diversity of opinion in regard to their affinities is directly due to their composite nature.

a. DILLENIUS AND LINNAEUS. The first systematists were chiefly impressed by their likeness to mosses, hepatics or algae. Dillenius[3] in the *Historia Muscorum* grouped them under the moss genera:—IV. *Usnea*, V. *Coralloides* and VI. *Lichenoides*. Linnaeus[4] classified them among algae under the general name *Lichen*, dividing them into eight orders based on thalline characters in all but one instance, the second order being distinguished from the first by bearing scutellae. The British botanists of the latter part of the eighteenth century—Hudson, Lightfoot and others—were content to follow Linnaeus and in general adopted his arrangement.

b. ACHARIUS. Early in the nineteenth century Acharius, the Swedish Lichenologist, worked a revolution in the classification of lichens. He gave first place to the form of the thallus, but he also noted the fundamental differences in fruit-formation: his new system appeared in the *Methodus Lichenum*[5] with an introduction explaining the terms he had introduced, many of them in use to this day.

Diagnoses of twenty-three genera are given with their included species. The work was further extended and emended in *Lichenographia Universalis*[6] and in the *Synopsis Lichenum*[7]. In his final arrangement the family "Lichenes" is divided into four classes, three of which are characterized solely by apothecial characters; the fourth class has no apothecia. They are as follows:

Class I. Idiothalami with three orders, Homogenei, Heterogenei and Hyperogenei: the apothecia differ in texture and colouration from the thallus: *Lecidea, Opegrapha, Gyrophora*, etc.

Class II. Coenothalami, with three orders, Phymaloidei, Discoidei and Cephaloidei.

[1] Tournefort 1694.   [2] Morison 1699.   [3] Dillenius 1741.   [4] Linnaeus 1753.
[5] Acharius 1803.   [6] Acharius 1810.   [7] Acharius 1814.

The apothecia are partly formed from the thallus: *Lecanora, Parmelia*, etc. The Pyrenolichens are also included by him in this class, because "the thallus surrounds and is concrete with the partly or wholly immersed apothecia."

Class III. Homothalami with two orders, Scutellati and Peltati. The apothecia are formed from the cortical and medullary tissue of the thallus: *Ramalina, Usnea, Collema*, etc.

Class IV. Athalami, with but one sterile genus, *Lepraria*.

The orders are thus based on the form of the fruit; the genera in the *Synopsis* number 41. Large genera such as *Lecanora* with 132 species are divided into sections, many of which have in turn been established as genera, by S. F. Gray in 1821, and later by other systematists.

The *Synopsis* was the text-book adopted by succeeding botanists for some 40 years with slight alterations in the arrangement of classes, genera, etc.

Wallroth[1] and Meyer[2] followed with their studies on the lichen thallus, and Wallroth's division into "Homoiomerous" and "Heteromerous" was accepted as a useful guide in the maze of forms, representing as it did a great natural distinction.

c. SCHAERER. This valiant lichenologist worked continuously during the first half of the nineteenth century, but with very partial use of the microscope. His last publication in 1850, an *Enumeration of Swiss Lichens*, was the final declaration of the older school that relied on field characters. His classification is as follows:

Class I. Lichenes Discoidei, with ten orders from Usneacei to Graphidei; fruits open.

Class II. Lichenes Capitati, with three orders: Calicioidei, Sphaerophorei and Cladoniacei; fruits stalked.

Class III. Lichenes Verrucarioidei, with three orders: Verrucarii, Pertusarii and Endocarpei: fruits closed.

An "Appendix" contains descriptions of Crustacei and Fruticulosi, all sterile forms, except *Coniocarpon* and *Arthonia*, which seem out of place, and finally a "Corollarium" of gelatinous lichens all classified under one genus *Collema*.

d. MASSALONGO AND KOERBER. As a result of their microscopic studies, these two workers proposed many changes based on fruit and spore characters, and Koerber in the *Systema Lichenum Germaniae* (1855) gave expression to these views in his classification. He also made use of Wallroth's distinctions of "homoiomerous" and "heteromerous," thus dividing lichens at the outset into those mostly with blue-green and those with bright-green gonidia.

---

[1] Wallroth 1825. [2] Meyer 1825.

The following is the main outline of Koerber's classification:

Series I. Lichenes Heteromerici.
    Order   I.   Lich. Thamnoblasti (fruticose).
    Order II.   Lich. Phylloblasti (foliose).
    Order III.   Lich. Kryoblasti (crustaceous).
Series II. Lichenes Homoeomerici.
    Order IV.   Lich. Gelatinosi.
    Order V.   Lich. Byssacei.

With the exception of Order V all are subdivided into two sections, "gymnocarpi" with open fruits and "angiocarpi" with closed fruits, a distinction that had long been recognized both in lichens and in fungi.

    e. NYLANDER. The above writers had been concerned with the inter-relationships of lichens; Nylander, who was now coming forward as a lichenologist of note, gave a new turn to the study by dwelling on their relation to other classes of plants. Without for a moment conceding that they were either algal or fungal, he yet insisted on their remarkable affinity to algae on the one hand, and to fungi on the other, and he sought to make evident this double connection by his very ingenious scheme of classfication[1]. He began with what we may call "algal lichens," those associated with blue-green gonidia in the family "Collemacei"; he continued the series to the most highly evolved foliose forms and then wound up with those that are most akin to fungi, that is, those with least apparent thalline formation —according to him—the "Pyrenocarpei."

    In his scheme, which is the one followed by Leighton and Crombie, the "family" represents the highest division; series, tribe, genus and species come next in order. We have thus:

    Fam.   I.   Collemacei.
    Fam. II.   Myriangiacei (now reckoned among fungi).
    Fam. III.   Lichenacei.

This last family, which includes the great bulk of lichens, is divided into the following series: I. Epiconiodei; II. Cladoniodei; III. Ramalodei; IV. Phyllodei; V. Placodei; VI. Pyrenodei. It is an ascending series up to the Phyllodei, or foliaceous lichens, which he considers higher in development than the fruticose or filamentous Ramalodei. The Placodei include four tribes on a descending scale, the Lecanorei, Lecidinei, Xylographidei and Graphidei. The classification is almost wholly based on thalline form, except for the Pyrenodei in which are represented genera with closed fruits, there being one tribe only, the Pyrenocarpei.

    Nylander claims however to have had regard equally to the reproductive system and was the first to give importance to the spermogonia. The classification is coherent and easy to follow, though, like all classifications

---

[1] Nylander 1854.

based on imperfect knowledge, it is not a little artificial; also while magnifying the significance of spermogonia and spermatia, he overlooked the much more important characters of the ascospores.

f. MÜLLER(-ARGAU). In preparing his lists of Genevan lichens (1862), Müller realized that Nylander's series was unnatural, and he found as he studied more deeply that lichens must be ranged in parallel or convergent but detached groups. He recognized three main groups:

1. Eulichens, divided into Capitularieae, Discocarpeae and Verrucaroideae.
2. Epiconiaceae.
3. Collemaceae.

He suggested that, in relation to other plants, Eulichens approach Pezizae, Hysteriaceae and Sphaeriaceae; Epiconiaceae have affinity with Lycoperdaceae, while Collemaceae are allied to the algal family Nostocaceae. These three groups of Eulichens, he held, advanced on somewhat parallel lines, but reached a very varied development, the Discocarpeae attaining the highest stage of thalline form. Müller accepted as characters of generic importance the form and structure of the fruiting body, the presence or absence of paraphyses, and the septation, colour, etc. of the spores.

A few years later (1867) the composite nature of the lichen thallus was announced by Schwendener, and, after some time, was acknowledged by most botanists to be in accordance with the facts of nature. Any system of classification, therefore, that claims to be a natural one, must, while following as far as possible the line of plant development, take into account the double origin of lichens both from algae and fungi, the essential unity and coherence of the class being however proved by the recurring similarity between the thalline types of the different phyla. As Müller had surmised: "they are a series of parallel detached though convergent groups."

g. REINKE. The arrangement of Ascolichens on these lines was first seriously studied by Reinke[1], and his conclusions, which are embodied[2] in the *Lichens of Schleswig-Holstein*, have been largely accepted by succeeding workers. He recognizes three great subclasses: 1. Coniocarpi; 2. Discocarpi; 3. Pyrenocarpi.

The Coniocarpi are a group apart, but as their fruit is at first entirely closed—at least in some of the genera—the more natural position for them is between Discocarpi and Pyrenocarpi. It is in the arrangement of the Discocarpi that variation occurs. Reinke's arrangement of orders and families in that subclass is as follows:

Subclass 2. Discocarpi.

Order I. *GRAMMOPHORI:* Fam. *GRAPHIDACEI* and *XYLOGRAPHACEI.*

[1] Reinke 1894, '95, '96.   [2] Darbishire and Fischer-Benzon 1901.

Order II. *LECIDEALES:* Fam. *GYALECTACEI, LECIDEACEI, UMBILICARI-ACEI*·and *CLADONIACEI.*

Order III. *PARMELIALES:* Fam. *URCEOLARIACEI, PERTUSARIACEI, PAR-MELIACEI, PHYSCIACEI, TELOSCHISTACEI* and *ACAROSPORACEI.*

Order IV. *CYANOPHILI:* Fam. *LICHINACEI, EPHEBACEI, PANNARIACEI, STICTACEI, PELTIGERACEI, COLLEMACEI* and *OMPHALARIACEI.*

The orders represent generally the principal phyla or groups, the families subordinate parallel phyla within the orders. The first three orders are stages of advance as regards fruit development; the Cyanophili are a group apart.

Wainio[1] rendered great service to Phylogeny in his elaborate work on Cladoniaceae, the most complicated of all the lichen phyla. He also drew up a scheme of arrangement in his work on Brazil Lichens[2]. There is in it some divergence from Reinke's arrangement, as he tends to give more importance to the thallus than to fruit characters as a guide. He places, for instance, Gyrophorei beside Parmelei and at a long distance from his Lecidei. The Cyanophili group of families he has interpolated between *Buelliae* (Physciaceae) and *Lecideae.* Many workers approve of Wainio's classification but it presents some difficult problems.

h. ZAHLBRUCKNER. The systematist of greatest weight in recent times is A. Zahlbruckner, who is responsible for the systematic account of lichens in Engler and Prantl's *Natürlichen Pflanzenfamilien.* It is difficult to express the very great service he has rendered to Lichenology, in that and other world-wide studies of lichens. The sketch of lichen phylogeny as given in the present volume owes a great deal to the sound and clear guidance of his work, though his conclusions may not always have been accepted. The classification in the *Pflanzenfamilien* is the one now generally followed.

The class *Lichenes* is divided by Zahlbruckner[3] into two subclasses, I. Ascolichens and II. Hymenolichens. He gives a third class, Gasterolichens[4], but as it was founded on error[5], it need not concern us here. The Ascolichens are by far the more important. These are subdivided into:

Series 1. **PYRENOCARPEAE**, with perithecial fruits.

Series 2. **GYMNOCARPEAE**, with apothecial fruits.

These are again broken up into families, and in the arrangement and sequence of the families Zahlbruckner indicates his view of development and relationship. They occur in the following order:

---

[1] Wainio 1887, '94, '97.   [2] Wainio 1890.   [3] Zahlbruckner 1907.
[4] Massee 1887.   [5] Fischer 1890.

Series 1. PYRENOCARPEAE

ALGAL CELLS PROTOCOCCACEAE OR *PALMELLA*.

I. *MORIOLACEAE*
II. *EPIGLOEACEAE* }. Thallus crustaceous, perithecia solitary.
III. *VERRUCARIACEAE*
IV. *DERMATOCARPACEAE*. Thallus squamulose or foliose.
V. *PYRENOTHAMNIACEAE*. Thallus fruticose.

ALGAL CELLS *PRASIOLA*.
VI. *MASTOIDIACEAE*.

ALGAL CELLS *TRENTEPOHLIA*.
VII. *PYRENULACEAE* }. Thallus crustaceous, perithecia occurring singly.
VIII. *PARATHELIACEAE*
IX. *TRYPELHELIACEAE* }. Thallus crustaceous, perithecia united (stromatoid).
X. *ASTROTHELIACEAE*
XI. *MYCOPORACEAE*. Thallus crustaceous, perithecia in compact groups with a common outer wall.
XII. *PHYLLOPYRENIACEAE*. Thallus minutely foliose.

ALGAL CELLS *PHYLLACTIDIUM* OR *MYCOIDEA*.
XIII. *STRIGULACEAE*. Tropical leaf-lichens.

ALGAL CELLS *NOSTOC* OR *SCYTONEMA*.
XIV. *PYRENIDIACEAE*. Thallus minutely squamulose or fruticose.

Series 2. GYMNOCARPEAE

Subseries 1. Coniocarpineae, with subperithecial fruits.
Subseries 2. Graphidineae, with elongate, narrow fruits.
Subseries 3. Cyclocarpineae, with round open fruits.

Subseries 1. CONIOCARPINEAE

This is a well-defined group, peculiar in the disappearance of the asci at an early stage so that the spores lie like a powder in the globose partly closed fruits. Algal cells, bright-green; Protococcaceae. There are only three families:

XV. *CALICIACEAE*. Thallus crustaceous, apothecia stalked.
XVI. *CYPHELIACEAE*. Thallus crustaceous, apothecia sessile.
XVII. *SPHAEROPHORACEAE*. Thallus foliose or fruticose, apothecia sessile.

Subseries 2. GRAPHIDINEAE

This subseries comes next in the form of fruit development; generally the apothecia are elongate, with a narrow slit-like opening, so that a transverse section shows almost a perithecial outline. Algal cells are mostly *Trentepohlia*.

XVIII. *ARTHONIACEAE*. Thallus crustaceous, apothecia oval or linear, flat.
XIX. *GRAPHIDACEAE*. Thallus crustaceous, apothecia linear, raised.
XX. *CHIODECTONACEAE*. Thallus crustaceous, apothecia generally immersed in a stroma.
XXI. *DIRINACEAE*. Thallus crustaceous, corticate above, apothecia round.
XXII. *ROCCELLACEAE*. Thallus fruticose, apothecia round or elongate.

Subseries 3. CYCLOCARPINEAE

A large and very varied group! In most of the families the algal cells are bright-green (Chlorophyceae), in some they are blue-green (Cyanophyceae), these latter corresponding to Reinke's order Cyanophili. The apothecia, as the name implies, are round and open; the "Cyanophili" have been placed by Zahlbruckner after those families in which the apothecium has no thalline margin. They form a phylum distinct from those that precede and those that follow.

The first family of the Cyclocarpineae, the Lecanactidaceae, is often placed under Graphidineae; in any case it forms a link between the two subseries.

1. *Leciaeine group* (apothecia without a thalline margin).

XXIII. *LECANACTIDACEAE*. Thallus crustaceous. Algal cells *Trentepohlia*. Apothecium with carbonaceous hypothecium or parathecium.

XXIV. *PILOCARPACEAE*. Thallus crustaceous. Algal cells Protococcaceae. Apothecia with a dense rather dark hypothecium.

XXV. *CHRYSOTHRICACEAE*. Thallus felted, loose in texture. Algal cells *Palmella*, Protococcaceae or *Trentepohlia*. Apothecia with or without a thalline margin. The affinity of the "Family" seems to be with Pilocarpaceae.

XXVI. *THELOTREMACEAE* ⎫
XXVII. *DIPLOSCHISTACEAE* ⎭ Thallus crustaceous. Algal cells in the first *Trentepohlia*; in the second Protococcaceae. In both there are prominent double margins round the apothecium.

XXVIII. *ECTOLECHIACEAE*. Thallus very primitive in type. Algal cells Protococcaceae. Apothecia with or without a thalline margin. Nearly related to Chrysothricaceae.

XXIX. *GYALECTACEAE*. Thallus crustaceous. Algal cells *Trentepohlia*, *Phyllactidium* or rarely *Scytonema*. Apothecia biatorine, *i.e.* of soft consistency and without gonidia.

XXX. *COENOGONIACEAE*. Thallus confusedly filamentous (byssoid). Algal cells *Trentepohlia* or *Cladophora*. Apothecia biatorine.

XXXI. *LECIDEACEAE*. Thallus crustaceous or squamulose. Algal cells Protococcaceae. Apothecia biatorine (soft), or lecideine (carbonaceous).

XXXII. *PHYLLOPSORACEAE*. Thallus squamulose or foliose. Algal cells Protococcaceae. Apothecia biatorine or lecideine.

XXXIII. *CLADONIACEAE*. Thallus twofold. Algal cells Protococcaceae. Apothecia biatorine or lecideine.

XXXIV. *GYROPHORACEAE*. Thallus foliose. Algal cells Protococcaceae. Apothecia lecideine.

XXXV. *ACAROSPORACEAE*. Thallus primitive crustaceous, squamulose or foliose. Algal cells Protococcaceae. Apothecia with or without a thalline margin; very various, but always with many-spored asci.

2. *Cyanophili group*.

In this group the classification depends almost entirely on the nature of the algal constituents. The apothecia are in most genera provided with a thalline margin.

a. *More or less gelatinous when moist*.

XXXVI. *EPHEBACEAE*. Algal cells *Scytonema* or *Stigonema*. Thallus minutely fruticose or filamentous.

XXXVII. *PYRENOPSIDACEAE*. Algal cells *Gloeocapsa* (*Gloeocapsa*, *Xanthocapsa* or *Chroococcus*). Thallus crustaceous, minutely foliose or fruticose.

XXXVIII. *LICHINACEAE*. Algal cells *Rivularia*. Thallus crustaceous, squamulose or minutely fruticose.

XXXIX. *COLLEMACEAE*. Algal cells *Nostoc*. Thallus crustaceous, minutely fruticose, or squamulose to foliose.

XL. *HEPPIACEAE*. Algal cells *Scytonema*. Thallus generally squamulose and formed of plectenchyma.

b. Not gelatinous when moist.

XLI.   *PANNARIACEAE.* Algal cells *Nostoc, Scytonema* or rarely bright-green, Protococcaceae. Thallus crustaceous, squamulose or foliose.

XLII. *STICTACEAE.* Algal cells *Nostoc* or Protococcaceae. Thallus foliose, and very highly developed, corticate on both surfaces.

XLIII. *PELTIGERACEAE.* Algal cells *Nostoc* or Protococcaceae. Thallus foliose, corticate above.

3. *Lecanorine group* (apothecia with a thalline margin).

The remaining families have all bright-green gonidia and nearly always apothecia with a thalline margin. The group includes several distinct phyla:

XLIV.   *PERTUSARIACEAE.* Thallus crustaceous. Apothecia, one or several immersed in thalline tubercles; spores mostly very large.

XLV.   *LECANORACEAE.* Thallus crustaceous or squamulose. Apothecia mostly superficial.

XLVI.   *PARMELIACEAE.* Thallus foliose, rarely almost fruticose or filamentous. Apothecia scattered over the surface or marginal, sessile.

XLVII. *USNEACEAE.* Thallus fruticose or filamentous. Apothecia sessile or shortly stalked.

XLVIII. *CALOPLACACEAE.* Thallus crustaceous, squamulose or minutely fruticose. Apothecia with polarilocular colourless spores.

XLIX.   *TELOSCHISTACEAE.* Thallus foliose or fruticose. Apothecia with polarilocular colourless spores.

L.   *BUELLIACEAE.* Thallus crustaceous or squamulose. Apothecia (lecideine or lecanorine) with two-celled, thick-walled brown spores (polarilocular in part).

LI.   *PHYSCIACEAE.* Thallus foliose, rarely partly fruticose. Apothecia with two-celled thick-walled brown spores (polarilocular in part).

Subclass 2. Hymenolichens.

There are only three closely related genera of Hymenolichens, *Cora, Corella* and *Dictyonema* with *Chroococcus* or *Scytonema* algae.

There is reason to dissent from the arrangement in one or two instances which will be pointed out in the following examination of families and genera.

B. Families and Genera of Ascolichens

The necessity for a well-reasoned and well-arranged system of classification is self-evident: without a working knowledge of the plants that are the subject of study no progress can be made. The recognition of plants as isolated individuals is not sufficient, it must be possible to place them in relation to others; hence the importance of a natural system. In identifying species artificial aids, such as habitat and substratum, are also often of great value, and a good working system should take account of all characteristics.

Lichen development is the result of two organisms mutually affecting each other, but as the fungus provides the reproductive system, it is the dominant partner: the main lines of classification are necessarily determined by fruit characters. The algae occupy a subsidiary position, but they also are of importance in shaping the form and structure of the thallus. The different phyla are often determined by the presence of some particular alga; it is in the delimitation of families that the algal influence is of most effect.

Zahlbruckner's system gives due weight to the inheritance from both fungus and alga with, however, the fungus as the chief factor in development, and as his work is certain to be generally followed by modern lichenologists, it is the one of most immediate interest. His scheme has been accepted in the following more detailed account of families and genera, and for the benefit of home workers those that have not so far been recorded from the British Isles have been marked with an asterisk.

It cannot be affirmed that nomenclature is as yet firmly established in lichenology. Both on historical grounds and on those of convenience, the subject is one of extreme importance, and interest in it is one of the main avenues by which we secure continuity with the past, and by which we are able to realize not only the difficulty, but the romance of pioneer work. Besides, there can be no exchange of opinion between students nor assured knowledge of plants, until the names given to them are beyond dispute. According to the ruling of the Brussels Botanical Congress in 1910, Linnaeus's[1] list of lichens in the *Species Plantarum* has been selected as the basis of nomenclature, but since his day many new families, genera and species have been described and often insufficiently delimited. It is not easy to decide between priority, which appeals to the historical sense, and recent use which is the plea of convenience. Here also it seems there can be no rigid decision; the one aim should be to arrive at a conclusion satisfactory to all, and accepted by all.

In the following necessarily brief account of families and genera, the "spermogonia" or "pycnidia" have in most cases been left out of account, as in many instances they vary within the family and occasionally even within the genus. Their taxonomic value is not without importance, but, in the general systematic arrangement, they are only subsidiary characters. An account of them has already been given, and for more detailed statements the student is referred to purely systematic works.

There are two main types of spore production in the "pycnidia" which have been shortly described by Steiner[2] as "exobasidial" and "endobasidial." In the former the sporophores are simple or branched filaments, at the apices of which a short process grows out and buds off a pycnidiospore; in the latter the spores are budded directly from cells lining the walls or filling the cavity of the pycnidium. The exobasidial type is more simply rendered in the following pages by "acrogenous," the endobasidial by "pleurogenous" spore production. In many cases the "spermogonia" or

---

[1] Linnaeus 1753.　　　　　　　　　　　[2] Steiner 1901.

"pycnidia" are still imperfectly known. In designating the gonidial algae, the more comprehensive Protococcaceae has been substituted for *Protococcus*, as in many cases the alga is probably not *Protococcus* as now understood, but some other genus of the family[1].

SUBCLASS I. ASCOLICHENS

SERIES I. PYRENOCARPINEAE

It is on mycological grounds that Pyrenocarpineae are placed at the base of lichen classification. There is no evidence that the series was first in time.

I. MORIOLACEAE

This family was described by Norman[2] in 1872 from specimens collected by himself in Norway or in the Tyrol, on soil or more frequently on trees. There seems to have been no further record, and Zahlbruckner, while accepting the family, suggests that an examination or revision may be necessary.

The thallus is crustaceous. The algal cells, Protococcaceae, occur either in groups (sometimes stalked) surrounded by a plectenchymatous wall and called by Norman "goniocysts," or they form nests in the thallus termed "nuclei" which are surrounded by a double wall of plectenchyma, colourless in the interior and brown outside. Norman invented the term "Allelositismus," which may be rendered "mutualism," to indicate this peculiar form of thallus. The species of *Spheconisca* are fairly numerous on poplars, willows and conifers:

Algae in "goniocysts".................. 1. *Moriola Norm.[3]
Algae in double-walled "nuclei" ... 2. *Spheconisca Norm.

II. EPIGLOEACEAE

The family consists of but one genus and one species, *Epigloea bactrospora*, and, according to Zahlbruckner, further examination is necessary to make certain as to the lichenoid nature of the plant.

Zukal[4] found the perithecia scattered over the leaves of mosses, and he alleges that hyphae connected with the perithecium were closely associated with the alga, *Palmella botryoides*, and were causing it no harm. Along with the perithecia he also found minute pycnidia. The "thallus" is of a gelatinous nature and homoiomerous in structure; the perithecia are soft and clear-coloured with many-spored asci and colourless one-septate spores.

The small globose pycnidia contain simple sporophores and acrogenous straight or slightly bent rod-like spores.

Asci many-spored; spores one-septate. 1. *Epigloea Zukal.

[1] See p. 56.　　　　　　　　　　[2] Norman 1872 and '74.
[3] Genera marked with an asterisk have not been found in the British Isles.　　[4] Zukal 1890.

III. *Verrucariaceae*

In all the genera of this family the thallus is crustaceous, and, with very few exceptions, the species are saxicolous or terricolous. The thallus is variable within the crustaceous limits, and may be superficial and very conspicuous, almost imperceptible, or wholly immersed in the substratum. The algal cells are Protococcaceae, and in two of the genera the green cells penetrate the hymenium and grow in rows alongside of the asci. The perithecia are small roundish structures scattered over the thallus, the base immersed, but the upper portion generally projecting. An outer dark-coloured wall surrounds the whole perithecium (entire) or only the upper exposed portion (dimidiate); it opens above by a pore or ostiole more or less prominent.

In some of the genera the paraphyses become dissolved at an early stage, and somewhat similar filaments near the ostiole, termed periphyses, aid in the expulsion of the spores. The spores vary in septation, colour and size, and these variations have served to delimit the genera which have been formed from the original very large genus *Verrucaria*. The ascus may be 1–2-, 4- or 8-spored. In only one genus is it many-spored (*Trimmatothele*).

The genera are as follows:

Perithecia with simple ostioles.
  Paraphyses disappearing early, or wanting.
    Spores simple, ellipsoid .... 1. Verrucaria Web.
    Spores simple, elongate vermiform .... 2. Sarcopyrenia Nyl.
    Spores simple, numerous in the ascus .... 3. *Trimmatothele Norm.
    Spores 1–3-septate... 4. Thelidium Massal.
    Spores muriform (with transverse and longitudinal divisions).
      Without hymenial gonidia .... 5. Polyblastia Massal.
      With hymenial gonidia.................................. 6. Staurothele Norm.
  Paraphyses present.
    Spores simple.
      Without hymenial gonidia .... 7. Thrombium Wallr.
      With hymenial gonidia.................................. 8. *Thelenidia Nyl.
    Spores 3-septate, broadly ellipsoid....................... 9. *Geisleria Nitschke.
    Spores acicular, many-septate.............................10. Gongylia Koerb.
    Spores muriform ....11. Microglaena Lönnr.
Perithecia with a wide ring round the ostiole.
    Spores muriform; paraphyses unbranched ....12. *Aspidothelium Wain.
    Spores elongate, many-septate; paraphyses branched 13. *Aspidopyrenium Wain.

IV. *Dermatocarpaceae*

In this family there is a much more advanced thalline development—generally squamulose or with some degree of foliose structure, though in tne genus *Endocarpon*, some of the species are little more than crustaceous.

The gonidia are bright-green Protococcaceae (according to Chodat, *Coccobotrys* in *Dermatocarpon*). In *Endocarpon* they appear in the hymenium.

The least developed in structure is *Normandina*: the thallus of the single species consists of delicate shell-like squamules which are non-corticate above and below. In the other genera there is a cortex of plectenchyma.

The perithecia are almost wholly immersed, and open above by a straight ostiole. The fructification of *Dacampia* is considered by some lichenologists to be only a parasite on the white thickish squamulose thallus with which it is associated.

Hymenial gonidia present.
    Spores muriform ....1. Endocarpon Hedw.
Hymenial gonidia absent.
    Thallus non-corticate ....2. Normandina Wain.
    Thallus corticate.
        Spores simple, colourless ....3. Dermatocarpon Eschw.
        Spores simple, brown ....4. *Anapyrenium Müll.-Arg.
        Spores elongate-septate, colourless ....5. *Placidiopsis Beltr.
        Spores elongate-septate, brown ....6. *Heterocarpon Müll.-Arg.
        Spores muriform, colourless.........................7. *Psoroglaena Müll.-Arg.
        Spores muriform, brown ....8. Dacampia Massal.

V. *Pyrenothamniaceae*

Thallus more or less fruticose and corticate on both surfaces. Algal cells Protococcaceae.

Only two genera are included in this family: *Nylanderiella* with one species from New Zealand, with a small laciniate thallus up to 15 mm. in height, partly upright, partly decumbent, and attached to the substratum by basal rhizinae; the other small genus, *Pyrenothamnia*, belongs to N. America; the thallus has a short rounded stalk which expands above to an irregular frond. The perithecia are immersed in the fronds.

Spores colourless, 1-septate..........................1. *Nylanderiella Hue[1].
Spores brown, muriform ....2. *Pyrenothamnia Tuckerm.

VI. *Mastoideaceae*

A family containing one genus and one species, with a wide distribution, having been found in Siberia, on the Antarctic continent (Graham's Land), as also in Tierra del Fuego, South Georgia, South Shetland Islands and Kerguelen. The thallus is foliose, of small thin lobes, and without rhizinae. Algal cells *Prasiola*[2]. The perithecia are globose and partly project from the thallus; the asci are 8-spored; the paraphyses are mucilaginous and partly dissolving.

Spores elongate-fusiform, simple, colourless ...1. *Mastoidea Hook. and Harv.

[1] Hue 1914.   [2] Hue 1909.

VII. PYRENULACEAE

This family of crustaceous lichens differs from Verrucariaceae chiefly in the gonidium which is a species of *Trentepohlia*. Genera and species are largely corticolous and the thallus is inconspicuous, often developing within the substratum. The perithecia, like those of *Verrucariae*, are immersed or partly emergent and have an entire or dimidiate outer wall. They are scattered over the thallus except in *Anthracothecium* where they are often coalescent. This genus is tropical or subtropical except for one species which inhabits S.W. Ireland.

Paraphyses are variable, and in some species tend to disappear, but do not dissolve in mucilage. The spores are generally colourless, only in one monotypic genus, *Coccotrema*, are they simple. The cells into which the spore is divided differ in form according to the genus.

Paraphyses branched and entangled or wanting.
  Perithecia opening above by stellate lobes .... 1. *Asteroporum Müll.-Arg.
  Perithecia opening by a pore.
  Spores variously septate.
    Spore cells cylindrical or cuboid.
    Spores colourless, elongate or ovate 1–5-septate 2. Arthopyrenia Massal.
    Spores colourless, filiform 1–multi-septate ...... 3. Leptorhaphis Koerb.
    Spores colourless, muriform.......................... 4. Polyblastropsis A. Zahlbr.
    Spores brown, ovoid or elongate 2–5-septate ... 5. Microthelia Koerb.
    Spore cells globose or lentiform, 3–multi-septate 6. *Pseudopyrenula Müll.-Arg.
Paraphyses unbranched free.
  Spore cells cylindrical or cuboid.
    Perithecia beset with hairs .... 7. *Stereochlamys Müll.-Arg.
    Perithecia naked.
    Asci disappearing; spores elongate multi-septate, colourless .... 8. *Belonia Koerb.
    Asci persistent.
      Spores simple, ellipsoid, colourless .... 9. *Coccotrema Müll.-Arg.
      Spores elongate, 1–multi-septate, colourless...10. Porina Müll.-Arg.
      Spores elongate, 1–multi-septate, brown ......11. Blastodesmia Massal.
      Spores muriform, colourless......................12. *Clathroporina Müll.-Arg.
      Spores elongate, 2–3-septate, colourless ....13. Thelopsis Nyl.
  Spore cells globose or lentiform.
    Spores elongate, 1–5-septate, brown ....14. Pyrenula Massal.
    Spores muriform, brown ....15. Anthracothecium Massal.

VIII. PARATHELIACEAE

This family is peculiar in that the perithecia open by a somewhat elongate ostiole that slants at an oblique angle. The algal cells are *Trentepohlia*. Genera and species are endemic in tropical or subtropical regions of the Western hemisphere, though a species of *Pleurotrema* has been found in subantarctic America. They are corticolous and the thallus is either superficial or embedded. The genera are arranged according to spore characters :

Spores elongate, 2- or more-septate.
   Spore cells cylindrical, colourless ....I. *Pleurotrema Müll.-Arg.
   Spore cells globose-lentiform.
      Spores colourless ....2. *Plagiotrema Müll.-Arg.
      Spores brown ....3. *Parathelium Müll.-Arg.
Spores muriform.
      Spores colourless ....4. *Campylothelium Müll.-Arg.
      Spores brown ....5. *Pleurothelium Müll.-Arg.

IX. TRYPETHELIACEAE

This and the following two families are distinguished by the pseudo-stroma or compound fruit, a character rare among lichens, though the true stroma is frequent in Pyrenomycetes in such genera as *Dothidea, Valsa,* etc. The genera are crustaceous and corticolous and occur with few exceptions in tropical or subtropical regions, mostly in the Western Hemisphere. Several grow on officinal bark (*Cinchona,* etc.). Algal cells are *Trentepohlia.* As in many tropical lichens, the spores are large. The genera are based chiefly on spore characters, on septation, and on the form of the spore cells :

Spore cells cylindrical or cuboid.
   Spores colourless, elongate, multi-septate...............I. *Tomasiella Müll.-Arg.
   Spores colourless, muriform ....2. *Laurera Rehb.
   Spores brown, muriform ....3. *Bottaria Massal.
Spore cells globose-lentiform.
   Spores colourless, elongate, multi-septate...............4. *Trypethelium Spreng.
   Spores brown, elongate, multi-septate ....5. Melanotheca Müll.-Arg.

X. ASTROTHELIACEAE

The perithecia are either upright or inclined, and occur usually in radiate groups. They are free or united in a stroma, and the elongate ostioles open separately or coalesce in a common canal. The genera are all crustaceous, with *Trentepohlia* gonidia. They are tropical or subtropical, mostly in the Western Hemisphere; but species of *Parmentaria* and *Astrothelium* have been recorded also from Australia.

The spores are all many-celled and the form of their cells is a generic character:

Spores elongate, multi-septate.
   Spore cells cylindrical ....I. *Lithothelium Müll.-Arg.
   Spore cells globose-lentiform.
      Spores colourless ....2. *Astrothelium Trev.
      Spores brown ....3. *Pyrenastrum Eschw.
Spores muriform.
      Spores colourless ....4. *Heufleria Trev.
      Spores brown ....5. *Parmentaria Fée.

XI. MYCOPORACEAE

A small family with only two genera which are found in both Hemi-spheres; species of both occur in Great Britain. They are all corticolous. The perithecia are united into a partially chambered fruiting body surrounded by a common wall, but opening by separate ostioles. The thallus is thinly crustaceous, with *Palmella* gonidia in *Mycoporum*, and *Trentepohlia* in *Mycoporellum*. The spores are colourless or brown in both genera:

Spores muriform ....1. Mycoporum Flot.
Spores elongate, multi-septate ....2. Mycoporellum A. Zahlbr.

XII. PHYLLOPYRENIACEAE

Thallus foliose with both surfaces corticate and attached by rhizinae. Algal cells *Trentepohlia*. There is but one genus, *Lepolichen*, which has a laciniate somewhat upward growing thallus. Two species, both from South America, have been described, *L. granulatus* Müll.-Arg. and *L. coccophora* Hue. The latter has been recently examined by Hue[1] who finds, on the thalli, cephalodia which are peculiar in containing bright-green gelatinous algae either *Urococcus* or *Gloeocystis*, one of the few instances known of chlorophyllaceous algae forming part of a cephalodium. *Gloeocystis* may be the only alga present in the cephalodium; *Urococcus* is always accompanied by *Scytonema*.

The perithecia are immersed in thalline tubercles:

Spores colourless, simple, ovoid or ovoid-elongate ....1. *Lepolichen Trevis.

XIII. STRIGULACEAE

A family of epiphyllous lichens inhabiting and disfiguring coriaceous evergreen leaves, or occasionally fern leaves in tropical or subtropical regions. The algae associated are *Mycoidea* and *Phycopeltis* (*Phyllactidium*). The only truly parasitic lichen, *Strigula*, belongs to this family: the alga precedes the lichen on the leaves and is gradually invaded by the hyphae of the lichen and altered in character. The small black perithecia are scattered over the surface. In *Strigula* the lichen retains the spreading rounded form of the alga. The other genera are more irregular.

Thallus orbicular in outline....................................1. *Strigula Fries.
Thallus irregular.
   Perithecia without hairs.
      Spores colourless.
         Spores elongate, multi-septate ....2. *Phylloporina Müll.-Arg.
         Spores muriform..3. *Phyllobathelium Müll.-Arg.
      Spores brown.
         Spores simple..4. *Haplopyrenula Müll.-Arg.
         Spores elongate, 1–3-septate ....5. *Microtheliopsis Müll.-Arg.
   Perithecia beset with stiff hairs ....6. *Trichothelium Müll.-Arg.

[1] Hue 1905.

XIV. *Pyrenidiaceae*

The only family of Pyrenocarpineae associated with blue-green algae. The genera of Pyrenidiaceae are all monotypic, only one is common and of wide distribution, *Coriscium* (*Normandina* Nyl.). *Pyrenidium* is the only member that has a fruticose thallus, and that is of minute dimensions. *Eolichen Heppii*, found and described by Zukal, is a doubtful lichen. "*Lophothelium*" Stirton is a case of parasitism of a fungus, *Ticothecium*, on the squamules of *Stereocaulon condensatum*.

Algal cells *Scytonema* or *Stigonema*.

Thallus crustaceous[1]; spores simple, colourless ......1. *Rhabdopsora Müll.-Arg.
Thallus crustaceous; spores 1-septate, colourless ......2. *Eolichen Zuk.
Thallus crustaceous; spores muriform, brown ....3. *Pyrenothrix Riddle[2].
Thallus squamulose; spores numerous, simple ....4. *Placothelium Müll.-Arg.

Algal cells *Nostoc*.

Thallus crustaceous; spores filiform, simple, colourless 5. *Hassea A. Zahlbr.
Thallus fruticose; spores elongate, 3-septate, brown ...6. Pyrenidium Nyl.

Algal cells *Microcystis* (*Polycoccus*).

Thallus squamulose; fructification unknown ....7. Coriscium Wainio.

SERIES II. **GYMNOCARPEAE**

SUBSERIES I. **Coniocarpineae**

This small subseries is marked by the peculiar "mazaedium" type of fruit with its disappearing asci. It forms a connecting link between the families with perithecia and those with apothecia. The thallus is crustaceous or fruticose, often poorly developed and sometimes absent. The algal cells are Protococcaceae or rarely *Trentepohlia*.

XV. *Caliceaceae*

The thallus is thinly crustaceous, sometimes brightly coloured, sometimes absent, taking no part in the formation of the fruits; these have upright stalks with a small capitulum, and often look like minute nails. One genus, *Sphinctrina*, is parasitic on the thallus of other lichens, mostly *Pertusariae*.

Fruits with slender stalks.
  Spores simple.
    Spores colourless ....1. Coniocybe Ach.
    Spores brown ....2. Chaenotheca Th. Fr.
  Spores septate, brown.
    Spores 1-septate.............................3. Calicium De Not.
    Spores 3–7-septate..........................4. Stenocybe Nyl.
Fruits with short thick stalks.
    Spores globose, brown (parasitic) ....5. Sphinctrina Fries.
    Spores 1-septate, brown ....6. *Pyrgidium Nyl.

[1] Zahlbr., in *Hedwigia*, LIX. p. 301, 1917.   [2] Riddle 1917.

XVI. Cypheliaceae

Thallus crustaceous. Algal cells Protococcaceae or *Trentepohlia*. Apothecia sessile, more widely open than in the previous family; in some genera the thallus forms an outer apothecial margin. The genera *Farriola* from Norway and *Tylophorella* from New Granada are monotypic. The British genus *Cyphelium* has been known as *Trachylia*.

Thallus with Protococcaceae.

Spores colourless, simple ....1. *Farriola Norm.
Spores brown, 1–3-septate (rarely simple or muriform) ...2.　Cyphelium Th. Fr.

Thallus with *Trentepohlia*.

Spores simple, many in the ascus ....3. *Tylophorella Wainio.
Spores 8 in the ascus.
　Apothecia with a thalline margin ....4. *Tylophoron Nyl.
　Apothecia without a thalline margin.....................5. *Pyrgillus Nyl.

XVII. Sphaerophoraceae

The most highly evolved family of the subseries, as regards the thallus. Algal cells Protococcaceae. In *Tholurna*, a small lichen endemic in Scandinavia, there is a double thallus: one of horizontal much-divided squamules, the other swollen, upright, terminating in the capitulum. The fruit is lateral in *Calycidium*, a squamulose form from New Zealand, and in *Pleurocybe* from Madagascar, with stiff strap-shaped fronds. All the genera are monotypic except *Sphaerophorus*, of which genus ten species are recorded, some of them with a world-wide distribution. The spores are brown and simple or 1-septate.

Thallus squamulose and upright................................1. *Tholurna Norm.
Thallus wholly squamulose ....2. *Calycidium Stirton.
Thallus fruticose.
　Fronds hollow in the centre....................................3. *Pleurocybe Müll.-Arg.
　Fronds not hollow.
　　Fruit without a thalline margin ....4. *Acroscyphus Lev.
　　Fruit inclosed in the tip of the fronds ....5.　Sphaerophorus Pers.

Subseries 2. **Graphidineae**

In this subseries are included five families that differ rather widely from each other both in thallus and apothecia; the latter are more or less carbonaceous and mostly with a proper margin only. Families and genera are widely distributed, though most abundant in warm regions. Algal cells mostly *Trentepohlia*.

A comprehensive study of the apothecia of this series by Bioret[1] gives some interesting results in regard to the paraphyses: in *Arthonia* they are irregular in direction and much-branched; in *Opegrapha*, the paraphyses are vertical and parallel with more regular branching; *Stigmatidium* (*Entero-*

---

[1] Bioret 1914.

grapha) resembles *Opegrapha* in this respect as does also *Platygrapha*, a genus of Lecanactidaceae, while in *Graphis* the paraphyses are vertical, unbranched and free; *Melaspilea* paraphyses are somewhat similar to those of *Graphis*.

XVIII. ARTHONIACEAE

The thallus of Arthoniaceae is corticolous with few exceptions and is very inconspicuous, being largely embedded in the substratum. The apothecia (ardellae) are round, irregular or stellate, without any margin, the hymenium being protected by the dense branching of the paraphyses at the tips.

Arthonia is abundant everywhere. The species of the other genera belong mostly to tropical or subtropical countries. *Arthoniopsis* is similar to *Arthonia* in the character of the fruits, but the gonidium is a *Phycopeltis*, and it is only found on leaves. *Synarthonia* with peculiar stromatoid fructification is monotypic; it occurs in Costa Rica.

Thallus with *Trentepohlia* gonidia.
Apothecia scattered.
Spores elongate 1- or pluri-septate ....1. Arthonia Ach.
Spores muriform ....2. Arthothelium Massal.
Apothecia stromatoid.
Spores elongate, multi-septate ....3. *Synarthonia Müll.-Arg.
Thallus with *Palmella* gonidia.
Spores 1- or more-septate ....4. Allarthonia Nyl.
Spores muriform ....5. *Allarthothelium Wain.
Thallus with *Phycopeltis* gonidia.
Spores elongate 1- or more-septate ....6. *Arthoniopsis Müll.-Arg.

XIX. GRAPHIDACEAE

Thallus crustaceous, inconspicuous, partly immersed, mainly growing on bark but occasionally on dead wood or stone. Algal cells chiefly *Trentepohlia*, very rarely *Palmella* or *Phycopeltis* (epiphyllous). Apothecia (lirellae) carbonaceous more or less linear, opening by a narrow slit with a well-developed proper margin except in *Gymnographa*, a monotypic Australian genus. In two genera, the fruit is of a compound nature, several parallel discs occurring in one lirella: these are *Ptychographa* (on bark in Scotland) and *Diplogramma* (Australia), both are monotypic. They must not be confused with *Graphis elegans* and allied species in which the sterile carbonaceous margin is furrowed. Two tropical genera associated with *Phycopeltis* are epiphyllous.

Graphidaceae are among the oldest recorded lichens, attention having been drawn to them since early times by the resemblance of the lirellae on the bark of trees to hieroglyphic writing.

Thallus with *Palmella* gonidia.

Apothecia single.

Hypothecium dark-brown.

Spores simple... 1. Lithographa Nyl.

Hypothecium colourless or brownish.

Spores colourless.

Spores simple .... 2. Xylographa Fries.

Spores elongate 3–8-septate......................... 3. *Aulaxina Fée.

Spores brown.

Spores 1-septate .... 4. Encephalographa Massal.

Spores pluri-septate, then muriform .... 5. *Xyloschistes Wain.

Apothecia compound.

Spores simple, colourless............................. 6. Ptychographa Nyl.

Spores pluri-septate, colourless .... 7. *Diplogramma Müll.-Arg.

Thallus with *Trentepohlia* gonidia.

Spores elongate 1–multi-septate, the cells longer than wide.

Spores brown.

Spores 1–(rarely more)-septate .... 8. Melaspilea Nyl.

Spores 3-septate (apothecia rudimentary)......... 9. *Gymnographa Müll.-Arg.

Spores colourless.

Spores acicular, coiled (many in the ascus) ......10. *Spirographa A. Zahlbr.

Spores fusiform, straight ....11. Opegrapha Humb.

Spores muriform.

Spores elongate, central cells finally muriform 12. *Dictyographa Müll.-Arg.

Spores elongate, septate, cells wider than long.

Paraphyses unbranched, filiform.

Spores multi-septate, colourless ....13. Graphis Adans.

Spores multi-septate, brown ....14. Phaeographis Müll.-Arg.

Spores muriform, colourless..........................15. Graphina Müll.-Arg.

Spores muriform, brown ....16. Phaeographina Müll.-Arg.

Paraphyses clavate, warted at tips....................17. *Acanthothecium Wain.

Paraphyses branched, interwoven above ....18. *Helminthocarpon Fée.

Thallus with *Phycopeltis* gonidia (epiphyllous).

Spores elongate, 3-9-septate, colourless ....19. *Opegraphella Müll.-Arg.

Spores elongate, 1-septate, brown ....20. *Micrographa Müll.-Arg.

XX. *CHIODECTONACEAE*

Specially distinguished in this subseries by the grouping of the somewhat rudimentary apothecia in pseudostromata in which they are almost wholly immersed. In form they are roundish or linear; the spores are septate or muriform. The thallus is thinly crustaceous and continuous: in *Glyphis*, *Sarcographa* and *Sarcographina* there is an amorphous upper cortex, the other genera are non-corticate. Algal cells are *Trentepohlia* with the exception of two epiphyllous genera associated with *Phycopeltis*.

Genera and species are mostly tropical. *Sclerophyton* with five species is represented in Europe by a single British specimen, *S. circumscriptum*.

The form of the paraphyses is a distinguishing character of the genera.

Thallus with *Trentepohlia* gonidia.
Paraphyses free, unbranched.
    Spore cells short or almost globose.
        Spores elongate, multi-septate, colourless .... 1. Glyphis Fée.
        Spores elongate, multi-septate brown .... 2. *Sarcographa Fée.
        Spores muriform, brown .... 3. *Sarcographina Müll.-Arg.
    Spore cells longer and cuboid.
        Spores muriform, colourless .... 4. *Enterodictyon Müll.-Arg.
    Paraphyses branched, interwoven above.
        Spores elongate, multi-septate, colourless .... 5. Chiodecton Ach.
        Spores elongate, multi-septate, brown .... 6. Sclerophyton Eschw.
        Spores muriform, colourless............................ 7. *Minksia Müll.-Arg.
        Spores muriform, brown .... 8. *Enterostigma Müll.-Arg.

Thallus with *Phycopeltis* gonidia (epiphyllous).
Paraphyses free.
        Spores unequally 2-celled, colourless................. 9. *Pycnographa Müll.-Arg.
Paraphyses branched, interwoven above.
        Spores elongate, multi-septate, colourless ....10. *Mazosia Massal.

XXI. DIRINACEAE

A small family, which is associated with and often included under Graphidaceae. The thallus is crustaceous and corticate on the upper surface, the cortex being formed of palisade hyphae. Algal cells *Trentepohlia*. Apothecia are rounded or with a tendency to elongation, and, in addition to a thin proper margin, possess a stout thalline margin; the hypothecium is thick and carbonaceous. There are two genera: *Dirina* with twelve species has a wide distribution; *Dirinastrum* is monotypic and occurs on maritime rocks in Australia. In both the spores are elongate-septate, differing only in colour:

        Spores colourless .... 1. Dirina Fr.
        Spores brown .... 2. *Dirinastrum Müll.-Arg.

XXII. ROCCELLACEAE

The Roccellaceae differ from the preceding Dirinaceae chiefly in the fruticose thallus which is more or less characteristic of all the genera, though in *Roccellographa* it expands into foliose dimensions and in *Roccellina* is reduced to short podetia-like processes from a crustose base. The fronds—mostly long and strap-shaped—are protected in most of the genera by a cortex of compact palisade hyphae; in a few the outer hyphae are parallel with the long axis. The medulla is of parallel hyphae, either loose or compact. The algal cells are *Trentepohlia*.

The apothecia are lateral except in *Roccellina* where they occur at the tips of the short upright fronds, and only in *Roccellaria* is there no thalline margin. They are superficial in all of the genera except *Roccellographa*, in which they are immersed and almost closed, recalling the perithecia-like fruits of *Chiodecton* (sect. *Enterographa*). The spores are elongate, narrow, pluri-septate, and colourless or brownish, except in *Darbishirella* in which they are ovoid, 2-septate and brown.

The affinity of Dirinaceae and Roccellaceae with Graphidaceae was first indicated by Reinke[1] and elaborated later by Darbishire[2] in his monograph of Roccellaceae. The apothecia in some species of *Dirina* are ellipsoid rather than round; in several genera of Roccellaceae they are distinctly lirellate, and in *Roccella* itself some species have ellipsoid fruits. The fruticose thallus is predominant in Roccellaceae, but its evolution from the crustaceous type may be traced through *Roccellina* which is partly crustaceous and only imperfectly fruticose.

In most of the genera only one species is recorded. *Roccella*, represented by twelve species, is well known for its dyeing properties, and has a wide distribution. Like other Graphidineae they are mainly plants of warm regions, many of them exclusively maritime rock-dwellers.

The following synopsis of the genera is the one given by Darbishire in his monograph.

Cortex fastigate, of palisade hyphae.
  Spores colourless.
    Hypothecium black-carbonaceous.
      Apothecia round.
        Thallus fruticose .... 1. Roccella DC.
        Thallus crustaceous-fruticose .... 2. *Roccellina Darbish.
      Apothecia lirellate .... 3. *Reinkella Darbish.
     Hypothecium colourless.
      Gonidia present under the hypothecium .... 4. *Pentagenella Darbish.
      Gonidia absent from hypothecium .... 5. *Combea De Not.
  Spores brown or brownish.
    Medulla of parallel somewhat loose hyphae...... 6. *Schizopelte Th. Fr.
    Medulla solid, black .... 7. *Simonyella Steiner.
Cortex fibrous, of parallel hyphae.
  Apothecia round.
    Hypothecium black-carbonaceous.
      Apothecia with thalline margin .... 8. *Dendrographa Darbish.
      Apothecia with proper margin .... 9. *Roccellaria Darbish.
    Hypothecium colourless ....10. *Darbishirella A. Zahlbr.
  Apothecia lirellate ....11. *Ingaderia Darbish.

SUBSERIES 3. CYCLOCARPINEAE

This last subseries includes the remaining twenty-nine families of Asco-lichens. They are very varied both in the fungal and the algal symbionts. The fruit is more or less a discoid open apothecium. The gonidia belong to different genera of Myxophyceae and Chlorophyceae, but the most frequent are Protococcaceae. Families are based largely on thalline structure.

[1] Reinke 1895.   [2] Darbishire 1898.

XXIII. LECANACTIDACEAE

By many systematists this family is included under Graphidineae on account of the fruit structure which in some of the forms is carbonaceous and almost lirellate, and also because the algal symbiont is *Trentepohlia*. The thallus is primitive, being thinly crustaceous and non-corticate; the apothecium has a black carbonaceous hypothecium in two of the genera, *Lecanactis* and *Schismatomma* (*Platygrapha*); in the third genus, *Melampydium*, it is colourless. The latter is monotypic, and the spores become muriform. In the other genera they are elongate and multi-septate.

Apothecia with prominent proper margin............ 1. Lecanactis Eschw.
Apothecia with thin proper margin .... 2. *Melampydium Müll.-Arg.
Apothecia with thalline margin .... 3. Schismatomma Flot.

XXIV. PILOCARPACEAE

A small family with but one genus, *Pilocarpon*. It is distinguished as one of the few epiphyllous genera of lichens associated with Protococcaceous gonidia and with a distribution extending far beyond the tropics. The best known species, *P. leucoblepharum*, encircles the base of pine-needles with a white felted crust, or inhabits coriaceous evergreen leaves. Another species lives on fern leaves. The fruit is a discoid apothecium with a dark carbonaceous hypothecium and proper margin, and with a second thalline margin. The paraphyses are branched and interwoven above.

Spores elongate, 3-septate, colourless .... 1. Pilocarpon Wain.

XXV. CHRYSOTRICHACEAE

This family now, according to Hue[1], includes two genera, *Crocynia* and *Chrysothrix*. In both there is a thallus of interlaced hyphae with Protococcaceous algae scattered through it or in groups. The structure is thus homoiomerous, and Hue has suggested for it a new series, "Intertextae." The only British species, *Crocynia lanuginosa*, first placed by Nylander[2] in *Amphiloma* and later transferred by him to *Leproloma*[3], has a soft crustaceous lobate thallus, furfuraceous on the surface; no fructification has been found. A West Indian species, *C. gossypina*, has discoid apothecia with a thalline margin. There is only one species of *Chrysothrix*, *Ch. nolitangere*, which forms small clumps or tufts on the spines of Cactus in Chili. The structure is somewhat similar to that of *Crocynia*.

Spores colourless, simple...... .... 1. Crocynia Nyl.
Spores colourless, 2–3-septate............................. 2. *Chrysothrix Mont.

[1] Hue 1909.   [2] Nylander 1855.   [3] Nylander 1883.

XXVI. *Thelotremaceae*

A tropical or subtropical family of which the leading characteristic is the deeply sunk disc of the apothecium: it has a proper hyphal margin, and, round that, an overarching thalline margin. The apothecia occur singly, or they are united in a kind of pseudostroma: in *Tremotylium* several grow together, while in *Polystroma* each new apothecium develops as an outgrowth from the thalline margin of the one already formed, so that an upright, branching succession of fruits is built up. It is a very unusual type of lichen fructification, with one species, *P. Ferdinandezii*, found in Spain and in Guiana.

The thallus in all the genera is crustaceous with an amorphous (decomposed) cortex; or it is non-corticate. The algal cells are *Trentepohlia* except in *Phyllophthalmaria*, an epiphyllous genus associated with the alga *Phycopeltis*. In *Polystroma* the alga is unknown.

Only one genus is represented in the British Isles.

Apothecia growing singly.
  Thallus with *Trentepohlia* gonidia.
    Paraphyses numerous, unbranched, free.
      Spores colourless.
        Spores elongate, 2- or multi-septate .... 1. *Ocellularia Spreng.
        Spores muriform .... 2. Thelotrema Ach.
      Spores brown.
        Spores elongate, septate .... 3. *Phaeotrema Müll.-Arg.
        Spores muriform .... 4. *Leptotrema Mont.
    Paraphyses scanty, branched.
      Spores muriform, brown .... 5. *Gyrostomum Fr.
  Thallus with *Phycopeltis* gonidia .... 6. *Phyllophthalmaria A. Zahlbr.
Apothecia in pseudostromata.
  Apothecia united in tubercles .... 7. *Tremotylium Nyl.
  Apothecia united by the margins .... 8. *Polystroma Clem.

XXVII. *Diploschistaceae*

Scarcely differing from the preceding family except in the gonidia which are Protococcaceous algae. The thallus is crustaceous and non-corticate. The apothecia have a double margin but the outer thalline margin is less overarching than in Thelotremaceae. The spores in the two genera are somewhat peculiar: in *Conotrema* they are exceedingly long and divided by parallel septa into thirty to forty small cells; in *Diploschistes* (*Urceolaria*) they are large, muriform and brown. *Conotrema* contains two corticolous species; *Diploschistes* about thirty species mostly saxicolous. Both genera are represented in the British Isles.

    Spores elongate, multi-septate, colourless .... 1. Conotrema Tuck.
    Spores muriform, brown .... 2. Diploschistes Norm.

XXVIII. *Ectolechiaceae*

A family of tropical epiphyllous lichens that are associated with Protococcaceous gonidia. The thallus is primitive in character, mostly a weft of hyphae with intermingled algal cells, described as homoiomerous.

The apothecia are without a thalline margin, and with a scarcely developed proper margin: their affinity is with the Lecideaceae, though in two genera, *Lecaniella* and *Arthotheliopsis*, there are gonidia below the hypothecium, a character of Lecanoraceae. The genera are nearly all monotypic; in *Sporopodium* has been included *Lecidea phyllocharis* Wainio (Sect. *Gonothecium*), which is distinguished by hymenial gonidia.

Apothecia at first covered by a "veil."
    Spores elongate, colourless, septate .... 1. *Asterothyrium Müll.-Arg.
Apothecia uncovered from the first.
  Gonidia not present below the hypothecium.
    Paraphyses unbranched, free.
      Spores muriform...................................... 2. *Lopadiopsis Wain.
    Paraphyses branched.
      Spores 1-septate.................................... 3. *Actinoplaca Müll.-Arg.
      Spores elongate, multi-septate .... 4. *Tapellaria Müll.-Arg.
      Spores muriform .... 5. *Sporopodium Mont.
  Gonidia present below the hypothecium.
    Spores elongate, 2-septate .... 6. *Lecaniella Wain.
    Spores muriform.................................... 7. *Arthotheliopsis Wain.

XXIX. *Gyalectaceae*

The algal cells in this family are filamentous; either Myxophyceae (*Scytonema*) or Chlorophyceae (*Trentepohlia* or *Phyllactidium*). The thallus is crustaceous, and in some cases homoiomerous, as in *Petractis*, where the alga, *Scytonema*, penetrates the substratum as deeply as the hyphae. *Monophiale*, a tropical genus, possesses two kinds of gonidia: the species that grow on bark or mosses are associated with *Trentepohlia*; others that have invaded the surface of leathery evergreen leaves resemble most epiphyllous lichens in being associated with the leaf alga *Phyllactidium* (*Phycopeltis*). Some species of *Trentepohlia* exhale when moist an odour of violets. This scent is retained in at least one genus, *Jonaspis*.

The apothecia are superficial, and are soft, waxy and bright-coloured, with prominent margins which are however entirely hyphal: the affinity is therefore with Lecideaceae. In one genus, *Sagiolechia*, the fruit is carbonaceous and dark coloured. The spores of all the genera are colourless.

Apothecia waxy, bright-coloured.
  Thallus with *Scytonema* gonidia.
    Spores elongate, 3-septate .... 1. Petractis Fr.

Thallus with *Trentepholia* gonidia.
  Asci 6–8-spored.
    Spores simple... 2. Jonaspis Th. Fr.
    Spores 1-septate .... 3. *Microphiale A. Zahlbr.
    Spores septate or muriform....................... 4. Gyalecta Ach.
  Asci 12–many-spored.
    Spores 1-septate................................... 5. *Ramonia Stizenb.
    Spores fusiform or acicular, many-septate ... 6. Pachyphiale Lönnr.
  Apothecia carbonaceous.
    Spores elongate, 2–3-septate .... 7. *Sagiolechia Massal.

XXX. Coenogoniaceae

There are only two genera in this small family, *Coenogonium* with *Trentepohlia* gonidia, and *Racodium* with *Cladophora*. Both genera follow the algal form and are filamentous. In *Coenogonium* the filaments are sometimes matted into a loose felted expansion. The genus is mainly tropical or subtropical and mostly rather light-coloured. There is only one British species, *C. ebeneum*[1], a sterile form, in which the hyphae are very dark-brown; it often covers large areas of stone or rock with its sooty-like creeping filaments.

Racodium includes 2 (?) species. One of these, *R. rupestre*, is sterile and resembles *C. ebeneum* in form and colour.

The apothecia of *Coenogonium* are waxy and light-coloured; they are borne laterally on the filaments; the spores are simple or 1-septate.

Thallus with *Trentepohlia* gonidia.................... 1. Coenogonium Ehrenb.
Thallus with *Cladophora* gonidia .... 2. Racodium Fr.

XXXI. Lecideaceae

One of the largest lichen families as regards both genera and species, and of world-wide distribution. The algal cells are Protococcaceae. The thallus is mostly crustaceous but it becomes squamulose in *Psora*, a section of *Lecidea*; and in *Sphaerophoropsis*, a Brazilian genus, there are small upright fronds or stalks with lateral apothecia. The prevailing colour of the thallus is some shade of grey, but it ranges from white or yellow to dark-brown or almost black. Cephalodia appear in some of the species.

The apothecia have a proper margin only, no gonidia taking part in the fruit-formation. They may be soft and waxy (biatorine) or hard and carbonaceous (lecideine). The genera are mainly based on spore characters which are very varied.

The arrangement of genera given below follows that of Zahlbruckner; in several instances, both as to the limitations of genera and to the nomenclature, it differs from that of British text-books, though the general principle of classification is the same.

[1] Lorrain Smith 1906.

Thallus crustaceous non-corticate.
  Spores simple.
    Spores small, thin-walled.
      Spores colourless .... 1. Lecidea Ach.
      Spores brown .... 2. *Orphniospora Koerb.
    Spores large, thick-walled .... 3. Mycoblastus Norm.
  Spores 1-septate.
    Spores small, thin-walled........................... 4. Catillaria Th. Fr.
    Spores large, thick-walled .... 5. Megalospora Mey. and Flot.
  Spores elongate, 3–multi-septate.
    Spores elongate, narrow, thin-walled.............. 6. Bacidia A. Zahlbr.
    Spores elongate, large and thick-walled .... 7. Bombyliospora De Not.
  Spores muriform.
    Spores colourless; on trees.......................... 8. Lopadium Koerb.
    Spores colourless to brown ; on rocks .... 9. Rhizocarpon Th. Fr.
Thallus warted or squamulose, corticate.
  Spores elongate, 1–7-septate, thin-walled ....10. Toninia Th. Fr.
Thallus of upright podetia-like small fronds.
  Spores ellipsoid, becoming 1-septate ....11. *Sphaerophoropsis Wain.

XXXII. PHYLLOPSORACEAE

A small family of exotic lichens with a somewhat more developed thallus than that of the Lecideaceae, being in both of the genera squamulose or almost foliose.

The apothecia are without a thalline margin ; they are biatorine or lecideine ; the hypothecium is formed of plectenchyma and is purple-red in one species, *Phyllopsora furfuracea*. The two genera differ only in spore characters. There are fifteen species, mostly corticolous, belonging to *Phyllopsora* ; only one, from New Zealand, is recorded for *Psorella*.

  Spores simple .... 1. *Phyllopsora Müll.-Arg.
  Spores elongate, septate .... 2. *Psorella Müll.-Arg.

XXXIII. CLADONIACEAE

Associated with Lecideaceae in the type of apothecium, but differing widely in thallus formation. The latter is of a twofold type : the primary thallus is crustaceous, squamulose, or very rarely foliose; the secondary thallus or podetium, upright, simple or branched, is terminated by the apothecia, or broadens upwards to cup-like scyphi. Algal cells, Protococcaceae, according to Chodat, *Cystococcus*.

Much attention has been given to the origin and development of the podetia in this family. They are superficial on granule or squamule except in the monotypic Himalayan genus *Gymnoderma* where they are marginal on the large leaf-like lobes. Though in origin the podetia are doubtless fruit stalks, they have become in most cases vegetative in function.

The fruits are coloured yellowish, brown or red (or dark and carbonaceous in *Pilophorus*), and are borne on the tips of the branches or on the margins of the scyphi. In *Glossodium* and *Thysanothecium*—the former from New Granada, the latter from Australia—the apothecia occupy one side of the widened surface at the tips.

Cephalodia are developed on the primary thallus of *Pilophorus,* and on the podetia of *Stereocaulon* and *Argopsis*.

Podetia simple, short, not widening upwards.
    Podetial stalks naked.
        Primary thallus thin, continuous .... 1. Gomphillus Nyl.
        Primary thallus granular or squamulose ... 2. Baeomyces Pers.
        Primary thallus foliose.
            Podetia superficial .... 3. *Heteromyces Müll.-Arg.
            Podetia marginal .... 4. *Gymnoderma[1] Nyl.
    Podetial stalks granular, squamulose .... 5. Pilophorus Th. Fr.
    Podetia short, widening upwards.
        Podetia simple above, rarely divided ... 6. *Glossodium Nyl.
        Podetia lobed, leaf-like .... 7. *Thysanothecium Berk. & Mont.
    Podetia elongate, variously branched, or scy-
        phous and hollow .... } 8. Cladonia Hill.
    Podetia elongate, not scyphous, the stalks solid.
        Spores elongate, septate .... 9. Stereocaulon Schreb.
        Spores muriform ....10. *Argopsis Th. Fr.

XXXIV. *Gyrophoraceae*

A small family of foliose lichens allied to Lecideaceae by the character of the fruit—a superficial apothecium in the formation of which the gonidia take no share. There are only three genera, distinguished by differences in spore and other characters. *Dermatiscum* has light-coloured thallus and fruits ; of the two species, one occurs in Central Europe, the other in North America. *Umbilicaria* and *Gyrophora* are British; they are dark-coloured rock-lichens and are extremely abundant in Northern regions where they are known as "tripe de roche." Algal cells Protococcaceae.

Umbilicaria, Dermatiscum, and some species of *Gyrophora* are attached to the substratum by a central point. Other species of *Gyrophora* are rhizinose. In all there is a cortex of plectenchyma above and below. In *Gyrophora* the thallus may be monophyllous as in *Umbilicaria*, or polyphyllous and with or without rhizinae. New lobes frequently arise from protuberances or warts on the older parts of the thallus. At the periphery, in most species, growth is equal along the margins, in *G. erosa*[2] the edge is formed of numerous anastomosing lobes with lateral branching, the whole forming a broadly meshed open network. Further back the tissues become continuous owing to the active growth of the lower tissue or hypothallus,

---

[1] *Neophyllis* Wils. is synonymous with *Gymnoderma*.   [2] Lindau 1899.

which grows out from all sides and meets across the opening. The overlying layers, with gonidia, follow more slowly, but they also in time become continuous, so that the "erose" character persists only near the periphery. This forward growth of the lower thallus occurs in other species, though to a much less marked degree.

There is abundant detritus formation in this family; the outer layers of the cortex are continually being sloughed, the dead tissues lying on the upper surface as a dark gelatinous layer, continuous or in small patches. On the under surface the cast-off cortex gathers into a loose confused mass of dead tissues.

Asci 8-spored.
    Spores mostly simple (disc gyrose) .... 1. Gyrophora Ach.
    Spores 1-septate.. 2. *Dermatiscum Nyl.
Asci 1–2-spored.
    Spores muriform .... 3. Umbilicaria Hoffm.

XXXV. *Acarosporaceae*

Thallus foliose, squamulose or crustaceous, sometimes scarcely developed. Algal cells Protococcaceae.

Into this family Zahlbruckner has gathered the genera in which the asci are many-spored, as he considers that a character of great importance in determining relationship, but he has in doing so overlooked other very great differences. The fruit-bodies are round and completely enclosed in a thalline wall in *Thelocarpon*, which has however no perithecial wall. They have a proper margin only (lecideine) in *Biatorella*, and a thalline margin (lecanorine) in the remaining genera. In *Acarospora* the apothecia are sunk in the thallus. Stirton's genus *Cryptothecia*[1] is allied to *Thelocarpon* in the fruit-formation, but the basal thallus is well developed and the spores are few in number and variously divided.

Thallus none.
    Apothecia (or perithecia) in thalline warts .... 1. Thelocarpon Nyl.
Thallus crustaceous.
    Apothecia lecideine; spores simple ....,.. 2. Biatorella Th. Fr.
    Apothecia lecanorine; spores septate .... 3. *Maronea Massal.
Thallus of small squamules.............................. 4. Acarospora Massal.
Thallus almost foliose, attached centrally.............. 5. *Glypholecia Nyl.

XXXVI. *Ephebaceae*

A family of very simple structure either filamentous, foliose or crustaceous. The algal cells which give a dark colour to the thallus are *Stigonema* or *Scytonema*, members of the blue-green Myxophyceae, and consist of minute simple or branched filaments—single cell-rows in *Scytonema*, compound in *Stigonema*.

[1] Stirton 1877, p. 164.

In some of the genera the lichen hyphae travel within the gelatinous sheath of the filaments, both algae and hyphae increasing by apical growth so that filaments many times the length of the alga are formed as in *Ephebe*. In others the filaments scarcely increase beyond the normal size of the alga as in *Thermutis* (*Gonionema*); or the gelatinous algal cells may be distributed in a stratum of hyphae.

The apothecia are minute and almost closed; they may be embedded in swellings of the thallus, or are more or less superficial. The spores are rather small, colourless and simple or 1-septate.

The lichens of this family are rock-dwellers and are mostly to be found in hilly or Alpine regions. A tropical species, *Leptogidium dendriscum*, occurs in sterile condition in south-west Ireland. There are few species in any of the genera.

Algal cells *Scytonema*.
    Thallus minutely fruticose, non-corticate .... 1. Thermutis Fr.
    Thallus minute, of felted filaments, cortex one cell thick .... } 2. *Leptodendriscum Wain.
    Thallus of elongate filaments, cortex of several cells 3. Leptogidium Nyl.
    Thallus foliose or fruticose, cellular throughout ...... 4. Polychidium Ach.
    Thallus crustaceous, non-corticate .... 5. Porocyphus Koerb.
Algal cells *Stigonema*.
    Thallus minutely fruticose, non-corticate .... 6. Spilonema Born.
    Thallus of long branching filaments.
        Spores septate; paraphyses wanting .... 7. Ephebe Fr.
        Spores simple; paraphyses present .... 8. Ephebeia Nyl.
    Thallus crustaceous; upper surface non-corticate, lower surface corticate .... } 9. *Pterygiopsis Wain.

XXXVII. *Pyrenopsidaceae*

In this family are included gelatinous lichens of which the gonidium is a blue-green alga with a thick gelatinous coat, either *Gloeocapsa* (including *Xanthocapsa*) or *Chroococcus*. In *Gloeocapsa* and *Chroococcus* the gelatinous envelope is often red, in *Xanthocapsa* it is yellow, and these colours persist more or less in the lichens, especially in the outer layers.

The thallus is in many cases a formless gelatinous crust of hyphal filaments mingling with colonies of algal cells as in *Pyrenopsis*; but small fruticose tufts are characteristic of *Synalissa*, and larger foliose and fruticose thalli appear in some exotic genera. A plectenchymatous cortex is formed on the thallus of *Forssellia*, a crustaceous genus from Central Europe, with two species only; the whole thallus is built up of a kind of plectenchyma in some others, but in most of the genera there is no tissue formed.

The apothecia, as in Ephebaceae, are generally half-closed.

Thallus with *Gloeocapsa* gonidia.
  Thallus crustaceous.
    Spores simple.................................. 1. Pyrenopsis Nyl.
    Spores 1-septate............................. 2. *Cryptothele Forss.
  Thallus shortly fruticose .... 3. Synalissa Fr.
  Thallus lobate, centrally attached .... 4. *Phylliscidium Forss.
Thallus with *Chroococcus* gonidia.
  Thallus crustaceous .... 5. Pyrenopsidium Forss.
  Thallus lobate, centrally attached .... 6. *Phylliscum Nyl.
Thallus with *Xanthocapsa* gonidia.
  Thallus crustaceous.
    Thallus non-corticate.
      Spores simple.
        Apothecia open, asci 8-spored.................... 7. Psorotichia Forss.
        Apothecia covered, asci many-spored .... 8. *Gonohymenia Stein.
      Spores 1-septate.
        Apothecia closed .... 9. *Collemopsidium Nyl.
    Thallus with plectenchymatous cortex ....10. *Forssellia A. Zahlbr.
  Thallus lobate, centrally attached.
    Spores simple.
      Thallus plectenchymatous throughout ....11. *Anema Nyl.
      Thalline tissue of loose hyphae ....12. *Thyrea Massal.
      Cortex of upright parallel hyphae ....13. *Jenmania Wächt.
    Spores 1-septate.
      Thalline tissue of loose hyphae ....14. *Paulia Fée.
  Thallus fruticose.
    Thallus without a cortex ....15. *Peccania Forss.
    Thallus with cortex of parallel hyphae ....16. *Phloeopeccania Stein.

XXXVIII. *Lichinaceae*

The only family of lichens associated with *Rivularia* gonidia, the trichomes of which retain their filamentous form to some extent in the more highly developed genera; they lie parallel to the long axis of the squamule or of the frond except in *Lichinella* in which genus they are vertical to the surface. The thallus may be crustaceous, or minutely foliose, or fruticose; in all cases it is dark-brown in colour, and the gelatinous character is evident in the moist condition. The best known British genus is *Lichina* which grows on rocks by the sea.

The apothecia are more or less immersed in the tissue; in *Pterygium* and *Steinera* they are open and superficial (the latter monotypic genus confined to Kerguelen). They are also open in *Lichinella* and *Homopsella*, both very rare genera. The spores are colourless and simple except in *Pterygium* and *Steinera* where they are elongate, and 1–3-septate.

Thallus crustaceous squamulose.
  Apothecia immersed in thalline warts .... 1. *Calothricopsis Wain.
  Apothecia superficial, with thalline margin .... 2. *Steinera A. Zahlbr.
  Apothecia superficial, without a thalline margin ...... 3. Pterygium Nyl.

Thallus of small fruticose fronds.
  Gonidia occupying the central strand .... 4. *Lichinodium Nyl.
  Gonidia not in the centre.
    Apothecia immersed .... 5. Lichina Ag.
    Apothecia superficial.
      Paraphyses present .... 6. *Lichinella Nyl.
      Paraphyses absent..................................... 7. *Homopsella Nyl.

XXXIX. COLLEMACEAE

The most important family of the gelatinous lichens and the most numerous. *Collema* is historically interesting as having first suggested the composite thallus. Algal cells, *Nostoc*, which retain the chain-like form except in *Leprocollema*, a doubtful member of the family. The thallus varies from indeterminate crusts to lobes of considerable size; occasionally the lobes are narrow and erect, forming minute fruticose structures. In the more primitive genera the thallus is non-corticate, but in the more evolved, the apical cells of the hyphae coalesce to form a continuous cellular cortex, one or more cells thick, well marked in some species, in others rudimentary; the formation of plectenchyma also occurs occasionally in the apothecial tissues of some non-corticate species.

The apothecia are superficial except in *Pyrenocollema*, a monotypic genus of unknown locality. They are generally lecanorine, with gonidia entering into the formation of the apothecium: in some genera they are lecideine or biatorine, being formed of hyphae alone. The spores are colourless and vary in form, size and septation.

Apothecia immersed; spores fusiform, 1-septate......... 1. *Pyrenocollema Reinke.
Apothecia superficial.
  Thallus without a cortex.
    Spores simple, globose or ellipsoid.
      Thallus crustaceous .... 2. *Leprocollema Wain.
      Thallus largely squamulose-fruticose.
        Apothecia lecideine (dark-coloured) .... 3. *Leciophysma Th. Fr.
        Apothecia lecanorine................................ 4. Physma Massal.
    Spores variously septate or muriform.
      Apothecia biatorine (light-coloured) .... 5. *Homothecium Mont.
      Apothecia lecanorine................................ 6. Collema Wigg.
  Thallus with cortex of plectenchyma.
    Spores simple.
      Spores globose .... 7. Lemmopsis A. Zahlbr.
      Spores ellipsoid, with thick subverrucose wall... 8. *Dichodium Nyl.
      Spores vermiform, spirally curved .... 9. *Koerberia Massal.
    Spores variously septate or muriform.
      Apothecia biatorine (light-coloured) ....10. *Arctomia Th. Fr.
      Apothecia lecanorine.................................11. Leptogium S. F. Gray.

XL. *Heppiaceae*

A family belonging to the "blue-green" series as it is associated with a gelatinous alga, *Scytonema*, but is of almost entirely cellular structure and is non-gelatinous. The thallus is squamulose or minutely foliose, or is formed of narrow almost fruticose lobes; the apothecia are semi-immersed; the asci are 4–many-spored.

Heppia is a wide-spread genus both in northern and tropical regions with about forty species that live on soil or rock. So far, no representative has been recorded in our Islands.

Spores simple, colourless, globose or ellipsoid......... 1. *Heppia Naeg.
Spores muriform, colourless,,ellipsoid .... 2. *Amphidium[1] Nyl.

XLI. *Pannariaceae*

The members of this family are also non-gelatinous, though for the most part associated with blue-green gelatinous algae, *Nostoc* or *Scytonema*. The gonidia are bright-green in the genera *Psoroma* and *Psoromaria*, the former often included under *Lecanora*, but too closely resembling *Pannaria* to be dissociated from that genus.

The thallus varies from being crustaceous to squamulose or foliose, and has a cortex of plectenchyma on the upper and sometimes also on the lower surface. The apothecia are superficial or lateral and with or without a thalline margin (lecanorine or biatorine), the spores are colourless.

Zahlbruckner has included *Hydrothyria* in this family. It is a monotypic aquatic genus found in North America and very closely allied to *Peltigera*. The British species of the genus, familiarly known as *Coccocarpia*, have been placed under *Parmeliella*, the former name being restricted to the tropical or subtropical species first assigned to *Coccocarpia* and distinguished by the cortex, the hyphae forming it lying parallel with.the surface though forming a regular plectenchyma.

An Antarctic lichen *Thelidea corrugata* with *Palmella* gonidia is doubtfully included: the thallus is foliose, the apothecia biatorine with colourless 1-septate spores.

Thallus with bright-green gonidia.
  With *Palmella* .... 1. *Thelidea Hue.
  With Protococcaceae.
    Apothecia non-marginate (biatorine)................. 2. *Psoromaria Nyl.
    Apothecia marginate....................................... 3. Psoroma Nyl.
Thallus with *Scytonema* gonidia.
  Apothecia marginate, spores 1-septate .... 4. Massalongia Koerb.
  Apothecia non-marginate ; spores simple.
    Upper surface smooth .... 5. *Coccocarpia Pers.
    Upper surface felted .... 6. *Erioderma Fée.

[1] A. Zahlbruckner, in *Oesterr. bot. Zeitschr.* 1919, p. 163.

Thallus with *Nostoc* gonidia.

    Apothecia marginate; spores simple .... 7.   Pannaria Del.

    Apothecia non-marginate; spores various.

        Thallus crustaceous or minutely squamulose ... 8.   Placynthium Ach.

        Thallus squamulose, cortex indistinct .... 9. *Lepidocollema Wain.

        Thallus squamulose or foliose, cortex cellular ...10.   Parmeliella Müll.-Arg.

        Thallus foliose, thin veined below ....11. *Hydrothyria Russ.

XLII. *STICTACEAE*

Thallus foliose, mostly horizontal, with a plectenchymatous cortex on both surfaces, a tomentum of hair-like hyphae taking the place of rhizinae on the lower surface. Algal cells Protococcaceae or *Nostoc*. Cephalodia and cyphellae or pseudocyphellae often present. Apothecia superficial or lateral; spores colourless or brown, variously septate.

The highly organized cortex and the presence of aeration organs—cyphellae or pseudocyphellae—which are almost solely confined to the genus *Sticta* give this family a high position as regards vegetative development. The two genera are of wide distribution, but *Sticta* is more abundant in the Southern Hemisphere. *Lobaria pulmonaria* is one of our largest lichens.

Under surface dotted with cyphellae or pseudo-cyphellae ....} 1.   Sticta Schreb.

Under surface without these organs .... 2.   Lobaria Schreb.

XLIII. *PELTIGERACEAE*

A family of heteromerous foliose lichens containing in some instances blue-green (*Nostoc*), in others bright-green (Protococcaceae) gonidia, and thus representing a transition between these two series. They have large or small lobes and grow on the ground or on trees.

Cephalodia, either ectotrophic (Peltidea) or endotrophic (Solorina), occur in the family and further exemplify the capacity of the fungus hyphae to combine with different types of algae.

The upper surface is a wide cortex of plectenchyma, which in some forms (*Nephromium*) is continued below. In the non-corticate under surface of *Peltigera*, the lower hyphae grow out in hairs or rhizinae, very frequently brown in colour. Intercalary growth of the upper tissues stretches the thallus and tears apart the lower under surface so that the hair-bearing areas become a network of veins, with the white exposed medulla between. In *Peltigera canina* there is further growth and branching of the hyphae in the veins, adding to the bulk of the interlacing ridges.

From all other foliose lichens Peltigeraceae are distinguished by the flat wholly appressed or peltate apothecia without a thalline margin which arise mostly on the upper surface, but in *Nephromium* on the extreme margin of the under surface, the tip of the fertile lobe in that case is turned back as the apothecium matures, so that the fruit eventually faces the light. In *Nephroma* has been included *Eunephroma* with bright-green gonidia and *Nephromium* with blue-green.

Bitter[1] has recorded the finding of apothecia on the under surface of *Peltigera malacea* and not at the margin, as in *Nephromium*. The plant was otherwise normal and healthy. *Solorinella*, from Central Europe and *Asteristion* from Ceylon are monotypic genera with poorly developed thalli.

Thallus poorly developed.
Asci 6–8-spored; spores 3–5-septate .... 1. *Asteristion Leight.
Asci many-spored; spores 1-septate .... 2. *Solorinella Anzi.
Thallus generally well developed.
Apothecia superficial, sunk in the thallus .... 3. Solorina Ach.
Apothecia terminal on upper surface of lobes .... 4. Peltigera Willd.
Apothecia terminal on lower surface of lobes .... 5. Nephroma Ach.

XLIV. *Pertusariaceae*

Thallus crustaceous, often rather thick and with an amorphous cortex on the upper surface. Algal cells Protococcaceae. Apothecia solitary or several immersed in thalline warts, generally with a narrow opening which barely exposes the disc, and which in one genus, *Perforaria*, is so small as almost to constitute a perithecium; spores are often very large and with thick walls; some if not all are multinucleate and germinate at many points.

In the form of the fruit, this family stands between Pyrenocarpeae and Gymnocarpeae, though more akin to the latter. *Perforaria*, with two species, belongs to New Zealand and Japan. *Pertusaria* has a world-wide distribution, and *Varicellaria*, a monotypic genus, with a very large two-celled spore, is an Alpine plant, recorded from Europe and from Antarctic America.

Spores simple.
Apothecia with pore-like opening .... 1. *Perforaria Müll.-Arg.
Apothecia with a wider opening .... 2. Pertusaria DC.
Spores 1-septate... 3. Varicellaria Nyl.

XLV. *Lecanoraceae*

Thallus mostly crustaceous, occasionally squamulose or very rarely minutely fruticulose. The squamulose thallus is corticate above, the under surface appressed and attached to the substratum by penetrating hyphae, often effigurate at the circumference. Algal cells Protococcaceae. Apothecia well distinguished by the thalline margin; spores colourless, simple or variously septate or muriform.

[1] Bitter 1904[2].

Lecanora, Ochrolechia, Lecania, Haematomma and *Phlyctis* are cosmo-politan genera, some of them with a very large number of species; the other genera are more restricted in distribution and generally with few species.

The genus *Candelariella* is of uncertain position; the spores are 8 or many in the ascus and are simple or 1-septate, and not unfrequently become polarilocular as in Caloplacaceae, but there is no parietin present.

Algae distributed through the thallus. Spores simple   1. *Harpidium Koerb.
Algae restricted to a definite zone.
   Spores simple.
      Thallus grey, white or yellowish.
         Spores rather small .... 2. Lecanora Ach.
         Spores large .... 3. Ochrolechia Massal.
      Thallus bright yellow.
         Spores simple or 1-septate .... 4. Candelariella Müll.-Arg.
   Spores 1-septate (rarely pluri-septate).
      Paraphyses free.
         Thallus squamulose, effigurate .... 5. Placolecania Zahlbr.
         Thallus crustaceous.
            Apothecial disc brownish........................... 6. Lecania Zahlbr.
            Apothecial disc flesh-coloured..................... 7. Icmadophila Trevis.
         Paraphyses branched, intricate .... 8. *Calenia Müll.-Arg.
   Spores elongate, pluri-septate.
      Apothecia superficial.................................... 9. Haematomma Massal.
      Apothecia immersed.
         Paraphyses free ....10. *Phlyctella Müll.-Arg.
         Paraphyses branched, intricate ....11. *Phlyctidia Müll-Arg.
   Spores muriform.
      Apothecia superficial....................................12. *Myxodictyon Massal.
      Apothecia immersed ....13. Phlyctis Wallr.

XLVI. PARMELIACEAE

A very familiar family of foliose lichens. Genera and species are dorsi-ventral and stratose in structure, though some *Cetrariae* are fruticose in habit. Algal cells are Protococcaceae; in *Physcidia* they are *Palmellae*. In every case the upper surface of the thallus is corticate and generally of plectenchyma, the lower being somewhat similar, but in *Heterodea* and *Physcidia*, monotypic Australasian genera, the upper cortex is of branching hyphae parallel with the surface, the lower surface being non-corticate.

The *Parmeliae* are mostly provided with abundant rhizinae; in *Cetrariae* and *Nephromopsis* these are very sparingly present, while in *Anzia* (including *Pannoparmelia*) the medulla passes into a wide net-like structure of anasto-mosing hyphae.

In *Heterodea*, cyphellae occur on the under surface as in Stictaceae; and in *Cetraria islandica* bare patches have been described as pseudocyphellae. The latter lichen is one of the few that are of value as human food. Special aeration structures are present on the upper cortex of *Parmelia aspidota*.

Thallus non-corticate below.
  Apothecia terminal .... 1. *Heterodea Nyl.
  Apothecia superficial... 2. *Physcidia Tuck.
Thallus spongy below .... 3. *Anzia Stizenb.
Thallus corticate below.
  Asci poly-spored... 4. Candelaria Massal.
  Asci 8-spored.
    Spermatia acrogenous .... 5. Parmeliopsis Nyl.
    Spermatia pleurogenous.
      Apothecia superficial................................ 6. Parmelia Ach.
      Apothecia lateral.
        Apothecia on upper surface .... 7. Cetraria Ach.
        Apothecia on lower surface .... 8. *Nephromopsis Müll.-Arg.

XLVII. *Usneaceae*

This also is a familiar family of lichens, *Usnea barbata* the "bearded moss" being one of the first lichens noted and chronicled. Algal cells Protococcaceae. Structure radiate, the upright or pendulous habit characteristic of the family securing all-round illumination. Special adaptations of the cortex or of the internal tissues have been evolved to strengthen the thallus against the strains incidental to their habit of growth as they are attached in nearly all cases by one point only, by a special sheath, or by penetrating hold-fasts.

Apothecia are superficial or marginal and sometimes shortly stalked; spores are simple or variously septate.

Ramalina and *Usnea*, the most numerous, are cosmopolitan genera; *Alectoria* inhabits northern or hilly regions.

The genus *Evernia*, also cosmopolitan, represents a transition between foliose and fruticose types; the fronds of the two species, though strap-shaped and generally upright, are dorsiventral and stratose, the gonidia for the most part lying beneath one surface; the other (lower) surface is either white or very dark-coloured. *Everniopsis*, formed of thin branching strap-shaped fronds, is also dorsiventral.

A number of genera, *Thamnolia*, *Siphula*, etc. are of podetia-like structure, generally growing in swards. Several of them have been classified with *Cladoniae*, but they lack the double thallus. One of these, *Endocena*, a sterile monotypic Patagonian lichen, with stiff hollow coralloid fronds, was classified by Hue[1] along with *Siphula*; recently he has transferred it to his family Polycaulionaceae[2] based on *Polycauliona regale* (*Placodium frustulosum* Darbish.), and allied to *Placodium* Sect. *Thamnoma*[3]. In recent studies Hue has laid most stress on thalline characters. He places the new family between "Ramalinaceae" and "Alectoriaceae." *Dactylina arctica* is a common Arctic soil-lichen.

[1] Hue 1892.   [2] Hue 1914.   [3] Tuckerman 1872, p. 107.

Thallus strap-shaped.
  Structure dorsiventral.
    Greyish-green above .... 1. Evernia Ach.
    Whitish-yellow above .... 2. *Everniopsis Nyl.
  Structure radiate alike on both surfaces.
    Fronds grey; medulla of loose hyphae.............. 3. Ramalina Ach.
    Fronds yellow; medulla traversed by strands ...... 4. *Letharia A. Zahlbr.
Thallus filamentous.
  Medulla a strong "chondroid" strand .... 5. Usnea Dill.
  Medulla of loose hyphae.
    Spores simple.. 6. Alectoria Ach.
    Spores muriform, brown .... 7. *Oropogon Fr.
Thallus of upright podetia-like fronds.
  Fronds rather long (about two inches), tapering, 8. Thamnolia Ach. (Cerania
    white...   S. F. Gray).
  Fronds shorter, blunt.
    Medulla solid .... 9. *Siphula Fr.
  Medulla partly or entirely hollow.
    Fronds swollen and tall (about two inches) ......10. *Dactylina Nyl.
    Fronds coralloid, entangled...........................11. *Endocena Cromb.
    Fronds short, upright ....12. *Dufourea Nyl.

XLVIII. CALOPLACACEAE

In this family Zahlbruckner has included the squamulose or crustaceous lichens with colourless polarilocular spores, relegating those with more highly developed thallus or with brown spores to other families. He has also substituted the name *Caloplaca* for the older *Placodium*, the latter being, as he considers, less well defined.

Algal cells are Protococcaceae. The thallus is mostly light-coloured, generally some shade of yellow, and, with few exceptions, contains parietin, which gives a purple colour on the application of potash. The squamulose forms are closely appressed to the substratum, and have often a definite rounded outline (effigurate). The spores have a thick median septum with a loculus at each end and a connecting canal[1].

In *Blastenia* the outer thalline margin is obscure or absent—though gonidia are frequently present below the hymenium. Caloplacaceae occur all over the globe; they are among the most brilliantly coloured of all lichens. *Polycauliona* Hue[2] possibly belongs here: though based on thalline rather than on spore characters, one species at least has polarilocular spores.

  Apothecia with a distinct thalline margin.............. 1. Caloplaca Th. Fr.
  Apothecia without a thalline margin .... 2. Blastenia Th. Fr.

[1] See p. 188.   [2] Hue 1908.

XLIX. *Teloschistaceae*

Polarilocular colourless spores are the distinguishing feature of this family as of the Caloplacaceae. Algal cells Protococcaceae. The thallus of Teloschistaceae is more highly developed, being either foliose or fruticose, though never attaining to very large dimensions. The cortex of *Xanthoria* (foliose) is plectenchymatous, that of *Teloschistes* (fruticose) is fibrous. The species of both genera are yellow or greenish-yellow due to the presence of the lichen-acid parietin.

Both genera have a wide distribution over the globe, more especially in maritime regions.

Thallus foliose .... 1. Xanthoria Th. Fr.
Thallus fruticose .... 2. Teloschistes Norm.

L. *Buelliaceae*

A family of crustaceous lichens distinguished by the brown two-celled spores. Algal cells Protococcaceae. Zahlbruckner has included here *Buellia* and *Rinodina*; the former with a distinctly lecideine fruit and with thinly septate spores; the latter lecanorine and with spores of the polarilocular type, with a very wide central septum pierced in most of the species by a canal which may or may not traverse the middle lamella of the wall. *Rinodina* is closely allied to Physciaceae, while *Buellia* has more affinity with Lecideaceae and is near to *Rhizocarpon*.

Both genera are of world-wide distribution.

Apothecia lecideine, without a thalline margin ...... 1. Buellia De Not.
Apothecia lecanorine, with a thalline margin .... 2. Rinodina Massal.

LI. *Physciaceae*

Thallus foliose or partly fruticose, and generally attached by rhizinae. Algal cells Protococcaceae. The spores resemble those of *Rinodina*, dark-coloured with a thick septum and reduced cell-lumina. As in that species there may be a second septum in each cell, giving a 3-septate spore; but that is rare.

Pyxine, a tropical or subtropical genus, is lecanorine only in the very early stages; it soon loses the thalline margin. *Anaptychia* is differentiated from *Physcia* by the subfruticose habit, though the species are nearly all dorsiventral in structure, only a few of them being truly radiate and corticate on both surfaces. The upper cortex of *Anaptychia* is fibrous, but that character appears also in most species of *Physcia* either on the upper or the lower side. *Physcia* and *Anaptychia* are widely distributed.

Thalline margin absent in apothecia..................... 1. *Pyxine Nyl.
Thalline margin present in apothecia.
    Thallus foliose .... 2. Physcia Schreb.
    Thallus fruticose... 3. Anaptychia Koerb.

C. *Hymenolichens

Fungus a Basidiomycete, akin to *Thelephora*. Algal cells *Scytonema* or *Chroococcus*. Thallus crustaceous, squamulose or foliose. Spores colourless, produced on basidia, on the under surface of the free thallus.

The Hymenolichens[1] are few in number and are endemic in tropical or warm countries. They inhabit soil or trees.

Thallus of extended lobes.
    Gonidia near the upper surface .... 1. *Dictyonema Zahlbr.
    Gonidia in centre of tissue .... 2. *Cora Fr.
Thallus squamulose, irregular .... 3. *Corella Wain.

II. NUMBER AND DISTRIBUTION OF LICHENS

1. ESTIMATES OF NUMBER

Calculations have been made and published, once and again, as to the number of lichen species occurring over the globe or in definite areas. In 1898 Fünfstück stated that about 20,000 different species had been described, but as many of them had been proved to be synonyms, and since many must rank as forms or varieties, the number of well-authenticated species did not then, according to his estimate, exceed 4000. Many additional genera and species have, however, been discovered since then. In Engler and Prantl's *Pflanzenfamilien*, over 50 families and nearly 300 genera find a place, but even in these larger groupings opinions differ as to the limits both of genera and families, and lichenologists would not all accept the arrangement given in that volume.

Fünfstück has reckoned that of his estimated 4000, about 1500 are European and of these at least 1200 occur in Germany. Probably this is too low an estimate for that large country. Leighton in 1879 listed, in his *British Lichen Flora*, 1710 in all, and, as the compilation includes varieties, it cannot be considered as very far astray. On comparing it with Olivier's[2] recent statistics of lichens, we find that of the larger fruticose and foliose species, 310 are recognized by him for the whole of Europe, 206 of these occurring in the British Isles. Leighton's estimate of similar species is about 145, without including varieties now reckoned as good species. In a more circumscribed area, Th. Fries[3] described for Spitzbergen about 210 different lichens, a number that closely approximates to the 206 recent records by Darbishire[4] for the same area.

A general idea of the comparative numbers of the different types of lichens may be gathered from Hue's compilation of exotic lichens[5], examined

---

[1] See p. 152.   [2] Olivier 1907.   [3] Th. Fries 1867.
     [4] Darbishire 1909.   [5] Hue 1892.

or described by Nylander, and now in the Paris herbarium. There are 135 genera with 3686 species. Of these, about 829 belong to the larger foliose and fruticose lichens (including *Cladoniae*); the remaining 2857 belong to the smaller kinds, most of them crustaceous.

2. GEOGRAPHICAL DISTRIBUTION

A. GENERAL SURVEY

The larger foliose and fruticose lichens are now fairly well known and described for Europe, and the knowledge of lichens in other continents is gradually increasing. It is the smaller crustaceous forms that baffle the investigator. The distribution of all lichens over the surface of the earth is controlled by two principal factors, climate and substratum; for although lichens as a rule require only support, they are most of them restricted to one or another particular substratum, either organic or inorganic. As organisms which develop slowly, they require an unchanging substratum, and as sun-plants they avoid deeply shaded woodlands: their occurrence thus depends to a large extent on the configuration and general vegetation of the country.

Though so numerous and so widely distributed, lichens have not evolved that great variety of families and genera characteristic of the allied fungi and algae. They conform to a few leading types of structure, and thus the Orders and Families are comparatively few, and more or less universal. They are most of them undoubtedly very old plants and were probably wide-spread before continents and climates had attained their present stability. Arnold[1] indeed considers that a large part of the present-day lichens were almost certainly already evolved at the end of the Tertiary period, and that they originated in a warm or probably subtropical climate. As proof of this he cites such genera as *Graphis, Thelotrema* and *Arthonia*[2] which are numerous in the tropics though rare in the colder European countries; and he sees further proof in the fact that many fruticose and gelatinous lichens do not occur further north than the forest belt, though they are adapted to cold conditions. Several genera that are abundant in the tropics are represented outside these regions by only one or few species, as for instance *Conotrema urceolatum* and *Bombyliospora incana*.

During the Ice age of the Quaternary period, not many new species can have arisen, and such forms as were not killed off must have been driven towards the south. As the ice retreated the valleys were again stocked with southern forms, and northern species were left behind on mountain tops all over the globe.

---

[1] Arnold 1890.

[2] These genera are associated with *Trentepohlia* algae which are numerous and abundant in tropical climates, and their presence there may possibly account for these particular lichens.

In examining therefore the distribution of lichens, it will be found that the distinction between different countries is relative, certain families being more or less abundant in some regions than others, but, in general, nearly all being represented. Certain species are universal, where similar conditions prevail. This is especially true of those species adapted to extreme cold, as that condition, normal in polar regions, recurs even on the equator if the mountains reach the limit of perpetual snow ; the vertical distribution thus follows on the lines of the horizontal.

In all the temperate countries we find practically the same families, with some few exceptions; there is naturally more diversity of genera and species. Genera that are limited in locality consist, as a rule, of one or few species. In this category, however, are not included the tropical families or genera which may be very rich in species: these are adapted to extreme conditions of heat and often of moisture, and cannot exist outside tropical or subtropical regions, extreme heat being more restricted as to geographical position than extreme cold.

In the study of distribution the question which arises as to the place of origin of such widely distributed plants is one that is difficult to solve. Wainio[1] has attempted the task in regard to *Cladonia*, one of the most unstable genera, the variations of form, which are dependent on external circumstances, being numerous and often bewildering. In his fine monograph of the genus, 132 species are described and 25 of these are cosmopolitan.

The distribution of Phanerogams is connected, as Wainio points out, with causes anterior to the present geological era, but this cannot be the case in a genus so labile and probably so recent as *Cladonia*, though some of the species have existed long enough to spread and establish themselves from pole to pole. Endemic species, or those that are confined to a comparatively limited area, are easily traced to their place of origin, that being generally the locality where they are found in most abundance, and as a general rule in the centre of that area, though there may be exceptions: a plant for instance that originated on a mountain would migrate only in one direction—towards the regions of greater cold.

The difficulty of determining the primitive stations of cosmopolitan, or of widely spread, species is much greater, but generally they also may be referred to their area of greatest abundance. Thus a species may occur frequently in one continent and but rarely in another, even where the conditions of climate, etc., are largely comparable. It may therefore be inferred that the plant has not yet reached the full extent of possible distribution in the less frequented area. As examples of this, Wainio cites, among other instances, *Cladonia papillaria*, which has a very wide distribution in Europe,

[1] Wainio 1897.

but, as yet, has been found only in the eastern parts of North America; and
Cl. pycnoclada, a plant which braves the climate of Cape Horn and the
Falkland Islands, but has not travelled northward beyond temperate North
America: the southern origin of that species is thus plainly indicated. Wainio
also finds that evidence of the primitive locality of a very widely spread
species may be obtained by observing the locality of species derived from
it, which are as yet of limited distribution; presumably these arose in the
ancestral place of origin, though this indication is not always to be relied
on. If, however, the ancestral plant has given rise to several of these rarer
related species, those of them that are most closely allied to the primitive
plant would be found near to it in the original locality.

A detailed account of species distribution according to these indications
is given by Wainio and is full of interest. No such attempt has been made
to deal with any other group, and the distribution of genera and species can
only be suggested. An exhaustive comparison of the lichens of different
regions is beyond the purpose of our study and is indeed impossible as,
except in some limited areas, or for certain species, the occurrence and distribution are not fully known. It is in any case only tentatively that genera
or species can be described as local or rare, until diligent search has been
made for them over a wider field. The study of lichens from a floristic point
of view lags behind that of most other groups of plants. The larger lichen
forms have received more attention, as they are more evident and more
easily collected; but the more minute species are not easily detected, and,
as they are largely inseparable from their substratum of rocks, or trees, etc.,
on which they grow, they are often difficult to collect. They are also in
many instances so indefinite, or so alike in outward form, that they are
liable to be overlooked, only a microscopic examination revealing the differences in fruit and vegetative structure.

Though much remains to be done, still enough is known to make the
geographical distribution of lichens a subject of extreme interest. It will be
found most instructive to follow the usual lines of treatment, which give the
three great divisions: the Polar, the Temperate and the Tropical regions
of the globe.

B. LICHENS OF POLAR REGIONS

Strictly speaking, this section should include only lichens growing within
the Polar Circles; but in practice the lichens of the whole of Greenland and
those of Iceland are included in the Arctic series, as are those of Alaska:
the latitudinal line of demarcation is not closely adhered to. With the
northern lichens may also be considered those of the Antarctic continent,
as well as those of the islands just outside the Antarctic Circle, the South

Shetlands, South Orkneys, Tierra del Fuego, South Georgia and the Falkland Islands. During the Glacial period, the polar forms must have spread with the advancing cold; as the snow and ice retreated, these forms have been left, as already stated, on the higher colder grounds, and representatives of polar species are thus to be found very far from their original haunts. There are few exclusively boreal genera: the same types occur at the Poles as in the higher subtemperate zones. One of the most definitely polar species, for instance, *Usnea* (*Neuropogon*) *melaxantha* grows in the whole Arctic zone, and, in the Antarctic, is more luxuriant than any other lichen, but it has also been recorded from the Andes in Chili, Bolivia and Peru, and from New Zealand (South Island).

Cold winds are a great feature of both poles, and the lichens that by structure or habit can withstand these are the most numerous; those that have a stout cortical layer are able to resist the low temperatures, or those that grow in tufts and thus secure mutual protection. In Arctic and Subarctic regions, 495 lichens have been recorded, most of them crustaceous. Among the larger forms the most frequently met are certain species of *Peltigera*, *Parmelia*, *Gyrophora*, *Cetraria*, *Cladonia*, *Stereocaulon* and *Alectoria*. Among smaller species *Lecanora tartarea* spreads everywhere, especially over other vegetation, *Lecanora varia* reaches the farthest limits to which wood, on which it grows, has drifted, and several species of *Placodium* occur constantly, though not in such great abundance. Over the rocks spread also many crustaceous Lecideaceae too numerous to mention, one of the most striking being the cosmopolitan *Rhizocarpon geographicum*.

Wainio[1] has described the lichens collected by Almquist at Pitlekai in N.E. Siberia just on the borders of the Arctic Circle, and he gives a vivid account of the general topography. The snow lies on the ground till June and falls again in September, but many lichens succeed in growing and fruiting. It is a region of tundra and sand, strewn more or less with stones. Most of the sand is bare of all vegetation; but where mosses, etc., have gained a footing, there are also a fair number of lichens: *Lecanora tartarea*, *Psoroma hypnorum*, with *Lecideae*, *Parmeliae*, *Cladoniae*, *Stereocaulon alpinum*, *Solorina crocea*, *Sphaerophorus globosus*, *Alectoria nigricans* and *Gyrophora proboscidea*. Some granite rocks in that neighbourhood rise to a height of 200 ft., and though bare of vegetation on the north side, yet, in sheltered nooks, several species are to be found. Stunted bushes of willow grow here and there, and on these occur always the same species: *Placodium ferrugineum*, *Rinodina archaea*, *Buellia myriocarpa* and *Arthopyrenia punctiformis*. Some species such as *Sphaerophorus globosus*, *Dactylina arctica* (a purely Arctic genus and species) and *Thamnolia vermicularis* are so abundant that they bulk as largely as other better represented genera such

[1] Wainio 1909.

as *Cladoniae, Lecanorae* or *Lecideae.* On the soil, *Lecanorae* cover the largest areas.

Wainio determined a large number of lichens with many new species, but the region is colder than that of Lappland, and trees with tree-lichens are absent, with the exception of those given above. In Arctic Siberia, Elenkin[1] discovered a new lichen *Placodium subfruticulosum* which scarcely differs from Darbishire's[2] Antarctic species *Pl. fruticulosum* (or *P. regale*); both are distinguished by the fruticose growth of the thallus, for which reason Hue[3] placed them in a new genus, *Polycauliona.*

The Antarctic Zone and the neighbouring lands are less hospitable to plant life than the northern regions, and there is practically no accumulation of detritus. Collections have been made by explorers, and several lists have been published which include a marvellous number of species common to both Poles, if the subantarctic lands are included in the survey. An analytic study of the various lists has been published by Darbishire[4]. He recognizes 106 true Antarctic lichens half of which are Arctic as well. The greater number are crustaceous and are plants common also to other lands though a certain number are endemic. The most abundant genera in species as well as individuals are *Lecidea* and *Lecanora.* Several bright yellow species of *Placodium—Pl. elegans, Pl. murorum,* etc., are there as at the North Pole. Among the larger forms, *Parmeliae, Cetrariae,* and *Cladoniae* are fairly numerous; *Usneae* and *Ramalinae* rather uncommon, while members of the Stictaceae are much more abundant than in the North. The common species of *Peltigera* also occur in Antarctica, though *P. aphthosa* and *P. venosa* are wanting; both of these latter are boreal species. Darbishire adds that lichens have so great a capacity to withstand cold, that they are only checked by the snow covering, and were bare rocks to be found at the South Pole, he is sure lichens would take possession of them. The most southerly point at which any plant has been found is 78° South latitude and 162° East longitude, in which locality the lichen *Lecanora subfusca* was collected by members of Scott's Antarctic expedition (1901–1904) at a height of 5000 ft.

A somewhat different view of the Antarctic lichen flora is indicated by Hue[3] in his account of the plants brought back by the second French Antarctic Expedition. The collection was an extremely favourable and important one: great blocks of stone with their communities of lichens were secured, and these blocks were entirely covered, the crustaceous species, especially, spreading over every inch of space.

Hue determined 126 species, but as 15 of these came from the Magellan regions only 111 were truly Antarctic. Of these 90 are new species, 29 of them belonging to the genus *Buellia.* Hue considers, therefore, that in Antarctica there is a flora that, with the exception of cosmopolitan species,

[1] Elenkin 1906.   [2] Darbishire 1905.   [3] Hue 1915.   [4] Darbishire 1912.

is different from every other, and is special to these southern regions. Darbishire himself described 34 new Antarctic species, but only 10 of these
are from true Antarctica; the others were collected in South Georgia, the
Falkland Islands or Tierra del Fuego. Even though many species are
endemic in the south, the fact remains that a remarkable number of lichens
which occur intermediately on mountain summits are common to both Polar
areas.

C. Lichens of the Temperate Zones

Regions outside the Polar Circles which enjoy, on the whole, cool moist
climates, are specially favourable to lichen growth, and the recorded numbers
are very large. The European countries are naturally those in which the
lichen flora is best known. Whereas polar and high Alpine species are
stunted in growth and often sterile, those in milder localities grow and fruit
well, and the more highly developed species are more frequent. *Parmeliae,
Nephromae, Usneae* and *Ramalinae* become prominent, especially in the
more northern districts. Many Arctic plants are represented on the higher
altitudes. A comparison has been made between the lichens of Greenland
and those of Germany: of 286 species recorded for the former country, 213
have been found in Germany, the largest number of species common to
both countries being crustaceous. Lindsay[1] considered that Greenland
lichens were even more akin to those of Scandinavia.

There is an astonishing similarity of lichens in the Temperate Zone all
round the world. Commenting on a list of Chicago lichens by Calkins[2],
Hue[3] pointed out that with the exception of a few endemic species they
resemble those of Normandy. The same result appears in Bruce Fink's[4]
careful compilation of Minnesota lichens, which may be accepted as typical
of the Eastern and Middle States of North Temperate America. The
genera from that region number nearly 70, and only two of these, *Omphalaria*
and *Heppia*, are absent from our British Flora. The species naturally present
much greater diversity. Very few Graphideae are reported. In other States
of North America there occurs the singular aquatic lichen, *Hydrothyria
venosa*, nearly akin to *Peltigera*.

If we contrast American lichens with these collected in South Siberia
near Lake Baikal[5], we recognize there also the influence of temperate
conditions. Several species of *Usnea* are listed, *U. barbata, U. florida,
U. hirta* and *U. longissima*, all of them also American forms, *U. longissima*
having been found in Wisconsin. *Xanthoria parietina*, an almost cosmopolitan lichen, is absent from this district, and is not recorded from Minnesota.
The opinion[6] in America is that it is a maritime species: Tuckerman gives

[1] Lindsay 1870.   [2] Calkins 1896.   [3] Hue 1898.   [4] Fink 1903.
[5] Wainio 1896.   [6] Comm. Heber Howe.

its habitat as "the neighbourhood of a great water," and reports it from near Lake Superior. In our country it grows at a good distance from the sea, in Yorkshire dales, etc., but all our counties would rank as maritime in the American sense. *Lecanora tartarea* which is rare in Minnesota is also absent from the Lake Baikal region. It occurs frequently both in Arctic and in Antarctic regions, and is probably also somewhat maritime in habitat. Many of the *Parmeliae, Nephromiae* and *Peltigerae,* common to all northern temperate climes, are Siberian as are also *Cladoniae* and many crustaceous species. There is only one *Sticta, St. Wrightii,* a Japanese lichen, recorded by Wainio from this Siberian locality.

A marked difference as regards species is noted between the Flora of Minnesota and that of California. Herre[1] has directed attention to the great similarity between the lichens of the latter state and those of Europe: many European species occur along the coast and nowhere else in America so far as is yet known; as examples he cites, among others, *Calicium hyperellum, Lecidea quernea, L. aromatica, Gyrophora polyrhiza, Pertusaria amara, Roccella fuciformis, R. fucoides* and *R. tinctoria.* The Scandinavian lichen, *Letharia vulpina,* grows abundantly there and fruits freely; it is very rare in other parts of America. Herre found, however, no specimens of *Cladonia rangiferina, Cl. alpestris* or *Cl. sylvatica,* nor any species of *Graphis*; he is unable to explain these anomalies in distribution, but he considers that the cool equable climate is largely responsible: it is so much more like that of the milder countries of Europe than of the states east of the Sierra Nevada. His contention is supported by a consideration of Japanese lichens. With a somewhat similar climate there is a great preponderance of European forms. Out of 382 species determined by Nylander[2], 209 were European. There were 17 Graphideae, 31 *Parmeliae,* and 23 *Cladoniae,* all of the last named being European. These results of Nylander's accord well with a short list of 30 species from Japan compiled by Müller[3] at an earlier date. They were chiefly crustaceous tree-lichens; but the *Cladoniae* recorded are the familiar British species *Cl. fimbriata, Cl. pyxidata* and *Cl. verticillata.*

With the Japanese Flora may be compared a list[4] of Maingay's lichens from China, 35 in all. *Collema limosum,* the only representative of Collemaceae in the list, is European, as are the two species of *Ramalina, R. gracilenta* and *R. pollinaria*; four species of *Physcia* are European, the remaining *Ph. picta* being a common tropical or subtropical plant. *Lecanora saxicola, L. cinerea, Placodium callopismum* and *Pl. citrinum* are cosmopolitan, other *Lecanorae* and most of the *Lecideae* are new. *Graphis scripta, Opegrapha subsiderella* and *Arthonia cinnabarina*—the few Graphideae collected—are

[1] Herre 1910.   [2] Nylander 1890.   [3] Müller 1879.
[4] Nylander and Crombie 1884.

more or less familiar home plants. Among the Pyrenocarpei, *Verrucaria* (*Pyrenula*) *nitida* occurs; it is a widely distributed tree-lichen.

It is unnecessary to describe in detail the British lichens. Some districts have been thoroughly worked, others have barely been touched. The flora as a whole is of a western European type showing the influence of the Gulf Stream, though there is also a representative boreal growth on the moorlands and higher hills, especially in Scotland. Such species as *Parmelia pubescens*, *P. stygia* and *P. alpicola* recall the Arctic Circle while *Alectoriae*, *Cetrariae* and *Gyrophorae* represent affinity with the colder temperate zone.

In the southern counties such species as *Sticta aurata*, *S. damaecornis*, *Phaeographis Lyellii* and *Lecanora* (*Lecania*) *holophaea* belong to the flora of the Atlantic seaboard, while in S.W. Ireland the tropical genera *Leptogidium* and *Anthracothecium* are each represented by a single species. The tropical or subtropical genus *Coenogonium* occurs in Great Britain and in Germany, with one sterile species, *C. ebeneum*. *Enterographa crassa* is another of our common western lichens which however has travelled eastwards as far as Wiesbaden. *Roccella* is essentially a maritime genus of warm climates: two species, *R. fuciformis* and *R. fucoides*, grow on our south and west coasts. The famous *R. tinctoria* is a Mediterranean plant, though it is recorded also from a number of localities outside that region and has been collected in Australia.

In the temperate zones of the southern hemisphere are situated the great narrowing projections of South Africa and South America with Australia and New Zealand. As we have seen, the Antarctic flora prevails more or less in the extreme southern part of America, and the similarity between the lichens of that country and those of New Zealand is very striking, especially in the fruticulose forms. There is a very abundant flora in the New Zealand islands with their cool moist climate and high mountains. Churchill Babington[1] described the collections made by Hooker. Stirton[2] added many species, among others *Calycidium cuneatum*, evidently endemic. Later, Nylander[3] published the species already known, and Hellbom[4] followed with an account of New Zealand lichens based on Berggsen's collections; many more must be still undiscovered. Especially noticeable as compared with the north, are the numbers of Stictaceae which reach their highest development of species and individuals in Australasia. They are as numerous and as prominent as are Gyrophoraceae in the north. A genus of Parmeliaceae, *Hetorodea*, which, like the *Stictae*, bears cyphellae on the lower surface, is peculiar to Australia.

A warm current from the tropical Pacific Ocean passes southwards along the East Coast of Australia, and Wilson[5] has traced its influence on the

[1] Babington 1855.   [2] Stirton 1875.   [3] Nylander 1888.   [4] Hellbom 1896.
[5] Wilson 1892.

lichens of Australia and Tasmania to which countries a few tropical species of *Graphis, Chiodecton* and *Trypethelium* have migrated. Various unusual types are to be found there also: the beautiful *Cladonia retepora* (Fig. 71), which spreads over the ground in cushion-like growths, with the genera *Thysanothecium* and *Neophyllis*, genera of Cladoniaceae endemic in these regions.

The continent of Africa on the north and east is in so close connection with Europe and Asia that little peculiarity in the flora could be expected. In comparing small representative collections of lichens, 37 species from Egypt and 20 from Palestine, Müller[1] found that there was a great affinity between these two countries. Of the Palestine species, eight were cosmopolitan; among the crustaceous genera, *Lecanorae* were the most numerous. There was no record of new genera.

The vast African continent—more especially the central region—has been but little explored in a lichenological sense; but in 1895 Stizenberger[2] listed all of the species known, amounting to 1593, and new plants and new records have been added since that day. The familiar genera are well represented, *Nephromium, Xanthoria, Physcia, Parmelia, Ramalina* and *Roccella*, some of them by large and handsome species. In the Sahara Steiner[3] found that genera with blue-green algae such as the Gloeolichens were particularly abundant; *Heppia* and *Endocarpon* were also frequent. Algeria has a Mediterranean Flora rather than tropical or subtropical. Flagey[4] records no species of *Graphis* for the province of Constantine, and only 22 species of other Graphideae. Most of the 519 lichens listed by him there are crustaceous species. South America stretches from the Tropics in the north to Antarctica in the south. Tropical conditions prevail over the central countries and tropical tree-lichens, Graphidaceae, Thelotremaceae, etc. are frequent; further West, on the Pacific slopes, *Usneae* and *Ramalinae* hang in great festoons from the branches, while the foliose *Parmeliae* and *Stictae* grow to a large size on the trunks of the trees.

Wainio's[5] *Lichens du Brésil* is one of the classic systematic books and embodies the writer's views on lichen classification. There are no new families recorded though a number of genera and many species are new, and, so far as is yet known, these are endemic. Many of our common forms are absent; thus *Peltigera* is represented by three species only, *P. leptoderma, P. spuriella* and *P. Americana*, the two latter being new species. *Sticta* (including *Stictina*) includes only five species, and *Coenogonium* three. There are 39 species of *Parmelia* with 33 of *Lecanora* and 68 of *Lecidea*, many of them new species.

[1] Müller-Argau 1884. [2] Stizenberger 1888–1895. [3] Steiner 1895. [4] Flagey 1892. [5] Wainio 1890.

D. Lichens of Tropical Regions

In the tropics lichens come under the influence of many climates: on the high mountains there is a region of perpetual snow, lower down a gradual change to temperate and finally to tropical conditions of extreme heat, and, in some instances, extreme moisture. There is thus a bewildering variety of forms. By "tropical" however the warmer climate is always implied. Several families and genera seem to flourish best in these warm moist conditions and our familiar species grow there to a large size. Among crustaceous families Thelotremaceae and Graphidaceae are especially abundant, and probably originated there. In the old comprehensive genus *Graphis*, 300 species were recorded from the tropics. It should be borne in mind that *Trentepohlia*, the alga that forms the gonidia of these lichens, is very abundant in the tropics. *Coenogonium*, a genus containing about twelve species and also associated with *Trentepohlia*, is scarcely found in Europe, except one sterile species, *C. ebeneum*. Other species of the genus have been recorded as far north as Algeria in the Eastern Hemisphere and Louisiana in the Western, while one species, *C. implexum*, occurs in the southern temperate zone in Australia and New Zealand.

Of exclusively tropical lichens, the Hymenolichens are the most noteworthy. They include three genera, *Cora*, *Corella* and *Dictyonema*, the few species of which grow on trees or on the ground both in eastern and western tropical countries.

Other tropical or subtropical forms are *Oropogon loxensis*, similar to *Alectoria* in form and habit, but with one brown muriform spore in the ascus; it is only found in tropical or subtropical lands. *Physcidia Wrightii* (Parmeliaceae) is exclusively a Cuban lichen. Several small genera of Pyrenopsidaceae such as *Jenmania* (British Guiana), *Paulia* (Polynesia) and *Phloeopeccania* (South Arabia) seem to be confined to very hot localities. On the other hand Collemaceae are rare: Wainio records from Brazil only four species of *Collema*, with nine of *Leptogium*.

Among Pyrenolichens, Paratheliaceae, Mycoporaceae and Astrotheliaceae are almost exclusively of tropical distribution, and finally the leaf lichens with very few exceptions. These follow the leaf algae, *Mycoidea*, *Phycopeltis*, etc., which are so abundant on the coriaceous long-lived green leaves of a number of tropical Phanerogams. All the Strigulaceae are epiphytic lichens. *Phyllophthalmaria* (Thelotremaceae) is also a leaf genus; one of the species, *Ph. coccinea*, has beautiful carmine-red apothecia. The genera of the tropical family Ectolechiaceae also inhabit leaves, but they are associated with Protococcaceae; one of the genera *Sporopodium*[1] is remarkable as having hymenial gonidia. Though tropical in the main,

[1] Wainio 1890, ii. p. 27 (recorded under *Lecidea*).

epiphyllous lichens may spread to the regions beyond: *Sporopodium Caucasium* and a sterile *Strigula* were found by Elenkin and Woronichin[1] on leaves of *Buxus sempervirens* in the Caucasus, well outside the tropics.

Pilocarpon, an epiphytic genus, is associated with Protococcaceae; one of the species, *P. leucoblepharum*, spreads from the bark to the leaves of pine-trees; it is widely distributed and has also been reported in the Caucasus[2]. *Chrysothrix*, in which the gonidia belong to the algal genus *Palmella*, grows on Cactus spines in Chili, and may also rank as a subtropical epiphyllous lichen.

A series of lichens from the warm temperate region of Transcaucasia investigated by Steiner[3] were found to be very similar to those of Central Europe. Lecanoraceae were, however, more abundant than Lecideaceae and Verrucariaceae were comparatively rare.

Much of Asia lies within tropical or subtropical influences. Several regions have received some amount of attention from collectors. From Persia there has been published a list of 59 species determined by Müller[4]; several of them are Egyptian or Arabian plants, 15 are new species, but the greater number are European.

A small collection of 53 species from India, near to Calcutta, published by Nylander[5], included a new genus of Caliciaceae, *Pyrgidium* (*P. bengalense*), allied to *Sphinctrina*. He also recorded *Ramalina angulosa* in African species, along with *R. calicaris*, *R. farinacea* and *Parmelia perlata*, f. *isidiophora*, which are British. Other foliose forms, *Physcia picta*, *Pyxine Cocoës* and *P. Meissnerii* are tropical or subtropical; along with these were collected crustaceous tropical species belonging to *Lecanorae*, *Lecideae*, Graphideae, etc.

Leighton[6] published a collection of Ceylon lichens and found that Graphideae predominated. Nylander[7] came to the same conclusion with regard to lichens referred to him: out of 159 species investigated from Ceylon, there were 36 species of Graphideae. In another list[8] of Labuan, Singapore and Malacca lichens, 164 in all, he found that 56 belonged to the Graphidei, 36 to Pyrenocarpei, 14 to Thelotremei and 11 to Parmelei; only 15 species were European.

On the whole it is safe to conclude from the above and other publications that the exceptional conditions of the tropics have produced many distinctive lichens, but that a greater abundance both of species and individuals is now to be found in temperate and cold climates.

III. FOSSIL LICHENS

In pronouncing on the great antiquity of lichens, proof has been adduced from physiological rather than from phytogeological evidence. It would have been of surpassing interest to trace back these plants through the ages,

---

[1] Elenkin and Woronichin 1908.   [2] Jaczewski 1904.   [3] Steiner 1919.   [4] Müller 1892.
[5] Nylander 1867.   [6] Leighton 1869.   [7] Nylander 1900.   [8] Nylander 1891.

even if it were never possible to assign to any definite period the first symbiosis of the fungus and alga; but among fossil plants there are only scanty records of lichens and even these few are of doubtful determination.

The reason for this is fairly obvious: not only are the primitive thalline forms too indistinct for recognizable preservation, but all lichens are characterized by the gelatinous nature of the hyphal or of the algal membranes which readily imbibe water. They thus become soft and flaccid and unfit to leave any impress on sedimentary rocks. It has also been pointed out by Schimper[1] that while deciduous leaves with fungi on them are abundant in fossil beds, lichens are entirely wanting. These latter are so firmly attached to the rocks or trees on which they grow that they are rarely dislodged, and form no part of wind- or autumn-fall. Trunks and branches of trees lose their bark by decay long before they become fossilized and thus all trace of their lichen covering disappears.

The few records that have been made are here tabulated in chronological order:

1. **Palaeozoic.** Schimper decides that there are no records of lichens in the earlier epochs. Any allusions[2] to their occurrence are held to be extremely vague and speculative.

2. **Mesozoic.** Braun[3] has recorded a *Ramalinites lacerus* from the Keuper sandstone at Eckersdorf, though later[4] he seemed to be doubtful as to his determination. One other lichen, an *Opegrapha*, has been described[5] from the chalk at Aix.

3. **Cainozoic.** In the brown-coal formations of Saxony Engelhardt[6] finds two lichens: *Ramalina tertiaria*, a much branched plant, the fronds being flat and not channelled "and of further interest that it is attached to a carbonized stem." The second form, *Lichen dichotomus*, has a dichotomously branching strap-shaped frond. "There is sufficient evidence that these fronds were cylindrical and that the width is due to pressure. In one place a channel is visible, filled with an ochraceous yellow substance."

Other records on brown coal or lignite are: *Verrucarites geanthricis*[7] Goepp., somewhat similar to *Pyrenula nitida*, found at Muskau in Silesia; *Opegrapha Thomasiana*[8] Goepp., near to *Opegrapha varia*, and *Graphis scripta succinea* Goepp.[9] on a piece of lignite in amber beds, all of them doubtful.

Schimper has questioned, as he well might, Ludwig's[10] records from lignite from the Rhein-Wetterau Tertiary formations; these are: *Cladonia rosea*, *Lichen albineus*, *L. diffissus* and *L. orbiculatus*; he thinks they are probably fungus mycelia. Another lichen, a *Parmelia* with apothecia,

1 Schimper 1869, p. 145. 2 Lindsay 1879. 3 Braun 1840. 4 Muenster 1846, p. 26.
5 Eltingshausen and Debey 1857. 6 Engelhardt 1870 (Pl. I. figs. 1 and 2).
7 Goeppert 1845, p. 195. 8 See Schimper 1869, pp. 145, etc.
9 Goeppert and Menge 1883, t. 1, fig. 3. 10 Ludwig 1859, p. 61 (t. 9, figs. 1–4), 1859–61.

which recalls somewhat *P. saxatilis* or *P. conspersa*, collected by Geyler also in the brown coal of Wetterau is accepted by Schimper[1] as more trustworthy.

More authentic also are the lichens from the amber beds of Königsberg and elsewhere collected by Goeppert and others. These deposits are Cainozoic and have been described by Goeppert and Menge[2] as middle Miocene. Schimper gives the list as: *Parmelia lacunosa* Meng. and Goepp., fragments of thallus near to *P. saxatilis*; *Sphaerophorus coralloides*; *Cladonia divaricata* Meng. and Goepp.; *Cl. furcata*; *Ramalina calicaris* vars. *fraxinea* and *canaliculata*; *Cornicularia aculeata, C. subpubescens* Goepp., *C. ochroleuca, C. succinea* Goepp., and *Usnea barbata* var. *hirta*. Schimper rather deprecates specific determinations when dealing with such imperfect fragments.

In a later work Goeppert and Menge[2] state that they have found twelve different amber lichens and that among these are *Physcia ciliaris, Parmelia physodes* and *Graphis* (probably *G. scripta succinea*) along with *Peziza resinae* which is more generally classified among lichens as *Lecidea (Biatorella) resinae*.

Another series of lichens found in recent deposits in North Europe has been described by Sernander[3] as "subfossil." While engaged on the investigations undertaken by the Swedish Turf-Moor Commission, he noted the alternation of slightly raised *Sphagnum* beds with lower-lying stretches of *Calluna* and lichen moor—in some instances dense communities of *Cladonia rangiferina*. In time the turf-forming *Sphagnum* overtopped and invaded the drier moorland, covering it with a new formation of turf. Beneath these layers of "regenerated turf" were found local accumulations of blackened remains of the *Cladonia* still recognizable by the form and branching. Some specimens of *Cetraria islandica* were also determined.

Of especial lichenological interest in these northern regions was the Calcareous Tufa or Calc-sinter in which Sernander also found subfossil lichens—distinct impressions of *Peltigera* spp. and the foveolae of endolithic calcicolous species.

In another category he has placed *Ramalina fraxinea, Graphis* sp. and *Opegrapha* sp., traces of which were embedded with drift in the Tufa. In the two Graphideae the walls of apothecia and pycnidia were preserved. Sernander considers their presence of interest as testifying to warmer conditions than now prevail in these latitudes.

---

[1] Schimper in Zittel 1890.   [2] Goeppert and Menge 1883.   [3] Sernander 1918.

CHAPTER IX

ECOLOGY

A. General Introduction

ECOLOGY is the science that deals with the habitats of plants and their response to the environment of climate or of substratum. Ecology in the lichen kingdom is habitat "writ large," and though it will not be possible in so wide a field to enter into much detail, even a short examination of lichens in this aspect should yield interesting results, especially as lichens have never, at any time, been described without reference to their habitat. In very early days, medicinal Usneas were supposed to possess peculiar virtues according to the trees on which they grew and which are therefore carefully recorded, and all down the pages of lichen literature, no diagnosis has been drawn up without definite reference to the nature of the substratum. Not only rocks and trees are recorded, but the kind of rock and the kind of tree are often specified. The important part played by rock lichens in preparing soil for other plants has also received much attention[1].

Several comprehensive works on Ecology have been published in recent times and though they deal mainly with the higher vegetation, the general plan of study of land plants is well adapted to lichens. A series of definitions and explanations of the terms used will be of service:

Thus in a work by Moss[2] we read "The flora is composed of the individual species: the vegetation comprises the groupings of these species into ensembles termed vegetation units or plant communities." And again:

1. "A *plant formation* is the whole of the vegetation which occurs on a definite and essentially uniform habitat."—All kinds of plants are included in the formation, so that strictly speaking a *lichen formation* is one in which lichens are the dominant plants. Cf. p. 394. The term however is very loosely used in the literature. A uniform habitat, as regards lichens, would be that of the different kinds of soil, of rock, of tree, etc.

2. "A *plant association* is of lower rank than a formation, and is characterized by minor differences within the generally uniform habitat."—It represents a more limited community within the formation.

3. "A *plant society* is of lower rank than an association, and is marked by still less fundamental differences of the habitat."—The last-named term represents chiefly aggregations of single species. Moss adds that: "*plant community* is a convenient and general term used for a vegetation unit of any rank."

Climatic conditions and geographical position are included in any consideration of habitat, as lichens like other plants are susceptible to external influences.

[1] See p. 392.   [2] Moss 1913.

Ecological plant-geography has been well defined by Macmillan[1] as "the science which treats of the reciprocal relation between physiographic conditions and life requirements of organisms in so far as such relations manifest themselves in choice of habitats and method of establishment upon them...resulting in the origin and development of plant formations."

B. EXTERNAL INFLUENCES

The climatic factors most favourable to lichen development are direct light (already discussed)[2], a moderate or cold temperature, constant moisture and a clear pure atmosphere. Wind also affects their growth.

a. TEMPERATURE. Lichens, as we have seen, can endure the heat of direct sunlight owing to the protection afforded by thickened cortices, colour pigments, etc. Where such heat is so intense as to be injurious the gonidia succumb first[3].

Lichens endure low temperatures better than other plants, their xerophytic structure rendering them proof against extreme conditions: the hyphae have thick walls with reduced cell lumen and extremely meagre contents. Freezing for prolonged periods does them little injury; they revive again when conditions become more favourable. Efficient protection is also afforded by the thickened cortex of such lichens as exist in Polar areas, or at high altitudes. Thus various species of *Cetrariae* with a stout "decomposed" amorphous cortex can withstand very low temperatures and grow freely on the tundra, while *Cladonia rangiferina*, also a northern lichen, but without a continuous cortex, cannot exist in such cold conditions, unless in localities where it is protected by a covering of snow during the most inclement seasons.

b. HUMIDITY. A high degree of humidity is distinctly of advantage to the growth of the lichen thallus, though when the moist conditions are excessive the plants become turgid and soredial states are developed.

The great abundance of lichens in the western districts of the British Isles, where the rainfall is heaviest, is proof enough of the advantage of moisture, and on trees it is the side exposed to wind and rain that is most plentifully covered. A series of observations on lichens and rainfall were made by West[4] and have been published since his death. He has remarked in more than one of his papers that a most favourable situation for lichen growth is one that is subject to a drive of wind with much rain. In localities with an average of 216 days of rain in the year, he found abundant and luxuriant growths of the larger foliose species. In West Ireland there were specimens of *Ricasolia laetevirens* measuring 165 by 60 cm. In West Scotland with an "average of total days of rain, 225," he found plants of *Ricasolia amplissima* 150 × 90 cm. in size, of *R. laetevirens* 120×90 cm., while *Pertusaria*

[1] Macmillan 1894. [2] See p. 240 et seq. [3] See p. 238. [4] West 1915.

globulifera formed a continuous crust on the trees as much as 120 × 90 cm. *Lecanora tartarea* seemed to thrive exceptionally well when subject to driving mists and rains from mountain or moorland, and was in these circumstances frequently the dominant epiphyte. Bruce Fink[1] also observed in his ecological excursions that the number of species and individuals was greater near lakes or rivers.

Though a fair number of lichens are adapted to life wholly or partly under water, land forms are mostly xerophytic in structure, and die off if submerged for any length of time. The *Peltigerae* are perhaps the most hydrophilous of purely land species. Many Alpine or Polar forms are covered with snow for long periods. In the extreme north it affords more or less protection; and Kihlman[2] and others have remarked on the scarcity of lichens in localities denuded of the snow mantle and exposed to severe winter cold. On the other hand lichens on the high Alpine summits that are covered with snow the greater part of the year suffer, according to Nilson[3], from the excessive moisture and the deprivation of light. Foliose and fruticose forms were, he found, dwarfed in size; the crustaceous species had a very thin thallus and in all of them the colour was impure. *Gyrophorae* seemed to be most affected: folds and outgrowths of the thallus were formed and the internal tissues were partly disintegrated. Lichens on the blocks of the glacier moraines which are subject to inundations of ice-cold water after the snow has melted, were unhealthy looking, poorly developed and often sterile, though able to persist in a barren state. Lindsay[4] noted as a result of such conditions on *Cladoniae* not only sterility but also deformity both of vegetative and reproductive organs; discolouration and mottling of the thallus and an increased development of squamules of the primary thallus and on the podetia.

c. WIND. Horizontal crustaceous or foliose lichens are not liable to direct injury by wind as their close adherence to the substratum sufficiently shelters them. It is only when the wind carries with it any considerable quantity of sand that the tree or rock surfaces are swept bare and prevented from ever harbouring any vegetation, and also, as has been already noted, the terrible winds round the poles are fatal to lichens exposed to the blasts unless they are provided with a special protective cortex. After crustaceous forms, species of *Cetraria*, *Stereocaulon* and *Cladonia* are best fitted for weathering wind storms: the tufted[5] cushion-like growth adopted by these lichens gives them mutual protection, not only against wind, but against superincumbent masses of snow. Kihlman[2] has given us a vivid account of wind action in the Tundra region. He noted numerous hollows completely scooped out down to the sand: in these sheltered nooks he

---

[1] Fink 1894.   [2] Kihlman 1890.   [3] Nilson 1907.
[4] Lindsay 1869.   [5] Sättler 1914.

observed the gradual colonization of the depressions, first by a growth of hepatics and mosses and by such ground lichens as *Peltigera canina, P. aphthosa* and *Nephromium arcticum* ; they cover the soil and in time the hollow becomes filled with a mass of vegetation consisting of Cladonias, mosses, etc. On reaching a certain more exposed level these begin to wither and die off at the tips, killed by the high cold winds. Then arrives *Lecanora tartarea,* one of the commonest Arctic lichens, and one which is readily a saprophyte on decayed vegetation. It covers completely the mound of weakened plants which are thus smothered and finally killed. The collapse of the substratum entails in turn the breaking of the *Lecanora* crust, and the next high wind sweeps away the whole crumbling mass. How long recolonization takes, it was impossible to find out.

Upright fruticose lichens are necessarily more liable to damage by wind, but maritime *Ramalinae* and *Roccellae* do not seem to suffer in temperate climates, though in regions of extreme cold fruticose forms are dwarfed and stunted. The highest development of filamentous lichens is to be found in more or less sheltered woods, but the effect of wind on these lichens is not wholly unfavourable. Observations have been made by Peirce[1] on two American pendulous lichens which are dependent on wind for dissemination. On the Californian coasts a very large and very frequent species, *Ramalina reticulata* (Fig. 64), is seldom found undamaged by wind. In Northern California the deciduous oaks *Quercus alba* and *Q. Douglasii* are festooned with the lichen, while the evergreen " live oak," *Q. chrysolepis,* with persistent foliage, only bears scraps that have been blown on to it. Nearer the coast and southward the lichen grows on all kinds of trees and shrubs. The fronds of this *Ramalina* form a delicate reticulation and when moist are easily torn. In the winter season, when the leaves are off the trees, wind- and rain-storms are frequent ; the lichen is then exposed to the full force of the elements and fragments and shreds are blown to other trees, becoming coiled and entangled round the naked branches and barky excrescences, on which they continue to grow and fruit perfectly well. A succeeding storm may loosen them and carry them still further. Peirce noted that only plants developed from the spore formed hold-fasts and they were always small, the largest formed measuring seven inches in length. Both the hold-fast and the primary stalk were too slight to resist the tearing action of the wind.

Schrenk[2] made a series of observations and experiments with the lichens *Usnea plicata* and *U. dasypoga,* long hanging forms common on short-leaved conifers such as spruce and juniper. The branches of these trees are often covered with tangled masses of the lichens not due to local growth, but to wind-borne strands and to coiling and intertwining of the filaments owing

---

[1] Peirce 1898.　　　　　　　　　　[2] Schrenk 1898.

to successive wetting and drying. Tests were made as to the force of wind required to tear the lichens and it was found that velocities of 77 miles per hour were not sufficient to cause any pieces of the lichen to fly off when it was dry; but after soaking in water, the first pieces were torn off at 50 miles an hour. These figures are, however, considered by Schrenk to be too high as it was found impossible in artificially created wind to keep up the condition of saturation. It is the combination of wind and rain that is so effective in ensuring the dispersal of both these lichens.

d. HUMAN AGENCY. Though lichens are generally associated with undisturbed areas and undisturbed conditions, yet accidents or convulsions of nature, as well as changes effected by man, may at times prove favourable to their development. The opening up of forests by thinning or clearing will be followed in time by a growth of tree and ground forms; newly planted trees may furnish a new lichen flora, and the building of houses and walls with their intermixture of calcareous mortar will attract a particular series of siliceous or of lime-loving lichens. A few lichens are partial to the trees of cultivated areas, such as park-lands, avenues or road-sides. Among these are several species of *Physcia*: *Ph. pulverulenta*, *Ph. ciliaris* and *Ph. stellaris*, some species of *Placodium*, and those lichens such as *Lecanora varia* that frequently grow on old palings.

On the other hand lichens are driven away from areas of dense population, or from regions affected by the contaminated air of industrial centres. In our older British Floras there are records of lichens collected in London during the eighteenth century—in Hyde Park and on Hampstead Heath—but these have long disappeared. A variety of *Lecanora galactina* seems to be the only lichen left within the London district: it has been found at Camden Town, Notting Hill and South Kensington.

So recently as 1866, Nylander[1] made a list of the lichens growing in the Luxembourg gardens in Paris; the chestnuts in the alley of the Observatory were the most thickly covered, and the list includes about 35 different species or varieties, some of them poorly developed and occurring but rarely, others always sterile, but quite a number in healthy fruiting condition. All of them were crustaceous or squamulose forms except *Parmelia acetabulum*, which was very rare and sterile; *Physcia obscura* var. and *Ph. pulverulenta* var., also sterile; *Physcia stellaris* with occasional abortive apothecia and *Xanthoria parietina*, abundant and fertile. In 1898, Hue[2] tells us, there were no lichens to be found on the trees and only traces of lichen growth on the stone balustrades.

The question of atmospheric pollution in manufacturing districts and its effect on vegetation, more especially on lichen vegetation, has received special attention from Wheldon and Wilson[3] in their account of the lichens of

[1] Nylander 1866.   [2] Hue 1898.   [3] Wheldon and Wilson 1915.

South Lancashire, a district peculiarly suitable for such an inquiry, as nowhere, according to the observations, are the evil effects of impure air so evident or so wide-spread. The unfavourable conditions have prevailed for a long time and the lichens have consequently become very rare, those that still survive leading but a meagre existence. The chief impurity is coal smoke which is produced not only from factories but from private dwellings, and its harmful effect goes far beyond the limits of the towns or suburbs, lichens being seen to deteriorate as soon as there is the slightest deposition of coal combustion products—especially sulphur compounds—either on the plants or on the surfaces on which they grow. The larger foliose and fruticose forms have evidently been the most severely affected. "While genera of bark-loving lichens such as *Calicium, Usnea, Ramalina, Graphis, Opegrapha, Arthonia* etc. are either wholly absent or are poorly represented in the district," corticolous species now represent about 15 per cent. of those that are left; those that seem best to resist the pernicious influences of the smoky atmosphere are, principally, *Lecanora varia, Parmelia saxatilis, P. physodes* and to a less degree *P. sulcata, P. fuliginosa* var. *laetevirens* and *Pertusaria amara*.

Saxicolous lichens have also suffered severely in South Lancashire; not only the number of species, but the number of individuals is enormously reduced and the specimens that have persisted are usually poorly developed. The smoke-producing towns are situated in the valley-bottoms, and the smoke rises and drifts on to the surrounding hills and moorlands. The authors noted that crustaceous rock-lichens were in better condition on horizontal surfaces such as the copings of walls, or half-buried stones, etc. than on the perpendicular or sloping faces of rocks or walls. This was probably due to what they observed as to the effect of water trickling down the inclined substrata and becoming charged with acid from the rock surfaces. They also observed further that a calcareous substratum seemed to counteract the effect of the smoke, the sulphuric acid combining with the lime to form calcium sulphate, and the surface-washings thus being neutralized, the lichens there are more favourably situated. They found in good fruiting condition, on mortar, cement or concrete, the species *Lecanora urbana, L. campestris, L. crenulata, Verrucaria muralis, V. rupestris, Thelidium microcarpum* and *Staurothele hymenogonia*. Some of these occurred on the mortar of sandstone walls close to the town, "whilst on the surface of the sandstone itself no lichens were present."

Soil-lichens were also strongly affected, the Cladoniae of the moorlands being in a very depauperate condition, and there was no trace of *Stereocaulon* or of *Sphaerophorus* species, which, according to older records. previously occurred on the high uplands.

The influence of human agency is well exemplified in one of the London districts In 1883 Crombie published a list of the lichens recorded from

Epping Forest during the nineteenth century. They numbered 171 species, varieties or forms, but, at the date of publication, many had died out owing to the destruction of the older trees; the undue crowding of the trees that were left and the ever increasing population on the outskirts of the Forest. Crombie himself made a systematic search for those that remained, and could only find some 85 different kinds, many of them in a fragmentary or sterile condition.

R. Paulson and P. Thompson[1] commenced a lichen exploration of the Forest 27 years after Crombie's report was published, and they have found that though the houses and the population have continued to increase round the area, the lichens have not suffered. " Species considered by Crombie as rare or sterile are now fairly abundant, and produce numerous apothecia. Such are *Baeomyces rufus, B. roseus, Cladonia pyxidata, Cl. macilenta* var. *coronata, Cl. Floerkeana* f. *trachypoda, Lecanora varia, Lecidea decolorans* and *Lecidea tricolor.*" They conclude that "some at least of the Forest lichens are in a far more healthy and fertile condition than they were 27 years ago." They attribute the improvement mainly to the thinning of trees and the opening up of glades through the Forest, letting in light and air not only to the tree trunks but to the soil. In 1912[2] the authors in a second paper reported that 109 different kinds had been determined, and these, though still falling far short of the older lichen flora, considerably exceed the list of 85 recorded in 1883.

C. Lichen Communities

Lichen communities fall into a few definite groups, though, as we shall see, not a few species may be found to occur in several groups—species that have been designated by some workers as "wanderers." The leading communities are:

1. **Arboreal**, including those that grow on leaves, bark or wood.
2. **Terricolous**, ground-lichens.
3. **Saxicolous**, rock-lichens.
4. **Omnicolous**, lichens that can exist on the most varied substrata, such as bones, leather, iron, etc.
5. **Localized Communities** in which owing to special conditions the lichens may become permanent and dominant.

In all the groups lichens are more or less abundant. In arboreal and terricolous formations they may be associated with other plants; in saxicolous and omnicolous formations they are the dominant vegetation. It will be desirable to select only a few of the typical communities that have been observed and recorded by workers in various lands.

[1] Paulson and Thompson 1911.   [2] Paulson and Thompson 1912.

I. ARBOREAL

Arboreal communities may be held to comprise those lichens that grow on wood, bark or leaves. They are usually the dominant and often the sole vegetation, but in some localities there may be a considerable development of mosses, etc., or a mantle of protococcaceous algae may cover the bark. Certain lichens that are normally corticolous may also be found on dead wood or may be erratic on neighbouring rocks: *Usnea florida* for instance is a true corticolous species, but it grows occasionally on rocks or boulders generally in crowded association with other foliose or fruticose lichens.

Most of the larger lichens are arboreal, though there are many exceptions: *Parmelia perlata* develops to a large size on boulders as well as on trees; some species of *Ramalinae* are constantly saxicolous while there are only rare instances of *Roccellae* that grow on trees. The purely tropical or subtropical genera are corticolous rather than saxicolous, but species that have appeared in colder regions may have acquired the saxicolous habit: thus *Coenogonium* in the tropics grows on trees, but the European species, *C. ebeneum*, grows on stone.

a. EPIPHYLLOUS. These grow on Ferns or on the coriaceous leaves of evergreens in the tropics. Many of them are associated with *Phycopeltis*, *Phyllactidium* or *Mycoidea*, and follow in the wake of these algae. Observations are lacking as to the associations or societies of these lichens whether they grow singly or in companies. The best known are the Strigulaceae: there are six genera in that family, and some of the species have a wide distribution. The most frequent genus is *Strigula* associated with *Phycopeltis* which forms round grey spots on leaves, and is almost entirely confined to tropical regions. Chodat[1] records a sterile species, *S. Buxi*, on box leaves from the neighbourhood of Geneva.

Other genera, such as those of Ectolechiaceae, which inhabit fern scales and evergreen leaves, are associated with Protococcaceae. *Pilocarpon leucoblepharum* with similar gonidia grows round the base of pine-needles. It is found in the Caucasus. In our own woods, along the outer edges, the lower spreading branches of the fir-trees are often decked with numerous plants of *Parmelia physodes*, a true "plant society," but that lichen is a confirmed "wanderer." *Biatorina Bouteillei*, on box leaves, is a British and Continental lichen.

b. CORTICOLOUS. In this series are to be found many varying groups, the type of lichen depending more on the physical nature of the bark than on the kind of trees. Those with a smooth bark such as hazel, beech, lime, etc., and younger trees in general, bear only crustaceous species, many of them with a very thin thallus, often partly immersed below the surface.

---

[1] Chodat 1912.

As the trees become older and the bark takes on a more rugged character, other types of lichens gain a foothold, such as the thicker crustaceous forms like *Pertusaria*, or the larger foliose and fruticose species. The moisture that is collected and retained by the rough bark is probably the important factor in the establishment of the thicker crusts, and, as regards the larger lichens, both rhizinae and hold-fasts are able to gain a secure grip of the broken-up unequal surface, such as would be quite impossible on trees with smooth bark.

Among the first to pay attention to the ecological grouping of corticolous lichens was A. L. Fée[1], a Professor of Natural Science and an Army doctor, who wrote on many literary and botanical subjects. In his account of the Cryptogams that grow on "officinal bark," he states that the most lichenized of all the *Cinchonae* was the one known as " Loxa," the bark of which was covered with species of *Parmelia*, *Sticta* and *Usnea* along with crustaceous forms of *Lecanora*, *Lecidea*, *Graphis* and *Verrucaria*. Another species, *Cinchona cordifolia*, was completely covered, but with crustaceous forms only: species of Graphidaceae, *Lecanora* and *Lecidea* were abundant, but *Trypethelium*, *Chiodecton*, *Pyrenula* and *Verrucaria* were also represented. On each species of tree some particular lichen was generally dominant:

A species of *Thelotrema* on *Cinchona oblongifolia*.
A species of *Chiodecton* on *C. cordifolia*.
A species of *Sarcographa* on *C. condaminea*.

Fries[2], in his geography of lichens, distinguished as arboreal and "hypophloeodal" species of Verrucariaceae, while the Graphideae, which also grew on bark, were erumpent. *Usnea barbata*, *Evernia prunastri*, etc., though growing normally on trees might, he says, be associated with rock species.

More extensive studies of habitat were made by Krempelhuber[3] in his *Bavarian Lichens*. In summing up the various "formations" of lichens, he gives lists of those that grow, in that district, exclusively on either coniferous or deciduous trees, with added lists of those that grow on either type of tree indifferently. Among those found always on conifers or on coniferous wood are: *Letharia vulpina*, *Cetraria Laureri*, *Parmelia aleurites* and a number of crustaceous species. Those that are restricted to the trunks and branches of leafy trees are crustaceous with the exception of some foliose Collemaceae such as *Leptogium Hildenbrandii*, *Collema nigrescens*, etc.

Arnold[4] carried to its furthest limit the method of arranging lichens ecologically, in his account of those plants from the neighbourhood of Munich. He gives " formation " lists, not only for particular substrata and in special situations, but he recapitulates the species that he found on the several different trees. It is not possible to reproduce such a detailed survey, which indeed only emphasizes the fact that the physical characters of the bark are the most important factors in lichen ecology: that on smooth bark,

---

[1] Fée 1824.   [2] Fries 1831.   [3] Krempelhuber 1861.   [4] Arnold 1891, etc.

whether of young trees, or on bark that never becomes really rugged, there is a preponderance of species with a semi-immersed thallus, and very generally of those that are associated with *Trentepohlia* gonidia, such as Graphidaceae or Pyrenulaceae, though certain species of *Lecidea*, *Lecanora* and others also prefer the smooth substratum.

Bruce Fink[1] has published a series of important papers on lichen communities in America, some of them similar to what we should find in the British Isles.

On trees with smooth bark he records in the Minnesota district:

Xanthoria polycarpa.
Candelaria concolor.
Parmelia olivacea, P. adglutinata.
Placodium cerinum.
Lecanora subfusca.
Bacidia fusca-rubella.
Lecidea enteroleuca.
Graphis scripta.
Arthonia lecideella, A. dispersa.
Arthopyrenia punctiformis, A. fallax.
Pyrenula nitida, P. thelena, P. cinerella, P. leucoplaca

On rough bark he records :

Ramalina calicaris, R. fraxinea, R. fastigiata.
Teloschistes chrysophthalmus.
Xanthoria polycarpa, X. lychnea.
Candelaria concolor.
Parmelia perforata, P. crinita, P. Borreri, P. tiliacea, P. saxatilis, P. caperata.
Physcia granulifera, Ph. pulverulenta, Ph. stellaris, Ph. tribacia, Ph. obscura.
Collema pycnocarpum, C. flaccidum.
Leptogium mycochroum.
Placodium aurantiacum, Pl. cerinum.
Lecanora subfusca.
Pertusaria leioplaca, P. velata.
Bacidia rubella, B. fuscorubella.
Lecidea enteroleuca.
Rhizocarpon alboatrum, Buellia parasema.
Opegrapha varia.
Graphis scripta.
Arthonia lecideella, A. radiata.
Arthopyrenia quinqueseptata, A. macrospora.
Pyrenula nitida, P. leucoplaca.

Finally, as generally representative of the commonest lichens in our woods of deciduous trees, including both smooth- and rough-barked, the community of oak-hazel woods as observed by Watson[2] in Somerset may be quoted:

Collema flaccidum.
Calicium hyperellum.

[1] Fink 1902.   [2] Watson 1909.

Ramalina calicaris, R. fraxinea with var. *ampliata, R. fastigiata, R. farinacea* and
R. pollinaria.
Parmelia saxatilis and f. *furfuracea, P. caperata, P. physodes.*
Physcia pulverulenta, Ph. tenella (hispida).
Lecanora subfusca, L. rugosa.
Pertusaria amara, P. globulifera, P. communis, P. Wulfenii.
Lecidea (Buellia) canescens.
Graphis scripta.

And on the soil of these woods :

Cladonia pyxidata, Cl. pungens, Cl. macilenta, Cl. pityrea, Cl. squamosa and *Cl.
sylvatica.*

Paulson[1], from his observations of lichens in Hertfordshire, has concluded
that the presence or absence of lichens on trees is influenced to a considerable degree by the nature of the soil. They were more abundant in woods
on light well-drained soils than on similar communities of trees on heavier soils,
though the shade in the former was slightly more dense and therefore less
favourable to their development; the cause of this connection is not known.

c. LIGNICOLOUS. Lichens frequenting the branches of trees do not long
continue when these have fallen to the ground. This may be due to the
lack of light and air, but Bouly de Lesdain[2] has suggested that the chemical
reactions produced by the decomposition of the bast fibres are fatal to them,
Lecidea parasema alone continuing to grow and even existing for some time
on the detached shreds of bark.

On worked wood, such as old doors or old palings, light and air are well
provided and there is often an abundant growth of lichens, many of which
seem to prefer that substratum : the fibres of the wood loosened by weathering
retain moisture and yield some nutriment to the lichen hyphae which burrow
among them. Though a number of lichens grow willingly on dead wood,
there are probably none that are wholly restricted to such a habitat. A few,
such as the species of *Coniocybe*, are generally to be found on dead roots of
trees or creeping loosely over dead twigs. They are shade lichens and fond
of moisture.

The species on palings—or " dead wood communities "—most familiar
to us in our country are :

Usnea hirta.	*Rinodina exigua.*
Cetraria diffusa.	*Lecanora Hageni, L. varia* and its allies.
Evernia furfuracea.	*Lecidea ostreata, L. parasema.*
Parmelia scortia, P. physodes.	*Buellia myriocarpa.*
Xanthoria parietina.	Cladoniaceae and Caliciaceae (several species).
Placodium cerinum.	

These may be found in very varying association. It has indeed been
remarked that the dominant plant may be simply the one that has first

[1] Paulson 1919.   [2] Lesdain 1912.

gained a footing, though the larger and more vigorous lichens tend to crowd out the others. Bruce Fink[1] has recorded associations in Minnesota:

On wood:

Teloschistes chrysophthalmus.	*Buellia parasema (disciformis), B. turgescens.*
Placodium cerinum.	*Calicium parietinum.*
Lecanora Hageni, L. varia.	*Thelocarpon prasinellum.*
Rinodina sophodes, R. exigua.	

On rotten stumps and prostrate logs: *Peltigera canina. Cladonia fimbriata* var. *tubaeformis, Cl. gracilis, Cl. verticillata. Cl. symphicarpia, Cl. macilenta, Cl. cristatella.*

Except for one or two species such as *Buellia turgescens, Cladonia symphicarpia,* etc., the associations could be easy paralleled in our own country, though with us *Peltigera canina, Cladonia gracilis* and *Cl. verticillata* are ground forms.

2. TERRICOLOUS

In this community other vegetation is dominant, lichens are subsidiary. In certain conditions, as on heaths, they gain a permanent footing, in others they are temporary denizens and are easily crowded out. As they are generally in close contact with the ground they are peculiarly dependent on the nature of the soil and the water content. There are several distinct substrata to be considered each with its characteristic flora. Cultivated soil and grass lands need scarcely be included, as in the former the processes of cultivation are too harassing for lichen growth, and only on the more permanent somewhat damp mossy meadows do we get such a species as *Peltigera canina* in abundance. Some of the earth-lichens are among the quickest growers: the apothecia of *Baeomyces roseus* appear and disappear within a year. *Thrombium epigaeum* develops in half a year; *Thelidium minutulum* in cultures grew from spore to spore, according to Stahl[2], in three months.

There are three principal types of soil composition: (1) that in which there is more or less of lime; (2) soils in which silica in some form or other predominates, and (3) soils which contain an appreciable amount of humus.

Communities restricted to certain soils such as sand-dunes, etc., are treated separately.

a. ON CALCAREOUS SOIL. Any admixture of lime in the soil, either as chalk, limy clay or shell sand is at once reflected in the character of the lichen flora. On calcareous soil we may look for any of the squamulose *Lecanorae* or *Lecideae* that are terricolous species, such as *Lecanora crassa, L. lentigera, Placodium fulgens, Lecidea lurida* and *L. decipiens.* There are also the many lichens that grow on mortar or on the accumulated debris mixed with lime in the crevices of walls, such as *Biatorina coeruleonigricans,* species of *Placodium,* several species of *Collema* and of Verrucariaceae.

---

[1] Fink 1896, etc.   [2] Stahl 1877.

Bruce Fink[1] found in N.W. Minnesota an association on exposed calcareous earth as follows:

Heppia Despreauxii.	*Biatora (Bacidia) muscorum.*
Urceolaria scruposa.	*Dermatocarpon hepaticum.*
Biatora (Lecidea) decipiens.	

This particular association occupied the slope of a hill that was washed by lime-impregnated water. It was normally a dry habitat and the lichens were distinguished by small closely adnate thalli.

There are more lichens confined to limy than to sandy soil. Arnold[2] gives a list of those he observed near Munich on the former habitat:

Cladonia sylvatica f. *alpestris.*	*Urceolaria scruposa* f. *argillacea.*
Cladonia squamosa f. *subsquamosa.*	*Verrucaria (Thrombium) epigaea.*
Cladonia rangiformis f. *foliosa.*	*Lecidea decipiens.*
Cladonia cariosa and f. *symphicarpa.*	*Dermatocarpon cinereum.*
Peltigera canina f. *soreumatica.*	*Collema granulatum.*
Solorina spongiosa.	*Collema tenax.*
Heppia virescens.	*Leptogium byssinum.*
Lecanora crassa.	

It is interesting to note how many of these lichens specialized as to habitat are forms of species that grow in other situations.

b. ON SILICEOUS SOIL. Lichens are not generally denizens of cultivated soil; a few settle on clay or on sand-banks. *Cladonia fimbriata* and *Cl. pyxidata* grow frequently in such situations; others more or less confined to sandy or gravelly soil are, in the British Isles:

Baeomyces roseus.	*Gongylia viridis.*
Baeomyces rufus.	*Dermatocarpon lachneum.*
Baeomyces placophyllus.	*Dermatocarpon hepaticum.*
Endocarpon spp.	*Dermatocarpon cinereum.*

These very generally grow in extended societies of one species only.

In his enumeration of soil-lichens Arnold[2] gives 40 species that grow on siliceous soil, as against 57 on calcareous. Many of them occurred on both. Those around Munich on siliceous soil only were:

Cladonia coccifera.	*Baeomyces rufus.*
Cladonia agariciformis.	*Lecidea gelatinosa.*
Secoliga (Gyalecta) bryophaga.	*Psorotichia lutophila.*

Mayfield[3] in his account of the Boulder Clay lichen flora of Suffolk found only four species that attained to full development on banks and hedgerows. These were: *Collema pulposum, Cladonia pyxidata, Cl. furcata* var. *corymbosa* and *Peltigera polydactyla.*

---

[1] Fink 1902, etc.   [2] Arnold 1891.   [3] Mayfield 1916.

On bare heaths of gravelly soil in Epping Forest Paulson and Thompson[1] describe an association of such lichens as :

Baeomyces roseus.	*Cladonia macilenta.*
Baeomyces rufus.	*Cladonia furcata.*
Pycnothelia papillaria.	*Cetraria aculeata.*
Cladonia coccifera.	*Peltigera spuria.*
Lecidea granulosa.	

And on flints in the soil: *Lecidea crustulata* and *Rhizocarpon confervoides*. They found that *Peltigera spuria* colonized very quickly the burnt patches of earth which are of frequent occurrence in Epping Forest, while on wet sandy heaths amongst heather they found associated *Cladonia sylvatica* f. *tenuis* and *Cl. fimbriata* subsp. *fibula*.

c. ON BRICKS, ETC. Closely allied with siliceous soil-lichens are those that form communities on bricks. As these when built into walls are more or less smeared with mortar, a mixture of lime-loving species also arrives. Roof tiles are more free from calcareous matter. Lesdain[2] noted that on the dunes, though stray bricks were covered by algae, lichens rarely or never seemed to gain a footing.

There are many references in literature to lichens that live on tiles. A fairly representative list is given by Lettau[3] of " tegulicolous " species.

Verrucaria nigrescens.	*Placodium elegans.*
Lecidea coarctata.	*Placodium murorum.*
Candelariella vitellina.	*Xanthoria parietina.*
Lecanora dispersa.	*Rhizocarpon alboatrum* var.
Lecanora galactina.	*Buellia myriocarpa.*
Lecanora Hageni.	*Lecidea demissa.*
Lecanora saxicola.	*Physcia ascendens.*
Parmelia conspersa.	*Physcia caesia.*
Placodium teicholytum.	*Physcia obscura.*
Placodium pyraceum.	*Physcia sciastrella.*
Placodium decipiens.	

Several of these are more or less calcicolous and others are wanderers, indifferent to the substratum. Though certain species form communities on bricks, tiles, etc., none of them is restricted to such artificial substrata.

d. ON HUMUS. Lichens are never found on loose humus, but rocks or stumps of trees covered with a thin layer of earth and humus are a favourite habitat, especially of *Cladoniae*. One such " formation " is given by Bruce Fink[4] from N. Minnesota ; with the exception of *Cladonia cristatella*, the species are British as well as American :

Cladonia furcata.	*Cladonia rangiferina.*
Cladonia cristatella.	*Cladonia uncialis.*
Cladonia gracilis.	*Cladonia alpestris.*
Cladonia verticillata.	*Cladonia turgida.*

[1] Paulson and Thompson 1913.   [2] Lesdain 1910[2].   [3] Lettau 1911,   [4] Fink 1903.

Cladonia coccifera.
Cladonia pyxidata.
Cladonia fimbriata.

Peltigera malacea.
Peltigera canina.
Peltigera aphthosa.

e. ON PEATY SOIL. Peat is generally found in most abundance in northern and upland regions, and is characteristic of mountain and moorland, though there are great moss-lands, barely above sea-level, even in our own country. Such soil is of an acid nature and attracts a special type of plant life. The lichens form no inconsiderable part of the flora, the most frequent species being members of the Cladoniaceae.

The principal crustaceous species on bare peaty soil in the British Isles are *Lecidea uliginosa* and *L. granulosa.* The former is not easily distinguishable from the soil as both thallus and apothecia are brownish black. The latter, which is often associated with it, has a lighter coloured thallus and apothecia that change from brick-red to dark brown or black; Wheldon and Wilson[1] remarked that after the burning of the heath it was the first vegetation to appear and covered large spaces with its grey thallus. Another peat species is *Icmadophila ericetorum*, but it prefers damper localities than the two *Lecideae.*

To quote again from Arnold[2]: 24 species were found on turf around Munich, 13 of which were *Cladoniae*, but only four species could be considered as exclusively peat-lichens. These were:

Cladonia Floerkeana.
Biatora terricola.

Thelocarpon turficolum.
Geisleria sychnogonioides.

The last is a very rare lichen in Central Europe and is generally found on sandy soil. Arnold considered that near Munich, for various reasons, there was a very poor representation of turf-lichens.

f. ON MOSSES. Very many lichens grow along with or over mosses, either on the ground, on rocks or on the bark of trees, doubtless owing to the moisture accumulated and retained by these plants. Besides *Cladoniae* the commonest "moss" species in the British Isles are *Bilimbia sabulosa, Bacidia muscorum, Rinodina Conradi, Lecidea sanguineoatra, Pannaria brunnea, Psoroma hypnorum* and *Lecanora tartarea*, with species of *Collema* and *Leptogium* and *Diploschistes bryophilus.*

Wheldon and Wilson[3] have listed the lichens that they found in Perthshire on subalpine heath lands, on the ground, or on banks amongst mosses:

Leptogrum spp.
Peltigera spp.
Cetraria spp.
Parmelia physodes.
Psoroma hypnorum.
Lecanora epibryon.
Lecanora tartarea.
Lecidea coarctata.

Lecidea granulosa.
Lecidea uliginosa.
Lecidea neglecta.
Bilimbia sabulosa.
Bilimbia ligniaria.
Bilimbia melaena.
Baeomyces spp.
Cladonia spp.

[1] Wheldon and Wilson 1907.   [2] Arnold 1892, p. 34.   [3] Wheldon and Wilson 1915.

As already described *Lecanora tartarea*[1] spreads freely over the mosses of the tundra. Aigret[2] in a study of *Cladoniae* notes that *Cl. pyxidata*, var. *neglecta* chooses little cushions of acrocarpous mosses, which are particularly well adapted to retain water. *Cl. digitata, Cl. flabelliformis* and some others grow on the mosses which cover old logs or the bases of trees.

g. ON FUNGI. Some of the fungi, such as Polyporei, are long lived, and of hard texture. On species of *Lenzites* in Lorraine, Kieffer[3] has recorded 15 different forms, but they are such as naturally grow on wood and can scarcely rank as a separate association.

3. SAXICOLOUS

Lichens are the dominant plants of this and the following formations, they alone being able to live on bare rock; only when there has been formed a nidus of soil can other plants become established.

a. CHARACTERS OF MINERAL SUBSTRATA. It has been often observed that lichens are influenced not only by the chemical composition of the rocks on which they grow but also by the physical structure. Rocks that weather quickly are almost entirely bare of lichens: the breaking up of the surface giving no time for the formation either of thallus or fruit. Close-grained rocks such as quartzite have also a poor lichen flora, the rooting hyphae being unable to penetrate and catch hold. Other factors, such as incidence of light, and proximity of water, are of importance in determining the nature of the flora, even where the rocks are of similar formation.

b. COLONIZATION ON ROCKS. When a rock surface is laid bare it becomes covered in time with lichens, and quite fresh surfaces are taken possession of preferably to weathered surfaces[4]. The number of species is largest at first and the kind of lichen depends on the flora existing in the near neighbourhood. Link[5], for instance, has stated that *Lichen candelarius* was the first lichen to appear on the rocks he observed, and, if trees were growing near, then *Lichen parietinus* and *Lichen tenellus* followed soon after. After a time the lichens change, the more slow-growing being crowded out by the more vigorous. Crustaceous species, according to Malinowski[6], are most subject to this struggle for existence, and certain types from the nature of their thallus are more easily displaced than others. Those with a deeply cracked areolated thallus become disintegrated in the older central areas by repeated swelling and contracting of the areolae as they change from wet to dry conditions. Particles of the thallus are thus easily dislodged, and bare places are left, which in time are colonized again by the same lichen or by some invading species. There may result a bewildering mosaic of

[1] See p. 358. [2] Aigret 1901. [3] Kieffer 1894. [4] Stahlecker 1906.
[5] Link 1795. [6] Malinowski 1911.

different thalli and fruits mingling together. Some forms such as *Rhizo-carpum geographicum* which have a very close firm thallus do not break away. In the course of time lichen communities come and go, and the plants of one locality may be different from those of another for no apparent reason.

The question of colonization[1] was studied by Bruce Fink[2] on a "riprap" wall of quartz, 30 years old, built to protect and brace a railway in Iowa. Near by was a grass swamp which supplied moisture especially to the lower end of the wall. A few boulders were present in the vicinity, but the nearest lichen "society" was on trees about 150 metres away and these bore corti-colous Parmelias, Physcias, Ramalinas, Placodiums, Lecanoras and Rinodines which were only very sparingly represented on the riprap. Moisture-loving species never gained a footing; the extreme xerophytic conditions were evidenced by the character of the lichens, *Biatora myriocarpoides* (*Lecidea sylvicola*) occupying the driest parts of the wall. Lower down where more moisture prevailed *Bacidia inundata* and *Stereocaulon paschale* were the dominant species. Some 30 species or forms were listed of which 11 were Cladonias that grew mainly on debris from the disintegration of the wall. With the exception of two or three species the number of individuals was very small.

Some of these lichens had doubtless come from the boulders, others from the trees; the Cladonias were all known to occur within a few miles, but most of the species had been wind-borne from some distance. The *Stereo-caulon* present did not exist elsewhere in Iowa; it had evidently been brought by the railroad cars, possibly on telegraph poles.

A similar wall on the south side of the railway, subject to even more xerophytic conditions but with less disintegration of the surface, had a larger number of individuals though fewer species. Only one *Cladonia* and one *Parmelia* had gained a footing, the rest were crustaceous, *Buellia myriocarpa* being one of the most frequent.

There are two types of rock of extreme importance in lichen ecology: those mainly composed of lime (calcareous), and those in which silica or silicates preponderate (siliceous). They give foothold to two corresponding groups of lichen communities, calcicolous and silicicolous.

c. CALCICOLOUS. The pioneer in this section of lichen ecology is H. F. Link, who was a Professor of Natural Science and Botany at Rostock, then at Breslau, and finally in Berlin. He[3] published in 1789, while still at Rostock, an account of limestone plants in his neighbourhood, most of them being lichens. In a later work he continues his Botanical Geography or "Geology" and gives more precise details as to the plants, some of which are essentially calcicolous though many of them he records also on siliceous rocks.

---

[1] See also p. 254.   [2] Fink 1904.   [3] Link 1789.

Most calcicolous lichens are almost completely dependent on the lime substratum which evidently supplies some constituent that has become necessary to their healthy growth. Calcareous rocks are usually of softer texture than those mainly composed of silica, and not only the rhizoidal hyphae but the whole thallus—both hyphae and gonidia—may be deeply embedded. Only the fruits are visible and they are, in some species, lodged in tiny depressions (foveolae) scooped out of the surface by the lichen-acids acting on the easily dissolved lime.

Those obligate lime species may be found in associations on almost any calcareous rock. Watson[1] has given us a list of species that inhabit carboniferous limestone in Britain. Wheldon and Wilson[2] have described in West Lancashire the "grey calcareous rocks blotched with black patches of Pannarias (*Placynthium nigrum*) and Verrucarias, or dark gelatinous rosettes of Collemas. White and grey *Lecanorae* and *Verrucariae* spread extensively, some of them deeply pitting the surface. These more sombre or colourless species are enlivened by an intermixture of orange-yellow *Physciae* (*Xanthoriae*) and *Placodii* by the ochrey films of *Lecanora ochracea* and lemon-yellow of *Lecanora xantholyta*. Amongst the greenish scaly crusts of *Lecanora crassa* may be seen the bluish cushions of *Lecidea coeruleo-nigricans*, the whole forming an exquisite blend of tints."

The flora recorded by Flagey[3] on the cretaceous rocks of Algeria in the Province of Constantine does not greatly differ, some of the species being identical with those of our own country. Placodiums and Rinodinas were abundant, as also *Lecanora calcarea*, *Acarospora percaenoides* and *Urceolaria actinostoma* var. *calcarea*. Also a few *Lecideae* along with *Verrucaria lecideoides*, *V. fuscella*, *V. calciseda* and *Endocarpon monstrosum*. The rocks of that region are sometimes so covered with lichens that the stone is no longer visible.

Bruce Fink[4] gives a typical community on limestone bluffs in Minnesota:

Pannaria (*Placynthium*) *nigra*.	*Placodium citrinum*.
Crocynia lanuginosa.	*Bacidia inundata*.
Omphalaria pulvinata.	*Rhizocarpon alboatrum* var.
Collema plicatile.	*Dermatocarpon miniatum*.
Collema pustulatum.	*Staurothele umbrinum*.
Leptogium lacerum.	

Forssell[5] pointed out an interesting selective quality in the Gloeolichens which are associated with the gelatinous algae, *Chroococcus*, *Gloeocapsa* and *Xanthocapsa*. The genera containing the two former grow on siliceous rocks with the exception of *Synalissa*. The genera *Omphalaria*, *Peccania*, *Anema*, *Psorotichia* and *Enchylium*, in which *Xanthocapsa* is the gonidium, grow on

[1] Watson 1918[2].   [2] Wheldon and Wilson 1907.   [3] Flagey 1901.
[4] Bruce Fink 1902[2].   [5] Forssell 1885.

calcareous rocks. *Collemopsidium* is the only *Xanthocapsa* associate that is silicicolous.

d. SILICICOLOUS. There is greater variety in the mineral composition and in the nature of the surface in siliceous than in calcareous rocks; they are also more durable and give support to a large number of slow-growing forms.

Silicon enters into the composition of many different types, from the oldest volcanic to the most recent of sedimentary rocks. Some of these are of hard unyielding surface on which only a few lichens are able to attach themselves. Such a rock is instanced by Servit[1] as occurring in Bohemia, and is known as Lydite or Lydian stone, a black flinty jasper. The association of lichens on this smooth rock was almost entirely *Acarospora chlorophana* and *Rinodina oreina*, which as we shall see occur again as a "desert" association in Nevada; these two lichens grow equally well in sun or shade, and either sheltered or exposed as regards wind and rain. *Acarospora chlorophana*, according to Malinowski[2], arrives among the first on rocks newly laid bare, and forms large societies, though in time it gives place to *Lecanora glaucoma* (*L. sordida*), a common silicicolous lichen.

A difference has been pointed out by Bachmann[3] between the lichens of acid and of basic rocks. The acid series, such as quartz- and granite-porphyry, contain 70 per cent. and more of oxide of silica; the basic—diabase and basalt—not nearly 50 per cent. He observed that *Rhizocarpon geographicum* was the most frequent lichen of the acid porphyry, while on basalt there were only small scattered patches. *Pertusaria corallina* was abundant only on granitic rocks. On the other hand *Pertusaria lactea* f. *cinerascens*, *Diploschistes scruposus*, *D. bryophilus* and *Buellia leptocline* preferred the basic substratum of diabase and basalt. In this case it is the chemical rather than the physical character of the rocks that affects the lichen flora, as porphyry and basalt are both close-grained, and are outwardly alike except in colouration.

Other rocks, such as granite, in which the different crystals, quartz, mica and felspar are of varying hardness, are favourite habitats as affording not only durability but a certain openness to the rhizoidal hyphae, though in Shetland, West[4] found the granitic rocks bare owing to their too rapid weathering. In these rocks the softer basic constituents such as the mica are colonized first; the quartz remains a long time naked, though in time it also is covered. Wheldon and Wilson[5] point out that the sandstone near to intrusive igneous rocks has become close-grained and indurated and bears *Lecanora squamulosa*, *L. picea*, *Lecidea rivulosa* and *Rhizocarpon petraeum*, which were not seen on the unaltered sandstone. It was also observed by Stahlecker[6], that, in layered rocks, the lichen chose the surface at right angles to the layering as the hyphae thus gain an easier entrance.

[1] Servit 1910.　　　[2] Malinowski 1911.　　　[3] Bachmann 1914.　　　[4] West 1912.
[5] Wheldon and Wilson 1913.　　　　　　[6] Stahlecker 1906.

It will only be possible to give a few typical associations from the many that have been published. Crustaceous forms are the most abundant. On granite and on quartzite not disintegrated Malinowski[1] listed :

Acarospora chlorophana.
Lecanora glaucoma.
Rhizocarpon viridiatrum.

Lecidea tumida.
Biatorella sporostatia.
Biatorella testudinea.

On granite and quartzite disintegrated :

Aspicilia cinerea.
Aspicilia gibbosa.
Aspicilia tenebrosa.
Buellia coracina.
Catillaria (Biatorina) Hochstetteri.
Rhizocarpon petraeum.
Rhizocarpon geographicum vars.
Biatorella cinerea.

Lecanora badia.
Lecanora cenisia.
Lecidea confluens.
Lecidea fuscoatra.
Lecidea platycarpa.
Lecidea lapicida.
Haematomma ventosum.

On these disintegrated rocks there is a constant struggle for existence between the various species ; the victorious association finally consists of *Lecanora badia, L. cenisia* and *Lecidea confluens* with occasional growths of the following species:

Aspicilia cinerea.
Haematomma ventosum.
Rhizocarpon geographicum vars.

Biatorella cinerea.
Lecidea platycarpa.

A number of rock associations have been tabulated by Wheldon and Wilson[2] for Perthshire. Among others they give some of the most typical lichens on granitic and eruptive rocks :

Sphaerophorus coralloides.
Sphaerophorus fragilis.
Platysma Fahlunense.
Platysma commixtum.
Platysma glaucum.
Platysma lacunosum.
Parmelia saxatilis.
Parmelia omphalodes.
Parmelia Mougeotii.
Parmelia stygia.
Parmelia tristis.
Parmelia lanata.
Gyrophora proboscidea.
Gyrophora cylindrica.
Gyrophora torrefacta.
Gyrophora polyphylla.

Gyrophora flocculosa.
Lecanora gelida.
Lecanora atra.
Lecanora badia.
Lecanora tartarea.
Lecanora parella.
Lecanora ventosa.
Lecanora Dicksonii.
Lecanora cinerea.
Lecanora peliocypha.
Pertusaria dealbata.
Stereocaulon Delisei.
Stereocaulon evolutum.
Stereocaulon coralloides.
Stereocaulon denudatum.
Psorotichia lugubris.

Lecidea inserena.
Lecidea panaeola.
Lecidea contigua.
Lecidea confluens.
Lecidea lapicida.
Lecidea plana.
Lecidea mesotropa.
Lecidea auriculata.
Lecidea diducens.
Lecidea aglaea.
Lecidea rivulosa.
Lecidea Kochiana.
Lecidea pycnocarpa.
Buellia atrata.
Rhizocarpon Oederi.

On siliceous rocks in West Lancashire the same authors[3] depict the lichen flora as follows: "There are many grey *Parmeliae* and *Cladoniae*

[1] Malinowski 1911. [2] Wheldon and Wilson 1915. [3] Wheldon and Wilson 1907.

with coral-like *Sphaerophorei* on the rocks, and on the walls smoky-looking patches of *Parmelia fuliginosa* and ragged fringes of *Platysma glaucum* and *Evernia furfuracea*. On the higher scars, flat topped tabular blocks exhibit black scaly *Gyrophoreae*, dingy green *Lecidea* (*Rhizocarpon*) *viridiatra* and mouse-coloured *L. rivulosa*. Suborbicular (whitish) patches of *Pertusaria lactea* and *P. dealbata* enliven the general sadness of tone, and everywhere loose rocks and stones are covered with the greyish-black spotted thallus of *Lecidea contigua*."

On the Silurian series of rocks in the same district they describe a somewhat brighter coloured flora: "First Stereocaulons invite attention, and greenish or yellowish shades are introduced by an abundance of *Lecanora sulphurea*, *L. polytropa*, *Rhizocarpon geographicum* and *Parmelia conspersa*, often beautifully commingled with grey species such as *Lecidea contigua* and *L. stellulata*, and reddish angular patches of *Lecanora Dicksonii*. Also an abundance of orbicular patches of *Haematomma ventosum* with its reddish-brown apothecia." A brightly coloured association on the cretaceous sand-rocks of Saxon Switzerland has been described as "Sulphur lichens." These have recently[1] been determined as chiefly *Lepraria chlorina*, in less abundance *Lecidea lucida* and *Calicium arenarium*, with occasional growths of *Coniocybe furfuracea* and *Calicium corynellum*.

4. OMNICOLOUS LICHENS

Some account must be taken in any ecological survey of those lichens that are indifferent to substrata. Certain species have become so adapted to some special habitat that they never or rarely wander; others, on the contrary, are true vagabonds in the lichen kingdom and settle on any substance that affords a foothold: on leather, bones, iron, pottery, etc. There can be no sustenance drawn from these supports, or at most extremely little, and it is interesting to note in this connection that while some rock-lichens are changed to a rusty-red colour by the infiltration of iron—often from a water medium containing iron-salts—those that live directly on iron are unaffected.

The "wanderers" are more or less the same in every locality and they pass easily from one support to another. Bouly de Lesdain[2] made a tabulation of such as he found growing on varied substances on the dunes round Dunkirk and they well represent these omnicolous communities. It is in such a no man's land that one would expect to find an accumulation of derelict materials, not only favourably exposed to light and moisture, but undisturbed for long periods and bordering on normal lichen associations of soil, tree and stones. Arnold[3] also noted many of these peculiar habitats.

---

[1] Schade 1916.   [2] Lesdain 1910.   [3] Arnold 1858.

The following were noted by Lesdain and other workers:

On iron—*Xanthoria parietina, Physcia obscura* and var. *virella, Ph. ascendens, Placodium (flavescens) sympageum, Pl. pyraceum, Pl. citrinum, Candelariella vitellinum, Rinodina exigua, Lecanora campestris, L. umbrina, L. galactina, Lecania erysibe, Bacidia inundata. Xanthoria parietina* is one of the commonest wandering species; it was found by Richard[1] on an old cannon lying near water, that was exfoliated by rust.

On tar—*Lecanora umbrina.*

On charcoal—*Rinodina exigua, Lecanora umbrina.*

On bones—*Xanthoria parietina, Physcia ascendens, Ph. tenella, Placodium citrinum, Pl. lacteum, Rinodina exigua, Lecanora galactina, L. dispersa, L. umbrina, Lecania erysibe, L. cyrtella, Acarospora pruinosa, A. Heppii, Bacidia inundata, B. muscorum, Verrucaria anceps, V. papillosa.*

In Arctic regions in Ellesmere Land and King Oscar Land, Darbishire[2] found on bones: *Lecanora varia, L. Hageni, Rinodina turfacea* and *Buellia parasema (disciformis)*. He could not trace any effect of the lichens on the substratum.

On charcoal—*Rinodina exigua, Lecanora umbrina.*

On dross or clinkers—*Parmelia dubia, Physcia obscura, Ph. ascendens* f. *tenella, Ph. pulverulenta, Xanthoria parietina, Placodium pyraceum, Pl. citrinum, Rinodina exigua, Lecanora dispersa, L. umbrina, Lecania erysibe.*

On glass[3]—*Physcia ascendens* f. *tenella, Buellia canescens*. Richard has recorded the same lichens on the broken glass of walls and in addition: *Xanthoria parietina, Lecanora crenulata, L. dispersa, Lecania erysibe, Rinodina exigua,* and *Buellia canescens.*

On earthenware, china, etc.—*Physcia ascendens* f. *tenella, Lecanora umbrina, L. dispersa, Lecania (? Biatorina) cyrtella, Verrucaria papillosa, Bacidia inundata.*

On leather—Nearly fifty species or varieties were found by Lesdain on old leather on the dunes. Cladonias, Parmelias and Physcias were well represented with one Evernia and a large series of crustaceous forms. He adds a note that leather is an excellent substratum: lichens covered most of the pieces astray on the dunes. Similar records have been made in Epping Forest by Paulson and Thompson[4] who found *Cladonia fimbriata* var. *tubaeformis* and *Lecidea granulosa* growing on an old boot. These authors connect the sodden condition of the leather with its attraction for lichens.

On pasteboard—Even on such a transient substance as this Lesdain found a number of forms, most of them, however, but poorly developed: *Cladonia furcata* (thallus), *Parmelia subaurifera* (beginning), *Xanthoria parietina* (beginning), *Physcia obscura, Placodium citrinum* (thallus), *Pl.*

[1] Richard 1877.   [2] Darbishire 1909.   [3] Cf. p. 234.   [4] Paulson and Thompson 1913.

pyraceum, Lecanora umbrina, Bacidia inundata and *Polyblastia Vouauxi* var. *charticola.*

On linoleum—*Xanthoria parietina, Physcia ascendens* f. *tenella, Rinodina exigua, Lecanora umbrina.*

On indiarubber—*Physcia ascendens* f. *tenella.*

On tarred cloth—*Xanthoria parietina, Placodium citrinum, Pl. pyraceum, Rinodina exigua, Lecanora umbrina, Lecania erysibe, Bacidia inundata.*

On felt—*Bacidia inundata, B. muscorum.*

On cloth (cotton, etc.)—*Bacidia inundata.*

On silk—*Physcia ascendens, Ph. obscura, Placodium citrinum* (thallus), *Lecanora umbrina, Bacidia inundata.*

On cord—*Physcia ascendens* f. *tenella, Placodium citrinum* (thallus).

On excreta—One would scarcely expect to find lichens on animal droppings, but as some of these harden and lie exposed for a considerable time, some quick-growing species attain to more or less development on what is, in any case, an extremely favourable habitat for fungi and for many minute organisms. Paulson and Thompson found tiny fruiting individuals of *Cladonia macilenta* and *Cl. fimbriata* var. *tubaeformis* growing on the dry dung of rabbits in Epping Forest. On the same type of pellets Lesdain records *Physcia ascendens* f. *leptalea, Cladonia pyxidata, Bacidia inundata* and *B. muscorum* ; and on sheep pellets : *Physcia ascendens* f. *leptalea* and *Placodium citrinum* ; while on droppings of musk-ox in Ellesmere Land Darbishire found *Biatorina globulosa, Placodium pyraceum, Gyalolechia subsimilis, Lecanora epibryon, L. verrucosa, Rinodina turfacea* and even, firmly attached, *Thamnolia vermicularis.*

It would be difficult to estimate the age of these lichens, but it seems evident that the "wanderers" are all more or less quick growers, and the lists also prove conclusively their complete indifference to the substratum, as the same species occur again and again on the very varied substances.

5. LOCALIZED COMMUNITIES

Lichens may be grouped ecologically under other conditions than those of substratum. They respond very readily to special environments, and associations arise either of species also met with elsewhere, or of species restricted to one type of surroundings. Such associations or communities might be multiplied indefinitely, but only a few of the outstanding ones will be touched on.

a. MARITIME LICHENS. This community is the most specialized of any, many of the lichens having become exclusively adapted to salt-water surroundings. They are mainly saxicolous, but the presence of sea-water is the factor of greatest influence on their growth and distribution, and they occur indifferently on any kind of shore rock either siliceous or calcareous. Wheldon and Wilson[1] noted this indifference to substratum on the Arran shores, where a few calcicolous species such as *Verrucaria nigrescens, V. maculiformis, Placodium tegularis* and *Pl. lobulatum,* grow by the sea on siliceous rocks. They suggest that the spray-washed habitat affords the conditions, which, in other places, are furnished by limestone.

The greater or less proximity of the salt water induces in lichens, as in other maritime plants, a distribution into belts or zones which recede gradually or abruptly according to the slope of the shore and the reach of the tide. Weddell[2] on the Isle d'Yeu delimited three such zones: (1) marine, those nearest the sea and immersed for a longer or shorter period at each tide; (2) semi-marine, not immersed but subject to the direct action of the waves, and (3) maritime or littoral, the area beyond the reach of the waves but within the influence of sea-spray. In the course of his work he indicates the lichens of each zone.

Fig. 122. *Ramalina siliquosa* A. L. Sm. Upper zone of barren plants (after M. C. Knowles, R. Welch, *Photo.*).

In Ireland, a thorough examination has been made of a rocky coast at Howth near Dublin by M. C. Knowles[3]. She recognizes five distinct belts

[1] Wheldon and Wilson 1913.   [2] Weddell 1875.   [3] Knowles 1913.

beginning with those furthest from the shore though within the influence of the salt water:

1. The Ramalina belt.
2. The Orange belt.
3. Lichina Vegetation.
4. Verrucaria maura belt.
5. The belt of Marine Verrucarias.

(1) **The Ramalina belt.** In this belt there are two zones of lichen vegetation: those in the upper zone consist mainly of barren plants of *Ramalina siliquosa*[1], rather dark or glaucous in colour with much branched fronds which are incurved at the tips (Fig. 122). They are beyond the direct action of the waves. The lower zone consists also mainly of the same *Ramalina*, the plants bearing straight, stiff, simple, or slightly branched fertile fronds of a pale-green or straw colour (Fig. 123). The pale colour may be partly due to frequent splashings by sea-spray.

Ramalina siliquosum in both zones takes several distinct forms, according to exposure to light, wind or spray, the effects of which are most marked in the upper zone. The plants growing above the ordinary spray zone generally form sward-like growths (Fig. 124); at the higher levels the sward growth is replaced by isolated tufts with a smaller more amorphous thallus which passes into a very small stunted condition. The latter form alone has gained and retained a footing on the steep faces of the hard and close-grained quartzite rocks. "On the western faces, indeed, it is the only visible vegetation." The dwarfed tufts with lacerated fronds measuring from $\frac{1}{4}$ to $\frac{1}{2}$ an inch in height are dotted all over the quartzites. On the sea faces the plants are larger, but everywhere they are closely appressed to the rock surface. At lower levels the fronds lengthen to more normal dimensions. "On these steep rock-faces there is a complete absence of any of the crustaceous species. The problem, therefore, as to how the *Ramalina* has obtained a foothold on these very hard precipitous rocks, which are too inhospitable even for crustaceous species is an interesting and puzzling one."

In the *Ramalina* zone along with the dominant species there occur occasional tufts of *R. Curnowii* and *R. subfarinacea*, the latter more especially in shady and rather moist situations. There are also numerous foliaceous and crustaceous lichens mingling with the *Ramalina* vegetation (Fig. 125), several Parmelias, *Physcia aquila*, *Xanthoria parietina*, *Buellia canescens*, *B. ryssolea*, *Lecanora atra*, *L. sordida*, *Rhizocarpon geographicum* and others. In the main these are arranged in the following order descending towards the sea:

1. *Parmeliae.*
2. *Physcia aquila.*
3. *Xanthoria parietina.*
4. Crustaceous species.

---

[1] The two morphologically similar plants *Ramalina cuspidata* and *R. scopulorum* are here united under the older name *R. siliquosa*. The distinction between the two is based on reaction tests with potash, which give very uncertain results.

Fig. 123. *Ramalina siliquosa* A. L. Sm. Lower zone of fertile plants (after M. C. Knowles, R. Welch, *Photo.*).

Fig. 124. Sward of young *Ramalinae* (after M. C. Knowles, R. Welch, *Photo.*).

Parmelia prolixa is the most abundant of the Parmelias: it covers large spaces of the rocks and frequently competes for room with the Ramalinas, or in other areas with *Physcia aquila* and *Lecanora parella*.

A number of crustaceous species which form the sub-vegetation of the *Ramalina* belt, and also on the same level, clothe the steeper rock faces where shelter and moisture are insufficient to support the foliose forms. "In general the sub-vegetation of the eastern and northern coasts is largely composed of species that are common in Alpine and upland regions. This

Fig. 125. Crustaceous communities in the *Ramalina* belt. *Lecanora atra* Ach. (grey patches) and *Buellia ryssolea* A. L. Sm. (dark patches). (After M. C. Knowles, R. Welch, *Photo.*)

is due to the steepness of the rocks and also to the colder and drier conditions prevailing on these coasts." An association of *Rhizocarpon geographicum*, *Lecanora (sordida) glaucoma* and *Pertusaria concreta* f. *Westringii* forms an almost continuous covering in some places, descending nearly to sea-level.

On sunnier and moister rocks with a south and south-west aspect the association is of more lowland forms such as *Buellia colludens, B. stellulata Lecanora smaragdula* and *L. simplex* f. *strepsodina*.

(2) **The Orange belt.** "Below the Ramalinas, and between them and the sea, several deep yellow or orange-coloured lichens form a belt of varying

width all round the coast. In summer, the colour of these lichens is so brilliant that the belt is easily recognized from a considerable distance." The most abundant species occur mainly in the following order descending towards the sea:

1. *Xanthoria parietina.*
2. *Placodium murorum.*
3. *Placodium tegularis.*
4. *Placodium decipiens.*
5. *Placodium lobulatum.*

"On the stones and low shore rocks that lie just above the ordinary high-tide level *Placodium lobulatum* grows abundantly, covering the rocks with a continuous sheet of brilliant colour." With these brightly coloured lichens are associated several with greyish thalli such as:

Lecanora prosechoides.
Lecanora umbrina.
Lecanora Hageni.
Rhizocarpon alboatrum.
Biatorina lenticularis.
Rinodina exigua var. *demissa.*
Opegrapha calcarea f. *heteromorpha.*

(3) **The Lichina vegetation**, and (4) **The Verrucaria maura belt.** These two communities are intermingled, and it will therefore be better to consider them together. There are only two species of *Lichina* on this or any other shore, *L. pygmaea* and *L. confinis*; the latter grows above the tide-level, and sometimes high up on the cliffs, where it is subject to only occasional showers of spray: it forms on the Howth coast a band of vegetation four to five inches wide above the **Verrucaria belt.** *Lichina pygmaea* occurs nearer the water, and therefore mixed with and below *Verrucaria maura.* Those three zones were first pointed out by Nylander[1] at Pornic, where however they were all submerged at high tide.

Verrucaria maura is one of the most abundant lichens of our rocky coasts, and is reported from Spitzbergen in the North to Graham Land in the Antarctic. It grows well within the range of sea-spray, covering great stretches of boulders and rocks with its dull-black crustaceous thallus. At Howth it is submerged only by the highest spring tides. Though it is the dominant lichen on that beach, other species such as *V. memnonia, V. prominula,* and *V. aquatilis* form part of the association, and more rarely *V. scotina* along with *Arthopyrenia halodytes, A. leptotera* and *A. halizoa.*

(5) **The belt of marine Verrucarias.** This association includes the species that are submerged by the tide for a longer or shorter period each day. The dominant species are *Verrucaria microspora, V. striatula* and *V. mucosa. Arthopyrenia halodytes* is also abundant; *A. halizoa* and *A. marina* are more rarely represented. Among the plants of *Fucus spiralis, Verrucaria mucosa,* the most wide-spreading of these marine forms, is "very conspicuous as a dark-green, almost black, band of greasy appearance stretching along the shore." When growing in the shade, the thallus is of a brighter green colour.

[1] Nylander 1861.

An examination[1] of the west coast of Ireland yielded much the same results, but with a still higher "white belt" formed mainly of *Lecanora parella* and *L. atra* which covered the rocks lying above high-water mark, "giving them the appearance of having been whitewashed." A more general association for the same position as regards the tide is given by Wheldon and Wilson[2] on the coasts of Arran as:

Physcia aquila.	*Placodium tegularis.*
Xanthoria parietina.	*Ramalina cuspidata.*
Lecanora parella.	*Physcia stellaris.*
Lecanora atra.	*Physcia tenella.*
Lecanora campestris.	*Verrucaria maura.*
Placodium ferrugineum var. *festivum.*	

A somewhat similar series of "formations" was determined by Sandstede[3] on the coast of Rügen. On erratic granite boulders washed by the tide he found:

Verrucaria maura.	*Lecanora prosechoides.*
Lichina confinis.	*Placodium lobulatum.*

While in a higher position on similar boulders:

Lecanora exigua.	*Lecanora parella.*
Lecanora dispersa.	*Lecidea colludens.*
Lecanora galactina.	*Lecidea lavata.*
Lecanora sulphurea.	*Lecidea nigroclavata* f. *lenticularis.*
Lecanora saxicola.	*Xanthoria parietina* and f. *aureola.*
Lecanora caesiocinerea.	*Physcia subobscura.*
Lecanora gibbosa.	*Physcia caesia.*
Lecanora atra.	

And more rarely a few species of *Lecidea*.

b. LICHENS OF SAND-DUNES. These lichens might be included with those of the, terricolous communities, but they really represent a maritime community of xerophytic type, subject to the influence of salt spray but not within reach of the tide. They are sun-lichens and react to the strong light in the deeper colour of the thallus. In such a sun-baked area at Findhorn a luxuriant association of lichens was observed growing among short grass and plant debris. It consisted chiefly of:

Parmelia physodes.	*Cladonia cervicornis.*
Evernia prunastri.	*Cladonia endiviaefolia.*
Cetraria aculeata.	*Peltigera* spp.

On very arid situations the species of *Cladonia* are those that have a well-developed rather thick primary thallus, probably because such a thallus is able to retain moisture for a prolonged period[4]. On shifting sand, as in the desert, there are no lichens; it is only on surfaces more or less fixed by marram

---

[1] Knowles 1915.   [2] Wheldon and Wilson 1913.   [3] Sandstede 1904.   [4] Aigret 1901.

grass that lichens begin to develop, though in the cool damp weather of autumn and winter, as observed by Wheldon and Wilson[1], certain species associated with Myxophyceae, such as Collemaceae, may make their appearance, among others *Leptogium scotinum, Collemodium turgidum* and *Collema ceranoides*. Watson[2] makes the same observation in his study of sand-dunes.

When the loose sand on the dunes of South Lancashire becomes cemented by algae and mosses several rare *Lecideae* are to be found on the decaying vegetation, and with further accumulation of humus *Cladoniae* appear and spread rapidly along with several species of *Peltigera* and the ubiquitous *Parmelia physodes*. The latter starts on dead twigs of *Salix repens* and spreads on to the surrounding soil where it forms patches some inches in diameter. The association also includes *Lecidea uliginosa* and *Bilimbia sphaeroides*.

On the more inland portions of the dunes numerous rather poorly developed *Cladoniae* and *Cetraria aculeata* were associated, while on the sides of "slacks" or "dune-pans" *Collema pulposum, Cladonia sylvatica* and several crustaceous lichens covered the soil. The wetter parts of the dunes were not found to be favourable to lichen growth.

Sandstede[3] found on the sandy shores of Rügen, from the shore upwards: first a stretch of bare sand, then a few dune grasses with scattered scraps of *Cladoniae, Peltigerae* and *Cetraria aculeata*. Next in order sandbanks with *Parmelia physodes, Cladonia sylvatica, Cl. alcicornis* and *Stereocaulon paschale*. All these are species that occur on similar shores in the British Islands. Sandstede adds an extensive list of maritime species observed by him in Rügen.

A very careful tabulation of lichens at Blakeney Point in Norfolk was made by McLean[4] and the table on p. 386 is reproduced from his paper. Sand, he writes, is present in all the associations and the presence or absence of stones marks the great difference between the two formations determined by dune and shingle.

(1) **Bare sand,** which is the first association listed, is an area practically without phanerogams; the few lichen plants, *Cladonia furcata* and *Cetraria aculeata* f. *acanthella*, are attached by slight embedding in the soil.

(2) **Grey dune.** The sand-loving lichens of the association grow in company with *Hypnum cupressiforme* and attain their greatest development. Other species which also occur there are *Parmelia physodes* and *Evernia prunastri* var. *stictocera*.

(3) **Derelict dune.** This part of the dune formation occurs here and there on the seaward margin where the grey dune has been worn down by the wind. It is more shingly, hence the presence of stone lichens; dune phanerogams are interspersed and with them a few fruticose lichens, such as *Cladonia furcata*.

[1] Wheldon and Wilson 1915. [2] Watson 1918[1]. [3] Sandstede 1904. [4] McLean 1915.

(4) **High shingle.** The term indicates shingle aggregated into banks lying well above all except the highest tides. A large percentage of sand may be mixed with the stones and if no humus is present and the stones of small size, lichens may be absent altogether. Those occurring in the "loose shingle" are saxicolous In the "bound shingle" where there is no grass the stones, fixed in a mixture of sand and humus, are well covered with lichens. With the presence of grass, a thin layer of humus covers the stones and a dense lichen vegetation is developed both of shingle and of dune species.

(5) **Low shingle.** This last association lies in the hollows among plants of *Suaeda fruticosa*. Stability is high and tidal immersions regular and frequent. The dominant factor of the association is the quantity of humus and mud deposited around and over the stones. The lichens cover almost every available spot on the firmly embedded pebbles. The characteristic species of such areas are *Lecanora badia* and *L. (Placodium) citrina* which effect the primary colonization. To these succeed *Lecanora atra* and *Xanthoria parietina*. In time the mud overwhelms and partly destroys the lichens, so that the phase of luxuriant growth is only temporary.

Lecanora badia is conspicuously abundant at the sand end of this formation. *Lecanora (Placodium) citrina* disappears as the mud is left behind. *Collema* spp. also occur frequently on the mixture of mud and sand round the stones. The species on "low shingle" are those most tolerant of submersion: *Verrucaria maura* is confined to this area, where it is covered by the tide several hours each day.

FORMATION	ASSOCIATION		PRINCIPAL SPECIES
Dune	1. Bare Sand		*Cetraria aculeata* f. *acanthella* / *Cladonia furcata*
	2. Grey Dune		*Cladonia rangiferina*, *Peltigera rufescens* / *Cladonia furcata*, *Cl. alcicornis*
	3. Derelict Dune		*Cladonia furcata*, *Parmelia fuliginosa* / *Rhizocarpon confervoides*
Shingle	4. High Shingle — Loose	With sand	*Lecanora atra*, *L. galactina* / *Rhizocarpon confervoides* / *Lecanora citrina*
		Without sand	*Physcia tenella*, *Lecanora citrina*, *Xanthoria parietina* / *Squamaria saxicola* / *Parmelia saxatilis*, *P. fuliginosa*
	Bound	With grasses	*Cladonia rangiferina*, *Cl. furcata*, *Cl. pungens* / *Cetraria aculeata*
		Without grasses	*Xanthoria parietina*, *Biatorina chalybeia*, *Lecanora atr* / *Aspicilia gibbosa*, *Buellia colludens*, *Verrucaria microspor* / *Physcia tenella*, *Lecanora atroflava*
	5. Low Shingle		*Rhizocarpon confervoides*, *Lecanora citrina* var. *incrustar* / *L. badia*, *L. atra*, *Xanthoria parietina* / *Verrucaria maura*

McLean adds that *Xanthoria parietina* in its virescent form on *Suaeda fruticosa* also endures constant immersion; *Lecanora badia* does not occur above the tidal line and *Lecanora galactina* does not descend below tidal limits; the latter is an arenicolous species and colonizes some of the loosest and sandiest areas of shingle. *Rhizocarpon confervoides* is ubiquitous.

c. MOUNTAIN LICHENS. On the mountain summits of our own and other lands are to be found lichens very similar to those of the far North the climatic conditions being the chief factors of importance in determining the formations. These regions are occupied by what Wheldon and Wilson[1] describe as "a zone of Arctic-Alpine vegetation," and they have recorded a series of lichen associations belonging to that zone on the schistose summits of the Perthshire mountains. The following is one of the most typical:

Euopsis granatina.	Parmelia saxatilis.	Parmelia alpicola.
Sphaerophorus coralloides.	Parmelia omphalodes.	Cetraria aculeata.
Sphaerophorus fragilis.	Parmelia lanata.	Cetraria crispa.
Gyrophora polyphylla.	Parmelia stygia.	Cetraria islandica.
Cetraria tristis.	Stereocaulon tomentosum.	Lecidea limosa.
Cetraria nivalis.	Stereocaulon alpinum.	Lecidea alpestris.
Lecanora tartarea var. frigida.	Cladonia coccinea.	Lecidea demissa.
Lecanora upsaliensis.	Cladonia gracilis.	Lecidea uliginosa.
Aspicilia oculata.	Cladonia uncialis.	Lecidea cuprea.
Pertusaria dactylina.	Cladonia destricta.	Lecidea Berengeriana.
Pertusaria glomerata.	Cladonia racemosa.	Lecidea cupreiformis.
Stereocaulon denudatum.	Lecidea arctica.	Lecidea atrofusca.

Again on the summit of Ben-y-Gloe the same authors[2] have recorded "*Gyrophora erosa, G. torrefacta* and *G. cylindrica, Parmelia alpicola, Lecanora tartarea* var. *frigida, Lecidea limosa* and *L. arctica*, the last two lichens thriving in the most bleak and exposed situations. *Cladonia cervicornis* grew in reduced squamulose cushions; *Stereocaulon* and *Sphaerophorus* in very compact forms, the outer stalks prostrate, the next inclined, the central ones erect so that points only are exposed and no lateral stress is caused by wind storms. Erect fruticose lichens are absent in this region, being represented only by *Parmelia lanata*, a semi-decumbent plant, and by *Thamnolia vermicularis* which is prostrate on the ground except where the points of the stalks turn up to catch the dew. Many of the *Lecideae* were observed to have large fruits and very little thallus: "the hyphae ramify in the minute interstices of the stone and the gonidia cluster under the lea of the apothecia; this is especially the case on loose stones where conditions are extremely dry."

On the Continent an interesting study of the lichens of high altitudes was made by Maheu[3] in the Savoyard Oberland. On the Great Casse at

[1] Wheldon and Wilson 1915. [2] Wheldon and Wilson 1914. [3] Maheu 1887.

a height of 3861 m. he collected four mosses and sixteen lichens. These
were :

Stereocaulon condensatum.	*Candelaria concolor.*	*Buellia discolor.*
Gyrophora cylindrica	*Caloplaca pyracea* var. *nivalis.*	*Buellia stellulata.*
Gyrophora spodochroa.	*Haematomma ventosum.*	*Lecidea contigua* var. *steriza*
Solorina·crocea.	*Acarospora smaragdula.*	*Lecidea confluens.*
Solorina saccata.	*Psora decipiens.*	*Dermatocarpon hepaticum.*
Parmelia encausta.		

He found that as he climbed higher and higher foliaceous species became
rarer and crustaceous more abundant. The colour of the lichens on the high
summits was slightly weakened and the thallus often reduced, but all were
fertile and the apothecia normal and sporiferous. Lichens at less high
altitudes where they emerge from the snow covering for longer periods and
enjoy light and sunshine are, as already observed, often very brightly
coloured and of luxuriant growth.

d. TUNDRA LICHENS. In phyto-geography the term "tundra" is given
to great stretches of country practically treeless and unsheltered within the
Polar climate; the tundra extends from the zone of dwarfed trees on to the
permanent ice or snow fields. The vegetation includes a few dwarfed trees,
shrubs, etc., but is mainly composed of mosses and lichens ; the latter being
the most abundant. These are true climatic lichen formations.

Leighton[1], in describing lichens from Arctic America brought home by
the traveller, Sir John Richardson, quotes from the latter that : "the terrestrial lichens were gathered on Great Bear, and Great Slave Lakes before
starting on our summer voyages after the snow had melted....The barren
grounds are densely covered for many hundreds of miles with *Corniculariae*
and *Cetrariae*, and where the ground is moist with *Cladoniae*, while the
boulders thickly scattered over the surface are clothed with *Gyrophorae*....
The smaller stones on the gravelly ridges of the Barren Grounds are
covered with lichens."

The accounts of tundra lichens that have been given by various travellers
deal chiefly with the more prominent terricolous forms. They have been
classified as "Cladina tundra," including *Cladonia rangiferina* and *Sphaerophorus coralloides*, "Cetraria tundra," and "Alectoria heath," the latter the
hardiest of all. Great swards of these lichens often alternate with naked
stony soil.

Kihlman[2] has noted, as characteristic of tundra formations, the compact
cushion-like growth of the mosses which are thus enabled to store up water
and to conduct it by capillarity throughout the mass to the highest stalks.
Certain tundra lichens take on the same growth character as adaptations to
the strenuous life conditions. *Cetraria glauca* f. *spadicea* with f. *congesta* and

[1] Leighton 1867.   [2] Kihlman 1890.

C. crispa are examples of this compact growth: they form a soft thick carpet of a yellowish-grey colour. *Cladoniae* also grow in crowded tufts, but are generally to be found in the more sheltered positions, in valleys between the tundra hills and in the clefts of the rocks, or between great boulders and stones where there is also more moisture.

The same kinds of lichens occur all over these northern regions. Birger Nilson[1] gives as the principal earth-lichens in Swedish Lappland, *Alectoria ochroleuca, A. nigricans, Cetraria nivalis, C. cucullata, Cladonia uncialis, Thamnolia (Cerania) vermicularis* and *Sphaerophorus coralloides*.

Darbishire[2] speaks of the extensive beds of various species of *Cetraria* in Ellesmere Land and King Oscar Land. *Alectoria nigricans* and *A. ochroleuca* were often found in pure communities, but even more frequently in close company with mosses. Though these fruticose lichens are not represented by many species in Arctic regions, they cover a very extensive area and form a very important feature in the vegetation.

Crustaceous lichens are not wanting: *Lecanora tartarea* f. *frigida*, *L. epibryon* and others are to be found in great sheets covering the mosses or the soil, or spreading over the stones and boulders. Cold has no deterrent effect, and their advance is only checked by the presence of perpetual snow.

e. DESERT LICHENS. The reduced rainfall of desert countries is unfavourable to general lichen growth and only the more xerophytic species— those with a stout cortex—can flourish in the adverse conditions of excessive light and dryness. Lichens, however, there are, in great numbers as far as individuals are concerned, though the variety is not great. The abundance of the crustaceous *Lecanora esculenta* in the deserts of Asia has already been noted. Flagey[3] found it one of the dominant species at Biskra in the Sahara where it grows on the rocks. Patouillard[4] in describing the flora of Tunis speaks of the great patches (societies) of *Lecanora crassa* f. *deserti* which at a distance look like milk spilled on the ground, or if growing on unequal surfaces take the aspect of plaster that has been passed over by some wheeled vehicle. At Biskra species of *Heppia* grow on the sand. Steiner[5] also records the frequency of *Heppia* and of *Endocarpon* in the Sahara as well as of Gloeolichens which, as they are associated with gelatinous blue-green algae, can endure extreme and long-continued desiccation. These lichens, however, only form communities in clefts among the rocks where these abut on the desert. In the great plains the sand is too mobile and too often shifted by the sirocco to enable them to settle.

Bruce Fink[6] discusses desert lichens and their adaptive characters: crustaceous species with a stout cortex are best able to withstand the long dry periods; conspicuously lobed thalli are lacking, as are lichens with

[1] Nilson 1907.   [2] Darbishire 1909.   [3] Flagey 1901.   [4] Patouillard 1897.
[5] Steiner 1895.   [6] Bruce Fink 1909.

fruticose structure though he thinks the latter are prevented from developing by the exposure to high winds and driving sand storms. Herre's[1] study of the desert lichen flora at Reno, Nevada, is full of interest. The district is situated at an altitude of 4500 feet east of the Sierra Nevada Mountains. The annual rainfall averages 8·21 inches, and a large part falls as snow during the winter months or as early spring rain. The summer is hot and dry and the diurnal changes of temperature are very great. Strong drying winds from the west or north are frequent.

At 5000 feet and upwards lichens are, in general, exceedingly abundant on all rock substrata and represent 57 species or subspecies, only three of these being arboreal: *Buellia triphragmia* occurs rarely, *Xanthoria polycarpa* is frequent on sage brush, while *Candelariella cerinella* though a rock-lichen grows occasionally on the same substratum. *Caloplaca (Placodium) elegans* is one of the most successful and abundant species and along with *Lecanora* (nine forms), *Acarospora* (seven forms) and *Lecidia* (five forms) comprises three-fourths of the rock surface occupied by lichens. The addition of *Rinodina* with two species and *Gyrophora* with four brings the computation of individuals in these desert rock formations up to nine-tenths of the whole. As the desert rocks pass to the Alpine, *Gyrophora* becomes easily the dominant genus followed by *Acarospora*, *Caloplaca* and *Lecidea*.

"The colouring characteristic of the rock ledges of the desert and cañon walls is often entirely due to lichens, and in a general way they form the only brilliant plant formations in a landscape notable for its subdued pale monotonous tones. Most conspicuous are *Acarospora chlorophana* and *Caloplaca elegans*, which form striking landmarks when covering great crags and rock walls. The next most conspicuous lichens are *Rinodina oreina* and *Lecanora rubina* and its allies, which often entirely cover immense boulders and northerly sloping rock walls." Herre concludes that though desert conditions are unfavourable to most species of lichens, yet some are perfectly at home there and the rocks are just as thickly covered as in regions of greater humidity and less sunshine.

f. AQUATIC LICHENS. There is only one of the larger lichens that has acquired a purely aquatic habit, *Hydrothyria venosa*, a North American plant. It grows on rocks[2] in the beds of streams, covering them often with a thick felt; it is attached at the base and the rather narrow fronds float freely in the current. The gonidium is *Nostoc* sp., and the thallus is of a bluish-grey colour; the fruits are small discoid reddish apothecia with an evanescent margin. It is closely allied to *Peltigerae*, some of which are moisture-loving though not truly aquatic.

The nearest approach to aquatic habit among the foliose forms in our

---

[1] Herre 1911[2].   [2] See p. 97.

country is *Dermatocarpon aquaticum*, with thick coriaceous rather contorted lobes; it inhabits rocks and stones in streams and lakes. Somewhat less continuously aquatic is *D. miniatum* var. *complicatum* which grows on damp rocks exposed to spray or occasionally to inundation. Lindsay[1] has described it " on boulders by the side of the Tay, frequently covered by the river when flooded, and of a deep olive colour when under water": both these lichens have a wide distribution in Europe, Africa, America and New Zealand.

In a discussion of lake shore plants Conway Macmillan[2] describes on the flat shores a *Dermatocarpon* zone on the wet area nearest the lake, behind that a *Biatora* zone and further landward a *Cladonia* zone. On rounded rocky shores the same zones followed each other but were less broad : they were so close together that the *Cladoniae*, which with *Stereocaulon paschale* grow in profusion on all such shores, occurred within a couple of feet of the high-water mark.

M. C. Knowles[3] reports concerning the lichen flora of some mountain lakes in Waterford, that a band of *Dermatocarpon miniatum* var. *complicatum* six feet wide grew all the way round the lakes between the winter and summer level of the water. Below that zone *D. aquaticum* formed another belt mingled with the moss *Fontinalis* and several species of crustaceous lichens *Staurotheleae*, *Polyblastiae*, etc.

Bruce Fink[4] gives as a typical "amphibious angiocarpous lichen formation" of wet rocks in Minnesota: *Dermatocarpon aquaticum*, *D. miniatum* var. *complicatum*, *Staurothele clopima* and *Verrucaria viridula*. These "formations," he says, "may be seen complete in places along the shores of Vermillion Lake and less well represented at other portions of the lake shore." Macmillan found that on the rocky shores of Lake Superior the *Dermatocarpon* zone also occurred nearest the water.

Species with closed fruits such as Pyrenolichens, or with apothecia deeply sunk in the thallus and thus also well protected, seem to be best adapted to the aquatic life. Such in our own country are *Lecanora lacustris*, *Bacidia inundata* and others, with a number of *Verrucariae*: *V. aethiobola*, *V. hydrela*, *V. margacea*, etc.

Lettau[5] gives as "formations" on rocks or boulders in the beds of streams in Thuringia :

Verrucaria aethiobola.　　　　　*Bacidia inundata.*
Verrucaria hydrela.　　　　　　*Lecanora aquatica.*
Dermatocarpon aquaticum.

In their ecological study of Perthshire lichens Wheldon and Wilson[6] give two "formations." The first is on rocks submerged for long periods,

---

[1] Lindsay 1856.　　　[2] Macmillan 1894.　　　Knowles *in litt.*　　　[4] Bruce Fink 1903.
[5] Lettau 1911.　　　　　　　　　　[6] Wheldon and Wilson 1915.

though in dry weather the lichens may be exposed, and can withstand desiccation for a considerable time :

Pterygium Kenmorensis.	*Lecidea contigua.*
Collema fluviatile.	*Lecidea albocoerulescens.*
Lecanora lacustris.	*Dermatocarpon miniatum* var. *complicatum.*
Lecanora epulotica.	*Dermatocarpon aquaticum.*
Bacidia inundata.	*Verrucaria laevata.*
Rhizocarpum obscuratum.	*Verrucaria aethiobola.*
Rhizocarpum petraeum.	*Verrucaria margacea.*

The second group of species usually inhabits damp, shaded rocks of ravines or large boulders by streams or near waterfalls. It includes species of *Collema, Sticta, Peltigera, Solorina, Pannaria,* etc., with *Opegrapha zonata, Porina lectissima* and *Verrucaria nigrescens.*

The last-mentioned lichen grows by preference on limestone, but in excessive moisture[1], as by the sea-side, the substratum seems to be of minor importance.

D. Lichens as Pioneers

a. Soil-formers. The part played by lichens in the "Economy of Nature" is of very real importance : to them is allotted the pioneer work of breaking down the hard rock surfaces and preparing a soil on which more highly developed plants can grow. This was pointed out by Linnaeus[2] who thus describes the succession of plants : "Crustaceous lichens," he writes, "are the first foundation of vegetation. Though hitherto we have considered theirs a trifling place among plants, nevertheless they are of great importance at that first stage in the economy of nature. When the rocks emerge from the seas, they are so polished by the force of the waves, that scarcely any kind of plant could settle on them, seen more especially near the sea. But very soon, in truth, the smallest crustaceous lichens begin to cover those arid rocks, and are sustained by minute quantities of soil and by imperceptible particles brought to them by rain and by the atmosphere These lichens in time become converted by decay into a thin layer of humus, so that at length imbricate lichens are able to thrust their rhizoids into it. As these in turn change to humus by natural decay, various mosses such as *Hypnum, Bryum* and *Polytrichum* follow, and find suitable place and nourishment. In time there is produced by the dying down of the mosses such a quantity of soil that herbs and shrubs are able to establish themselves and maintain their existence."

Similar observations have been made since Linnaeus's day, among others by Guembel[3] in his account of *Lecanora ventosa.* Either by the excretion of carbon dioxide which acidifies the surrounding moisture, or by the mechanical

---

[1] Wheldon and Wilson 1913.   [2] Linnaeus 1762.   [3] Guembel 1856.

action of hyphae and rhizinae, the component particles of rocks such as granite are gradually dissolved and broken up. Rocks exposed to weather alone are unchanged, while those covered with lichens have their surface disintegrated and destroyed.

The decaying parts of the lichen thallus add to the soil material as observed by Linnaeus, and in time mosses follow, and, later, phanerogams. Goeppert[1] has pointed out the succession observed on roofs of houses as : "first some lichen such as *Lecanora saxicola*, then the moss *Grimmia pulvinata*, which forms compact cushions on which later grow *Poa compressa*, small crucifers, etc."

Goeppert[1] has noted as special rock-destroyers some foliaceous species, *Parmelia saxatilis*, *P. stygia* and *P. encausta*, the underlying rock being roughened and broken up by their rhizoids. Species of *Gyrophora* and *Sphaerophorus* have the same disintegrating effect, so that the surface of the rock may in time lose its coherence to a depth of 2 to 4 inches. Crustaceous species such as *Lecanora polytropa*, *Candelariella vitellina*, etc., exercise an equally powerful solvent action, while underneath closely appressed growers like *Lecanora atra* and *Acarospora smaragdula* the stone is converted to a friable substance that can be sliced away with a knife.

Salter[2] concluded that oxalic acid was the principal agent in disintegration. He found that it acted more or less rapidly on minerals and almost any class of saline compounds; it even attacked glass finely powdered, though silica remained unchanged.

Bachmann[3] found that granite was reduced by lichens to a clay-like granular yellow mass in a comparatively short time, the lichen seizing on the particles of mica first; but the spread of the lichen over the rock, he observes, is largely directed by the amount of humidity and by the chance of gaining a foothold. In the case of calcareous rocks he[4] tested the relative dampness of those containing lichens and those that were lichen-free. In the former case water was absorbed more freely and retained much longer than in the barren rock, thus encouraging further vegetation.

Lucy E. Braun[5] has described the successive colonization of limestone conglomerate in Cincinnati. The rock is somewhat resistant to erosion and stands out in irregular outcrops on the hillsides of the region. The first plants to gain a footing are certain crustaceous lichens, *Lecidea* sp., *Pertusaria communis*, *Staurothele umbrina*, *Verrucaria muralis* and *Placodium citrinum* which occur as patches on the smoother and more exposed rock faces. With these were associated small quantities of a moss, *Grimmia apocarpa*. In the second stage of growth *Dermatocarpon miniatum*, and, to a lesser degree, a gelatinous *Omphalaria* sp. were the most prominent plants,

---

[1] Goeppert 1860.   [2] Salter 1856.   [3] Bachmann 1911.
[4] Bachmann 1913.   [5] Braun 1917.

but mosses were more in evidence, and the next stage consisted almost exclusively of mosses and hepatics with *Peltigera canina*. A thick layer of humus was gradually built up by these plants on which Phanerogamous plants were able to flourish.

In tropical countries the first vegetation to settle on bare rocks would seem to be blue-green gelatinous algae. Three years after the eruption of Krakatoa, dark-green layers of these plants were found by Treub[1] on the surface of the pumice and ash, and on the loose stones in the ravines of the mountain. It was only at a later stage that lichens appeared.

b. OUTPOSTS OF VEGETATION. Lichens are the only plants that can survive extreme conditions of cold or of heat. They grow in Polar regions where no other vegetation could obtain sustenance; they are to be found at great heights on mountains all over the globe; and, on arid desert rocks they persist through long dry seasons, depending almost entirely on night dews for the supply of moisture. Here we have true lichen formations in the sense of modern ecology.

[1] Treub 1888.

CHAPTER X

ECONOMIC AND TECHNICAL

A. Lichens as Food.

a. Food for Insects, etc. Some of the earlier botanists made careful observations on the important place occupied by lichens in nature as affording food to many small animals. In 1791 Jacques Brez[1] wrote his *Flore des Insectophyles*, and in the list of food-plants he includes seven species of lichens. The "insects" that frequented these lichens were species of the genera *Acarus* (mites) and *Phalena* (moths). A few years later Persoon[2] noted that lichens formed the main food supply of many insects, slugs, etc. Zukal[3], quoting from Otto Wilde (*Die Pflanzen und Raupen Deutschlands*, Berlin, 1860), gives a list of caterpillars that are known to feed on and destroy lichens.

A very considerable number of small creatures feed eagerly on lichens, and traces of their depredations are constantly to be seen in the empty fruit discs, and in the cortices eaten away in patches so as to expose the white medulla. It has been argued by Zukal[4] that the great formation of acid substances in lichens is for shielding them against the attacks of animals; Zopf[5] on the contrary insists that these substances afford the plants no real protection. He made a series of experiments with snails, feeding them with slices of potato smeared with pure lichen acids. Many snails ate the slices with great readiness even when covered with bitter acids such as cetraric, or with those which are poisonous for other animals such as rhizo-carpic and pinastrinic. The only acid they refused was vulpinic, which is said to be poisonous for vertebrates. The crystals of the acids passed unchanged through the alimentary canal of the snails, and were found in masses in the excreta. They were undissolved, but, enclosed in slime, their sharp edges did no damage to the digestive tract.

Stahl[6] however upholds Zukal's theory of the protective function of lichen acids against the attacks of small animals. Some few snails, cater-pillars, etc., that are omnivorous feeders consume most lichens with impunity, and the bitter taste seems to attract rather than repel them ; but many others he contends are certainly prevented from eating lichens by the presence of the acids. He proved this by soaking portions of the thalli of certain bitter species for about twenty-four hours in a one per cent. soda solution, which was sufficiently strong to extract the acids. He found that

---

[1] Brez 1791.   [2] Persoon 1794.   [3] Zukal 1895, p. 1317 (note).   [4] Zukal 1895, p. 1315.
[5] Zopf 1896.   [6] Stahl 1904.

these treated specimens were in most cases preferred to fresh portions that had been simply moistened with water.

Even the omnivorous snail, *Helix hortensis*, was several times observed to touch the fresh thallus and then creep away, while it ate continuously the soda-washed portion as soon as it came into contact with it. Calcium oxalate, on the other hand, formed no protection; omnivorous feeders ate indifferently calcicolous lichens such as *Aspicilia calcarea* and *Lecanora saxicola*, whether treated with soda or not, but would only accept lichens with acid contents, such as *Parmelia caperata*, *Evernia prunastri*, etc., after they had been duly soaked.

Experiments were also made with wood-lice (*Oniscus murarius*), and with earwigs (*Forficula auricularia*), and the result was the same: they would only eat bitter lichens after the acids had been extracted by the soda method. Stahl therefore concludes that acids must be regarded as eminently adapted to protect lichens which otherwise, owing to their slowness of growth, would scarcely escape extinction.

The gelatinous Collemaceae, as also *Nostoc*, the alga with which these are associated, are unharmed by snails, etc., on account of their slippery consistency when moist, which prevents the creatures from getting a foothold on the thallus. These lichens however do not contain acids, and if, when dry, they are reduced to powder and then moistened, they are eagerly eaten both by snails and by wood-lice. *Peltigera canina*, on account of a disagreeable odour it acquires on being chewed, is avoided to a certain extent, but even so it is frequently found with much of the thallus eaten away.

Hue[1] in his study of Antarctic lichens, comments on the abundance and perfect development of the lichens, especially the crustaceous species, which cover every inch of rock surface. He ascribes this to the absence of snails and insects which in other regions so seriously interfere with the normal and continuous growth of these plants.

Snails do not eat lichens when they are dry and hard, but on damp or dewy nights, and on rainy days, all kinds, both large and small, come out of their shells and devour the lichen thalli softened by moisture. Large slugs (*Limax*) have been seen devouring with great satisfaction *Pertusaria faginea*, a bitter crustaceous lichen. The same *Limax* species eats many different lichens, some of them containing very bitter substances. Zopf[2] observed that *Helix cingulata* ate ten different lichens, containing as many different kinds of acid.

Other creatures such as mites, wood-lice, and the caterpillars of many butterflies live on lichens, though, with the exception of the caterpillars, they eat them only when moist. Very frequently the apothecial discs and the soredia are taken first as being evidently the choicest portions. All lichens

[1] Hue 1915.   [2] Zopf 1907.

are, however, not equally palatable. Bitter[1] observed that the insect *Psocus* (*Orthoptera*) had a distinct preference for certain species, and restricted its attention to them probably because of their chemical constitution. He noted that in a large spreading thallus of *Graphis elegans* on holly, irregular bare spots appeared, due to the ravages of insects—probably *Psocus*. In other places, the thallus alone had been consumed, leaving the rather hard black fruits (lirellae) untouched. In time the thallus of *Thelotrema lepadinum*, also a crustaceous lichen, invaded the naked areas, and surrounded the *Graphis* lirellae. The new comer was not to the taste of the insects and was left untouched.

Petch[2] says that lichens form the staple food of *Termes monoceros*, the black termite of Ceylon. These ants really prefer algae, but as the supply is limited they fall back on lichens, though they only consume those of a particular type, or at a particular stage of development. Those with a tough smooth cortex are avoided, preference being given to thalli with a loose powdery surface. At the feeding ground the ants congregate on the suitable lichens. With their mandibles they scrape off small fragments of the thallus which they form into balls, varying in size from 1·5 mm. to 2·5 mm. in diameter. The workers then convey these to the nests in their mandibles. It would seem that they carry about these balls of food, and allow the ants busy in the nest to nibble off portions. Lichen balls are not used by termites as fungi are, for "gardens."

Other observations have been made by Paulson and Thompson[3] in their study of Epping Forest lichens: "Mites of the family Oribatidae must be reckoned among the chief foes of these plants upon which they feed, seeming to have a special predilection for the ripe fruits. We have had excellent specimens of *Physcia parietina* spoiled by hidden mites of this family, which have eaten out the contents of the mature apothecia after the lichens have been gathered. One can sometimes see small flocks of the mites browsing upon the thallus of tree-dwelling lichens, like cattle in a meadow." The Oribatidae, sometimes called beetle-mites, a family of Acarinae, are minute creatures familiar to microscopists. They live chiefly on or about mosses, but Michael[4] is of opinion that a large number frequent these plants for the fungi and lichens which grow in and about the mosses. In Michael's *Monograph of British Oribatidae*, four species are mentioned as true lichen-lovers, *Leiosoma palmicinctum* found on *Peltigera canina* and allied species; *Cepteus ocellatus* and *Oribata parmeliae* which live on *Physciae*, the latter exclusively on *Physcia* (*Xanthoria*) *parietina*; and *Scutovertes maculatus* which confines itself to lichens by the sea-shore. Another species, *Notaspis lucorum*, frequents maritime lichens, but it is also found on other substrata;

[1] Bitter 1899.   [2] Petch 1913.   [3] Paulson and Thompson 1913.
[4] Michael 1884.

while *Tegeocranus labyrinthicus*, though usually a lichen-eating species, lives either on mosses or on lichens on walls. Zopf[1] reckoned twenty-nine species of lichens, mostly the larger foliose and fruticose kinds, that were eaten by mites. Lesdain[2] in his observations on mite action notes that frequently the thallus round the base of the perithecia of *Verrucaria* sp. was eaten clean away, leaving the perithecia solitary and extremely difficult to determine.

J. A. Wheldon[3] found the eggs of a species of mite, *Tetranychus lapidus*, attached to the fruits of *Verrucaria calciseda*, *Lecidea immersa* and *L. Metzleri*, calcicolous lichens of which the thallus not only burrows deep down into the limestone, but the fruits form in shallow excavated pits (Fig. 126). The

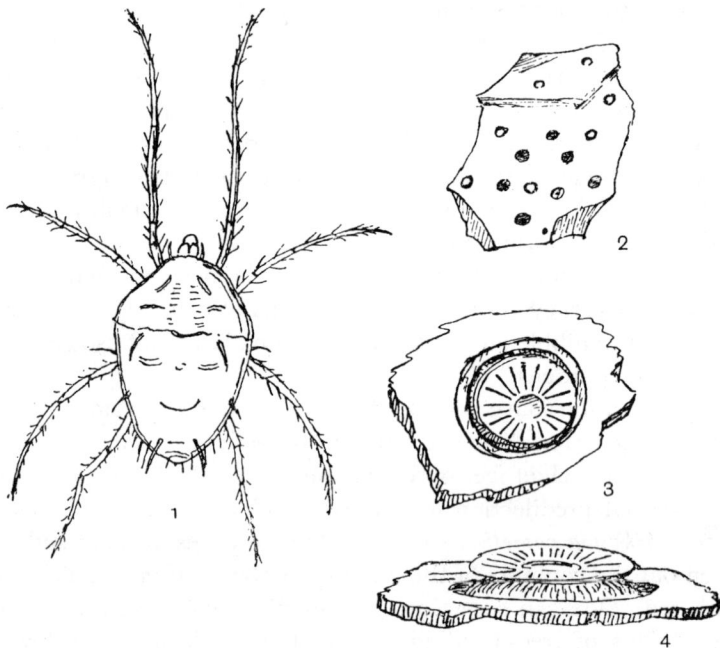

Fig. 126. 1, *Tetranychus lapidus*, enlarged; 2, *Verrucaria calciseda* with eggs *in situ*, slightly enlarged; 3 and 4, eggs attached to lichen fruits, much magnified (after Wheldon).

eggs of this stone mite are found fairly frequently on exposed limestone rocks, bare of vegetation, except for a few crustaceous lichens. "There is usually a single egg, rarely two, in each pit apparently attached to the old lichen apothecium. The eggs are very attractive objects under a lens; they measure ·5 mm. in diameter, and are disc-like with a central circular depression from which numerous ridges radiate to the circumference, like the spokes of a wheel. When fresh, they have a white pearly lustre, becoming chalk-white when dry and old." Wheldon's observations were made in the Carnforth and Silverdale district of West Lancashire.

[1] Zopf 1907.   [2] Lesdain 1910.   [3] Wheldon 1914.

A minute organism, *Hymenobolina parasitica*[1], first described by Zukal and doubtfully grouped among the mycetozoa, feeds, in the plasmodium stage, on living lichens. The parasitic habit is unlike that of true mycetozoa. It has recently been recorded from Aberdeenshire.

b. INSECT MIMICRY OF LICHENS. Paulson and Thompson[2] give instances of moth caterpillars, which not only feed on lichens, but which take on the coloration of the lichens they affect, either in the larval or in the perfect moth stage. "One of the most remarkable examples of this protective resemblance to lichens is that of the larva of the geometrid moth, *Cleora lichenaria*, which feeds upon foliose lichens growing upon tree-trunks and palings, and being of a green-grey hue, and possessed of two little humps on many of their body-segménts, they so exactly resemble the lichens in colour and appearance as to be extremely difficult of detection." Several instances are recorded of moths that resemble the lichens on which they settle : perfect examples of such similarity are exhibited at the Natural History Museum, South Kensington, where *Teras literana*, *Moma orion*, and other moths are shown at rest on lichen-covered bark from which they can hardly be distinguished.

Another curious instance of suggested mimicry is recorded by G. E. Stone[3]. He spotted a number of bodies on the bark of some sickly elms in Massachusetts. They were about $\frac{1}{8}$ of an inch in diameter "with a dark centre and a drab foliaceous margin." They were principally lodged in the crevices of the bark and Stone collected them under the impression that they were the apothecia of a lichen most nearly resembling those of *Physcia hypoleuca*. Some of the bodies were even attached to the thallus of a species of *Physcia*; others were on the naked bark and had every appearance of lichen fruits. Only closer examination proved their insect nature, and they were identified as belonging to a species *Gossypina Ulmi*, an elm-leaf beetle common in Europe where it causes a disease of the tree. It had been imported into the United States and had attacked American elms.

It is stated by Tutt[4] that the larvae of many of the Psychides (*Lepidoptera*) live on the lichens of trees and walls, such as *Candelaria concolor*, *Xanthoria parietina*, *Physcia pulverulenta* and *Buellia canescens*, and that their larvae pupate on their feeding grounds. Each species makes a "case" peculiar to itself, but those of the lower families are usually covered externally with grains of sand, scraps of lichens, etc. The "case" of *Narcyria monilifera*, for instance, is somewhat raised on a flat base and is obscured with particles of sand and yellow lichen, giving the whole a yellow appearance. That of *Luffia lapidella* is roughly conical and is held up at an angle of 30° to 45° when the larva moves. The "cases" of *Bacotia sepium* are always upright; they measure about 5·5 mm. in height and 2·75 mm. in width and

[1] See also p. 267. [2] Paulson and Thompson 1913. [3] Stone 1896. [4] Tutt 1900, p. 107.

present a hoary appearance from the minute particles of lichen with which they are covered, so that the structure is not unlike the podetium of a *Cladonia.*

c. FOOD FOR THE HIGHER ANIMALS. It has been affirmed, especially by Henneguy, that many lichens, if deprived of the bitter principle they contain, by soaking in water, or with the addition of sodium or potassium carbonate, might be used with advantage as fodder for animals. He cites as examples of such, *Lobaria pulmonaria, Evernia prunastri, Ramalina fraxinea, R. farinacea,* and *R. fastigiata,* all of which grow abundantly on trees, and owe their nutritive quality to the presence of lichenin, a carbohydrate allied to starch.

Fig. 127. *Cladonia rangiferina* Web. (S. H., *Photo.*).

Cladonia rangiferina (Fig. 127), the well-known "reindeer moss," is, however, the lichen of most economic importance, as food for reindeer, cattle, etc. It is a social plant and forms dense tufts and swards of slender, much branched, hollow stalks of a greenish-grey colour which may reach a height of twelve inches or even more; the stalks decay slowly at the base as they increase at the apex, so that very great length is never attained. In normal conditions they neither wither nor die, and growth continues indefinitely. It is comparatively rare in the northern or hilly regions of the British Isles, and is frequently confused with the somewhat smaller species *Cl. sylvatica* which is very common on our moorlands, a species which Zopf[1] tells us reindeer absolutely refuse to eat.

[1] Zopf 1907, p. 372.

The true reindeer moss is abundant in northern countries, more especially in forest regions[1] and in valleys between the tundra hills which are more or less sheltered from the high winds; it is independent of the substratum and flourishes equally on barren sand and on wet turf; but grows especially well on soil devastated by fire. For long periods it may be covered with snow without injury and the reindeer are accustomed to dig down with horns and hoofs in order to reach their favourite food. Though always considered as peculiarly "reindeer" moss, deer, roebuck and other wild animals, such as Lemming rats[2], feed on it largely during the winter. In some northern districts it is collected and stored as fodder for domestic cattle ; hot water

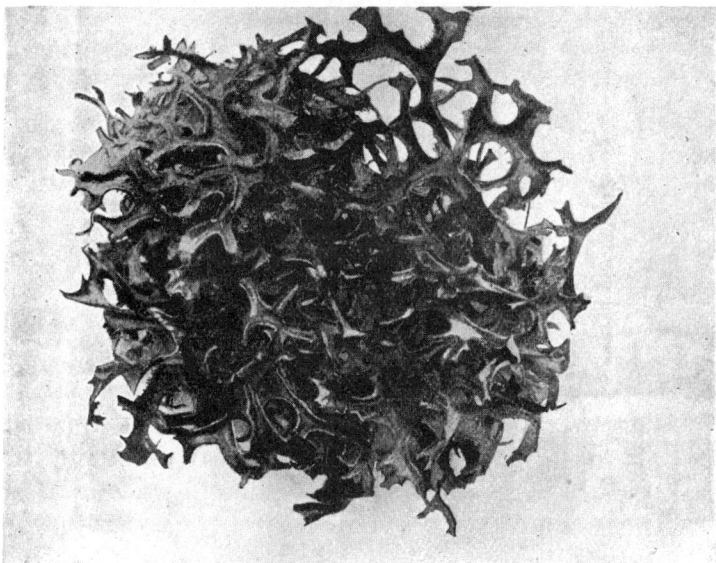

Fig. 128. *Cetraria islandica* Ach. (S. H., *Photo.*).

is poured over it and it is then mixed with straw and sprinkled with a little salt. Johnson[3] has reported that the richness of the milk yielded by the small cows of Northern Scandinavia is attributed by some to their feeding in great measure on the "reindeer moss."

When *Cladonia rangiferina* is scarce, a few other lichens[4] are made use of, *Alectoria jubata*, a brownish-black filamentous tree-lichen being one of the most frequent substitutes. *Stereocaulon paschale*, which grows in large dense tufts on the ground in mountainous regions, is also eaten by reindeer and other animals; and Iceland moss, *Cetraria islandica*, is stored up in large quantities by the Icelanders and used as fodder. Willemet[5] reports it as good for horses, oxen, cows and pigs.

[1] Kihlman 1890.   [2] Linnaeus 1762.   [3] Johnson 1861.
[4] Lindsay 1856.   [5] Willemet 1787.

It is interesting to recall a discovery of prehistoric remains at the Abbey of Schussenried on the Lake of Constance and described by F. Keller[1]: under successive beds of peat and crumbly tufa, there was found a layer, 3 feet thick, containing flints, horns of reindeer and bones of various animals, and, along with these, masses of reindeer moss ; a sufficient proof of its antiquity as a fodder-plant.

d. FOOD FOR MAN. Lichens contain no true starch nor cellulose, but the lichenin present in the cell-walls of the hyphae has long been utilized as a food substance. It is peculiarly abundant in *Cetraria islandica* (Fig. 128), which grows in northern countries, covering great stretches of ground with its upright strap-shaped branching fronds of varying shades of brown. In more southern lands it is to be found on high hills or on upland moors, but in much smaller quantities. Commercial " Iceland moss " is supplied from Sweden, Norway or Iceland. In the last-named country the inhabitants harvest the lichen preferably from bare stony soil where there is no admixture of other vegetation. They revisit the locality at intervals of three years, the time required for the lichen to grow to a profitable size ; and they select the wet season for the ingathering of the plants as they are more easily detached when they are wet. If the weather should be dry, they collect it during the night. When gathered it is cleansed from foreign matter and washed in water to remove as much as possible of the bitter principle. It is then dried and reduced to powder. When required, the powder is put to macerate in water for 24 hours, or it is soaked in a weak solution of soda or of carbonate of potassium, by which means the bitter cetraric acid is nearly all eliminated. When boiled[2] it yields a jelly which forms the basis of various light and easily digested soups or of other delicacies prepared by boiling in milk, which have been proved to be valuable for dyspeptics or sufferers from chest diseases. The northern nations also make the powder into bread, porridge or gruel. Johnson[3] states in his account of " Useful Plants" that considerable quantities of Iceland moss were formerly employed in the manufacture of sea biscuit, and that ship's bread mixed with it was said to be less liable to the attacks of weevil than when made from wheat flour only.

An examination of the real food value of the mucilaginous extract from "Iceland moss" has been made by several workers. Church[4] states that for one part of flesh formers, there are eight parts of heat-givers reckoned as starch. Brown[5] isolated the two carbohydrates, lichenin and iso-lichenin. The former, a jelly which yields on hydrolysis a large quantity of a reducing sugar, dextrose, ferments with yeast and gives no phloroglucin reaction ; it is unaffected by digestion and probably does not form glycogen.

[1] Keller 1866.   [2] Proust 1906.   [3] Johnson 1861.
[4] Church 1880.   [5] Brown 1898.

Iso-lichenin is much less abundant and resembles soluble starch, but on digestion yields only dextrins—no sugar. It may be concluded, judging from the chemical nature of the mucilage, from the resistance of its constituents to digestion and from the small amount present in the jelly, that its nutritive value is practically nil[1].

It has been stated that "reindeer moss" in times of food scarcity is powdered and mixed with "Iceland moss" and rye to make bread in North Finland. Johnson confirms this and cites the evidence of a Dr Clarke that: "to our surprise we found we might eat of it with as much ease as of the heart of a fine lettuce. It tasted like wheat-bran, but after swallowing it, there remained in the throat and upon the palate a gentle heat, or sense of burning, as if a small quantity of pepper had been mixed with the lichen."

The Egyptians[2] have used *Evernia prunastri*, more rarely *E. furfuracea*, in baking. In the eighteenth century fermentative agents such as yeast were unknown to them, and these lichens, which were imported from more northern lands, were soaked in water for two hours and the solution then mixed with the flour to give a much appreciated flavour to the unleavened bread.

In India[3] a species of *Parmelia* (near to *P. perlata*) known in the Telegu language as "rathapu" or rock-flower has been used as a food, generally prepared as a curry, by the natives in the Bellary district (Madras Presidency), and is esteemed as a delicacy. It is also used medicinally. The collecting of rathapu is carried on during the hot weather in April and May, and forms a profitable business.

A note has been published by Calkins[4], on the authority of a correspondent in Japan, that large quantities of *Endocarpon* (*Dermatocarpon*) *miniatum* (Fig. 56) are collected in the mountains of that country for culinary purposes, and largely exported to China as an article of luxury. The local name is "iwataka," meaning stone-mushroom. Properly prepared it resembles tripe. It is possibly the same lichen under a different name, *Gyrophora esculenta*, which is described by Manabu Miyoshi[5] as of great food value in Japan where it is known as "iwatake." It is a greyish-brown leathery "monophyllous" plant of somewhat circular outline and fairly large size, measuring 3 to 13 cm. across. Fertile specimens are rare, and are smaller than the sterile. It grows generally on the steep declivities of damp granitic rocks and is common in various districts of Japan, being especially abundant on such mountains as Kiso, Nikko, Kimano, etc. The face of the precipices is often thickly covered with the lichen growth. The inhabitants collect the plants in large quantities. They dry them and send them to the towns, where they are sold in all vegetable stores; some are even exported to other countries.

---

[1] Hutchinson 1916. [2] Forskål 1875, p. 193. [3] Watt 1890. [4] Calkins 1892.
[5] Miyoshi 1893.

These lichens are not bitter to the taste, nor are they irritating as are other species of the genus. They are on the contrary quite harmless and are much relished by the Japanese on account of their agreeable flavour, in spite of their being somewhat indigestible. Though only determined scientifically in recent times, this edible lichen has long been known, and the risks attending its collection have frequently been described in Old Chinese and Japanese writings.

Other species of *Gyrophora* including *G. polyrhiza* (Fig. 129) and *Umbilicaria*, black leathery lichens which grow on rocks in northern regions,

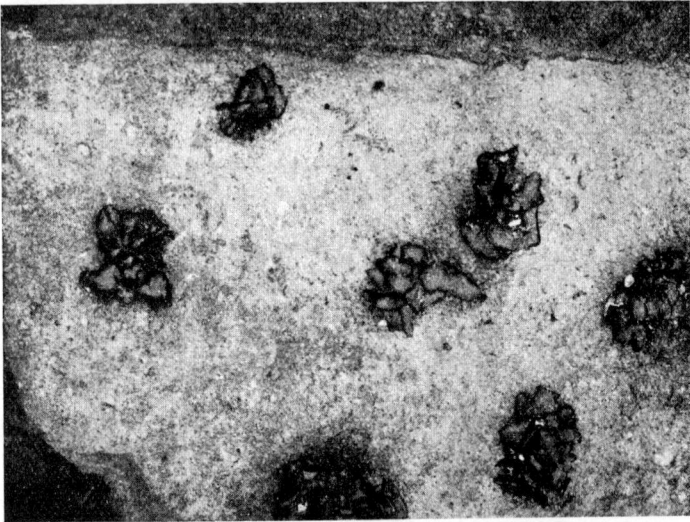

Fig. 129. *Gyrophora polyrhiza* Koerb. (S.H., *Photo.* reduced).

have also been used as food. They are the "Tripe de Roche" or Rock Tripe of Arctic regions, a name given to the plants by Canadian fur-hunters. They have been eaten by travellers and others in desperate straits for food; but though to a certain extent nutritious, they are bitter and nauseous, and cause severe internal irritation if the bitter acids are not first extracted by boiling or soaking.

Of more historical interest is the desert lichen *Lecanora esculenta*, supposed to be the manna[1] of the Israelites, and still called "bread from heaven." Eversmann[2] wrote an account of its occurrence and qualities, and fuller information was given by Berkeley[3]: when mixed with meal to a third of its weight it is made into bread and eaten by the desert tribes. It grows abundantly in North Africa and in many parts of Western Asia, on the rocks or on soil. It is easily broken off and driven into heaps by the wind; and has been reported as covering the soil to a depth of 15 cm. to

[1] See p. 422.   [2] Eversmann 1825.   [3] Berkeley 1849.

20 cm. with irregular contorted lumps varying in size from a pea to a small nut (Fig. 130). Externally these are clear brown or whitish; the interior is white, and consists of branching interlaced hyphae, with masses of calcium oxalate crystals, averaging about 60 per cent. or more of the whole substance.

A still more exhaustive account is given by Visiani[1], who quotes the experience of a certain General Jussuf, who had tested its value in the Sahara as food for his soldiers. When bread

Fig. 130. *Lecanora esculenta* Eversm. Loose nodules of the sterile thallus.

was made from the lichen alone it was friable and without consistency; when mixed with a tenth portion of meal it was similar to the soldiers' ordinary bread, and had something of the same taste. The General also gave it as fodder to the horses, some of them being nourished with the lichen and a mixture of barley for three weeks without showing any ill effects. It is also said that camels, gazelles and other quadrupeds eat it with advantage, though it is in any case a very defective food.

A remarkable deposit of the lichen occurred in recent times in Mesopotamia during a violent storm of hail. After the hail had melted, the ground was seen to be covered, and specimens were sent to Errera[2] for examination. He identified it as *Lecanora esculenta*. In his opinion two kinds of manna are alluded to in the Bible: in one case (Exodus xvi.) it is the sweet gum exuded from the tamarisk that is described; the other kind (Numbers xi.), he thinks, plainly refers to the lichen. He considers that its nutritive value must be very low, and it can only be valued as food in times of famine.

B. Lichens as Medicine

a. Ancient Remedies. An interesting note has been published by Müller-Argau[3] which seems to trace back the medicinal use of lichens to a very remote age. He tells us that Dr Schweinfurth, the distinguished traveller, who made a journey through the valley of the Nile in 1864, sent to him from Cairo a piece of lichen thallus found in a vase along with berries of *Juniperus excelsa* and of *Sapindus*, with some other undetermined seeds. The vase dated from the 18th Dynasty (1700 to 1600 B.C.), and the plants contained in it must thus have lain undisturbed over 3000 years. The broken pieces of the lichen thallus were fairly well preserved; they were extremely soft and yellowish-white and almost entirely decorticate, but on the under surfaces there remained a few black patches, which, on microscopical examination, enabled Müller to identify them as scraps of *Evernia furfuracea*. This lichen does not grow in Egypt, but it is still sold there along with

[1] Visiani 1867.   [2] Errera 1893.   [3] Müller-Argau 1881, p. 526.

Cetraria islandica and some other lichens as foreign drugs. Dr Schweinfurth considered his discovery important as proving the use of foreign remedies by the ancient Egyptians.

b. DOCTRINE OF "SIGNATURES." In the fifteenth century A.D. there was in the study and treatment of disease a constant attempt to follow the guidance of nature. It was believed that Providence had scattered here and there on plants "signatures," or resemblances more or less vague to parts of the human body, or to the diseases to which man is subject, thus indicating the appropriate specific.

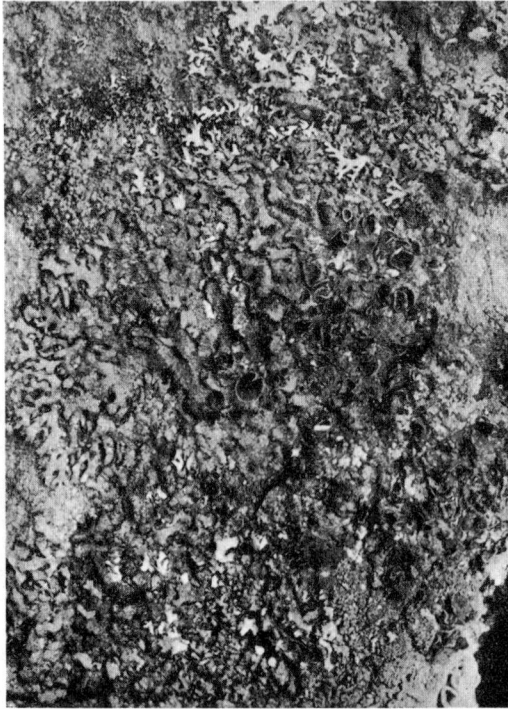

Fig. 131. *Parmelia saxatilis* Ach. (S. H., *Photo.*).

Lichens among other plants in which any "signature" could be detected or imagined were therefore constantly prescribed: the long filaments of *Usnea barbata* were used to strengthen the hair; *Lobaria pulmonaria*, the true lung-wort, with its pitted reticulate surface (Fig. 72), was marked as a suitable remedy for lung troubles; *Xanthoria parietina* being a yellow lichen was supposed to cure jaundice, and *Peltigera aphthosa*, the thallus of which is dotted with small wart-like tubercles[1], was recommended for children who suffered from the "thrush" eruption.

[1] See p. 138.

The doctrine reached the height of absurdity in the extravagant value set on a lichen found growing on human skulls, "Muscus cranii humani" or "Muscus ex cranio humano." There are a number of lichens that grow indifferently on a variety of substances, and not infrequently on bones lying in the open. This skull lichen[1], *Parmelia saxatilis* (Fig. 131) or some other, was supposed to be worth its weight in gold as a cure for epilepsy. Parkinson[2] tells us in all confidence "it groweth upon the bare scalps of men and women that have lyen long...in former times much accounted of because it is rare and hardly gotten, but in our own times much more set by, to make the 'Unguentum Sympatheticum' which cureth wounds without the local application of salves...but as Crollius hath it, it should be taken from the sculls of those that have been hanged or executed for offences." Ray[3] says that the same gruesome plant "is celebrated by several authors as useful in haemorrhages and is said to be an ingredient of the famous 'Unguentum Armarium[4],' reported to have been invented by Paracelsus." Another lost ointment!

c. CURE FOR HYDROPHOBIA. Still another lichen to which extraordinary virtue was ascribed, was the very common ground species *Peltigera canina* (Fig. 54), a preparation of which was used in the cure of rabies. Dillenius[5] has published in full the prescription as "A certain Cure for the Bite of a Mad Dog" which was given to him by a very celebrated physician of that day, Dr Richard Mead, who had found it effective:

"Let the patient be blooded at the arm, nine or ten ounces. Take of the herb called in Latin *Lichen cinereus terrestris*, in English Ash-coloured ground liverwort, clean'd, dry'd and powder'd half an ounce. Of black pepper powder'd two drachms.

"Mix these well together and divide the Powder into four Doses, one of which must be taken every Morning, fasting, for four Mornings successively in half a Pint of Cow's Milk warm. After these four Doses are taken, the Patient must go into the cold bath, or a cold Spring or River, every Morning fasting, for a Month. He must be dipt all over but not stay in (with his head above water) longer than half a minute, if the Water be very cold. After this he must go in three Times a Week for a Fortnight longer."

Lightfoot[6], some forty years later, refers to this medicine as "the once celebrated 'Pulvis antilyssus,' much recommended by the great Dr Mead." He adds that "it is much to be lamented that the success of this medicine has not always answered the expectation. There are instances where the application has not prevented the Hydrophobia, and it is very uncertain

---

[1] From an examination of old figures of the *Muscus cranii*, Arnold (1892, p. 53) has decided that several kinds of lichens or hepatics are included in this designation.

[2] Parkinson 1640, p. 1313.   [3] Ray 1686, p. 117.   [4] Amoreux 1787, p. 46.

[5] Dillenius 1741, p. 202.   [6] Lightfoot 1777, II. p. 846.

whether it has been at all instrumental in keeping off that disorder." Belief in
the efficacy of the powder died out before the end of the century but the echo
of the famous remedy remains in the name *Peltigera canina*, the dog lichen.

  d. POPULAR REMEDIES. Lichens with very few exceptions are non-
poisonous plants. They owed their repute as curative herbs to the presence
in the thallus of lichenin and of some bitter or astringent substances, which,
in various ailments, proved of real service to the patient, though they have
now been discarded in favour of more effective drugs. Some of them, on
account of their bitter taste, were frequently used as tonics to replace

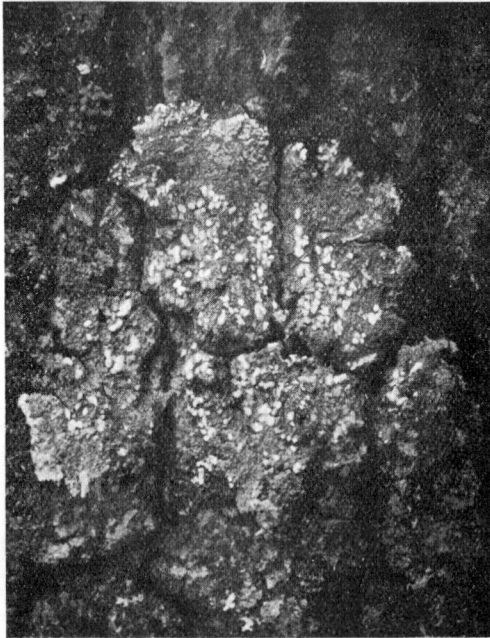

Fig. 132. *Pertusaria amara* Nyl. on bark (S. H., *Photo.*).

quinine in attacks of fever. Several species of *Pertusaria*, such as the bitter
P. amara (Fig. 132), and of *Cladonia* as well as *Cetraria islandica* (Fig. 128),
were recommended in cases of intermittent fever; species of *Usnea* and
others, as for instance *Evernia furfuracea*, were used as astringents in
haemorrhages; others were given for coughs, *Cladonia pyxidata* (Fig. 69)
being supposed to be specially valuable in whooping cough.

  One of the most frequently prescribed lichens was the tree lung-wort
(*Lobaria pulmonaria*) (Fig. 72). It was first included among medical plants
by Dorstenius[1], a Professor at Marburg; he gives a good figure and supplies

[1] Dorstenius 1540.

directions for its preparation as a cure for chest complaints. The doctrine of "signatures" influenced practitioners in its favour, but it contains lichenin which acts as an emollient. In England, it was taken up by the famous Dr Culpepper[1], who, however, believed in astrology even more than in signatures. He says: "it is of great use with many physicians to help the diseases of the lungs and for coughs, wheesings and shortness of breath which it cureth both in man and beast." He adds that " Jupiter seems to own the herb." A century later we find Dr John Hill[2], who was a physician as well as a naturalist, stating that the great tree lung-wort has been at all times famous in diseases of the breast and lungs, but by that time "it was not much used owing to change in fashions."

The only lichen that has stood the test of time and experience as a real remedy is *Cetraria islandica*, and even the " Iceland moss " is now rarely prescribed. The first mention in literature of this famous plant occurs in Cordus[3] as the *Muscus* with crisp leaves. Some years later it figures among the medicinal plants in Sibbald's[4] *Chronicle of the Scottish Flora*, and Ray[5] wrote of it about the same time as being known for its curative and alimentary properties. It was Linnaeus[6], and later Scopoli[7], who gave it the important place it held so long in medicine. It has been used with advantage in many chronic affections as an emollient and tonic. Cramer[8] in a lengthy dissertation gathered together the facts pertaining to its use as a food, a medicine and for dyeing, and he gives recipes he had himself prescribed with marked success in many different maladies. It has been said that if "Iceland moss" accomplished all the good it was alleged to do, it was indeed a " Divine gift to man."

The physiological action of cetrarin (acid principle of the lichen) on living creatures has been studied by Kobert[9] and his pupils. It has not any poisonous effect when injected into the blood, nor does it work any harm when taken into the stomach even of small animals, so that it may be safely given to the most delicate patients. Nearly always after small doses peristaltic movements in the intestines are induced which indicate that as a drug it might be of service in the case of enfeebled organs. In larger doses it may cause collapse in animals, but if administered as free cetraric acid it passes through the stomach unchanged to become slowly and completely dissolved in the intestine. The mucous membrane of the intestine of animals that had been treated with an overdose, was found to be richer in blood so that it seems as if cetrarin might be of service in chlorosis and in assisting digestion.

Cetrarin has also been proved to be a nerve excitant which might be used with advantage in mental maladies.

[1] Culpepper 1652.   [2] Hill 1751.   [3] Cordus 1561.   [4] Sibbald 1684.   [5] Ray 1686.
[6] Linnaeus 1737.   [7] Scopoli 1760.   [8] Cramer 1880.   [9] Kobert 1895.

C. Lichens as Poisons

Though the acid substances of lichens are most of them extremely irritating when taken internally, very few lichens are poisonous. Keegan[1] writing on this subject considers this quality of comparative innocuousness as a distinctive difference between fungi and lichens and he decides that it proves the latter to be higher organisms from a physiological point of view: "the colouring matters being true products of deassimilation, whereas those of fungi are decomposition or degradation waste products of the albuminoids akin to alkaloids."

The two outstanding exceptions to this general statement are the two Alpine species *Letharia vulpina* and *Cetraria pinastri*. The former contains vulpiniç acid in the cortical cells, the crystals of which are lemon-yellow in the mass. *Cetraria pinastri* produces pinastrinic acid in the hyphae of the medulla and the crystals are a beautiful orange or golden yellow.

These lichens, more especially *Letharia vulpina*, have been used by Northern peoples to poison wolves. Dead carcasses are stuffed with a mixture of lichen and powdered glass and exposed in the haunts of wolves in time of frost. Henneguy[2], who insists on the non-poisonous character of all lichens, asserts that the broken glass is the fatal ingredient in the mixture, but Kobert[3], who has proved the poisonous nature of vulpinic acid, says that the wounds caused by the glass render the internal organs extremely sensitive to the action of the lichen.

Kobert, Neubert[4] and others have recorded the results of experiments on living animals with these poisons. They find that *Letharia vulpina* either powdered or in solution has an exciting effect on the mucous membrane. Elementary organisms treated with a solution of the lichen succumbed more quickly than in a solution of the acid as a salt. Kobert concluded that vulpinic acid is a poison of protoplasm.

He further tested the effect of the poison on both cold- and warm-blooded animals. Administered as a sodium salt, 4 mg. proved fatal to frogs. The effect on warm-blooded animals was similar. A sodium salt, whether swallowed or administered as subcutaneous or intravenous injections, was poisonous. Cats were the most sensitive—hedgehogs the least—of all the animals that were subjected to the experiments. Volkard's[5] synthetic preparation of vulpinic acid gave the same results as the solution directly extracted from the lichens.

---

[1] Keegan 1905.   [2] Henneguy 1883.   [3] Kobert 1895.   [4] Neubert 1893.
[5] See p. 228

D. Lichens used in Tanning, Brewing and Distilling

The astringent property in *Cetraria islandica* and in *Lobaria pulmonaria* has been made use of in tanning leather. The latter lichen grows commonly on oak and could hardly be gathered in sufficient quantity to be of commercial importance. Like many other lichens it develops very slowly. *Lobaria pulmonaria* has also been used to replace hops in the brewing of beer. Gmelin[1] in his journey through Siberia visited a monastery at Ussolka where the monks employed it for this purpose. The beer tasted exactly like that made with hops, but was more intoxicating. The lichen in that country grew on pine-trees.

Lichens have in more modern times been used in the preparation of alcohol. The process of manufacture was discovered by Roy of Tonnerre, early in the nineteenth century, and was described by Léorier[2]. It was further improved by Stenberg[3], a Professor of Chemistry in Stockholm. Roy had worked with *Physcia ciliaris*, *Ramalina fraxinea*, *R. fastigiata*, *R. farinacea* and *Usnea florida*, but Stenberg and distillers after his time[4] made more use of *Cladonia rangiferina* (Fig. 127), *Cetraria islandica* (Fig. 128) and *Alectoria jubata*.

By treatment with weak sulphuric or nitric acid the lichenin of the thallus is transformed into glucose which on fermentation forms alcohol. Stenberg found that 68 per cent. of the weight in *Cladonia rangiferina* was a "sugar" from which a good brandy could be prepared : a kilogramme of the lichens furnished half a litre of alcohol. The Professor followed up his researches by establishing a distillery near Stockholm. His papers contain full instructions as to collecting and preparing the plants. Henneguy[5], writing in 1883, stated that the fabrication of alcohol from lichens was then a large and increasing industry in Sweden. The whole industry seems, however, to have fallen into disuse very soon : Wainio[6], quoting Hellbom[7], states that the various distilleries were already closed in 1884, because of the exhaustion of the lichen in the neighbourhood, and the impossibility of obtaining sufficient supplies of such slow-growing plants.

E. Dyeing Properties of Lichens

a. Lichens as Dye-plants. Knowledge as to the dyeing properties of lichens dates back to a remote antiquity. It has been generally accepted that lichen-colours are indicated by the prophet Ezekiel in his denunciation of Tyre: "blue and purple from the Isles of Elishah was that which covered thee." Theophrastus describes certain plants as growing in Crete, and being

[1] Gmelin 1752, p. 425. [2] Léorier 1825. [3] Stenberg 1868. [4] Richard 1877.
[5] Henneguy 1883. [6] Wainio 1887, p. 47. [7] Hellbom 1886, p. 72.

used to dye wool, etc., and Pliny in his *Phycos Thalassion* is also understood as referring to the lichen *Roccella*, "with crisp leaves, used in Crete for dyeing garments."

Information as to the dyeing properties of certain lichens is given in most of the books or papers dealing with these plants from the herbals onwards. Hoffmann[1] devoted a large part of his *Commentatio de vario Lichenum usu* to the dye-lichens, and, illustrating his work, are a series of small rectangular coloured blocks representing samples of woollen cloth dyed with different lichens. There are seventy-seven of these samples with the colour names used by French dyers.

An important treatise on the subject translated into French was also contributed by Westring[2]. He desired to draw attention to the tinctorial properties of lichens other than the *Roccellae* which do not grow in Sweden. The Swedes, he states, already used four to six lichens as dye-plants, but only for one colour. He demonstrated by his improved methods that other colours and of finer tint could be obtained. He describes the best methods both of extraction and of dyeing, and then follows with an account of the different lichens likely to be of service. The treatise was subsequently published at greater length in Swedish[3] with twenty-four very fine coloured illustrations of the lichens used, and with sample blocks of the colours to be obtained.

b. THE ORCHIL LICHEN, ROCCELLA. The value of *Roccella* as a dye-plant had been lost sight of until it was accidentally rediscovered, early in the fourteenth century, by a Florentine merchant called Federigo. He introduced its use into Florence, and as he retained the industry in his own hands he made a large fortune, and founded the family of the Orcellarii, called later the Rucellarii or Rucellai, hence the botanical name, *Roccella*. The product was called *orseille* for which the English name is orchil or archil. Another origin suggested for orchil is the Spanish name of the plant, *Orcigilia*. There are a number of different species that vary in the amount of dye-product. Most of them grow on rocks by the sea-side in crowded bluish-grey or whitish tufts of strap-shaped or rounded stiff narrow fronds varying in length up to about six inches or more. The main supply of "weeds" came from the Levant until the fifteenth century when supplies were obtained from the Canaries (long considered to produce the best varieties), Cape Verd and the African coasts. The geographical distribution of the *Roccellae* is very wide: they grow on warm sea-coasts all over the globe, more particularly in Angola, the Cape, Mozambique, Madagascar, in Asia, in Australia, and in Chili and Peru.

Zopf[4] has proved the existence of two different colouring substances among the Roccellas: in *R. fuciformis* (Fig. 57) and *R. fucoides* (both

[1] Hoffmann 1787. [2] Westring 1792 and 1793. [3] Westring 1805–1809. [4] Zopf 1907.

British species), in *R. Montagnei* and *R. peruensis* the acid present is erythrin; in *R. tinctoria*, *R. portentosa* and *R. sinuensis* it is lecanoric acid. In *R. tinctoria* (Fig. 133), according to Ronceray[1], the acid is located chiefly in the gonidial layer and the soredia but is absent from the cortex and centre. In *R. portentosa* it is abundant in the cortex and central layer, while scarcely to be detected in the gonidial layer, and it is wanting altogether in the soredia. In *R. Montagnei* it is chiefly found in the cortex and the gonidial layer, and is absent from the soredia and from the medulla.

c. PURPLE DYES: ORCHIL, CUDBEAR AND LITMUS. Orseille or orchil is formed not only from erythrin and lecanoric acid (orseillic acid), but also from erythrinic, gyrophoric, evernic and ramalic acids[2] and may be obtained from any lichen containing these substances. By the action of ammonia the acids are split up into orcin and carbonic acid. In time, under the influence of ammonia and the oxygen of the air[3], orcin becomes orcein which is the colouring principle of orchil; the perfecting of the process may take a month. The dye is used for animal fibres such as wool and silk; it has no effect on cotton.

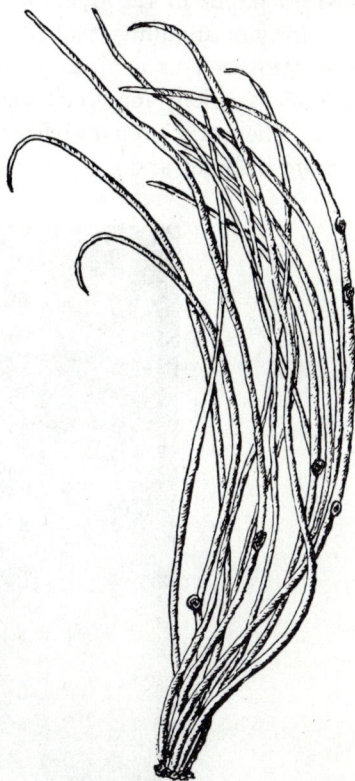

Fig. 133. *Roccella tinctoria* Ach. From the Cape of Good Hope.

There are several different preparations on the market, chiefly obtained from France and Holland; orchil or orseille in the form of a solution, cudbear (persio of Germany) almost the same, but manufactured into a violet-reddish powder, and litmus (tournesol of France) which is prepared in a slightly different manner. At one time the lichen, broken into small pieces, was soaked in urine; a fermentation process was set up, then lime and potash with an admixture of alum were added. The mass of material when ready was pressed into cubes and dried in the air. Commercial litmus contains three substances, erythrolein, erythrolitmin and azolitmin; the last named, which is the true litmus, is a dark brown amorphous powder soluble in water, and forming a blue solution with alkalies.

[1] Ronceray 1904. [2] Zopf 1907.
[3] Zahlbruckner (1905, p. 109) quotes from Czapek a statement that orchil fermentation is brought about by an obligate aerobic bacillus.

An aqueous solution of litmus when exactly neutralized by an acid is violet coloured; it becomes red with the smallest trace of free acid, or blue with free alkali. Litmus paper is prepared by steeping specially prepared unsized paper in the dye solution. It is as a ready and sensitive indicator of acidity or alkalinity that litmus is of so much value. According to Zopf[1] it is also used as a blueing agent in washing and as a colouring of wine. Litmus is chiefly manufactured in Holland. Still another substance some-what differently prepared from the same lichens is sold as French purple, a more brilliant and durable colour than orchil.

Fig. 134. *Lecanora tartarea* Ach. (S. H., *Photo.*).

d. OTHER ORCHIL LICHENS. Though species of *Roccella* rank first in importance as dye-plants, purple and blue colours are obtained, as indicated above, from other very different lichens. Lindsay[2] extracted orchil from about twenty species. Those most in use in northern countries are on the whole less rich in colouring substances; they are: *Umbilicaria pustulata*, species of *Gyrophora*, *Parmelia* and *Pertusaria*, and above all *Lecanora tartarea* (Fig. 134). The last named, one of the hardiest and most abundant

[1] Zopf 1907, p. 393.   [2] Lindsay 1855.

of rock- or soil-lichens, is chiefly used in Scotland and Sweden (hence the name "Swedish moss") to furnish a red or crimson dye. In Scotland all dye-lichens are called "crottles," but the term "cudbear" was given to *Lecanora tartarea* (either the lichen or the dye-product); it was acquired from a corrupt pronunciation of the Christian name of Dr Cuthbert Gordon, a chemist, who, according to Bohler[1], obtained a patent for his process of producing the dye, or who first employed it on a great scale in Glasgow. Johnson[2] remarks that the colour yielded by cudbear, if well prepared, is a fine, clear, but not very bright purple. It is, he alleges, not permanent. Like other orchil substances it is without effect on cotton or linen.

e. PREPARATION OF ORCHIL. A general mode of treatment of dye-lichens recommended by Lauder Lindsay[3] for home production of orchil, cudbear and litmus is as follows:

1. Careful washing, drying and cleansing to separate earthy and other impurities.

2. Pulverization into a coarse or fine pulp with water.

3. Repeated addition of ammoniacal liquor of a certain strength, obtainable from several sources (*e.g.* putrid urine, gas liquor, etc.).

4. Frequent stirring of the fermenting mass so as to ensure full exposure of every part thereof to the action of atmospheric oxygen.

5. Addition of alkalies in some cases (*e.g.* potash or soda), to heighten or modify colour; and of chalk, gypsum and other substances to impart consistence.

f. BROWN AND YELLOW DYES. The extracting of these colours from lichens is also a very old industry. Linnaeus found during his journey to Lappland[4], undertaken when he was quite a young man, that the women in the northern countries made use of a brown lichen for dyeing which is evidently *Parmelia omphalodes* (Fig. 135). He describes it as a "rich *Lichenoides* of a brown stercoraceous colour," and he has stated that it grew' in such abundance in the Island of Aland, that every stone was covered, especially near the sea. In the *Plantae tinctoriae*[5] there is a record of six other lichens used for dyeing: *Lichen Roccella, L. tartareus, L. saxatilis, L. juniperinus, L. parietinus* and *L. candelarius*. The value of *Lichen omphalodes* was also emphasized by Lightfoot; the women of Scotland evidently appreciated its dyeing properties as much as other northern peoples.

A series of memoirs on the utility of lichens written by Willemet[6], Amoreux and Hoffmann, and jointly published at Lyons towards the end of the eighteenth century, represents the views as to the economic value of lichens held by scientific botanists of that time. All of them cite the

---

[1] Bohler 1835, N. 10.   [2] Johnson 1861.   [3] Lindsay 1855.   [4] Linnaeus 1711.
[5] Linnaeus 1760.   [6] Willemet etc. 1787.

various dye-species, and Hoffmann, as already stated, gives illustrations of colours that can be obtained. It has been once and again affirmed that *Parmelia saxatilis* yields a red colour, but Zopf[1] denies this. It contains saxatillic acid which is colourless when extracted but on boiling gives a clear reddish-yellow to reddish-brown solution which dyes wool and silk directly without the aid of a mordant. Zopf[1] observed the process of dyeing

Fig. 135. *Parmelia omphalodes* Ach. (S. H., *Photo.*).

followed in South Tyrol: a layer of the lichen was placed in a cooking pot, above this a layer of the material to be dyed, then lichen and again the material until the pot was filled. It was covered with water and boiled three to four hours, resulting in a beautiful rust-brown and peculiarly fast dye.

Reddish- or rust-brown dye is also obtained from *Haematomma ventosum* and *H. coccineum*, a yellow-brown from *Parmelia conspersa* (salazinic acid), and other shades of brown from *Parmelia perlata*, *P. physodes*, *Lobaria pulmonaria* and *Cetraria islandica*.

Yellow lichens in general furnish yellow dyes, as for instance *Xanthoria parietina* which gives either brown or yellow according to treatment and *Cetraria juniperina* which forms a beautiful yellow colouring substance on

[1] Zopf 1907.

boiling. *Teloschistes flavicans* and *Letharia vulpina* yield very similar yellow dyes, and from *Lecanora parella* (Fig. 39), *Pertusaria melaleuca* and *Usnea barbata* yellow colours have been obtained. *Candelariella vitellina* and *Xanthoria lychnea* both contain yellow colouring agents and have been employed by the Swedes for dyeing the candles used in religious ceremonies.

g. COLLECTING OF DYE-LICHENS. Lauder Lindsay[1] made exhaustive studies of dye-lichens both in the field and in the laboratory, and recorded results he obtained from the micro-chemical examination of 540 different specimens. He sought to revive and encourage the use of their beautiful colour products among country people; he has given the following practical hints to collectors:

1. That crustaceous dwarf pale-coloured species growing on rocks, and especially on sea-coasts, are most likely to yield red and purple dyes similar to orchil, cudbear or litmus; while on the other hand the largest, most handsome foliaceous or fruticose species are least likely.

2. That the colour of the thallus is no indication of colorific power (in orchil lichens), inasmuch as the red or purple colouring substances are the result of chemical action on crystalline colo..iic "principles" previously devoid of colour.

3. That alterations in physical characters, chemical composition and consequently in dyeing properties are very liable to be produced by modification in the following external circumstances:

    (i)   Degree of moisture.
    (ii) Degree of heat.
    (iii) Degree of exposure to light and air.
    (iv) Climate.
    (v) Elevation above the sea.
    (vi) Habitat; nature of basis of support.
    (vii) Age.
    (viii) Seasons and atmospheric vicissitudes, etc.

August has been recommended as the best month for collecting dye-lichens: *i.e.* just after the season of greatest light and heat when the accumulation of acids will be at its maximum.

Some of the acids found useful in dyeing occur in the thalli of a large number of lichens, many of which are too scantily developed to be of any economic value. Thus salazinic acid which gives the effective yellow-brown dye in *Parmelia conspersa* was found by Zopf in 13 species and varieties. It has since been located by Lettau[2] in 72 different lichens, many of them, however, with poorly developed or scanty thalli, so that no technical use can be made of them.

[1] Lindsay 1855.   [2] Lettau 1914.

h. LICHEN COLOURS AND SPECTRUM CHARACTERS. In a comparative study of vegetable colouring substances, Sorby[1] extracted yellow colouring matters from various plants distinguished by certain spectrum characters. He called them the "lichenoxanthine group" because, as he explains, "these xanthines occur in a more marked manner in lichens than in plants having true leaves and fronds. Orange lichenoxanthine he found in *Peltigera canina*, *Platysma glaucum*, etc., when growing well exposed to the sun. Lichenoxanthine he obtained from the fungus *Clavaria fusiformis*; it was difficult to separate from orange lichenoxanthine. Yet another, which he terms yellow lichenoxanthine, he obtained most readily from *Physcia* (*Xanthoria*) *parietina*. The solutions of these substances vary according to Sorby in giving a slightly different kind of spectrum. He did not experiment on their dyeing properties.

F. LICHENS IN PERFUMERY

a. LICHENS AS PERFUMES. There are a few lichens that find a place in Gerard's[2] *Herball* and that are praised by him as being serviceable to man. Among others he writes of a "Moss that partakes of the bark of which it is engendered. It is to be used in compositions which serve for sweet perfumes and that take away wearisomeness." At a much later date we find Amoreux[3] recording the fact that *Lichen* (*Evernia*) *prunastri*, known as "Moussé de Chêne," was used as a perfume plant.

Though lichens are not parasitic, the idea that they owed something of their quality to the substratum was firmly held by the old herbalists. It appears again and again in the descriptions of medicinal lichens, and still persists in this matter of perfumes. Hue[4] states in some notes to a larger work, that French perfumers extract an excellent perfume from *Evernia prunastri* (Fig. 59) known as "Mousse des Chênes" (Oak moss), and it appears that the plants which grow on oak contain more perfume than those which live on other trees. The collectors often gather along with *Evernia prunastri* other species such as *Ramalina calicaris* and *R. fraxinea*, but these possess little if any scent. A still finer perfume is extracted[5] from *Lobaria pulmonaria* called "moss from the base of the oaks," but as it is a rarer lichen than *Evernia* it is less used. Most of the Stictaceae, to which family *Lobaria* belongs, have a somewhat disagreeable odour, but this one forms a remarkable exception, which can be tested by macerating the thallus and soaking it in spirit : it will then be found to exhale a pleasant and very persistent scent. These lichens are not, however, used alone; they are combined with other substances in the composition of much appreciated perfumes. The thallus possesses also the power of retaining scent and, for this reason, lichens frequently form an ingredient of potpourri.

[1] Sorby 1873.   [2] Gerard 1597.   [3] Amoreux 1787.   [4] Hue 1889.   [5] Hue 1900.

b. LICHENS AS HAIR-POWDER. In the days of white-powdered hair, use was occasionally made of *Ramalina calicaris* which was ground down and substituted for the starch that was more commonly employed.

In older books on lichenology constant reference is made to a hair-powder called " Pulvis Cyprius " or " Cyprus powder " and very celebrated in the seventeenth century. It was believed to beautify and cleanse the hair by removing scurf, etc. *Evernia prunastri* was one of the chief ingredients of the powder, but it might be replaced by *Physcia ciliaris* or by *Usnea*. The virtue of the lichens lay in their capacity to absorb and retain perfume. The powder was for long manufactured at Montpellier and was a valuable monopoly. Its composition was kept secret, but Bauhin[1] (J.) published an account of the ingredients and how to mix them. Under the title " Pulvis Cyprius Pretiosius" a more detailed recipe of the famous powder was given by Zwelser[2], a Palatine medical doctor. The lichen employed in his preparation, as in Bauhin's, is *Usnea*, but that may include both *Evernia* and *Physcia* as they are all tree plants. He gives elaborate directions as to the cleaning of the lichen from all impurities—it is to be beaten with a stick, washed repeatedly with limpid and pure water, placed in a linen cloth and dried in the sun till it is completely bleached and deprived of all odour and taste.

When well dried it was placed in a basket in alternate layers with freshly gathered, entire flowers of roses and jasmine (or flowers of orange and citrus when possible). The whole was compressed by a heavy weight, and each day the flowers were renewed until the "Usnea" was thoroughly impregnated with a very fragrant odour. It was then reduced to a fine powder and ready for other ingredients. To each pound should be added:

1½ oz. powdered root of white Iris.

1½ oz. of *Cyperus* (a sedge).

1 scruple or half drachm of musk reduced to a pulp with fragrant spirit of roses.

½ drachm of ambergris dissolved in a scruple of genuine oil of roses, or oil of jasmine or oranges as may be preferred.

Zwelser adds :

"This most fragrant royal powder when sprinkled on the head invigorates by its remarkably pleasant odour; by its astringency and dryness it removes all impurities, and, since it operates with no viscosity nor sticks firmly either to skin or hair, it is easily removed from the hair of the head."

[1] Bauhin 1650, p. 88.   [2] Zwelser 1672.

G. Some minor Uses of Lichens

The possibility of extracting gum or mucilage from lichens was demonstrated by the Russian scientist, Professor Georgi[1], and later by Amoreux[2], the method employed being successive boiling of the plants. The larger foliose or fruticose forms were specially recommended.

At a later date, during the Napoleonic wars, the "ingenious Lord Dundonald[3]," of great fame as an inventor, published an account of the extraction process and of the application of the gum to calico-printing, staining and manufacture of paper, dressing and stiffening silks. Lord Dundonald's aim was to replace the gum Senegal, then a monopoly of the French, who were in possession of the Settlement of Senegambia. He took out a patent for his invention, but whether the gum was successfully used is not recorded.

According to Henneguy[4], lichen mucilage, as a substitute for gum arabic, has been used at Lyons with advantage in the fabrication of dyed materials.

---

[1] Georgi 1779.   [2] Amoreux 1787.   [3] Dundonald 1801.   [4] Henneguy 1883.

APPENDIX

POSTSCRIPT TO CHAPTER VII[1]

IN a remarkable paper on *The Symbiosis of Lichens*[2], Dr A. Henry Church has presented a new and striking view of the origin and development of lichens: he has sought to link them up with other classes of vegetation that, in the great transmigration, passed from sea to land. As we know from his *Thalassiophyta*[3] *and the subaerial transmigration*, he holds that primeval algae of advanced form and structure were left exposed on dry land by the gradually receding waters, and those that successfully adapted themselves to the changed conditions formed the basis of the land flora. A certain number of the algae lost their surface tissues containing chlorophyll and they had perforce to secure from other organic sources the necessary carbohydrates: they adopted a heterotrophic existence as saprophytic or parasitic fungi. Fungi are a backward race (deteriorated according to Dr Church) as regards their soma, but in number, distribution and variety of spore-production, they are eminently successful plants.

Lichens are similarly regarded by Dr Church as derived from stranded contemporaneous types of marine algae—crustaceous, foliose and fruticose, that had also lost their chlorophyll, but by taking into association green algal units of a lower grade they established a vicarious photosynthesis. But, to quote his own words[4], "as the alga-lichen-fungus left the sea, so it remained: it might deteriorate, but it certainly never advanced, once the sea factors which produced it were eliminated, it simply stopped along these lines."

And again[5]: "Lichens thus present an interesting case of an algal race deteriorating along the lines of a heterotrophic existence, yet arrested, as it were, on the somatic down-grade, by the adoption of intrusive algal units of lower degree to subserve photosynthesis (much in the manner of the marine worm *Convoluta*). Thus arrested, they have been enabled to retain more definite expression of more deeply inherent factors of sea-weed habit and construction than any other race of fungi; though closely paralleled by such types as *Xylaria* (Ascomycete) and *Clavaria* (Basidiomycete), which have followed the full fungus progression as holosaprophytic on decaying plant residues."

Dr Church's theory is of vivid interest and might be convincing were there no possibility and no proof of advance within the symbiotic plant, but

---

[1] See p. 302.   [2] *Journ. Bot.* LVIII. pp. 213–9; 262–7, 1920.   [3] *Bot. Memoirs*, 3, Oxford, 1919.
[4] Church *in litt.*   [5] *Journ. Bot. l.c.*

in numbers of crustaceous thalli, there is evident, by normal or abnormal[1] development, the first advance to the formation of rudimentary squamules, a condition diagnosed as subsquamulose. "Deterioration" of the lichen plant—when it occurs owing to unfavourable conditions—is a reversion to the leprose early stage of the association; there is no evidence of reversion from fruticose or foliose to squamulose. A glance at the table of lichen phyla[2] shows progression again and again from the crustaceous forms onwards. In such a phylum as Physciaceae (with colourless polarilocular spores) there is a clear example of a closely connected series; the different types of thallus—crustaceous, squamulose, foliose and fruticose—are all represented and form a natural sequence, being well delimited by the unusual form of the spore and by the presence of parietin in thallus or apothecium.

That there has been development seems absolutely certain, and that along the lines sketched in the chapter on phylogeny. Progress has been mainly in the thallus, but there has also been change and advance in the reproductive organs, more especially in the spores which in several families reach a size and septation unparalleled in fungi. That association with green algal cells stimulated the fungus to new development is the view taken of the lichen plant and emphasized in the present volume. But it seems more in accordance with the polyphyletic origin and recurring parallel development in the phyla that association began at the elementary crustaceous stage, and that the lichen soma was gradually evolved within what is after all a very limited and simple structure.

ADDENDUM

FOOT-NOTE TO PAGE 404

E. M. Holmes[3] has published recently an account of a substance which seems in some respects to answer to the description of manna (Exodus xvi.; Numbers xi.) more nearly than the generally accepted *Lecanora esculenta*. The information is quoted from Swann's book: *Fighting the slave-hunters in Central Africa*. The author writes (p. 116): "I was shown a curious white substance similar to porridge. It was found early in the morning before the sun rose. On examination it was found to possess all the characteristics of the manna......of the Israelites. In appearance it resembled coriander seed, was white in colour like hoar frost, sweet to the taste, melted in the sun and if kept over night was full of worms in the morning. It required to be baked if you intended to keep it for any length of time. It looked as if it was deposited on the ground in the night." The writer has suggested that "the substance might be mushroom spawn as, on the spot where it melted tiny fungi sprung up the next night." Swann's statement has been confirmed by Dr Wareham, a medical missionary from the same district, who states, however, that it is of rare occurrence.

[1] See p. 271 *ante*.   [2] See p. 302 *ante*.
[3] *Chemist and Druggist*, XCII. pp. 25–26, 1920; *Bot. Abstracts*, N. 903, p. 135, 1920.

BIBLIOGRAPHY

OF BOOKS AND PAPERS CITED IN THE TEXT

Acharius, Erik. Lichenographiae Suecicae Prodromus. Linköping, 1798.
—— Methodus Lichenes. Stockholm, 1803.
—— Lichenographia Universalis. Göttingen, 1810.
—— Synopsis Methodica Lichenum. Lund, 1814.
Acton, E. Botrydina vulgaris Bréb., a Primitive Lichen. Ann. Bot. XXIII. pp. 579–587, 1909.
Adanson, M. Famille des Plantes. Paris, 1763.
Agardh, C. A. Dissertatio de Metamorphosi Algarum. Lund, 1820.
Aigret, Clém. Monographie des Cladonia de Belgique. Bull. Soc. Roy. Bot. Belgique, XL. pp. 43–213, 1901.
Allescher, Andreas. Rabenhorst Krypt. Flora, I. 7. Leipzig, 1901–3.
Almquist, S. Monographia Arthoniarum Scandinaviae. K. Svensk. Vet.-Akad. Handl. XVII. No. 6, 69 pp., 1880.
Amoreux, D. M. Recherches et expériences sur les divers Lichens. Lyon, 1787.
Arcangeli, G. Sulla Questione dei Gonidi. Nuovo Giorn. Bot. Ital. VII. p. 270, 1875.
Archer, W. A Résumé of Recent Views respecting the Nature of Lichens. Quart. Journ. Microsc. Sci. XIII. pp. 217–235 (2 pls.), 1873.
—— A Further Résumé of Recent Observations on the "Gonidia-Question." Op. cit. XIV. pp. 115–139, 1874.
—— On apothecia occurring in some Scytonematous and Sirosiphonaceous Algae, in addition to those previously known. Op. cit. XV. p. 27 (1 pl.), 1875.
Arnaud, G. Sur la Cytologie du Capnodium meridionale et du mycelium des Fumagines. Comptes Rendus CLV. pp. 726–728 (figs.), 1912.
Arnold, F. Lichenologische Fragmente XVI. Flora, LVII. pp. 81–89, etc., etc., 1874.
—— Die Lichenen des Fränkischen Juras. Flora, XLI. etc., pp. 81, etc., 1858–1885. Separate publication, Regensburg, 323 pp., 1885.
—— Die Lichenen des Fränkischen Jura. Denkschr. R. Bayer. Bot. Ges. Regensburg, VI. pp. 1–61, 1890.
—— Zur Lichenenflora von München (Issued with the Ber. Bayer. Bot. Ges. München), Abth. I. 147 pp., 1891; II. 76 pp., 1892; III. 45 pp., 1897; IV. 82 pp., 1898; V. 100 pp., 1900; VI. 24 pp., 1901.
Artari, A. Ueber die Entwickelung der grünen Algen unter Ausschluss der Bedingungen der Kohlensäure-assimilation. Bull. Soc. Imp. Nat. Moscou. Nouv. sér. XIV. pp. 39–47, 1899.
—— Zur Ernährungsphysiologie der grünen Algen. Ber. Deutsch. Bot. Ges. XIX. pp. 7–9, 1901.
—— Zur Frage der physiologischen Rassen einiger grüner Algen. Ber. Deutsch. Bot. Ges. XX. pp. 172–175, 1902.
—— Ueber die Bildung des Chlorophylls durch grüne Algen. Ber. Deutsch. Bot. Ges. XX. pp. 201–207, 1902[2].
Babikoff, J. Du Développement des céphalodies sur le thallus du lichen Peltigera aphthosa Hoffm. Bull. Acad. Imp. Sci. St Pétersbourg, XXIV. pp. 548–559 (1 pl.), 1878.
Babington, Churchill. Lichenes in the Botany of the Antarctic Voyage by Joseph Dalton Hooker. II. Flora Novae-Zelandiae, pp. 266–311 (8 pls.). London, 1855.

Bachmann, E. Ueber nichtkrystallisirte Flechtenfarbstoffe, ein Beitrag zur Chemie und Anatomie der Flechten. Pringsh. Jahrb. Wiss. Bot. XXI. pp. 1–61 (1 pl.), 1890.

—— Der Thallus der Kalkflechten. Wiss. Beil. Realsch. Plauen I. v. 26 pp. (1 pl.), 1892, and Ber. Deutsch. Bot. Ges. X. pp. 30–37 (1 pl.), 1892.

—— Zur Frage des Vorkommens von ölfuhrenden Sphaeroidzellen bei Flechten. Ber. Deutsch. Bot. Ges. XXII. pp. 44–46, 1904.

—— Die Beziehungen der Kieselflechten zu ihrem Substrat. Tom. cit. pp. 101–104 (1 pl.), 1904.

—— Die Rhizoidenzone granitbewohnender Flechten. Jahrb. Wiss. Bot. XLIV. pp. 1–40 (2 pls.), 1907.

—— Die Beziehungen der Kieselflechten zu ihrer Unterlage. II. Granat und Quarz. Ber. Deutsch. Bot. Ges. XXIX. pp. 261–273 (figs.), 1911. III. Bergkristall und Flint. Op. cit. XXXV. pp. 464–476, 8 figs., 1917.

—— Der Thallus der Kalkflechten. II. Flechten mit Chroolepusgonidien. Ber. Deutsch. Bot. Ges. XXXI. pp. 3–12 (1 pl.), 1913.

—— Zur Flechtenflora des Erzgebirges. I. Rittersgrün. Hedwigia, LIII. pp. 99–123, 1913. II. Allenburg. Hedwigia, LV. pp. 157–182, 1914.

Bachmann, Freda M. A New Type of Spermogonium and Fertilization in Collema. Ann. Bot. XXVI. pp. 747–760 (1 pl.), 1912.

—— The Origin and Development of the Apothecium in Collema pulposum. Arch. Zellforsch. X. 4, pp. 369–430 (7 pls.), 1913.

Baranetzky, J. Beitrag zur Kenntniss des selbständigen Lebens der Flechtengonidien. Bull. Acad. Imp. Sci. St Pétersbourg XII. pp. 418–431 [1867], 1868.

—— Beitrag zur Kenntniss des selbständigen Lebens der Flechtengonidien. Pringsh. Jahrb. Wiss. Bot. VII. pp. 1–18 (1 pl.), (1868), 1869–70.

Bary, Anton de. Morphologie und Physiologie der Pilze, Flechten und Myxomyceten. Leipzig, 1866.

—— Ueber die Keimung einiger grosssporiger Flechten. Pringsh. Jahrb. Wiss. Bot. v. pp. 201–216 (3 pls.), 1866–7.

—— Die Erscheinung der Symbiose. Naturf. Vers. Cassel, LI. Tagebl. p. 121, 1879.

—— Vergleichende Morphologie und Physiologie der Pilze. Leipzig, 1884.

Bauhin, J. and Cherler, J. H. Historiae Plantarum Universalis I. Lib. II. Yverdun, 1650.

Bauhin, Kaspar. Pinax Theatri botanici, etc. Basle, 1623.

Baur, Erwin. Zur Frage nach der Sexualität der Collemaceen. Ber. Deutsch. Bot. Ges. XVI. pp. 363–367 (1 pl.), 1898.

—— Die Anlage und Entwickelung einiger Flechtenapothecien. Flora, LXXXVIII. pp. 319–332 (2 pls.), 1901.

—— Untersuchungen über die Entwickelungsgeschichte der Flechtenapothecien I. Bot. Zeit. LXII. pp. 21–44 (2 pls.), 1904.

Bayrhoffer. Einiges über Lichenen und deren Befruchtung. Bern. 44 pp. (4 pls.), 1851.

Beckmann, Paul. Untersuchungen über die Verbreitungsmittel von gesteinbewohnenden Flechten im Hochgebirge mit Beziehung zu ihrem Thallusbau. Engler, Bot. Jahrb. XXXVIII. Beibl. pp. 1–72 (10 figs.), 1907.

Berg, Th. Zur Kenntniss des in der Cetraria islandica vorkommenden Lichenins und jodbläuenden Stoffes. Russ. Zeitschr. Pharm. 1873, pp. 129 and 161. See Jahresber. Chemie (1873), p. 848, 1875.

Berkeley, M. J. Note on Lecanora esculenta. Gard. Chron. p. 611 (figs.), 1849.

—— Introduction to Cryptogamic Botany. London, 1857.

Berzelius, J. J. Versuche über die Mischung des Isländischen Mooses und seine Anwendung als Nahrungsmittel. Schweigger Journ. VII. pp. 317–352, 1813.

Beyerinck, M. W. Culturversuche mit Zoochlorellen, Lichenengonidien und anderen niederen Algen. Bot. Zeit. XLIII. pp. 725–739, 741–754, 757–768 781–785 (1 pl.), 1890.

BIBLIOGRAPHY 425

Beyerinck, M. W. Das Assimilationsprodukt der Kohlensäure in den Chromatophoren der Diatomeen. Rec. Trav. Bot. Néerl. I. pp. 28–33, 1904.

Bialosuknia, W. Sur un nouveau genre de Pleurococcacées. Bull. Soc. Bot. Genève. Sér. 2, I. pp. 101–104 (figs.), 1909.

Bioret, G. Contributions à l'étude de l'apothécie chez les Graphidées. Rev. Gén. de Bot. XXVI. pp. 249–252 (1 pl.), 1914.

Bitter, G. Ueber das Verhalten der Krustenflechten beim Zusammentreffen ihrer Ränder. Pringsh. Jahrb. Wiss. Bot. XXXIII. pp. 47–127 (14 figs.), 1899[1].

—— Ueber maschenförmige Durchbrechungen der untern Gewebeschichte oder des gesammten Thallus bei verschiedenen Laub- und Strauchflechten. Botan. Untersuch., Festschrift für Schwendener. Berlin, pp. 120–149 (8 figs.), 1899[2].

—— Ueber die Variabilität einiger Laubflechten und über den Einfluss äusserer Bedingungen auf ihr Wachsthum. Pringsh. Jahrb. Wiss. Bot. XXXVI. pp. 421–492 (7 pls. and figs.), 1901[1].

—— Zur Morphologie und Systematik von Parmelia, Untergattung Hypogymnia. Hedwigia, XL. pp. 171–274 (2 pls., 21 figs.), 1901[2].

—— Zur Soredienbildung. Hedwigia, XLIII. pp. 274–280, 1904[1].

—— Peltigeren-Studien I und II. Ber. Deutsch. Bot. Ges. XXII. pp. 248–254 (1 pl.), 1904[2].

Blackman, V. H. On the Fertilization, Alternation of Generations, and General Cytology of the Uredineae. Ann. Bot. XVIII. pp. 323–373 (3 pls.), 1904.

Blackman, V. H. and Welsford, E. J. The Development of the Perithecium of Polystigma rubrum DC. Ann. Bot. XXVI. pp. 761–767 (2 pls.), 1912.

Bohler, J. Lichenes Britannici. Sheffield, 1835.

Bonnier, Gaston. Recherches expérimentales sur la synthèse des lichens dans un milieu privé de germes. Comptes Rendus, CIII. p. 942, 1886.

—— Germination des spores des lichens sur les protonémas des Mousses et sur des Algues différent des gonidies du Lichen. Comptes Rendus Soc. Biol., Sér. 8, V. pp. 541–543, 1888.

—— Germination des lichens sur les protonémas des Mousses. Rev. Génér. Bot. I. pp. 165–169 (1 pl.), 1889[1].

—— Recherches sur la synthèse des lichens. Ann. Sci. Nat., Sér. 7, IX. pp. 1–34 (5 pls.), 1889[2].

Bornet, Ed. Description de trois lichens nouveaux. Mém. Soc. Sci. Nat. Cherbourg, IV. pp. 225–234 (4 pls.), 1856.

—— Sur les gonidies des Lichens. Comptes Rendus, Paris, LXXIV. p. 820, 1872.

—— Recherches sur les gonidies des Lichens. Ann. Sci. Nat., Sér. 5, XVII. pp. 45–110 (11 pls. col.), 1873.

—— Deuxième note sur les gonidies des Lichens. Op. cit. XIX. pp. 314–320, 1874.

Borzi, A. Intorno agli offici dei Gonidii de Licheni. Nuovo Giorn. Bot. Ital. VII. pp. 193–204, 1875.

—— Studii sulla sessualità degli ascomiceti. Nuovo Giorn. Bot. Ital. X. pp. 43–78 (2 pls.), 1878.

Braconnot, Henri. De la présence de l'oxalate de chaux dans le règne minéral ; existence du même sel en quantité énorme dans les plantes de la famille des Lichens, et moyen avantageux d'en extraire l'acide oxalique. Ann. Chim. Phys. XXVIII. pp. 318–322, 1825.

Brandt, Theodor. Beiträge zur anatomischen Kenntniss der Flechtengattung Ramalina. Hedwigia, XLV. pp. 124–158 (5 pls.), 1906.

Braun, Fr. Verzeichniss der in der Kreis.-Nat.-Samml. Bayreuth Petrefacten. Leipzig, p. 94, 1840.

Braun, Lucy E. The vegetation of conglomerate rocks of the Cincinnati region. Plant World, XX. pp. 380–392, 1917, and Bryologist, XXI. p. 93, 1918.

Brefeld, Oscar. Untersuchungen aus dem Gesammtgebiete der Mykologie, VIII. Leipzig, 1889.
—— Untersuchungen aus dem Gesammtgebiete der Mykologie. Münster, IX., 1891.
Brez, Jacques. La Flore des Insectophiles. Antrecht, 1791.
Britten J. and Boulger, G. S. A Biographical Index of British and Irish Botanists. London, 1893. Suppls. 1899, 1905, 1908.
Brooks, F. T. The Development of Gnomonia erythrostoma Pers. Ann. Bot. XXIV. pp. 585–605 (2 pls.), 1910.
Brown, Ernest W. Notes on Cetraria islandica (Iceland Moss). Amer. Journ. Physiol. I. pp. 455–460, 1898.
Brown, W. H. The Development of the Ascocarp of Lachnea scutellata. Bot. Gaz. LII. pp. 275–305 (figs. and pl.), 1911.
Buchet, Gaston. Les Lichens attaquent le verre et, dans le vitreux, semblent préférer certaines couleurs. C. R. Soc. Biol. Paris, Sér. 9, II. p. 13, 1890.
Buddle, Adam. Hortus siccus Plantarum Angliae, quo continetur curiosa Muscorum collectio (in Herb. Sloane in Brit. Mus.). 1690–1700.
Buxbaum, J. C. Enumeratio Plantarum, etc. Halle, 1721.
—— Plantarum minus cognitarum, complectens Plantas circa Byzantium in Oriente observatas. Cent. II. St Petersburg, 1728.
Calkins, W. W. An edible lichen not heretofore noted as such. Bot. Gaz. XVII. p. 418, 1892.
—— The Lichen Flora of Chicago and vicinity. Bull. Geol. Nat. Hist. Survey. Chicago, 58 pp., 1896.
Camerarius, Joachimus. De plantis Epitome utilissima iconibus, etc. 1586.
Candolle, A. P. de and Lamarck, J. B. P. A. de M. de. Flore Française, II. Paris, 1805.
Carrington, B. Dr Gray's Arrangement of the Hepaticae. Trans. Bot. Soc. Edinb. X. pp. 305–309, 1870.
Cassini, Henri. Doutes sur l'origine et la nature du Nostoc. Journ. de Phys. Chim. Hist. Nat. Paris, LXXXIV. pp. 395–399, 1817.
Chambers, C. O. The relation of algae to dissolved oxygen and carbon dioxide, with special reference to carbonates. Missouri Bot. Gard. Ann. Rep. 23, pp. 171–207, 1912.
Chevallier, F.-T. Histoire des Graphidées. Paris, 1824.
Chodat, Robert. On the Polymorphism of the Green Algae and the Principles of their Evolution. Ann. Bot. XI. pp. 97–121, 1897.
Chodat, R. Lichens épiphylles des environs de Genève. Verh. Schweiz. Naturf. Ges. XCV. pp. 209–210, 1912.
—— Monographies d'Algues en Culture Pure. Berne, 1913.
Church, A. Herbert. Food, some account of its sources, constituents, and uses. South Kensington Museum Science Handbooks, Chapman and Hall, Piccadilly, 1880.
Claassen, E. Caloplaca pyracea, eine Krustenflechte auf den Sandstein-Fuszsteigen zu East Cleveland, Ohio. Hedwigia, LIV. pp. 217–218, 1914.
Colonna, Fabio. Minus cognitarum Stirpium aliquot, ac etiam rariorum nostro coelo orientium [Ecphrasis], etc. Rome, 1606.
Comère, J. Les algues d'eau douce. Paris, 1912.
Corda, A. C. I. Icones Fungorum. Prague, 1837–1854; III., 1839.
Cordus, Valerius. Historiae Stirpium. Strasburg, 1561.
Cramer, C. Ueber das Verhaltnis von Chlorodictyon foliosum J. Ag. und Ramalina reticulata (Noehden). Ber. Schweiz. Bot. Ges. I. pp. 100–123 (3 pls.), 1891.
Cramer, G. C. P. De Lichene Islandico (Diss.). Erlangen, 1780.
Crombie, J. M. On the Lichen-Gonidia question. Popular Science Review, 18 pp. (1 pl.), July, 1874.
—— Dr Nylander on gonidia and their different Forms (translation). Grevillea, VI. pp. 39–48, 1877.

Crombie, J. M. On the Lichens of Dillenius's "Historia Muscorum," as illustrated by his Herbarium. Journ. Linn. Soc. XVII. pp. 553–581, 1880.
—— On the Algo-Lichen Hypothesis. Journ. Linn. Soc. XXI. pp. 259–283 (2 pls.), 1885.
—— Recent observations of Dr Nylander on Schwendenerism (translation from Nylander). Grevillea, XX. pp. 60–62, 1891.
—— A Monograph of Lichens found in Britain, I. London, 1894.
Culpepper, Nicolas. The English Physician, etc. London, 1652.
Cunningham, D. D. On Mycoidea parasitica, a new genus of Parasitic Algae and the Part which it plays in the Formation of certain Lichens. Trans. Linn. Soc. Ser. 2, I. p. 301 (1 pl.), 1879.
Cutting, E. M. On the Sexuality and Development of the Ascocarp in Ascophanus carneus Pers. Ann. Bot. XXIII. pp. 399–417 (1 pl.), 1909.
Czapek, Friedrich. Biochemie der Pflanzen. 2 vols. Jena, 1905.
Dangeard, P. A. Recherches sur la structure des Lichens. Le Botaniste, Sér. 4, fasc. I and 2, 1894.
—— La Reproduction sexuelle des Ascomycètes. Tom. cit. pp. 21–58 (figs.), 1894.
Danilov, A. N. Ueber das gegenseitige Verhältnis zwischen den Gonidien und dem Pilzkomponenten in der Flechtensymbiose. Bull. Jard. Imp. Bot. St Pétersbourg, X. pp. 34–66 (German Résumé, pp. 66–70), (3 pls.), 1910.
Darbishire, O. V. Kritische Bemerkungen über das Microgonidium. Hedwigia, XXXIV. pp. 181–190, 1895.
—— Dendrographa, eine neue Flechtengattung. Ber. Deutsch. Bot. Ges. XIII. pp. 313–326 (1 pl.), 1895[2].
—— Botanische Ergebnisse. Flechten aus dem Umanakdistrikt. Bibliotheca Botanica, Heft 42, VI. pp. 55–61, 1897.
—— Die deutschen Pertusariaceen mit besonderer Berücksichtigung ihrer Soredienbildung. Engler, Bot. Jahrb. XXII. pp. 593–671, 1897[2].
—— Monographia Roccelleorum. Bibliotheca Botanica, Heft 45, 103 pp. (30 pls., 29 figs.). Stuttgart, 1898.
—— Ueber die Apothecienentwickelung der Flechte Physcia pulverulenta. Pringsh. Jahrb. Wiss. Bot. XXXIV. pp. 322–345, 1900.
—— The lichens of the South Orkneys. Trans. and Proc. Bot. Soc. Edinburgh, XXIII. pp. 1–6 (1 pl.), 1905.
—— Report of the second Norwegian expedition in the Fram 1898–1902, N. 21, Lichens. Kristiania, 68 pp. (2 pls.), 1909.
—— The lichens of the Swedish Antarctic Expedition. Wissenschaftliche Ergebnisse der Schwedischen Südpolar-Expedition 1901–1903. IV. Lief. 11, 73 pp. (1 fig., 3 pls.), 1912.
—— The Development of the Apothecium in the Lichen Peltigera (abstract). Trans. Brit. Ass. Adv. Sci. pp. 713–714, 1913.
Darbishire, O. V. and Fischer-Benzon, R. V. Die Flechten Schleswig-Holsteins. Kiel und Leipzig, 1901.
Davies, Hugh. Welsh Botanology. London, 1813.
Dawson, Maria. On the Biology of Poronia punctata. Ann. Bot. XIV. pp. 245–262 (2 pls.), 1900.
Deckenbach, Const. Ueber den Polymorphismus einiger Luftalgen. Scripta Botanica. Hort. Univ. Imp. Petrop. IV. pp. 32–40 (1 pl.), 1893.
Delise, D. Histoire des Lichens. Genre Sticta. Caen, 1822.
Desfontaines, R. L. Flora Atlantica, etc. Paris, 1798–1800.
De-Toni, G. V. Sylloge Algarum, I. Pavia, 1889.
Dickson, J. J. Plantarum Cryptogamicarum Britanniae. 4 Fasc. (Illus.). London, 1785–1801.

Dillenius, Johann Jakob. Catalogus Plantarum sponte circa Gissam nascentium, etc. Frankfurt am Main, 1719.
—— Ray's Synopsis Methodica, etc. Ed. 3, 1724.
—— Historia Muscorum. Oxonii (1740), 1741.
Dodoens, R. Stirpium historiae pemptades. Antwerp, 1583.
Dorstenius, Theodoricus. Botanicon, continens Herbarum, aliorumque Simplicium, quorum usus in medicinis est, etc. Frankfurt, 1540.
Druce, G. Claridge and Vines, S. H. The Dillenian Herbaria. Oxford, 1907.
Dufrenoy, J. Les conditions écologiques du développement des champignons parasites. Bull Soc. Mycol. France, XXXIV. pp. 8–26, 1918.
Dundonald, Lord. Process for extracting a gum from Lichens. Phil. Mag. London, X. pp. 293–299, 1801.
Edinburgh Encyclopaedia (Brewster's). Lichen, XII. pp. 729–741, 1830.
Egeling, Gustav. Ein Beitrag zur Lösung der Frage bezüglich der Ernährung der Flechten. Oesterr. Bot. Zeitschr. XXXI. pp. 323–324, 1881.
Elenkin, A. A. Wanderflechten der Steppen und Wüsten. Bull. Jard. Imp. Bot. St Pétersbourg, I. pp. 16–38 and 52–72 (4 pls., 7 figs.), 1901[1].
—— Les Lichens facultatifs. Bull. Jard. Imp. Bot. St Pétersbourg, I. pp. 129–154 (1 pl. and figs.), 1901[2]. (Russian with French résumé.)
—— Zur Frage der Theorie des "Endosaprophytismus" bei Flechten. Bull. Jard. Imp. Bot. St Pétersbourg, II. pp. 65–84, 1902.
—— Neue Beobachtungen über die Erscheinungen des Endosaprophytismus bei heteromeren Flechten. Bull. Jard. Imp. Bot. St Pétersbourg, IV. pp. 25–39 (2 col. pls.), 1904[1].
—— Zur Frage der Theorie des "Endosaprophytismus" bei Flechten. Bull. Soc. Imp. Nat. Moscou, p. 164, 1904[2].
—— Notes Lichenologiques. Bull. Jard. Imp. Bot. St Pétersbourg, V. pp. 121–133, 1905.
—— Species novae lichenum in Sibiria arctica, etc. Ann. Mycol. IV. pp. 36–38, 1906[1].
—— Die Symbiose als abstracte Auffassung des beweglichen Gleichgewichts der Symbionten. (Russian with German résumé.) Bull. Jard. Imp. Bot. St Pétersbourg, VI. pp. 1–19, 1906[2].
Elenkin, A. A. and Woronichin, N. N. Epiphylle Flechten im Kaukasus. Trav. Soc. Imp. Nat. St Pétersbourg, XXXIX. pp. 252–258, 1908.
Elfving, F. Ueber die Flechtengonidien. Förh. Nordisk. Nat.-forsk. och Läk. Helsingfors, 1902, 5 pp., 1903. Ann. Mycol. II. pp. 304–305, 1904.
—— Untersuchungen über die Flechtengonidien. Act. Soc. Sci. Fenn. XLIV. n. 2, 71 pp. (8 pls.), 1913.
Engelhardt, Hermann. Flora der Braunkohlenformation im Königreich Sachsen. Leipzig 1870.
Ernst, A. (Trans. by A. C. Seward). The new Flora of the volcanic Island of Krakatau. Cambridge, 1908.
Errera, Leo. Ueber den Nachweis des Glykogens bei Pilzen in Bot. Zeit. XLIV. pp. 316–320, 1886.
—— "Pain du ciel" provenant de Diarbekir. Bull. Acad. Roy. Belg. Sér. 3, XXVI. pp. 83–91, 1893.
—— L'épiplasme des Ascomycetes et le glycogène des végétaux (Thèse. Bruxelles, 1882). Rec. Inst. Bot Univ. Brux. I. pp. 1–70, 1906.
Eschweiler, F. G. Systema Lichenum, genera exhibens, etc. Nuremberg (1 pl.), 1824.
Escombe, F. Chemistry of Lichenic and Fungal Membranes. Ann. Bot. X. pp. 293–294, 1896.
—— Beitrag zur Chemie der Membranen der Flechten und Pilze. Zeitschr. Physiolog. Chemie, XXII. p. 288, 1896.

Etard and Bouilhac. Présence des chlorophylles dans un *Nostoc* cultivé à l'abri de la lumière. Comptes Rendus, CXXVII. pp. 119–121, 1898.

Ettingshausen C. and Debey, M. H. Die urweltlichen Thallophyten des Kreidegebirges von Aachen und Maestricht. Sitzungsb. K. Akad. Wiss. Wien, pp. 507–512, 1857; and Bull. Soc. Bot. France, v. pp. 304–306, 1858.

Euler, H. Grundlagen und Ergebnisse der Pflanzenchemie. Braunschweig, 1908.

Eversmann, E. In Lichenem esculentum Pallasci. Nova Acta Leop. XV. pp. 349–362 (1 pl.), 1825.

Famintzin, A. Die Symbiose als Mittel der Synthese von Organismen. Biol. Centralbl. XXVII. p. 353, 1907.

Famintzin, A. and Baranetzky, J. Zur Entwickelungsgeschichte der Gonidien und Zoosporenbildung der Flechten. Mem. Acad. Imp. Sci. St Pétersbourg, Sér. 7, XI. No. 9, 7 pp. (1 pl.) (1867), 1868. Ann. Sci. Nat., Sér. 5, VIII. pp. 137–144 (1 pl.), 1867.

Faull, J. H. The Cytology of the Laboulbeniales. Ann. Bot. XXV. pp. 649–654, 1911.

Fee, A. L. A. Essai sur les Cryptogames des écorces exotiques officinales. Paris, 1824.

—— Matériaux pour une Flore Lichénologique du Brésil. Bull. Soc. Bot. Fr. XX. pp. 307–319, 1873.

Fink, Bruce. Lichens of Minneapolis and Vicinity. Minn. Bot. Stud. I. pp. 703–725, 1894.

—— Contributions to a knowledge of the lichens of Minnesota, I.–VII. Minn. Bot. Stud. I.–III., 1896–1903.

—— Lichens of the Lake Superior region. Minn. Bot. Stud. II. pp. 215–276, 1898–1902.

—— Lichens of the Minnesota Valley. Tom. cit. pp. 277–329[2].

—— Lichens of N.W. Minnesota. Tom. cit. pp. 657–709[3].

—— Lichens of the Northern Boundary. Op. cit. III. pp. 167–236, 1903.

—— Composition of a Desert Lichen Flora. Mycologia, I. pp. 87–109, 1909.

—— Some Common Types of Lichen Formations. Torrey Bot. Club, XXX. pp. 412–418, 1903.

—— A Lichen Society of a Sandstone Rip-rap. Bot. Gaz. XXXVI. pp. 265–284 (5 figs.), 1904.

—— The Nature and Classification of Lichens. I. Mycologia, III. pp. 231–269, 1911; II. Op. cit. V. pp. 97–116, 1913.

—— The rate of Growth and Ecesis in Lichens. Mycologia, IX. pp. 138–158, 1917.

—— A new genus and species of the Collemaceae. Mycologia, X. pp. 235–238 (1 pl.), 1918.

Fischer, Ed. Beiträge zur Kenntniss exotischen Pilze. Hedwigia, XXIX. pp. 161–171 (1 pl.), 1890.

Fitting, N. Ueber die Beziehungen zwischen den epiphyllen Flechten und den von ihnen bewohnten Blättern. Ann. Jard. Bot. Buitenzorg, Suppl. 3, pp. 505–519, 1910.

Fitzpatrick, Henry Morton. Sexuality in Rhizina undulata. Bot. Gaz. LXV. pp. 201–226 (2 pls.), 1918.

Flagey, C. Lichenes algeriensis exsiccati. Rev. Mycol. XIII. pp. 83–87 and 107–117, 1901; pp. 70–79, 1892.

—— Catalogue des Lichens. Battandier and Trabut, Flore de l'Algérie. Algiers, Part 2, I. pp. XII. and 139, 1896.

Flörke, H. G. Deutsche Lichenen. 10 Lief. Berlin, 1815–19.

—— De Cladoniis, etc. Rostock, 1828.

Flotow, Julius von. Mikroskopische Flechtenstudien. Bot. Zeit. VIII. pp. 361–369, 377–382, 1850.

Forskål, P. Descriptiones Plantarum Florae Aegyptiaco-Arabicae (5). Hauniae, 1775.

Forssell, K. B. J. Studier öfver Cephalodierna. Bihang K. Svensk. Vet.-Akad. Handl. VIII. n. 3, 112 pp. (2 pls.), 1882.

Forssell, K. B. J. Lichenologische Untersuchungen. I. Ueber die Cephalodien. Flora, LXVII. pp. 1–8, 33–46, 58–63, 177–193, 1884.

—— Anatomie und Systematik der Gloeolichenen. Nov. Act. Reg. Soc. Sci. Upsal. Sér. 3, 118 pp., 1885[1].

—— Die anatomische Verhältnisse und die phylogenetische Entwicklung der Lecanora granatina Sommerf. Bot. Centralb. XXII. pp. 54–58 and 85–89, 1885[2].

—— Ueber den Polymorphismus der Algen (Flechtengonidien), etc. Flora, LXIX. pp. 49–64, 1886.

Forster, T. F. Flora Tonbrigensis. London, 1816.

Frank, A. B. Ueber die biologischen Verhältnisse des Thallus einiger Krustenflechten. Cohn's Beiträge zur Biologie der Pflanzen, II. pp. 123–200 (1 pl.), 1876

Fraser, H. C. I. On the Sexuality and Development of the Ascocarp in Lachnea stercorea Pers. Ann. Bot. XXI. pp. 349–360 (2 pls.), 1907.

French, G. H. Mounting Lichens. Journ. Applied Microscopy. Rochester N. Y. I. p. 135 1898.

Friederich, Albert. Beiträge zur Anatomie der Silikatflechten. Fünfstück's Beitr. Wiss. Bot. v. pp. 377–404, 1906.

Fries, Elias. Systema orbis vegetabilis, I. Lund, 1825.

—— Primitiae Geographiae Lichenum. Lund, 1831.

—— Lichenographia Europaea reformata. Lund, 1831.

Fries, Th. M. Monographia Stereocaulorum et Pilophororum. Act. Reg. Soc. Sci. Upsala, Ser. 3, II. pp. 307–380 (4 pls.), 1858.

—— Genera Heterolichenum Europeae recognita. Upsala, 1861.

—— Lichenes Arctoi. Nova Act. Soc. Sci. III. pp. 103–398, 1861.

—— Beiträge zur Kenntniss der sogenannten Cephalodien bei den Flechten. Flora, XLIX. pp. 17–25, 1866.

—— Lichenes Spitsbergenses. K. Sv. Vet.-Akad. Handl. VII. n. 2, 1867.

Fritsch, F. E. The Rôle of Algal Growth in the colonization of new ground, etc. Geographical Journal, XXX. pp. 531–547, 1907.

Fuisting, W. Beiträge zur Entwickelungsgeschichte der Lichenen. Bot. Zeit. XXVI. pp. 641, etc. (1 pl.), 1868.

Fünfstück, M. Beiträge zur Entwickelungsgeschichte der Lichenen. Eichler's Jahrb. Bot. Gart. Berlin, III. pp. 155–174 (3 pls.), 1884.

—— Die Fettabscheidung der Kalkflechten in Fünfstück s Beitr. Wiss. Bot. I. pp. 157–220 (3 pls.), 1895 and Nachtrag, pp. 316–321, 1896.

—— Lichenes (Allgemeiner Teil). Engler und Prantl, Die Natürlichen Pflanzenfamilien, I. 1*, pp. 1–48, 1898.

—— Weitere Untersuchungen über die Fettabscheidung der Kalkflechten. Bot. Untersuch., Festschrift für Schwendener, pp. 341–356. Berlin, 1899.

—— Der gegenwärtige Stand der Flechtenforschung nebst Ausblicken auf deren voraussichtliche Weiterentwickelung. Ber. Deutsch. Bot. Ges. XX. 19te General-Versammlung, pp. 62–77, 1902.

Galløe, O. Danske Likeners Ökologi. Botan. Tidsskrift, XXVIII. pp. 285–372 (3 pls.), 1908.

—— Forberedende Undersøgelser til en almindelig Likenølogi. Dansk Botanisk Arkiv, I. n. 3, 119 pp. (240 figs.), 1913–15.

Garjeaune, A. J. M. Die Verpilzung der Lebermoosrhizoiden. Flora, CII. pp. 147–185 (2 pls. and figs.), 1911.

Gautier, Armand. Présence de l'iode en proportions notables dans tous les végétaux à chlorophylle de la classe des Algues et dans les sulfuraires. Comptes Rendus, CXXIX. pp. 191–194, 1899.

Georgi, I. G. Scrutamen chemicum Lichenum parasiticorum. Acta Acad. Sci. Imp. Petropol. III. Pars II. pp. 282–292 [1779], 1783.

Gerard, John. The Herball or generall historie of Plantes, etc. London, 1597.

Gibelli, Giuseppe. Sugli Organi Riproduttori del genere Verrucaria. Memorie della Soc. Ital. Sci. Nat. Milano, I. n. 5 (1 pl.), 1866.

Gilson, E. La cristallisation de la cellulose et la composition chimique de la membrane cellulaire végétale. La Cellule, IX. fasc. 2, 1893.

—— Recherches chimiques sur la membrane cellulaire des Champignons. La Cellule, XI. fasc. 1. pp. 7–15, 1894.

Gleditsch, J. G. Einleitung in die neuere Forstwissenschaft, I. Berlin, 1775.

Glück, Hugo. Entwurf zu einer Vergleichenden Morphologie der Flechten-Spermogonien. Verh. Naturhist.-Med. Ver. VI. 2. Heidelberg, pp. vi. and 136 (2 pls.), 1899.

Gmelin, J. F. Systema Naturae, II. Leipzig, 1791.

Gmelin, J. G. Reise durch Sibirien. Göttingen, 1752.

Goeppert, H. R. Uebersicht der fossilen Flora Schlesiens 1844–45 (in Wimmer's Flora von Schlesien, Breslau, 1845).

—— Ueber den Einfluss der Pflanzen auf felsige Unterlage. Flora, XLIII. pp. 161–171, 1860.

Goeppert, H. R. and Menge, A. Die Flora des Bernsteins, I. Danzig, 1883.

Gray, S. F. A Natural Arrangement of British Plants, I. London, 1821.

Greville, R. K. Scottish Cryptogamic Flora, etc. I.–VI. Edinburgh, 1823–28.

—— Flora Edinensis. Edinburgh, 1824.

Guembel, C. W. Mittheilungen über die neue Färberflechte Lecanora ventosa Ach. Denkschr. K. Akad. Wiss. Math.-Natur. Cl. Wien, XI. Abth. 2, pp. 23–40 (1 pl.), 1856.

Guérin-Varry, R. J. Mémoires sur deux Produits naturels de la Végétation considérés comme des Gommes. Ann. Chim. Phys. Sér. 2, LVI. pp. 225–252, 1834.

Guilliermond, A. Formation des Asques et de l'épiplasme des Ascomycètes. Rev. Gén. Bot. XVI. pp. 49–66, 1904.

Haberlandt, G. Ueber die Beziehungen zwischen Function und Lage des Zellkernes bei den Pflanzen. Jena, pp. viii, 135 (2 pls.), 1887.

—— Physiologische Pflanzenanatomie, ed. 2. Leipzig, 1896.

Haller, Alb. von. Enumeratio Methodica Stirpium Helvetiae indigenarum, etc. Göttingen, 1742.

—— Historia Stirpium indigenarum Helvetiae, III. Berne, 1768.

Halsey, A. Synoptical view of the Lichens, growing in the vicinity of the city of New York. Ann. Lyceum Nat. Hist. New York, I. pp. 3–21, 1824.

Hamlet, W. M. and Plowright, C. B. On the occurrence of Oxalic Acid in Fungi. Chemical News, XXXVI. pp. 93–94, 1877.

Harmand, J. Lichens de France. Fasc. I. II. 1905; III. 1907; IV. 1909; V. 1913.

Harper, R. A. Cell-Division in Sporangia and Asci. Ann. Bot. XIII. pp. 467–525, 1899.

—— Sexual reproduction in Pyronema confluens, etc. Ann. Bot. XIV. pp. 321–400 (3 pls.), 1900.

Hassall, A. H. A History of the British Freshwater Algae. London, 1845.

Hedlund, T. Kritische Bemerkungen über einige Arten der Flechtengattungen Lecanora, Lecidea und Micarea. Bih. K. Svensk. Vet.-Akad. Handl. XVIII. Afd. III. n. 3, 104 pp. (1 pl.), 1892.

—— Ueber Thallusbildung durch Pyknokonidien bei Catillaria denigrata und C. prasina. Bot. Centralbl. LXIII. pp. 9–16, 1895.

Hedwig, Johann. Microscopisch-Analytische Beschreibungen und Abbildungen neuer und zweifelhafter Laub-Moose, II. Leipzig, 1789.

—— Theoria generationis et fructificationis plantarum cryptogamicarum. St Petersburg, 1784. Enlarged edition. Leipzig, 1798.

Hellbom, P. J. Norrlands Lafvar. K. Svensk. Vet.-Akad. Handl. XX. n. 8, 131 pp., 1884.

Hellbom, P. J. Lichenaea Neo-Zeelandica, etc. Bihang K. Svensk. Vet.-Akad. Handl. XXI. Afd. III. n. 13, 150 pp., 1896.

Henneguy, Félix. Les Lichens Utiles. Paris, 114 pp. (20 figs.), 1883.

Herbal. The Grete Herball, etc., translated from the French, printed by Peter Treveris. London, 1526.

Herberger, J. E. Ueber den Bitterstoff des isländischen Mooses (Cetraria islandica). Buchner's Repertorium für Pharmacie, XXXVI. pp. 226–237, 1830.

Herissey, H. Sur la présence de l'émulsine dans les Lichens. Comptes Rendus Soc. Biol. Sér. 10, V. pp. 532–534, 1898 ; Bull. Soc. Mycol. France, XV. pp. 44–48, 1899.

Herre, A. C. The growth of Ramalina reticulata. Bot. Gaz. XXXVIII. pp. 218–219, 1904.

—— Suggestions as to the origin of California's Lichen Flora. Plant World, XIII. pp. 215–220, 1910.

—— The Gyrophoraceae of California. Contrib. U.S. Nat. Herb. XIII. 10, pp. 313–321 (5 pls.), 1911[1].

—— The desert Lichens of Reno, Nevada. Bot. Gaz. LI. pp. 286–297, 1911[2].

Hesse, O. Beitrag zur Kenntniss der Flechten und ihrer charakteristischen Bestandteile, 9 Mitth. Journ. prakt. Chem. LXX. pp. 449–502, 1904.

Hicks, J. Braxton. Contributions to the knowledge of the Development of the Gonidia of Lichens in relation to the Unicellular Algae. Quart. Journ. Micros. Sci. VIII. p. 239, 1860. New series, I. p. 15, 1861.

—— Observations on the Gonidia and Confervoid Filaments of Mosses, and on the relation of their Gonidia to those of Lichens and of certain freshwater Algae. Trans. Linn. Soc. London, XXIII. pp. 567–588 (2 pls.), 1862.

Hill, Sir John. History of Plants. London, 1751.

—— Flora Britannica. London, 1760.

Hoffmann, G. Fr. Enumeratio Lichenum iconibus et descriptionibus illustrata. Erlangen, 1784.

—— Commentatio de vario Lichenum usu. Lyon, 1787.

—— Descriptio et Adumbratio plantarum e classe cryptogamica Linnaei quae Lichenes dicuntur. Leipzig, 1790–1801.

—— Deutschland's Flora, etc. Erlangen, 1795.

Hofmann, W. Parasitische Flechten auf Endocarpon miniatum. Fünfstück's Beitr. Wiss. Bot. V. pp. 259–274, 1906.

Holle, G. von. Zur Entwickelungsgeschichte von Borrera ciliaris. Inaug.-Diss. Göttingen, 43 pp. (2 pls.), 1849.

Hooker, W. J. Flora Scotica. London, 1821.

—— English Botany Supplement. London, 1831.

—— Smith's Engl. Fl. V. pp. 129–241, 1833.

Hooker, Sir W. J. and Arnott, G. A. Walker. The Botany of Captain Beechey's Voyage, etc. London, 1841.

Hornschuch, Friedrich. Einige Beobachtungen über das Entstehen der Algen, Flechten und Laubmoose. Flora, II. pp. 140–144, 1819.

—— Einige Beobachtungen und Bemerkungen über die Entstehen und Metamorphose der niedern vegetabilischen Organismen. Acad. Caes. Leop. Nov. Act. X. p. 544, etc., 1821.

How, William. Phytologia Britannica. London, 1650.

Howe, R. Heber. Classification de la Famille des Usneaceae dans l'Amérique du Nord. 32 pp. (10 pls.), Paris, 1912.

—— North American Species of the genus Ramalina. Bryologist, XVI. pp. 65–74, etc. 1913.

Hudson, W. Flora Anglica. London, ed. 1, 1762 ; ed. 2, 1778.

Hue, A. M. Lichenes exoticos a professore W. Nylander descriptos, etc., etc. Paris, 1892.

—— Revue des Travaux sur la description et la géographie botanique des Lichens. Rev. Gén. Bot. I. pp. 397-403, 1888 ; II. pp. 403-411, 1889; IV. pp. 31-39, 1890 ; V. pp. 36-48, 1891 ; VI. pp. 174-185, etc. 1894 ; X. pp. 125-128, etc. 1898[1].

—— Causerie sur les Parmelia. Journ. de Bot. XII. pp. 177-189, 239-250, 1898[2].

—— William Nylander with portrait and lists of publications. Bull. Soc. Bot. Fr. XLVI. pp. 153-165, 1899.

—— Lichenes extra-Europaei, etc. Nouv. Arch. Mus. Hist. Nat. Paris, Sér. 3, X. pp. 213-280, 1898 ; Sér. 4, I. pp. 27-220, 1899 ; II. pp. 49-122, 1900 ; III. pp. 21-146 (18 pls.), 1901.

—— Description de deux espèces de Lichens et de céphalodies nouvelles. Ann. Ass. Nat. Levallois-Perret, p. 31, 1904 ; Bot. Centralbl. XCIX. p. 34, 1905.

—— Lichens Tarbelliens. Bull. Soc. Bot. Fr. LV. Mém. 12, 19 pp., 1908.

—— Le Mastoidea tessellata Hook. fil. et Harv. Bull. Soc. Bot. France, LVI. pp. 315-322 (5 figs.), 1909[1].

—— Lichenes morphologice et anatomice disposuit. Nouv. Arch. Mus. Hist. Nat. Paris, Sér. 4, VIII. pp. 237-272 (figs.), 1906 ; op. cit. X. pp. 169-224 (figs.), 1908 ; Sér. 5, I. pp. 110-166 (figs.), 1909 ; II. pp. 1-119 (figs.), 1910.

—— Lichenum Generis Crocyniae Massal, etc. Mém. Soc. Sci. Nat. Cherb., Sér. 4, VII. pp. 223-254, 1909[2].

—— Sur la variation des gonidies dans le genre Solorina. Comptes Rendus Acad. Sci. Paris, CLI. pp. 332-334, 1910.

—— Monographiam Generis Solorinae Ach., etc. Mém. Soc. Sci. Nat. Cherb. XXXVIII. pp. 1-56, 1911[1].

—— Notice sur les spores des "Licheni blasteniospori" Massal. Bull. Soc. Bot. France, LXIII. pp. lxvii-lxxxvi (2 pls.), 1911[2].

—— Lichenes novos vel melius cognitos. Ann. Mycol. XII. pp. 509-534, 1914.

—— Expédition Antarctique Française (1903-1905). Dr J. Charcot, Lichens. Paris, 1908.

—— Deuxième Expédition (1908-1910). Dr J. Charcot, Lichens. Paris, 1915.

Hulth, J. M. Ueber Reservestoffbehälter bei Flechten. Bot. Centralbl. XLV. pp. 209-210 and 269-270, 1891.

Hutchinson, Robert. Food and the Principles of dietetics. Ed. 4. London, Arnold, 1916.

Istvanffi, Gy. von. Ueber die Rolle der Zellkerne bei der Entwickelung der Pilze. Ber. Deutsch. Bot. Ges. XIII. pp. 452-467, 1895.

Itzigsohn, Hermann. Die Antheridien und Spermatozoën der Flechten. Bot. Zeit. VIII. pp. 393-394 and 913-919, 1850.

—— Wie verhält sich Collema zu Nostoc und zu den Nostochineen. Bot. Zeit. XII pp. 521-527, 1854.

—— Gloeocapsa und Cladonia. Bot. Zeit. XIII. pp. 203-207, 1855.

—— Cultur der Glaucogonidien von Peltigera canina. Bot. Zeit. XXVI. pp. 185-196, [1867], 1868.

Jaczewski, A. Specimina Pilocarpi leucoblephari e Caucaso. See A. Elenkin in Bull. Jard. Imp. Bot. St Pétersb. IV. pp. 3-8, 1904.

Jatta, A. Monographia Lichenum Italiae Meridionalis. Trano, 1889.

Jennings, A. Vaughan. On two new species of Phycopeltis from New Zealand. Proc. Roy. Irish Acad. Ser. 3, III. pp. 753-766 (2 pls.), 1895.

John, T. F. Ueber die Ernährung der Pflanzen. Berlin, 1819.

Johnson, Charles Pierpoint. The Useful Plants of Great Britain. Illustrated by J. E. Sowerby. London, 1861 [62].

Johow, Friedrich. Die Gruppe der Hymenolichenen, etc. Pringsh. Jahrb. Wiss. Bot: XV. pp. 360–409 (5 pls.), 1884.

Jumelle, Henri. La vie des Lichens pendant l'Hiver. Mém. Soc. Biol. Paris, Sér. 9, II pp. 115–119, 1890.

—— Recherches Physiologiques sur les Lichens. Rev. Gén. Bot. IV. pp. 49–64, 103–121, etc. Résumé général, p. 316 (2 pls.), 1892.

Kajanus, Birger (früher Nilson). Morphologische Flechtenstudien. Ark. Bot. X. n. 4, 47 pp. (2 pls.), 1911.

Kappen, Hubert. Kristallographisch-optische Untersuchungen einiger Flechtensäuren. Zeitschr. Kristallogr. XXXVII. pp. 151–170, 1903.

Keeble, F. Plant-Animals. A study in Symbiosis. Cambridge, 1910.

Keegan, P. Q. The Chemistry of some Common Plants. Naturalist, pp. 274–275, 1905; pp. 24–25, 1907.

Keiszler, Karl von. Zwei neue Flechtenparasiten aus Steiermark. Hedwigia, L. pp. 294–298, 1911.

Keller, F. The Reindeer Age on the Lake of Constance. Athenaeum, p. 500, 1866.

Kerner von Marilaun, A. and Oliver, F. W. The Natural History of Plants. Vols. I. and II. London, 1894.

Kieffer, J. J. Die Flechten Lothringens. Hedwigia, XXXIII. pp. 101–122, 1894.

Kienitz-Gerloff, F. Neue Studien über Plasmodesmen. Ber. Deutsch. Bot. Ges. XX p. 93 (1 pl.), 1902.

Kihlman, A. Osw. Pflanzenbiologische Studien aus Russisch-Lappland. Act. Soc. Faun. and Fl. Fenn. VI. 3, XXIV. 263 pp., 1890.

Knop, W. Chemisch-physiol. Untersuchung über die Flechten. Ann. Chem. XLIX. pp. 103–124, 1844.

—— Chemischer Beitrag zur Physiologie der Flechten. Chem. Zentralbl. III. pp. 172–176, 1872.

Knop, W. and Schnederman, G. Chemisch-physiologische Untersuchung der Flechten und zwar der Cetraria islandica. Flora, XXIX. pp. 238–239, 1846.

—— Chemisch-physiologische Untersuchungen über die Flechten. Erdm. Journ. prakt. Chem. XXXIX. pp. 363–367, 1846.

Knowles, Matilda C. The maritime and marine Lichens of Howth. Sci. Proc. Roy. Dublin Soc. XIV. (N.S.), No. 6, pp. 79–143 (7 pls.), 1913.

—— Results of a Biological Survey of Blackrod Bay, Co. Mayo. Lichenes. Dept. Agric. Techn. Instr. Ireland, pp. 22–26, 1915.

Kobert, R. Ueber Giftstoffe der Flechten. Sitzungsb. Naturf. Ges. Dorpat, X. pp. 157–166, 1895.

Koelreuter, J. G. Das entdeckte Geheimnisz der Cryptogamie. Carlsruhe, 1777.

Koerber, G. G. De Gonidiis Lichenum. Berlin, 1839.

—— Einige Bemerkungen über individuelle Fortpflanzung der Flechten. Flora, XXIV. pp. 6 and 17, 1841.

—— Systema Lichenum Germaniae. Breslau, 1855.

Kotte, J. Einige neue Fälle von Nebensymbiose (Parasymbiose). Inaug.-Diss., G. Fischer, Jena, 1909. (Bot. Centralbl. XXIII. p. 19, 1910.)

Krabbe, G. Entwickelung, Sprossung und Theilung einiger Flechtenapothecien. Bot. Zeit. XL. pp. 65–83, 89–99, 105–116, 121–142 (2 pls.), 1882.

—— Morphologie und Entwickelungsgeschichte der Cladoniaceen. Ber. Deutsch. Bot. Ges. I. pp. 64–77, 1883.

—— Entwickelungsgeschichte und Morphologie der polymorphen Flechtengattung Cladonia. Leipzig (12 pls.), 1891.

Kratzmann, E. Der microchemische Nachweis und die Verteilung des Aluminiums im Pflanzenreiche. Sitzungsb. K. Akad. Wiss. Math.-Nat. Cl. Wien, XXVII. 2, Abt. I. pp. 311–336, 1913. (Mycol. Centralbl. V. p. 36, 1914.)

Krempelhuber, August von. Die Lichenen-Flora Bayerns. Regensburg, 1861.
—— Geschichte und Litteratur der Lichenologie, I. 1867; II. 1869–1872.
—— Beitrag zur Kenntniss der Lichenen-Flora der Südsee-Inseln. Journ. Mus. Godeffroy, Hamburg, IV. pp. 93–100 (1 pl.), 1873.
Kützing, F. T. Phycologia Generalis. Leipzig, 1843.
Lacour, E. Analyse chimique du Lichen esculentus manne du désert ou manne des Hébreux. Just. Bot. Jahresb. für 1880, I. p. 463, 1883.
Lang, Eugen. Beiträge zur Anatomie der Krustenflechten. Fünfstück's Beitr. Wiss. Bot. V. pp. 162–188 (13 figs.), 1903.
Laubert, R. Ein interessanter neuer Pilz an absterbenden Apfelbäumen. Gartenflora, LX. p. 76, 1911.
Leighton, W. A. The British Species of Angiocarpous Lichens elucidated by their sporidia. 101 pp. (30 pls.). London, 1851.
—— Monograph of British Graphideae. Ann. Mag. Nat. Hist., Ser. 2, XIII. pp. 81–97, etc. (4 pls.), 1854.
—— Monograph of the British Umbilicariae. Ann. Mag. Nat. Hist., Ser. 2, XVIII. pp. 273–297 (1 pl.), 1856.
—— Notes on Lichens collected by Sir John Richardson in Arctic America. Journ. Linn. Soc. Bot. IX. pp. 184–200 (1 pl.), 1867.
—— Notulae Lichenologicae, No. XXX. Further Notes on the Lichens of Cader Idris, North Wales. Ann. and Mag. Nat. Hist., Ser. 4, IV. pp. 198–202, 1869.
—— The Lichens of Ceylon collected by G. H. K. Thwaites. Trans. Linn. Soc. XXVII. pp. 161–185 (2 pls.), 1869.
—— The Lichen Flora of Great Britain, Ireland and the Channel Islands. Shrewsbury, 1871; ed. 3, 1879.
Léorier. Rapport fait à la Société Linnéenne sur le procédé de M. Roy de Tonnerre pour retirer de l'alcool des Lichens. Soc. Linn. Paris, IV. pp. 219–225, 1825.
Lesdain, Bouly de. Lichens de Dunkerque. Dunkerque, 1910[1].
—— Végétation de l'argile des Polders. Comptes Rendus Congrès, Soc. Savantes, 1909. Sciences, 8 pp. Paris, 1910[2].
—— Écologie d'une petite panne dans les dunes des environs de Dunkerque. Bull. Soc. Bot. France, Sér. 4, XII. pp. 177–184, 207–284, 1912.
Lett, H. W. Report on the Mosses, Hepatics and Lichens of the Mourne Mountains district. Proc. Roy. Irish Acad. Ser. 3, I. pp. 319–325, 1890.
Lettau. G. Beiträge zur Lichenographie von Thüringen. Hedwigia, LI. pp. 176–220, 1915.
—— Nachweis und Verhalten einiger Flechtensäuren. Hedwigia, LV. pp. 1–78, 1914.
Lightfoot, John. Flora Scotica, II. London, 1777.
Lindau, G. Ueber die Anlage und Entwickelung einiger Flechtenapothecien. Flora, LXXI. pp. 451–489 (1 pl.), 1888.
—— Die Beziehungen der Flechten zu den Pilzen. Hedwigia, XXXIV. pp. 195–204, 1895[1].
—— Lichenologische Untersuchungen, Heft I. Ueber Wachstum und Anheftungsweise der Rindenflechten. 4to, 66 pp. (3 pls.), Dresden, 1895[2].
—— Beiträge zur Kenntniss der Gattung Gyrophora. Festschrift für Schwendener, pp. 19–37 (2 pls.), 1899. (Hedwigia, XXXVIII. Beibl. p. 101, 1899.)
Lindsay, W. Lauder. Experiments on the Dyeing Properties of Lichens. Edin. New Phil. Journ. LVII. pp. 228–249, 1854, and LVIII. pp. 56–80, 1855.
—— A Popular History of British Lichens. London, 1856.
—— Monograph of the genus Abrothallus. Trans. Brit. Assoc., 41 pp. (2 col. pls.), 1856.
—— Memoir on the Spermogones and Pycnides of Filamentous, Fruticulose, and Foliaceous Lichens. Trans. Roy. Soc. Edin. XXII. pp. 101–303 (11 pls.), 1859.

Lindsay, W. Lauder. Observations on new Lichenicolous Micro-Fungi. Trans. Roy. Soc. Edinb. XXV. pp. 513–555 (2 pls.), 1869[1].

—— Observations on the Lichens collected by Dr Robert Brown in West Greenland in 1867. Trans. Linn. Soc. XXVII. pp. 305–368 (5 pls. col.), 1869[2].

—— The Lichen Flora of Greenland. Trans. Bot. Soc. Edinb. X. pp. 32–65, 1870[1].

—— Experiments on Colour-Reaction as a specific character in Lichens. Tom. cit. pp. 82–98, 1870[2].

—— Enumeration of Micro-Lichens parasitic on other Lichens. Quart. Journ. Micr. Sci. IX. pp. 49–57, etc., 1869[2].

—— Observations on Lichenicolous Micro-Parasites. Op. cit. XI. pp. 28–42, 1871.

—— Memoir on the Spermogones and Pycnides of Crustaceous Lichens. Trans. Linn. Soc. XXVIII. pp. 189–318 (8 pls.), 1872.

—— The true Nature of Lichens. Nature XIII. p. 247, 1876.

—— Fossil Lichens. Gard. Chron. VIII. p. 566, 1877.

—— Fossil Lichens. Trans. and Proc. Bot. Soc. Edinb. XIII. pp. 160–165, 1879.

Link, H. F. Florae Goettingensis Specimen sistens vegetabilia saxo calcareo propria. Hildesheim, 1789.

—— Einige Bemerkungen über den Standort (loca natalia) der Pflanzen. Usteri, Ann. Bot. XIV. pp. 1–17, 1795.

Linkola, K. Ueber die Thallusschuppen bei Peltigera lepidophora. Ber. Deutsch. Bot. Ges. XXXI. pp. 52–54 (1 pl.), 1913.

Linnaeus, Carolus. Flora Lapponica. Amsterdam, 1737.

—— Genera Plantarum, etc. Leyden, 1737.

—— Species Plantarum. Stockholm, 1753.

—— Plantae Tinctoriae (E. Jörlin, Upsala, 1759). Amoenitates Academicae, Holmiae, v. pp. 314–342, 1760.

—— Oeconomia Naturae (Isacus J. Biberg, Upsala, 1749). Amoenitates Academicae, Holmiae, ed. 2, II. pp. 1–52, 1762.

—— Lachesis Lapponica or a Tour in Lappland...translated by J. E. Smith. 2 Vols. illust. London, 1811.

Lister, Gulielma. A Monograph of the Mycetozoa, ed. 2. Brit. Mus., London, 1911.

—— Haunts of the Mycetozoa. Essex Naturalist, XVIII. pp. 301–321, 1918.

Lloyd, C. G. Synopsis of some genera of the large Pyrenomycetes. Cincinnati, Ohio. 17 pp. (pls. and figs.). Jan. 1917.

L'Obel, Mathias de (Lobelius). Plantarum seu Stirpium Historia, etc. *illust.* Antwerp, 1576.

Lotzy, J. P. Beiträge zur Biologie der Flechtenflora des Hambergs bei Göttingen. Diss. Göttingen, 1890.

Ludwig, R. Fossile Pflanzen aus der ältesten Abtheilung der Rheinisch-Wetterauer Tertiär-Formationen. Meyer, Palaeontographica, VIII. pp. 39–154, 1859–1861.

Lutz, K. G. Ueber die sogenannte Netzbildung bei Ramalina reticulata Krplhbr. Ber. Deutsch. Bot. Ges. XII. pp. 207–214 (figs.), 1894.

Luyken, J. A. Tentamen Historiae Lichenum, etc. Göttingen, 1809.

McLean, R. C. Ecology of Maritime Lichens at Blakeney Point, Norfolk. Journ. Ecol. III. pp. 129–148 (1 pl. and figs.), 1915.

Macmillan, Conway. Observations on the Distribution of Plants along the shore at Lake of the Woods. Minn. Bot. Stud. I. pp. 949–1022 (pls.), 1894.

Maheu, Jacques. Contribution à l'Étude de la Flore souterraine de France. Ann. Sci. Nat. Sér. 9, III. Chap. IV. Lichens, pp. 98–101, 1906.

—— Les Lichens des hauts Sommets du Massif de la Tarentaise (Savoie). Bull. Soc. Bot. France, LIV. pp. 232–240, 1907.

Maire, René. Recherches cytologiques sur quelques Ascomycètes. Ann. Mycol. III. pp. 123–154 (3 pls.), 1905.

Malinowski, E. Sur la biologie et l'écologie des lichens épilithiques. Bull. Acad. Sci. Cracovie, Sér. B. Sci. Nat. pp. 349–390 (1 pl., 6 figs.), 1911.

Malme, G. O. Ein Fall antagonistischer Symbiose zweier Flechtenarten. Bot. Centralbl. LXIV. pp. 46–49, 1895.

Malpighi, Marcello. Opera Omnia, II. Londini, 1686.

Martius, Ph. V. Flora Brasiliensis, etc. I. Stuttgart and Tübingen, 1833.

Massalongo, A. B. Synopsis Lichenum blasteniospororum. Flora, XXXV. pp. 545–576, 1852.

—— Ricerche sull' autonomia dei Licheni crostosi. Verona, 1852.

—— Monografia dei Licheni blasteniospori. Atti Ist. Sci. Lett. ed Arti, Ser. 2, III. Appendice III. 131 pp. (6 pls.), 1852. (Reprint, Venezia, 1853.)

Massee, G. On Gasterolichenes, a new type of the Group Lichenes. Philos. Trans. Roy. Soc. London, CLXXVIII. pp. 305–309 (2 pls.), 1887.

Mattirolo, Oreste. Contribuzioni allo studio del genere Cora Fr. Nuovo Giorn. Bot. Ital. XIII. pp. 245–267 (2 pls.), 1881.

Mäule, C. Ueber die Fruchtanlage bei Physcia pulverulenta. Ber. Deutsch. Bot. Ges. IX. pp. 209–213, 1891.

Mayfield, A. The Lichens of a Boulder-Clay Area. Journ. Ipswich, etc. Field Club, V. pp. 34–40, 1916.

Mereschkovsky, Const. Note sur une nouvelle forme de Parmelia vivant à l'état libre. Bull. Soc. Bot. Genève, Sér. 2, X. pp. 26–34, 1918.

Merrett, Christopher. Pinax rerum naturalium Britannicarum, continens Vegetabilia, Animalia, etc. London, 1666.

Metzger, Otto. Untersuchungen über die Entwicklung der Flechtenfrucht. Fünfstück's Beiträge Wiss. Bot. V. pp. 108–144 (7 figs.), 1903.

Meyer, Arthur. Die Plasmaverbindungen und die Fusionen der Pilze der Florideenreihe. Bot. Zeit. LX. pp. 139–178 (1 pl.), 1902.

Meyer, G. F. W. Die Entwickelung, Metamorphose und Fortpflanzung der Flechten. Goettingen, 1825.

Michael, A. D. British Oribatidae. London Ray Society, 2 vols. (pls.), 1884.

Michaux, André. Flora Boreali-Americana, II. p. 320 etc., Paris and Strasburg, 1803.

Micheli, Pier Antonio. Nova Plantarum Genera. Florence, 1729.

Minks, Arthur. Das Microgonidium. Flora, LXI., Nos. 14–20, pp. 209, etc., 1878.

—— Das Microgonidium. Ein Beitrag zur Kenntniss des wahren Wesens der Flechten. Basel, V. and 249 pp., 6 pls. col., 1879.

Miyoshi, Manabu. Die essbare Flechte Japans, Gyrophora esculenta n. sp. Bot. Centralbl. LVI. pp. 161–163, 1893.

—— Ueber die Sporocarpenevacuation und darauf erfolgendes Sporenausstreuen bei einer Flechte. Journ. Coll. Sci. Imp. Univ. Tōkyo, XV. pp. 367–370 (1 pl.), 1901.

Moebius, M. Ueber einige in Portorico gesammelte Süsswasser und Luft-Algen. Hedwigia, XXVII. pp. 221–249 (3 pls.), 1888.

Mohl, Hugo. Einige Bemerkungen über die Entwickelung und den Bau der Sporen der Cryptogamischen Gewächse. Flora, XVI. p. 55, 1833.

Molisch, H. Die Pflanze in ihren Beziehungen zum Eisen. Jena, 1892.

Möller, Alfred. Ueber die Cultur flechtenbildender Ascomyceten ohne Algen. Unters. aus Bot. Inst. K. Akad. Münster i. W., 52 pp., 1887.

—— Ueber die sogenannten Spermatien der Ascomyceten. Bot. Zeit. XLVI. pp. 421–425, 1888.

—— Ueber die eine Thelephoree, welche die Hymenolichenen, Cora, Dictyonema und Laudatea bildet. Flora, LXXVII. pp. 254–278, 1893.

Montagne, Cam. Cryptogamia Guyanensis, etc. Ann. Sci. Nat. XVI. pp. 47–63, 1851.

Moreau, Fernand (M. and Mme). L'évolution nucléaire et les phénomènes de la sexualité chez les lichens du genre Peltigera. Comptes Rendus, CLX. pp. 526–528, 1915.

Moreau, Fernand (M. and Mme). Les phénomènes de la sexualité chez les Lichens du genre Solorina. Op. cit. CLXII. pp. 793–795, 1916[2].

—— Quelques observations sur un Ascomycète parasite du Peltigera polydactyla. Bull. Soc. Mycol. Fr. XXXII. pp. 49–53 (3 figs.), 1916[3].

—— La Biomorphogénèse chez les Lichens. Bull. Soc. Mycol. France, XXXIV. pp. 84–85, 1918.

Moreau, Fernand. Sur le rôle de l'amyloide des asques et son utilisation éventuelle comme matière de réserve. Bull. Soc. Mycol. Fr. XXXII. pp. 25–26, 1916[2].

Morison, Robert. Plantarum Historiae Universalis Oxoniensis III. Oxford, 1699.

Moss, C. E. Vegetation of the Peak District. Cambridge, 1913.

Mudd, W. A Manual of British Lichens. Darlington, 1861.

—— Monograph of British Cladoniae. Cambridge, 1865.

Mühlenberg, H. Catalogue of the Plants of North America. Philadelphia, 1813.

Mulder, G. J. Ueber das Inulin und die Moosstärke. Erdm. Journ. Chem. XV. pp. 299–302, 1838.

Müller, Jean (Müller-Argau). Principes de Classification des Lichens. Mém. Soc. Phys. et Hist. Nat. Genève, XVI. 2, pp. 343–435 (3 pls.), 1862.

—— Notice sur la nature des lichens. Archiv Soc. Phys. Nat. Genève, I. pp. 49–55, 1878.

—— Lichenes japonici. Flora, LXII. pp. 481–487, 1879.

—— Enumeratio Lichenum Aegyptiacorum. Roumeguère Rev. Mycol. II. pp. 73–83, 1880.

—— Lichenologische Beiträge, XII. and XIV. Flora, LXIV. p. 111 and pp. 513–527, 1881 ; Beiträge, XXI. op. cit. LXVIII. p. 345, 1885 ; Beiträge, XXXIII. op. cit. LXXIII. p. 202, 1890.

—— Lichens de Palestine. Rev. Mycol. VI. pp. 12–13, 1884.

—— Enumeratio Lichenum aegyptiacorum. Tom. cit. pp. 13–20, 1884.

—— Lichenes Persici, etc. Hedwigia, XXXI. pp. 151–159, 1892.

Müller, Karl. Die chemische Zusammensetzung der Zellmembranen bei verschiedenen Kryptogamen. Zeitschr. Phys. Chemie, XLV. pp. 265–298, 1905.

Münster, Georg, Count. Beiträge zur Petrefacten-Kunde. Heft VI., 1846.

Necker, N. J. de. Methodus Muscorum, etc. Mannheim, 1771.

Nees von Esenbeck. Handbuch der Botanik, I. Nürnberg, 1820.

Neubert, Adolf. 1. Toxikologische Studien über einige organische Säuren. Diss. Dorpat (Jurjew), 1893. See Zopf, Die Flechtenstoffe, p. 376, 1907.

Neubner, Eduard. Untersuchungen über den Thallus und die Fruchtanfänge der Calycieen. Wiss. Beil. IV. Jahresber. K. Gymnas. Plauen I. v. 12 pp., 1893.

Nienburg, W. Beiträge zur Entwickelungsgeschichte einiger Flechtenapothecien. Flora, XCVIII. pp. 1–40 (7 pls., 3 figs.), 1908.

—— Ueber die Beziehungen zwischen den Algen und Hyphen im Flechtenthallus. Zeitschr. für Bot. IX. pp. 529–543 (1 pl., 6 figs.), 1917.

Nilson, Birger. Zur Entwickelungsgeschichte, Morphologie und Systematik der Flechten. Bot. Not. pp. 1–33, 1903.

—— Die Flechtenvegetation des Sarekgebirges. Hamberg's Nat. Wiss. Untersuch. Sarekgebirges in Schwedisch-Lappland, III. pp. 1–70 (9 pls.), Stockholm, 1907 ; Bot. Centralbl CV. p. 309, 1907.

Norman, J. M. Conatus praemissus redactionis novae generum, etc. Nyt. Mag. Naturvid. VII. pp. 213–252, 1852.

—— Fuligines lichenosae Moriolei. Bot. Not. pp. 9–20, 1872.

—— Allelositismus eller det forhold, etc. K. Norsk. Vid. Selsk. Skrift. VII. pp. 243–255 [1872], 1874.

Notaris, G. de. Frammenti lichenografici di un lavoro inedito. Giorn. Bot. Ital. II. pp. 174–224 and 299–330, 1846.

Nylander, W. Conspectus Florae Helsingforsiensis. Helsingfors Act. Soc. Sci. Fenn. III. p. 62, 1852.

—— Observationes aliquot ad Synopsin Lichenum Holmiensium. Bot. Not. pp. 175–180, 1852.

—— Essai d'une nouvelle classification des Lichens. Mém. Soc. Sci. Nat. Cherbourg, II. pp. 5–16, 1854.

—— Second Mémoire. Op. cit. III. pp. 161–202, 1855.

—— Synopsis Lichenum. Paris, 2 vols. 1858–1860 and 1885.

—— Lichenes adnotati in Armorica, ad Pornic. Bull. Soc. Bot. Fr. VIII. pp. 753–759, 1861.

—— Adhuc circa characteres quosdam Lichenum. Flora, XLIX. pp. 177–181, 1866[1].

—— Circa novum in studio Lichenum criterium chemicum. Flora, XLIX. pp. 198–201 (1866)[1].

—— Les Lichens du Jardin du Luxembourg. Bull. Soc. Bot. Fr. XIII. pp. 364–371, 1866.

—— Lichenes Kurziani e Calcutta. Flora, L. pp. 3–9, 1867.

—— Exemplum cephalodiorum in Sphaerophoro. Flora, LII. pp. 68–69, 1869.

—— Animadversio de theoria gonidiorum algologica. Flora, LIII. pp. 52–53, 1870.

—— Review, including notes, on the Algo-Lichen hypothesis. Flora, LVII. pp. 56, etc., 1874. Translation by Crombie. Grevillea, II. pp. 145–152, 1874.

—— Addenda nova ad Lichenographiam Europaeam. Flora, LVII. p. 306, 1874.

—— Céphalodies. Baillon's Dictionnaire de Botanique, IX. p. 69, 1878.

—— Addenda nova ad Lichenographiam Europaeam. Flora, LXVI. pp. 97–109, 1883.

—— Lichenes Novae Zelandiae. Paris, 1888.

—— Lichenes Japoniae. Paris, 1890.

—— Sertum Lichenææ Tropicæ, Labuan et Singapore. Paris, 1891.

—— Lichenes Ceylonenses, etc. Act. Soc. Sci. Fenn. XXVI. n. 10, 33 pp., 1900.

Nylander, W. and Crombie. J. M. On a collection of Lichens made in Eastern Asia by the late Dr A. C. Maingay. Journ. Linn. Soc. XX. pp. 48–69, 1884.

Ohlert, Arnold. Lichenologische Aphorismen, II. Schrift. Naturf. Ges. Danzig. Neue Folge 2, III., Heft 4, 34 pp., 1871.

Olivier, H. Lichens d'Europe. Cherbourg, Fasc. 1 and 2, 1907, 1909.

Parkinson, John. Theatrum Botanicum : The Theater of Plants, or, an Herball of a large extent, etc. London, 1640.

Patouillard, N. Plantes Cellulaires de la Tunisie. (Lichens by A. Hue, pp. 136–151.) Paris, 1897.

Paulson, R. Notes on the Ecology of Lichens. Essex Naturalist, XVIII. pp. 276–286 (2 pls.), 1918.

—— The Lichen Flora of Hertfordshire. Trans. Herts. Nat. Hist. Soc. XVII. pp. 83–96 (1 pl.), 1919.

Paulson, R. and Hastings, Somerville. A wandering Lichen. Knowledge, XXXVII. pp. 319–323, 1914.

—— The Relation between the Alga and Fungus of a Lichen. Journ. Linn. Soc. XLIV. pp. 497–506 (2 pls.), 1920.

Paulson, R. and Thompson, P. G. Reports on the Lichens of Epping Forest (First paper), Essex Naturalist, XVI. pp. 136–145, 1911 ; (Second paper), op. cit. XVII. pp. 90-105, 1913.

Peirce, G. J. Fixing and Imbedding Lichens. Journ. Applied Microscopy. Rochester, N.Y. I. pp. 99–100, 1898.

—— On the mode of dissemination and on the reticulations of Ramalina reticulata. Bot. Gaz XXV. pp. 404–417, 1898.

—— The Nature of the Association of Alga and Fungus in Lichens. Proc. Calif. Acad. Sci. Ser. 3, I. pp. 207–240 (1 pl.), 1899.

Peirce, G. J. The Relation of Fungus and Alga in Lichens. The American Naturalist, XXXIV. pp. 245–253, 1900.

Persoon, C. H. Einige Bemerkungen über die Flechten, etc. Usteri, Ann. Bot. VII. pp. 1–32, 1794.

—— Synopsis Methodica Fungorum. Göttingen, 1801.

Petch, T. The black termite of Ceylon. Ann. Roy. Bot. Gardens, Peradeniya, V. part 6, pp. 395–420, 1913.

Petiver, J. Musei Petiveriani. Cent. II. and III. London, 1695.

—— Pterigraphia Americana (Gazophylacium, Vol. II.). London, 1712.

Pfaff, C. H. Ueber eine neue eigenthümliche Säure in dem isländischen Moose (Cetraria islandica). Schweigger Journ. Chem. Phys. XLVII. pp. 476–483, 1826. See Berzelius, Jahresb. VII. pp. 216–217, 1828.

Pfeffer, W. Die Oelkörper der Lebermoose. Flora, LVII. pp. 2–6, etc. (1 pl.), 1877.

Phillips, W. Lichens, their rate of Growth. Gard. Chron. n.s. IX. p. 624, 1878.

Plot, Robert. The Natural History of Staffordshire. Oxford, 1686.

Plowright, C. B. British Uredineae and Ustilagineae. London, 1889.

Plukenet, Leonard. Phytographia. London, 1691–1696.

Porta, Joh. Bapt. Phytognomonica...octo libris contenta. Naples, 1588.

Porter, Lilian. Attachment Organs of corticolous Ramalinae. Proc. Roy. Irish Acad. XXXIV. pp. 17–32 (3 pls.), 1917.

—— On the attachment organs of some common Parmeliae. Proc. Roy. Irish Acad. XXXIV. pp. 205–211 (3 pls.), 1919.

Proust, J. L. L'utilité du Lichen d'Islande comme Aliment. Journ. Phys. Chim. Hist. Nat. LXIII. pp. 81–96, 1806.

Raab, —. Excursion in die Gegend von Muggendorf. Flora, II. pp. 289–304, 1819.

Radais, M. Sur la culture pure d'une algue verte ; formation de chlorophylle à l'obscurité. Comptes Rendus, CXXX. pp. 793–796, 1900.

Rave, P. Untersuchung einiger Flechten aus der Gattung Pseudevernia in Bezug auf ihre Stoffwechselprodukte. Inaug.-Diss. von Münter i. W. Borna, Leipzig, 1908. (Hedwigia, XLVII. (171), 1908.)

Ray, John. Catalogus Plantarum Angliae, etc. London, 1670.

—— Historia Plantarum. London, I. 1686 ; II. 1688 ; III. 1704.

—— Synopsis Methodica Stirpium Britannicarum. London, ed. 1, 1690 ; ed. 2, 1696 ; ed. 3 (edited by Dillenius), 1724.

Rees, Max. Ueber die Entstehung der Flechte Collema glaucescens Hoffm. Monatsber. K. Acad. Wiss. Berlin, pp. 523–533 (1 pl.), 1871.

Rehm, H. Die Pilze Deutschlands, etc., Ascomyceten. Rabenhorst's Krypt.-Flora, I. 3, 1887–1896.

Reinke, J. Ueber die anatomische Verhältnisse einiger Arten von Gunnera. Göttingen, Nachrichten, pp. 100–108, 1872.

—— Morphologische Abhandlungen. Leipzig, 1873.

—— Abhandlungen über Flechten, I. and II. Jahrb. Wiss. Bot. XXVI. pp. 495–542, 1894; Abh. III. and IV. op. cit. XXVIII. pp. 39–150 and 359–486, 1895; Abh. V. op. cit. XXIX. pp. 171–236, 1896.

Reinke, J. and Grisebach, A. H. R. A. S. Oersted's System der Pilze Lichenen und Algen. Leipzig, 1873.

Relhan, Richard. Flora Cantabrigiensis. Cambridge, 1785 ; ed. 3, 1820.

Richard, O.-J. Catalogue des Lichens des Deux-Sèvres. Niort, 1877.

Riddle, Lincoln Ware. The North American species of Stereocaulon. Bot. Gaz. pp. 285–304, 1910.

—— Pyrenothrix nigra, gen. et sp. nov. Bot. Gaz. LXIV. pp. 513–515 (4 figs.), 1917.

Ronceray, P. L. Contribution à l'étude des Lichens à orseille. Paris, 94 pp. (3 pls.), 1904.

—— Orseille (Translation). The Pharmaceutical Journal, Ser. 4, XIX. p. 734, 1904.

Rosendahl, F. Vergleichend anatomische Untersuchungen über den braunen Parmelien., Dissertation Münster 1907, and in Nova Acta Abh. K. Leop.-Carol. Deutsch. Akad. Naturf. LXXXVII. 3, pp. 403-459 (4 pls.), 1907.

Ruel, J. (Ruellius). De natura stirpium, etc. Paris, 1536.

Ruppius, Heinr. Bernh. Flora Jenensis. Frankfurt and Leipzig, 1718.

Sachs, Jul. Zur Entwickelungsgeschichte des Collema pulposum Ach. etc. Bot. Zeitung, XII. pp. 1-9 (1 pl.), 1855.

Salter, J. H. Protoplasmic connections in Lichens. Journ. Bot. XL. p. 48, 1902.

Salter, J. W. On some Reactions of Oxalic acid. Chem. Gaz. XIV. pp. 130-131, 1856.

Sandstede, H. Rügen's Flechtenflora. Verh. Bot. Ver. Prov. Brandenburg, XLV. pp. 110-140, 1904.

Sappin-Trouffy, P. Recherches histologiques sur la famille des Urédinées. Le Botaniste, Sér. 5, pp. 59-244, 1896.

Sättler, Hans. Untersuchungen und Erörterungen über die Ökologie und Phylogenie der Cladoniapodetien. Hedwigia, LIV. pp. 226-263 (5 pls.), 1914.

Schade, A. Die Schwefelflechte der Sachseschen Schweiz. Abh. Naturw. Gesell. "Isis" in Dresden 1916, pp. 28-44. See also Ann. Mycol. XV. p. 511, 1917.

Schaerer, Ludov. Eman. Lichenum Helveticorum Spicilegium. Bern, 1823-1842.

Schellenberg, H. Beiträge zur Kenntniss der verholtzten Zellmembran. Jahr. Wiss. Bot. XXIX. p. 249, 1896.

Schikorra, Walter. Ueber die Entwickelungsgeschichte von Monascus. Zeitschr. Bot. I. pp. 378-410 (1 pl., 1 fig.), 1909.

Schimper, W. P. Traité de Paléontologie Végétale, I. Paris, 1869.

Schneider, Albert. A Text-Book of General Lichenology. Binghampton, N.Y., 1897.

Schreber, J. C. D. Linnaei...Genera Plantarum, ed. 8, II. Frankfurt am Main, 1789-1791.

Schrenk, Hermann von. On the Mode of Dissemination of Usnea barbata. Trans. Acad. Sci. St Louis, VIII. pp. 189-198 (1 pl.), 1898.

Schulte, Fritz. Zur Anatomie der Flechtengattung Usnea. Beih. Bot. Centralbl. XVIII. 2, pp. 1-22 (3 pls. and figs.), 1904.

Schwarz, Fr. Chemische-botanische Studien über die in den Flechten vorkommenden Flechtensäuren. Cohn's Beitr. Biol. III. pp. 249-265, 1880.

Schwenckfeld, Caspar. Stirpium et fossilium Silesiae catalogus, etc. Leipzig, 1600.

Schwendener, S. Untersuchungen über den Flechtenthallus, Naegeli's Beitr. Wiss. Bot. Leipzig, II. pp. 109-186 (7 col. pls.), 1860.

—— Op. cit. III. pp. 127-198 (4 col. pls.), 1863.

—— Op. cit. IV. pp. 161-202 (2 col. pls.), 1868.

—— Ueber die Entwickelung der Apothecien von Coenogonium Linkii. Flora, XLV. pp. 225-234 (1 pl.), 1862.

—— Ueber die "Apothecia primitus aperta" und die Entwickelung der Apothecien im Allgemeinen. Flora, XLVII. pp. 321-332, 1864.

—— Ueber den angeblichen Protothallus der Krustenflechten. Flora, XLIX. pp. 401-412 (1 pl.), 1866.

—— Ueber den Bau des Flechtenthallus. Verh. Schweiz. Naturf. Ges. Aarau, p. 88, 1867.

—— Die Algentypen der Flechtengonidien. Basel (3 col. pls.), 1869.

—— Erörterungen zur Gonidienfrage. Flora, LV. pp. 161-166; 177-183; 193-202; 225-234 (1 pl.), 1872.

—— Die Flechten als Parasiten der Algen. Verh. Schweiz. Naturf. Ges. Basel, V. pp. 551-557, 1873[1].

—— Erörterungen zur Gonidienfrage. Flora, LV. pp. 161, etc., 1872. Translated Archer, Quart. Journ. Micros. Sci. XIII. pp. 235-251 (2 pls.), 1873[2].

Scopoli, J. A. Flora carniolica. Vienna, 1760; ed. 2, 1772.

—— Anni historico-naturales, II. Lichenis islandici vires medicae. Leipzig, pp. 107-118, 1769.

Scott-Elliot, G. F. Notes on the Trap Flora of Renfrewshire. Ann. Anders. Nat. Hist. Glasgow, III. Reprint, 10 pp., 1907.

Senft, E. Ein neues Verfahren zum mikrochemischen Nachweis der Flechtensäuren. Phar. Praxis. Vienna and Leipzig, VI. 12, 9 pp. (text figs.). 1907. Hedwigia, XLVIII. Beibl. pp. 24–25, 1908.

Sernander, R. On förekomsten af stentafvar på gammalt trä. Bot. Notis. pp. 17–33, 1891.
—— Om de buskartade lafvarnes hapterer. Bot. Notis. 1901, pp. 21 and 107, etc. See also Bot. Centralbl. LXXXVIII. p. 293, 1901.
—— Om några former för art och varietets-bildnung hos lafvarna. Svensk. Bot. Tidskr. I. pp. 97–115 and 135–186 (5 pls.), 1907.
—— Subfossile Flechten. Flora, CXII. pp. 703–724 (7 figs.), 1918.

Servettaz, Camille. Recherches expérimentales sur le Developpement et la nutrition des Mousses en milieux stérilisés. Ann. Sci. Nat., Sér. 9, XVII. p. 111, 1913.

Servit, Mir. Zur Flechtenflora Böhmens und Mährens. Hedwigia, L. pp. 51–85, 1910.

Sibbald, Robert. Scotia illustrata. Part 2, I. De Plantis Scotiae, etc. Edinburgh, 1684.

Sibthorp, J. Flora Oxoniensis, etc. Oxford, 1794.

Sievers, F. Ueber die Wasserversorgung der Flechten. Wiss. Beil. 38 Jahresber. Ber. Landw. Schule Marienberg, 52 pp., 1908. (Bot. Centralbl. CXIII. p. 22, 1910.)

Sloane, Hans. Catalogus Plantarum quae in Insula Jamaica sponte proveniunt. London, 1696.
—— A voyage to...Jamaica with the Natural History of Herbs, Trees, etc. London, 1707.

Smith, A. Lorrain. British Coenogoniaceae. Journ. Bot. XLIV. pp. 266–268, 1906.
—— Fungal parasites of Lichens. Trans. Brit. Mycol. Soc. III. pp. 174–178, 1910.
—— Monograph of British Lichens, Part II. London, 1911. Part I., 1918.

Smith, J. E. English Botany. London, 1790–1814.
—— Linnaeus' Lachesis Lapponica or a Tour in Lappland. 2 Vols. London, 1811.

Sorby, H. C. Comparative Vegetable Chromatology. Proc. Roy. Soc. XXI. pp. 442–483 (1873).

Speerschneider, J. Zur Entwickelungsgeschichte der Hagenia ciliaris. Bot. Zeit. XI. pp. 705, etc., 1853.
—— Zur Anatomie und Entwickelungsgeschichte der Usnea barbata dasypoga Fr. Bot. Zeit. XII. pp. 193, etc. (1 pl.), 1854.

Spiegel, A. Ueber die Vulpinsäure. Ber. Deutsch. Chem. Ges. XIII. pp. 1629–1635, 1880; tom. cit. pp. 2219–2221 ; op. cit. XIV. pp. 1686–1696, 1881.

Sprengel, K. Einleitung in das Studium der kryptogamischen Gewächse, 1804. Eng. ed. London (Letter XXV.), 1807.

Stahel, Gerold. Stickstoffbildung durch Pilze bei gleichzeitiger Ernährung mit gebundenem Stickstoff. Jahrb. Wiss. Bot. XLIX. pp. 579–615, 1911.

Stahl, E. Beiträge zur Entwickelungsgeschichte der Flechten. Heft I. and II. 55, and 32 pp. (4 pls. 2 col.). Leipzig, 1877.
—— Die Schutzmittel der Flechten gegen Tierfrass. Festschrift zum siebzigsten Geburtstage von Ernst Haeckel. Jena, pp. 357–375, 1904.

Stahlecker, Eugen. Untersuchungen über Thallusbau in ihren Beziehungen zum Substrat bei siliciseden Krustenflechten. Fünfstück's Beitr. Wiss. Bot. V. pp. 405–451 (10 figs.), 1906.

Steiner, J. Verrucaria calciseda, Petractis exanthematica, ein Beitrag zur Kenntniss des Baues und der Entwickelung der Krustenflechten. Programm K.K. Staatsobergymn. Klagenfurt, XXXI. 50 pp. (1 pl.), 1881.
—— Ein Beitrag zur Flechtenflora der Sahara. Sitzungsb. K. Akad. Wiss. Wien, Math.-Nat. Cl. CIV. pp. 384–393, 1895.

Steiner, J. Beitrag zur Flechtenflora Sudpersiens. Sitzungsb. K. Akad. Wiss. Wien, Math.-Nat. Cl. CV. Abth. I. pp. 436–446, 1896.

—— Ueber die Function und den systematischen Wert der Pycnoconidien der Flechten. Festschr. zur Feier des zweihundert Jahr. Best. K.K. Staatsgymn. im VIII. Bezirke Wiens, pp. 119–154, 1901.

—— Flechten auf Madeira und den Kanaren, etc. Oesterr. Bot. Zeitschr. LIV. pp. 333–336, 1904.

—— Flechten aus Transkaukasien. Ann. Mycol. XVII. pp. 1–32, 1919.

Stenberg, Sten. Om användandet af Lafvar rason material för framställning af Drufsocker och Alkohol. Oefv. K. Vetensk. Akad. Förh. pp. 17–28, 1868.

—— Om Tillverkning af Lafbränvin. Stockholm, 52 pp., 1868.

—— See also Flora LII. pp. 517–522, 1869.

Stenhouse, J. and Groves, C. E. Picroroccellin. Proc. Roy. Soc. XXV. pp. 60–68, 1877.

Stirton, J. Additions to the Lichen-Flora of New Zealand. Journ. Linn. Soc. XIV. pp. 458–474, 1875.

—— Description of recently discovered foreign Lichens. Proc. Phil. Soc. Glasgow, X. pp. 156–164, 1874.

Stizenberger, E. Lichenaea Africana. Jahresb. Naturw. Ges. St Gallen, 1888–1895.

—— Die Grübchenflechten (Stictei) und ihre geographische Verbreitung. Flora, LXXXI. pp. 88–150, 1895.

Stone, G. E. Resemblance of an Insect Larva to a Lichen Fruit. Torrey Bot. Club, XXIII. pp. 454–455, 1896.

Stüde, Fr. Ueber Everniin, Pectin und eine neue Glycogene Substanz. Ann. Chem. Pharm. CXXXI. pp. 241–251, 1864.

Sturgis, W. C. On the Carpologic Structure and Development of the Collemaceae and allied groups. Proc. Amer. Acad. Arts Sci. XXV. pp. 15–52 (8 pls.), 1890.

Sutherland, G. K. New Marine Fungi on Pelvetia. New Phytologist, XIV. pp. 33–42, 1915.

Swartz, O. Nova genera et species plantarum, etc. Stockholm, 1788.

—— Observationes Botanicae quibus Plantae Indiae occidentalis, etc. Erlangen, 1791.

Tabernaemontanus, Jac. Theodor. Eicones plantarum seu stirpium, etc. Frankfurt, 1590.

Taylor, T. Lichenes in Mackay's Flora Hibernica, II., 1836.

Thaxter, R. Preliminary Descriptions of new species of Rickia and Trenomyces. Proc. Amer. Acad. Arts and Sci. XLVIII. pp. 365–386, 1912.

Thomas, Nesta. Notes on Cephaleuros. Ann. Bot. XXVII. pp. 781–792 (1 pl.), 1913.

Thwaites, G. H. K. On the gonidia of Lichens. Ann. Mag. Nat. Hist., Ser. 2, III. pp. 219–222, 1849.

—— Note on Cystocoleus, a new genus of minute plants. Tom. cit. pp. 241–242.

Tieghem, Ph. van. Traité de Botanique, I. and II. Paris, 1891.

Tobler, F. Das physiologische Gleichgewicht von Pilz und Alge in den Flechten. Ber. Deutsch. Bot. Ges. XXVII. pp. 421–427 (1 fig.), 1909.

—— Zur Ernährungsphysiologie der Flechten. Ber. Deutsch. Bot. Ges. XXIX. pp. 3–12, 1911[1].

—— Zur Biologie von Flechten und Flechtenpilzen, I., II. Pringsh. Jahrb. Wiss. Bot. XLIX. pp. 389–416 (1 pl.), 1911[2].

Torrey, J. A Catalogue of plants growing spontaneously within 30 miles of the city of New York. Albany, 1819.

Tournefort, Joseph Pitton de. Élémens de Botanique. Paris, 1694.

—— Institutiones Rei Herbariae. Paris, 1700.

Treboux, O. Organische Säuren als Kohlenstoffquelle bei Algen. Ber. Deutsch. Bot. Ges. XXIII. pp. 432–441, 1905.

—— Die freilebende Alge und die Gonidie Cystococcus humicola in Bezug auf die Flechtensymbiose. Ber. Deutsch. Bot. Ges. XXX. pp. 69–80, 1912.

Treub, M. Lichenencultur. Bot. Zeit. XXXI. pp. 721–727 (1 pl.), 1873.

—— Notice sur la nouvelle Flore de Krakatau. Ann. Jard. Bot. Buitenzorg, VII. pp. 213–223, 1888.

Tuckerman, E. An Enumeration of some Lichens of New England with Remarks. Boston Journ. Nat. Hist. II. pp. 245–261, 1839.

—— Genera Lichenum (North American). Amherst, 1872.

—— Lichens of Kerguelen's Land. Bull. Torrey Bot. Club, VI. pp. 57–59, 1875.

Tulasne, L. R. Note sur l'appareil reproducteur dans les Lichens et les Champignons. Comptes Rendus, XXXII. pp. 427 and 470, etc., 1851.

—— Mémoire pour servir à l'Histoire Organographique et Physiologique des Lichens. Ann. Sci. Nat., Sér. 3, XVII. pp. 5–128 and 153–249 (16 pls.), 1852.

Tutt, J. W. British Lepidoptera. London, vol. II., 1900.

Uhlíř, V. Ueber Isolation der Algen aus dem Collemacaeen. Živa [1914] (1915), p. 233. See also Bot. Centralbl. CXXIX. p. 379, 1915.

Ulander, A. Untersuchungen über die Kohlenhydrate der Flechten. Inaug.-Dissert. Göttingen, 8°, 59 pp., 1905.

Uloth, W. Beiträge zur Flora der Laubmoose und Flechten von Kurhessen. II. Flechten. Flora, XLIV. pp. 565, etc., 1861.

Vaillant, Sebastien. Botanicon Parisiense, etc. Leyden and Amsterdam, 1727.

Vallot, J. Sur la vitesse de croissance d'un lichen saxicole. Rev. Gén. Bot. VIII. pp. 201–202, 1896.

Ventenat, E. P. Tableau du règne végétal. Paris, vol. II. p. 36, 1794.

Villars, M. Histoire des Plantes de Dauphiné. Grenoble, Lyon, Paris, 1786–1789.

Visiani, de. Bericht über einen Regen einer vegetabilischen Nahrungs-Substanz, etc. (1864), translated by Krempelhuber. Flora, L. pp. 197, etc., 1867.

Volkard, J. Synthese und Constitution der Vulpinsäure. Ann. Chemie, CCLXXXII. pp. 1–21, 1894.

Vouaux, Léon. Synopsis des Champignons parasites de Lichens. Bull. Soc. Mycol. France, XXVIII. pp. 177–208, etc., etc., 1912–1914.

Wąhlberg, A. Ueber die Apothecienentwicklung bei einigen Flechten der Gattungen Anaptychia und Physcia. Öfvers. Finsk. Vet.-Soc. Förh. XLIV. 30 pp. (1 pl.), 1902.

Wahrlich, W. Zur Anatomie der Zelle bei Pilzen und Fadenalgen. Script. Bot. Hort. Univ. Imp. Petrop. IV. pp. 41–100, German résumé (3 pls.), 1893.

Wainio, E. A. Tatkimus Cladoniein phylogenetillisesta, etc. Inaug.-Diss. Helsingfors, 62 pp. (1 pl.), 1880.

—— Lichens du Brésil. I. II. Helsingfors, 1890. (Act. Soc. Faun. et Fl. Fenn. VII.)

—— Lichenes Sibiria Meridionali collecti. Act. Soc. Faun. and Fl. Fenn. XIII. n. 6, 20 pp., 1896.

—— Monographia Cladoniarum universalis. Helsingfors, I. 1887 ; II. 1894 ; III. 1897.

—— Lichenes in Caucaso, etc. Termész. Füz. XXII. pp. 269–343, 1899.

—— Expédition Antarctic Belge. Résultats du voyage du S.Y. Belgica en 1897–1899, etc. Lichens, 46 pp. (4 tab.), Anvers, 1903.

—— Lichenes...Pitlekai in Sibiria septentrionali a E. Almquist collecti. Arkiv Bot. VIII. n. 4, 175 pp., 1909.

Waite, M. B. Experiments with Fungicides in the removal of Lichens from Pear trees. Journ. Mycol. VII. pp. 264–268 (2 pls.), 1893.

Wallroth, F. W. Naturgeschichte der Flechten. 2 vols. Frankfurt am Main, 1825–1827.

—— Naturgeschichte der Säulchen-Flechten. Naumburg, 1829.

Ward, Marshall. On the structure, development and life-history of a tropical epiphyllous lichen (Strigula complanata Fée, fide Rev. J. M. Crombie). Trans. Linn. Soc., Ser. 2, II. pp. 87–119 (4 pls.), 1884.

Watson, Sir W. An Historical Memoir concerning a Genus of Plants called Lichen, etc. Phil. Trans. L. 2 [1758], pp. 652–688. London, 1759.

Watson, W. The Distribution of Bryophytes in the woodlands of Somerset. New Phytologist, VIII. pp. 60–96, 1909.

—— Cryptogamic Vegetation of the Sand-Dunes of the West coast of England. Journ. Ecol. VI. pp. 126–143, 1918[1].

—— The Bryophytes and Lichens of calcareous soil. Tom. cit. pp. 189–198, 1918[2].

Watt, George. A Dictionary of the Economic Products of India, IV. pp. 635–639, 1890.

Weber, G. H. Wiggers' Primitiae Florae Holsaticae. Kiel, 1780.

Weddell, H. A. Les Lichens des promenades publiques et, en particulier, du Jardin de Blossac, à Poitiers. Bull. Soc. Bot. Fr. XVI. pp. 194–203, 1869.

—— Les Lichens du massif granitique de Ligugé, etc. Bull. Soc. Bot. Fr. XX. pp. 142–155, 1873.

—— Excursion lichénologique dans l'île d'Yeu sur la côte de la Vendée. Mém. Soc. Sci. Nat. Cherb. XIX. pp. 251–316, 1875[1].

—— Remarques complémentaires sur le rôle du substratum, etc. Comptes Rendus, LXXX. pp. 1434–1438, 1875[2].

—— Les substratum neutres. Op. cit. LXXXI. pp. 211–214, 1875[3].

—— Remarques sur le rôle du substratum dans la distribution des Lichens saxicoles. Ann. Sci. Nat. Sér. 6, I. pp. 394–398, 1875[4].

Wehmer, Carl. Entstehung und physiologische Bedeutung der Oxalsäure im Stoffwechsel einiger Pilze. Bot. Zeit. XLIX. pp. 611–620 and 630–638, 1891.

Weir, James R. Concerning the introduction into the United States of extra-limital wood-destroying fungi. Mycologia, XI. pp. 58–65, 1919.

West, G. S. A Treatise on the British Freshwater Algae. Cambridge, 1904.

—— Cambridge Botanical Handbooks. Algae, vol. I. Cambridge, 1916.

West, W. Physcia parietina. Journ. Bot. XLIII. p. 31, 1905.

—— Ecological Notes; chiefly Cryptogamic. Journ. Linn. Soc. XLIII. pp. 57–85, 1915.

Wester, D. A. Studien über das Chitin. Arch. Pharm. CCXLVII. pp. 282–307, 1909. (Bot. Zeit. LXVII. pp. 293–294, 1909.)

Westring, J. P. Sur la propriété tinctoriale des Lichens. Ann. Chimie, XV. pp. 267–297, 1792 ; XVII. pp. 67–84, 1793.

—— Svenska Lafvarnes Farghistoria. Stockholm (24 col. pls.), 1805–1809.

Wettstein, F. V. Geosiphon Fr. Wettst., eine neue interessante Siphonee. Oesterr. Bot. Zeitschr. pp. 145–156 (2 pls.), 1915. See also Bot. Centralbl. CXXXI. pp. 131–132, 1916.

Wheldon, J. A. Stone Mites in West Lancashire. Lancashire and Cheshire Naturalist, pp. 31–32 (4 figs.), 1914.

Wheldon, J. A. and Travis, W. G. The Lichens of South Lancashire. Journ. Linn. Soc. XLIII. pp. 87–136, 1915.

Wheldon, J. A. and Wilson, A. The Flora of West Lancashire. Eastbourne, 1907.

—— Inverness and Banff Cryptogams. Journ. Bot. XLVIII. pp. 123–129, 1910.

—— Lichens of Arran. Journ. Bot. LI. pp. 248–253, 1913.

—— The Lichens of Perthshire. Journ. Bot. LIII. Suppl. 73 pp., 1915.

Wiesner, J. Untersuchungen über den Lichtgenuss der Pflanzen, etc. Sitzungsb. K. Akad. Wiss. Wien, Math.-Naturw. Cl. CIV. pp. 606–711, 1895.

—— Die Rohstoffe des Pflanzenreichs, I. pp. 668–671, 1900.

Wille, N. Algologische Notizen, XXII. Nyt. Magazin Naturv. LI. I, pp. 1–26 (1 pl.), 1913.

Willemet, M. Lichenographie Économique ou Histoire des Lichens utiles. Lyon, 1787.

Wilson, A. and Wheldon, J. A. Alpine Vegetation of Ben-y-Gloe, Perthshire. Journ. Bot. LII. pp. 227–235, 1914.

Wilson, F. R. M. The Climate of Eastern Tasmania indicated by its lichen flora. Papers and Proc. Roy. Soc. Tasmania for 1892, p. 131, 1893.

Winter, Georg. Ueber die Gattung Sphaeromphale und Verwandte. Ein Beitrag zur Anatomie der Krustenflechten. Pringsh. Jahrb. Wiss. Bot. x. pp. 245–274 (3 pls.), 1876.

—— Lichenologische Notizen. I. Cephalodien von Sticta und Solorina. Flora, LX. pp. 177–184, 193–203, 1877[1]. II. Flechtenparasiten. tom. cit. pp. 209–214, 1877[2].

Winterstein, E. Zur Kenntniss der Pilzcellulose. Ber. Deutsch. Bot. Ges. XI. pp. 441–445, 1893.

Wisselingh, C. van. Mikrochemische Untersuchungen über die Zellwände der Fungi. Pringsh. Jahrb. Wiss. Bot. XXXI. pp. 618–687 (pl.), 1898.

Withering, W. A Botanical Arrangement, etc. ed. 1. Birmingham, 1776.

Wolff, Gertr. P. Beiträge zur Entwicklungsgeschichte der Flechtenapothecien. Flora, XCV. pp. 31–57 (figs.), 1905.

Woodward, T. J. Observations upon the Generic Characters of Ulva with Descriptions of some new species. Trans. Linn. Soc. III. pp. 46–58, 1797.

Woronin, M. Recherches sur les gonidies du Lichen Parmelia pulverulenta Ach. Ann. Sci. Nat. Sér. 5, XVI. pp. 317–325 (1 pl.), 1872.

Zahlbruckner, A. Studien über brasilianische Flechten. Sitzungsb. K. Akad. Wiss. Wien, Math.-Naturw. Cl. CXI. pp. 357–432 (2 pls.), 1902.

—— Lichenes (Specieller Teil). Engler and Prantl, Die Natürlichen Pflanzenfamilien, LI*. pp. 49–249, 1903–1907.

Zittel, A. Handbuch der Palaeontologie. Abt. II. von W. Ph. Schimper und A. Schenk. München und Leipzig, 1890.

Zopf, W. Die Pilze. Schenk's Handbuch der Botanik, IV. pp. 271–775, 1890.

—— Beitr. Phys. Morph. niederer Organismen. Leipzig, 1892.

—— Die Weissfärbung von Thamnolia vermicularis, etc. Hedwigia, XXXII. pp. 66–69, 1893.

—— Uebersicht der auf Flechten schmarotzenden Pilze. Hedwigia, XXXV. pp. 312–366, 1896.

—— Ueber Nebensymbiose (Parasymbiose). Ber. Deutsch. Bot. Ges. XV. pp. 90–92, 1897.

—— Zur biologischen Bedeutung der Flechtensäuren. Biol. Centralbl. XVI. No. 16, pp. 593–610, 1896.

—— Untersuchungen über die durch parasitische Pilze hervorgerufene Krankheiten der Flechten. Nova Acta Acad. Caes. Leop.-Carol. LXX. No. 2, pp. 97–190 (pl.), 1897, and tom. cit. No. 4, pp. 243–288 (fig.), 1898.

—— Vergleichende Untersuchungen über Flechten in Bezug auf ihre Stoffwechsel-produkte. Beih. Bot. Centralbl. XIV. pp. 95–126 (4 pls.), 1903.

—— Biologische und morphologische Beobachtungen an Flechten. Ber. Deutsch. Bot. Ges. XXIII. pp. 497–504 (1 pl.), 1905.

—— Zur Kenntniss der Flechtenstoffe. Lieb. Ann. Chemie, CCLXXXIV.–CCCLII., 1895–1907.

—— Die Flechtenstoffe in chemischer botanischer pharmakologischer und technischer Beziehung. Jena, 1907.

—— Biologische und morphologische Beobachtungen an Flechten. Ber. Deutsch. Bot. Ges. XXV. pp. 233–238 (1 pl.), 1907.

—— Beiträge zu einer chemischen Monographie der Cladoniaceen. Ber. Deutsch. Bot. Ges. XXVI. pp. 51–113 (4 pls.), 1908.

—— Die Flechtenstoffe. Liebig's Ann. Chemie, CCCLXIV. pp. 273–313, 1909.

Zschacke, H. Ein Beitrag zur Flechtenflora des unteren Saaletales. Zeitschr. Naturwiss. LXXX. pp. 231–253, 1908.

Zukal, H. Das Zusammenleben von Moos und Flechten. Oesterr. Bot. Zeitschr. XXIX. pp. 189–191, 1879.

—— Flechtenstudien. Denkschr. K. Akad. Wiss. Math.-Nat. Cl. Wien, XLVIII. II. pp. 249–292 (1 pl.), 1884.

—— Ueber das Vorkommen von Reservestoffbehältern bei Kalkflechten. Bot. Zeit. XLIV. pp. 761–770, 1886.

—— Ueber einige neue Ascomyceten. Verh. K. K. Zool.-Bot. Ges. Wien, XXXVII. pp. 39–46 (1 pl.), 1887.

—— Epigloea bactrospora. Verh. K. K. Zool.-Bot. Ges. Wien, XXXIX. p. 78, 1889 and Österr. Bot. Zeitschr. XL. pp. 323–328 (1 pl.), 1889.

—— Halbflechten. Flora, LXXIV. pp. 92–107 (1 pl.), 1891.

—— Ueber zwei neue Myxomyceten. Oesterr. Bot. Zeitschr. XLIII. pp. 73–77 and 133–137 (1 pl.). 1893.

—— Morphologische und biologische Untersuchungen über die Flechten. Sitzungsb. K. Akad. Wiss. Math.-Naturw. Cl. Wien, CIV. pp. 529–574 and 1303–1395 (2 pls.), 1895 ; op. cit. CV. pp. 197–264, 1896.

Zwelser, Joanne. Pharmacopæa augustana reformata cum ejus mantissa, etc. (p. 578), 1672.

INDEX

CAMBRIDGE: PRINTED BY J. B. PEACE, M.A., AT THE UNIVERSITY PRESS

SUPPLEMENTARY INDEX

This Supplementary Index provides the currently accepted names of lichen genera and species (and some other organisms) where these differ from those employed in the text in *Lichens:* in cases of controversy British usage of the names has been followed. Names of lichens in the text not listed here (other than those published prior to 1753 or referring to fossil lichens) are still accepted in modern lichen literature or are of very uncertain application. Typographical errors are cited in quotation marks; if a name has been commonly misapplied "p.m.p." is used before the name of the taxon to which it usually (incorrectly) referred. In cases where generic names or specific epithets remain unchanged these have been abbreviated to their initial letters.

Abrothallus cetrariae = *A. parmeliarum*
A. oxysporus = *Lecidea o.*
A. peyritschii = *A. parmeliarum* f. p.
A. smithii = *A. parmeliarum* ?
Acanthothecium = *Acanthothecis*
Acarospora pruinosa = *Sarcogyne regularis·is*
Acolium = *Cyphelium*
Acrocordia gemmata = *Arthopyrenia g.*
Actinoplaca = *Echinoplaca*
Alectoria implexa p.m.p. = *A. capillaris*
A. jubata p.m.p. = *A. fuscescens*
A. thrausta = *Ramalina t.*
Allarthonia = *Arthonia*
Allarthothelium = *Arthothelium*
Amphiloma = *Caloplaca* and *Xanthoria*
Arnoldia minutula = *Pyrenocollema m.*
Arthonia astroidea = *A. tumidula*
A. cinnabarina = *A. tumidula*
A. gregaria = *A. tumidula*
A. pruinosa = *A. impolita*
A. subvarians = *A. clemens*
Arthoniopsis = *Arthonia*
Arthopyrenia halizoa = *Verrucaria microspora*
A. leptotera = *Stigimidium marinum*
A. macrospora = *A. finkii*
A. marina = *Stigmidium m.*
Arthotheliopsis = *Echinoplaca*
Ascophanus carneus = *Iodophanus c.*
Aspicilia atroviolacea = *Lecanora a.*
A. flavida = *Lecanora f.*
Aspidopyrenium = *Aspidothelium*
Asteristion = *Phaeotrema*

Bacidia flavovirescens = *Arthrorhaphis citrinella*
Biatora = *Lecidea*
Biatorella cinerea = *Sporastatia c.*
B. pruinosa = *Sarcogyne regularis*
B. resinae = *Tromera r.*
B. simplex = *Sarcogyne s.*
B. testudinea = *Sporastatia t.*
Biatorina = *Catillaria*
B. bouteillei = *Catillaria b.*
B. chalybeia = *Catillaria c.*
B. coeruleonigricans = *Toninia c.*
B. globulosa = *Catillaria g.*
B. lenticularis = *Catillaria l.*
B. prasina = *Micarea p.*
B. synothea = *Micarea denigrata*

Bilimbia aromatica = *Toninia a.*
"*B. incana*" = *Bombyliospora i.* =
  B. pachycarpa
B. microcarpa = *Bacidia m.*
B. obscurata = *Bacidia o.*
B. sabulosa = *Toninia lobulata*
B. sphaeroides = *Bacidia s.*
Bombyliospora incana = *B. pachycarpa*
Borrera = *Anaptychia* or *Teloschistes*
Bryopogon = *Alectoria*
Buellia colludens = *Rhizocarpon hochstetteri*
B. coracina = *B. moriopsis*
B. discolor = *Rinodina d.*
B. myriocarpa = *B. punctata*
B. parasema = *B. disciformis*
B. parmeliarum = *Abrothallus p.*
B. punctiformis = *B. punctata*
B. ryssolea = *B. subdisciformis*

Calcium hyperellum = *C. viride*
C. parietinum = *Mycocalicium subtile* var. p.
C. trachelinum = *C. salicinum*
Callopisma = *Caloplaca*
C. aurantia var. *callopisma* = *C. a.*
C. interveniens = *C. circumalbata*
C. pyracea = *C, holocarpa*
"*Calothricopsis*" = *Calotrichopsis*
Candelariella cerinella = *C. aurella*
Catillaria hochstetteri = *Rhizocarpon h.*
Celidium stictarum = *Lichenomyces lichenum*
Cerania = *Thamnolia*
C. vermicularis = *Thamnolia v.*
Cetraria aculeata = *Cornicularia a.*
C. caperata = *C. pinastri*
C. crispa = *C. islandica* subsp. *crispa*
C. diffusa = *Parmeliopsis aleurites* s
C. tristis = *Cornicularia normoerica*
Cinchona cordaminea = *C. officinalis*
Cladina = *Cladonia*
C. agariciformis = *C. caespiticia*
C. aggregata = *Cladia a.*
C. alcicornis = *C. foliacea*
C. alpestris = *C. stellaris*
C. degenerans = *C. phyllophora*
C. endiviaefolia = *C. convoluta*
C. flabelliformis = *C. polydactyla*
C. leptophylla = *C. capitata*
C. papillaria = *Pycnothelia p.*

C. racemosa = C. furcata
C. "retepora" = Cladia retipora
C. sullivanii = Cladia s.
C. sylvatica = C. arbuscula
Cleora lichenaria = Cleodares l.
Coenogonium ebeneum = Cystocoleus niger
Collema ceranoides = C. tenax var. c.
C. cheileum = C. crispum
C. granuliferum = C. cristatum
C. hildenbrandii = Leptogium h.
C. microphyllum = C. fragrans
C. plicatile = Leptogium p.
C. pulposum = C. tenax
C. pustulatum = C. cristatum
C. pycnocarpum = C. conglomeratum
  var. crassiusculum
Collemodes = Collema
C. bachmannianum = Collema b.
Conida = Arthonia
C. rubescens ?= Arthonia clemens
Coniocarpon = Arthonia
Cornicularia ochroleuca = Alectoria o.
Crocynia p.m.p. = Lepraria
C. lanuginosa = Lepraria membranacea
Cyphella aeruginascens = Pyrenotrichum
  splitgerberi

"Dacampia" = Decampia = Pleospora
Dermatocarpon aquaticum = D. fluviatile
Dichodium = Physma
Didymosphaeria pulposi = Didymella p.
Diplosphaera = Stichococcus
Dufourea = Dactylina

Endocarpon monstrosum = Dermatocarpon m.
Ephebe pubescens p.m.p. = E. lanata
Ephebeia = Ephebe
Eunephroma = Nephroma
Euopsis granatina = Lecanora g.
Evernia furfuracea = Pseudevernia f.

Gongylia viridis = G. sabuletorum
Gonothecium = Gyalectidium
Gyalecta cupularis = G. jenensis
G. rubra = G. ulmi
Gyalolechia = Candelariella
G. subsimilis = Candelariella aurella
Gyrophora = Umbilicaria
G. cylindrica = Umbilicaria c.
G. erosa = Umbilicaria torrefacta
G. esculenta = Umbilicaria e.
G. flocculosa = Umbilicaria deusta
G. murina = Umbilicaria m.
G. polyphylla = Umbilicaria p.
G. "polyrhiza" = Umbilicaria polyrrhiza
G. proboscidea = Umbilicaria p.
G. spadochroa = Umbilicaria s.
G. torrefacta = Umbilicaria t.
G. vellea = Umbilicaria v.

Haematomma coccineum = H: ochroleucum
Hagenia ciliaris = Anaptychia c.
Haplopyrenula = Vizella
Helix hortensis = Cepaea h.
Heppia despreauxii = H. lutosa

H. guepinii = Peltula euploca
H. virescens = H. lutosa
Heufleria = Asterothelium

Isidium = Pertusaria
I. corallinum = Pertusaria c.
I. westringii = Pertusaria pseudocorallina

"Jonaspis" = Ionaspis

Karschia = Buellia
K. destructans = Buellia d.
K. lignyota = Buellia l.

Lachnea scutellata = Scutellinia s.
L. stercorea = Cheilymenia s.
Laudatea = Dictyonema
Lecania candicans = Solenopsora c.
L. holophaea = Solenopsora h.
Lecaniella = Byssolecania
Lecanora aquatica = L. amphibola
L. atroflava = Caloplaca a.
L. aurella = Candelariella a.
L. citrina = Caloplaca c.
L. crassa = Squamarina c.
L. dicksonii = Lecidea atrata
L. epulotica = Ionaspis e.
L. ferruginea = Caloplaca f.
L. galactina = L. dispersa
L. gelida = Placopsis g.
L. glaucoma = L. rupicola
L. glaucoma var. corrugata = L. rupicola
L. hageni p.m.p. = L. dispersa
L. lentigera = Squamarina l.
L. ochracea = Caloplaca o.
L. pallescens = Ochrolechia p.
L. parella = Ochrolechia p.
L. "peliocypha" = Acarospora pelicypha
L. prosechoides = L. helicopis
L. rugosa = L. chlarotera
L. saxicola p.m.p. = L. muralis
L. simplex = Sarcogyne s.
L. smaragdula = Acarospora s.
L. sophodes = Rinodina s.
L. sordida = L. rupicola
L. subfusca p.m.p. = L. chlarotera
L. sulphurea = Lecidea s.
L. tartarea = Ochrolechia t.
L. umbrina = L. dispersa
L. upsaliensis = Ochrolechia u.
L. urbana = L. dispersa
L. varia p.m.p. = L. conizaeoides
L. xantholyta = Leproplaca x.
Lecidea arctica = L. caesioatra
L. aromatica = Toninia a.
L. atrofusca = L. templetonii
L. coarctata = Trapelia c.
L. coeruleonigricans = Toninia c.
L. colludens = Rhizocarpon hochstetteri
L. contigua = L. macrocarpa
L. cupreiformis = L. berengeriana
L. fumosa = L. fuscoatra
L. grisella = L. fuscoatra var. grisella
L. herbidula = Bacidia h.
L. immersa = Protoblastenia i.

[ii]

L. *irregularis* = Fungus (identity uncertain)
L. *lavata* = *Rhizocarpon l.*
L. *metzleri* = *Protoblastenia m.*
L. *nigroclavata* = *Catillaria n.*
L. *ostreata* = *L. scalaris*
L. *parasema* = *Lecidella elaeochroma*
L. *phyllisiocarpa* = *L. auriculata*
L. *"phyllocaris"* = *L. phyllocharis* =
  Sporopodium p.
L. *platycarpa* = *L. macrocarpa*
L. *rivulosa* = *Fuscidea cyathoides*
L. *sanguinarius* = *Mycoblastus s.*
L. *stellulata* = *Buellia s.*
L. *sulphurella* = *L. atrosulphurea* var. *biformis*
L. *testacea* = *Protoblastenia t.*
L. *tricolor* = *Catillaria griffithii*
Lepidocollema = *Collema*
Lepolichen coccophora = *L. coccophorus*
Lepra p.m.p. = *Lepraria*
L. *viridis* = *Lepraria botryoides*
Leproloma = *Lepraria*
Leptodendriscum = *Polychidium*
Leptogidium = *Polychidium*
L. *dendriscum* = *Polychidium d.*
Leptogium lacerum = *L. lichenoides*
L. *myochroum* = *L. saturninum*
L. *scotinum* = *L. sinuatum* var. *s.*
Lichen candelarius = *Xanthoria c.*
L. *juniperinus* = *Cetraria j.*
L. *parietinus* = *Xanthoria p.*
L. *roccella* = *Roccella tinctoria*
L. *saxatilis* = *Parmelia s.*
L. *tartareus* = *Ochrolechia t.*
L. *tenellus* = *Physcia tenella*
Lithoicea lecideoides = *Verrucaria l.*
Lobaria laciniata = *L. amplissima*
Lopadiopsis = *Gyalectidium*

Micrographa ? = *Lembosia* or *Melaspilea*
Microphiale = *Dimerella*
Mycocalicium parietinum = *M. subtile* var. *p.*
Mycoconiocybe ? = *Coniocybe*
Mycoidea = *Cephaleuros*
M. parasitica = *Cephaleuros p. ?* = *C. virescens*
Mycoporum = *Mycoporellum*

Neophyllis = *Gymnoderma*
Nephromium = *Nephroma*
N. laevigatum p.m.p. = *Nephroma bellum*
N. lusitanicum = *Nephroma laevigatum* s.s.
N. tomentosum = *Nephroma t.*
Neuropogon = *Usnea*
Nylanderiella = *Siphula*

Obryzum ? = *Guignardia*
Omphalaria = *Thyrea*
O. heppii = *Thyrea h.*
O. pulvinata = *Thyrea p.*
Oospora = *Oidium*
Opegrapha hapalea = *O. atra*
O. subsiderella = *O. niveoatra*
Opegraphella = *Opegrapha*
Orbilia coccinella ? = *Hyalina rubella*

Pannaria brunnea = *P. pezizoides*

P. *triptophylla* = *Parmeliella corallinoides*
Pannoparmelia anzioides = *Anzia a.*
Parathelium = *Campylothelium*
Parmelia adglutinata = *Physciopsis a.*
P. *aleurites* = *Parmeliopsis a.*
P. *aspidota* = *P. exasperata*
P. *dubia* p.m.p. = *P. subrudecta*
P. *encausta* = *Hypogymnia intestiniformis*
P. *enteromorpha* = *Hypogymnia e.*
P. *farinacea* = *Hypogymnia bitteriana*
P. *fuliginosa* = *P. glabratula* subsp. *f.*
P. *glomellifera* = *P. verruculifera*
P. *hyperopta* = *Parmeliopsis h.*
P. *"kamtschadalis"* = *P. camtschadalis*
P. *lanata* p.m.p. = *Alectoria pubescens*
P. *obscurata* = *Hypogymnia bitteri*
P. *papulosa* = *P. exasperatula*
P. *pertusa* = *Menegazzia terebrata*
P. *physodes* = *Hypogymnia p.*
P. *pilosella* = *P. crinita*
P. *proboscidea* = *P. crinita*
P. *pubescens* = *Alectoria p.*
P. *scortea* p.m.p. = *P. tiliacea*
P. *tristis* = *Cornicularia normoerica*
P. *vittata* = *Hypogymnia duplicata*
Paulia = *Umbilicaria*
Peltigera americana = *P. austroamericana*
P. *leptoderma* = *P. spuria*
P. *spuriella* = *P. spuria*
Perforaria = *Coccotrema*
Pertusaria communis = *P. pertusa*
P. *faginea* = *P. amara*
P. *globulifera* = *P. albescens*
P. *lutescens* = *P. flavida*
P. *melaleuca* = *P. pustulata*
P. *wulfenii* = *P. hymenea*
Petractis exanthematica = *P. clausa*   .
Peziza resinae = *Tromera r.*
Phialopsis rubra = *Gyalecta ulmi*
Phyllactidium = *Phycopeltis*
P. *tropicum* = *Cephaleuros virescens*
Phyllophthalmaria = *Metasphaeria*
P. *coccinea* = *Chroodiscus coccineus*
Phylloporina = *Porina*
Physcia aquila = *Anaptychia fusca*
P. *ascendens* = *P. adscendens*
P. *ciliaris* p.m.p. = *Anaptychia c.*
P. *granulifera* = *Anaptychia g.*
P. *hispida* = *P. tenella*
P. *hypoleuca* p.m.p. = *Anaptychia obscura*
P. *intricata* = *Tornabenia i.*
P. *leucomelas* = *Anaptychia leucomeleana*
P. *obscura* p.m.p. = *P. orbicularis*
P. *parietina* = *Xanthoria p.*
P. *sciastrella* = *P. nigricans*
P. *stellaris* var. *tenella* = *P. tenella*
P. *villosa* = *Teloschistes v.*
Physma = *Lempholemma*
P. *chalazanum* = *Lempholemma c.*
P. *compactum* = *Lempholemma myriococcum*
P. *franconicum* = *Lempholemma chalazanum*
Pilocarpon = *Byssoloma*
P. *leucoblepharum* = *Byssoloma l.*
Placodium = *Caloplaca*
P. *atroflavum* = *Caloplaca a.*

P. *aurantiacum* = *Caloplaca a.*
P. *bicolor* = *Placopsis b.*
P. *callopismum* = *Caloplaca aurantia*
P. *cerinum* = *Caloplaca c.*
P. *citrinum* = *Caloplaca c.*
P. *decipiens* = *Caloplaca d.*
P. *elegans* = *Xanthoria e.*
P. *ferrugineum* = *Caloplaca f.*
P. *flavescens* = *Caloplaca heppiana*
P. *fructiculosum* = *Caloplaca regalis*
P. *fulgens* = *Fulgensia f.*
P. *lacteum* = *Caloplaca l.*
P. *lobulatum* = *Caloplaca marina*
P. *luteoalbum* = *Caloplaca l.*
P. *murorum* = *Caloplaca saxicola*
P. *nivale* = *Caloplaca n.*
P. *pyraceum* = *Caloplaca holocarpa*
P. *rupestre* = *Protoblastenia r.*
P. *teicholytum* = *Caloplaca t.*
P. *garovaglii* = *Lecanora muralis* var. *g.*
P. *"saxicolum"* = *P. saxicola* =
   Lecanora muralis
Placolecania = *Solenopsora*
Platygrapha = *Schismatomma*
Platysma = *Cetraria*
P. *commixtum* = *Cetraria c.*
P. *fahlunense* p.m.p. = *Cetraria hepatizon*
P. *glaucum* = *Platismatia g.*
P. *lacunosa* p.m.p. = *Platismatia norvegica*
Pleospora collematum = *P. hookeri*
Pleurothelium = *Parathelium*
Polyblastia catalepta = *Staurothele c.*
Polycauliona = *Caloplaca*
P. *regale* =, *Caloplaca r.*
Polystictus versicolor = *Coriolus v.*
Protococcus = *Pleurococcus*
P. *viridis* = *Pleurococcus v.*
Psora decipiens = *Lecidea d.*
Psorotichia lugubris = *Lecidea cinereorufa*
Pterygium = *Placynthium*
P. *kenmorensis* = *Porocyphus k.*
Pycnographa = *Schneepia*
Pyrenothamnia = *Endocarpon*
P. *spraguei* = *Endocarpon s.*
Pyrenothea = *Dimerella*
Pyrenula cinerella = *Microthelia micula*
P. *thelena* = *Microthelia t.*
Pyxine meissneri = *P. berteriana*

Ramalina cuspidata = *R. siliquosa*
R. *dilacerata* = *R. minuscula*
R. *gracilenta ?* = *R. farinacea*
R. *landroensis* = *R. sinensis*
R. *reticulata* = *R. menziesii*
R. *strepsilis* = *R. capitata*
Rhizocarpon alboatrum = *Buellia a.*
R. *concentricum* = *R. petraeum*
R. *confervoides* = *R. constrictum*
R. *epipolium* = *Buellia e.*
Rhymbocarpus punctiformis =
   Phacopsis geographici
Ricasolia = *Lobaria*
R. *amplissima* = *Lobaria a.*
R. *laetevirens* = *Lobaria l.*
Rinodina oreina = *Dimelaena o.*

Roccella fucoides = *R. phycopsis*
R. *"sinuensis"* = *R. sinensis*

Sagedia = *Porina*
S. *declivum* = *Porina mammillosa*
Secoliga bryophaga = *Gloeolecta b.*
Sirosiphon pulvinatus ? = *Stigonema* sp.
Sphaerophorus coralloides = *S. globosus*
Sphyridium byssoides = *Baeomyces rufus*
S. *fungiforme* = *Baeomyces rufus*
"Sprocladus" lichenicola = *Sprocadus l.* =
   Seimatosporium l. (conidial *Clathridium
   corticola*)
Sporodinia = *Syzygites*
Sporopodium caucasium = *Gyalectidium
   filicinum*
Squamaria p.m.p. = *Lecanora*
Staurothele umbrinum = *S. catalepta*
Stereocaulon coralloides = *S. dactylophyllum*
Stereochlamys = *Trichothelium*
Sticta aurata = *Pseudocyphellaria a.*
S. *crocata* = *Pseudocyphellaria c.*
S. *damaecornis* p.m.p. = *S. canariensis*
'S. *intricata* = *Pseudocyphellaria i.*
S. *oregana* = *Lobaria o.*
Stictina = *Sticta*
Stigmatea = *Stigmea*
Strigula buxi = *S. elegans*

Thamnonia = *Caloplaca*
Thelidium minutulum ? = *T. mesotropum*
   (p.m.p. = *T. impressum*)
Thelocarpon prasinellum = *T. laureri*
T. *turficola* = *T. superellum*
Trematosphaeropsis ? = *Homostegia*

Usnea dasypoga = *U. filipendula*
U. *melaxantha* = *U. aurantiaco-atra* s.s.
U. *taylori* = *U. sulphurea* ·

Varicellaria microsticta = *V. rhodocarpa*
Verrucaria anceps = *Polyblastia a.*
V. *hoffmanii* f. *purpurascens* = *V. marmorea*
V. *maculiformis* = *Thelidium m.*
V. *rupestris* = *V. muralis*
Verrucula ? = *Guignardia*
V. *aegyptica* = *Guignardia a.*
V. *cahirensis* = *Guignardia aegyptiacum*

Xanthocaspa = *Gloeocapsa*
Xanthoria lychnea = *X. candelaria*
Xylographa spilomatica = *X. vitiligo*